Freud's Theory of Psychoanalysis

PSYCHOANALYTIC CROSSCURRENTS
General Editor: Leo Goldberger

FREUD'S THEORY
OF PSYCHOANALYSIS

OLE ANDKJÆR OLSEN
and
SIMO KØPPE

TRANSLATED BY
Jean-Christian Delay and Carl Pedersen
with the assistance of Patricia Knudsen

NEW YORK UNIVERSITY PRESS
New York and London

Translation of this book from the original Danish was paid for by the Danish Research Council for the Humanities and by the Danish Medical Research Council.

Library of Congress
Library of Congress Cataloging-in-Publication Data

Olsen, Ole Andkjaer.
    [Freuds psykoanalyse. English]
    Freud's theory of psychoanalysis / Ole Andkjaer Olsen and Simo Koppe; translated by Jean-Christian Delay and Carl Pedersen with the assistance of Patricia Knudsen.
    p. cm.—(Psychoanalytic crosscurrents)
    Translation of: Freuds psykoanalyse.
    Bibliography: p.
    Includes index.
    ISBN 0-8147-6167-4
    1. Psychoanalysis. 2. Freud, Sigmund, 1856–1939. I. Koppe, Simo. II. Title. III. Series.
BF173.O53 1988   87-28270
150.19'52—dc19   CIP

New York University Press books are Smyth-sewn
and printed on permanent and durable acid-free paper.

CONTENTS

FOREWORD

The *Psychoanalytic Crosscurrents* series presents selected books and monographs that reveal the growing intellectual ferment within and across the boundaries of psychoanalysis.

Freud's theories and grand-scale speculative leaps have been found wanting, if not disturbing, from the very beginning and have led to a succession of derisive attacks, shifts in emphasis, revisions, modifications, and extensions. Despite the chronic and, at times, fierce debate that has characterized psychoanalysis, not only as a movement but also as a science, Freud's genius and transformational impact on the twentieth century have never been seriously questioned. Recent psychoanalytic thought has been subjected to dramatic reassessments under the sway of contemporary currents in the history of ideas, philosophy of science, epistemology, structuralism, critical theory, semantics, and semiology as well as in sociobiology, ethology, and neurocognitive science. Not only is Freud's place in intellectual history being meticulously scrutinized, his texts, too, are being carefully read, explicated, and debated within a variety of conceptual frameworks and sociopolitical contexts.

The legacy of Freud is perhaps most notably evident within the narrow confines of psychoanalysis itself, the "impossible profession" that has served as the central platform for the promulgation of official orthodoxy. But Freud's contributions—his original radical thrust—reach far beyond the parochial concerns of the clinician psychoanalyst as clinician. His writings touch on a wealth of issues, crossing traditional boundaries—be they situated in the biological, social, or humanistic spheres—that have profoundly altered our conception of the individual and society.

A rich and flowering literature, falling under the rubric of "applied psychoanalysis," came into being, reached its zenith many decades ago, and then almost vanished. Early contributors to this literature, in addition to Freud himself, came from a wide range of backgrounds both within and outside the medical/psychiatric field, many later became psychoanalysts themselves. These early efforts were characteristically reductionistic in their attempt to extrapolate from psychoanalytic theory (often the purely clinical theory) to explanations of phenomena lying at some distance from the clinical. Over the years, academic psychologists, educators, anthropologists, sociologists, political scientists, philosophers, jurists, literary critics, art historians, artists, and writers, among others (with or without formal psychoanalytic training) have joined in the proliferation of this literature.

The intent of the *Psychoanalytic Crosscurrents* series is to apply psychoanalytic ideas to topics that may lie beyond the narrowly clinical, but its essential conception and scope are quite different. The present series eschews the reductionistic tendency to be found in much traditional "applied psychoanalysis." It acknowledges not only the complexity of psychological phenomena but also the way in which they are embedded in social and scientific contexts that are constantly changing. It calls for a dialectical relationship to earlier theoretical views and conceptions rather than a mechanical repetition of Freud's dated thoughts. The series affirms the fact that contributions to and about psychoanalysis have come from many directions. It is designed as a forum for the multidisciplinary studies that intersect with psychoanalytic thought but without the requirement that psychoanalysis necessarily be the starting point or, indeed, the center focus. The criteria for inclusion in the series are that the work be significantly informed by psychoanalytic thought or that it be aimed at furthering our understanding of psychoanalysis in its broadest meaning as theory, practice, and sociocultural phenomenon; that it be of current topical interest and that it provide the critical reader with contemporary insights; and, above all, that it be high-quality scholarship, free of obsolete dogma, banalization, and empty jargon. The author's professional identity and particular theoretical orientation matters only to the extent that such facts may serve to frame the work for the reader, alerting him or her to inevitable biases of the author.

The *Psychoanalytic Crosscurrents* series presents an array of works from the multidisciplinary domain in an attempt to capture the ferment of scholarly activities at the core as well as at the boundaries of psychoanalysis. The books and monographs are from a variety of sources: authors will be psychoanalysts—traditional, neo- and post-Freudian, existential, object-relational, Kohutian, Lacanian, etc.—social scientists with quantitative or qualitative orientations to psychoanalytic data, and scholars from the vast diversity of approaches and interests that make up the humanities. The series entertains works on critical comparisons of psychoanalytic theories and concepts as well as philosophical examinations of fundamental assumptions and epistemic claims that furnish the base for psychoanalytic hypotheses. It includes studies of psychoanalysis as literature (discourse and narrative theory) as well as the application of psychoanalytic concepts to literary criticism. It will serve as an outlet for psychoanalytic studies of creativity and the arts. Works in the cognitive and the neurosciences will be included to the extent that they address some fundamental psychoanalytic tenet, such as the role of dreaming and other forms of unconscious mental processes.

It should be obvious that an exhaustive enumeration of the types of works that might fit into the *Psychoanalytic Crosscurrents* series is pointless. The studies comprise a lively and growing literature as a unique domain; books of this sort are frequently difficult to classify or catalog. Suffice it to say that the overriding aim of the editor of this series is to serve as a conduit for the identification of the outstanding yield of that emergent literature and to foster its further unhampered growth.

Leo Goldberger
Professor of Psychology
New York University

INTRODUCTION

In this book, we propose a way to read—or reread—the works of Sigmund Freud. As the years passed during which we studied Freud's own body of work and its historical context, as well as a fair share of the more recent psychoanalytic literature, we came to feel that the newer literature by and large did not reflect an advance over Freud's psychoanalysis. The more recent works seem dishearteningly sterile when compared with the wealth of ideas that flowed from Freud, the spark of his contradictions, his open-ended formulations. Freud's choice of words, phrasing, and style are intimately bound to all that falls under his analytic scrutiny. Furthermore, we noticed that there were fundamental aspects of Freud's psychoanalysis that had been ignored or outright suppressed in most of the English and, in particular, American psychoanalytic literature, aspects brought to our attention by contemporary French psychoanalysts such as Jacques Lacan and Jean Laplanche. In this book we hope to reintroduce these aspects of Freud's work and establish (or reestablish) the stimulating field within which Freud made his observations, the field that made them so pervasively dialectical. Our contention is that Freud's ideas cannot be wrenched out of context without suffering great loss, and that consequently it is important to gain an understanding of how these ideas fit into the whole body of his work. To this end, we will make use of a number of theoretical formalizations in an attempt to establish the Freudian alphabet, so to speak, so that it will again be possible for attentive readers to spell their way through Freud's writings.

An important concept that will be set in sharper focus by this proposed rereading of Freud's works is that of the human subject, the word *subject* replacing more traditional terms such as *individual, person,* or *human being,* for reasons that will become apparent in the course of the book. The treatment of this concept constitutes the main secondary axis of this book. We will discuss the nature of the new subject from three different perspectives: first, from the perspective of psychoanalysis itself, that is, of metapsychology and clinical psychoanalysis; second, from the perspective of the subject's social conditions, hoping thereby to shed light on the relationship between the socially determined subject and the subject studied by Freud in psychoanalysis; and third, from the perspective of the history of science, in order to explore the extent to which not only the subject, but also sciences dealing with the subject (including psychoanalysis) are themselves socially and historically determined. We feel that these three perspectives dovetail quite well, leading to a fruitful appraisal of the psychoanalytic study of the subject both as a study of a socially and historically determined subject and also as a socially and historically determined study of that subject. We will briefly expand these comments by taking up our three approaches separately.

(1) In his theoretical work, Freud sought to elucidate the nature of the subject's structure, as well as of its genesis. The common interpretation of this work sets these two aspects in close causal relation; the earliest stages in the genesis of the subject form the basis for the deepest layers of the subject's structure. The further back one goes in development, the deeper one goes into the unconscious, and the more decisive causes one finds for the subject's behavior. We suggest another reading of Freud's concepts; we stress the idea that one element of a structure has no meaning except in relation to another. Thus, as two fundamental elements of Freud's theory are the conscious and the unconscious, his study of the subject's structure concerns itself with all the ways in which the unconscious acts decisively upon the conscious, where the relation of the conscious and the unconscious does not follow the laws of simple linear causality, but rather takes on the form of overdetermination. In overdetermination, perception in the present may exert influence on memory presentations by a process of deferred action; thus, there is no simple conformity between structure and genesis. Impressions from the earliest phases of development are processed according to certain rules before being encoded in the unconscious as structural elements, and these impressions are, in principle, able to create new psychological constellations in the mind throughout life. Hence, we have reason to seek other than purely ontogenetic explanations for the subject's structure.

(2) Freud himself hoped to find in phylogenesis what he had not found in ontogenesis. It is on this point that he made what seems to us to be his only fundamental mistake. He was fascinated by the developmental theories of Haeckel, Darwin, and notably Lamarck, and believed that their new ideas about biology could be transferred to psychology, a maneuver Darwin

himself had attempted. If ontogenesis, as Haeckel maintained, was an abbreviated repetition of phylogenesis, then it should be possible to apply information stemming from phylogenesis to ontogenesis. Freud proceeded to do just this. The phylogenetic core of psychoanalytic theory harbors far-reaching ideas to the effect that the deepest layers of the unconscious contain material reaching back to the origin of mankind, even of biological life itself. The operational modes of the unconscious are thought to have been handed down from generation to generation to the present-day subject in the form of inborn reflexes that are beyond the control of will power. These reflexes are supposed to represent inherited impressions and experiences from the origin of life, from the first human beings' struggle against the elements in primeval times, and from events that took place in the earliest social orders.

In the course of our own study, we wondered whether it was not possible to exchange the theoretical core of psychoanalytic subject theory with one other than the phylogenetic. Indeed, on many points, Freud's phylogenetic explanations can be replaced or supplemented with sociogenetic explanations, that is, explanations on the social history of the subject through the past centuries, rather than based on its biological history. This leads us to the conclusion that psychoanalytic theory is not a general theory of the subject, but a theory whose validity is restricted to a specific subject, namely the subject as it has evolved within the confines of a sphere of intimacy. The sphere of intimacy is that part of society that attends to reproduction, in a broad sense of the term: private life, care of children, leisure time, rest, and so forth. About two hundred years ago the sphere of intimacy became characterized by the emergence of the nuclear family. Concomitantly, the functions of the sphere of intimacy became subject to the increasing influence of the spheres of production and circulation in an expanding capitalist society and to a great extent determined by them. The subjects of the sphere of intimacy, primarily housewives and children, were in turn affected by these changes. The monotonous nature of the housewife's tasks, the intensified care of children, the necessity of being at close quarters all day, the absence of the father from the home, all contributed to establish what could be called a frictional sexuality between these subjects (housewives and children). In short, the sphere of intimacy generated increasing amounts of nervousness and irritability, not to mention the binding of heightened emotional and imaginative activity.

The fact is incontrovertible that Freud made his way to psychoanalysis from the biological sciences. In what we will call the adaptive register, we show that Freud studied fundamental psychobiological laws and that he took great interest in the relationship of adaptation between organism and environment. This, however, does not undercut our contention, for, as we will also show, Freud did often take into consideration the above-mentioned origin of sexuality. In what we call the psychosexual register, he worked with sexuality as a fairly clearly delineated field of inquiry, governed by rules as a whole different from those commanding the adaptive register. Sexuality, or the sexual drives, are organized in clusters with goals very different from, though not entirely independent of, their biological and social functions. The Oedipus complex, one of Freud's central concepts, is a remarkable tool with which to analyze the nuclear family's particular emotional ties and entanglements, their implantation in childhood, and the all-too-obvious imprint they leave on the adult. Hence, Freud's concept of the unconscious does not have as much bearing on inheritance that goes back to the origin of the species as it does on the psychological structures passed on to a child immediately after birth, and bound to and transmitted by the institutions and traditions of the nuclear family.

However true that may be, our point is *not* to suggest that a simple one-to-one correlation can be established between the content of the Freudian unconscious and the past three or four centuries of social history. No social-historical analysis, no matter how precise, can determine how the unconscious operates. The unconscious is not identical to a certain quantum of specific historical material derived from the sphere of intimacy. This material is subject to distortion as it is incorporated into the unconscious in accordance with a set of rules that cannot be assimilated to the idea of ideological distortion. It is the initiation of the child into language and intersubjectivity that distorts preverbal experiences into active unconscious fantasies. Eventually, it became Freud's opinion that fantasies in the unconscious arose by way of deferred action *(nachträglichkeit)*; they behaved like memories of events that have taken place even though the events never had. Hence, besides phylogenesis, ontogenesis, and sociogenesis, we must pay attention to genesis in the structure itself. As a child grows up, acquiring language, learning to orient itself in physical and social space, as well as in a linear time continuum, a utopic identity based on narcissistic and oedipal experiences is encapsulated in the unconscious. But the unconscious form taken by these oedipal experiences, the Oedipus complex, is not an accurate image of the child's true family relationships; instead, it is a fantasy image that for better or worse leaves its imprint on the entire life history of the subject, who never quite learns to comprehend the nature of this somewhat obscure and mythic, though very active, force within him. Since the unconscious Oedipus complex is determinant for both the anxieties and desires of the subject, it has a psychological reality that distinguishes it from both biological and social reality.

As just mentioned, the child's initiation to language and intersubjectivity is the structural prerequisite for the distortion of experiences from the sphere of intimacy that takes place in the unconscious. Language and intersubjectivity permit subjects to relate meanings to formal systems of signs and to combine linguistic elements in such a way as to let them take on new meanings, as well as to give them access to the active-passive polarity. Since both this polarity and others interchangeable with it are made to carry great emotional valence by a strong Oedipus complex, it seems to us that psychoanalytic insight into these matters has special bearing on capitalist society, where an independent sphere—the sphere of intimacy—has been set apart to care for socialization. This is where the active-passive polarity is instilled in children in countless variations: not only as what pertains to love and hate, but also to questions concerning power, authority, freedom; concerning hiding knowledge from others and obtaining access to their secret knowledge; concerning property ownership, presents, inheritance, debt, and affects related to these experiences, such as guilt, envy, pride, ambition, and so on. What is historically specific about the subject studied by psychoanalysis is the fact that its initiation to the active-passive polarity has taken place within the confines of the sphere of intimacy. Other historical contexts for this initiation to the active-passive polarity has taken place within the confines of the sphere of intimacy. Other historical contexts for this initiation can be imagined.

(3) Finally, we were led to inquire into the conditions that encouraged the appearance of psychoanalysis at a precise juncture of history, to study our object from the point of view of the history of science. Both before psychoanalysis and contemporaneously with it, other attempts were made to formulate coherent explanations for the subject's multifaceted experiences in the sphere of intimacy. The first of these was ostensibly the cultural-historical movement generally known as romanticism. Romantic writers portrayed their characters as vortices of emotion and desire, following the actual fate of these in their works. As mentioned earlier, this intensification of affect was in part due to the new role ascribed to the sphere of intimacy and to its isolation from and subservience to the other spheres of society. The understanding of this shown by the romantics, however, was very poor. They dwelt on the purported divinity of human nature, an idea vastly

inadequate to stem the rising tide of the expanding capitalist social system's encroachment upon the sphere of intimacy. If anything, they imagined that further isolation of this sphere would somehow free it from its shackles, as if its values could be self-determined and exist independently of the rest of society. From a psychoanalytic point of view, this romantic idea of a boundless paradisiacal natural state must be called narcissistic.

Like the romantics, Freud studied the expression of feelings in the sphere of intimacy, but unlike them his approach was concrete. He was a clinician trying to respond to the complaints addressed to him by his patients. Furthermore, he gave his work a scientific turn, thereby making it at once more accessible and practically useful. The first hypotheses of psychoanalysis became tools with which it was possible to gain more insight into the workings of the subject for a number of years. Though more successful with his project than the romantics were with theirs, Freud's success cannot simply be attributed to superior genius. One reason for this is that the subject's crisis had worsened during the course of the nineteenth century. It had simply become easier to see that something was going wrong. Literature itself had evolved accordingly. Naturalistic writers such as Flaubert, Zola, Ibsen, and J. P. Jacobsen (author of the novel *Niels Lyhne,* see I.B.6.b) had come to the fore. Freud knew the works of these writers. Another reason is that Freud had access to a vast body of empirical knowledge gathered during the course of the nineteenth century from many fields: from physics and neurophysiology, through psychology and psychiatry, to philosophy and literature. Freud had a striking gift for combining information from these many sources into a whole. This led him to forge a theory that has the great advantage of being applicable to the problems of the sphere of intimacy without isolating this sphere ideologically from the rest of society. Already in the 1890s, Freud pointed out that socially determined sexual morality was in part responsible for the existence of neurosis. Thus psychoanalysis became a more useful tool than romantic literature and philosophy with which the subject of the sphere of intimacy could reflect or act upon his problems.

The question now is how useful a tool psychoanalysis has continued to be since. Our overall appraisal of the status of psychoanalysis is a cautious one, as neither is psychoanalysis an unambiguous phenomenon, nor has the nature of its theory or its analytic and therapeutic methods been fully clarified. Freud was the founder of a movement that has radiated in many directions and some of his followers have taken it far from its point of departure. Not all of this can still be called psychoanalysis, and Freud cannot be blamed for the mistakes his successors have made. If we focus our attention on psychoanalysis as a therapeutic method of treatment for neurotic afflictions, then we find that its results are not particularly uplifting. As institutional models, psychoanalytic institutions are not particularly inspiring either: most psychoanalysts are politically conservative; Freud's ideas on the neutrality of the analyst and the, in principle, self-determination of the analysand have been reinterpreted as positivistic and liberalistic dogma; and little has been done by psychoanalysts themselves to open the doors of psychoanalysis to the general public.

It is not, however, our intention with this book to discuss the present status of psychoanalysis, but merely to point out that much remains to be discovered in Freud's writings. This is true notwithstanding the fact that society, the sphere of intimacy in particular, has undergone great change during the past fifty years. It seems to us that in times of social change such as ours we might find support in Freud's psychoanalysis to help us avoid falling back on romantic and politically useless, if not outright dangerous, positions as we grope our way to a new society.

Having given an account of how we have approached the object of our research and, consequently, of how we have treated it, we will end with a few remarks on the way the book has been designed. In a presentation such as this one no matter where we begin we have to suppose prior knowledge of something that will be clarified only later. It seems no one has yet succeeded in giving a flawless account of psychoanalysis, not even Freud himself. We have opted for the simplest solution by moving forward chronologically in the first two parts before making a thorough review of Freud's psychoanalytic work in the last three. In part 1, we place psychoanalysis in its historical context by presenting the major social, scientific, and cultural events contemporaneous with its beginnings. There, we will take a closer look at the genesis of the sphere of intimacy. In part 2, we paint a portrait of Freud's life, emphasizing his remarkable talent for the integration of social, scientific, and cultural experience, his creation of psychoanalysis almost alone in the 1890s and the expansion of psychoanalysis into a vast movement after the turn of the century. Then, inspired by Freud himself (1923a), we take up his analytic, therapeutic, and theoretical work, in that order, in the last three parts of the book. The analytic work treated in part 3 covers topics such as dreams, literary works, and social behavior, all of which might be called applied psychoanalysis, as opposed to clinical psychoanalysis where living subjects are analyzed. Psychopathology and the psychoanalytic classification of mental diseases, mostly neuroses, will be presented in part 4 along with Freud's therapeutic work. Finally, part 5 will take the form of an in-depth reading of Freud's metapsychological concepts and of his views on the subject's genesis and structure.

This scheme allows the book to be used for reference or to be read as an unbroken essay. It is not an elementary introduction to psychoanalysis, so readers only slightly familiar with the subject will get more out of reading parts 2, 3, and 4 first. These parts are more accessible and the theoretical concepts used in part 5 are defined in them.

Instead of using footnotes, we have put references directly into the text. Moreover, we have worked out a section of bibliographical notes, citing and in some cases discussing, chapter by chapter, the most important secondary literature. In the introductory note to the bibliography proper, we have given a more complete explanation of the principles guiding our system of reference and of the structure of the bibliography itself. The many diagrams should be useful in study situations, but they may be skipped during a less committed reading of the book.

Some of our better-informed readers will perhaps feel that too little space has been allotted to our study of sociogenesis and the place of psychoanalysis in the history of science. We would like to say in our defense that additions would not significantly have altered our basic contentions, and that we have felt it incumbent upon us first of all to underscore the importance of a thorough reading of Freud's texts. Having carefully studied many of the leading Freud interpreters available on the market today, we dare affirm that numerous authors tend to go to the other extreme, that is, to base their works on at times strikingly inaccurate or insufficient readings of his writings. Those readers who find this book useful may be interested to know that we are planning a similar book about leading schools of psychoanalysis since Freud. It is in this second book that we plan to make a more detailed appraisal of the social status and political implications of psychoanalysis.

I

THE HISTORICAL ORIGINS
OF PSYCHOANALYSIS

INTRODUCTION
TO PART I

In part 1 of this book, we will present the historical origins of psychoanalysis and follow these up to the time of its inception as an independent science in the 1890s. In order to understand the nature of psychoanalysis, it is necessary to be familiar with both what preceded it and the social conditions and scientific ideas from which it arose. Since we consider psychoanalysis to be a science primarily concerned with the human subject, we will concentrate our efforts on describing the characteristics of this social subject, on the changes it has undergone through history, as well as on the philosophical, scientific, and esthetic disciplines that, in the service of sundry ideologies, have contributed to shaping its image.

Section A of part 1 begins with our analysis of the shaping of the subject in capitalist society. The evolution of society led to the fragmentation of the subject into parts corresponding to the functions it had to fulfill (production, circulation, and reproduction). This three-part fragmentation in turn generated three typical subject concepts, of which we will describe the essential aspects. In section B, we will examine ideas stemming from philosophy, literature, the natural sciences, and medicine, ideas presumed to have influenced Freud around the time of the inception of psychoanalysis. Finally, in section C, we will show how the three basic subject concepts began to influence each other in the latter part of the nineteenth century, and how the psychoanalytic theory of the subject is a critical continuation of the humanistic subject concept.

In our account, we have attempted to remedy an important weakness in the existing literature on the historical origins of psychoanalysis, in that we have tried to "include everything" instead of focusing on a few chosen fields. It is not possible to single out one chief source for psychoanalysis, so the following variegated, though nonetheless coherent, portrayal of the background of psychoanalysis is necessary if one is to make intelligible the conditions surrounding its birth. Freud himself went beyond the narrow confines of his own field when he created psychoanalysis, and this is precisely what we must also do in order to understand his work.

A.

THE SHAPING
OF THE SUBJECT
IN CAPITALIST SOCIETY

It is our intention here to outline the societal background of psychoanalysis as a psychological theory of the subject. It seems necessary to suppose that when psychoanalysis arises as a "new" theory of the subject, it does so because society has in fact given rise to a "new" subject. The component parts of the new theory are of course fragments of older theories, but in the last analysis it is not this fragmentation of the older theories, but the changed conditions of the subject that make theoretical renewal necessary. It is difficult to say with any certainty whether a particular subject concept is a forerunner to, ideologically paving the way for, the subject's real evolution, or if, on the contrary, concepts first emerge in the wake of real changes, perhaps even long after these have taken place. On one hand, the free-will hypothesis, to which we shall soon return, was used in the political struggle for a free and democratic society; on the other, the negative consequences of the subject's changed conditions (the repression of feelings and the organization of neurosis) were first recognized much later. Although unable to solve this theoretical difficulty now, we conjecture that at precise moments in history, trenchantly new subject concepts arose that included both a theory of the subject's structure and an ideological program for its upbringing, and that each concept so conceived was closely related to the social practice from which it originated. A precisely formulated conception of what the subject *should* be like often makes it easier to understand how the subject really is and how it can be forced to change, repress, and nurture different parts of itself in order to live up to the demands of society. By basing our analysis of various subject concepts on our prior knowledge of the evolution of capitalist society, it is possible for us to present a reasonably coherent picture of both the evolution of the subject itself and its concept, as well as to place psychoanalysis within this picture.

The essence of our prior knowledge of the subject consists of the fact that capitalist society was increasingly subdivided into spheres each with its specific function. With increasing division of labor, the individual was no longer able to carry out all the tasks necessary to support life, but instead found himself forced to specialize; in return, specialization led to increasing efficiency. We will operate with three general functions, namely production, circulation, and reproduction. It is easy to imagine a primitive society where one, in a manner of speaking, lives from hand to mouth, that is, lives off the plants and animals that are at hand. In capitalist society, functional compartmentalization has taken place. Production takes place almost exclusively in a sphere of production, a place of work where the subject is only present during working hours and with the sole aim of producing commodities. Commodities circulate, are purchased and sold, in a sphere of circulation, in principle merely a large market to which everyone has access, but in fact also including the rules, regulations, and laws that govern it, that is, the entire state apparatus. Finally, reproduction takes place in a sphere of intimacy including the home and family and where eating, procreation, rest, and other similar activities take place during the subject's spare time.

Though a subject may move freely from one sphere to another, it will inevitably change character in doing so, just as it takes off its work clothes when coming home from work or dresses accordingly when going out. A particular subject will often feel greater affinity for the sphere that most completely defines his or her identity. The typical housewife, if there are any left, sees her entire life from the standpoint of the sphere of intimacy, its functions, and terminology. Sensitivity, love, manners, authority, and all the other terms that go hand in hand with a life with husband and children comprise the basic building blocks of her self-understanding. She takes these concepts with her wherever she goes, to the polls, for example. It is our intention to apply this point of view to the historical evolution of capitalism, and to demonstrate how the three spheres of society and their functions have generated three distinct subject concepts that retain much of their resilience even in our day.

1. THE LIBERALISTIC SUBJECT CONCEPT

Capitalistic modes of production began to replace feudal ones in the 1500s. This was partly a consequence of the massive influx of wealth from colonies overseas. Great quantities of capital were accumulated that made it possible to reorganize modes of production from handicraft to the manufacture of commodities. Work was simplified and rationalized; the small shops of craftsmen gave way to vast halls where artisans practicing various trades were gathered. Each step in the production of a particular article was entrusted to a group of persons, which made it possible for these persons to carry out the task more quickly and more effectively than had been the case before. In order to keep up with this trend, it became necessary for craftsmen to relinquish the independence they had hitherto enjoyed. Through a century-long process, they became wage earners, which, of course, radically changed their lives.

However, the spread of capitalist modes of production depended on the salability of the commodities produced, and consequently the first profound social changes occurred in the sphere of circulation. The first owners of capital were trade capitalists who made their profits by buying low and selling high. This was also true when they invested some of their capital in means of production. They were not interested in producing commodities for their use value, but only in producing exchange values, i.e., financially profitable commodities. In order to reach this goal, it was necessary for them to ensure that commodities as well as labor could circulate freely on the market; this necessity prompted the awakening of the trade capitalists political consciousness. If the laws in force forbade free trade, there was no advantage to be gained from producing commodities cheaper than those of their competitors. The many isolated, protected, and relatively self-sufficient local communities characteristic of feudal times were unfit for larger commercial intercourse.

Hence, the capitalist's first task was political, namely to ensure free trade. Precisely this task was at the root of the liberal ideology expounded during the seventeenth and eighteenth centuries. The common denominator of the capital-strong bourgeoisie's political and ideological program is the concept of freedom. The first freedom demanded was freedom of trade, which meant the freedom to trade anywhere, without regard to the privileges of guilds and castes. Furthermore, free competition and free trade were demanded, specifically the elimination of all tax restrictions as well as of all measures protecting weak professions. Everyone was to have equal access to the market and equal opportunity to purchase the cheapest commodities (the capitalist was interested in buying the cheapest labor). This liberalistic way of thinking was extrapolated to matters concerning the state: political freedom, freedom of assembly, freedom of expression, freedom of faith, and so on, were all demanded. The state was to attend to the wishes of the people and not the other way around. This conceptual edifice was crowned by the idea of free will, according to which nature had endowed the individual with the ability to make free choices and this endowment, in the final analysis, was the essence of his personality. Thus, inner freedom (free will) is the core of the liberalistic subject concept, just as external (social) freedom is the core of liberalism's political program.

But the rights of the bourgeoisie were not won without a struggle. The political and ideological struggle concomitant with the spread of capitalist means of production lasted for centuries, from the birth of the first ideas on freedom in the seventeenth century to the bourgeois revolutions of 1789, 1830, and 1848. The struggle was in part centered around and led by the so-called bourgeois public, at first a kind of news agency for businessmen that gradually became a debate forum for the entire bourgeoisie. On a small scale the bourgeois public exemplified the ideal social structure as seen by the bourgeoisie. Any topic could be brought up there, although matters of general ongoing concern had priority. Any opinion could be expressed, even if it challenged the church and state monopolies on truth and power. With these facts in mind, it is clear that for a long time the bourgeois public only existed as an underground movement at the heart of autocratic social systems. Far-sighted philosophers and writers who expressed new ideas on man and society were censured and otherwise persecuted. Examples are Pascal, Spinoza, Montesquieu, and Voltaire. Newspapers and magazines expressing liberal ideas were also subject to censure. The real opposition to absolute monarchy was seated in secret societies and lodges, where people met under the pretext of pursuing harmless activities to discuss political questions. Members were mostly academics and businessmen, and it is among them we find the future political leaders of the bourgeoisie. Parliamentary democracy, instituted in most of Europe during the nineteenth century, is the direct descendant of the bourgeois public. In the bourgeois states of Europe, public debate is still considered a guarantee of freedom itself.

As stated previously, the core of the liberalistic subject concept is the idea of free will. For most of the far-sighted philosophers of the time, nothing was more self-evident than the idea that the individual was equipped with an ego representing the ultimate reasoning agency behind all choice. The English philosopher John Locke (1632–1704) expressed his blind faith in the idea that the individual is directed by his conscious ego in a manner characteristic of the time:

> The *idea* of the beginning of motion we have only from reflection on what passes in ourselves, where we find by experience that barely by willing it, barely by a thought of the mind, we can move the parts of our bodies which were before at rest. [. . .] This, at least, I think evident; that we find in ourselves a power to begin or forbear, continue or end several actions of our minds and motions of our bodies, barely by a thought or preference of the mind ordering or, as it were commanding, the doing of such or such a particular action. This power which the mind has thus to order the consideration of any idea, or the forbearing to consider it, or to prefer the motion of any part of the body to its rest, and vice versa, in any particular instance, is that which we call the will. (Locke 1690, p. 195)

This way of looking at the human subject had been given its modern dress half a century earlier by René Descartes (1596–1650). Descartes believed that all life could be reduced to *res cogitans* (thinking things) and *res extensa* (extended things), or simply things of the mind and things of the body. They are distinct properties, in principle able to exist autonomously, but combined in humans in the *sensorium commune* located in the pineal gland. Impulses traveling between the body and the mind must pass through the gland. The extended world, of which the body is a part, is seen as a machine entirely subject to the laws of causality; it is furthermore characterized by divisibility. The ego or the mind *(res cogitans),* on the other hand, cannot be divided. Even if the ego is able to carry out different tasks, it is still "one and the same soul, always in operation, regardless of whether I want something, sense something, or understand something" (Descartes 1641, p. 797). The mind is able both to receive impulses from and send impulses to the body, and hence the surrounding world, but it is not a reflex apparatus such as those we know from the nervous systems of animals. Animals are able both to sense and react to the world, though they are unable to choose how to do so; they are living machines of a kind. Conversely, the human mind is not causally determined, but rather guided by free will. This dualistic conception of body and mind as two independent parameters nonetheless able to exert mutual influence is generally called the theory of psychophysical interaction. This theory was already criticized during Descartes's lifetime for letting the soul, as a cause itself without cause, interfere in the mechanistic processes of the material world. Notwithstanding, Descartes's theory enjoyed wide circulation until long after his death, and it gave incipient liberalistic thought a philosophical and psychological basis.

Let us now take a closer look at what is entailed by the idea of free will. The theory of psychophysical interaction tells us that the seat of freedom is in the mind and not in the body. Mind and body are in conflict. When the mind dominates the body, the subject is free, and it is unfree when the opposite is true. The impulses of the body are called feelings and passions and should be controlled by the impulses of the mind, emanating from reason and intellect. The subject is then split into two fundamentally different parts. This split is reflected by the liberalistic subject concept in the sense that reason is clearly placed above feelings. If reason does not have a firm grip on feelings, freedom itself is lost: first free will, then also social and political freedom. The Danish dramatist Holberg's views on peasants are a typical example of this way of considering the problem. Peasants are, according to Holberg, unable to emancipate themselves from their daily tasks and family lives, even when these are not particularly satisfying. They lack a broader understanding of their own social condition and are characteristically apathetic and inert. They are short-sighted in their calculations, wanting in their productivity, and lax in the face of their feelings and passions. To their advantage, Holberg claims that this is not their true nature, that they are able to learn to understand and to live up to the new social ideals as well as anyone else, on the sole condition that they be given more freedom and more responsibility.

Hence, we see that a slightly lofty ideal of freedom implies a far more concrete educational ideal. The external coercion of feudalism is replaced by an internal coercion based on self-control and logical calculation, whose aim is to make the individual perform more efficiently. This disciplinary process begins within the bourgeoisie's own ranks and gradually spreads so as to include all those who partake or are to partake in the capitalist economic system. The new work ethic spreads from places of work to schools and homes, and the pedagogy of the 1600s and 1700s is filled with rules of common sense the ego is expected to be brought up to obey. Far-sighted and courageous businessmen became the ideal of an otherwise static society, and the myth of the great capitalist who earns his wealth by diligence, thrift, and shrewdness lives on even in our day. We assume that the influence of this educational philosophy led to the appearance of a new psychological personality structure. During the period when childhood emerged as a concept (the idea of childhood hardly existed before the advent of capitalism), the years of childhood were resolutely turned into years of disciplinary apprenticeship and learning that stood in sharp contrast to primitive feelings and reaction patterns. It might even be argued that feelings and passions first came into being when an attempt was made to repress them.

In summary, it can be said that there is a certain logical relation between the liberalistic subject concept, whose essence is the idea of free will, and the changes in the subject's character structure that in fact took place during early capitalism. Freedom seen in a liberalistic perspective is not the freedom to choose anything one pleases. On the free market there is only one choice, namely the cheapest commodity. Any sensible person will only be able to make that one choice. In fact, the unreasonable, short-sighted, and passionate choice is not a choice at all, for it is simply determined by body chemistry. Even a philosopher like Spinoza (1632–1677), who denied the existence of free will, was, in the final analysis, still in agreement with liberalistic ideals when he claimed that the reasonable ego would "be very little disposed to seek a good which was present, but which would be a cause of any future evil" (Spinoza 1677, p. 342). The idea of free will is, as we have suggested, an ideological figurehead. It does not say the whole truth about the subject, though it was a good point of reference in the political struggle that took place in Europe from the sixteenth century on, and an effective argument in favor of discipline for the subject.

2. THE HUMANISTIC SUBJECT CONCEPT

At the end of the eighteenth century and at the beginning of the nineteenth an alternative to the liberalistic subject concept appeared. In what follows we will call this alternative the humanistic subject concept. Two causes may be cited for this development, both related to the upsurge of capitalism, namely society's increasing differentiation into sharply delineated spheres of activity and the changed economic conditions of the petite bourgeoisie.

Before the advent of capitalism it was customary for work to be done in or near the home. This was true of peasants and craftsmen, where employers housed their employees. Everyone took part in all phases of production, both grownups and children, young and old, men and women. This was possible because work processes were not particularly specialized and did not require complex organizational structures. With the capitalist mode of production, things changed. To begin with, production and reproduction were separated, production taking place in factories or other sites of collective enterprise, whereas reproduction was isolated in the home. It is this separation that now makes it possible to distinguish between a production sphere and a sphere of intimacy where only an undifferentiated "private sphere" existed before. In many walks of life, it became customary for the man of the house to earn his living away from home, while his wife stayed home to take care of the house and children. This division of labor was not class specific. The factory owner, the accountant, and the factory worker all worked away from home. It can be said that this process drained the home of many of its earlier functions. However, entirely new ones were acquired, and these were especially obvious where the petite bourgeoisie was concerned.

The bourgeoisie succeeded in its political struggle partly because it symbolized the struggle for freedom of all. The bond between the bourgeoisie and the lower classes was strong, though it was again broken when the bourgeoisie won its economic and political foothold. The working class, or the proletariat, was not primarily oppressed by the nobility or by absolute monarchs as was the case of the bourgeoisie, but by the employers who sought to buy their labor as cheaply as possible. Hence, the petite bourgeoisie gradually stood in increasing opposition to the upper bourgeoisie. Marx and Engels fittingly described the petite bourgeoisie in *The Communist Manifesto* as follows: "The lower strata of the middle class—the small tradespeople, shopkeepers, and retired tradesmen generally, the handicraftsmen and peasants—all these sink gradually into the proletariat, partly because their diminutive capital does not suffice for the scale on which modern industry is carried on, and is swamped in the competition with the large capitalists, partly because their specialized skill is rendered worthless by new methods of production" (Marx and Engels 1848, pp. 17–18). Historically, the petite bourgeoisie considered itself part of the bourgeoisie. It fought with zeal for the same ideals of freedom and forged its identity on the basis of the same cultural models. It was a particularly bitter experience for the petite bourgeoisie to be ruined and suffer social setbacks as a consequence of the economic upsurge of the upper bourgeoisie, and it is not surprising that members of the petite bourgeoisie were the first to criticize capitalism.

The most graphic example of the petite bourgeoisie's criticism of capitalism is romanticism. Romanticism made its breakthrough as a cultural movement at the beginning of the nineteenth century. It is often seen as a reaction to the bourgeois French revolution of 1789, although it was also a reaction against both capitalism in general and industry and finance in particular. It was reactionary when it took sides for the nobility and absolute monarchy against liberalism and democracy, but was also progressive insofar as it criticized negative sides of capitalism. Romantics held the view that nature was a source of positive norms and that society and its products were unnatural. Children were considered to be in harmony with nature and it was the goal of education to maintain this harmony (see Rousseau's *Emile* from 1762). Qualities lacking in the present were attributed to the past. Feelings and spontaneity were revalued while speculation and calculation were depreciated. Capitalists and businessmen were considered unfeeling and greedy persons without any sense of true life and basic values, whose emotions had been perverted in their pursuit of profit and career. It was primarily the nouveaux riches, that is, the rising bourgeoisie, that became the object of the hatred of the petite bourgeoisie, while the "old rich," i.e., nobility and royalty, were seen as possessors of truly humane characteristics.

That what has been called the bourgeois family in fact arose from petite bourgeois ideological premises is particularly clear when one compares it with other family models. Intimacy and positive emotionality limited to the family made its appearance during the latter half of the eighteenth century and was not found earlier. There was no tradition in the nobility to separate what was public from what was private. Nobles could hardly escape their lackeys and servants even in their bedchamber, and intercourse between spouses was often very limited. It was not uncommon that they lived separately on their own respective estates with a lover or mistress, and such situations were always a matter of public knowledge. Nor was a sharp distinction made between public and private in the lower classes. One room served as a bedroom, kitchen, dining room, and bathroom for everyone. The functions of the home became more specialized and privatized as capitalistic division of labor and suppression of bodily and sensual expression increased. Special rooms were designed for sleep, children, and washing, and one did not wish to be disturbed while carrying out intimate functions. The suppression and castigation of sensuality continued, but it was counterbalanced as internalized sensitivity was held forth as a positive ideal that found a particularly high degree of expression in the relationship between the members of a family.

There was a general tendency to seek compensation for reverses suffered in society within the family. The home became a cultural reservoir where as much education was given to children as could be afforded. The only small capital left to the petite bourgeoisie as it gradually lost its means of production was its children. They were to be taken care of, nurtured, and educated in view of social careers that would perhaps permit the family to regain its lost dignity. It followed that the new class of technicians and academics was largely recruited from the petite bourgeoisie. Logically enough, educational tasks were to be carried out by women in the home, eventually assisted by a whole staff of nurses, tutors, and kitchen help. Children were thoroughly prepared for society, and the romantic value system was unhesitatingly implanted in their minds as the unshakable ideological and moral basis of their lives. But at the same time, more interest than ever was taken in their manners, digestion, sexuality, and health in general. Such constant watching over, prying, and reprimanding led to much more intense emotional ties between children and their parents than earlier. Often pent-up and entangled feelings resulted in various fantasies and longings that expressed, if anything, the adult's romantic wish to return to his family and childhood.

The (petit) bourgeois nuclear family satisfied the needs of family fathers to a significant degree. In the family, they both found physical and emotional restitution and got moral support and confirmation of their feelings about themselves before going out to confront the chaos of social life. Humiliation on the job could be counterbalanced by the authority exercised within the family, and if everything else failed, they still had loyal family relations to fall back on. In the family, one was not simply judged according to one's success in society, but also as the person one was. In contrast, the condition of women was more ambiguous. On one hand, they were called upon to carry out comprehensive and fairly monotonous household tasks, while on the other were considered the noblest incarnation of sensitivity. In literary works, women were portrayed as the nearly inaccessible object of man's deepest longings, representing all that was most authentically and fundamentally human. Romantic love stories where economic calculation clashes with feelings are not uncommon. In the most fortunate cases, a couple is formed, as when a calculating man falls in love with a warm, sensitive woman, whereby the man's cold and cautious nature gives way to less tempered feelings. The fact is, however, that romantic ideals had a hard time of it, since overwrought feelings could not find natural release and their neurotic forms could not be realized on account of internal contradictions. The emotional freedom proclaimed as the correlate of lib-eralistic freedom did not hinder marriages of convenience, and one contin-ued to marry within one's social class even as one imagined the possibility of doing otherwise. For women, there was no freedom in marriage. On the contrary, if a woman wanted to accede to the social security marriage offered, she had to give up her personal and emotional freedom and swear obedience to her husband. In this sense, the family remained a backward, authoritarian structure, a remnant of feudalism that did not at first follow the liberalistic developmental tendencies of the sphere of circulation and of public life.

In summary, we are able to note, as has been the case in the preceding section, a certain relationship between the humanistic subject concept stressing the importance of feelings at the expense of reason on one side, and the character structure that emerged in consequence of the social delimitation of both the family and private spheres on the other. Thus what in fact took place was internalization and heightened emotional and imaginative activity, even if we would describe and explain this process differently today than we would have at the time it actually took place. Today, we would choose as significant causes specific conditions concern-ing the breakthrough of capitalism and industrialism, while it was then thought that an original sensitivity about to be lost in man had been rediscovered. In romantic utopias, societies were invented where feelings would find a natural place without being warped or suppressed. It was thought that such feelings held all the proper principles necessary to run a happy and healthy society. In view of this, it is not surprising that the term *romantic* has become synonymous with *naive*. The myth of the family as the cradle of love, spontaneity, and education—humanity, in one word (Habermas 1962, p. 44)—lives on even today. Humanistic ways of viewing the subject have always been akin those of the romantics.

3. THE MECHANISTIC SUBJECT CONCEPT

The mechanistic subject concept is the third we will treat here. In a sense, it is as old as the other two, although it first seriously came to the fore during the middle of the nineteenth century. The general background for this progression lies in the increasing independence of the sphere of pro-duction and its subjugation of both the spheres of circulation and intimacy.

A more specific cause is the advance of the medical and particularly the neurobiological sciences and their incorporation into the worldview of the natural sciences.

Changes in the structure of society concomitant with the advent of capitalism may be seen as processes whereby preponderance is shifted from the sphere of circulation to the sphere of production. During early capitalism (trade capitalism) the circulation of commodities exerted its obvious influence on the rest of society. It was the buying and selling of commodities that made society more homogeneous, turning it into one huge market, and it was commerce that demanded that society be given an organizing superstructure. Workshops and factories were considered small, privately owned islands in an otherwise free society. This situation was reversed as more was invested in the expansion of production (transition from trade capitalism to industrial capitalism). The logic of the sphere of production, according to which surplus value was created through the exploitation of the work force, became dominant in all of society. The spheres of intimacy and circulation became simple service organs for productive capital. Sensibility and love in the sphere of intimacy served to reproduce and restitute the work force, and the democratization of the state apparatus and the liberalization of public life took place based on the demands of capitalism, a fact which is attested by the laws passed against unions and strikes, for instance.

One of the conditions for the expansion of the sphere of production was advancing technology. In order to increase productivity it was necessary to develop ever more complex machines. The most striking example of this is the industrial exploitation of the steam engine to make steam-driven looms, locomotives, and so on. Capitalists were forced to take an interest in these matters if they wished to remain competitive. This is the background for the extraordinary rise of the natural sciences during the eighteenth and nineteenth centuries. Here, the mechanistic way of thinking was put to its most severe test, since no machine could be built without precise calculations concerning all its causal relations. The medical sciences followed a similar pattern of development and attempts were made to understand diseases as damage suffered by the mechanical relations of the body. Descartes had already given a unified mechanical description of the blood's circulation and the function of muscles and the senses, attuned to his view of the human body as a machine, as opposed to the human mind. But it was first during the 1800s that a thorough mapping out of the nervous system according to these principles was undertaken (see I.B). This paved the way for the mechanistic subject concept according to which man as a whole could be reduced to a machine, abolishing both the soul and free will. A new generation of researchers appeared in the natural sciences during the middle of the nineteenth century who took pride in eliminating all metaphysics from their thoughts. Emil du Bois-Reymond wrote in 1842 about himself and his friend Ernst Brücke, who was later to become Freud's mentor at the University of Vienna, that they had sworn an oath to show that no forces were active in the human organism other than common physiochemical ones. The goal was to undertake a mapping-out of the factors at play in the functioning of the body so thorough that nothing would be left that could be attributed to either chance or purely psychological causes.

We have said of the liberalistic and humanistic subject concepts that they reflected both general trends in the evolution of society and more specific changes in the character structure of the subject, and that they served as concrete ideological models in the organization of the spheres of circulation and intimacy. As we have seen, there is also evident correlation between the evolution of the sphere of production and the mechanistic subject concept, although it cannot be said that the mechanistic subject concept reflects any change in the subject's character structure, or that it serves as an ideological model for the organization of the production sphere or the subject's participation in production.

It would be tempting to conclude that the ever more monotonous and specialized tasks of the industrial worker, as depicted in Chaplin's *Modern Times* from 1936, led to changes in the worker's character structure. Although this is certainly true, it must also be kept in mind that the working class had not been the one to formulate the mechanistic subject concept, nor did it use it as a basis for positive self-understanding. Such extreme alienation would be unthinkable. Conversely, industrialists did not rally around the mechanistic subject concept either. Although they had nothing against making calculations placing manpower as an objective parameter of the production process alongside machines, they preferred to see workers as free subjects who sold their commodities (in this case, their labor power) for the highest price, and they seldom expressed any wish to curtail this freedom built into the market. In general, capitalists realized that their economic power was most effectively safeguarded by discretion.

Hence, neither workers nor capitalists were advocates of the mechanistic subject concept. The true standard-bearers of the new ideas came from the intellectual petite bourgeoisie, who neither had experience from the sphere of production nor was interested in it. Its views were based on the natural sciences, the expansion of which followed in the wake of the expansion of the sphere of production. The most decided mechanists were biologists who considered their research to be an end in itself. They were supported by a broader cultural movement, namely naturalism, whose ideal was the natural sciences. This movement emerged around 1860 and exerted some influence for the remainder of the century. The use of mechanism to combat religious dogma and bourgeois moral norms was a trait the naturalists had in common. It is difficult to say if they understood the social compulsion of capitalism, since they pointed out the freedom lacking in society even more radically than the liberalists. This was a logical consequence of the contradiction between feeling and the freedom of reason (as ideals of the romantic and liberalistic subject concepts, respectively). The naturalists imagined that a positive synthesis was possible with the help of the natural sciences, a social system where both feelings and reason would have their place.

In practice, however, it was not easy to imagine even in a distant future a realm of freedom placed within the worldview of the natural sciences. It was, after all, necessary to choose between freedom and determinism, and there was a tendency (for example, in Brandes, Ibsen, and Nietzsche) to attribute freedom to an intellectual elite and determinism to the broad masses, that is, to solve the problem by working for a political system in which the elite took major decisions on behalf of the masses. Let us likewise note that in our century the mechanistic subject concept has gained the widest extension in corporative and totalitarian social systems (behaviorism in the United States and neurobiological reductionism in the Soviet Union).

During the nineteenth century the mechanistic subject concept took the form in part of concrete studies of the human nervous system (reflexes, brain centers, and so on) and in part of tentative attempts to place all earlier experiences concerning human beings in the polarity of heredity and environment. The work done by the philosophical psychology of the 1600s and 1700s with rules of reason and thought associations could be pursued by studying how people adapted to the environment, how they learned from experience, and how they surmounted dangers and difficulties. Correspondingly, the interest in emotional life was taken over from the romantics by describing feelings as inherited instincts and reflexes. Excessive or perverted feelings were ascribed by many to faulty heredity (so-called degeneration). It is easy to show the ideological principles behind the would-be scientific objectivity and neutrality. Normality and health were not themselves put into question, and physicians obviously held adaptation and effectivity as ideals of health. They endeavored to make their patients fit so as to be able to fulfill the demands made on them by society.

4. COMPARISON OF
THE THREE SUBJECT CONCEPTS

We have now delineated the main contours of the three subject concepts that emerged over a period of two to three hundred years coextensive with the rise of capitalism. Obviously, their views on the human subject differ. Nonetheless they are comparable because they seem to be based on the same division of the subject. The subject is comprised of two parts; one is inborn, the other acquired during childhood and adolescence. Throughout life, the two parts are in latent or manifest conflict with each other. The question is whether one of the two parts will dominate the subject or whether a compromise can be reached between them.

In the liberalistic subject concept, emotions and reason are opposed. Emotions are the expression of the body's needs, and are already active at birth. It was posited by some of the philosophers of the time that reason was also inborn as a *res cogitans* that first manifested itself after being activated by education and discipline. Free will is the very essence of the operational mode of reason. One is only free when guided by reason, while unfree, or determined, in one's actions when carried away by one's feelings. The typical conflict can be formulated by the question of whether one must choose what is immediately pleasurable or pursue a more distant goal, tolerating the temporary unpleasure that comes from not yielding to an inclination for pleasure.

The humanistic subject concept moves in a diametrically opposed direction saying one does best in letting oneself be guided by one's feelings, because feelings cannot lie. Man's true and original nature is found in children and women, while in man himself it has been perverted by cool calculation. Man has devoted himself to reason and utility to such an extent that he has forgotten his feelings and all of mankind has been led astray by this.

In the mechanistic subject concept, the above contradiction and conflict has been somewhat neutralized, since emotions and reason are considered to be objective and causally determined phenomena. Emotions are a result of inherited instincts and reflexive actions, while reason is derived from adaptation to the environment. It is no longer a question of preferring one to the other. In any case the subject is the product of the interaction between inheritance and environment, and both factors may lead to illness and thus unsettle the subject as a whole. It is possible to be tainted by both inheritance and environment. In each case the goal is normalization.

This schematic survey perforce erases all individual differences within each of the three subject concepts, just as it leaves mixed forms out of consideration. On the other hand, we get a picture of the logical extremes of the discussion on the nature of the subject and will venture to present a comparative scheme based on this. The three subject concepts are decidedly

	inborn	acquired
LIBERALISTIC SUBJECT CONCEPT	feelings, passions determination the uncultivated	reason, self-control free will the cultivated
HUMANISTIC SUBJECT CONCEPT	feelings, spontaneity freedom, self-determination the natural	insensitivity, calculation coercion, exploitation the unnatural
MECHANISTIC SUBJECT CONCEPT	heredity species, instincts nature	environment individual, adaptation culture

ideological. They do not tell us the truth about the subject, but rather something about what the subject looks like when seen from specific and narrowly defined points of view. If one wishes to understand why they have arisen and why they have taken precisely the form they have, it is necessary to explore their societal backgrounds. In the preceding section, we have called attention to a number of traits concerning structural changes in society under capitalism (division into spheres attending to specific functions), concerning the political and ideological functions of each subject concept, and concerning changes in the subject's character structure. Carrying out such an analysis can be rendered difficult by the fact that a subject concept can be determined by specific, mutually opposed factors. This seemed to be the case for the mechanistic subject concept, to which we shall shortly return. Here again, it is necessary for us to accept imprecisions and simplifications in order to get a general view.

The expansion of the sphere of circulation contemporaneous to trade capitalism is the background from which the liberalistic subject concept emerged. It was imperative for the new class of trade capitalists to break down the societal barriers hindering the free flow of capital and commodities. The spirit of liberty was an ideological rallying point for the bourgeoisie and lower classes in their struggle against absolute monarchy. The liberalistic subject concept functioned in a similar manner as a model for the bourgeoisie's self-understanding and for the disciplining of the lower classes. The idea that freedom was linked to responsibility, and therefore that freedom had to be purchased with renunciation and privation, was the essence of bourgeois self-understanding. Finally, the liberalistic subject concept reflected changes in the subject's character structure that were a consequence of his increased self-disciplining. Using psychoanalytic terminology, a strengthening of the superego must have taken place; self-esteem and selfishness were on the rise, it is true, but not at the expense of significant efforts made to reach transindividual political goals.

The creation of the sphere of intimacy where reproductive functions were to be attended to provided the social background of the humanistic subject concept. Within the new (petit) bourgeois nuclear family a context was established in which the subject could unfold its intimate sides, where sensitivity and intimacy had a central position. These new values formed the ideological rallying point for the reaction against capitalism. Romanticism thus created a paradoxical alliance between the economically pressed petite bourgeoisie and the politically pressed apparatus of the absolute state. Internally, humanistic ideas served as ideological models of education for the organization of the sphere of intimacy. Women and children especially found an easy and positive possibility for self-understanding in the humanistic subject concept. However, only the unreflective belief in authority (of the family, the king, and God) took the sting out of outwardly directed criticism. Renewed interest in children in the family probably intensified their emotional life, strengthening their dependency on infantile fantasies and reaction patterns. This real change in their character structure in itself made them more susceptible to humanistic self-understanding.

As stated earlier, the mechanistic subject concept is difficult to explain. The mechanistic way of thought originates in the natural sciences, whose advance in the eighteenth and nineteenth centuries is again related to the sphere of production and its explosive development after the breakthrough of industrialism. The mechanistic subject concept did not function, however, as a medium through which any group or class achieved positive self-understanding. It follows therefore that its ideological function is less transparent than is the case for the other two subject concepts. Scientists and intellectuals from the humanities were the first to come into line with it. At first they used it to criticize the hypocrisy of bourgeois society, but it later came to serve the interests of the industrial bourgeoisie. By turning questions regarding the subject into purely scientific matters, it contributed in a number of cases to neutralizing political and ideological discussions concerning, for example, the inhumanity of work in factories, the right to own the means of production, and the democratic rights of the population. Much has been legitimatized and explained by science under the cover of neutrality and objectivity. During the nineteenth century, ideas concerning disease and man's (biological) nature were grossly manipulated to serve purely political interests. It is difficult to say whether it is also possible to note a real change in the character structure of the subject as a consequence of the mechanistic subject concept. In any case, such a change hardly affected those who formulated it, but rather the wage earners who became more and more alienated in the production process as a result of giving up self-determination and the fragmentation of their lives. In their case, it can be said that life took on such an automatic, causally determined, and mechanical quality that it must also have exerted some influence on their character structure. Psychoanalytically speaking, this would correspond to a psychosis where people are perceived as machines and where the subject even perceives itself as a machine.

B.
THE SUBJECT IN PHILOSOPHY, NATURAL SCIENCE, AND LITERATURE

This section will attempt to show how the three concepts of the subject find expression in fields bordering on psychoanalysis that may have exerted some influence on it. We can in each field trace the same pattern of development that we roughly sketched in section A, that is, the transition from rationalism (with a liberalistic concept of the subject) through romanticism (with a humanistic concept of the subject) to naturalism (with a mechanistic concept of the subject). There are, of course, considerable individual differences. For example, the sciences in particular were not measurably affected by romanticism. Moreover, there are a number of specialized discussions motivated by concrete research, which should not therefore be traced back to any single concept of the subject. Such reservations apply, for example, to the case of several philosophers in the 1600s who became mechanists because as such they were better able to describe the laws of thought associations, even though they, in league with other contemporary philosophers, otherwise granted the subject the ability to make rational choices.

In choosing material for this section, we have only included writers with whom we are certain or presume Freud was familiar before the turn of the century. We would like to emphasize that the main contours of psychoanalytic theory were formulated as early as 1897, and we have therefore attempted to trace all the theoretical fragments with which Freud grappled up to this point. In our presentation of the result we move in the opposite direction, considering not only psychoanalysis as a product of a number of internally heterogeneous sources, but in addition as a logical stage in the historical development of these sources themselves. We therefore treat the development of, for example, neurophysiology, psychology, and psychiatry as well. Naturally, we did not grant priority to individual fields or individual writers according to their intrinsic significance, but rather in relation to their importance for psychoanalysis. This section does not therefore pretend to be a general introduction to the natural sciences and humanities in the 1800s. Furthermore, we could not include all the writers who in one way or another are "related" to Freud. Such an undertaking would be futile. We do not deal with Kierkegaard, Schopenhauer, or Nietzsche. They did not influence Freud, even though it can be argued that they expressed in philosophical terminology some of the ideas that Freud expressed scientifically.

This section consists, therefore, of sources of psychoanalysis placed in their historical context. Our discussion of these sources by fields (philosophy, biology, physics, neurophysiology, and so forth), might seem traditional and cumbersome, but it serves to clarify the general argument and there is really no alternative when attempting to give a sober presentation of such a large corpus of material.

1. PHILOSOPHY

Freud never studied philosophy systematically. During his student years, he attended a number of lectures on the history of philosophy from Descartes to Kant (see II.A.2). By his own admission, however, he did not keep abreast of contemporary philosophy. In this section, therefore, we have selected the philosophical problems of the seventeenth and eighteenth centuries that we believe to be related to psychoanalysis. We can only conjecture as to whether these problems exerted any direct influence on psychoanalytic thought.

Having already discussed Descartes' dualism (res cogitans and res extensa) and his theory of interaction (see I.A.1), we will start with another example of how the liberalistic concept of the subject was converted into a psychological theory: a treatise by Thomas Hobbes (1588–1679) entitled Human Nature or the Fundamental Elements of Policy (written in 1640, but not published until 1650). Hobbes was, of course, hardly a liberal. He denied the existence of free will and believed that dictatorship was the best form of government. However, his psychological theory contained the same

division of the subject into passions and reason as the more liberal philosophers, and he saw his primary task as describing how reason was capable
of controlling the emotions.

Hobbes believed that the psychical mediated between the body and the
world. As mentioned before, the psychical was itself divided into passions
and reason. The passions represented the impulses of the body, while reason
represented the impulses of the world. Following the precepts of ancient
philosophy, Hobbes located the passions in the heart and reason in the
brain (a localization that persists in figurative language). Heart and brain
were thought to be connected by a large number of nerve fibers through
which "the animal spirits" circulated. Nerves were perceived as hollow
tubes and the animal spirits as gases. Psychical activity involved the movement of the animal spirits either by the transference of oscillations from
the world or by warming the heart. A simple model of the psychic apparatus
will serve to illuminate the interaction of the different elements. Sense

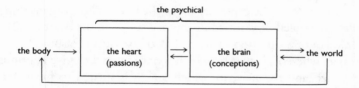

perception involved the transference of oscillations from an external object
to the mind. For Hobbes, ". . . image and color is but an apparition to us
of that motion, agitation, or alteration which the object worketh in the
brain or spirits, or some *internal* substance in the head" (Hobbes 1650, p.
186). Only when the object was present was the conception called a sense;
when it was absent, it was called a memory. Fantasy or memory was the
blurred image that remained and gradually faded after the sense perception
process had been completed. Hobbes used the image of rings in water that
do not stop appearing after the stone causing them has sunk to the bottom
of the lake. The theory of movement perceived thought and association
processes as types of chain reactions. The sequence of conscious ideas could
be both random and ordered. It was random in the dream state, but ordered
in the waking state. Temporal and spacial contact was the most fundamental
law of association. Other associations consisted of the nexus of cause and
effect and means and ends. Compared with later associationist psychology,
Hobbes's association theory is touchingly primitive, as the following quote
illustrates:

> The *cause* of the *coherence* or consequence of one conception to another, is their first *coherence* or consequence at the *time* when they are produced by sense: as for example, from St. Andrew the mind runneth to St. Peter, because their names are read together; from St. Peter to a *stone,* for the same cause; from *stone* to *foundation,* because we see them together; and for the same cause, from foundation to *church,* and from church to *people,* and from people to *tumult;* and according to this example, the mind may run almost from anything to anything (Hobbes 1650, p. 193).

Oscillations causing conceptions and associations in the brain did not stop in the brain but continued on to the heart, where they either facilitated or impeded the so-called vital motion. Pleasure arose when the vital motion was facilitated. When it was impeded; unpleasure arose. Every idea in the mind was thus potentially linked with a passion in the heart: pleasure combined with the object causing desire was called love, while unpleasure combined with its object was hate.

However, passions did not chiefly stem from the external sense perception, but rather from the other organs of the body. These organs impeded or facilitated, cooled or warmed the animal spirits in the heart in different ways. It was not a question of need, but of "sensual pleasures," ". . . the *greatest* part whereof, is that by which we are invited to give continuance to our *species;* and the *next,* by which a man is invited to meet, for the preservation of his *individual* person" (Hobbes 1650, p. 209). The idea was that corporal conditions influenced the heart, which in turn caused the brain to oscillate. It was the brain that provoked a movement possibly able to procure the object the body was lacking. Pleasure and unpleasure or "appetite" and "fear" were for Hobbes *"the first unperceived beginnings of our actions"* (Hobbes 1650, p. 237) and consequently made up the *will.*

> This motion, in which consisteth *pleasure* or *pain,* is also a *solicitation* or provocation either to draw *near* to the thing that pleaseth, or to *retire* from the thing that displeaseth; and this solicitation is the *endeavor* or internal beginning of *animal* motion, which when the object *delighteth,* is called *appetite;* when it *displeaseth,* it is called *aversion,* in respect to the displeasure *present;* but in respect of the displeasure *expected, fear"* (Hobbes 1650, p. 207).

Hobbes attempted to sustain the tenet of pleasure/unpleasure in detail and this same classification lay behind the description of other well-known emotions as pride, humility, hope, despair, compassion, indignation, shame, and bliss.

Volitional impulses did not lead directly to action, but were first considered in the brain. If the goal was the procurement of a specific object or condition, the objective of reasoning was to discover the shortest route to this object or condition, that is, to devise the series of means by which the end could be achieved, "as, when a man, from a thought of *honor* to which he hath an appetite cometh to the thought of *wisdom,* which is the next means thereunto; and from thence to the thought of *study,* which is the next means to wisdom" (Hobbes 1650, p. 193). Consideration passed through ideas, which in turn involved desire and repugnance or fear, in other words, the wish to achieve pleasure and avoid unpleasure. The goal would often be pleasurable and the means unpleasurable. The strength of reasoning lay in resisting immediate unpleasure by imagining future pleasure. By the same token, reasoning was able to impede an immediate pleasurable action by imagining future unpleasure. The educational ideal of early capitalist culture is reflected here in the one-sided tribute to reason, self-control, and calculation.

We can trace two relatively separate themes in Hobbes. First, the question of how external objects are perceived and how associational paths are formed between the representational elements. This question is dealt with in epistemological theories. Second, the question of how the thoughts and actions of the subject are related to emotions. This question is treated in ethics. Epistemology regards man as a knowing or observing subject. It is generally preoccupied with the question of the possibility and veracity of cognition. Psychology influenced by epistemological theory is based on themes such as sensation, perception, memory, and reasoning. This tradition became increasingly popular within the field of experimental psychology emerging in the latter half of the nineteenth century, which consequently was marked by associationistic ideas (associations between elements of representation stemming from the senses). Ethics, or moral philosophy, regards man as a desiring subject forced to control his desire and adjust his behavior according to various moral and social laws. Psychological theory influenced by ethics seeks to comprehend the nature and origins of desire. Such theories became a part of scientific psychology and later psychoanalysis via neurophysiology.

(a) The Philosophy of Knowledge and Association Psychology

The most important area of epistemological discussion in the seventeenth and eighteenth centuries concerned to what extent the knowing ego (reason) was innate. Rationalists like Descartes claimed that the subject was equipped with certain innate ideas already prior to the first sense perception. Of course, these were not ideas about houses, trees, and the like, but rather ideas about common logical contexts. Kant employed twelve common categories used by the intellect to know and classify the outside world. These twelve categories were classified in four groups—quantity, quality, relation, and modality—each containing three categories. Empiricists like Hobbes, on the other hand, believed that the isolated subject was nothing more than an empty form receiving sense impressions. Locke went so far as to characterize the subject as a *tabula rasa* (empty blackboard) that was gradually filled with ideas.

From our critical view of the subject, this discussion of innate ideas is not so important. Both rationalists and empiricists embraced the educational ideals and pedagogy of what we have called the liberalistic concept of the subject. The claim that the subject has innate characteristics is only influenced by ideology when it is used to classify subjects in races or classes, or when it leads to assumptions of psychic differences between the sexes.

We will instead focus on how the division of the subject into emotion and reason finds expression in epistemology. Epistemological philosophers intended to discover true knowledge of the world by eliminating subjective sources of error. Francis Bacon (1561–1626) had already pointed to the illusions of the human spirit, that is, characteristics of human subjectivity leading to the admission of mistakes and distortion of the truth. One example of this is individual interests: the subject only sees what he wants to see. To make a correct observation, the subject must forget himself, in order that the world be perceived as lucidly as possible. This division of the subject became even more pronounced after Bacon. It was claimed that the subject perceived with the senses and reason, not with the emotions and desire. The emotional part of the subject should therefore be eliminated. Most writers could give examples of how people possessed of violent passions were also robbed of their normal sense of judgment. Intense infatuation exempted the loved one from all faults, while strong hatred made the hated person worse than he really was. However, sources of error could also appear with sense perception. When the subject sensed a knife, characteristics like shape and size were objective sensations, while the pain experienced by being cut was a subjective sensation, not an innate characteristic of the knife.

But how does perception function after the emotional part of the subject has been removed and the rational part has been isolated? In *An Essay*

Concerning Human Understanding from 1690, John Locke argued that the characteristics of the world passed through the senses as simple ideas ("ideas of one sense"), for example, "yellow," "warm," "hard," and "bitter"; "the coldness and hardness which a man feels in a piece of *ice* being distinct *ideas* in the mind as the smell and whiteness of a lily, or as a taste of sugar, and smell of a rose" (Locke, 1690, p. 90). When simple ideas had been established, reasoning could commence. Reasoning consisted of consciousness moving from element to element, in other words, of associations between elements. Locke used somewhat the same types of association as Hobbes. Thus similarity was a principle for thought; two substances resembling each other or having something in common were naturally connected by an association. Another principle was proximity in time and space: if the subject had experienced two things simultaneously and/or concurrently with each other, he would automatically think of the other when experiencing the one thing in isolation. A third principle was causality, that is, the way thought combines cause and effect, means and ends. Associations generally served to imitate relations found in the world. Judgment determined what characteristics an object possessed, whether or not it could be the cause of a certain effect, and so forth. While sense perception of simple ideas was regarded as an objective process, thought was vulnerable to the disruptive influences of emotions, for judgment was an act of will. In principle, true knowledge was only possible if the will to true knowledge was present in addition to other volitional impulses of the subject.

Another question preoccupying epistemological philosophers was that of nonrealized properties in the world. It became common practice to assume that objects in one way or another possessed an essence that could not be apprehended. This essence could be something in the objects themselves or in their mutual relations. We will give an example of how nonrealized properties in the world are placed positively as nonknowledge in the psychic sphere. In this lies a nascent concretization of the unconscious, which of course plays an important role in psychoanalysis. The example is taken from the Leibniz philosophy.

G. W. Leibniz (1646–1716) is known primarily for his theory of monads, which holds that the material world is composed of indivisible infinitesimal particles, the so-called monads. These monads are incorporeal and can be compared to souls. Each one of them in the entire universe contains an image of all the others and comprises therefore its own miniature world. The differences between them are due to their different positions in the totality. The contents of each monad correspond to its particular perspective vis-à-vis the other monads. Thus no two monads are alike. The movements of the monads are not causal, but rather determined by the goal they are attempting to reach. They are incapable of exerting any influence on each other and develop in harmony like a number of clocks synchronized always to tell the same time.

Leibniz transferred this train of thought to psychology by regarding man as a multitude of monads with the soul functioning as the "leading monad." In Leibnitz's theory the perceptions of the soul (a concept devoid of its common meaning) are extremely comprehensive, for they must contain the image of the entire universe, all that has occurred and will occur in it. Such comprehensive knowledge is of course not directly contained in the individual soul, where only few perceptions are clearly evident at any one time. Leibniz's theory, however, employs several levels of consciousness, and can thus argue that at any given time residual knowledge is present in a kind of unconscious form as "small perceptions." Actual consciousness need not come to a halt in front of the object of its immediate perception, but can by association continue to travel to the cause of the object, then further on to the cause of the cause in an endless chainlike structure linking the entire universe in a synthesis of time and space. Leibniz provided academic examples of his theory. When observing a crowded street, for instance an image of the whole is apparent, but the endless numbers of details comprising this image are not all clearly evident. The same applies to the very weak perceptions of the initial hidden causes and the more or less predictable prospective effects. They form a swarm of unclear thoughts. It is these "small perceptions" that have been called the first philosophical formulation of the unconscious.

(b) Ethics and Dynamic Psychology

Emotions and desire faced sense perception and reason in the divided subject. The predominant philosophers of the seventeenth and eighteenth centuries attempted to intensify knowledge by isolating sense perception and reason and eliminating emotions and desire. Their paramount task was to determine what was true and false in cognition of the world. However, there were still philosophers preoccupied with ethical questions, that is, questions of what was good and evil for man and in man. These questions focused on emotions and desire, while cognition of the world was relegated to an instructive function. Emotions and desire determined the ends of human action, while the senses and reason calculated the means by which to achieve this end. Thus ethics came to be preoccupied with human desire and emotions. Many theories on what man actually desired were formulated. Some of these theories spoke of the pursuit of happiness and bliss, others of the pursuit of pleasure and the avoidance of unpleasure. An example of the latter, Hobbes's theory of pleasure/unpleasure, has already been mentioned: when bodily needs were not satisfied, the result was increasing unpleasure, which was only replaced by a feeling of pleasure when the satisfaction of needs had been initiated. This line of thought was almost predominant in ethics as religious dogma gradually lost its influence. Pleasure and unpleasure defined good and evil respectively, not vice versa.

The most important question for Enlightenment philosophers was how to learn to control the emotions when immediate satisfaction of needs was impossible or deleterious. Both Hobbes and Spinoza acknowledged that reason alone could accomplish nothing. Emotions were involved in rejecting immediate gratification by thinking of the unpleasure that would result from it. Inhibition proceeded from this unpleasure and not from reason itself, as Spinoza made clear in his *Ethics* from 1677 in which he claimed that a feeling could not be inhibited without a stronger feeling opposed to it.

According to Spinoza's theory, emotion and reason are actually intertwined. Emotions were a primitive form of thought, while reason is a highly developed form of emotion. Passionate emotions are primitive thoughts leaping from one idea to another without logical sequence. Logical thought is passive emotion moving from one idea to another without appreciable fluctuations. In their purest form emotions can thus be regarded as quantitative and mobile psychic energy linking ideas by different rules. In order to control any given emotion, it is necessary to attempt to separate it from the idea by thinking of something else; the emotion is then destroyed. For example, in order to control a passionate love for another person, the subject can try to think of God and see whether his passion is then subdued (and his love for God increased). The quantitative and economical view is also evident in Spinoza's recommendation to lead one confused emotion toward a coherent set of quiet emotions. The confused emotion will then either disrupt thought or be incorporated into the other emotions. This process is equivalent to the tenet that a passive feeling is no longer passive as soon as we form a clear idea about it.

We have already noted the connection between the establishment of the sphere of intimacy at the end of the 1700s and beginning of the 1800s and the internalization of emotions and the intensification of emotional life. In philosophy, Spinoza's description of emotions contributed to their reevaluation, and it is no accident that Spinoza was "rediscovered" during the romantic period. This new current of thought was expressed by Rousseau in the 1760s, when he changed his attitude toward the nature of emotions in a number of important works. He believed that emotions were not primarily destructive and asocial urges reducing men to the level of animals, but rather impulses leading to the expression of positive characteristics. Society destroyed these impulses and altered their content. The positive values of life—sensitivity, childhood, nature, and the national past—were emphasized as a positive bulwark against a society hostile to the emotions.

Romanticism embodied a serious attempt to reconstitute unappreciated and underrated emotions. In Romanticism, the ancient humanist injunction "know thyself" is leveled against the hypocrisy of society. Man should be known by his emotions and will inevitably find something of value by searching the depths of his soul. Suppressed emotions should find release in fantasy, and poetry can serve as a model of how these hidden treasures can once again be unearthed. Much symbolism is associated with archeology. However, emotions must not be distorted and used against their original intention, that is, the unearthed treasures must not be worshipped merely for their exchange value. (Mining was especially condemned by Romantic poets; see I.B.6 on literature.)

The rehabilitation of the emotions in philosophy caused a number of philosophers to stop isolating the cognition of the world from the emotions, as the Empiricists had attempted to do. The result was that there was no pure or true cognition of the world before desire, because desire determined interest in knowledge. Knowledge was intentional, that is, it was dependent on the intentions of the subject. Different versions of this view can be found in Hegel, Kierkegaard, Marx, Schopenhauer, and Brentano. This view is also found in Freud, but we will venture the conjecture that it came to him indirectly: from Herbart to Fechner, perhaps from Schopenhauer to von Hartmann, and perhaps inspired by Brentano's lectures on the history of philosophy. (We do not believe that Freud was directly influenced by Brentano's phenomenological theories. The lectures were about the history of philosophy and Freud's own theoretical development shows no sign of any phenomenological influence.)

J. F. Herbart (1776–1841) succeeded Kant as professor of philosophy at Göttingen. He intended to make philosophy an independent discipline based on experience, metaphysics, and mathematics. Basing his theories on Leibniz, he created a tangible concept of the unconscious in which he united the unperceived in the world and the unperceived in the subject (part of the emotions and desire). The soul was thought of as a mass composed of ideas, which in turn were regarded as forces. Moreover, the soul contained a threshold of consciousness. That which crossed over this threshold was conscious, that which lay under it was unconscious. The main rule was that strong ideas, because of their inherent strength, were able to force their way to a position over the threshold of consciousness. Psychic processes could, however, release individual ideas from the position of equilibrium they held relative to their strength. There was a constant struggle among ideas attempting to cross over the threshold of consciousness. In this struggle, strong ideas could temporarily be forced down into the unconscious, while weak ideas could unite and become conscious thanks to their collective strength. Strong ideas that remained for a longer period of time under the threshold were conspicuous as emotions and desire without representational content. These emotions enabled them to fight their way back to consciousness. Herbart attempted to describe the mathematical relationship between the conscious idea and the unconscious ideas it repressed. In principle, this description paved the way for a dynamic understanding of the dependence of consciousness on the unconscious. Herbart, however, did not succeed in his endeavor partly because he relied more on Leibniz's metaphysics than on concrete experience and analyses. Although Herbart is largely forgotten today, he exerted considerable influence on German psychology in the 1800s. For example, G. T. Fechner drew on his concept of the threshold of consciousness (see I.B.4 on psychology).

Like Herbart, Schopenhauer's pupil E. von Hartmann (1842–1906) is known for his attempt to conceptualize the unconscious. In 1868 he published the comprehensive and at the time widely read *Philosophie des Unbewussten (Philosophy of the Unconscious)*. In this work, von Hartmann classified different forms of the unconscious, from the unconscious in physical processes to the unconscious in biological evolutionary systems and instincts, ending with the psychical unconscious. Among the characteristics of the unconscious were the inability to be sick, become tired, doubt, or make mistakes. It could initiate actions with great precision, but without being conscious of the goal. On the whole, the impression is one of a superior, noncorporeal, and somewhat mystical intelligence, a romantic attempt to hold natural laws responsible for a universal metaphysical essence. Von Hartmann's sudden fall to obscurity in our century bears witness to the inconsistency and transient nature of his theories. However, von Hartmann's and Herbart's preoccupation with the unconscious might well have inspired Freud to develop just this concept.

2. PHYSICS AND BIOLOGY

The scientific investigation of man was conducted in biology. Consequently, biology became the battleground for different views on the subject. From the seventeenth century onward, conscious attempts were made to transfer the concepts of mechanical physics to biology (for example, in the description of the circulatory system, sensory motor reflexes, and muscle functions). These attempts formed the beginning of the modern mechanistic view of the subject. Opposed to this view was the so-called vitalist view that the living organism is fundamentally different in structure from dead matter. According to vitalism, biological laws differ from physical laws. Biological phenomena such as reproduction and growth can never be reduced to physical or chemical laws. Organic matter (plants, animals, and people, for example) contains mutually heterogeneous structures, each with their own distinctive features.

The conflict between mechanism and vitalism is historically displaced. The mechanists of the 1600s have much in common with the vitalists of the 1800s, an illustration of how mechanism gained ground at the expense of vitalism. In the 1600s and the greater part of the 1700s, both mechanists and vitalists believed that man had a soul and that that soul was related to God. For mechanists like Hobbes and Spinoza, however, God existed only as the first cause of all movements. When these movements were activated, they proceeded causally. In this scheme of things, God was present in equal measure in inorganic and organic matter. The animal spirits of living organisms were material. They were gases, liquids, or the like, circulating in the body like blood and following the laws of physics. They were present in the entire body and their task was to receive sense impressions and initiate muscle reactions. They could be affected by both heat and mechanical shock, and their movements corresponded to emotions (see the discussion of Hobbes in the section on philosophy). The vitalists believed that the soul was composed of animal spirits given to each individual directly by God. They were consequently regarded as "spiritual" and immaterial. They were at times referred to as "vital force" or "life force," and functioned teleologically, not causally.

The vitalists dominated biology in the beginning of the nineteenth century, but they had, as mentioned earlier, incorporated many mechanistic views. Only the most romantic vitalists espousing the philosophy of nature claimed that nature was animated and sought a higher goal. Vitalists with a more scientific bent could agree that the animal spirits were matter and could be subject to scientific investigation. They nevertheless clung to the view that organic matter was not controlled by causal mechanisms, but rather by its own intrinsic expediency. Furthermore, they believed that it was possible to show characteristics in organic matter totally lacking in inorganic matter, therefore making it impossible to reduce the former to the latter. Examples used were sensibility (a characteristic of the tissue of sensory organs) and irritability (a characteristic of muscle tissue).

The reaction against vitalism made itself felt in earnest at about the middle of the nineteenth century. Many of the concepts of vitalism were so speculative and metaphysical that they could be disproved with the help of empirical observations. For example, proof that the animal spirits in the nerves could not be gases was established by holding a severed frog's leg under water and observing that it didn't produce any bubbles. Another example can be taken from the study of organic cells. In 1839, Schleiden and Schwann advanced independently of each other a cell theory for all organisms based on microscopic investigations of different types of tissue. They showed that all living matter—from plants to primitive animals to man—were biologically constructed by the same type of substance: cells. Schwann also postulated that cells were constructed as crystals and had therefore the same structure as inorganic matter. Theoretically, there was thus a continuous development from the simplest particles in nature to man.

The success of mechanism was not completely grounded in empirical observation. There was a tendency to generalize and theorize from rather flimsy foundations. The new scientific theories, which were a reaction to the philosophy of nature, thus had philosophical overtones. We move now to the two mechanist theories that exerted the greatest influence on naturalists for the remainder of the nineteenth century and were defended with the greatest fanaticism. The first is Helmholtz's theory of energy, which did away with the vital forces in all organisms in favor of physical and chemical forces. The second is Darwin's theory of evolution, which rejected theories of expediency in favor of causal interpretations. Helmholtz and Darwin were both careful not to make generalizations from their theories, but their caution did not prevent their followers from focusing exclusively on the mechanistic aspects of these theories. In Freud we can see a typical example of this in that his fascination with ideas from romanticism and the philosophy of nature in his secondary school years was transformed into enthusiasm for extreme forms of mechanism in his university years.

(a) The Theory
of the Conservation of Energy

During industrialization, some handicrafts were replaced by machines. Part of the efficiency of these machines lay in their size. They could not be operated by people or the draught animals formerly used almost exclusively as an energy source, but were based on steam energy. The first steam engines were not very efficient. Most of the energy was wasted, partly because the boilers were badly insulated. Gradual improvements in machine construction led to a better understanding of the value of the energy source. If coal were employed more efficiently, less would be needed. The discovery of new and better energy sources would reduce the cost of production and increase productivity.

It was as a result of such considerations, which seem almost self-evident today, that the new energy theories flourished in the nineteenth century. It was formerly assumed that "forces" in nature caused movement. However, these forces were thought to vary qualitatively. Thus there could be a "tension force," a "chemical force," and special "vital forces" in man. Those proposing the industrial exploitation of different energy sources did not take these differences into account to the same degree. They wanted instead to compare the labor capability of these energy sources, in other words, their ability to move a given mass. To this end, formulas were worked out to gauge the relationship between, for example, kinetic energy, heat energy, and electric energy.

Hermann von Helmholtz (1821–1894) is usually thought of as representing the crossroads between the old and the new energy theory. In 1847 he advanced a mathematical theory of the conservation of energy. This theory was based on the discovery that one form of energy could be transformed into another according to certain rules. For example, kinetic energy in a steam engine could be achieved through the use of heat energy. Heat energy was derived from the chemical energy of coal, which in turn came from solar energy. Kinetic energy was usually produced from potential energy but could also be transformed into potential energy. It was as if the energy had continued to exist in one form or another and could not have been used up. On the other hand, it was impossible to create energy from nothing. Helmholtz thus chastised inventors who thought they could construct a perpetual motion machine. According to Helmholtz, energy could neither be created nor destroyed. It could only be transformed from one form to another. His theory was therefore based on the proposition that energy was conserved in a closed system.

Helmholtz's theory did not solve the problems facing industry, however. Enormous amounts of energy were apparently still wasted. When coal has been consumed and steam has done its job, no energy remains, because the machines have transferred their energy to the surrounding air. The air has been both set in motion and heated. This new energy cannot once again be transformed into labor power, but experiments show that this energy is as great as the energy admitted. This phenomenon forms an addendum to the principle of the conservation of energy: heat can only be transformed into mechanical labor power after it has been transferred from a warmer to a colder body. In a sense, it is then correct to regard the heat given off by machines to the air as wasted heat. It cannot be reused but seeps out into the atmosphere. Helmholtz called all usable forms of energy *free energy* (in the sense of available energy) and unavailable heat energy *bound energy*. Helmholtz's work was elaborated by a theory stating that all energy in the universe will eventually be transformed into latent heat energy leading to the end of all movement and all forms of life (the thermal death of the universe). Fechner advanced similar theories based on his belief that all movements try to attain a state of absolute stability (see I.B.4).

Helmholtz's general theory of energy had ramifications for biology and neurophysiology. The temperature of organisms (especially the question of how it was possible for the organism to maintain a constant temperature considerably higher than its surroundings) had long been a subject of contention among biologists. Their understanding of this phenomenon was broadened by regarding the organism as a machine for the transformation of energy. Food and drink served the same function for man as coal and water did for the steam engine. Similarly, attempts were made to juxtapose the energy of the nervous system with forms of energy found in physical nature. Consequently, the former life of spirits and vital forces was replaced by chemical and electrical impulses. Moreover, Helmholtz himself contributed to this field in 1850 by gauging the speed of nerve impulses with an electric measuring instrument. This simple experiment enabled Helmholtz to demonstrate that the nerve impulse did not move at astronomical speed, as previously thought, but at about 110 feet per second. He thus succeeded in clarifying a problem that had been the subject of much speculation for centuries.

(b) The Theory of Evolution

Until about 1800 it was commonly believed that plants and animals had been created in precisely the form they had. When the remains of extinct animals were found it was assumed that the species in question had disappeared after a natural catastrophe, and that God had then created new variations of the same species. J. B. Lamarck (1744–1829) was one of the first scientists to assert that the species were not unchanging but had attained their current forms by a process of evolution. According to this theory, the organism's motive for development lay in the needs it sought to satisfy. Through these needs the organism developed fixed patterns of behavior adapted to its environment. If the environment changed, making it more difficult for the organism to satisfy its needs, it adopted new patterns of behavior. In the course of several generations, these would become permanent characteristics that could be inherited. The best-known example states that the giraffe has literally stretched its neck to be able to reach the green leaves on the highest treetops. For Lamarck, the use (or disuse) of any given organ determined which characteristics would be inherited. Lamarck's theory can be summarized by two theses: first, that species become more highly developed as a result of an "inner will," and second, that acquired characteristics can be inherited.

These are the two theses Charles Darwin (1809–1882) rejected in his principal work from 1859 on the origin of the species and natural selection. According to Darwin's theory, an organism is only the carrier of a given heredity and that heredity is unaffected by the characteristics and abilities the organism might acquire in the course of its life. Actual changes in heredity are by contrast caused by random genetic mutations, to use contemporary terminology. These mutations do not obey any fixed principle. Most result in harmless changes in detail. Others are the direct cause of the death of the offspring, and only few provide the organism with better means of survival than its fellow members of the species. This last type is crucial for the development of the entire species because it determines which organisms actually survive. To take an example: in a large industrial region in England, a certain type of butterfly changed color from speckled white to coal black in the course of about one century. The white-speckled butterfly was originally perfectly adapted to the bark of birch trees. It was impossible to see and was therefore safe from predators. Then the factories came and their smoke and soot destroyed and blackened the bark of the birch trees. About one hundred years later, it was discovered that 99 percent of the butterflies in the region had black wings. Darwinist theory proposed that the reason for this transformation was not that the species as a whole had adapted to the new environment (as Lamarck thought the necks of giraffes had adapted to reach the treetops), but rather that several black mutations had come into being by accident and had survived in greater numbers than the white-speckled variant. A butterfly with black wings appeared accidentally and managed to survive. In the struggle for survival, organisms best able to adapt under any given condition survive, while those who cannot, die out.

As mentioned above, Darwin rejected not only Lamarck's theory that acquired characteristics were inherited, but his theory of the expediency of development as well. This point is especially important in connection with human evolution. According to Lamarck's theory, man undergoes a progressive evolution toward ever greater perfectibility or toward an ever greater control of nature by an inner will. Darwin refused to accept such a principle of evolution. For him, man's evolution was exclusively regulated by natural selection and the survival of the fittest. Evolution had no goal, but was determined by the blind chance of mutation, perhaps in harmony with changes in the environment. This theory is based on causality, not teleology (in other words, causal relations, not expedient relations). The scope of the debate raised by Darwinism can be better understood by adding to this theory Darwin's teaching on the descent of man, that is, the direct chain of evolution from prehistoric apes to modern man. This theory of man totally eliminated the humane as a self-evident aim and principle, and lumped man together with animals.

In Germany, evolutionary theory became especially popular in Ernst Haeckel's version. In 1866, Haeckel advanced the theory that ontogeny reproduced phylogeny, in other words, that a picture of the evolution of the human race from the first protoplasm could be attained by studying the development of a fertilized egg cell. This theory of recurrence has often been found in philosophy, for example, in Hegel, illustrating that natural science and philosophy had not yet become two distinct fields at that time. Another German Darwinist was August Weismann, who formulated a theory of heredity based on Darwin in the 1880s. In this theory, he differentiated between germ plasma and somatic plasma, germ plasma being the hereditary material and somatic plasma the remaining cells in the body, which were generated by germ plasma in every new organism. Germ plasma was theoretically immortal. All inherited characteristics were transmitted from the germ plasma to the somatic plasma, but characteristics acquired by somatic plasma could not be transmitted to the germ plasma. Acquired characteristics that appeared through the influence of the environment were caused by the direct influence of germ plasma. A good example of this is modern-day uranium radiation which measurably affects heredity.

Particularly in France and Germany, an inverted theory of evolution gained popularity. This was the so-called degeneration theory advanced by B. A. Morel in 1857. Degeneration was defined as inherited corporal or spiritual dissolution, which was steadily progressive if degenerates intermarried. The first generation had perhaps only nervous symptoms, the second hysteria or epilepsy, the third psychoses, the fourth idiocy, after which the family died out. Degeneration was thought to have been caused by alcohol and narcotics abuse, venereal disease, and even masturbation. Signs of degeneration appeared not only in the mind, but also in the body, for example, deformity of the cranium, deformed sexual organs, and clubfoot. According to degeneration theory, these signs could appear not only among the insane but also among criminals. Degeneration theory was particularly popular in psychiatry (see I.B.5) and served obvious moral, educational, and racial hygienic aims: people were frightened into leading more moral lives when the causes for degeneration were made known. Modern genetics has not been able to prove a single aspect of degeneration theory. It can therefore be concluded that this theory lacks any real foundation.

3. NEUROPHYSIOLOGY AND NEUROANATOMY

Research on the nervous system made considerable progress during the first decades of the nineteenth century. An important discovery found that sensory nerve paths (from the sense organ to the spinal cord) were anatomically separate from motor nerve paths (from the spinal cord to the muscle). It was previously believed that reflexes moved back and forth along the same path. Scientists then started to investigate which functions were carried out by the separate parts of the nervous system. The results of

the brain that alone determines the reflex of a single finger. The functions of the finger are controlled from several different centers simultaneously. However, the cortical centers control the spinal cord centers.

Taking his inspiration from Darwin and especially Herbert Spencer, Jackson called the progressive course of development of the nervous system *evolution* and used the term *dissolution* (corresponding to the terms *devolution* and *involution* used by other theorists) to describe the opposite course of development, where the functions of the higher centers were suspended and control of man was transferred to the lower centers. Jackson thus noted that when the brain was damaged, functions learned at a late stage of development were almost always lost, while functions learned early remained intact for the longest period. Severely enfeebled old people became as children again. They lost the ability to coordinate their actions and remember events from the distant past better than recent events.

(b) Instinct, Drive, and Affect

Associationist psychology was relatively easily assimilated into neurophysiology. However, this was not the case with dynamic psychology, which dealt with motivation. To be sure, motivation could be integrated into reflex theory: external stimulation could motivate flight, for example, while internal stimulation could motivate satisfaction of needs. The only problem was that reflexes developing from needs could not be demonstrated empirically. It was not known how the internal organs of the body influenced the nervous system or why the nervous system reacted as it did to stimulation. In attempting to answer the latter question, neurophysiologists employed the tenets of philosophical hedonism, which held that the affects—and in the last analysis pleasure and unpleasure—were the motivating factors. However, not much was known about the neurophysiological causes of these affects. As a rule, affect was placed somewhere in the middle of the nerve path and was not thought to have any independent ability to sever or deflect a reflex. The determining factor for affect lay in internal stimulation itself and in an abstract assumption that the function of the nervous system was to ensure the survival of the organism. By striving for pleasure and avoiding unpleasure, the nervous system also provided for the satisfaction of needs and a correct reaction to the dangers of the world as well as an opportunity for achieving satisfaction.

The difficulties underlying academic research into motivation caused many nineteenth-century neurophysiologists simply to avoid the issue. Müller thus openly admitted his ignorance of the subject. However, a smaller group of neurophysiologists constructed hypothetical models of motivation without recourse to empirical verification. They often used such terms as instinct, need, drive, affect, emotion, and feeling. We will in the following attempt to describe some of these theories, emphasizing those known to Freud. We have divided these theories into two groups: instinct theories and drive theories. However, they are not necessarily mutually exclusive; a person can have both instincts and drives.

The founders of modern evolutionary theory, Darwin and Spencer, were typical exponents of instinct theory. They claimed not only continuity in the development of animals and humans, but continuity in physical characteristics as well. It was unacceptable to regard animal behavior as determined by reflexes and human behavior as determined by the will as Descartes and many others had done. In reality, animal and human behavior could be regarded as a continuum ranging from simple spinal reflexes and relatively complex reflexes, which Spencer identified as instincts, to the most complex reflexes comprising the will. The difference between instincts and the will was that the former were innate and the latter was acquired. It had long been recognized that an entire animal species exhibited the same instinctive behavior regardless of environmental influences. For example, several fish from the same species could be placed in different environments along with other species of fish. In spite of the change in environment, they retained all the typical behavioral features of their species such as feeding habits; nest building, care of offspring, and the like. Since they could not learn this behavior by observing other fish, their behavior had to be innate. The theory was that the species retained or further developed the same reflex paths through heredity. Every one of the species had the same paths running from the sense organs and internal organs of the animals to the active muscles, and they therefore reacted in the same way. They could not act otherwise. Instincts were characterized by automatic, involuntary reactions.

In 1872, Darwin wrote a book on emotions in animals and man. He claimed that emotions were purely secondary attributes of instincts. Darwin was not interested in the subjective side of emotions, but rather in their objective expression, for example, smiling, blushing, frowning, and crying. A rather primitive neurophysiological model based on Müller's textbook was used for theoretical background: the sense organs and the internal organs stimulated the nervous system, creating nervous energy. This nervous energy then traveled through prefabricated paths until it caused an expedient reaction, such as flight, attack, or approach. Surplus nervous energy was produced in especially embarrassing situations. This nervous energy had to abreact in the closest nerve paths, and since facial muscles were closest to the eyes and ears, emotional expression would almost always produce facial reactions. There were special facial muscles for, for example, laughter and sorrow. In the course of phylogenesis, the instincts might lose their original function because higher centers in the nervous system would incorporate their functions. However, they were sometimes retained as superfluous emotional expressions. For example, drawing the lips back from the teeth as an expression of anger and aggression was a superfluous holdover from the time when our animal ancestors prepared to attack or bite their opponents in similar situations. Metaphorically speaking, the history of man could be subjected to archeological study by observing facial expressions.

While instinct theories explored inherited instincts typical of species, drive theories focused on individually acquired impulses of will, that is, those reflexes passing through cerebral hemispheres whose course was determined by its experiences there. Drive theories were especially well represented at German universities. Even though German neurophysiologists generally accepted Darwin's theory of evolution, they did not believe that man was supposed to be equipped with innate instincts to any great degree. In principle, man entered the world as a *tabula rasa*. He was helpless at birth and unlike animals could not immediately fend for himself. Only the lower reflexes were innate, but they did not guarantee survival. Drives were also innate, but they compelled without pointing in any one direction (today we would refer to *drives* as *corporal needs*).

Lotze (1852) pointed out that hunger and thirst were not originally drives for nourishment, but rather feelings of discomfort appearing when the internal organs of an organism transferred stimulation to the nervous system in a situation of want. Only when hunger and thirst were satisfied was an association made between discomfort and ideas about the object of satisfaction and the necessary muscle reaction. While this association was a reflex, it could be substituted by new reflexes and was therefore not as rigid as innate instincts. Drive was only determined by the functions of internal organs and a spectrum of external objects able to fulfill these functions. In accordance with this view, Lotze used the normal and regular functions of the body to characterize the emotions. Processes promoting the health of the body were felt as pleasure, while those disturbing health were felt as unpleasure. It was clear that there was a connection between nervous tension and unpleasure on the one hand and relaxation and pleasure on the other. However, Lotze did not believe that this connection should be overly stressed. First, unpleasure could arise from loss of energy, because equilibrium of tension was the norm for the organism. Second, emotions always possessed specific qualities depending on which external objects promoted or disturbed life functions. In summary, Lotze did not come much further than Hobbes had a couple of centuries before. Their psychological models have striking similarities (see I.B.1).

Meynert (1884) elaborated and clarified several of Lotze's views. Furthermore, he rejected the idea that man was equipped with instincts in the sense of "innate reflexes," and he thus contributed to a shift in interest from phylogeny to ontogeny. Meynert believed psychic reactions in children originally consisted of several wholly uniform reflexes. Pain caused a primary reflectory defense action, while the sight of a nipple caused an attack action. These two actions were the sources of unpleasure and pleasure respectively. The original reflexes were transferred to the cerebral cortex as memory traces, which allowed the more subtle reflexes of thought. Original emotions of pleasure and unpleasure were here represented as affects defined as "emotions without bodily pain." In other words, even the thought of objects able to arouse emotions could influence thought as affects. Moreover, Meynert believed that there was a physiological connection between inhibition and unpleasure on the one hand, and the free release of tension and pleasure on the other. He gave as an example a botanist who found a strange plant. The botanist instinctively attempted to classify the plant in his botanical system. This attempt was accompanied by different "moods." If a characteristic of the plant could be classified, association was inhibited, causing unpleasure. However, if it succeeded, the course of association was free, thus causing pleasure.

It should be noted that Meynert divided the central nervous system into cortex and subcortex. The subcortex managed the blind impulses of need in the body (and represented the evil and egoistical in man). Acquired characteristics (the good and social in man) were developed in the cortex. Through this development, first a primary and then a secondary self were formed. The primary self was the nucleus of the individual and consisted of ideas of the individual's body. However, the primary self was weak and passive and lacked the ability to impede the impulses of need. The secondary self consisted of ideas reproducing the outside world, through which active inhibition was made possible. Individuality was defined as the sum of all association paths between stabile images of memory. This sum also comprised individual character.

Not all neurophysiologists made a clear distinction between instinct and drive. Bastian (1880) and Exner (1894) attempted to combine the two. Although they valued the work of Spencer and Darwin, they recognized that human behavior could not always be explained on the basis of species-specific behavioral patterns. They therefore placed instincts in the reflex paths in the spinal cord and the medulla oblongata, where they fulfilled goals acquired by phylogeny, while letting drives and needs construct reflex paths in the cortex, where they enabled the individual to adapt to particular circumstances of life. The subject was thus under the sway of a conflict between the instincts and reason formed on the basis of the drives. However, reason usually emerged victorious from this conflict. It was difficult to give a precise definition of reason. Apart from the mere ability to think and associate, a kind of biological common sense and expediency were also apparent. The liberalistic concept of the subject, with its conflict between emotion and reason, reappeared under the guise of the mechanistic concept of the subject.

In discussing affects or emotions, Exner introduced the theory of special emotional centers whose function was to adapt incoming stimulations in such a way so that consciousness would experience them as specific emotions. Unlike Lotze and Meynert, Exner believed that pleasure and unpleasure were not dependent on the inhibition of tension, but only on whether the paths led to the center of pleasure or that of unpleasure. Most animal species had acquired through phylogeny a path from the sexual organs to the center of pleasure, which promoted sexual activity. In conclusion, it can be noted that both Exner and Bastian divided instincts into three groups: (1) instincts of self-preservation (nourishment, protection of the individual), (2) sexual instincts (procreation, care of the young), and (3) social and moral instincts. Because localization of the reflex paths as well as the sources of their stimulation in the organism caused insurmountable difficulties, it is understandable that many other writers exaggerated the use of instincts and drives. Scientists invented all sorts of instincts and drives to explain visible behavior with the result that their theoretical hypotheses ended by explaining nothing.

4. PSYCHOLOGY

We will open this section by discussing some of the factors that contributed to the development of psychology as an independent branch of science. We can then distinguish scientific psychology from philosophical psychology and neurophysiological psychology, which we have already examined.

Philosophical psychologists such as Locke, Hume, and Herbart called themselves empiricists. Herbart went so far as to attempt to separate psychology from philosophy as an independent empirical discipline. He did not succeed, partly because he limited his field of research to isolated striking and easily recognizable examples taken from self-observation. Neurophysiological psychology developed scientific methods in vivisection, microscopy, electrostimulation, chemical stimulation, and so forth. The problem here was explaining psychical phenomena as neurophysiological processes. The closest neurophysiological psychology came to a satisfactory explanation was in incorporating known psychical phenomena in the neurophysiological reflex path running through the brain.

Gustav Theodor Fechner (1801–1887) is commonly associated with the development of scientific psychology. Like Herbart, he insisted that psychology deal with data given by consciousness, instead of attempting to translate these data into neurophysiological terms. But he subjected the data as best he could to procedures developed in the natural sciences. He organized the data he collected systematically, used people and complex measuring instruments in his experiments, and attempted to calculate margins of error and take them into account. Fechner made psychology experimental.

Fechner was a very versatile scientist. In the course of his academic career, he managed to specialize in neurophysiology, physics, mathematics, philosophy, and aesthetics as well as psychology and became a professor in several of these subjects. His contribution to psychology rests primarily on his so-called theory of psychophysics (published in book form in 1860). However, Freud was also influenced by his more philosophically minded ideas on the pleasure principle and the principle of the tendency toward stability.

No examination of the development of psychology would be complete without mentioning Wilhelm Wundt (1832–1920), who more than anyone was instrumental in disseminating the study of experimental psychology at the end of the nineteenth century. Wundt systematized experiments by creating a university milieu for psychology, and he taught the entire generation of psychologists who became leaders in the field in Germany, England, and the United States at the close of the nineteenth century. However, Freud characteristically knew very little of experimental psychology. He remained an admirer of Fechner all his life, but had little sympathy for Wundt and his followers. Freud's admiration for Fechner was certainly based for the most part on Fechner's versatility and philosophical perspective. We will attempt to illustrate the scope of Fechner's work by examining his psychophysics and his theory of regulatory principles.

(a) Psychophysics

As already mentioned, Fechner was the first to complete an experimental study of psychical phenomena without referring back to neurophysiology. In describing his work, he focused on the psychophysical problem in philosophy, that is, the relationship between soul and body, and sought a scientific solution to this dilemma. He could not accept the traditional conflict between idealism and materialism, and believed instead that soul and body were two aspects of the same—not holding one aspect as more real than the other—just as a circle observed from the inside looks different from a circle observed from the outside, even if it is the same circle. Fechner explicitly agreed with what is known in philosophy as the 'identity hypothesis,' but apparently he did not believe that soul and body possessed 'identity.' He believed the psychical and the physical ran parallel to each other, and consequently the theory can be regarded as part of psychophysical parallelism.

Fechner divided psychophysics into two parts: internal psychophysics was concerned with what we normally regard as a psychophysical relation, that is, the direct relationship between consciousness and its corollary in the nervous system; external psychophysics explored the relationship between external stimulation and the sense perception it excited in consciousness. These two aspects of psychophysics can be described in the following reflex model:

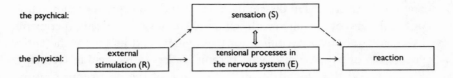

We use the abbreviations *R (Reiz)* for stimulation, *S (Sinnesempfindung)* for sensation and *E (Erregung)* for tension or tensional processes in the nervous system. Internal psychophysics thus deals with the relationship between *E* and *S*, while external psychophysics deals with the relationship between *R* and *S*. Reflexive motor reactions play no role in Fechner's experiments.

Let us first examine external psychophysics. In his work in this field, Fechner was influenced by E. H. Weber, who had conducted various investigations into how little differences in stimulation the senses are able to register. For example, if you put your finger into 10°C water, how much must the temperature be increased before you feel a difference? Every time a difference is registered, a threshold of stimulation is transgressed. Weber claimed that these thresholds of stimulation for a given sense organ formed a *quotient series,* that is, the next unit in the series could be determined by multiplying it by the same factor. To take a hypothetical example, if you could feel that the water were warmer at 12°, the constant factor would be 1.2 (because 12 is 10 times 1.2) and the next difference thresholds would therefore be at 14.4°, 17.3°, 20.7°, and so forth. Fechner improved upon Weber's experiments and worked with the sensation of weight, distance between lines, light intensity, sound intensity, and the like. As a physicist, he was aware of the conditions necessary for the precise measurement and manipulation of these sources of stimulation. However, he did not possess a standard for sensations. Only two factors could be accurately measured: (1) whether stimulations resulted in sensations, and (2) whether one sensation was greater, equal to, or smaller than another. Fechner therefore chose to use the number of successive difference thresholds as a measure of sensation. At the bottom was the absolute threshold, where a sensation was first registered by consciousness (for example, the sensation of sound and light). Next came a series of difference thresholds with the numerical values 1, 2, 3, and so on. The distance between two successive thresholds was assumed to be equal. This scale then formed a difference series.

It was then possible to coordinate external stimuli *(R)* with sensations *(S)*. *R* values formed a quotient series when *S* values formed a difference series. The common equation in external psychophysics was thus (because a function that converts a quotient series to a difference series is called a logarithmic function in mathematics):

$$S = k \log R.$$

In other words, the quantity of a sensation *(S)* could be calculated as a constant *(k)* times the logarithm of the quantity of external stimulation *(R)*. The constant expressed the sensitivity of the sense organ. When the quotient series increased "slowly," sensitivity was relatively great (small differences could be felt), while sensitivity was less the faster the quotient series increased.

External psychophysics was the prerequisite for internal psychophysics, which Fechner usually regarded as the more important of the two. In internal psychophysics, the problem was finding the relationship between conscious phenomena and psychophysical tensional processes in the nervous system, that is, finding the unknown middle link, *E*, in relation to *R* and *S*, which were already known. Fechner solved this problem by claiming that the relationship between external stimulations and the tensional processes of the brain were proportional because one physical medium transferred vibrations to another. It followed that the equation for internal psychophysics was, like external psychophysics, logarithmic. The only difference was the constant:

$$S = k' \log E.$$

This result was perhaps not particularly interesting in and of itself, but the problem did bring Fechner to a much more interesting discussion of cerebral localization. At first, Fechner denied that consciousness could be located at one central point in the brain. He gave many examples of such a localization, Descartes's localization of the soul in the pineal gland being the most well known. Fechner's rejection of localization was partly based on the experimental fact that a sensory consciousness was part of the medulla oblongata, while consciousness of thought was a part of the cerebral cortex. He concluded that the nervous system was a whole made up of mutually limited parts. Nevertheless, he probably believed that with time a relatively precise localization of consciousness could be determined, because consciousness appeared in those areas of the nervous system where the psychophysical tensional process *(E)* exceeded the absolute threshold of consciousness. Tensional value was a result of wave movements in the nervous system. There was a basic wave for sleep and the waking state and a more superficial wave connected to the intensity of sense impressions. These two waves could be combined in different ways so that they either impeded or strengthened each other. When the basic wave (or the subwave as Fechner called it) reached its zenith in one part of the nervous system, it would reach the nadir in another part and vice versa.

The wave theory can be illustrated by Fechner's concept of the psychology of dreams. Dream consciousness was not merely a weakened version of wakened consciousness that appeared as a result of a lowering of the level of tension. Even if one closed one's eyes and relaxed, one retained one's rational consciousness because it had its own anatomical place in the nervous system. Rational consciousness only disappeared when the level of tension fell below the threshold of consciousness, which normally occurred in sleep. Dream consciousness then resulted, because the tensional wave (subwave) had been displaced to another anatomical system whose threshold of consciousness it transgressed. As Fechner put it, dreams occurred on another scene of action *(Schauplatz)*. Thus the spatially or topically separated parts of the nervous system set different rules for conscious processes. Dream rules were similar to consciousness in children or primitive man. Indeed, Fechner compared the transition from waking consciousness to dreaming consciousness with the transition from city to country (from culture to nature): in the city one walked down straight streets along numbered houses, while in the country one could wander freely. There were also two different ways of living in the city and the country. Although it was possible to adapt, it was impossible to live a country way of life in the middle of a city. Only the creative artist who could invent an entire fantasy world in his waking consciousness was able to adapt in this way.

(b) The Pleasure Principle and the Principle of the Tendency Toward Stability

Fechner turned to religion after an extended emotional crisis lasting from 1840–1843 (in other words many years *before* his work on psychophysics), and he attempted to combine religious metaphysics with natural science. In the 1840s, he wrote extensively about a universal principle containing the truth as well as salvation: the pleasure principle. Fechner examined this principle in a book from 1846 on "the highest good" and in a shorter article from 1848 on "the pleasure principle of action."

Superficially, the pleasure principle was identical to the hedonistic principle that man acted to achieve pleasure and avoid unpleasure. However, Fechner believed that he superseded classical hedonism by not positing the goal as the decisive factor, but rather the amount of pleasure and unpleasure contained in each single thought: a soldier could die for his country without achieving pleasure or reward. The question was whether ideas such as loyalty and heroism were so pleasurable for him that they could control his actions. It is difficult to feel that Fechner's concept added anything new to the work of philosophers like Hobbes, Hume, and Herbart. Like Herbart, Fechner allowed the affects to be constantly bound by thoughts. Like Hobbes, he allowed these affects to be based on experience, and like all three philosophers he calculated the resulting will from the diverse forces connected to the individual thoughts. The similarity with Herbart is apparent in another sense as well. Fechner conceived of a kind of unconscious consideration: A person did not make a conscious decision on all the pleasurable and unpleasurable thoughts agitating for or against a particular action. Decision making often took place by itself without involving consciousness, as when an artist after what seemed to be a sudden impulse added a brush stroke to his canvas. In reality, this sudden impulse was made up of innumerable small motives arising from the artist's perception of his motif, his knowledge of the technique of other artists, and his state of mind at the time.

Fechner's considerations were based on the concept that pleasure and unpleasure could in some way be assigned the same standard. The only problem was that it was difficult to compare the pleasure contained in, for example, a good meal, the perception of a work of art, the "yes" of a loved one, and the achievement of honor. There was no quantitative scale to determine which one of these experiences afforded the greatest pleasure. This might be the reason why Fechner abandoned work on the pleasure principle for a period and instead preoccupied himself with psychophysics, which, as we have seen, was better able to be measured quantitatively.

Fechner did not resume work on the pleasure principle until the 1870s, and when he did, he conducted his studies in an abstract philosophical context. The nineteenth century had witnessed many different evolutionary theories encompassing many fields and many divergent perceptions of the course of evolution. Some saw perfection and salvation ahead; others saw death and destruction. Fechner considered Darwin and Helmholtz to be pessimists because of their mechanistic and materialistic views. He considered these views with his own religious optimism in books such as *Einige*

Ideen zur Schöpfungs- und Entwicklungsgeschichte der Organismen (1873) and *Die Tagesansicht gegenüber der Nachtansicht* (1879), whose titles alone bear witness to his wideranging interests.

Man, society, even the entire universe were, in Fechner's view, moving toward a final stability. Absolute stability would be the state where all movement in the universe had ceased and energy had reached the lowest possible level of tension. This concept was obviously inspired by thermodynamics and its theory of the thermic death of the universe. Fechner placed full stability on a lower level. The term *full stability* described a condition of regularly recurring movements. This stability set the norm for most processes, even though it was only a stop on the way toward absolute stability. Full stability had not yet been realized in any system, but all movements could be said to be controlled by a tendency toward stability, appearing most lucidly in the regular movements of celestial bodies and the regular functions of organisms. In keeping with these assumptions, Fechner called his principle the principle of the tendency toward stability. The pleasure principle was now regarded as a special instance of this principle, because there was a tendency in the world to increase the amount of pleasure and decrease the amount of unpleasure. As early as 1825, Fechner had proposed an evolutionary theory stating that the human species would soon grow wings and become angels. This optimism reappeared in the new theory, where, for example, the pleasure principle was directly perceived to be attainable in the gradually improving and more ordered social conditions. Stability did not bring death and destruction, but eternal bliss.

Fechner had a vision that phenomena such as repetition, time, regularity, stability, fluctuation, wave, harmony, and rhythm were common to everything in the universe, from the regularities in the oscillations of a sound wave to the regularity of the movement of the planets around the sun. Such interdisciplinary and universal theories were very popular at the time. We have already mentioned E. von Hartmann's theory of the unconscious, and we could also point out that Ewald Hering, who at one time worked with Freud's friend Josef Breuer, tried to discover a general connection between repetition and memory. Another friend of Freud's, Wilhelm Fliess, exploited the concept of time in a universal (and almost astrological) theory. As we shall see, even Freud was not averse to these kinds of speculations.

5. PSYCHIATRY

Most cultures draw a line between reason and madness. On the one side lie rules and thoughts defining a given social community as a totality. On the other side lies everything regarded as insane and incomprehensible, which cannot be placed in this totality. Primitive societies often ascribe magical powers to the unknown. The unknown is contrasted with man's helplessness and ignorance, and attains the status of a source of power and knowledge. It is not uncommon for half crazy medicine men to function as mediators between a tribe and the unknown, thus assuming a kinship between insanity and the divine. In Christianity, the opposite is the case. The divine is identified with social reason, while insanity is identified with the devil. The insane become scapegoats for internal social conflicts with social reason being defined in relation to insanity.

This section will focus on nineteenth-century thought, in which madness became mental illness, and where psychiatry was developed as a science of mental illness with its own classification system (nosology), its own understanding and explanation of the causes of mental illness (etiology), and its own form of treatment (therapy). However, we will first sketch the contours of earlier developments that form the basis for the genesis of psychiatry.

Medieval and Renaissance society was dominated by a feudal and static hierarchy with a clerical and a secular power structure. Cases abound of the Church's fighting its opponents by accusing them of being in league with the devil. The insane did not constitute any dangerous opposition to the Church per se, but, because of their peculiar gestures and manner of speech, they provided convincing examples of the devil's existence, and could therefore serve as scapegoats. The many witch trials, which facilitated the consolidation of clerical power, also laid the groundwork for an entire folk mythology of being possessed by the devil, making a pact with the devil, or being sold to the devil. Many were executed in order to scare and warn potential deviants from reason. Taken in isolation, secular power was less restrictive. We have all heard of the tales of village idiots, who could wander unaccosted among the gaudy throngs of the towns, and Renaissance works (like those of Bosch, Shakespeare, and Cervantes) bear witness to an interest in madness and a willingness to comprehend it.

These conditions changed with the emergence of capitalism in northern

Europe and the literal expulsion of Catholicism. Devil mythology as well as tolerance gave way to a massive disciplinary effort, where emotion and reason were defined as opposites. Social morality became a part of capitalist accumulation and emphasized diligence, frugality, self-control, and long-term calculation. This new morality was foisted upon society by singularly tangible means (see I.A). Discipline became the order of the day in school, the workplace, and the military. Laws were passed that punished failure to work for whatever reason by incarceration (such a law was on the books in France from 1657 to 1794). Every large city had a house of correction or prison for the incarceration of disruptive elements, the indolent, criminals, the deformed, invalids, and the unemployed; all of whom were incarcerated together. Only those able to work were separated and forced to produce different commodities. This production was often quite profitable and these institutions were therefore a lucrative business for the absolute monarchs. The insane were among the worst off in this system insofar as they could not adapt to the required work ethic. They were often chained to the walls of dark prison cellars or crowded together in large cages and exhibited for money on Sundays. Madness was simply defined as bestiality, a state thought to be immune to change and certainly not curable.

However, in the latter half of the eighteenth century a change occurred. In some institutions experiments were conducted on the imprisoned or hospitalized insane that revealed that their condition was not immutable. Finding a treatment that would improve the health of the patient was the only concern, in keeping with the model of medical science. This view marked the beginning of a definition of insanity as an illness. Bourgeois political ideals of freedom and human rights were eventually extended to include the insane. They were now regarded not as divine, nor as possessed by the devil or bestial, but as sick people. The years immediately following the French Revolution in 1789 were a decisive turning point. First, the sick were released from their chains, and second, a psychiatric science emerged. Several different developments took place in psychiatry during this period. We will now briefly examine four of these developments.

(1) The use of hypnosis was systematized in the 1770s by the Austrian F. A. Mesmer. He was able to cure psychic and psychosomatic illnesses without knowing the precise cause of the ailment. Thus he persisted in regarding hypnosis as a transferral of magnetic forces (see I.B.5.b).

(2) As mentioned above, experiments with different kinds of therapy were conducted in some institutions. Contemporary medical theories served as a point of departure, which naturally influenced the conception

of mental illness. According to some theories, mental illness was caused by animal spirits or improperly circulating blood, clumped together in different parts of the body. Therapists went so far as to claim that all mental disorders could be categorized as coming from somatic disorders in the same way as high fever caused a loss of mental clarity. Brutal cures were developed as a result of a rather primitive mechanistic view of mental illness. Manic patients were strapped in the same position for days on end in order to calm the life spirits; depressive patients were tied to revolving beds in order to ameliorate poor circulation. In addition, various shock cures were employed, for example, suddenly letting a patient fall into a tub through a hidden trapdoor. These cures were mitigated somewhat in the course of the nineteenth century, but were retained to a degree in the form of hydrotherapy (hot and cold baths), electrotherapy (stimulation by a weak electrical current), massage, and diets.

(3) Another group of therapists regarded mental illness as a psychological and moral problem. Their therapy has been called moral therapy, and simply attempted to reeducate the insane by creating a relationship of trust between the patient and the therapist and his fatherly authority. Many mentally ill patients suffered from an exaggerated sensitivity and an inability to control their emotions. It was previously thought that this condition was caused by the lack of a soul, and the insane were therefore regarded as no better than animals. However, moral therapists believed that the insane were underdeveloped, having for some reason stagnated at an early stage of development. In order to teach them how to make conscious choices, to learn responsibility and administer their own lives, the insane were allowed to live under relatively free conditions. Institutions were furnished as simply as possible so that the patient could understand their rules and norms. Only mild forms of punishment and reward were used. The most well-known moral therapists were Tuke in England and Pinel in France, both of whom started their reform work in the 1790s. Tuke, a deeply religious Quaker, established an asylum in the country, believing that rural labor and close contact with nature would provide the best opportunities for development. On this point he agreed with Rousseau and the Romantics, even though his concept of the subject cannot otherwise be called romantic. Exemplary of Tuke's therapy were his "tea parties," where the sane and insane participated as equals. The insane would then, under "social pressure" from the sane, compete in conforming to cultural norms as well as possible. Pinel held similar therapeutic ideas, but is especially known for his thorough description and classification of types of illnesses. He em-

ployed five main categories: melancholy, monomania, mania, dementia, and idiocy.

(4) The German natural philosophers also had a keen interest in mental illness. They criticized the liberalistic subject concept for representing only narrow-minded social reason. They instead stressed desire and emotion as primordial savagery and madness in all mankind. Pure madness was an expression of early stages in human evolution, but could of course never be accepted as such. The positive expression of madness could be found in artistic creativity, where the artist realized some of man's primordial essence in his work. Taking Schelling's writings on natural philosophy as their point of departure, philosophers and writers commonly became preoccupied with mental illness. However, their abstract sympathy for the plight of the mentally ill was not translated into practice because of the lack of a therapeutic dimension.

We do not intend to go into more detail with these first stages of the history of psychiatry, but will instead examine more closely areas in nineteenth-century philosophy directly concerned with the development of psychoanalysis: neuropathological psychiatry, originating in the 1840s; the interest in hypnosis and hysteria in the 1880s; and increased attention to sexuality as a subject for psychiatry toward the end of the century.

(a) Neuropathology and Psychiatry

Advances in neuropathology in the nineteenth century affected psychiatry by making it more homogeneous. At the same time that neurophysiology and neuroanatomy defined the human subject as a combination of the features and functions of the nervous system, it became common for psychiatrists to regard psychic disorders as expressions of malfunctions in the nervous system. During the period from the mid 1840s to the mid 1880s, there was no clear boundary between psychiatry and neuropathology (the science of diseases of the nervous system).

The leading figure behind this development was Wilhelm Griesinger (1817–1868). He was a doctor and through his practice had become acquainted with the latest findings in neurophysiological research, including those published in Müller's textbook (Müller 1834–1840). In 1840, he got a job in a psychiatric institution, where he specialized in the psychiatric theories of the somatics. He also sought a broader theoretical perspective and to this end published the first edition of his psychiatric textbook in 1845. This textbook defined psychic disorders in relation to the nervous system. Griesinger's view gained credence in certain circles and developments in neurophysiology (the discovery of reflex paths through the brain, cerebral localization) confirmed his hypothesis. In 1867, after several years of absence from psychiatry, he became a university professor of psychiatry in Berlin.

Griesinger made the famous statement that all mental diseases were brain diseases. He was not so rigid in his views in his practical work, where he employed psychological and clinical descriptions besides his theoretical models. This procedure was evident in his concept of etiology, which claimed that mental illness developed as a result of the interaction of several different causes, for example, innate weaknesses in the nervous system, other somatic ailments, extraordinary psychic experiences or states, and certain provoking situations. In his therapeutic work, Griesinger stressed preventive measures because he did not believe that an advanced mental illness could be cured. He felt that mechanical treatments, which were often violent, should be abandoned and replaced in part by chemical drugs (opium, prussiates) and baths. Griesinger did not believe that mental illness was self-imposed, and was therefore opposed to narrow-minded moral instruction of the mentally ill. On the other hand, he saw the goal of therapy as a strengthening of the self.

Classification of diseases was probably Griesinger's weakest point. He persisted in supporting Zeller's theory of a so-called unity psychosis. This theory held that there was really only one kind of mental illness. Consequently, different manifestations of mental illness were simply more or less advanced forms of this one illness. The Frenchman Morel used this model for his notorious degeneration theory that mental illness was hereditary and increased in severity with each generation, resulting eventually in idiocy (see I.B.2.b). According to Zeller and Morel this process was irreversible. Consequently, no effort was made to cure advanced cases, because it was felt that the patients would never recover from their illnesses anyway. Griesinger supported degeneration theory. The positive aspect of Griesinger's adherence to this theory and was that he attempted to classify milder mental disorders considered by the two theories to be intermediate stages of actual mental illness. He thus became the first psychiatrist to complete a study of neurotic symptoms, and he tried to understand them by comparing them to a number of well-known borderline cases in the normal psyche, such as dreams, inebriation, and delirium from fever. The first genuine stage of illness was depression, which Griesinger interpreted as a sign that mental illness in its original form could not be regarded as exaggerated emotional activity. On the contrary, he interpreted depression from the reflex model as the inhibition of energy release. He was also aware of similar psychological mechanisms, while he regarded inhibition as an inexpedient retention of emotional reactions. In a larger sense, the self or reason as the instrument controlling inhibition, calculation, and self-control entered the spotlight as the cause of mental illness.

For Griesinger, psychiatry and neuropathology were almost identical. This view enabled him better to understand organic psychoses, which could be traced to brain damage (for example, by poisoning), but it also entailed a certain confusion on other points. It gradually became increasingly necessary to distinguish between psychic and neuropathological illnesses, for there were psychic illnesses without demonstrable organic defects and neuropathological illnesses without psychic defects (such as child paralysis, aphasia, and epilepsy). A more pronounced separation of the two disciplines resulted. Psychiatry and neuropathology eventually became independent disciplines, with Kraepelin regarded as the leading psychiatrist and Charcot as the leading neuropathologist at the turn of the century. Freud's teacher Theodor Meynert was one of the few who developed Griesinger's theories and attempted to bridge the gap between psychiatry and neuropathology. Meynert was not successful in this endeavor, but it can perhaps be said that he inspired Freud to retain elements from psychiatry and neuropathology in his work. This aspect of the beginnings of psychoanalysis will be discussed in section IV.A on the psychoanalytical classification of diseases.

(b) Hypnosis and Hysteria

Hysteria has been known since antiquity, when it was thought to have been caused by the uterus's wandering about in a woman's body (the term *hysteria* is derived from the Greek word for *uterus*). Hysteria appears as cramps, paresis, or pains in various parts of the body accompanied by an exaggerated anxiety or fear of harmless objects or situations. Because no precise organic causes of hysteria could be found, it eventually became common to regard it as conscious simulation, that is, pretending to be ill. Milder cases of hysteria were seldom treated, because it was thought to be one of the typical weaknesses of character in women (hysterical symptoms in men were called hypochondria). Physicians refused to treat hysteria, considering it playacting, an attempt to attract attention. Despite these attitudes, hysteria became the object of much discussion, probably because the incidence of hysteria was more widespread after the independent development of the sphere of intimacy at the end of the eighteenth century. As already mentioned, women's work then became increasingly bound up with family life and the sphere of intimacy. Before her marriage, a woman served her parents, after marrying she became a servant for her husband and small children. At the same time she was supposed to be the repository of sensitivity and refinement. Freud's and Breuer's work with hysterical women contributed to the discovery of how these conditions generated mental illness.

The treatment of nervous disorders such as hysteria goes back to the exorcisms of the Middle Ages and the Renaissance. The magnetizer Franz Anton Mesmer (1734–1815), a Vienna physician and a personal friend of Mozart and Haydn, had witnessed an exorcism where a priest had produced violent cramps in a possessed person by invoking the devil and God. The priest had explained the alleviation of the possessed person's condition by saying that the devil had left the body. Mesmer rejected this explanation and claimed that he could effect the same cure without religious overtones. He regarded this illness as materially conditioned and had a theory that there were magnetic forces at play. His treatment consisted of letting the patient consume a ferruginous mixture and then placing two to four magnets on different parts of her body. He then sat opposite the patient, pressed his knees against the patient's knees and stared deeply into her eyes. Mesmer also sometimes rubbed his fingers against the patient's fingers. After a while a change occurred. The patient felt something like a strange fluid passing through her body accompanied by some pain. Verbal communication was strictly forbidden and the patient was therefore forced to abreact her tensions with a somatic attack. The patient had perhaps had these attacks in other situations, but under Mesmer's direction and influence they had a soothing and therapeutic effect. When the same treatment was repeated several days in a row, the symptoms gradually weakened and finally disappeared.

In 1778, Mesmer was forced to leave Austria because of his controversial practice. He settled in Paris, where he continued his therapy and developed it theoretically. He called it *animal magnetism*, because he interpreted his therapeutic treatment as the manifestation of magnetic forces. He believed that the universe contained magnetic forces affecting all life on earth. Pathological states were caused by an imbalance in the distribution of magnetic fluid in the body. Consequently, the cure was supposed to restore this balance. Mesmer used magnets, mixtures, and metallic objects to channel energy into the right paths again. He eventually came to regard himself as an unusually potent magnetic force with special abilities to control the course of fluid in the body. His therapeutic talents were thus supposed to consist of his ability to localize and treat unhealthy accumulations of energy and unblock circulation. It was therefore necessary for the patient to relive the crises that had caused the illness.

Mesmer's therapy caused a great stir, and he had many students and imitators. Extensive studies were published on the subject, which resulted in the appointment of an official commission to investigate Mesmer's methods more closely. The investigation led to a charge against Mesmer for quackery, because the commission rightfully doubted the existence of a magnetic fluid in the body. However, a contributing factor to the commission's findings was the view that magnetism was a threat to common sense and social mores. The fanatical cult surrounding Mesmer was not without sexual overtones. Many female patients apparently worshipped Mesmer and scenes of mass hysteria ensued when he placed a large group of patients in a tub in order to cure them simultaneously (one of Mesmer's students was apparently so preoccupied with his "magnetic stroking" that his patient became pregnant). Mesmer's most peculiar exploit was to magnetize a tree outside of Paris, which subsequently became a Mecca for the sick just like the healing springs of ancient times.

It is clear that Mesmer performed a kind of hypnosis, and that he had mastered the technique of putting his patients into a trance. His theory of the accumulation of magnetic energy in the body corresponded to the way his patients experienced their illnesses. One of the characteristics of hysteria is that symptoms manifest themselves as imaginary pains having some kind of psychic content in the diseased organs. By employing his unusual methods, Mesmer was able to enter the unconscious structures that caused the symptoms. However, his belief in a magnetic fluid was false, and it blinded him to a theoretical understanding of his discovery.

In 1841, Braid, a Scot, formulated a more advanced theory and was the first to employ the term *hypnosis,* which meant *the sleeping state.* Braid's scientific "purification" of magnetism reduced the significance of the relationship of the hypnotist to the patient by claiming that therapy took place in the patient's own imagination. The technique was now being used in many situations, for example, as an anesthetic in surgery. In the latter half of the nineteenth century, hypnosis enjoyed considerable popularity in

France especially, where it was used by Broca, Azam, and others. Despite this popularity, however, many doctors persisted in regarding hypnosis as nothing more than quackery. Most were only acquainted with hypnosis from public exhibitions, where the more conspicuous effects—such as actions performed while in a trance and under posthypnotic suggestion— were demonstrated along with other circus acts.

The French country doctor Liébeault was one of the first to devote himself entirely to hypnosis. A modest inheritance allowed him to retire from his practice in the 1870s. He settled in Nancy, where he gave free treatment to the poor. Like Mesmer, he used hypnosis to treat a wide range of illnesses, including purely organic disorders. His incontrovertible results quickly made him a controversial figure, which won him new supporters. One was Hippolyte Bernheim (1840–1919), a professor of medicine who in 1882 joined the Nancy school and became its theorist. The views of the Nancy school were thus disseminated through Bernheim's books. He once again changed the terminology of the treatment, substituting the term *suggestion* for hypnosis, thus underscoring the psychological perspective and the importance of interpersonal relations. Among the psychosomatic illnesses he successfully treated were constipation and anorexia in children, and insomnia, anxiety, and other hysterical symptoms in adults. Bernheim's method consisted of convincing the patient of the correctness and reason- ableness of the doctor's views. When the doctor told patients that they ought to be healthy and abandon their symptoms, they sometimes followed his orders. Bernheim made no attempt to explain his technique theoreti- cally, but instead underscored the therapeutic aspect of suggestion. Unlike Mesmer, Bernheim regarded language as the most important medium for contact with a patient, who literally had to be convinced. Objections were not accepted, and patients not responding to suggestions were blamed for not doing so, for Bernheim believed that anyone could respond to sugges- tion in principle, a view that was later strongly criticized.

We have already mentioned Jean Martin Charcot (1825–1893) as the leading neuropathologist of the century. For example, he made important contributions to sclerosis research. In this light, his sudden interest in hypnosis and hysteria in the 1880s has been regarded as a digression from more serious pursuits. He was introduced to the subject in 1876, when he became a member of a commission investigating the validity of hypotheses formulated by a contemporary magnetizer. The investigation unexpectedly found merit in the magnetizer's hypotheses, recognizing that certain me- tallic substances could induce cramps by touch. The reason for Charcot's positive attitude toward magnetism and hypnosis is thought to have been that he gained new insight into his hysterical patients. He had encountered an unusually high number of hysterical patients as the head of the great Parisian hospital for mentally ill women, La Salpêtrière. He was struck by the fact that hypnotized individuals exhibited the same symptoms of cramps as hysterical patients. As a neuropathologist, Charcot felt that a psychological explanation for this similarity was inadequate. He therefore argued that only those having a particular organic disposition were responsive to hypnosis as well as hysteria. The same minority made up both groups. By stimulating certain "hysterogenic zones" in the body, a series of states could be induced, including trances, violent muscle spasms, and spasmatic theatrical poses.

One of Charcot's most important discoveries was that individuals with hysterical tendencies reacted differently from others to traumatic experiences. His most well-known example was a bricklayer who had fallen from a scaffold and later became paralyzed in one arm without having any demonstrable organic defects. Charcot presumed that such posttraumatic neuroses were caused by special "dynamic functional lesions," which could not be localized in the same way as normal lesions. His psychological explanation for this phenomenon was that during the period after the trauma (the shock of the fall), the bricklayer had isolated the motor functions of the arm from the group of psychically active functions (by so-called autosuggestion), causing the arm to be exempt from the influence of the will for a time. In some of these cases, the patient was cured after an affect-dominated crisis, which meant that the abreaction was therapeutically effective. It is difficult to determine whether Charcot was aware of this connection. At any rate, he apparently pointed out that hysterical attacks, because of their similarity to orgasms, had sexual overtones, and that "the genital" played a role in the etiology of hysteria.

Charcot's theory of hysteria and hypnosis caused quite a stir. During his weekly lectures, he was fond of exhibiting hysterical patients alongside hypnotized individuals in order to demonstrate the similarities between the two. Unlike the Nancy school, he did what he could to relate hypnosis to physically induced phenomena. He thus experimented with magnets and metallic substances, making the same basic mistake as Mesmer: clouding genuine knowledge of psychic mechanisms with a more-than-dubious physical theory. On the whole, Charcot stimulated great public interest in mental disorders, and many well-known writers of the time are known to have attended his lectures.

For the time being, we can summarize the differences between Bernheim and Charcot with the following points: (1) Charcot regarded receptivity to hypnosis as a sign of weakness in the nervous system, while Bernheim believed that anyone could be hypnotized (respond to suggestion); (2) Charcot maintained a physical and neurophysiological view of hypnosis, while Bernheim stressed the psychic and interpersonal aspects of suggestion; and (3) Charcot only rarely used hypnosis in therapy, while Bernheim devoted himself exclusively to the therapeutic possibilities of suggestion. At an important congress in 1889, supporters of Charcot and Bernheim clashed. On the whole, the views of the Nancy school emerged victorious. The consequences of this conflict were negligible, however, because interest in hypnosis once again faded after the turn of the century. Charcot's most prominent discipline, Janet, was able to draw important conclusions from Charcot's theories (he adopted a psychological approach and described psychic splits), but his work was tarnished by his support for Morel's degeneration theory.

Bernheim's and Charcot's enduring significance lies in the inspiration they gave to Freud, who used their theories in his formulation of psychoanalysis. Moreover, Charcot's work also exerted considerable influence on neuropathology.

(c) Sexology and Psychiatry

Much of what we have said about madness applies to an even greater degree to sexuality. Many features of Christianity and capitalist culture can only be understood in light of their sexual origins. Sexuality itself changes character with social development. It underwent a strong differentiation during the rise of capitalism, becoming a versatile and mobile instrument for many different functions. In psychoanalytic terms, sexuality can attach itself to the superego and to external, socially determined ideals, it can bring people together in pairs or in groups, and it can constitute a transgressive desire based on utopian fantasies. We will not attempt to review these functions and their historical transformations here.

The ideological history of sexuality roughly follows the history of the concept of the subject discussed in section I.A. Having been considered divine and/or satanic in various mythologies, sexuality in the seventeenth and eighteenth centuries was, for better or worse, adapted to the hierarchy separating the emotional from the rational and innate from acquired characteristics. Like the emotions, sexuality was regarded as an innate and animal element in man, something that should be excluded from society like madness, and which was in any case only tolerated in its adult, disciplined manifestations. In the eighteenth century, a veritable crusade was started against children's masturbation. Ingenious alarm and surveillance systems were employed to prevent sexual activity among children, which only served to excite their interest in sexuality. During the Romantic era, emotions and sexuality were to some degree integrated as a positive element in the human subject. At the same time, a romantic myth of sex as the most valuable and the most fragile and sensitive part of man gained currency. Sex was seen as a potential source of sickness because it was especially vulnerable to the omniscient moral depravity in society. Public attention was therefore primarily directed at pathological and abnormal sexuality, making a cure for such disorders imperative.

Research in sexuality during most of the nineteenth century was generally conducted in light of moral dogmas. Church authorities were traditionally interested in sexual issues. The positive aspect of this interest was that the subject could be discussed from a psychological perspective, for example, in terms of sin and temptation, the dangers of succumbing to sinful thoughts, fantasies, and the struggle against passion and carnal desire. Behind this attitude lay considerable insight into many psychic mechanisms and a knowledge of conflicting inclinations in the psyche. Research in sexuality in the natural sciences might have been expected at the time the mechanistic subject concept developed, around 1850, but deeply religious scientists continued to dominate the field. The subject was apparently taboo around this period, which is remarkable in light of how the materialistic natural sciences dismissed God and the human soul.

Throughout the nineteenth century, research in sexuality was marked by two pseudoscientific theories: Gall's phrenology in the first half of the century and Morel's degeneration theory in the latter half. We have already discussed Morel's theory (see I.B.2.b). Phrenology was in many ways a precursor of degeneration theory. It held that typical human characteristics such as destructiveness, *joie de vivre,* self-esteem, altruism, and calculation all had a permanent place in the brain. The shape of the cranium thus corresponded to the relative strength of these characteristics: a projection indicated well-developed characteristics, an indentation defective capacity. According to this theory, phrenologists believed it possible to measure an individual's personality (and, for example, single out potential criminals).

Sexual instinct was located in the cerebellum. Consequently, a corpulent neck was a sign of overdeveloped sexual instinct.

In the nineteenth century, sexuality was generally explained as a three-way interdependence of the nervous system, heredity, and the genitals, without much knowledge of any of them. Gall emphasized the localization of sexuality in the nervous system, while Morel stressed heredity. A number of sporadic causes of sexuality were formulated with the help of vitalist ideas. The view of the evils of masturbation was retained and elaborated. Sperm was considered the same substance as animal spirits and the life force, so masturbation was believed to lead to lethargy and apathy. Some even held that there was a connection between sperm and spinal marrow, and that masturbation could cause a fatal waste of spinal marrow. Similar connections could not be made with women. Instead, masturbation was linked to irregularities in menstruation, sterility, and so on. Moreover, it was thought that masturbation of the clitoris caused it to grow, producing male features in women and converting them to lesbianism.

Venereal disease was a favorite subject as evidence of a direct relationship between sexuality and disease. One mistake could lead to madness (from syphilis) and could be passed on to future generations. Gradual degeneration caused distortions of the genitals and madness and perversion. Morel, who was very religious, described perversions in moralistic terms as sexual relations with persons of the same sex, children, animals, corpses, and dolls. Only toward the end of the century was there any discussion of whether these perversions were innate or acquired. However, leading sexologists such as Krafft-Ebing and Havelock Ellis did not entirely abandon degeneration theory. Krafft-Ebing, who succeeded Meynert as professor of psychiatry in Vienna, is often mentioned as the first to systematize psychosexual disorders. His textbook *Psychopathia Sexualis* (Krafft-Ebing 1889) was reprinted twelve times in increasingly large numbers. In his book, Krafft-Ebing called perversions "cerebral neuroses." Moreover, he constructed the terms *sadism* and *masochism* from the fiction writers Sade and Sacher-Masoch. He made extensive descriptions of all the clinical symptoms, but nevertheless persisted in explaining perversions as an expression of innate disorders of the nervous system. He regarded masturbation as pathological, and supposedly went so far as to claim that he could detect signs of degeneration in all women who had had sexual relations outside of marriage.

Darwinism provided an important contribution to research in sexuality.

In his book on the descent of man (Darwin 1871), Darwin expressed the idea of a common bisexuality. Noting that most primitive organisms were neuter, he concluded that sexual differentiation had come about at a certain stage of development. Man was neuter in the first stages of embryonic development, or rather, the fetus had both male and female sex anlages. Therefore, either the male or the female anlages became dominant during the development of the fetus. This area of hereditary theory was elaborated in Germany by Weismann (see I.B.2.b) and became part of sexual pathology. Just as hermaphrodites could be born as a result of mutation, it was believed that a perverse course of psychosexual development could lead to homosexuality and bisexuality. This theory was based on the assumption that psychosexual attitudes were controlled by male and female brain centers. Perverse development was therefore the result of an imbalance in the natural relationship between these two centers.

After the turn of the century, sexology became more a part of scientific discourse, partly because sexologists became aware of the significance of Mendel's laws of heredity and could therefore root out the many myths surrounding inherited characteristics. Several bodies of work had enduring importance in the field of sexology: Krafft-Ebing's and Havelock Ellis's descriptions of perversions, Iwan Bloch's incorporation of cultural, historical, and anthropological perspectives, Wilhelm Fliess's and Magnus Hirschfeld's theories of bisexuality, and Freud's demonstration of the connection between sexuality and neurosis. Among these scientists Freud rapidly emerged as the one best able to incorporate new ideas in a general theory of sexuality.

6. LITERATURE

There are significant differences between the psychology found in philosophy and science, and that found in literature. Philosophers and scientists search for abstract and universal concepts and universal laws. Writers of fiction, however, are compelled to express their experiences. Philosophers and scientists usually regard psychological connections from the outside and try to objectify them. Writers, however, often invite the reader to follow the thoughts and actions of fictional characters subjectively. Philosophers and scientists divide the study of man into compartmentalized interests and disciplines, while writers attempt to depict individual lives as a totality. They are able to follow their characters from cradle to grave, describe their hopes and frustrations and show how their personalities are created and developed in a larger context. Although plot and action are fictional, a literary work can encompass an entire *Weltanschauung* (a theory of human life) comparable to any philosophical or scientific theory. We do not intend to set literature against philosophy or science. They have influenced each other, and we shall examine some of the literary tendencies that influenced Freud and through him psychoanalysis as the science of the subject.

We have decided to focus on themes in nineteenth-century literature. Although Freud knew and valued earlier writers like Shakespeare, Cervantes, and Milton, it is clear that, from a psychoanalytical viewpoint, the more recent literature provided a key to understanding the earlier writers. Moreover, nineteenth-century literature consistently developed a psychological viewpoint. Romantic writers gave a dynamic description of psychic conflicts and charted new territory in the personality, while naturalistic writers searched for genetic explanations of the personality using the criteria of heredity and environment. We find in Romanticism and Naturalism the greatest psychological insight into the tragic chain of events related to the failure of synthesis between emotion and reason, past and present. This chain of events leads to a psychological personality divided into the separate parts that normally create a balance in the healthy personality. This division brings features to the fore that are otherwise hidden.

(a) Romantic Literature:
The Eruption of the Hidden Forces of the Soul

Romantic literature would not be very interesting if it focused exclusively on the emphasis of emotion at the expense of reason in a symmetrical inversion of the *Weltanschauung* of rationalism. This motif does mark most romantic works, with their rapid idealization of emotion, nature, and the glorious national past. However, several writers did attempt to trace the actual fate of emotions in contemporary capitalist society, creating a less idyllic image. Emotional and sexual demands maintained uncompromisingly were adversely affected in the encounter with the environment and in frustration withdrew back to the soul as abnormal fantasies. Writers were now able to describe how these fantasies were mobilized as demonic forces able to strike anywhere at any time. They had personally observed nature in the process of being destroyed by industry, and a bourgeois society controlled by money and therefore took the side of the violated emotions to the extent of pathological hyperbole. The clash between mining and mountain demons was an often-used image of the conflict. It showed that the inherent forces of nature became dangerous adversaries when provoked. On the psychological level, the conflict was expressed as a split in the personality. The personality was no longer a monadic ego able to control emotions from its self-conscious vantage point. It contained unknown depths where powerful emotions and fantasies lived independent lives. The rational ego was in reality weak and disjointed and was as a rule driven to madness or suicide when it was unable to integrate the deeper layers of the personality. Indeed, many romantic writers had split personalities. Kleist, Hoffman, Hölderlin, Byron, and Poe are just a few examples.

Some of the finest illustrations of psychological insight in romantic literature are found in E. T. A. Hoffmann's tales. We will discuss Freud's analysis of them later (see III.C.2.b). Hoffmann's fictional universe houses animated dolls, fortune-tellers, magnetizers, and substitute children. The plot is developed in such a way that the reader gradually comprehends that the demonic characters and strange turns of events in reality are expressions of the unconscious fantasies and incipient madness of the main protagonist. His ever-changing states of consciousness range from situations where the ego acts against its will without understanding why to purely psychotic states where objects begin to talk and mysterious doubles physically attack the ego in order to destroy it. The genesis of self-reflection in Hegel's philosophy becomes in Hoffmann pathological self-observation and narcissism. Mirror images are transformed into living doubles, the total incarnation of psychic characteristics repressed by the superficial and conventional ego and the ideals and norms it attempts to live up to. The deeper layers of the personality are thus not merely primitive and inarticulate drives. They are mobilized as an independent subject. The madman acts as if he were possessed by the devil and the devil is portrayed as the product of the madman's fantasies. The depiction of these features illustrates the development of the psychological concept of the superego.

Edgar Allan Poe continued the romantic tradition by constructing his criminal mysteries in such a way that only knowledge of the unconscious intelligence and its methods—for example, a knowledge of cryptography and rebus riddles and the ability to put oneself in another's shoes by intersubjective identification could reveal the truth. Poe's doubles are also supernatural figures who cannot be repelled by normal means: one kills one's double, one kills oneself. Later variations on this theme can be found in Stevenson, Dostoevsky, and Hamsun. In their works, the appearance of the double is a sign of madness.

The French writer Stendhal should also be mentioned as a relatively realist psychologist in the romantic tradition. In his novel *The Red and the Black* (Stendhal 1830), there are no supernatural doubles and the like, and the plot unfolds in a historically correctly depicted milieu. However, the main protagonist, Julien, possesses quite extraordinary psychic characteristics: on the one hand he has remarkable intelligence and will power, which he cynically employs for egoistic goals, and on the other he is subjected to irrational impulses, which he carries out without knowing why. The double has in this case been transformed into an internal ego ideal (Napoleon himself) controlling all of Julien's actions. It is clear that emotional and sexual drives combined with particularly intense experiences and ideas comprise the deeper layers of his personality. Hate and love for the same person alternate in characteristic patterns without being able to be traced back to an unequivocal ego desiring the one or the other. The personality is split into conflicting parts and inclinations, the most important being precisely those which Enlightenment literature did everything to trivialize.

(b) Naturalist Literature: Life History and the Return of the Past

Naturalism in the 1860s was a reaction to Romanticism, as was natural science to natural philosophy. Literature was analyzed in the context of contemporary scientific and philosophical trends. Pioneers such as Hippolyte Taine and Georg Brandes created a broader radical Enlightenment movement, giving equal praise to philosophers like Comte, Mill, and Nietzsche, scientists like Darwin, and writers like Flaubert, Zola, Ibsen, and J. P. Jacobsen. Behind the praise for the writers was a political aim. Literature was to forge an alliance with the natural sciences in the struggle against prejudices and illusions. No important issue was to be passed over in silence. Literature was to debate controversial subjects, especially the sore points of bourgeois society, for example, religion, the family, sexual morality, and social injustice.

Taine collected some of these features in a psychological analytical model according to which the personality was primarily determined by race and milieu. Many writers attempted to incorporate precise causal relationships in their fictional plots. Some emphasized race or heredity, others milieu. Emile Zola belongs to the former group. He attempted to incorporate the methods of experimental biology in the novel. He believed that the novelist should experiment with his characters by successively placing them in different contexts and situations and then observing their reactions (despite the fact that the novelist himself could create whatever reactions he desired). Darwin's biological theory of evolution was transformed in the novel into a vulgar social Darwinism where the biologically fittest won the struggle for existence. Degeneration theory was also frequently incorporated into literary works, and numerous fictional characters fought in vain against fate, only because they belonged to a degenerate family. Social conflicts were portrayed as racial conflicts, where the healthiest race triumphed. The other group of naturalist writers, those who stressed environmental factors, are more interesting from a psychological perspective. In addition to family history, these writers took as their theme life history, and attempt to understand it as a coherent totality by regarding it in terms of causal relations between crucial experiences on the one hand and the formation of individual character on the other.

The Goncourt brothers in their novel, *Germinie Lacerteux* (Goncourt and Goncourt 1865), offered an example of such a scrupulous portrayal of a life history. The basis for the novel was the authors' discovery that their servant girl had been leading a double life for many years. She had apparently served her masters loyally and was liked and respected by all. However, she had secretly led a depraved life of drunkenness, prostitution, and theft. The only visible sign of this double life was a pronounced nervous behavior during which she sometimes collapsed in a spastic attack. In the novel, the authors attempted to construct a coherent life history of her disorder from information they gathered after her death. She came from a destitute rural family and early in her life lost the two people she really cared for and who had protected her—her mother and brother. Her sisters then got her a job as a servant in a Parisian public house where the men made crude advances to her. Her only friend and guardian was an old man named Joseph. However, one day when they were home alone he raped her. Her next tragedy came when her confessor, with whom she was unconsciously in love, rejected her. Her most traumatic experience was a relationship to a somewhat younger man who exploited her economically and sexually. In order to appease him, she had to steal from the old lady she worked for and was forced to abandon herself to all kinds of debauchery, which shattered her spirits and corrupted her morals. As a history of an illness, the novel was not successful (Charcot allegedly whistled in disapproval from his box seat when a dramatized version of the novel was staged). The characteristic changes between "good" and "evil" in Germinie fail to describe a split personality and cannot be explained as a manifestation of typical fluctuations of mood common to hysterical patients (see II.A.2, B.1, on Breuer's patient, Anna O.). However, the novel clearly illustrates how repeated traumatic experiences (the loss of loved ones and especially the rape) undermined Germinie's chances of realizing her emotions, and the connection between her rape and nervous attacks is well developed.

In the Danish writer J. P. Jacobsen's novel, *Niels Lyhne* (Jacobsen 1880), we are presented with an intimate psychological description of a split personality, where emotions and reason are in constant conflict. The emotions manifest themselves as fantasies, dreams, and longing, which can lead to madness and self-destruction if they are not realized. Reason is expressed by down-to-earth activities providing gratification unaccompanied by extreme emotional fluctuations. This conflict is regarded from both sides, and the novel claims that it is just as impossible and unbearable to live in dreams without reality as it is to live in reality without dreams. This dilemma plagues Niels Lyhne's mother from the beginning of the novel. She feels an emotional frustration in her marriage:

> She sank back into the dreams of her girlhood, but with the difference that now they were no longer illumined by hope. Moreover, she had learned that they were only dreams—distant, illusive dreams, which no longing in the world could ever draw down to her earth. When she abandoned herself to them now, it was with a sense of weariness, while an accusing inner voice told her that she was like the drunkard who knows that his passion is destroying him, that every debauch means strength taken from his weakness and added to the power of his desire. But the voice sounded in vain, for a life soberly lived, without the fair vice of dreams, was no life at all—life had exactly the value that dreams gave it and no more (Jacobsen 1880, pp. 26–27).

The cause of her frustration is the materialistic views of her husband. She compensates for this frustration by transferring her longings and hopes to her son, who throughout his childhood is constantly involved in the conflict between his mother's lyrical dream world and his father's down-to-earth labor. This conflict marks Niels Lyhne for the rest of his life. After he has been exposed to these dreams and longings and has inculcated them in his mind, nothing can diminish the strength of this psychic pole. Even though this development does not fully explain his life history, the novel nevertheless demonstrates a wide spectrum of possibilities for the realization of emotions. Niels's mother turns to religion, a friend becomes an artist, and Niels himself turns into an idealistic atheist and through his atheism is able to anchor his longing in reality. Niels declares his atheism on his deathbed, and this part of his personality creates a certain coherence in his life. The novel shows that it is impossible to escape from one's emotional background. The consequences of this emotional makeup must be endured for better or worse. When Freud read *Niels Lyhne* in 1895, he characterized the ending as classic and the novel as the most moving he had read in nine years.

Our last example is Henrik Ibsen's so-called contemporary dramas (1877–1899), which became the subject of much discussion around the turn of the century. Many of them treated political and social issues, but there was always a psychological dimension as well. The plots open in a harmless atmosphere seemingly free of conflict, which is then revealed to conceal inner tension. Past events, which have become a heavy burden for one or more of the characters, are gradually exposed. The more the main protagonist attempts to adjust to the present behind an honorable facade, the more the past is revealed as a dangerous threat to this facade. The problem is always that the present is built on the past and the whole edifice might collapse if the lies and sins of the past are not exposed and reputed.

In *Pillars of Society* (Ibsen 1877), Lona tells consul Bernick: a lie made him what he is. When he later tries to excuse himself for what he has become by saying that his son should create a society based on truth, she objects that it will be based on a lie because of the inheritance he gives his son. Similarly, in *An Enemy of the People* (Ibsen 1882), when Doctor Stockmann tirelessly demands that a past mistake be redressed, he asks the mayor if the town's prosperity must be founded on a lie. The mistake of the past is that the town's water supply has been contaminated because the town did not want to finance an expensive water pipe. Symbolically, the past mistake is that the sources of the town's spiritual life were poisoned, and that the whole community was founded on a lie. In *Rosmersholm* (Ibsen 1886), Rosmer states that no victory was ever won by guilty men. His affair with Rebekka can never be realized because she must face the fact that she—partly unknowingly—has had a sexual relationship with her father and has murdered Rosmer's wife: she would have only to stretch out her hand to seize happiness but that her past stands in the way.

The almost monotonous repetition of this pattern indicates that it should not be regarded as a result of circumstance, but as a necessity, an unavoidable challenge in the development of every human being. It is noteworthy that Ibsen sometimes absolves his characters from taking the entire blame for their misfortunes. In *A Doll's House* (Ibsen 1879), Nora commits a crime out of love for her husband. The crime is regarded as right, while the opinions of society and Nora's husband are seen as wrong. The theme of *The Wild Duck* (Ibsen 1884) is living a lie in order to retain a sense of sanity. An evil fate is always justified by past events: (1) it is inherited, as we see it in *Ghosts* (Ibsen 1881) when Osvald inherits his father's syphilis; (2) fateful acts are committed, without realizing that they are incompatible with one's life goals; or (3) characters are forced to submit to social norms, which leads them to condemn their own past. Conflict develops when the present is superimposed on the past, and breaks out when the past returns and demands to be integrated into the present.

In Ibsen's work, the past event is as a rule a crime or a lie, but the plot structure would have been the same if it had revolved around a sexual trauma as in *Germinie Lacerteux* or emotional overexposure in childhood as in *Niels Lyhne*. In this context, Ibsen's most penetrating psychological drama is *The Lady from the Sea* (Ibsen 1888). Ellida Wangel suffers from a nervous disease and has no sexual relations with her husband. It is gradually revealed that her thoughts focus around a lengthy past liaison with a sailor. She is drawn toward the sea and the sailor, who appeals to her unfulfilled sexual inclinations, which gives her guilt feelings for betraying her husband. The conflict reaches a climax when the sailor appears and wants Ellida back. She is then given a choice, and by "freely" choosing her husband she is released from the threatening power of the past. The primitive sexual fantasies that had previously expressed themselves by an attraction to the sea and "abnormal ideas" can now be fulfilled in her relationship with her husband.

Ibsen's drama resembles in some respects Freud's case histories of hysterical patients from the 1890s. Here too, nervous disease expressed itself as sexual anxiety and "abnormal ideas." Many young girls entered marriage with strong but ambivalent ties to their parents, ranging from jealous infatuation to seduction and rape fantasies. When these ties were transferred to the future husband, they became overtly neurotic. Under this surface lay the repression of forbidden sexual fantasies, for example, infantile masturbation, and the eventual cure consisted of rooting out sexual repression and becoming aware of and developing primitive sexual fantasies. Ibsen's play would follow this pattern if we substituted the mysterious sailor whom Ellida met when she still lived with her father in an isolated lighthouse, with the father himself. Whatever passed between father and daughter (and Ibsen had described an incestuous relationship two years earlier in *Rosmersholm*) has blocked Ellida's feelings for her husband. In her mind, past events have assumed pathological dimensions: she sees "the stranger" in her mind, sees the pearl in his brooch as a dead fish eye staring at her, sees his eyes in the eyes of her dying child. This is the "ghastly crime" that both attracts and repels, her, and that resembles a drifting toward the sea and death. Ibsen's cure consists of bringing the representative of the past to life, so that Ellida can make a new choice between him and her husband. She chooses her husband, because he lets her choose "freely," thus allowing her to escape the oppression of her marriage, which was one of the causes of her hysteria.

Throughout his writings, Freud continued to search for new explanations for the phenomenon we have called *the return of the past*. We will review this phenomenon in part 5 in the section on development and repetition (see V.B.3).

C.

THE CRISIS OF THE SUBJECT AND CRITIQUE OF SIMPLIFIED SUBJECT CONCEPTS

We will conclude the first section dealing with the historical origins of psychoanalysis with a review of subject concepts developed in the last third of the nineteenth century. These were formulated as a result of genuine changes in the subject, and criticized each of the three simplified subject concepts that we examined in section A and summarize below.

We have schematically placed these three subject concepts in relation to three historical periods and three social spheres. The liberalistic subject concept was developed in relation to the relative dominance of the sphere of circulation in early capitalism. Free trade thus became the social model for the rationalistic concept of a free and rational subject. What we now call the humanistic subject concept developed as a reaction to capitalism and its rigid rationalistic ideology, where freedom became increasingly occulted by calculation and multiple considerations. Particularly during the Romantic period, spontaneous emotions were considered to constitute the core of the subject, preconditioned by the confinement of the family in a sphere of intimacy determined by functional considerations that isolated the reproduction of the subject. Finally, we discussed the mechanistic subject concept, which came to the fore along with the natural sciences (especially the biological and medical sciences) in the middle of the nineteenth century. According to this concept, the subject was nothing more than a machine. The social model for this concept was to be found in the sphere of production and its development of industrial technology.

The chronological order presented here does not indicate that one subject concept disappeared when another appeared. The liberalistic subject concept was more widely accepted in the nineteenth century than in the eighteenth century when it was developed. Much the same time lapse applies to the humanistic subject concept. Bourgeois societies established in a number of countries in the nineteenth century did not actually favor any one of the three concepts, but let them develop side by side. The reason for this is that capitalist society can only function when the three social spheres (the sphere of circulation, the sphere of intimacy, and the sphere of production) are kept separate and each fulfills a necessary social function (circulation, reproduction, and production). The three spheres must be *separate* and must adapt *to each other* in order for society to function. These two demands cause social crises and consequently the crisis of the subject.

The spheres are isolated from each other in order to fulfill a certain function. Consequently, the sphere is organized *as if* it were autonomous, *as if* its function were an aim in itself, and *as if* its values were universal. The formulation of a fixed subject concept is an important part of the internal organization of the sphere and perhaps the very part that permits the sphere to close itself off from the others, because the essence of the subject has no need for external recognition. The three simplified subject concepts are all represented in capitalist society. Although they contradict each other, they have a remarkable ability to coexist. Child care and education, the media, and political ideologies have all developed many clichés about the subject, a truism for every occasion. A person must intermittently be able to be sensitive and reasonable and regard any part of himself as a medical problem; he must be able to be spontaneous and reflective, altruistic and fiercely independent. The latent contradiction does not express itself as long as individual identity adheres to a single subject concept: housewives, artists, and pedagogues are usually "humanists," while scientists, doctors, and generals are "mechanists," and so on. However, there are historical reasons for the failure of the individual identity to adhere to any one concept.

These reasons result from the fact that the three social spheres must constantly cooperate for society as a whole to function. Production and consumption *must* balance ideally, the sphere of intimacy *must* provide the labor power necessary for the sphere of production. When this cooperation fails, economic crises develop that mercilessly penetrate the fragile autonomy of the separate spheres, thus causing subjective crises in which the subjects lose their ideological points of reference. Fixed values become fluid when economic considerations interfere with the closed world of ideologies. A typical example is when women during an economic boom are encouraged to enter the labor market. This development is justified by the liberalistic subject concept (women have equal opportunity, they can support themselves and be trained in the laws of reason and calculation). During a slump, however, women are sent back to the confines of the sphere of intimacy and society then emphasizes the blessings of womanhood, motherhood, and spontaneity.

In the last thirty years of the nineteenth century, there was a general tendency for the simple subject concepts to change character. Having previously described subjects who were immutable and determined by their own essence, the simple concepts of the subject now described subjects who were historically changeable and whose essence was environmentally determined. The new and more complex subject concepts did not define the subject as an autonomous being, but rather as if its functions were socially determined, in other words, dependent on other functions. The mind of the subject began to be seen as containing active processes that it could not control and of which it was hardly aware. The formulation of these new subject concepts sought to achieve a theoretical understanding of these active processes. This led to the abandonment of a great number of illusions concerning the subject and to a more constant adjustment of the understanding of the subject in relation to its actual life.

We have discussed these new complex subject concepts in the plural, because no new global subject concept as a whole was developed. Instead, the outdated subject concepts were criticized and attempts were made to update them. These attempts focused on broadening the understanding of *separate* functions of the subject in the context of other functions. Thus, the subject in the sphere of production, the sphere of circulation, and the sphere of intimacy still had to be differentiated. Although we are aware of the dangers of simplification and generalization, we will in the following sections discuss (1) how the concept of the subject in the sphere of production (or the subject seen from the perspective of the sphere of production) was transformed from being purely mechanistic to positivistic, (2) how the concept of the subject in the sphere of circulation (or the subject seen from the perspective of the sphere of circulation) was transformed from being liberalistic to being Marxist, and finally (3) how the concept of the subject in the private sphere (or the subject seen from the perspective of the private sphere) was transformed from being humanistic to being psychoanalytical. We will then have tentatively characterized the psychoanalytic subject concept and placed the development of psychoanalysis in a historical and social context.

1. THE POSITIVISTIC DEVELOPMENT
OF THE MECHANISTIC SUBJECT CONCEPT

In 1845, several students of the physiologist Johannes Müller formed the Berliner Physikalische Gesellschaft (The Physical Society of Berlin). The most well-known members were Hermann Helmholtz, Emil du Bois-Reymond, Ernst Brücke, and Carl Ludwig. The society was interested in natural science based on materialistic, reductionistic, and mechanistic views. Everything in the universe including all aspects of human consciousness was regarded as the result of physical matter and its processes. There are rumors of a Helmholtz school, where mostly young scientists championed the new ideals with fanatical zeal. During the 1850s and 1860s, disciples of Helmholtz appeared at most European universities. For example, Brücke became a professor in Vienna ("our ambassador in the Far East," as his Berlin friends called him) where for a number of years he taught Freud. Together with Darwin and his disciples, the Helmholtz school also inspired naturalist writers, critics, and philosophers, seemingly an indication that mechanistic materialism was to flourish over a long period.

However, this was not to be the case; questions were asked that mechanistic materialism was unable to answer. For example, in neurophysiology, the localization of even the simplest psychic mechanisms in the nervous system was a problem. In the 1870s, the natural sciences underwent a crisis. In 1872, du Bois-Reymond created a stir by publicly renouncing his former views. He rejected the possibility of explaining the human subject by using physics and chemistry and claimed that there were limits to human knowledge. Among the seven riddles of the universe were the origins of consciousness and the question of free will.

The natural sciences survived the crisis thanks to new developments in the field. These developments have been summarized in the statement "Matter disappears." A theory of knowledge replaced mechanistic materialism, which was now regarded as speculative, not empirical. It was founded on the existence of matter, despite the fact that the only givens were subjective sensory impressions. Sensory impressions formed the new basis for the natural sciences, a basis more limited, but at the same time more secure, than that of materialism. Different positivistic schools emerged from this new view. In Germany, Ernst Mach was a typical example. In

1872, he formulated three aims for scientific research: (1) to study the laws of the connections between ideas, (2) to discover the laws of the connections between perceptions, and (3) to clarify the laws of the connections between perceptions and ideas. Mach called these three aims psychology, physics, and psychophysics. His formulations were accepted by psychologists and physicists alike (however, it should be noted that Fechner's and Mach's psychophysics differed).

Positivism did not, however, affect the research methods of the natural sciences. A descriptive classification method and an experimental method (and a clinical pathological method in medicine) still dominated the field. However, the positivists refrained from creating general hypothetical models on the basis of the results of their research, and the natural sciences therefore lost some of their former uniform character. Innumerable research laboratories were established where specific problems were meticulously investigated. In the field of psychology, the great pioneer was Wilhelm Wundt who continued Fechner's work by performing numerous experiments on human psychic and psychophysical reactions. The consideration of the subject as a totality, which even Fechner had maintained, was thus abandoned. A similar tendency can be traced in psychiatry, where Emil Kraepelin's work dominated the field. Kraepelin abandoned comprehensive anatomical and etiological theories in favor of a description of symptoms and classification of mental illness according to these symptoms.

Positivism meant doing away with materialism, but not with mechanism. Comprehensive materialistic theories were abandoned and Theodor Meynert was considered a prescientific brain mythologist because he based his work on general hypothetical models. However, data were regarded as objective knowledge and therefore subjected to mathematical and statistical examination. The reintroduction of the observing subject was thus only a reintroduction of a passive and mechanical subject.

The question is then what relation the positivistic version of the mechanistic subject concept has to the sphere of production, and why the original materialistic version was replaced. We have already indicated that the mechanistic subject concept is not the basis for the self-knowledge of any group or class. Its function is not to isolate the sphere of production and protect it from outside influence. Its function is more to safeguard the sphere of production's control of the sphere of circulation and the sphere of intimacy. Materialistic mechanism was not suited to this task because it totally destroyed the ideological basis and consequently the viability of these spheres. Without some ideological basis in religious, moral, or democratic ideals, these spheres collapse—at any rate in the form they assume in capitalist society. Mechanistic materialism thus originally emerged as a threat to bourgeois norms and values. Conversely, the sphere of production could not bar itself from influencing the two other spheres. This would risk dangerous political organization around the self-evident democratic and humanistic ideals of these spheres leading to a democratization and humanization of the sphere of production.

Positivistic mechanism thus remains the most effective instrument the sphere of production has to control the two other spheres ideologically. First, it is not offensive since it only answers the questions it is asked. All ideological values posing no threat to the sphere of production are thus left intact. Second, positivistic mechanism surrounds itself with an aura of scientific objectivity. It only determines what is true or false and not what is desirable or reprehensible, and it is presumed to serve any political interest with an equal amount of loyalty. Third, it has been able to provide desired results in research by selecting questions, generating concepts and categories, and determining norms a priori.

An important cause of the triumph of positivism over materialism at the end of the nineteenth century was the massive support industry gave to many new research laboratories, which were very flexible in the selection of research projects. The entire research process followed scientific norms to the letter, but there was no method for determining *what* was to be the subject of research. Research projects therefore often served industry. In psychology laboratories toward the end of the century only rather harmless experiments were conducted in perception and association. However, the scientific apparatuses developed as a result of these experiments were later used to classify individuals according to intelligence and labor capacity.

2. MARXISM AND THE CRITIQUE OF THE LIBERALISTIC SUBJECT CONCEPT

The democratic constitutions of the nineteenth century owed much to liberal ideology. Citizens and especially businesses were granted freedom in the sphere of circulation. However, this freedom was based on private property, so that only citizens owning a certain amount of property could vote for parliament. Freedom was not, even in the long term, extended to include the sphere of production and the sphere of intimacy. In the sphere of production, the employer had absolute power to manage and delegate labor power, and in the sphere of intimacy fathers could evoke the sanctity of private life and tyrannize over the family. If this limited freedom in the sphere of circulation had any value whatsoever, it accrued to the employers and male heads of families. Freedom was nevertheless regarded as something to be defended by all. The liberalistic subject concept, which emphasized free will, reason, and responsibility, was in principle universal. In the name of liberalism, those without property were brought up to exhibit self-discipline and responsibility toward employers and the state.

In his seminal work, *Capital* (Marx, K. 1867–1894), Karl Marx criticized the entire basis of liberal economics. His analysis showed that the "free" circulation of commodities on the market actually served the accumulation of capital. The better free circulation functioned, the more capital was accumulated at the expense of the workers. This fundamental critique of liberal economics was consistently repeated as a critique of the bourgeois state and the liberalistic subject concept. Marx did not formulate an independent psychological theory, but he did recognize some connections between the consciousness of the subject and its social status, which can be regarded as a new subject concept. While the liberalistic concept of the subject has free will as its official trademark, the Marxist subject concept is seemingly characterized by mechanism. This may appear paradoxical in light of Marx's support for the emancipation of the working class and his emphasis on the coercive nature of capitalist society. However, this paradox is only apparent. The liberalistic concept of the subject disguises the actual coercion. Marx with his mechanism attempted to expose this coercion in the context of a future emancipation. For Marx, the freedom to buy and sell commodities at market price was fundamentally a false freedom.

The primary focus of the Marxist subject concept is alienation. It originates in Hegelian philosophy and indicates a state in which the subject has created an object over which it loses control; this object then starts to control the subject. In religion, alienation develops when man creates a God who determines what man should do, and sometimes even controls his actions. In politics, alienation arises when the citizen creates a state that not only suppresses his interests, but starts to control him. In economics, alienation appears when a worker produces commodities that the capitalist transforms into a huge capital apparatus suppressing and impoverishing the worker. It is especially this last form of alienation that Marx analyzed. For Marx, the essence of the subject was to work and produce commodities but in capitalist society this essence is not identical with the consciousness of the subject, that is its understanding of itself and society. The subject works, but does not perceive itself as a working soul. Through labor it loses part of itself in the product. Labor has become reified, and in the sphere of circulation the subject cannot recognize itself in the form of the product. The product appears as an independent being, a fetish. It exerts an almost mystical magical power and enthralls its creator in passive fascination. In any case something of value has been lost through this process. It has been accumulated as dead labor in capital, which as an independent overlapping subject regulates production as well as circulation. Alienation

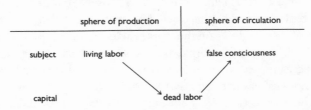

implies that the consciousness of the subject has been separated from its essence. False consciousness is the ideological self-perception of the sphere of circulation (free will, reason, self-discipline) and social perception (free circulation of commodities, private property, democracy, equality before the law). The sphere of circulation is a closed system functioning as if it were autonomous, thus fulfilling its primary function as a tool of capital. The workers cannot resist because their false consciousness prevents them from breaking away from capitalist ideology. However, they experience blatant injustices in their daily lives inconsistent with liberal ideals. Marx concluded from this economic analysis that the workers had a moral right to capitalist wealth. This right could be realized by repossessing the alienated labor through the formation of unions and political organizations. Democracy and freedom should not be limited to the sphere of circulation, but rather extended to encompass the sphere of production. This view brings us to the confrontation between socialism and liberalism, which lies outside the scope of this book.

The Marxist subject concept considers labor the essence of the subject. These analyses imply that this essence can be hidden from the subject or can be expressed in a distorted form. Although false consciousness is a result of capital, capital is produced by labor. Consequently, the worker must understand the dependence of capital on his labor. Criticism of consciousness leads to criticism of free will, which is closely linked to consciousness in the liberalistic subject concept. If you do not know the causes of your actions, you cannot claim that you are acting freely. Workers are alienated and not free because they see an explanation for the causes of their labor in ideological terms. They can explain why they go to work, why they bring up their children the way they do, and why they join a particular political party, but this awareness is only coherent because of ideologies. Abolishing alienation and recapturing freedom can only come about if the workers obtain a correct understanding of their position in society and if they remove the external barriers preventing them from acting freely.

The Marxist subject concept can be regarded as an alternative to the liberalistic one because it is based on a different analysis of the sphere of circulation. The Marxist and liberalistic analyses both employ commodity exchange as a model for the subject concept but Marxism extends this perspective by regarding labor power as a commodity. The explanation for surplus value is thus no longer in the sphere of circulation, but in the sphere of production, because value is created by labor. Both the Marxist and liberalistic subject concepts hold that the subject is bound to satisfy its needs under the guidance of reason. However, Marxist analysis sees this reason not only as the narrow, ideological reason of the sphere of circulation, but as the reason of society as a whole. Both concepts employ the term *freedom*. Liberalistic freedom is individual, based on competition between individuals, and only limited by the legal rights of other individuals. Marxist freedom is collective and consists of the greatest possible satisfaction of natural needs. This view comes close to Spinoza's definition of freedom as insight into necessity.

As in the mechanistic subject concept, Marx tended to create mechanistic general models where nature, society, and the subject were included as objective entities. However, Marx believed that the subject had the power to change history if it became aware of its own determination. Marx's concept of history therefore contained an element of freedom.

In relation to the humanistic subject concept, there are many similarities especially between Hegel and Marx. Both employed a dialectical model in which the subject realized itself through alienation and a reintegration of the alienated object. For Marx, labor constituted the essence of the subject, and it was through labor that the subject realized itself. For Hegel, labor was only the manifestation of a deeper desire that could be expressed in other ways. On this issue Hegel was a genuine representative for the humanistic concept of the subject in attempting to isolate emotions and desire as the sources of an understanding of the essence of the subject. By choosing labor as a category, Marx placed the subject in the sphere of production. He was then able to analyze phenomena relating to the spheres of production as well as circulation. However, he reduced the sphere of intimacy to a reproductive sphere simply bending to the coercion of economic processes. This prevented him from analyzing the consequences of the symptoms of crisis in the sphere of intimacy such as the pathological organization of desire, which in turn pointed to sexuality as a factor in the social dynamic.

3. PSYCHOANALYSIS AND THE CRITIQUE OF THE MECHANISTIC SUBJECT CONCEPT

The goal of the empirical and later positivistic theory of knowledge was to purge the disruptive influence of emotions from the knowledge of the world. The ideal for the scientific observer was a passive and neutral consciousness without personal expectations and biases. The views of most fanatic romantics were diametrically opposed to this. According to them, consciousness could first enter the emotional depths when it was isolated from its environment. They did not regard emotions as part of the organic condition of the body, but instead thought of them as spiritual and timeless. Emotions were like buried treasure hardly able to bear the intolerant curiosity of the present and sure to die out if attempts were made to convert them into something of concrete value. They were vulnerable and fragile and therefore had to be protected against the degradation that was all too often their fate in society.

We have already argued that romantic sensitivity was actually a result of the pedagogy of capitalism with its emphasis on surveillance and self-discipline and on the separation and delimitation of the sphere of intimacy from the other social spheres. The sphere of intimacy was developed around internalized sexuality and the consequent tense emotional ties within the family. Romantic ideology and the humanistic subject concept contributed to making the sphere of intimacy a closed and autonomous system. In romantic utopias, the sphere of intimacy was extended to encompass a self-contained paradisiacal state of nature where negative emotions and cold calculation were banished. The realization of such a paradise necessitated knowledge of how emotions were expressed before the fall into the materialistic contemporary world. Poets and philosophers became self-proclaimed prophets of true emotion. It is characteristic that they did not provide a subtle empirical description of the emotions (for example, listing different emotions by name), choosing instead to posit the ideal essence of emotions before contact with concrete objects. According to this view, the sensual components of emotions were also irrelevant.

In light of the development of the sphere of intimacy in the course of the nineteenth century, it is understandable that romantic ideas could not continue to function as a basis for the self-perception of family members. As a result of the constant pressures of society and new demands on the sphere of intimacy, crises and conflicts developed in family life, the consequences of which affected women first and foremost. The intense emotions described in books were there, to be sure, but they were linked to fantasies and longings, the realization and satisfaction of which the books ignored. The beauty of this distant world did not appear and was difficult to see in daily life. Upper-class women may have passed the time with reading and music and lower-class women with hard and monotonous housework, but both groups could not express their emotions socially or sexually. Taking the boundaries of sexual life at the time into account, it is clear that women were reduced to being childbearers and passive objects of male sexuality. Sexual gratification for women was hardly a subject of discussion. Couples who did not want children were virtually prevented from having sexual contact because of the lack of contraceptives.

Generally, marriage and the nuclear family seem to have been an extremely unsatisfactory arrangement for emotional and sexual life. The more the woman expected from marriage, the greater was her disappointment in her trivial daily existence and her husband's lack of emotion. From the middle of the nineteenth century, fiction began to deal specifically with this problem and to describe different possibilities for emotional development. The possibility of divorce was thus treated by Flaubert in *Madame Bovary* (Flaubert 1857) and later by writers such as Herman Bang in *Ved Vejen (By the Road)* (Bang 1886). Flight from marriage was described by J. P. Jacobsen in *Marie Grubbe* (Jacobsen 1876) and by Henrik Ibsen in *A Doll's House* (Ibsen 1879). We have already discussed some examples in section I.B.6: Jacobsen's examination of the life-long consequences of a mother-child relationship in *Niels Lyhne* (Jacobsen 1880) and the descriptions by the Goncourt brothers and Ibsen of the transformation of emotions into nervousness and neuroses.

Marriage and the nuclear family were also criticized from the perspective of the man and child. Most of August Strindberg's work depicts marriage as a catastrophe for the husband (because of the criminal nature of women). In his autobiographical *The Son of a Servant* (Strindberg 1886), the nuclear family is brutally criticized.

It is more difficult to find a similar theoretical assessment of the romantic emotional ideology. The natural sciences reduced emotions to a psychic expression of different corporal states, primarily examined in connection with the question of how instincts and needs could be controlled, regulated, and satisfied in a more rational manner. Psychological subtleties were thus lost, of course, and no natural scientist could explain the paradoxes and crises of emotional life as they were expressed in the sphere of intimacy. Hysteria and other neuroses were dismissed as exhibitionism and at best treated by diets and cures in health resorts. Only in philosophy can we see the beginnings of a theoretical elaboration and critique of romanticism on its own terms. We are referring to the nascent phenomenology and existentialism of Hegel and Kierkegaard. Both recognized emotions and desire as the basis for the subject's interest in the world. They did not regard desire as an internal immutable essence existing prior to its encounter with its surroundings, but acknowledged the existence of alienated desire. The subject could not develop by holding desire within itself (or in the sphere of intimacy, for that matter), but was forced to risk it in the world in order to attain self-realization. Emotions expressed during this process were real, not alienated desire.

We have thus come to what we will call the *scientific* critique of the romantic and humanistic subject concept—psychoanalysis. Like the romantics, Freud was interested in emotions and affects, anxiety, hate, and desire. Because of his training in the natural sciences, he tended to assign the affects to corporal drives and instincts, but he carefully avoided narrow causal explanations. A focal point of his concept was his belief that drives were first developed as partial drives during the encounter between the individual and his environment. For the child, this encounter took place in the sphere of intimacy, or "in the bosom of the family." Emotions, perceptions, and impulses appearing in the conscious ego could, of course, be traced back to a drive, but drives developed in the unconscious according to a complex set of rules. Freud formulated a number of scientific hypotheses on the unconscious, its genesis, its function, and its ability to influence consciousness. One causal chain led back to the functions of the body and the biologically inherited reflexes of the nervous system. However, another led out toward the sphere of intimacy and society. Concrete experiences from the sphere of intimacy and the other social spheres settled under given circumstances in the unconscious in the form of repressed ideas and fantasies, thereby attaining equal status with biological inheritance as internal parts of the subject's being.

Psychoanalytic concepts are composed so as not to close the sphere of intimacy despite the fact that they are similar to traditional psychological concepts in many respects. Any conscious emotion or thought always has unconscious roots. The unknown and unconscious in the subject is constantly interacting with the unknown and unconscious in society. All the structures affecting the subject, all the rules the subject obeys, exist as elements in the unconscious. Freud therefore believed that the essence of the subject was not comprised of the conscious ego or of a scientifically indefinable metaphysical individuality. A disharmonious relationship between the unconscious and the conscious in the subject—as known in neuroses—is rooted in the same causes as the disharmonious relationship between the social spheres. The economic crises of society make it impossible for the subject to isolate and consolidate itself in the sphere of intimacy around some "eternally human" values. Sooner or later economic crises manifest themselves as subjective crises. The development of psychoanalysis is thus merely a necessary historical reaction to the crisis of the subject in capitalist society, an attempt to replace the obsolete humanistic concept of the subject with a new and more appropriate one.

II

FREUD AND THE DEVELOPMENT OF PSYCHOANALYSIS

INTRODUCTION
TO PART II

We have chosen to begin our presentation of psychoanalysis with a chronological examination of Freud's life. This biographical outline will afford us the opportunity to show how Freud acquired the personal, social, and academic assumptions for his work, and how he combined his experiences in the formation of psychoanalytic theory. This part of the book does not contain any analysis of theory or comparison of psychoanalytic concepts with their historical background, which will be treated later. However, a chronological presentation of the inception of psychoanalysis in particular can contribute to an understanding of what psychoanalysis is, because it illustrates the logical relationship between the problems Freud encountered, his attempts to solve these problems, and the appearance of new problems. Freud's conceptual framework was constructed in stages, which enables us to comprehend why old and new concepts sometimes contradict each other.

We do not intend to emphasize Freud's personality in our presentation by explaining the development of psychoanalysis as a result of his genius, stubbornness, or incorruptibility, as some have done. Freud and psychoanalysis are inextricably linked for other, more concrete reasons. First, Freud united the necessary prerequisites for the development of psychoanalysis: he belonged to a petite bourgeoisie whose identity was threatened by social developments; he had himself experienced the neurotic constrictions of the petit bourgeois family and the strict sexual mores of bourgeois society; he had learned the basic views of the rapidly developing natural sciences and the socially critical ideals of the naturalist enlightenment; he effortlessly combined his specialist training in neuroanatomy and neuropathology with a deep and all-consuming interest in art, literature, and philosophy; and, due to various circumstances, he was forced to abandon his career in the natural sciences at the university and devote himself to work with private neurotic patients. Second, it is evident that Freud always seemed to make the right decisions on the development of psychoanalysis in difficult situations. Freud stood alone during the entire period of the inception of psychoanalysis because his closest colleagues, Breuer and Fliess, each objected to crucial aspects of psychoanalytic theory. During the establishment of the psychoanalytic movement, it was Freud who consistently rejected Jung's and Adler's theories. Only toward the end of the 1920s and in the 1930s did Freud lose his steady grip on psychoanalysis and it was during this period that the seeds were sown for the various Freudian schools that still exist today.

We have decided to end our presentation with Freud's death in 1939, leaving for another book the fate of psychoanalysis after Freud. For the same reason, we do not discuss writers who were already active in the field in the 1920s and 1930s, but who did not come into their own and form schools until after World War II: ego psychologists such as Anna Freud, Wälder, Nunberg, and Hartmann; the Freudian Marxist Wilhelm Reich; and fantasy- and symbol-oriented analysts like Melanie Klein and Jacques Lacan.

A.
FREUD'S BACKGROUND

During Freud's lifetime, Austria was a world power on the wane. Once the dominant state in the German coalition after the Vienna Congress in 1815, Austria was gradually outdistanced by Prussia. Headed by Metternich, the political leadership of Austria was extremely conservative, crushing all liberal movements with an iron fist. In 1848, when much of Europe erupted in revolt in the wake of the French February Revolution, the liberals took power in Vienna. Metternich fled the country, and the kaiser abdicated in favor of his nephew, the self-proclaimed liberal Franz Joseph. In June 1848, radical groups took power and Vienna was transformed into a veritable "Paris Commune," which, however, was short-lived. The city was besieged in October and then attacked, culminating in the slaughter of radical workers and students. As a grim reminder of this massacre, mutilated bodies could be found in the trenches long after the event. Kaiser Franz Joseph I, who soon revealed his deeply reactionary views, occupied the throne until 1916. During his reign, Austria was governed in turn by conservative and liberal ministers. Behind the scenes, however, the capitalist bourgeoisie wielded the real power. Among its reforms was improving the educational system. Schooling was obligatory for all children between six and fourteen years of age. The secondary school system was extended and improved. Influential circles in industry primarily supported the technological disciplines, but the natural sciences were also considered in a positive light.

Prussia's Bismarck declared war on Austria in 1866. Prussia emerged victorious, despite the initial support Austria received from the other member states of the German coalition. Austria was excluded from the coalition after the war, which crippled its power. To ease the pressure of growing nationalist sentiment, the Magyars were granted partial autonomy in the establishment of the Austro-Hungarian Empire in 1867. Nationalist conflicts involving other minorities (Czechs, Slovaks, Serbs, and Croats) persisted, however, and the country teemed with terrorists, who murdered prominent political figures in the name of one cause or another. In 1914, the Austrian crown prince was assassinated in Sarajevo, which was the spark that ignited World War I. After the war, the dual monarchy was abolished, and Austria, drastically reduced, emerged in its present form.

During the period of national crisis after 1848, industry in Austria expanded at a rapid rate. The ever-growing working class began to express its aims politically, and many academics are said to have harbored socialist sympathies. This development precipitated pronounced reactionary tendencies among the bourgeoisie and the petite bourgeoisie of the 1880s and 1890s. Particularly in Vienna, a lively cultural atmosphere flourished, with movements and schools of every stripe. The reactionary bourgeoisie closed ranks around Victorian mores, while radical leftist elements plunged headlong into all sorts of sectarianisms. As a whole, cultural life grew increasingly decadent, and the universities became the scenes of fatal conflicts among competing theories. One could compare *fin de siècle* Vienna with Paris in the 1960s and 1970s, where the dissolution of a former great power also fostered many different cultural and political activities.

1. CHILDHOOD AND YOUTH
(1856–1873)

Freud (his first name Sigismund was later modernized to Sigmund) was born in 1856 in Freiberg, about 150 miles from Vienna. His family belonged to the German-speaking Jewish lower middle class. His father, Jacob Freud, was in the wool trade, an industry which was based on local production. The 1848 revolution had brought about an increase in national liberation movements throughout Austria, and the German minority in Moravian Freiberg could not ignore the growth of Czech nationalism (Freiberg is now part of Czechoslovakia). The revolution had also generated industrial development, which adversely affected the many small wool manufacturers in the rural districts. Freiberg, once a prominent trade city located on a main trade route, underwent a steady decline after a new railway was built bypassing the city in the 1840s. Local wool production gradually came to a standstill, affecting the wool trade, which was the primary means of subsistence for the Freud family. Rampant inflation in the 1850s further impoverished it. During the 1859 economic crisis, a result of Austria's war with Italy, the family moved to Vienna, where anti-Semitic legislation had been partially repealed in 1848. In Vienna, the family apparently managed to subsist on a modest income from the interest on savings from the sale of Freud's father's business. The rest of the savings were given to Jacob Freud's two adult sons from his first marriage. They emigrated to England, where they managed quite well.

The little information we have on Freud's childhood comes from his books and letters. He was the first child of Jacob Freud's third marriage. His father was forty when Freud was born; his mother, Amalie, only twenty. His mother lavished love and affection on him (he always remained her "*goldener* Sigi"), and Freud regarded his father and half brothers as dangerous rivals. He was also very close to an old Czech nanny, a Catholic, who took him to church. His imagination was stimulated by her hair-raising tales of heaven and hell, guilt and punishment. She was dismissed for theft when Freud was two and a half years old. Freud's half brother Philipp reported the theft, which earned him hatred in the fantasies of his younger brother. Freud also had two playmates his age, Emil and Gisela Fluss, who later appeared in a memory from childhood (see III.B.1.a).

Leaving Freiberg was a traumatic experience for Freud. The family's first stop was Leipzig, where Freud's father planned to continue his business. At the train station in Breslau, Freud saw gaslights for the first time. He associated these lights with burning souls in hell. After several months in Leipzig, Freud's mother and her children traveled to Vienna alone. One night during the trip, Freud saw his mother naked, which aroused sexual desire in him. From that time on, he had a neurotic anxiety of train trips (see the analysis of the forgetting of the name Signorelli, III.B.1.b).

Freud's early childhood was profoundly engraved in his memory, because it formed a sharp contrast to his life in Vienna. The move to Vienna from Freiberg was in no way an improvement. Freud had moved from an open rural environment to a confining apartment in a big city, from relative economic prosperity to poverty, from prestige and respect to anonymity. The fate of Freud's family is typical of the historical proletarianization of the petite bourgeoisie. This proletarianization did not result in any political consciousness, although Freud's father was a warm supporter of the liberal ministeries that from time to time were given power in Austria. Freud regarded his childhood years in Vienna as harsh, and preferred not to be reminded of them. He did occupy, however, a privileged position in the household, with five younger sisters and one brother who was ten years younger. All the available evidence points to rigid gender roles. The oldest son became the hope of the family, while the girls were left to cope for themselves. One of Freud's sisters played the piano, but it was sold because her playing disturbed his studying.

Even though Freud's father was not so strict or authoritarian, Freud nevertheless regarded him as the epitome of rules and punishment and as an ideal worthy of emulation (he later wrote that for the son, the father is "the most powerful, the wisest, and the richest"). The fact that his father soon revealed himself to be weak, pathetic and somewhat of a failure only confirmed Freud's desire to succeed. His choice of childhood heroes illustrates how he identified with outsiders who succeeded in society on their own: Alexander the Great, Hannibal, Cromwell, and Napoleon. Freud was somewhat of a rebel and despised his father's humility toward those who were stronger. It was especially shocking to hear his father relate an episode from his youth, when a passerby, greeting him with the words "Jew, get off the pavement," knocked his hat into the gutter. His father apparently put up no resistance to this abuse.

In his youth, Freud developed a passionate interest for literature, which steered his fantasies and dreams along new paths. His knowledge of art and literature was unusually broad. He could read several languages and many literary classics counted among his favorite reading (Shakespeare, Cervantes, Milton, Goethe, and so on). Interestingly enough, at the gymnasium Freud received a prize for his translation of Sophocles' Greek verse on King Oedipus, a figure who, of course, profoundly marked psychoanalytic theory.

Austrian industry enjoyed an upswing after the 1848 revolution but in 1873 the so-called Black Friday suddenly halted the boom. Too many stocks had been issued in unstable businesses, and the crash brought financial catastrophe for many small stockholders. The industrial bourgeoisie and financiers prospered while the petite bourgeoisie and the workers suffered. Freud's father lost the rest of his savings. The family apparently managed to survive with the help of relatives on his mother's side.

It was in this year of crisis that Freud was to choose his career after graduating from the gymnasium. Thus 1873 was in many respects a break in his life. For the previous six years he had been first in his class. The curriculum in the gymnasium consisted of a classical humanist education, which certainly contributed to safeguarding the illusions of the pauperized petite bourgeoisie, but did not provide any guidelines for a future career. Languages and the arts held out no hope for the future. There was a tradition in Jewish circles to pursue a career in industry, trade, law, and medicine. Business did not attract Freud, since it was the cause of his father's penury, and moreover, it did not sit well with his humanistic ideals. Law and medicine remained, and for a time Freud was inclined to choose law on the advice of his friend, the future socialist leader Heinrich Braun. According to Freud, his decision to choose medicine instead was motivated by a lecture he heard on Goethe's concept of nature. He found in this concept a combination of the humanities and the natural sciences and thus a compromise between his personal interests and economic necessity. He did not have any fundamental interest in curing the sick, only a passion for exploring the riddle of man.

2. UNIVERSITY STUDIES
AND HOSPITAL TRAINING
(1873–1886)

Freud maintained close contact with his family throughout most of his student years. He lived at home until he was twenty-seven. In 1883, he got a room at the hospital ward where he worked. During this period, his personal development was to a great degree influenced by his financial status. His family suffered privation because of his studies, and Freud borrowed considerable sums from friends and teachers at the university. His only luxury was books. Some of the dreams analyzed in *The Interpretation of Dreams* (Freud 1900a) stem from his financial problems, such as the dream about the botanical monograph, which will be discussed later (see III.A.2.b). Freud probably did not have sexual relations before his marriage, and he underwent several personal neurotic crises, which may have contributed to his later understanding of the nature of neuroses. During his student years, he spoke of his own neurasthenia (an emotional and psychic disorder characterized by easy fatigability). At the time he believed that his neurasthenia was caused by overexertion, but he later developed the theory that the loss of tension in the nervous system was caused by excessive masturbation. He attempted to treat these symptoms by using cocaine and almost became an addict. In spite of fatigability and occasional lapses in concentration, Freud was, as a whole, a very diligent student, tackling even the most trivial academic tasks effectively when it was demanded of him. Many of his teachers and friends came to play a father role for him, and some of the impetus behind his grandiose ambitions and many collaborations followed by estrangement assumedly stemmed from his father tie. The tumultuous nature of these relationships formed the personal background for Freud's discovery of the Oedipus complex.

During his first years of study, Freud showed a many-sided interest in social and political issues. As could be expected of someone who had personally witnessed the petite bourgeoisie being deprived of its economic foundation, Freud was attracted by the radical ideas that flourished at the university. He belonged to a reading circle that held discussions on political and philosophical issues. There was a great deal of pan-German sentiment in these discussions. The circle felt that Austria should be reunited with Germany. German culture would save the "degenerate" Austrian empire and would point the way to social equality and justice. When this pan-German movement assumed fascist characteristics (totalitarian organization, anti-Semitism) at the end of the 1870s, Freud was understandably disappointed, and subsequently confined himself to a bourgeois democratic view with no connection to political extremism.

Especially in the 1870s, the academic standard at the University of Vienna was high. The university boasted internationally renowned experts in several fields and had also imported a number of prominent scholars from leading German universities. Darwin's and Helmholtz's theories were widely accepted, and, as already mentioned, the university provided a climate conducive to political and philosophical discussions. In 1873, when Freud embarked on his study of medicine at age seventeen, it was natural that he attempt to broaden his horizons after his gymnasium period. He therefore attended Franz Brentano's lectures on the history of philosophy during his first years at the university. Up until 1872, philosophical lectures had been obligatory, but Freud attended them voluntarily. Letters from this period indicate that he grappled with issues in the history of philosophy. At the time, Freud most admired Kant, and not Brentano's favorite philosophers, Descartes and Leibniz (Brentano has since been recognized as Husserl's teacher and one of the founders of phenomenology). Freud's philosophical interests as well as his passion for literature indicate that he was in no way a narrow-minded natural scientist. Moreover, Freud, at Brentano's urging, translated some of John Stuart Mill's essays (including those on women's liberation and socialism) in 1880. Freud was also attracted by Enlightenment currents in European radicalism, whose proponents included Mill and Georg Brandes. "The truth must out" was a paramount demand even if it threatened accepted religious and moral norms.

The medical curriculum was rather loosely structured. Required courses included chemistry, botany, minerology, and more traditional subjects in the field of biology. During his early student years, Freud had an ambitious curriculum, choosing more courses than required. His study plan was especially remarkable in light of his financial straits, as he had to pay for every course he took. As early as his third year, Freud conducted independent scientific experiments. This was a time of great scientific discoveries, and Freud obviously hoped to achieve instant renown by his experiments. He was assigned by his teacher Carl Claus to investigate whether there were male gonads in eels. Freud dissected about four hundred eels and came to the conclusion that Syrski's hypothesis on the location of the testicles in eels was probably correct. He published his findings in a short article (Freud 1877b) that did not, however, win him any recognition. In the fall of 1876, Freud began work at Brücke's physiological laboratory. Here too he received independent research assignments. His research was still in marine biology, and his investigations showed how certain nerve cells in a lower species of fish should be placed in an evolutionary perspective, and that there was no measurable difference between the nerve cells of lower and higher organisms. Moreover, Freud invented a method for coloring nerve tissue, thus facilitating the study of anatomical specimens. Alongside his research, he attended survey courses in medicine without, however, exhibiting great interest in them (with the exception of Meynert's lectures in psychiatry). According to Freud, when he took his medical finals in 1880–1881, three years late, he passed only thanks to his eidetic memory. He almost failed botany because he could not recognize the plants he was asked to comment on.

It is not difficult to see the direction Freud's studies were taking. His teacher Ernest Brücke (1819–1892) was a member of the famous group of four in Berlin headed by Helmholtz, which had formulated the basis for a break with vitalism in the 1840s. Brücke himself was a student of Johannes Müller, whose physiological textbook from the 1830s Freud also studied. He supported the use of Helmholtz's principle of constant energy in physiology, and believed in Darwin's evolutionary theory. Unlike du Bois-Reymond, he maintained his materialistic views and did not believe, as it became increasingly common to do, that concrete empirical investigations and general materialistic theories were inexorably opposed. Brücke and Meynert were two of the last great materialists in the natural sciences of their time. Under their tutelage, Freud thus avoided being blinded by the incipient positivism of scientists like Wundt and Kraepelin. Freud, who had been a humanist in the spirit of Goethe during his gymnasium years, became a radical materialist thanks to Brücke. The comprehensive view of the universe survived in this form, and Freud defended materialism so vehemently that he at one point during his student years was almost involved in a duel on this issue.

Freud was with Brücke for six years (1876–1882), until a year after he had taken his finals. Had he been given the opportunity, he would probably have pursued a traditional academic career in physiology. As we have mentioned, he was not interested in becoming a physician. However, Brücke already had two assistants, Fleischl-Marxow and Exner, who were both about ten years older than Freud. In 1882, Brücke therefore advised Freud to become a general practitioner and Freud followed this advice immediately. A contributing factor to his sudden decision might have been his recent engagement to Martha Bernays. As an assistant at a university, Freud could not support a family. Most assistants had to wait ten to twenty years before attaining tenure.

Martha Bernays came from a Jewish family somewhat better off than Freud's. Freud's passion for her resulted in an increasing interest in his private life at the expense of his career. The aim of his work in the following years was to establish a family, both socially and economically. Strong family ties were a Jewish tradition originating in the social discrimination of the Jews, and Freud believed that his difficulties at the university were caused by anti-Semitism. His decision to start a family may have also been to help him pursue his career. Freud's letters to Martha show that despite her lack of knowledge of his work, he shared his intrigues, hopes, and disappointments with her. However, she never became an equal partner in the relationship. For example, when she expressed an interest in Freud's translation of Mill's essay on women's liberation, Freud replied that the essay was off the mark. If women were to enter public life and compete on an equal footing with men, how would they have the time to take care of the household and the children?

After graduating from the university, Freud applied to the Vienna *Allgemeiner Krankenhaus* (General Hospital), at the time one of the leading medical centers in Europe, where he remained for three years (1882–1885). Up until then he had had no experience with patients, and needed this medical training in order to become a general practitioner. His work encompassed the following fields: surgery (two months), internal medicine (six months), psychiatry (five months), dermatology (three months), neuropathology (fourteen months), and ophthalmology (three months). Nervous diseases obviously interested Freud most. He stayed with this discipline for so long that he never completed studying the subjects that would have qualified him as a general practitioner. The most rewarding period for Freud were the five months he spent in Meynert's psychiatric clinic (May–October 1883). He had the time to read the classics of psychiatry and generally supported Griesinger's and Meynert's neuropathologically oriented psychiatry. His work at the Department of Nervous Diseases (1884) was less rewarding theoretically. The department economized on light as well as medicine, so Freud only managed to complete minor experiments, among them a study of cerebral hemorrhages. Freud admitted having once diagnosed a neurotically induced headache as an indication of meningitis, so it is clear that at the time he was still greatly influenced by traditional neuropathological thought.

Throughout this period at the General Hospital, Freud devoted much of his energy to attempts at making a scientific discovery that would provide a shortcut to a career. The most well-known attempt is Freud's so-called cocaine episode (1884–1885), in which he was one of the first to investigate the medical effects of cocaine. This episode is revealing because of Freud's total ignorance of the dangers of cocaine. He gave it to anyone in need of a pick-me-up (even to Martha to make her strong and redden her cheeks) and used it himself to combat fatigue and depression. The result was that Freud was regarded in certain circles as the person who had given humanity a third scourge after alcohol and morphine (his friend Fleischl-Marxow from Brücke's laboratory died in 1891, partly as a result of cocaine abuse), while Freud's colleague Koller reaped the glory of being the first to use cocaine as a local anesthetic in eye operations. Freud's use of cocaine, like hypnosis, probably served as a point of departure for psychoanalysis, especially in his study of unusual conscious states.

In his academic studies at the hospital, Freud constantly sought to use his considerable knowledge of neuroanatomy in his work in neuropathology and psychiatry. His work was strongly supported by Theodor Meynert (1833–1892), who was professor in both brain anatomy and psychiatry (and in his last years in neuropathology as well). For a time, Meynert thus assumed Brücke's role as Freud's academic ideal. Like Brücke, he was an inveterate materialist, a great admirer of Fechner (in spite of his materialism), but was opposed to Darwin's evolutionary theory. He supported Lotze's theory of drives as well as the theory of cerebral localization. His psychiatric studies were heavily influenced by Griesinger, and focused more on research than therapy, probably a significant reason for the ultimate failure of his work. Meynert regarded the therapeutic work conducted at various sanatoriums as unscientific. The conflict between research and therapy was so extreme that Freud, after serving as an intern at a private sanatorium for nervous diseases in the summer of 1885, was afraid to ask for a recommendation from the head of the sanatorium, Leidesdorf, whom he knew Meynert despised.

We have not yet mentioned the figure who was decisively instrumental in Freud's personal and academic development—Josef Breuer (1842–1925). Breuer was a physician and was highly respected for his academic abilities. He had abandoned a university career, but still participated in scientific research projects alongside his medical practice. He was thus a regular visitor to Brücke's laboratory, and it was probably there that he and Freud became acquainted around 1880. In theoretical matters, he was a disciple of Helmholtz and Fechner, but he also possessed a broad cultural background. He was the private physician of Freud's philosophy instructor Brentano and corresponded with him on philosophical subjects. Moreover, at one point he collaborated with the physiologist Ewald Hering, with whose speculative theory of memory as a universal attribute of matter Freud also became acquainted. Together with Hering, Breuer charted the self-regulation of respiration and later laid bare the connection between corporal coordination and the organ of equilibrium in the ear.

Breuer's significance for psychoanalysis rests on his treatment, from 1880–1882, of a woman suffering from hysteria. Anna O., as she was called in the case history published in 1895 (Freud [and Breuer] 1895d), was a gifted young girl from the upper class. Her illness, which appeared while she nursed her dying father, was characterized by alterations between two states of consciousness. On the one hand, she was the normal Anna, although more fatigued and in pain than before her illness, and on the other the sick Anna, who suffered from hysterical attacks and was intractable and malicious. The normal Anna and the sick Anna knew literally nothing of each other's existence. During his treatment, Breuer discovered that Anna in her abnormal state could speak several languages and could translate fluently from one to the other, while she refused to speak German. Talking calmed her, and Breuer therefore let her talk as much as possible. In the beginning she told simple fairy tales, but gradually more and more concrete memories of the past emerged. These memories were usually accurate renderings of her father's illness. After relating these episodes, Anna was more lively and suffered less pain in her normal state and remained in this state for longer periods of time. Anna O. called this treatment the "talking cure" or "chimney sweeping" (which she said in English), while Breuer spoke of "catharsis." In the fall of 1882, Breuer informed Freud of this strange case history. It did not at first fit into Freud's academic conceptual system based on neuroanatomy, but in the long term it became instrumental for his own work in psychotherapy and his first steps toward the development of psychoanalysis.

During this period, Brücke, Meynert, and Breuer supported Freud's career when he applied for the position of *Privatdozent* and for a government-sponsored traveling fellowship. A *Privatdozent* was only loosely associated with the university, and received no salary, but had the right to give a few lectures. The appointment was important because it was considered a step on the way to a tenured position. Freud received the appointment in 1885 after long negotiations, with the backing of his three supporters. Freud also received the traveling fellowship thanks to the intercession of his friends on the faculty of medicine. The future looked bright and promising for Freud when he went to Paris in the fall of 1885 to study with Charcot.

His stay in Paris was somewhat different from what he had expected. As mentioned earlier, Charcot's fame rested on his successful description and classification of a number of nervous diseases, while his work on hysteria in the 1880s was widely regarded as charlatanism. However, Freud became quickly enraptured by the atmosphere prevailing at Charcot's lectures. While Breuer had only used hypnosis sparingly in his treatment of Anna O., Charcot employed it as a general tool for understanding hysteria. His demonstrations and case histories provided Freud with a good idea of how the same abnormal conscious states and attacks could be induced (and sometimes abolished) by traumatic experiences, hypnosis, and even auto-hypnosis. Charcot and his students believed that hysteria and hypnosis could only appear in people with innate weaknesses in the nervous system. In a clinical sense, they were talking about a pathological constriction of consciousness and an inability to integrate as causes of the disease. Charcot inspired Freud to embark on a comparative investigation of organic and hysterical paralyses. His results underscored the need for a psychological theory to supplement neurophysiological theory. Moreover, he once heard Charcot say that the genital *(la chose génitale)* always played an etiological role in hysterical women with impotent husbands, a remark made out of context, which later fitted in nicely with Freud's general theory of the sexual etiology of neuroses. For the moment, however, Freud was preoccupied with learning new ideas. In order to promote work on these ideas, he started to translate Charcot's lectures into German. The first volume was published in 1886.

Freud returned to Vienna in the spring of 1886, and was apparently very eager to pass on his new-found knowledge. To this end he visited various academic organizations, including the physiological association and the medical association, but he was not received enthusiastically. A lecture on hypnosis caused only embarrassment because it was still regarded as quackery in medical circles, on a level with mind reading and spiritualism. A lecture on Charcot's theory of hysteria focusing on male hysteria and the traumatic etiology of hysteria met with a similar fate. Some scientists attempted to trivialize the novelty of the theory by remarking that cases of male hysteria were already known, but extremely rare. Others denied that hysterical symptoms had anything to do with shock (for instance, after a train accident) as Charcot claimed. Freud was encouraged to come with clinical examples, but was not allowed to find them in Meynert's department. He did manage to find a case of male hysterical blindness in Germany and published findings on the case. This evidence was politely received, but did not generate much interest. Thus, in the fall of 1886, Freud had to acknowledge that after one year he had jeopardized a considerable part of the goodwill of his teachers and colleagues. A university position was now out of the question, and Meynert henceforth became a bitter opponent. In connection with a discussion of Charcot, Meynert wrote that Freud had traveled to Paris a well-educated neurophysiologist, but had returned a fanatical disciple of suggestion.

B.

THE INCEPTION
OF PSYCHOANALYSIS

The crisis of the subject in the sphere of intimacy formed the general framework for the inception of psychoanalysis. Capitalist society made ever-increasing, mutually exclusive demands on the functions of the sphere of intimacy. This pressure on the subject led to increasing "nervousness," neurotically complex behavioral patterns where the conscious ego no longer controlled its actions, and strange states of consciousness exposing formerly unknown aspects of the subject. This entire abundant complex of symptoms and problems could not be redressed or understood in the framework of the humanistic subject concept. The firm belief in the idea of an original and undistorted essence of the subject only obscured the search for what this essence was. There was little consolation in sharing a "universally human" essence if it was obscured in philosophical clouds. To the extent that the subjective crisis actually threatened the functions of the sphere of intimacy, a new basis of understanding for the transformation of these functions was needed. In the latter half of the nineteenth century, new theories for such a basis were formulated: phenomenology and existentialism, which retain the humanistic subject concept; the attempt to define the problem from a medical standpoint by prescribing a normalizing treatment of one kind or another; fanatical modernism in art that made the division of the subject into a virtue (Baudelaire, Rimbaud, Lautréamont); and finally psychoanalysis, whose advantages over the other theories were its scientific synthesis of theory and praxis and its conscious critique of ideology.

We have mentioned that Freud was well trained to deal with the problems of the subject. He knew them from his own experience and by a lucky coincidence came to work with them as a physician. Moreover, he had a wide-ranging knowledge of medical, psychological, and literary descriptions of the subject as well as a considerable talent for combining these descriptions in an undogmatic way in the formulation of a new concept. In this connection, he made the right choices on at least three points, choices that pointed him in the direction of psychoanalysis, while his colleagues made the wrong choices and were either led astray or made no progress.

(1) Freud always attempted to incorporate his training in pathology in a general theory of normal and pathological phenomena. Obviously, a specialist in fractures must know what a healthy bone looks like, and must furthermore be aware of the functions of the bone, its resistence capabilities, and so on. Similarly, it might be assumed that a psychiatrist should not only know about mental disorders, but also about the normal functions of the mind. After the rise of positivism, however, there was a marked tendency for psychiatrists to preoccupy themselves exclusively with madness, while consciously neglecting to formulate general psychological theories (see Kraepelin and his followers). It is noteworthy that of Freud's teachers, Charcot only wrote about pathological phenomena, assuming familiarity with the healthy nervous system and the sound mind, while Meynert conducted a thorough investigation into normal psychic processes (association, thought, and learning), and attempted to understand the various types of psychic illnesses as specific damage to these processes. Following Meynert's example, Freud expressed an interest in general theory, in part because he felt that Meynert's theory and his investigations into mental disorders needed to be improved. Freud's work can therefore be regarded as an attempt to change general theory by making it more receptive to new discoveries in pathology and therapy.

(2) In choosing a general theoretical framework, Freud gradually distanced himself from concepts of evolutionary theory and neurophysiology (Darwin, Fechner, and Meynert) and moved toward a psychological and literary approach, in which subjective experiences were linked to each other in the context of a life history. However, in making this transition, Freud continued to employ theories of natural science as abstract models without their former biological or neurophysiological content. Such a formal transferral of models from one field to another is known from other scientific advances, for example, when Darwin derived the idea for the principles of evolution from Malthus's population theory. Moreover, by abandoning the possibility for translating psychological theory to neurophysiological concepts, Freud was able to combine many different models. Generally,

Freud's attempt to place subjective data in hypothetical models led to an understanding of the unconscious which in turn distanced psychoanalysis from any form of psychology of consciousness.

(3) It must be stressed that Freud searched consistently for the causes of illness in the subject's milieu rather than in its organism. Unlike most psychiatrists of his time, Freud was not content to use degeneration theory as an explanation of the causes of mental illness. Instead, following scientists like Charcot, he emphasized the role of trauma in mental illness, and like the naturalist writers Jacobsen, Ibsen, and the Goncourt brothers stressed milieu at the expense of heredity. Freud's etiological explanations were related to life history, which, as he himself admitted, gave his case histories a literary feel.

The inception of psychoanalysis was the result of Freud's attempt to understand and treat the crises of the subject, and the process of inception developed as a step-by-step harmonization of concrete theoretical and therapeutic investigations. Each phase in this development can be compared to a plateau maintaining a certain equilibrium between general theory, the etiological model, and the applied therapy. When this equilibrium is threatened by new findings that the theory cannot explain or the therapy is unable to treat, the appropriate adjustments in one or several areas are made until equilibrium is restored. In the process of establishing psychoanalytic theory, Freud thus developed new concepts and new therapeutic procedures. In doing so, he became aware of new aspects of the symptoms of his patients (the traditional interaction of theory and praxis). We have divided the process of inception of psychoanalysis into four phases, each marked by progress in therapeutic techniques and the addition of new concepts to general theoretical models. The final form of psychoanalytic theory thus developed by a gradual addition of new concepts and hypotheses to the rather simple model Freud worked with toward the end of the 1880s.

1. FIRST PHASE: HYPNOID THEORY AND THE SPLITTING OF CONSCIOUSNESS (1886–1892)

In April 1886, Freud started his own medical practice as a specialist in neuropathological diseases, and in September of the same year he married Martha after a four-year engagement. They eventually had six children, born between the years 1887 and 1895 (the youngest of them, Anna Freud, became a well-known psychoanalyst). Freud's paramount problem was how to provide for his family. He was forced to supplement his income from his medical practice by working three afternoons a week as the head of Kassowitz's children's hospital. This work was a natural extension of his neuropathological training. He had already done some work on the nervous system of children, and in time his practical work made him the leading specialist in the field. From 1891 to 1897 he published three books dealing in part with child paralysis and spastic paralysis, but these subjects preoccupied him less and less. Moreover, during his first years as a physician, he had planned to write textbooks on neuroanatomy and neuropathology. However, these ambitious plans only materialized as short articles in lexicons and handbooks. One of his articles published in a lexicon in 1889 examined aphasia, which apparently impelled Freud to embark on a more comprehensive study of the available literature on the subject. In 1891, he published a monograph dealing exclusively with aphasia (Freud 1891b). Aphasia denotes impairment of the power to use or comprehend words. There are different kinds of aphasia classified according to which functions in the patient have been impaired, the ability to repeat what is heard, to talk, to write, and or to form sentences. Freud argued that these abilities could not be localized in specific cerebral centers and conducting nerve paths, as had been attempted in light of Broca's discovery of the speech center (see I.B.3.a). In this connection he sharply criticized Meynert, who was one of the most prominent exponents of localization theory, while praising the work of Hughlings Jackson and Charcot. Moreover, the monograph contained many psychological considerations of word and thing presentations, their mutual association, and genetic relationships in language learning. However, these general considerations were first related to the psychology of neuroses in Freud's "A Project for a Scientific Psychology" from 1895 (Freud, 1950a).

In his private practice, Freud primarily treated "nerve patients" who were referred to him by other doctors because of his reputation as a neuropathologist. Breuer probably contributed the most patients and on many occasions also helped Freud out of his acute financial straits. Freud came into contact with the milder cases of nervous disorder, patients who sought medical help on either their own initiative or that of their families but did not require hospitalization or commitment to psychiatric institutions. As private patients, they had to be able to pay for treatment, and consequently most of Freud's patients came from the middle and upper classes. They were often housewives who had developed their "nervous-ness" out of idleness. There were some hysterical patients, but doubtless also many with thinly disguised psychosomatic symptoms. These mild nervous disorders had previously been neglected by researchers who considered them an expression of affectation and exaggerated anxiety or as the result of an innate neuropathological constitution. They had not been adequately classified, and until Griesinger and Charcot, their etiology was little known (or at any rate incorrectly perceived). Besides hysteria, the most frequent explanations for these mild nervous disorders were neurasthenia (fatigability, lack of motivation, and so on), hypochondria, and epilepsy. Freud persisted in his research only because in the beginning of the 1890s he succeeded in classifying these disorders in two different groups: actual neuroses (neurasthenia, anxiety neurosis) and psychoneurosis (hysteria, obsessional neurosis). Only the latter group was susceptible to psychoanalytic treatment (see IV.B). Freud had previously made only little progress. However, he had studied intensively the available literature on hysteria and translated three books, two by Bernheim and one by Charcot.

Freud's slow progress was undoubtedly also caused by his reluctance to abandon the neuropathological perspective. His private patients did not interest him theoretically because he could not dissect them in order to confirm or reject his diagnosis. He was also hard put to conduct therapy with them, and therefore he initially used traditional and accepted, but not very effective, methods such as baths, massage, and electrotherapy supplemented by rest, diets, and sea air. However, he felt he had to do something to make his patients feel that they were getting their money's worth. He remarked sarcastically that he could not make a living by sending his patients to a sanatorium after one consultation. Beginning in 1887, Freud, inspired by Bernheim's books, began to use hypnosis. This treatment consisted of suggesting a restoration to health, in other words, ordering patients under hypnosis to surrender their difficult or unreasonable symptoms, whether they were obsessions, anxiety, or imaginary pain. The patients were often cured when they came out of hypnosis. They followed the doctor's orders, but remembered nothing of having received them.

This finding was very significant. It implied an understanding that neuroses had a psychic dimension alongside the organic dimension. Freud had now embraced psychotherapy and subsequently employed a dualistic division of man into a psychic and an organic entity. As a therapeutic technique, however, hypnosis never satisfied him. Some of his patients were immune to hypnosis, others suffered a relapse shortly after treatment. Bernheim had claimed that in principle everyone could be hypnotized, not only potentially hysterical patients. Freud therefore suspected that he was a poor hypnotist. In the summer of 1889, he traveled to Nancy to study with Bernheim. At first he was very impressed with Bernheim's methods, but became disappointed when even Bernheim was unable to deal with a particularly difficult patient Freud had brought with him from Vienna. We cannot be sure if this disappointment was the reason that Freud gradually renounced suggestion technique. He later remarked that he had been uncomfortable with the psychic violence of Bernheim's suggestion technique. A third reason might have been that under hypnosis, patients related strange events they otherwise never mentioned. At any rate, Freud, after a seven-year delay, became once again interested in Breuer's catharsis method. This method seemed to a great degree to have a soothing effect on the nervous state of the patient when he was given the opportunity to speak freely under hypnosis. This would hardly have surprised a Catholic confessor, though the patient could not remember what he had said after hypnosis. The strongest effect was attained when the patient's revelations could be directed toward the origins of the symptoms. When did the anxiety or paralysis appear for the first time? Often a traumatic memory caused the neurotic symptoms. Charcot and others had already uncovered traumas, such as train accidents, falls from scaffolds, and so on in the etiology of hysteria, but Freud and Breuer discovered that traumas could also be of a more specifically psychic nature, such as disappointments, indignities, and so on.

Freud and Breuer now embarked on a more active cooperation in order to formulate a concept of the therapy and etiology of hysteria and to clarify the conflict between Charcot and Bernheim. That this conflict preoccupied Freud is evident from the foreword to his translation of Bernheim's book on the therapeutic effects of suggestion (Freud 1888–1889). Charcot and Breuer generally agreed in their original conception of hysteria as a series of fluctuating states of consciousness, some of which were similar to hypnotic states. Toward the end of the 1880s, Charcot's student Janet classified these symptoms as a splitting of consciousness. A controversy later arose as to whether it was Breuer or Janet who had first introduced this concept. Breuer treated Anna O. in 1880 to 1882 but the case history was first published in 1895. In spite of this controversy, it is clear that the concept of splitting was not unknown in contemporary psychological and literary works. In psychiatry, E. E. Azam had described "multiple personalities" where the same person could assume different identities interchangeably. We have already mentioned the theme of the double in literature. In Stevenson's novel from 1886, *Doctor Jekyll and Mr. Hyde,* the theme is spelled out in no uncertain terms: the main protagonist changes from an intellectual scientist by day to a bestial murderer at night—not unlike Anna O. It is noteworthy that Janet and Breuer disagreed about the evaluation of secondary consciousness. Janet connected the splitting of the mind with degeneration, regarding it as the first step toward the total dissolution and disassociation of the human intellect. Breuer opposed this view, and in keeping with the romantic subject concept believed that the split part of the personality had almost an independent intelligence not necessarily inferior to the normal intelligence: In the state of secondary consciousness, Anna O. spoke fluent English, French, and Italian; another hysterical patient became an excellent chess player.

Breuer and Freud were inclined to dismiss degeneration as an explanation for the etiology of hysteria. As a family physician, Breuer knew the relationships of his patients well, and found no reason to assume that heredity played a role in hysteria. On the other hand, Charcot's theory of trauma seemed to accord with his findings on Anna O. Charcot believed that the trauma attained a pathogenic effect by releasing an autosuggestion toward which the hysterical patient was especially disposed. During autosuggestion, groups of motor perceptions are isolated, resulting in paralysis or loss of feeling in the affected parts of the body. Instead of biologically conditioned autohypnosis, Breuer worked with a socially conditioned hypnoid state, in other words, a sleeping state. Breuer had apparently been inspired by Fechner's wave theory (see I.B.4.a), which held that the tensional wave of the nervous system culminated in one of the cerebral systems in the waking state and in another in the sleeping state. The latter process could generate dreams, which, according to Fechner, appeared on another scene. Breuer now believed that the pathological split in hysteria separated the two scenes from one another. A contributing factor to Anna O.'s illness was her daydreaming or "private theater" as she called it. While fantasizing (apparently because of boredom), she artificially induced a secondary conscious state similar to the hypnotized state. If she, while in this state, was suddenly confronted with an unexpected event, she was unable to respond to it normally. The experience was instead retained as memory in the dream system and, like a dream, was forgotten when the hypnoid state was replaced by the normal conscious state.

Freud and Breuer compared the traumatic memory in the dream system to a foreign body causing symptoms of hysteria. The experience itself was associated with strong affects, which had been incompletely or incorrectly abreacted. The therapy therefore aimed to obtain a correct abreaction resulting in the removal of the disruptive foreign body. The idea behind Breuer's catharsis method was to encourage the patient to recount the traumatic events in a way that made them the object of associative work, so as to reintegrate them into normal consciousness. For example, Anna O.'s hysterical paralysis of the arm was traced back to the time when she nursed her sick father. In a half-waking state, she imagined seeing a snake with a hideous death's head, but could not move her arm; subsequently one of her hysterical symptoms was paralysis of the arm. In other cases where hysterical attacks expressed themselves in the form of violent contortions of the body (*"attitudes passionelles"*), they could be analyzed as abortive and belated attempts to react to the trauma. Generally, Freud and Breuer believed that hysterical patients suffered from "reminiscences" (Freud [and Breuer] 1893a, p. 7). Their interpretational method could very well have been inspired by Darwin's theory of the expression of affect in animals and humans (see I.B.3.b). The affect, consisting of an accumulation of energy in the nervous system, traveled either through the first available channel (such as grimaces) or set off a specific reaction (as when animals expose their teeth in anger before attacking). When modern man— and thus the hysterical patient—used an incomprehensible expression of affect, the problem became one of trying to uncover the situation (in the past history of the species or the individual) where it first appeared.

We can summarize the first phase in the inception of psychoanalysis by underscoring the obvious topographical and economic aspect of Freud's (and, up to this point, Breuer's) theory. The topographical, or spatial, aspect is linked to the theory of a split personality, consisting of a normal consciousness and a dreaming consciousness. These two systems or "scenes" are made up of separate perceptions and associations as if they each had their own intelligence. Normally, they are active in the waking state and sleeping state respectively, but the "dream state" of hysterical patients is likely to last for longer periods and control behavior. The economic aspect refers to the fact that the energy in the systems is regarded quantitatively. The energy is distributed according to a sensorimotor reflex scheme. When a trauma generates a sudden (sensory) energy increase, problems develop if the energy cannot be abreacted (by a motor reaction). During hysteria, either reaction has been retained (retention hysteria) or there has been an inexpedient abreaction in the hysterical attack. This rather simple topographical-economic reflex model formed the basis of Freud's and Breuer's understanding when they, in December 1892, wrote their preliminary notes on the psychic mechanism of hysterical phenomena (Freud [and Breuer] 1893a). According to Freud, there was considerable conflict between the two colleagues in writing it and it was indeed during this time that the partnership of the two men actually deteriorated, even though they preserved a public facade of agreement for several more years. Their disagreement is commonly believed to be grounded in two issues: first, Freud's insistence on the sexual nature of trauma, and second, his rejection of Breuer's hypnoid theory in favor of his own theory of defense (*Abwehr*) as the explanation for the psychic split. He developed these two aspects of his theory without Breuer's help in the years that followed.

While the partnership with Breuer grew increasingly strained, Freud gradually developed a close relationship with the Berlin physician Wilhelm Fliess, whom he had met through Breuer in 1887. Fliess (1858–1928) was a nose and throat specialist, but was also well read on most issues of natural science. He is known for an astrological periodicity theory claiming that fate was determined by the interference between the female cycle (the menstrual period) of twenty-eight days and a male cycle of twenty-three days. He perceived these two periods as sexual biological forces, virtually controlling human development (biological maturation processes, psychic features, and gender) from their inception and also determining when a person would die. Furthermore, he had a theory that attempted to show a profound relationship between female sexual organs and the nose, and between nose bleeds and menstruation. He supported Freud's interest in sexuality, but was less enthused with Freud's inclination to abandon biology and neurophysiology in favor of psychology. For his part, Freud admired Fliess as a genius, and despite Fliess's age considered him a father figure and in general lavished attention on him. Only Freud's half of the extensive correspondence between the two, which lasted from 1887 to 1902, has been preserved, but his letters contain extremely detailed information on his theoretical development during this period. This correspondence was first published in 1950 (Freud 1950a), and even then only in extracts. A complete version appeared in 1985. It shows that most of the conceptual building blocks of psychoanalysis had been thought out by 1897, as will become apparent in the following sections.

2. SECOND PHASE: THE THEORY OF DEFENSE AND THE PSYCHIC PRIMARY AND SECONDARY PROCESSES (1892–1895)

Freud found Breuer's hypnoid theory unsatisfactory for several reasons. The idea of therapy was that the hypnoid state, during which the patient had been caught unawares by the trauma for the first time, should be artificially reestablished through hypnosis, thereby disclosing the trauma. However, even in those cases where Freud successfully used this procedure to enable the patient to reveal traumatic events, it did not necessarily have a therapeutic effect. If the patient revealed the trauma while under hypnosis, he often refused to accept it in the waking state. From 1892 to 1896, Freud therefore stopped using hypnosis and instead introduced a special technique of pressure and concentration. Freud would press the patient lightly on the forehead and ask him to tell him what came to mind at this moment. This thought was seldom directly related to the trauma, but by systematically tracing new thoughts and associations generated by the first thought, Freud usually succeeded in uncovering the traumatic experience. Use of this technique in analysis usually resulted in a permanent cure.

Through his analytic work, Freud realized that a trauma always consisted of an experience that was embarrassing or intolerable to the patient. Even after the trauma had been revealed, the patient would be extremely reluctant to think or talk about it. Freud concluded that the primary cause of the split was not due to the hypnoid state of the patient before the traumatic experience, but to the traumatic experience itself. Only embarrassing experiences caused a split, releasing a conscious attempt to forget what had happened. This attempt, which Freud called defense and sometimes repression, was thus the direct cause of the split. Freud's conclusion replaced Breuer's etiological model: hypnoid state/trauma/split, with his own: trauma/defense/split. After having been hinted at in the preliminary notes from 1892, the new theory was officially advanced in the short article "The Neuro-Psychoses of Defence" from 1894 (Freud 1894). In this article, Freud described defense in economic terms as a mechanism whereby affect became separated from idea. He based his theory on the idea that something could be forgotten by shifting attention to something else. An embarrassing experience could be forgotten by attaching the affect to something else. The affect then lost its qualitative content, but continued to exist as a purely quantitative "tensional space," which consequently had to be abreacted in one way or another. During hysteria the affect was transferred to the body, causing cramps, paralysis, and pain. Compulsive ideas indicated that the affect had remained in the psychic area, where it became attached to relatively innocent ideas that were then transformed into *"idées fixes."*

In April 1895, Freud and Breuer finished editing *Studies on Hysteria* (Freud [and Breuer] 1895d). Their book was important because it contained theory and clinical examples, but was also a book full of ambiguities concealing the conflict between Freud's theory of defense and Breuer's hypnoid theory. In their introduction, the authors reiterated their preliminary notes from 1892. Breuer wrote the case history of Anna O. and a theoretical chapter based on hypnoid theory. Freud contributed four case histories and a therapeutic chapter based on the theory of defense. Freud's own case histories were also ambiguous: the material for them had been collected over a number of years in which Freud had used several different techniques (suggestion, hypnosis, catharsis, pressure and concentration, sudden ideas, and free associations).

We will review Freud's case history of Miss Lucy R. as a clear example of the theory of defense. Lucy was a 30-year-old Englishwoman who worked as a governess in Vienna. She fell in love with the children's father who was the head of a factory. She discovered that her infatuation was not reciprocated when he threatened to dismiss her for letting a lady visitor kiss his children on the mouth, which he had strictly forbidden. Later, the father reprimanded another guest who wanted to kiss the children after dinner while the men were smoking cigars. The last episode Lucy related was her receiving a letter from her mother asking her to return home. She was interrupted by the children who tried to prevent her from reading the letter and who wanted to keep her in the family. Immediately afterwards she smelled a dessert that had burned. After this episode she suffered from olfactory hallucinations and depression. Lucy related these symptoms to Freud at the start of treatment, and using his pressure technique, Freud traced the associative wandering of the affect back to its origin: the smell of the burnt dessert was linked to the smell of cigar smoke, and the father's reprimand of the guest was linked to his reprimand of Lucy. The illness was caused by a defense against unrequited love and the affect was displaced along this chain of associations until it manifested itself as an incurable and inexplicable olfactory hallucination. Freud's analysis had two results: it removed the symptoms and cured the illness, and it taught Lucy not to harbor false expectations. As far as Lucy's expectations were concerned,

Freud could not abolish the social barrier between governess and master, but he could, as he himself claimed, transform hysterical misery into common unhappiness. By merely acknowledging unhappiness, one was already better prepared to fight it.

Freud's next step was to relate the etiological theory of defense to a general psychological theory. He took this step in September to October of 1895, when he wrote a manuscript of almost one hundred pages entitled *A Project for a Scientific Psychology* (Freud 1950a). He sent the manuscript to Fliess, and it was therefore first published with the other letters and manuscripts of their correspondence in 1950. Freud was already aware of several neurophysiological outlines of psychological theories, including those of Jackson, Meynert, Exner, and, most recently, Breuer in his theoretical section in the studies on hysteria. It was therefore only natural to take the step from a purely psychological presentation in clinical work to a neurophysiological presentation of a general theory. It was not a big step because Freud, in the model he constructed, was generally more loyal to his clinical findings than to his previous work in dissection and microscopy. This neurophysiological model entailed changes in terminology: *idea* became *neuron* (nerve cell), *affect* became *quantity* (nerve energy), and *association* became *facilitation* (breaking down the contact barriers between two nerve cells).

In *A Project for a Scientific Psychology,* Freud elaborated on his previous work with hysteria by adding a dynamic and genetic aspect. The reflex model he had formerly used had only encompassed the relationship between the external sense impression (especially the trauma) and the motor reaction (especially the abreaction). Freud now added stimulations of drives or needs originating inside the body, which he had earlier only included in connection with the exploration of actual neurosis. Associationist psychology thus received a dynamic aspect. Moreover, Freud attempted to describe the genetic structure of psychic functions, that is, the helpless baby's learning to satisfy his needs without outside help. Emotional processes initially dominated this course of development. The so-called primary processes represented an unbridled tendency to take over pleasurable memories and avoid unpleasurable ones (wishful attraction and reflexive defense). Secondary processes were biologically taught. These processes were normal reality-oriented processes that could tolerate genuine unpleasure and force a postponement of pleasure. We recognize here the main foundations of the typical psychological model that had existed since Hobbes.

For the moment, we are interested in how Freud succeeded in placing the etiology of hysteria in this model. Initially, he remarked that pathological defense in hysteria was similar to primary reflexive defense: the hysterical person was just as reluctant to think of the traumatic experience as the baby was to think of unpleasant things that had once caused pain. A mere hint of this experience was enough to produce those grimaces and expressions of affect associated with the original trauma. Unlike the hysterical person, however, the baby could gradually learn to control his feelings. He could learn to think of unpleasant things in order to avoid them better in future. The hysterical person continued to produce incomprehensible symptoms without being able to deal with them alone. Freud's task was to find out why a hysterical person used a primitive and inexpedient defense against the traumatic memory, and why he was unable to turn it into a normal defense. We can demonstrate this solution by taking another clinical example.

Emma was a young girl who suffered from a phobia: she was afraid to go into stores alone. She traced this hysterical compulsion back to an experience she had when she was twelve, during puberty. She had entered a store and seen two clerks talking and laughing together. Suddenly she had panicked and run out of the store. She imagined that they had laughed at her clothes and felt that one of the men had attracted her sexually. Freud believed that her reaction was irrational. Even if the clerks had laughed at her clothes, that was no reason to stop going to stores. His analysis uncovered another episode Emma had experienced at the age of eight. She had twice gone into a general store to buy candy. The first time the owner had grinned at her and put his hand on her crotch through her clothes. In spite of this incident, she went back to the store one more time. The experience did not produce a defense because Emma did not comprehend its sexual overtones. The later episode resulted in an associative identification of the two experiences: the two stores, the grinning store owner and the laughing clerks, the clothes that played a part in both incidents and the sexual overtones of the two episodes. The memory of the store owner had suddenly appeared and was now associated with a violent affect against which Emma could not defend herself. The affect was therefore separated from the original idea and transferred to the idea of the clothes. The clothes symbolized the episode at the general store and led to the false idea that it was her clothes the clerks were laughing at. However, this primitive defense had been effective, because Emma had totally forgotten the episode at the general store until Freud uncovered it.

For Freud, the significance of this example was the "incubation period" between the traumatic experience and the outbreak of the illness. The experience attained its traumatic character a long time after the event and this relationship explained the use of the primitive and pathological defense. Had Emma been aware of the sexual nature of the store owner's advances, she could have then run out of the store or at least refrained from going back a second time, but these reactions did her no good *afterward*. Whatever she did, she could not change the past, but could only defend herself against it by forgetting or repressing it and displacing the affect to the deferred symptomatic acts: running out of the store and subsequently avoiding stores altogether. This deferral *(Nachträglichkeit)* between the trauma and the defense (or between the actual experience and its assuming a traumatic character) was the real cause for the release of a pathological defense instead of a normal one. The deferral was thus indisputably necessary for the development of hysteria. Freud explained this deferred action by the late appearance of puberty in human development, which implied that only sexual experiences could become hysterical traumas.

In conclusion, Freud replaced Breuer's hypnoid theory with his own theory of pathological defense in the second phase of development as an explanation of the etiology of hysteria, and incorporated the concept of defense into general psychological theory. In doing so he added a dynamic and genetic aspect to the topographical-economic reflex model from the first phase of inception. The dynamic aspect entailed relating defense to those thought processes through which the individual normally satisfied his needs. The genetic aspect showed how typical gratification and defense processes developed from totally primitive reflexes in a newborn baby to reality-oriented thinking and calculation in an adult. As far as psychopathology was concerned, this extension of theory occurred to some degree at the expense of the topographical aspect. The romantic model of two separate intelligences (like Dr. Jekyll and Mr. Hyde) was replaced by a more rationalistic model of two genetic stages of development. Likewise, pathological processes were not placed in a separate system any more, but were defined as a return to a more primitive psychic functional mode. Pathological defense meant that all affects were removed from embarrassing ideas. These ideas did not comprise any coherent system, but occurred as scattered and segregated gaps in a superior ego structure.

3. THIRD PHASE: THE UNCONSCIOUS AND THE PRECONSCIOUS (1895–1896)

In the third phase of the inception of psychoanalysis, Freud succeeded in reincorporating the topographical aspect while retaining the other aspects. The result was a rough sketch of a genetic-functional reflex model of the psychic apparatus which came to comprise the core of psychoanalytical theory, so-called metapsychology.

After sending *A Project for a Scientific Psychology* (Freud 1950a) to Fliess in October 1895, Freud pursued his efforts at making the model function. His letters to Fliess reveal that his thoughts on the project fluctuated between optimism and pessimism. However, his continued considerations of sexual development, especially the relationship between "premature" sexual experiences in childhood and delayed defense in puberty, led to new discoveries. According to Freud, the etiology of hysteria consisted of sexual child abuse—the so-called seduction theory. Opposed to this was another neurosis previously overshadowed by hysteria—obsessional neurosis. On 15 October, Freud wrote to Fliess that obsessional neurosis was the result of "presexual sexual pleasure." Freud grappled with this assumption in many letters. In theory there was no defense against pleasurable memories, yet the experience had been repressed. Freud tackled this problem in "Manuscript K" from December 1895 (Freud 1950a and Freud 1985b), in which he formulated a new hypothesis: the original pleasure associated with the experience must have been transformed into unpleasure. A transformation of affect, as it was later called, must have occurred. Freud suggested several reasons for this transformation, the most crucial being that children apparently felt pleasure in things that caused unpleasure in adults, for example, feces and a number of sexual activities. It was not difficult to imagine how the "presexual sexual pleasure" of masturbation could turn into unpleasure as a result of adult disapproval, and Freud's investigations consequently focused on this problem in the period that followed. It can be said that transformation of affect is the basic principle behind every upbringing; what was new in Freud was only that he focused on the sexual affects.

Freud also attempted to illuminate the difference between the etiology of hysteria and obsessional neurosis by studying the appearance of trauma in child development. Without being too precise, he assumed that the hysterical trauma originated in the period from zero to four years, while obsessional neurosis originated in the period from four to eight years. He abandoned this time scheme later, but for the time supported the idea that the repetition of the trauma during illness was a repetition of typical thought processes a child commanded at the time the traumatic experience took place. The symptoms of obsessional neurosis were more complex than symptoms of hysteria, so the trauma could be thought to originate at a later period when the child's mental activity was more developed. Another pervasive characteristic of these symptoms was that they were always associated with innocuous memories originating at the same time as the trauma. For example, Emma (see II.B.2) avoided stores because she had experienced the trauma in a store. On the whole, a picture emerged of memory traces from the same period topographically placed alongside each other in the psyche. Freud expressed this theory in his famous letter to Fliess from 6 December 1896:

> As you know, I am working on the assumption that our psychical mechanism has come into being by a process of stratification: the material present in the form of memory-traces being subjected from time to time to a *re-arrangement* in accordance with fresh circumstances—to a *re-transcription*. Thus what is essentially new about my theory is the thesis that memory is present not once but several times over, that it is laid down in various species of indications. . . . I should like to emphasize the fact that the successive registrations represent the psychical achievement of successive epochs of life. (Freud 1950a, pp. 233–35).

Freud thus believed that the psychic apparatus was composed of separate memory systems whose spatial relationship corresponded to their temporal deposits, similar to the way archeological findings and geological deposits were older the deeper one dug. Freud did not determine how many systems existed, but in time only two genuine memory systems remained: the unconscious and the preconscious. The unconscious was the older of the two systems. It contained the so-called thing presentations, that is, the immediate sense impression of things or objects in the world. Their mutual organization was very loose: all associations fulfilling the demand for similarity and contiguity in time and space were possible. The actual processes of the unconscious were identical with the aforementioned primary processes. The term *the unconscious* was used because presentation could not become conscious by themselves but could only enter consciousness by transferring their impulses to the overlying system called *the preconscious*. This system contained so-called word presentations enabling thought by logical rules and the creation of the main concepts for the classification of perceived things. These thought processes could, if necessary, impede impulses and find new and safer ways to the given goal and corresponded to the aforementioned secondary processes. Ideas in the preconscious were adjacent to consciousness and could become conscious every time they were cathected by an impulse.

Jackson and Meynert held similar views. During development the superior reflex centers were created (Jackson) as well as the secondary ego (Meynert) which impeded and directed the lower reflexes. During illness the superior main reflex centers were suspended and the more primitive and older reflexes could once again function unimpeded. The originality of Freud's theory was his belief that the unconscious could influence thought and behavior without suspending the preconscious (the official ego). This process was similar to neurosis, and Freud's successful description of this process was due to the fact that his concept of defense could finally be incorporated in the general topographical model of the unconscious and preconscious. There were actually at least three kinds of defense: (1) The unconscious was dominated by a primitive, reflexive defense which immediately erased the unpleasurable ideas of the cathexis they had experienced; (2) the preconscious was dominated by a more highly developed defense which could anticipate a future unpleasure and a present unpleasure and in doing so guarantee a more expedient mode of function for the individual; (3) pathological defense or repression occurred when certain impulses from the unconscious were denied access to the preconscious. In obsessional neurosis, which of course formed the basis of these theoretical advances, unconscious memory was associated with pleasure. For example, a small child derived great pleasure from masturbation. However, a transformation affect then occurred as a result of upbringing, and during puberty the memory assumed a dangerous and traumatic character. Even the words and concepts in the preconscious that were supposed to express the traumatic memory and to adapt it were now so unpleasurable that they could not be cathected. This prevented the pleasurable memory of masturbation in the unconscious from entering consciousness by a direct passage through the preconscious. Instead, its cathexis was displaced to the surrounding ideas in the unconscious that had a peripheral relationship with the trauma (in Emma's case from sexuality to clothes and stores) and these ideas were mixed with the preconscious processes as inexplicable neurotic symptoms.

Thus, pathological defense was a primitive reflexive defense (a primary process) being initiated in the preconscious. It was still a question of some, preconscious, ideas' being drained of cathexis, but it was now also a question of other, unconscious, ideas' being prevented from releasing their functions normally. The unconscious was henceforth not merely a number of scattered and segregated ideas in the psyche (as in the second phase of inception); it was an independent psychic system partly representing an early stage in individual development, and partly controlling its own memories and thought processes. With this model, Freud combined the topographical-economic aspects of the first phase of inception with the genetic-dynamic aspects of the second phase. He thus achieved his goal: to construct a general psychological model that applied to normal as well as pathological phenomena.

4. FOURTH PHASE: THE OEDIPUS COMPLEX AND INFANTILE SEXUALITY (1896–1897)

The broad psychological model was created by generalizing certain features of obsessional neurosis: the "presexual sexual pleasure" and the transformation of affect. It was less applicable to hysteria in which no original sexual pleasure was at stake, but only the unpleasure caused by the traumatic experience. Throughout the fourth phase of inception Freud continued to study hysteria and made crucial revisions of his earlier views. These revisions led to the formulation of the last and most original part of psychoanalytic theory: the Oedipus complex, infantile sexuality, and the formulation of a general theory of neurosis. The development of Freud's insights took two different directions that were first brought together in September 1897. On the one hand he continued his work in seduction theory, supplemented by analyses of typical hysterical fantasies. On the other hand he started to analyze himself for a mild hysterical phobia, which resulted in a general insight into a child's experience of his relationship with his parents.

Freud's letters to Fliess reveal that as late as the spring of 1897 Freud maintained his belief in seduction theory as the etiology of hysteria. He constantly encountered cases directly or indirectly pointing to paternal sexual abuse of children. Some patients with hysterical symptoms told of their fathers' taking them to bed up until puberty and forcing them to provide some kind of sexual satisfaction. When Freud found the same symptoms in other patients, he concluded that they had been subjected to the same type of experiences and had repressed them. A number of hysterical patients who could not remember their own traumas had nevertheless vivid fantasies of seduction scenes in general. Freud concluded that these fantasies were psychic creations inserted between the traumatic memory and consciousness as a defense. The interpretation of these fantasies might uncover the trauma. Without this interpretation, patients often believed that their fantasies were the expression of actual events. Superstition could thus be demonstrated to stem from neurotic fantasies. In the literature from the Middle Ages on witches possessed by the devil, Freud believed he could see typical cases of hysterical women. Often the witches themselves admitted to having been raped by the devil, even though the real reason for their attacks of hysteria was not possession by the devil, but repressed memories of sexual abuse in childhood. On the whole, Freud saw no contradiction between seduction theory and hysterical fantasies. Even so, he did admit to Fliess that he had discovered hysterical symptoms in his younger brother and several of his sisters, which necessarily had to make him suspect his father of indecency.

Freud began his self-analysis in the summer of 1897. He acknowledged that he had some neurotic psychic problems including fear of train travel and he thought that self-analysis would help him. Freud was of course aware that self-analysis was more difficult than analysis of his patients. He therefore prepared himself with all his analytic concepts of repression, seduction, and resistance without attempting to make himself better than his patients. The barrier between analyst and patient that had characterized classical "objective" psychiatry was replaced by another barrier of principle in the analyst himself: the barrier between his own preconscious and unconscious. We regard it as important that Freud removed the first barrier by attempting to "understand" his patients, but we find it even more important that he acknowledged the existence of the other barrier and thereby the limitation imposed by the unconscious on any knowledge, be it self-knowledge or knowledge of others.

Freud hoped with his self-analysis finally to grasp the mystery of the unconscious. He had never succeeded in conducting such a thorough analysis of his patients; there had always been loose ends or lacked decisive memories, but Freud apparently believed he would succeed with himself as the patient. One must imagine that, guided by his hypotheses, he searched for genuine traumatic experiences behind his fantasies and symptoms, some kind of indecency on the part of his father or others. An important tool in his work was dream analysis. Since the summer of 1895, Freud had analyzed his own dreams, which could without difficulty be equated with fantasies. After his father's death in 1896, most of Freud's dreams were about him. Dream analysis uncovered many childhood memories but none that could definitely be called traumatic. As in other dreams, they were wish fulfillments. A wish that his father were wrong and Freud right on a specific issue could generate a dream that clearly showed that Freud was right despite the fact that the opposite might have been the case in reality. Consequently, it was not possible to trace actual events from dreams. There was still a missing link of interpretation, but Freud had gradually come to suspect that this link might not be sexual abuse in childhood after all. On 21 September 1897, Freud wrote to Fliess that he no longer believed in his theory of hysteria. It was impossible for so many children to have been sexually abused in childhood. He had only analyzed the fantasies of his hysterical patients. However, he did not know what caused these fantasies.

Out of the ruins of the seduction theory soon emerged a general theory of neurosis, which held that neurosis was not caused by genuine repressed traumatic memories, but by unconscious wish fantasies. On 15 October 1897, Freud informed Fliess that he could trace his own wishes back to a love for his mother and jealousy toward his father. This insight was the nucleus of the realization of the Oedipus complex as the fundamental structure of the unconscious. Although his ideas had not yet fallen into place, Freud started working on the assumption that oedipal fantasy was nourished by infantile sexuality. He had already introduced "presexual sexual pleasure" in the form of infantile masturbation in connection with the etiology of obsessional neurosis, and he could now likewise conclude that hysterical patients had also masturbated, but had defended themselves against this memory by the creation of a seduction fantasy. On 14 November 1897, he sent Fliess the first real outline of the theory of infantile sexuality in which he maintained that small children have many of the same abilities for sexual activity as adults. However, sexuality is not so narrowly localized, but instead associated with zones around the mouth and anus, perhaps even the entire surface of the body.

In light of the heated debate on this issue in recent years, it should be emphasized that there is no antagonistic relationship between seduction theory and the Oedipus complex. Seductions and other traumatic experiences *can* be included in the series of factors determining Oedipal wish fantasies and anxieties. Thus, Freud often referred to seduction in his writings after 1897, not least in the important case histories which we will examine in part 4. The new development in his thinking was merely that he did not in all cases refer sexual desires and neurotic and psychotic defense mechanisms to sexual abuse of children. Moreover, he used the concept "seduction" to cover everything from criminal child abuse to totally innocent sexual games. Freud employed the later term *attachment*, or *anaclisis*, to mean that all aspects of child care seemed sexual to the child: even having baby powder put on his bottom produced sexual pleasure and a desire for repetition. It must also be stressed that Freud never excused sexual abuse of children, even while pointing out that all children had their own sexuality. During criminal abuse the adult only thinks of his own perverted desire and never considers the child, above all ignoring the child's protests.

Freud had started his self-analysis in order to uncover his unconscious traumas and to rid himself of his neurotic symptoms. Instead, he discovered the Oedipus complex as an unconscious structure of wish fantasies that continued to be active. This structure could never be entirely eliminated and never fully acknowledged. It was expressed through continued new fantasies, symptoms, and actions, and thus constantly demanded new analyses. As far as is known, Freud analyzed himself throughout his life. He acknowledged that his infantile emotional ties to his parents often affected his current emotional ties. It was especially apparent when he transferred his father tie to his teachers and friends: initially, his admiration for them knew no bounds, but later he regarded them as dangerous rivals and took advantage of every given opportunity to oppose their views. His relationship with Fliess was characterized by such a father identification and did lead to estrangement. Freud's self-analysis probably helped to reveal that he had idealized and overrated Fliess, and made it possible for him to disengage himself from their friendship. The formal occasion for their estrangement was when Freud was reluctant to recognize Fliess's periodicity theory and integrate it into his psychological theory. In the summer of 1900, the two friends had a decisive quarrel, and in 1902 they stopped corresponding. In the same year, Freud took the initiative in establishing a private study group. In the following decades, the psychoanalytic movement was to emerge from this group.

C.

THE ORGANIZATION
OF PSYCHOANALYSIS

In the previous section on the inception of psychoanalysis, we discussed Freud's personal background and his scientific development. The structure of this section does not permit such a discussion. We have therefore decided to continue our chronological presentation, emphasizing Freud's most important publications, his recruitment of colleagues, and the formation of a scientific movement. A more in-depth examination of the analytic, therapeutic, and theoretical aspects of psychoanalysis can be found in the last three parts of the book.

1. THE MAKING
OF THE PSYCHOANALYTIC MOVEMENT
(1897–1918)

Freud's colleagues knew very little of psychoanalysis in 1897. Freud was a relatively well-known figure, but his reputation rested primarily on his neuropathological work. The hysteria theory had not caused a great stir, but rather evoked irritation among his fellow colleagues. Freud did however enjoy their respect to the extent that he was recommended as "professor extraordinarius" at the university. The sexologist Krafft-Ebing, Meynert's successor as professor of psychiatry, was among those who recommended Freud. However, it is characteristic that these two prolific contributors to sexual research did not have any real contact with each other. Krafft-Ebing belonged to the old school. He had totally rejected Freud's theory of the sexual etiology of hysteria, but he did respect Freud's scientific qualifications and was honorable enough not to place obstacles in the way of an academic opponent as Meynert had done. Five years passed after the recommendation before Freud was appointed, it was said, partly, because the minister responsible for such appointments, a certain Freiherr von Härtel, was opposed to Freud and his theory of sexuality (see III.B.1.b). The position of professor extraordinarius was unsalaried, as was the position of *Privatdozent,* but the title alone was to help Freud. He received more patients, and as a lecturer came into contact with a number of his later supporters. Freud lectured without a manuscript or notes, and his at once intimate conversational and ironically reserved manner fascinated his audience, giving it the impression of belonging to a small select group.

As has been mentioned, Freud had already made a rough formulation of psychoanalysis in 1897, and he now had to work on the details and find the proper form for the practice and further development of his theory. He chose to begin with general psychological themes in order to emphasize that psychoanalysis contained a general theory of the human psyche and was not merely a psychopathology and a supplement to psychiatry. Three important works emerged from this period. They emphasized in different respects the existence of unconscious psychic processes in *all* people, and consisted primarily of analyses of these unconscious processes using the same psychological model. The first work was *The Interpretation of Dreams* (Freud 1900a), written in 1897 to 1899 and published in 1899 (though dated 1900). It is still considered by many to be the magnum opus of psychoanalysis and expresses the view that dreams are generated from unconscious wishes that enter consciousness in a distorted form by way of complex association processes. Using countless interpretations of his and others' dreams, Freud showed that a knowledge of these processes was the key to interpreting dreams and uncovering unconscious wishes. The last chapter of the book contains a general psychological theory explaining the formation of the psyche, its structure consisting of systems, and the typical processes these systems perform. This chapter is actually a slightly simplified but more lucid version of the psychological model from *A Project for a Scientific Psychology* from 1895 (Freud 1950a). In his next book *The Psychopathology of Everyday Life* (1901b), Freud examined another general field: the slips of the tongue, lapses in memory, and symptomatic acts usually regarded as the result of coincidence and not considered very significant. Freud argued that these phenomena could also be traced back to unconscious but active motives that indirectly and in a distorted form gained access to consciousness and the motor function. Unlike *The Interpretation of Dreams,* this book quickly became popular because it shed new light on everyday problems using accessible theoretical language. The last book in this series was *Jokes and Their Relation to the Unconscious* (Freud 1905c), which, like the two previous works, revealed repressions and unconscious primary processes behind jokes and puns.

Two other pieces from this period had a more direct bearing on neurosis theory and psychopathology. The first was a case history, "Fragment of an Analysis of a Case of Hysteria" (Freud 1905e), which supplemented the material from the studies on hysteria. This case concerned a female patient, Dora, who was treated by Freud for a few months in the fall of 1900. He wrote down her case history in 1901, but had problems getting it published. Various publishers believed that it would violate the medical vow of confidentiality. Nevertheless, after four years, the book was finally published. Its most significant finding in relation to the studies on hysteria was the importance of transference in analysis. Moreover, Freud made extensive use of Dora's dreams. He showed the close connection between the structure of neurosis and dreams while giving an example of the practical use of dream analysis in therapy. The other work was *Three Essays on the Theory of Sexuality,* which was also published in 1905 (Freud 1905d). In these essays, Freud collected his views on sexuality in a general theory of sexuality, placing the theory of the sexual etiology of neurosis in a larger perspective. The three essays dealt with (1) sexual perversions, (2) infantile sexuality, and (3) adult sexuality. The first subject was rather traditional. Most contemporary sexologists were preoccupied with perversions or "sexual deviations" (homosexuality, sadism, masochism, and so on). Similarly, infantile sexuality was not an unknown quantity judging by the repeated warnings, security measures, and surveillance methods described in pedagogical literature. The originality of Freud's theory was that he did not trace the essence of sexuality back to a sexual instinct directed toward reproduction (an instinct which could manifest itself as a perversion or as infantile sexuality when it was developed unnaturally or prematurely), but regarded infantile sexuality, which had nothing to do with reproduction, as the basis of sexuality. According to this view, infantile sexuality develops positively into perversions and negatively (in its repressed form) into neuroses. Genital sexuality directed toward reproduction lies between these two extremes. It does not originally exist in the child but develops by a shift in sexual sensitivity from the mouth and the anal zone to the genital zone.

Having quit his job at the children's hospital, Freud made his living almost exclusively from his private patients. The income from his publications was negligible and despite a handsome hourly fee for analysis, the family budget was often shaky because new patients did not come regularly. Consequently, Freud was to some extent forced to give preference to patients from the bourgeoisie and the aristocracy, who had the time and money for a lengthy treatment. Freud analyzed his patients in an apartment connected to the family's private quarters in Berggasse No. 19. Like other specialists, Freud had a waiting room, but his office had the character of a private room. During analysis, the patient lay on a couch while Freud sat behind the couch, out of sight of the patient. Every patient had fifty-five minutes with Freud. He received about ten patients a day between 8 A.M. and 8 P.M. He studied and wrote his books and articles in the evening and at night. Family life therefore was almost exclusively centered around mealtimes.

In the beginning of the 1900s, Freud started to recruit supporters among students and younger doctors who wanted to extend their practice to treat nervous patients. The result of Freud's efforts was the beginning of the psychoanalytic movement. In October 1902, Freud invited four people to attend private weekly discussions (the so-called Wednesday club). The two most well-known figures were Alfred Adler and Wilhelm Stekel, who were both physicians. This circle was gradually expanded to thirty members by 1910. The most prominent members joined in the following order: Paul Federn (1903), Eduard Hitschmann (1905), Otto Rank and Isidor Sadger (1906), Sandor Ferenczi (1908), and Ludwig Jekels and Hanns Sachs (1910). At these weekly meetings, the members discussed practical and theoretical problems, such as each other's patients, newly published books relevant to psychoanalysis, and new theoretical advances. Otto Rank's minutes of meetings from 1906 to 1918 have now been published in four volumes (Nunberg and Federn 1962–75).

The first endorsement of psychoanalysis outside of Vienna came from Switzerland, where one of the leading training centers for psychiatry, Burghölzli, was located. The previous head of Burghölzli, Auguste Forel, had been one the first outside France to use suggestion therapy, and his successor, Eugen Bleuler, is known for coining the terms *schizophrenia*, *ambivalence*, and *autism*. Bleuler's immediate subordinate at Burghölzli was Carl Gustav Jung. Jung had already become acquainted with Freud's theories around the turn of the century, and had incorporated certain aspects of them in his psychiatric work, for instance, in tests with free association. Jung contacted Freud in 1906 and after meeting in 1907 they formed a fast friendship. Jung contributed to the growth of the psychoanalytic movement by bringing a number of his colleagues and assistants, and, for a time, his boss, Bleuler, into its ranks. Some of these men became the most fervid supporters of psychoanalysis in the following years. The first group of supporters included Max Eitingon, Karl Abraham, and Ludwig Binswanger. Later members were Abraham Brill (from the United States), and Ernest Jones (from England). In 1907, Jung established a Freud society in Zurich similar to Freud's Wednesday club in Vienna, and in 1908 it was decided to hold a meeting for all psychoanalysts and sympathizers. The meeting took place in Salzburg and has since been called the first International Psychoanalytic Congress. There were forty-two participants from six countries, and although the "congress" had a somewhat private character, it was a step toward the formation of an international psychoanalytic movement. It was decided to publish a yearbook with Jung as editor. However, already at this juncture the seeds for future rivalry were being sown. Abraham, who had been Jung's assistant, did not trust the Swiss group because of its ties with classical psychiatry. He was thus the first to anticipate the future rivalry between Freud and Jung. Abraham settled in Berlin, where he established a small psychoanalytic group that included the sexologists Iwan Bloch and Magnus Hirschfeld.

The dissemination of psychoanalysis was not without problems. To be sure, it quickly gained a certain amount of notoriety, but this was mainly due to the more sensation-hungry segment of the public, who gave a distorted picture of psychoanalysis. Soon an aura of sensation was associated with Freud's name, whom supporters and detractors alike labeled with misleading epithets ranging from "mystic" to "prophet of sex" and "revolutionary." Malicious campaigns were conducted against psychoanalysts, who were accused of violating pornography laws, getting their patients in trouble, and leading them down the road to sexual depravity. Taking into account that Victorian sexual mores expressly prohibited public discussion of sexuality except to warn against it, it is understandable that feelings ran high. However, the personal attacks on Freud usually backfired, for no one more respected the bourgeois norms he was accused of violating than he. It was far easier for Freud to find supporters among artists and intellectuals than among physicians and scientists. In Vienna, his colleagues tried to ignore him and pretended that psychoanalysis did not exist. Although he was later awarded various honors, he never felt totally accepted in his native city. However, it was not until Nazi occupation that psychoanalysis was subjected to direct abuse.

After the alliance with Swiss psychiatry, the next advance for psychoanalysis came when Freud was invited on a lecture tour of the United States with Jung and Ferenczi. The tour lasted from August to September 1909, and Freud was surprised at his warm reception by psychologists and neuropathologists alike. Upon his return to Vienna, he took steps toward a more permanent establishment of psychoanalysis. He intended to make Zurich the international center of the movement. He did not have much faith in his supporters in Vienna. At the second psychoanalytic congress in Nuremberg in 1910, Ferenczi functioned as Freud's mouthpiece. He proposed the formation of an International Psychoanalytic Association with Jung as president (Freud did not aspire to this position because of its administrative tasks and moreover regarded Jung as well suited to represent the association publicly), and spoke in disparaging terms of the Vienna group. His final proposal, which assumedly also had Freud's blessing, was that anyone publishing books or articles on psychoanalysis should first have them approved by the leadership of the association. This proposal rankled the members of the Vienna group. Many who had supported Freud for years felt unjustly treated. They did not want to work in Jung's shadow or take orders from Zurich. Adler and Stekel arranged a protest meeting, and Freud just barely succeeded in avoiding a total split. The Congress ended by establishing an international association with Jung as president, and—to counterbalance the influence of the association—a journal, *Zentralblatt für Psychoanalyse*, with Adler and Stekel as editors. The stage was set for the conflicts of the next four years.

Freud had obviously intended to create an effective movement that could promote the broader interests of psychoanalysis. He did not foresee that many members of the movement would develop psychoanalysis in different directions in their theoretical work. Much has been said and written about Freud's indignation toward these "dissenters," but it seems clear that the International Association would have been quickly reduced to a discussion group if he had tolerated them. Psychoanalysis could only survive and develop by educating new analysts. This work necessitated the formulation of a minimum program dealing with theory and therapy. In order to ensure continuity, the association soon demanded that new analysts should be psychoanalyzed as part of their training. This practice resulted in a certain stability, but also gave the association a somewhat hierarchical structure. An analyst's position in the hierarchy was determined by whether he or she had been analyzed by Freud himself or only by someone whom Freud had already analyzed. Bearing in mind the revelation of intimate details during analysis, it is understandable that analyzing other analysts could put a new analyst in a position of influence. It would be difficult for an analyst to oppose another analyst in organizational issues if the other analyst were privy to his innermost thoughts and problems. The conflicts that nevertheless did break out within the association were personal and intimate, even if they were based on weighty theoretical disagreements.

Freud concentrated on clinical work during the period of the formation of the International Association. At meetings and congresses and in the internal debate he provided searching analyses of individual patients, giving other analysts a standard of reference for their own work. The most famous case histories were written during these years. After "Dora" (1905e), Freud analyzed "Little Hans" (1909b). The material for this analysis of a five-year-old boy's phobia as provided by Max Graf, a member of the Vienna group, who under Freud's guidance treated his son for a fear of horses. In the same year, Freud published an intensive analysis of the "Rat Man's" obsessional neurosis (1909d) and years later Freud attempted for the first time to give a thorough analysis of a psychosis: the case of Schreber (1911c). Freud did not treat this patient himself, basing his analysis instead on Schreber's published book, *Memoirs of My Nervous Illness* (Schreber 1903). In the field of psychoanalysis, the psychiatrists from Burghölzli had previously had a monopoly on the study of psychoses. Freud now entered the discussion, motivated in part by his impression of an increasingly serious disagreement between Jung and Abraham. Freud's last major case history was based on a long and complicated analysis of the "Wolf Man" from 1910 to 1914, which was first published after World War I (1918b). In the same period, he also wrote a number of articles on therapy, including transference, which had a more direct bearing on the training of new analysts. Moreover, Freud attempted to limit the use of psychoanalytic therapeutic methods by doctors outside the association by attacking them for discrediting psychoanalysis by randomly employing its concepts in their work. Freud accused them of conducting "wild" psychoanalysis (1910k).

The period from 1910 to 1914 was marked by internal dissensions in the psychoanalytic movement. The course of events during this period has since been the subject of significant interest. However, we will not dwell on these dissensions, since the formation of opposing schools of psychoanalysis lies outside the scope of this book. We will take a brief look at three dissenters from the movement: Adler, Stekel, and Jung. Freud's estrangement from them was complicated by the fact that he had placed them in influential positions in the association. It was fortunate for Freud that the three did not join forces.

Alfred Adler (1870–1937) joined Freud early on, around the turn of the century. Freud acknowledged his intellectual gifts, but never developed a close personal relationship with him. Adler felt disregarded in light of Freud's unqualified and open favoring of Jung. There were also theoretical conflicts between the two men. Adler proclaimed himself a socialist, considering it his goal to formulate a synthesis of Marxism and psychoanalysis. Comparing him to later Freudian Marxists, however, it is difficult to uncover any clear traces of Marxism in his theories apart from his general emphasis of social influences in his work. After the Nuremberg congress in 1910, Adler's relationship with Freud seriously deteriorated. It did not improve even after Freud let Adler be elected president of the Vienna Psychoanalytic Society and editor of *Zentralblatt*. Freud provoked a break in 1911 by claiming that Adler's views were incompatible with his membership in the society. Freud was especially annoyed at Adler's declining interest in sexuality and the unconscious. Adler had replaced the sexual drive with a theory of "the will to power." The will to power developed as a compensation for an original inferiority complex (caused, for example, by an anatomical abnormality). The great men of society often had innate abnormalities. In Western civilization, compensational activity was associated with the male, and consequently Adler regarded what he called "masculine protest" as the source of the will to power. It should be noted that Adler did not, like Nietzsche, consider the will to power as something positive, but rather as an expression of neurosis. Not many in the Vienna group shared Adler's views, but the majority supported his right to express them. Freud's adamant attitude resulted in about half of the membership's leaving with Adler in 1911. Adler established a new Society for Free Psychoanalysis, emphasizing the right to independent research. Later the name of the Adlerian approach was changed to "individual psychology," which became quite popular, especially in the United States.

Wilhelm Stekel (1868–1940) was Adler's immediate subordinate in the Vienna society. He had supported Freud for as long as Adler, and had been the one to propose to Freud the formation of the Wednesday club in 1902. His most significant similarity to Adler was his view that members should have the right to their own opinions. However, he remained in the society after Adler left and as a reward was promoted to president. He is thought to have influenced Freud's theory of symbols in dreams, and he had a remarkable ability to analyze unconscious symptoms. In retrospect, moreover, his work contains the seeds of a theory of the death wish, anticipating an aspect of Freud's theory of the death drive, just as Adler had anticipated the theory of aggressive tendencies in the death drive.

Freud's conflict with Stekel was apparently caused by the latter's unreliability. If Stekel did not have the clinical material he needed at his disposal, he invented examples himself. Psychoanalysis was especially vulnerable on this point, because analyses of neurotic symptoms were widely regarded in scientific circles as pure fantasy. In 1912, Freud found an opportunity to get rid of Stekel. As the chief editor of *Zentralblatt,* Stekel had refused to print articles by Victor Tausk, one of the young hopes of the society, and Freud therefore asked him to resign. When Stekel refused, Freud persuaded the other editors to resign and form a new journal, *Internationale Zeitschrift für ärztliche Psychoanalyse.* Freud's maneuver proved successful: Stekel's *Zentralblatt* soon closed, while the new journal, along with *Imago,* established in 1911, became the most important mouthpiece for psychoanalysis in the following years. Freud had called Adler a pygmy, apparently a sarcastic reference to his theory of the inferiority complex's causing the will to power. Stekel readily admitted to being Freud's intellectual inferior, but, using an analogy, observed that a dwarf on the back of a giant could see farther then the giant alone. Freud is said to have agreed, adding, however, that the analogy did not apply to a louse sitting on the head of an astronomer.

Carl Gustav Jung (1876–1961) was in Freud's opinion the most talented of his students. Moreover, he had a solid position in contemporary psychiatry, and as a non-Jew he could safeguard psychoanalysis from anti-Semitic prejudices. Freud chose him as his successor (as Moses had chosen Joshua to lead the Jews to the promised land), and in 1910 Jung was officially appointed president of the International Psychoanalytic Association, which was the main coordinating body for the local groups. However, it was not long before insurmountable conflicts arose between the two men. Jung's work gradually drew him away from psychiatry in the direction of a universal cultural analysis and anthropology. He did not believe that psychoanalytic concepts could be broadly applied in the analysis of psychoses because they usually had an organic cause. In 1911, he published the first part of *Symbols of Transformation,* which made it clear that he did not agree with Freud's views on sexuality and the Oedipus complex. He regarded the libido as a universal life energy, while Freud the year before had for the first time explicitly divided drives into two groups, sexual drives and drives of self-preservation. Instead of a universal application of the Oedipus complex, Jung studied mythology to find other basic structures applicable to clinical material. Freud responded to Jung's studies by embarking on a major anthropological project to prove the universality of the

Oedipus complex. The result of his efforts was *Totem and Taboo* (Freud 1912–1913), which Freud considered one of his best books. Jung's concept of introversion also compelled Freud to broaden his horizons by incorporating the earliest stages of the ego, first in the Schreber case history (Freud 1911c) and later in his work on narcissism (Freud 1914c). The final split between Freud and Jung came in 1912. In September, Jung traveled to the United States, and there openly criticized Freud and psychoanalysis. A dramatic meeting between Freud and Jung in November did not lead to a reconciliation, and in December, at Freud's suggestion, they decided to end their personal correspondence. However, Jung's position and influence in the association were so strong that Freud and his supporters could not prevent Jung's reelection as president at the congress in Munich in September 1913. Plans were made to employ the same tactics as had been used against Stekel—that is, letting local societies resign from the International Psychoanalytic Association and form a new organization—but they were not carried out. In 1914, Freud wrote a vehemently polemical article on the history of psychoanalysis (1914d), in which he underscored his role as the creator of psychoanalysis and demanded the right to determine its content personally. However, Jung, apparently of his own free will, resigned as president in April 1914, before he had read the article, and created his own school of "analytical psychology" together with the majority of the Swiss group. This school, as we know, since developed into one of the most serious challenges to psychoanalysis and even today enjoys widespread support.

These many conflicts prompted Ernest Jones in 1912 to propose the formation of a special committee comprised of Freud's most loyal followers. Jones envisioned this committee as a bulwark to defend Freud and his ideas from criticism. The committee had five members: Jones, Sandor Ferenczi, Karl Abraham, Otto Rank, and Hanns Sachs. These five were given the practical task of implementing Freud's proposals in the International Psychoanalytic Association without consulting the democratic organs. They did fail, of course, to depose Jung at the 1913 congress, but they later encountered little resistance in carrying out proposals agreed on beforehand, especially in the years after World War I. Abraham was already the head of the Psychoanalytic Society in Berlin, and in 1913 Ferenczi and Jones established similar societies in Budapest and London respectively (moreover, during a visit to Canada in 1911, Jones provided the impetus for the formation of an American psychoanalytic association). These societies remained the most faithful in their support of Freud, while the Swiss society—even after Jung had left—followed its own course to a greater degree.

The conflicts with Adler and Jung affected the development of psychoanalysis in another way. Freud realized that he had to clarify psychoanalytic theory further in order to avoid future misconceptions. As in the 1890s, when he made his first theoretical—or metapsychological—advances by sketching a general psychological theory, Freud worked on theoretical questions again from 1910 to 1915. We have elsewhere called this period Freud's second metapsychological thrust. Among the subjects he examined were the clarification of drive categories (1910i), the pleasure principle and the reality principle (1911b), the unconscious (1912g), and the narcissistic developmental phase of the ego (1914c). However, the most significant work of these years, which compiled these concepts, were the twelve monographs from 1915. In this work, Freud attempted to clarify all the main concepts of psychoanalysis in individual essays. He had had the time for this work because of the isolation of the war, which, however, also complicated publication of his articles. Three were published in 1915, and dealt with drives (1915c), repression (1915d), and the unconscious (1915e). Two other articles followed in 1917, and examined dream theory (1917d) and the connection between narcissism, grief, and melancholy (1917e). The remaining seven essays were not published, probably because Freud thought them outdated after the war, when he had already made significant changes in his theory. It would undoubtedly have caused considerable confusion if they had been published at the same time as the major works from the beginning of the 1920s. Nevertheless, Freud's destruction of these manuscripts was, of course, a serious loss for students of his theoretical development, especially in light of the high quality of the five published essays. A rough draft of these essays was once sent to Sandor Ferenczi and has recently been found and published (Freud 1985a). It discusses transference neuroses placed in an evolutionary perspective.

The war was a serious threat to the already divided psychoanalytic movement. Many psychoanalysts, including Abraham and Ferenczi, were ordered to do their service as physicians and potential patients had problems other than analysis on their minds. Publication of books and journals was difficult and international cooperation almost suspended completely. Before the American entry into the war, Brill in New York was the only contact between Freud and the English group, and after 1917, all channels were cut off. Moreover, a conflict arose between Freud and Jones, because they sympathized with the war effort of their respective countries. Toward the end of the war, Freud became increasingly despondent, and he and his family suffered from hunger and cold. His most important work next to metapsychology was his lectures on the introduction to psychoanalysis, which in a more coherent form than the metapsychological essays gave a picture of what psychoanalysis was. Freud gave these lectures in 1915 to 1916 and 1916 to 1917, and they provide, along with the "new lectures" (1933a) the best general introduction to psychoanalysis. Freud had apparently retained his superstition from the Fliess period that he would die in February 1918, and the lectures were thus conceived as a testament. As we know, his superstition was false and at the war's end, Freud started a new phase in his work that would prove just as important as his previous endeavors.

2. THE ESTABLISHMENT OF PSYCHOANALYSIS AS AN INTERNATIONAL MOVEMENT (1918–1939)

Psychoanalysis began to flourish again surprisingly quickly after the end of World War I. Soldiers returning from the front suffered a manifold number of psychic disorders that established psychiatry was at a loss to cope with (the same phenomenon would repeat itself after World War II). There were not only cases of shell shock and related disorders, but emotional crises caused by constant anxiety, changes in environment, and iron discipline in the army. The military authorities were generally of the opinion that soldiers simulated emotional stress in order to escape military duty. A harsh "treatment" including strong electrical shocks was used, if for no other reason, to instill in soldiers a desire to be released from the hospital and return to active duty. However, Hungarian military authorities acknowledged the problem even before the war's end and urged a number of psychoanalysts to evaluate its scope, which in turn prompted the convening of a congress in Budapest in September 1918. The many different kinds of disorders were grouped under the heading "war neuroses." As early as 1919, several psychoanalysts published a book on the subject with a foreword by Freud (Freud 1919d). Freud was later commissioned as an expert to evaluate possible maltreatment of patients by Austrian psychiatrists during the war. However, his conception of war neuroses as a reactivation of infantile conflicts provoked by external causes was too remote from prevalent views to exert any influence, and his participation in this program made him, if possible, even less respected among traditional psychiatrists than previously. The main achievement for psychoanalysis was that it had survived the war and had been revived as an international movement.

In discussing postwar psychoanalysis, it is necessary to draw a sharp distinction between Freud's work and the work of the psychoanalytic movement in general. Freud's work became more exclusive, while rank-and-file members were assigned more menial tasks. Freud's writings during the 1920s were a demanding challenge to many psychoanalysts who had just become comfortable with earlier concepts, but the positive effect of Freud's work was that psychoanalysis did not degenerate into a stagnant system. Freud was especially prolific in the years 1920 to 1925, which we call his third metapsychological thrust. The most important works of this period were *Beyond the Pleasure Principle* (1920g), *Group Psychology and the Analysis of the Ego* (1921c), and *The Ego and the Id* (1923b). Among the other works from this period was *Inhibitions, Symptoms, and Anxiety* (1926d) written in 1925. These works contained extensive revisions of drive theory, development theory, and the model of the psychic apparatus, although the tendency of these revisions is the same. The death drive was introduced as the generic term for all the features in human behavior having goals other than the attainment of pleasure and adaption to the environment. Freud attempted to explain the death drive as a biologically based effort in all living things to return to the serene state of inorganic matter. He described the expression of the death drive in part as an outwardly directed aggressiveness in some cases guaranteeing the survival of the individual, and in part as a destructiveness directed inwardly at the ego. The death drive was expressed psychologically by the superego—the other new concept—and contributed to the preservation of utopian norms and ideals, which could plague the individual. The superego was generally accepted as an important concept among psychoanalysts, whereas the death drive met with resistance. Some chose to understand it as simply an aggression drive, while others continued to prefer the old division of drives into sexual drives and drives of self-preservation.

By the middle 1920s, the local psychoanalytic societies had joined the International Psychoanalytic Association, which had a total of about three hundred members, a third of which were in England and the United States. The most prominent members, however, were in continental Europe. The membership of the Vienna Psychoanalytic Society included Lou Andreas-Salomé, Siegfried Bernfeld, Edward Bibring, Helene Deutsch, Paul Federn, Otto Fenichel, Anna and Sigmund Freud, Heinz Hartmann, Eduard Hitschmann, Ludwig Jekels, Ernst Kris, Herman Nunberg, Otto Rank, Wilhelm Reich, Theodor Reik, Robert Wälder, and Edoardo Weiss. In Berlin the most important members were Karl Abraham, Franz Alexander, Max Eitingon, Georg Groddeck, Karen Horney, Melanie Klein, Rudolf Löwenstein, Sandor Rado, and Hanns Sachs. In Hungary, members included Sandor Ferenczi, Geza Roheim, and later Michael Balint, and in Switzerland, Ludwig Binswanger, Oskar Pfister, Jean Piaget, and Raymond de Saussure (son of the linguist Ferdinand de Saussure). It is noteworthy that Piaget, who was to become famous as a developmental psychologist, started his career in psychoanalysis. Moreover, the Soviet group included two of his colleagues in linguistic and developmental psychology, Luria and Vygotsky. Ernest Jones was the undisputed leader of the English group. His most well-known colleagues were Edward Glover, Susan Isaacs, Joan Riviere, and James Strachey. Strachey was later responsible for the excellent critical edition of Freud's collected works in English. Abraham Brill led the psychoanalytic group in the United States, which included Abram Kardiner and Harry S. Sullivan, who, however, later achieved prominence outside of orthodox psychoanalysis.

Freud stopped participating in international congresses in the beginning of the 1920s, partly for health reasons. The leadership of the organization was increasingly transferred to the committee, which was expanded to include Max Eitingon after the war. The presidency was occupied in shifts by committee members. Freud concentrated some of his energies on developing a psychoanalytic publishing company, seeing it as a necessary prerequisite for guaranteeing the independence of psychoanalysis. Because of financial problems with fluctuating rates of exchange the establishment of such a publishing company was well nigh impossible. In spite of several gifts of money, and in spite of the fact that Freud put his income from his own books into the company, it was usually in the red. The Nazis finally confiscated and destroyed the entire business. While the publishing company functioned, however, several journals and a number of books were published. Taken as a whole, they gave a good idea of developments in psychoanalysis. These developments were not totally harmonious. Aside from the conflicts arising from Freud's new theories and the geographic dispersal of the movement, the members of the committee also developed in different directions. We can give an impression of these differences by discussing the four most important members: Abraham in Berlin, Rank in Vienna, Ferenczi in Budapest, and Jones in London.

Karl Abraham (1877–1925) is regarded as Freud's most loyal follower, but his support for Freud does not mean he lacked his own views. He was the first to warn Freud of the dissenting opinions of Jung and later Rank. If later events had not confirmed his suspicions, he would probably have been regarded as a troublemaker. As a theorist he was the most prominent in the committee after Freud. He was originally trained at Burghölzli and understood better than Bleuler and Jung how psychoses could be viewed in relation to the developmental theory of psychoanalysis. His most important work (Abraham 1924) contains a clarification of Freud's theory of the oral and anal stages of development and the hitherto most thorough examination of the manic-depressive psychosis. Abraham died suddenly in 1925 after a mysterious disorder in the bronchial tubes. He was treated by Freud's old friend, the throat doctor Wilhelm Fliess, but in spite of Fliess's periodicity theory, Abraham could not be saved. It has been speculated that the diagnosis was wrong and Abraham suffered from lung cancer. During the 1920s, Berlin became an increasingly important center for psychoanalysis, and its prominent position was maintained after Abraham's death. One of the reasons was that a proper training center for psychoanalysis was established there, making the study of psychoanalysis more effective.

Otto Rank (1884–1939) was not medically trained. He was a man of letters and contributed early on in applying psychoanalysis to the analysis of literature and myths. He originally served as a kind of secretary to Freud and after the war advanced to the position of Freud's right-hand man and probable successor. He also headed the psychoanalytic publishing company. In 1923, he published a book on the birth trauma, in which he claimed that neurotic conflicts thought to stem from the Oedipus complex, in reality had deeper roots and stemmed from the state of anxiety during birth. Freud was initially receptive to Rank's theory. However, Abraham contended that Rank's theory, like those of Adler and Jung, was incompatible with the sexual theory of psychoanalysis. The final break did not come before 1924, when Rank, during a prolonged stay in the United States, claimed that his theory would shorten the long and difficult periods of analysis to about three months by focusing on the birth trauma instead of circumventing it by dwelling on the Oedipus complex. Upon his return from the United States, Rank decided after some hesitation to stand by his theory. Freud could not tolerate this open "treason" and Rank was forced to leave the psychoanalytic movement.

Sandor Ferenczi (1873–1933) was for many years Freud's closest colleague and personal friend. It is evident from their correspondence that Freud always confided his secrets to Ferenczi first, and Ferenczi was usually given the task of realizing Freud's ideas when Freud himself wanted to be dissociated from them. After the war there were plans to make Budapest the center of psychoanalysis, but political developments soon put an end to them, and Ferenczi became more isolated in his native city than Freud ever was in Vienna. Ferenczi was not so prominent as a theorist. His only major work was a somewhat speculative book on the ontogeny and phylogeny of genitality (Ferenczi 1924). Yet he was perhaps the most prominent therapist in psychoanalysis, developing new ideas in this field that Freud accepted in part. They are usually discussed under the heading "active analysis" and hold that the analyst should not merely be a passive listener, but should participate actively in the analysis at certain points. Freud did not believe that an analyst should force his own views on the patient in any way. The patient had to change his life by his own choice. However, Freud acknowledged that it might be necessary to give the patient certain instructions to prevent actions harmful to the analysis and the patient himself. In the late 1920s, Ferenczi expanded his "active analysis" and Freud then directly opposed it. Ferenczi thought that childhood traumas should be taken more seriously than Freud generally took them. Most psychic conflicts could be uncovered as an expression of maltreatment of one kind or another of the child by his parents. Analysis should therefore proceed as an attempt by the analyst to recreate a good parent-child relationship by playing the role of the good parent. Ferenczi went so far as to kiss and touch his patients, letting them feel "real" love in contrast to the cool transference of emotions in Freudian analysis. Freud accused Ferenczi condescendingly of "playing mother and child" with his patients, but their differences did not lead to any open estrangement, as in Rank's case.

Ernest Jones (1879–1958) is known primarily for his three-volume work on Freud's life and work (Jones 1953, 1955, and 1957). His contribution to psychoanalysis rests mainly on his organizational work. He was instrumental in the dissemination of psychoanalysis in England and the United States. His most important theoretical contribution was his theory of symbols (1916), where he studied a subject that later became significant in psychoanalysis. As a representative of English common sense, Jones consistently criticized the more speculative features of Freud's theory, including the death drive and Freud's belief in telepathy and Lamarck's evolutionary theories. However, their most serious disagreement arose in connection with Freud's theory of the phallic phase, which he formulated in the 1920s. Several female analysts, including Karen Horney and Melanie Klein, could not wholeheartedly accept Freud's concept of penis envy in girls. Horney claimed that phallic sexuality in girls (clitoris sexuality) was a secondary development caused by a defense of the vagina, which was the primary erogenous zone. Klein moved the Oedipus and castration complexes back to the first year of life, so that the question of the presence of a penis became a question of the presence of the mother's breast and the child's fantasies of the breast. Jones, who had invited Klein from Berlin to London after Abraham's death, became a warm supporter of her theories, to Freud's regret. However, Jones was always so moderate in his views that his support for Klein did not lead to a break between him and Freud.

During the 1920s and 1930s, the center of psychoanalysis moved from Central Europe to England and the United States. This development was not only a transfer of power but a transfer of analysts. There were two main reasons for this development. First, there was an enormous interest in psychoanalysis in the two countries, especially in the United States. Americans were already accustomed to a health system based on private enterprise, which also created a market for individual psychotherapy. Second, political developments in Europe led to the banning of psychoanalysis in several countries. In the Soviet Union, psychoanalysis met with widespread acceptance and was supported by Trotsky. However, it was totally purged under Stalin in the 1930s and has never been rehabilitated. It was accused of being "bourgeois," "idealistic," "individualistic," and "decadent." In Germany, Hitler's assumption of power put a sudden stop to psychoanalysis, which was accused of being a Jewish psychology. Psychiatry was put under the aegis of the Nazis, and was headed by Hermann Göring's cousin and Jung, who had earlier characterized his psychology as "Aryan." Jung resigned in 1939, but his cooperation with the Nazis stigmatized him once and for all, especially among Jewish psychoanalysts.

In the 1920s, the English and American groups provided a lucid example of their power in the international organization. In 1926, Freud successfully defended Theodor Reik in Vienna against an accusation of quackery. The reason for this accusation was that Reik had practiced psychoanalysis without medical training. Freud did not see anything wrong in this because he believed that psychoanalytic training was sufficient. In 1927, Ferenczi visited the United States, and was almost ostracized after attempting to form a group of analysts with no medical training. The Americans and the English consistently refused to accept nonphysicians as analysts. This was the beginning of a lengthy dispute in which Freud and Ferenczi fought energetically for their views. Freud even attempted unsuccessfully to have the American society excluded from the international association. His strong feeling about this dispute was probably caused by his fear that the group of medical doctors would come to influence psychoanalysis in a limited and narrow-minded direction. However, he was only able to reach a compromise under which analysts with no medical training could be approved under certain special circumstances, for example, as child analysts. After World War II, American analysts totally dominated psychoanalysis with the result that psychoanalytic training was primarily reserved for physicians. Of course, prominent personalities with no medical training such as Anna Freud, Erik H. Erikson, and David Rapaport were tolerated.

The flow of analysts to the United States was started by Sandor Rado, who in 1931 was invited to become the head of the psychoanalytic training center in New York, which had just opened (paid for by a gift of fifty thousand dollars). Hanns Sachs emigrated in 1932. After 1933 a large part of the Berlin group left Germany, and the Vienna group was also drained. Freud was terribly upset to see his immediate surroundings being depleted of talented scholars seeking better financial opportunities abroad. He had finally lost his personal influence on the development of psychoanalysis, and his best work from his last years concerns issues on the periphery of traditional psychoanalytic problems, for example, the examination of trends in modern civilization in *Civilization and Its Discontents* (1930a) and the analysis of the religious father figure in the major work on Moses (1939a). During this time, writers like Heinz Hartmann, Wilhelm Reich, and Jacques Lacan, who were to gain prominence in various psychoanalytic schools after World War II, were starting their work. After Hitler's invasion of Austria in 1938, Freud chose to emigrate, moving with his family to England the same year. He died in London in September 1939 from cancer of the jaw, from which he had suffered for sixteen years.

III

THE ANALYTIC WORK

INTRODUCTION
TO PART III

In the general introduction, we explained how Freud distinguished three dimensions in psychoanalysis: analysis, therapy, and theory. In general, the subject of analytic work is "completed" psychic manifestations, which are expressed in one way or another in consciousness or behavior. Analytic work can focus on dreams, psychic functional disorders, and jokes, some of the more specialized areas Freud studied around the turn of the century, but it can also involve works of art, religion, and social behavior, subjects with which Freud became increasingly preoccupied in his later years. All forms of analysis resemble each other by revealing unconscious sexual motives behind conscious thoughts and actions. However, they never become trivial, because every single analysis demands a meticulous study of the extremely complex primary and secondary processes that mediate the transition from unconscious to conscious.

Freud himself chose what he considered "privileged" expressions for the unconscious when he presented psychoanalysis publicly. These expressions were particularly distinct examples designed to provoke discussion with specialists in other fields. It was imperative for Freud to demonstrate the universal application of psychoanalysis as a tool of analysis. That he achieved this goal is evident from the fact that today most humanistic and sociological disciplines have been inspired by psychoanalysis. The examples of analysis in section C should be seen in this light. They do not adequately depict the analytic capabilities of psychoanalysis because Freud did not, of course, master the subjects in question as well as his own. They do, however, contain significant qualities by consistently searching for explanations for truths and norms that are usually taken for granted. Freud concentrated his efforts on exposing religion and its illusions, but the method he created by doing so can be used just as rewardingly in analyzing political, ideological, and moral concepts.

Freud's method of analysis can be characterized as interpretive or decoding. Like the Romantics, he was fascinated by ancient symbols, characters, and myths whose meaning had been lost. If the code could not be broken, the message could not be interpreted. The task was therefore to deduce the code and the message in the writings available. The interpretation of hieroglyphics especially was an example to be emulated. For a long time scholars were unable to interpret them because they thought that the hieroglyphics concerned the animals, plants, and celestial beings that the individual characters depicted. The solution was that these characters were not to be understood literally but rather as phonemes or syllables that could be freely combined to form new and more complicated words. We know this phenomenon today from rebus language: for example, the two words *in* and *deed* together form *indeed*.

Freud became acquainted with decoding in many different contexts, ranging from the natural sciences to literature to fun at the fair. We have discussed Darwin's interpretation of the affects, in which he traced their physiological expressions (facial expressions indicating sorrow, happiness, anger, and so on) back to functional reflexes in more primitive animal species. Reflex has gradually lost its function and therefore seems at times to be superfluous and meaningless in man if its origins are unknown. In literature, mystery writers like Poe and Conan Doyle involved their protagonists in decoding. Detective work was in itself a form of interpretation in which an idea of the crime and not least the criminal could be pieced together by examining drops of blood, footprints, and so on. Freud was, not without reason, popularly regarded as the Sherlock Holmes of psychology because his work consisted of making guesses, drawing conclusions, and analyzing the unconscious of a person using only little information. Even during Freud's lifetime, there were many examples of the misuse of decoding technique. Fortune-tellers read fortunes using coffee grinds, playing cards, crystal balls, and the lines of the palm. Spiritualists interpreted knocking sounds as messages from the dead. Astrologists thought that human destiny was determined by the position of celestial bodies. Many felt that Freud was too receptive to these ideas. For example, he believed that one day psychoanalysis would be able to explain various occult phenomena, and we have mentioned that he never entirely abandoned his fatalistic beliefs, as he had believed Fliess's astrologically based prediction of the day of his death.

These examples cannot stand alone, however. Freud's analytic method was naturally also influenced by a psychiatric dimension found in the work of Meynert, Charcot, and Breuer. In 1897, when Freud started to systematize his dream interpretation in earnest, he already had a method for the interpretation of neurotic symptoms and a hypothetical model of the psychic apparatus to work from. Without this method and this model, he would hardly have achieved what he did with his analysis.

A.

DREAMS

In 1900, when *The Interpretation of Dreams* (Freud 1900a) was finally published, Freud imagined, half in jest, that one day a marble tablet would be erected at Bellevue, the family's summer residence for many years, which would read: "Here the secret of dreams was revealed to Dr. Sigm. Freud on 24 July 1895." Although this was the day that Freud interpreted the dream about Irma's injection, which we will discuss later in this section, the chronology implied by the inscription is not entirely accurate. Judging from *A Project for a Scientific Psychology,* (1950a), Freud, in the fall of 1895, regarded dreams exclusively as an expression of a hallucinatory wish fulfillment. For example, if while asleep one developed a thirst, one would simply dream that one was drinking a glass of water. Such a direct wish fulfillment was, to be sure, unusual. Most dreams seemed disjointed and incomprehensible, but Freud explained that that was due to the fact that more complex desires left no room in dreams for the ideas that comprised the wish fulfillment. The cathexes therefore joined together in units of ideas, which then performed with particular intensity in the dream even though they perhaps had nothing to do with the wish fulfillment. On this point, Freud's theory still resembled Herbart's (see I.B.4.b). When several ideas competed to transgress the threshold of consciousness, Herbart assumed that random weak ideas could become conscious by joining together. Freud did improve on Herbart's theory by allowing primary processes to determine which ideas attained the greatest cathexis, but he had yet to integrate the defense concept in his dream theory. This integration occurred in two stages during the third and fourth phase of inception (see II.B on the inception of psychoanalysis). In the third phase (1895–1896), Freud managed to present pathological defense or repression in obsessional neurosis as a strong reaction of unpleasure in the preconscious directed toward a pleasure-oriented idea in the unconscious. A child repressed the idea of infantile masturbation and hence the wish to continue to masturbate because the idea of masturbation had been associated in the child's upbringing with extreme unpleasure. In the long term, therefore, wish was expressed as symptoms of obsessional neurosis via primary processes. At this time, repression was a purely pathological defense, according to Freud. However, he abandoned this view in the fourth phase (1896–1897) primarily due to the findings of his self-analysis. We can summarize the result in two points: (1) both normal and neurotic persons had active repressed wishes (including those suffering from hysteria and obsessional neurosis); (2) repressed wishes did not necessarily stem from real (traumatic) events, but could exist as wish fantasies, first and foremost oedipal fantasies of possessing the mother sexually and murdering the father.

In the fall of 1897, the fact that repressed wish fantasies were found in all normal people and were particularly active in dreams was a new element in Freud's thinking. This discovery naturally led to a radical change of previous dream theory so that now repression was placed at the center of the so-called dream censorship. The following two years were devoted almost exclusively to work on *The Interpretation of Dreams,* and it is understandable that Freud called the interpretation of dreams the royal road to a knowledge of the unconscious, because he had in his own dreams empirical material more readily accessible and more reliable than the accounts of neurotic patients.

Even the first edition of *The Interpretation of Dreams* was very long with a meticulous structure. Freud clearly intended to advance the idea of dreams as an everyday experience to a general theory of not only the formation of dreams, but of the psychic apparatus as a whole, that is, its genesis and function. Chapter by chapter he gradually expanded his terminological table, so that it was not until the end of chapter 6 that he had introduced all the concepts relating to dreams. He then took a final leap to the general psychological theory in the long final chapter. Our presentation will now move in the opposite direction. In the first section we will examine the process of the formation of dreams, and in the second section we will give examples of dream interpretation using all the concepts of dream theory. We will first focus on general psychological theory in part 5.

1. THE FORMATION OF DREAMS

Freud distinguished between manifest and latent dream content. Manifest dream content was what was normally called a dream, in other words, the conscious phenomena occasionally appearing during sleep that could be recounted afterward. It was impossible to make a scientific distinction between the recounted dream and the actual dream. The latter had always disappeared by the time interpretation began, so one had instead to take the recounted dream as the object of inquiry. Freud accepted this because recounting also produced valuable information for interpretation. The actual dream was primarily visual and could therefore be recounted in many ways, but the manner in which the dreamer recounted the dream also said something about his personality, just as the way he dreamt did. Latent dream content was all the sources of the dream uncovered during interpretation. It comprised so-called day residues (memories from the day before the dream), other memories (such as childhood memories), wish and drive impulses, and every physiological impulse affecting the senses during dreams (hunger, thirst, light, noise, heat, cold, and so on). Dream interpretation was the work performed by the dreamer or psychoanalyst to uncover latent dream thoughts from the manifest dream. This work resembled the deciphering of a message and the goal was, in the last analysis, to find the unconscious wish fantasy that had attained consciousness in the dream by a complex network of associations. Although interpretation, or deciphering, proceeded from the manifest to the latent content, Freud assumed that the manifest dream was formed by a work process traveling in the opposite direction: the so-called dream work whose function was to translate the unconscious wish fantasy to the code language of the manifest dream. In principal, dream work could employ all the memory ideas in the psyche, so without some knowledge of the personality of the dreamer, it was impossible to interpret his dreams. Freud therefore primarily used his own or his patients' dreams.

(a) The Three Phases of Dream Formation

The topographical model constructed by Freud in the third phase of the inception of psychoanalysis (as described in a letter to Fliess from 6 December 1896) was also the basis for the theory of the formation of dreams in *The Interpretation of Dreams*. We will discuss this in detail in section V.A.1, and will only deal with its main features here. The psyche, or psychic apparatus is divided into systems with different characteristics. The perception system (system *P*) records external sensory impulses that are then transmitted to the unconscious *(Ucs)*. The system *Ucs* contains the earliest received memory ideas, the so-called thing presentations, and processes passing between thing presentations called primary processes. Some impulses are transmitted to the preconscious *(Pcs)* containing word presentation received later, and the processes passing between them are called secondary processes. Compared to primary processes, the secondary processes are more logical and reality oriented. They usually perform in the conscious system *(Cs)*, while all impulses from *Ucs* must pass through *Pcs* to reach *Cs*. *Pcs* can under normal circumstances inhibit and in exceptional circumstances repress impulses from *Ucs* that threaten its integrity by awakening anxiety and unpleasure. During dream formation the repressive part of *Pcs* becomes a censor, censuring all unconscious impulses before they are allowed to enter *Pcs*.

Dream formation has three phases through which the impulse issuing from the unconscious wish fantasy must pass before attaining consciousness in the form of the manifest dream.

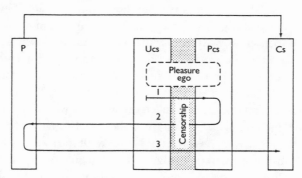

After 1920, when Freud altered his topographical model for good, dream theory was changed as well. We can for the time being observe that the system *Ucs* was renamed the *id*, while the systems *P*, *Cs*, and *Pcs* were joined to form the *ego*. The system of censorship was included in a new psychic system called the superego.

The sleeping state is a precondition for dreaming. Freud was directly inspired by Fechner when he said that the dream occurred on another scene (see I.B.4.a) or, in Freud's terminology, in another psychic system. However, Freud differed from Fechner regarding the influence of the sleeping state on dreams. Fechner believed that the energy of the nervous system fluctuated in such a way that it supplied the system of normal thought with energy in the waking state and the dream system with energy in the sleeping state. Freud thought that the level of excitation generally fell throughout the entire psychic apparatus during sleep. After introducing the concept of narcissism in the second metapsychological thrust (1910–1915), Freud compared the sleeping state with the narcissistic state in which the individual ceased to be interested in his environment and was only preoccupied with himself. Expressed in metapsychological terminology, all energy cathexis is, as far as possible, withdrawn to the narcissistic pleasure ego. The pleasure ego is an early psychic formation differing from the actual ego, and containing some of the elements contributing to the development of the id *(Ucs)*, the superego (censorship), and the ego *(Pcs)*. To illustrate Freud's line of reasoning we have tentatively included the pleasure ego in the above model.

The most striking effect of the pleasure ego's sleep wish is the decathexis of the conscious system, making it unreceptive to impressions—in other words, put out of action. However, Freud believed that the repressed wish fantasies in *Ucs* were not subject to the sleep wish and therefore retained some of their cathexes. A certain level of excitation was maintained in censorship as a reaction against them. Moreover, some day residues could keep their cathexes in *Pcs*. Dream formation could then proceed after this changed distribution of energy in the psychic apparatus.

During the first phase of dream formation, wish impulses in *Ucs* cathect some of the day residues in the *Pcs*, causing the development of the preconscious dream wish. This process has perhaps already started in the waking state, while some day residues (experiences during the day) have hardly become conscious because they have immediately been attracted by unconscious impulses and linked by association to unconscious wish fantasies. A typical formation of dream wish proceeds as follows: during the day, a person has been worried, disappointed, or had problems he has not been able to solve. If he is annoyed over a mistake he has made, he cannot help having a number of futile wishes ("if only I hadn't done it," "if only someone else were at fault," "if only it weren't anything important"), but they are usually not constructive enough to be used for solving the problem at hand. However, actual dream wishes are crystalized around these incipient wishes, when the preconscious day residues are reinforced during sleep by unconscious impulses. Normal preconscious wishes can usually be distinguished from dream wishes because the latter are more openly egoistical, more asocial, and less moral. This is because censorship, which controls morals (the superego), is weakened during sleep. According to its location in the psychic apparatus, censorship is primarily directed toward the unconscious wish fantasies, which have a sexual content. When these wish fantasies are merely converted to egoistical thoughts in the preconscious, they are usually allowed to pass. Freud sometimes designated the unconscious reinforcement of day residues and the formulation of the dream wish in *Pcs* as two successive phases in dream formation, while we have chosen to treat them as two aspects of the same process.

The second phase in dream formation is thus based in the preconscious wish fantasy (the dream wish). In referring to the topographical model, Freud observed that this impulse could either progress or regress. In the waking state a progression will normally take place because the impulse continues from *Pcs* to *Cs* where it becomes conscious and is perhaps converted into action. However, during sleep the system *Cs* is put out of action by the retraction of its cathexes to the narcissistic pleasure ego. In rare instances, the impulse can be converted into motor actions (sleepwalking), but Freud did not treat this phenomenon in depth. When progression is impossible, the wish impulse is forced to choose regression, that is, the movement back through the psychic apparatus. We have already discussed how unconscious thoughts and ideas can be conscious when thing presentations and the primitive and superficial associations in the system *Ucs* are translated to word presentations (concepts) and logical relations between them in the system *Pcs*. Now the task of the wish impulse is conversely to find its way back to thing presentations (especially visual), which are equivalent to dream thoughts in *Pcs*. Freud compared this task to the work of a political cartoonist, who expressed the content of a political editorial by a caricature. If well-known political figures were dressed as clowns, the meaning was clear. Dreams also employ expressions like this. The final link in regression is the movement from the system *Ucs* back to the system *P,* the system in which external sensory impulses normally become conscious. Unlike the system *Cs* this system has been able to function during sleep, as is evident by the fact that a strong sense impression can arouse the sleeper. The paradox of dreams is that wish impulses cathect the system *P* from the inside, while sensory impulses cathect it from the outside. Dreams perform with the same sense quality as external sensations, unlike waking thought in which the ability to imagine the thing or person one is thinking of is reduced.

The third phase in dream formation is a new progressive movement guiding the visualized dream from P to Cs. In the diagram above, we have drawn a direct path between the two systems causing the system Cs to be connected whenever the system P is activated. This path, which Freud introduced in *A Project for a Scientific Psychology,* must be assumed to raise the level of excitation in Cs causing the dream impulse to become conscious on its second attempt. The question arises as to whether the dream has not already become conscious when it is visualized in the system P. The answer is that it has in a way, but it has not yet attracted attention to itself and thus has not been conceptually revised. We sense an infinite number of things in our daily lives that never actually become conscious because we forget them the moment we have sensed them. Only things that are singled out for one reason or another can attract attention to themselves by a new passage through Ucs and Pcs. When we are awake we sometimes experience the difference between sense perception and mental revision if we are suddenly placed in an unexpected situation: for a few seconds we are clearly conscious that something unusual has happened, but we need time to think before we can understand what it really is. Freud called the second progressive movement in dreams the secondary revision and noted that it attempted to give the flickering dream images some form of rational coherence. This sometimes occurs by expanding on the dream and filling the gaps in it. In other cases a direct interpretation occurs, for example, the sound of an alarm clock (in the system P) is interpreted as church bells (in the system Cs). The secondary revision can also be expressed as the voice of a commentator more or less accurately explaining what is going on in a film strip. It can, for example, express surprise at the dream, even commenting that "it's only a dream." Such means are employed in an attempt to make the dream acceptable so that the (pleasure) ego can continue its narcissistic sleep. Secondary revision also continues, however, after awakening by the tendency, in recounting the dream, to add new goals and intentions to the murky passages in the dream.

We have followed Freud in sketching the three phases of dream formation. The main point is that repressed wish impulses trapped inside the system Ucs use the dream as an opportunity to escape. Their wanderings through the psychic apparatus in three different directions express the simplest path to discharge. Freud often found it necessary to employ even more zigzag movements to present all the ingredients in dream formation, or, as he observed in *The Interpretation of Dreams*, "but what happens in reality is no doubt a simultaneous exploring of one path and another, a swinging of the excitation now this way and now that, until at last it accumulates in the direction that is most opportune and one particular grouping becomes the permanent one" (Freud 1900a, p. 576).

Only when a form is found that takes everything from censorship to representability into account can the dream be discharged. "It is like a firework, which takes hours to prepare but goes off in a moment" (Freud 1900a, p. 576).

(b) The Logic of Dream Work

Dream work is made up of all the processes contributing to the transformation of the unconscious wish fantasy into the manifest dream. The three phases of dream formation are the skeleton of dream work. However, each phase contains innumerable individual associations, which we will now examine. They form a complex network or mycelium in which the threads are disseminated and gathered together according to specific rules. The regressive phase is characterized by association threads emanating from the preconscious dream wish in all directions and miraculously once again brought together in a new center, the visualized dream in the system *P*. Every single association is overdetermined, that is, determined by several different factors. Freud compared overdetermination to the restraint a poet exercised when he wanted to express a specific meaning and maintain the verse feet and rhyme of the poem at the same time. The determining factors that dream associations obey can be divided into two groups: (1) the relative strength of the agencies in the psychic apparatus, and (2) the means of expression at the disposal of dream work when the dream wish has to be formulated in a visual and relatively concentrated manner. If dream work cannot somehow meet these demands, there is no dream.

The relative strength of the psychic agencies is, as already mentioned, altered during sleep. The repressed wish fantasies in the system *Ucs* (the id) are relatively stronger, and cause the dream to appear as a hallucinatory wish fulfillment, inasmuch as the system *Ucs* makes no distinction between the wish and its fulfillment. Censorship (the superego) usually cannot totally stop wish impulses, but is able to produce an overall distortion of the fantasies. A great deal of dream work therefore involves distortion, which aims at camouflaging those features of wish fantasies that offend censorship. This distortion concerns primarily the sexual content, but also the more openly egotistical tendencies in wishes. The system *Pcs* (the ego) gives the dream the most coherent and realistic character possible (the secondary revision), but also represents the sleep wish of the pleasure ego and contributes to the formation of compromises between *Ucs* and censorship that guarantee continued sleep. We know of one example of a clear failure of this process: the nightmare. During a nightmare, the sleep wish must be abandoned in order to prevent the conflict between *Ucs* and censorship from producing more anxiety. The pleasure ego and the system *Pcs* also contribute directly to the dream content, making all dreams rigidly narcissistic and egotistic. The dreamer is always the main character, and dreams always compliment the dreamer, often in conflict with reality. The sense of reality is the psychic capability most obviously lacking in dreams. So-called reality testing, in which we distinguish between reality and fantasy while awake, does not function. The dreamer steadfastly believes that the dream is reality until he can convince himself that the opposite is the case after he has been awake for a few minutes. During this time, the relative strength of agencies in the psychic apparatus is once again altered. Reality testing starts to function and repression is augmented, so we often experience that we have forgotten the entire dream before we can repeat it to ourselves or write it down.

We have established that the dream wish cannot be directly expressed in consciousness. Its elements, either collectively or individually, must displace their cathexes along complex association chains until they reach elements having access to consciousness. From this perspective the problem is the same as finding a way out of a labyrinth. Elements appearing in a manifest dream represent elements in the dream wish. However, it is extremely unusual for an element in one area to correspond directly to an element in the other area. Association chains infiltrate each other and cross each other in innumerable places. Simple representation, in which element represents element, ceases after passage through centers and new ramifications in favor of structural representation in which one totality represents the other. For example, horse means penis because stable means vagina, and vice versa.

Dream work associations can for the most part be characterized as primary processes, because dream processes are emitted from the system *Ucs*. The only goal of energy cathexes is to attain discharge through consciousness, and there is no feedback from consciousness or the outside world to indicate whether the discharge process in question has had any result. Dream work therefore employs every association path imaginable. The only criterion for their use is whether they provide the necessary outlet for cathexes. This process stands in stark contrast to reality-oriented secondary process thinking in the system *Pcs* in which only associations having an actual counterpart in the outside world are permitted.

In order to provide a more detailed picture of dream processes, Freud usually divided dream work into four separate stages: condensation, displacement, visualization, and secondary revision. The manifest dream is produced by these component processes. They are primarily regarded as means of expression (and therefore also as discharge paths) for the dream wish, but the concept of overdetermination entails that they secondarily also fulfill the demands of censorship as well as the sleep wish, while they distort the dream wish and find useful compromises between the repressed wish fantasies and censorship. Freud's fourfold division is not rigidly systematic—the stages overlap. However, an improvement of this division would entail a rather detailed revision of the entire dream theory. We have therefore used it with certain modifications, which include employing dream symbols as an example of displacement.

The main principle of condensation is that latent dream thoughts are more extensive than the manifest dream. Only a small part of them is included, which results in compression or compromise. This often occurs by omission or selection, but the most characteristic means is the fusion of two or more ideas into one. For example, dreams can include mixed figures made up of characteristics from several different persons. Freud dreamt that a colleague had his uncle's long face, which meant that his colleague, like his uncle, was a blockhead *(Schwachkopf)* (Freud 1900a, pp. 119–25). Another dream was about a colleague whose style he called *norekdal*. This word was a condensation of *Nora* and *Ekdal*, protagonists in Ibsen's *A Doll's House* and *The Wild Duck* respectively. Freud had just seen two articles by his colleague, one on Ibsen and one in which a rather insignificant physiological discovery was praised in exaggerated terms. *Norekdal* described the style of the article, which referred especially to the hopelessly bragging visionary Hjalmar Ekdal in *The Wild Duck* (1900a, p. 296).

All psychic processes can, as mentioned, be considered displacements. However, in connection with the interpretation of dreams, *displacement* refers especially to the primary processes in which the relationship between the represented and the representing element is very loose. The primary-process displacement makes it easier for the dream both to find expression and to pass censorship, because it often distorts the original dream wish beyond recognition. Even a very slight similarity or proximity between two groups of ideas is sufficient to make displacement possible. A memory of an embarrassing argument, for example, can be expressed in the dream by a table in the house where the argument occurred, or by one of the persons who was present, or by specific sounds in the background, and so on. Displacement occurs especially between thing presentations, albeit names (see above) and words impressed on the mind are also treated as things. More extended primary-process displacements between the sound image and the written images of word presentations are known from jokes and psychoses. Reversals are a special group of displacements, in which, for example, big is represented by small, high by low, and good by evil. Freud had a theory that antonyms had developed linguistically from the same "primal words," which explained why antonyms could replace one another (1910e). *Sacer* thus means holy and cursed; *stumm* (mute) and *Stimme* (voice) are similar; *siccus* means dry, while *succus* means juice. Philologists have not confirmed Freud's theory, which has not, however, prevented the occurrence of reversals in dreams.

Inspired by Stekel, Freud introduced the term *symbol* to describe displacements that were relatively stable, not only from dream to dream in one individual, but of every individual in the same cultural milieu. The symbolized can usually be found inside the Oedipal fantasy universe. We can mention some of the more typical symbols: parents are pictured as kings and queens; the male genitals become canes, staffs, knives, and the like, and also the number 3; the female genitals become empty and open objects such as houses, rooms, cans, and suitcases. Intercourse is symbolized by walking on steps, dancing, and traffic accidents, while death is often symbolized as a departure. Freud provided a series of other examples that followed the same pattern. Symbol interpretations generally should not be exaggerated. There is some probability that symbols do apply because dream work always chooses the easiest solutions, but that does not prevent canes and cans in dreams from symbolizing things completely different from the genitals. A common indication of a poor interpretation of a dream is that only the symbols are interpreted without taking the structural totality of the dream into account.

Visualization converts the conceptual content of dream thoughts to images. Visualization is easiest to imagine with people, buildings, landscapes, and the like, where it permits seeing things and persons of which and whom one is thinking. Visualization of concepts is more difficult, and dream work must often take a detour. Freud observed that the breakup of a marriage could be visualized as the breaking of a leg (a displacement from one break to another), and ownership by someone sitting on what he owned. The whole dream wish can sometimes be expressed by a single word or a figure of speech, for example a proverb or a line of verse. As an exception, the part of the displacement leading from the dream wish to the linguistic expression is a secondary process, insofar as it is only associated with meaning: if you are awaiting an important decision about something, and you dream that you are in good spirits and are dragging a corn sheaf around, you have perhaps visualized the figure of speech "to draw the longest straw." The visualization itself does not respect the original meaning of the figure of speech, translating instead "draw" (drag) and "long straw" (corn sheaf) separately. Logical relations can in the same way only be visualized indirectly. If you "place one person higher than another" in regard, he might be visualized on a raised platform. A causal chain is visualized by the unification of cause and effect (or their visual representatives). Alternatives (either/or) are usually expressed by both possibilities' appearing side by side. A striking example of such an alternative is the dream of "Irma's injection" (see III.A.2.a).

We have already discussed the secondary revision as the third phase of dream formation. According to Freud's theory it is an expression of the demands of censorship. The secondary revision is the primary source of the nonvisual and nonsense concrete content of dreams. During a dream you reflect upon what you are dreaming. In special cases the secondary revision inserts explanatory links, makes connections, and interprets the visual dream so it becomes acceptable to reason. It then resembles rationalization, which is also known from neurotics' treatment of their own symptoms. Attempts are made to adapt the symptoms that are given expression to the conscious ego's rationality. For example, if a person washes his hands many times a day, he attempts to conceal the neurotic aspect of his actions by referring to hygiene, prevention of infection, and so on, as normally accepted practices. Secondary revision is distinguished from actual dream work by being controlled by the secondary process. The part of this process performed after awakening does not belong to dream work. Conversely, the remainder is integrated in the other processes of dream work in the sense that censorship would probably wake the sleeper and prevent the continuation of the dream if it were not there.

2. THE INTERPRETATION OF DREAMS

In principle, the interpretation of dreams attempts to follow dream formation in the opposite direction, that is, from manifest content to latent content and, in the last analysis, to the repressed wish fantasy. Freud usually began his analysis by clarifying the day residues, which often contained more distant memories, sometimes even memories from childhood. No matter how distorted the day residues have become, it is always possible to rediscover people, experiences, problems, and thoughts from the previous day. Distortion on first sight consists in familiar people and surroundings' changing character. They look different, perform unexpected acts, and appear in unusual situations. If the memory source and the manifest dream are known, the aim of interpretation is to comprehend the principle or tendency in the distortion. The preconscious dream wish can then be deduced. Memories have been transformed to portray the wish as fulfilled.

In some cases Freud considered the interpretation finished when the preconscious dream wish had been revealed. In principle, however, there is always another link in the interpretation, while the preconscious dream wish itself is a compromise formation between the repressed wish fantasy in the system *Ucs* and censorship. Regular psychoanalysis is usually necessary to uncover these factors because it entails a more systematic analysis of the psychic structures in the unconscious. In this section we will demonstrate Freud's method of analysis by using his interpretation of a couple of his own dreams. He only uncovers the preconscious dream wish, so we must add any information on the unconscious. In a later section we will return to how Freud analyzed the dreams of others in connection with the case histories of Dora and the "Wolf Man" (IV.C.I and IV.C.5).

(a) The Dream of Irma's Injection

The following dream from July 1895 is interesting because Freud himself regarded it as the first he was able to interpret. This dream led him to the recognition that dreams are wish fulfillments. However, he still lacked the concepts of the system *Ucs,* the system *Pcs,* and the censorship between them, so it can be assumed that his initial analysis was less complete than the analysis included as chapter 2 of *The Interpretation of Dreams* (1900a), which is also apparent from the outline of an interpretation in the "Project" (1950a). The content of the dream relates directly to Freud's personal and professional development up until 1895 (see part 2).

The prehistory of the dream is as follows: Freud had for a time treated a young widow, Irma, a close friend of the family, for symptoms of hysteria. At this time, around the time Freud completed his studies on hysteria (1895d), the etiological model and the therapeutic procedure had not been entirely worked out, and Freud was afraid of not being able to proceed correctly with his treatment. Moreover, the treatment was complicated by Freud's personal friendship with Irma and her family, because he feared that an unsuccessful treatment would affect this friendship. Freud none-theless succeeded in curing Irma's hysterical anxiety, but not her somatic symptoms. He had suggested an analysis (probably following the pattern: trauma/defense/conversion), which Irma did not accept. The treatment was interrupted because of summer vacation with Freud and Irma still disa-greeing. Freud traveled with his family to Bellevue outside Vienna. On 23 July, a younger colleague from Kassowitz hospital named Otto came to visit. Otto had just visited Irma and her family, and Freud therefore asked how she was. Otto replied that she was better but not quite well. Freud interpreted this answer as a reproach, a sign that Otto had let him down when he needed him. In the evening he wrote the clinical history of Irma's case to give to Dr. M., apparently in order to justify himself. Dr. M. was highly respected for his academic qualifications and his support would help Freud. On the night of 24 July Freud had the following dream, which he recorded and interpreted:

Dream of 23rd–24th July 1895

A large hall—numerous guests, whom we were receiving.—Among them was Irma. I at once took her to one side, as though to answer her letter and to reproach her for not having accepted my 'solution' yet. I said to her: 'If you still get pains, it's really only your fault.' She replied: 'If you only knew what pains I've got now in my throat and stomach and abdomen—it's choking me'—I was alarmed and looked at her. She looked pale and puffy. I thought to myself that after all I must be missing some organic trouble. I took her to the window and looked down her throat, and she showed signs of recalcitrance, like women with artificial dentures. I thought to myself that there was really no need for her to do that.—She then opened her mouth properly and on the right I found a big white patch; at another place I saw extensive whitish grey scabs upon some remarkable curly structures which were evidently modelled on the turbinal bones of the nose.—I at once called in Dr. M., and he repeated the examination and confirmed it. . . . Dr. M.

looked quite different from usual; he was very pale, he walked with a limp and his chin was clean-shaven. . . . My friend Otto was now standing beside her as well, and my friend Leopold was percussing her through her bodice and saying: 'She has a dull area low down on the left.' He also indicated that a portion of the skin on the left shoulder was infiltrated. (I noticed this, just as he did, in spite of her dress.) . . . M. said: 'There's no doubt it's an infection, but no matter; dysentery will supervene and the toxin will be eliminated.' . . . We were directly aware, too, of the origin of the infection. Not long before, when she was feeling unwell, my friend Otto had given her an injection of a preparation of propyl, propyls . . . propionic acid . . . trimethylamin (and I saw before me the formula for this printed in heavy type). . . . Injections of that sort ought not to be made so thoughtlessly. . . . And probably the syringe had not been clean. (Freud 1900a, p. 107)

The first step of the interpretation was to uncover the memories comprising the dream: the regular day residues and a number of older memories that Freud might have thought of when he recorded Irma's clinical history and that thereby had acquired the character of day residues. These memories concerned episodes in which Freud had met adversity and opposition in his scientific and academic work, and in which he had seriously to consider whether it was he or his critics who were wrong. The theme of these different anecdotes of erroneous diagnoses and treatments illustrates the conflict between academic career and failure. There are really no limits to how many memories can be unraveled during dream interpretation. However, considerations of space and clarity limit us to a concise discussion of the most important memories.

Receiving guests and the conversation with Irma. Freud's wife Martha had talked about inviting some guests for her birthday, among them Irma. Freud had just received a letter of complaint from a male patient he had sent on a sea voyage. His reproach of Irma for not having accepted the "solution" and his remark that the illness was therefore her own fault could have been made during treatment, since Freud at the time thought his therapeutic problem solved when he had informed the patient of his analysis. Irma's pains were not one of her main symptoms, which were primarily feelings of nausea. Constriction of the throat and pains in the neck were rather the symptoms of Irma's friend, another young widow, whom Freud regarded highly. The false teeth referred to a governess who was reluctant to have her throat examined because of her dentures. The pale, puffy appearance and the abdominal pains led Freud to Martha.

Freud's examination of Irma. Freud's dismay over Irma's somatic systems naturally caused him to speculate about whether he had overlooked an organic illness. His constant problem as a psychoanalyst was that he might confuse a hysterical with a somatic symptom. His examination of Irma by the window resembled another episode in which Freud had observed Irma's friend standing by the window while Dr. M. was explaining that she had a diphtheritic membrane. Freud suspected that her symptoms were hysterical and imagined how it would be to have her as a patient. She would probably be reluctant to do so, but because she was more intelligent than Irma, she would be able to understand his analyses more easily. The white spot in the throat recalled diphtheria, the presumed illness of Irma's friend. The scabby turbinal bones appeared to have associations with many ramifications: Freud had had problems with his nose, which he treated with cocaine, and a female patient who had done the same had irreparably damaged her nasal mucous membrane. Freud had reproached himself bitterly when his friend Fleischl-Marxow had died of cocaine abuse. However, Freud had only advised his friend to eat cocaine, but Fleischl-Marxow had decided to use injections. His friend Wilhelm Fliess also had a nasal disorder, which worried Freud, and Fliess, a nose specialist, had performed a nasal operation on another one of Freud's patients several months before (see below). The main link of these associations, however, was Fliess's theory of an anatomical similarity between the nose and the female genitals.

The examination of Irma by Freud's colleagues. Freud had called on Dr. M. earlier when he had given a female patient a fatal overdose of sulphonal (Freud had acted in good faith, because this drug was not believed to be dangerous at the time). Dr. M. bore some resemblance to Freud's older half brother in England, and both had just rejected proposals made by Freud. Leopold, like Otto, was Freud's assistant at Kassowitz hospital. He was Otto's rival, slower but more thorough. Freud had, in the hospital while examining children, experienced episodes like the one in the dream in which Leopold revealed characteristics in the patient that Otto had overlooked.

The diagnosis. Dysentery sounds like diphtheria, which Dr. M. had discovered in Irma's friend. Dr. M. had once told Freud that he had visited a patient with a colleague. His colleague had maintained his optimism regarding the case of a seriously ill woman even after Dr. M. had found albumen in the patient's urine. He believed (like Dr. M. in the dream) that the albumen would soon be excreted. Moreover, dysentery reminded Freud of a letter he had just received from the patient he had sent on a sea voyage. The patient complained of renewed intestinal trouble which a doctor in Egypt had diagnosed as dysentery. Freud believed that his intestinal trouble was hysterical, but reproached himself for putting his patient in a position to contract some organic disorder in addition to his psychic one.

The injection. Several of the aforementioned memories have already dealt with the injection: Fleischl-Marxow's cocaine injection, Freud's treatment of the female patient with the dangerous sulphonal, Fliess's theory of sexuality, which (aside from granting the significance of the nose) put trimethylamin in relation to sexual metabolism. While visiting Irma's family, Otto was called away to give an injection to someone who had been taken ill. Otto had given the Freud family a bottle of liqueur that smelled of fusel oil (amyl). *Propyl* reminded Freud of Fliess because the word sounded like *propylaea* (vestibules), which Freud had seen in Munich where he had met Fliess. The fact that the syringe was probably not clean made Freud think of an old lady whom he had given morphine injections over a long period of time. He had always taken care to make sure that the syringe was clean, but he had just heard that the lady had contracted phlebitis. He surmised that her affliction was caused by the carelessness of another doctor who did not use clean syringes.

In order better to comprehend Freud's relationship to the characters in his dream, it must be assumed that Dr. M. was Breuer, the coauthor of the studies on hysteria. Otto was Oscar Rie, coauthor of one of Freud's neuropathological studies (1891a), doctor of Freud's children, and Freud's lifelong close friend. Irma's real name was Anna Hammerschlag. She was the daughter of Freud's old religion teacher from the gymnasium, who, like Breuer, had supported him financially on several occasions. Irma's friend might have been Freud's sister-in-law Minna, whom he considered to be very intelligent. Even though she was not a widow, she never married after her fiancé died of tuberculosis (the illness Freud believed that Irma's friend imitated hysterically). Some commentators have conjectured that Freud and Minna had a sexual relationship. In addition, we can mention that the daughter to whom Martha gave birth five months after the Irma dream was named after "Irma" (Anna Freud).

Wilhelm Fliess is an unseen presence throughout the entire dream. His presence has been evident especially after the publication of letters from Freud to Fliess omitted in the 1950 edition (Freud 1985b). The unreasonable accusations against Oscar Rie in the dream must be seen as an expression of a displacement of extremely well-founded charges against Fliess. These charges stemmed from an episode that had occurred some months before the dream. Freud had requested Fliess to assist him in treating a hysterical patient by the name of Emma Eckstein, probably the

same Emma we have already mentioned in the second part of the book
(see II.B.2). Fliess believed that he could cure "sexual" disorders, including
hysteria and bleeding in the internal female sexual organs, from which
Emma suffered, by a form of zone therapy. However, Fliess's zone therapy
was performed not on Emma's feet, but on her nose! Confronted with
Emma's persistent symptoms, Freud and Fliess agreed that a nasal operation was in order. The operation was performed in the beginning of
February 1895. Fliess surgically removed some tissue from the nose and
also removed a piece of the turbinate bone. However, the wound did not
heal after the operation, and Freud was forced to call in more competent
doctors. To their general dismay, one of the doctors discovered a half-
meter strip of iodoform gauze left—and forgotten—inside the patient's
nasal cavity. When the gauze was removed, blood gushed out and the
bleeding was uncontrollable. For several weeks Emma hovered between
life and death, and although she survived, her nose was permanently damaged. Freud's prolonged hesitation in accepting Fliess's monstrous mistake
was an obvious explanation of why Oscar Rie was instead chosen to be the
scapegoat.

It is only at this point that the actual interpretation of the dream can
begin. In the dream events were arranged as Freud wished. By comparing
the memories with the manifest dream, Freud could deduce the dream
wishes active in the rearrangement of the memories. This provided no real
solution to the problems, but rather a primitive refutation of them. Freud
attributed flaws he might have had to those who doubted his theories or
therapeutic abilities, in the same way one child says to another "You're
dumb" and the other replies "So are you." Dreams encourage projective
defense mechanisms of this nature. They are concretized *ad absurdam* in
the dream because of the absence of reality's criticism. Taking the problems
surrounding Irma's illness as a whole, Freud was able to distinguish at least
five dream wishes, each of which either solved or rejected his problems in
a different way. In waking thought, alternative solutions can be employed
if only they are kept separate. Dream work, on the other hand, combines
every possible solution without taking their mutually conflicting interests
into consideration, and this explains some of the absurd nature of dreams.

(1) Irma's disease was her own fault, because she refused to accept
Freud's analysis. Freud believed this when awake as well, but dream work
defined the wish for a successful treatment by substituting the less compliant and intelligent Irma with her more compliant and intelligent friend.

If only she had been Freud's patient, the treatment would have been successful.

(2) The disease was organic, and Freud could therefore in good conscience refer Irma to other specialists for treatment. Dream work managed to define the organic disease (a possible diphtheritic infection) and to provide three doctors to cure it.

(3) Dr. M. was a clown because he had rejected Freud's theory of the sexual etiology of hysteria. The dream work ridiculed Dr. M. by putting an incompetent colleague's remarks in his mouth. Another aspect of the criticism of Dr. M. (Breuer) will be treated in point 5.

(4) Otto had really caused Irma's illness by most probably making Irma doubt Freud's "solution." In this instance, the dream work managed to gather together all the threads. Otto's coincidental injection while visiting Irma, his influence on her (she has been "infected" by his opinions), and his poisonous liqueur are brought together in the idea of Irma's injection with the wrong serum, which at the same time absolved Freud from wrongdoing in his unfortunate use of cocaine and sulphonal. Otto's *"Lösung"* (solution [of propyl]) was no better than Freud's *"Lösung"* (solution [his analysis]).

(5) Irma could not be cured by medical treatment because her hysteria was caused by her lack of a sex life. Freud deduced this solution from the word *trimethylamin,* which via Fliess referred to Freud's theory of the sexual etiology of hysteria. In this sense the interpretation seems a trifle contrived but can be further supported by other memories Freud omitted, although they must have been used by the dream work. First, we have seen that the dream must have been motivated to a great extent by Freud's desire to absolve Fliess of blame for the unsuccessful treatment of Emma Eckstein. Freud undoubtedly wanted to protect Fliess because Fliess was the only one of his colleagues prepared to accept the theory of the sexual etiology of hysteria. Second, Freud probably compared his treatment of Anna H. (Irma) to Breuer's treatment of Anna O. (see II.A.2,B.1). Freud never stopped reproaching Breuer for fleeing Anna O. in panic because of her sexual advances during treatment. For Freud, the most medically indefensible act was to leave a sick patient in time of need. Breuer's irresponsibility was expressed in the dream by Dr. M.'s belief that the illness would pass by itself. What really offended Freud was that Breuer's supposed sexual anxiety also caused him to reject the theory of the sexual etiology of hysteria. Third, Freud gained some insight into hysterical sexuality from an episode

in 1886, in which he visited a female patient together with the gynecologist Chrobak. At the time, Chrobak explained that the woman was still a virgin after eighteen years of marriage, because her husband was impotent, and consequently her hysterical anxiety demanded the following cure: *penis normalis dosim repetatur!* These repeated doses of a normal penis—intercourse—could not be administered by the doctor and she could therefore not be cured (see Freud 1914d, pp. 11–14). The dream clearly revealed Freud's fear of not being able to withstand Irma's sexual attraction (her willingness to open her mouth-vagina), but instead of shirking his responsibility as Breuer had done, he called for outside assistance, requesting Otto to perform the risky injection (insertion of the penis). An eventual marriage between Otto and Irma would solve the problem. Interestingly enough, Freud took the opportunity in *The Interpretation of Dreams* (1900a) to mention that Otto was unmarried (expressing the hope that his future wife would cure him of the habit of giving foolish gifts all the time), and that Irma's family would like to see her marry again soon. The dream did not end with this "solution," but continued by hinting that the syringe was apparently unclean (that improper intercourse could result in syphilis). Thus Irma's infection resembled both diphtheria and syphilis, a disease with which Freud, in his work as a dermatologist, was well acquainted (note the scabs on the noselike genitals in the dream). Moreover, the German word for *phlebitis, Venen-entzündung* (which the old lady had apparently contracted from an unclean syringe), and that for *venereal disease, Venerisches Leiden* resemble each other. It is natural for dream work to associate "sexually caused disease" with "venereal disease," that is, hysteria with syphilis.

The last phase of interpretation normally consists of pointing out the repressed wish fantasies in the unconscious that have strengthened the preconscious day residues and formed the dream wishes. Freud did not complete this last phase, instead mentioning twice in the text that discretion prohibited him from tracing his associations any farther. However, it is not difficult to see the elements comprising Freud's own Oedipus complex: a fantasy involving sexual possession of his mother and rivalry with his father (Freud's rivalry with male colleagues to obtain the favors of female patients). The analysis examined in the following sections will reveal this pattern with increasing clarity, which indicates that the active unconscious structures of a person are in one sense the central element of his personality. These unconscious structures are constant and intervene in order to organize the different episodes of everyday life, whether they concern family life, work, or personal conflicts.

(b) The Dream of the Botanical Monograph

Freud did not date this dream, but, judging from his correspondence with Fliess, it probably occurred in the beginning of March 1898. Compared to the dream about Irma, it is much more condensed and its origins more difficult to trace. On the other hand, the associations of this dream led Freud further back in his life history and deeper into his unconscious.

The dream was as follows: "I had written a monograph on a certain plant. The book lay before me and I was at the moment turning over a folded coloured plate. Bound up in each copy there was a dried specimen of the plant, as though it had been taken from a herbarium" (Freud 1900a, p. 169).

The uncovering of the day residues and other memories was at first complicated by the fact that Freud's most significant experience the day before the dream was apparently not represented in the manifest dream at all. It soon becomes clear, however, that all associations emanating from the dream joined together in this incident, which was an hour-long, extremely agitated conversation with his good friend Leopold Königstein, the eye specialist. Königstein probably tried to give Freud some good advice: why waste time on over-specialized and irrelevant psychological theories when one could become a skilled physician with a good income? Freud was not able to complete his reply to Königstein's advice, because their conversation was interrupted by Professor Gärtner, who dropped by with his wife. However, what Freud would have answered had he had the chance was contained in the dream. Before we examine his reply more closely, it is necessary to discuss the other memories of the dream.

"I had written a monograph on a certain plant." The day before the dream Freud had seen a monograph on the plant cyclamen in the window of a bookstore. The cyclamen was his wife's favorite flower, which he all-too-seldom remembered to give her. One of Freud's female patients, who had just visited Freud's wife, was once sadly disappointed that her husband had forgotten to bring her flowers on her birthday. Freud had explained to friends that such an oversight was the expression of unconscious intentions. In the conversation with Königstein, the patient in question was

mentioned, and Königstein may have been prompted to criticize Freud's theory of forgetting. Another association could also be traced back to Königstein: in 1884, Freud had actually written something like a monograph on the coca plant (1884e). As already mentioned, this monograph almost made a name for Freud, but instead it was Carl Koller who, inspired by Freud, was given the credit for discovering the use of cocaine as a local anesthetic. One of the first times cocaine was used as an anesthetic was in 1885, when Königstein operated on Freud's father for an eye disease. Shortly before his dream, Freud had seen in a *Festschrift* that Koller had been praised for his discovery and Professor Gärtner, who interrupted Freud's conversation with Königstein, was coauthor of this *Festschrift*. In order to underscore further the credibility of the association between the conversation and the botanical monograph, Freud mentioned that he had praised Gärtner's wife for her "blooming" appearance, and that he and Königstein had talked about a patient named Flora.

"The book lay before me." This reminded Freud of a letter from Fliess in which he had written that he could already imagine Freud's book on the interpretation of dreams lying before him completed. This letter was written long before Freud finished the book. The dream can be dated because Freud answered Fliess's letter on 10 March 1898 (Freud 1950a, pp. 262–63).

"I was at the moment turning over a folded coloured plate." Colored plates and pictures in books aroused many memories in Freud. He traced his great passion for books back to an incident that took place when he was five years old. His father gave him and his younger sister a travel book with colored plates which they could tear apart if they wished. This unusual and exciting incident was subsequently remembered as a lapse in his father's otherwise strict authoritarian manner and Freud's sexual desire for his mother was probably displaced to books in this way. This development was supported by an anxiety dream Freud had when he was between six and seven years old, and which he did not himself relate to the dream of the botanical monograph. In the dream Freud saw "my beloved mother, with a peculiar peaceful, sleeping expression on her features, being carried into the room by two (or three) people with birds' beaks and laid upon the bed." (Freud 1900a, p. 583). Before this dream, Freud had seen a picture of gods with birds' beaks (colored plates) in Phillipson's illustrated Bible. An older friend named Phillipp had taught him the word *vögeln* (to screw; the german word for *bird* is *Vogel*, plural *Vögeln*). The anxiety in the dream was not anxiety over his mother's death, but an anxiety awakened

by repressed sexual fantasies about his mother. During this time Freud became a very avid Bible reader, which his father remembered when he later gave him the family Bible, Jacob Freud's most precious object next to his wife. The symbolic displacement from mother to book was further underscored, and books, a point we shall return to in due course, were a central element in Freud's solution of his own Oedipal conflict. However, back to the colored plates for now: During his first student years Freud enjoyed looking at medical books containing beautiful colored plates, especially monographs, which he assumed contained the most thorough study of a single topic. He recalled an embarrassing experience in which his father sharply reproached him for the huge bills he received from bookstores because of Freud's love of books. Freud heard similar reproaches for one-sided and economically unsound interests from Königstein. This association was further encouraged by the fact that it was Königstein who, using cocaine as an anesthetic had operated on Freud's father for the eye disease.

"Bound up in each copy there was a dried specimen of the plant, as though it had been taken from a herbarium." In the gymnasium, the director had once called the pupils together to remove the book worms in the herbarium. Freud received only a few pages to clean because botany was his weakest subject. The pages Freud cleaned contained crucifers, a plant related to the artichoke, which Freud, half in jest, called his favorite flower. The special quality of the artichoke is that it is edible: the leaves are pulled off one by one and their contents sucked out. Thus the artichoke became the focal point of Freud's association chain, referring to his childhood destruction of the travel book page by page as well as to Martha's favorite flower, the cyclamen. A third association led to the coca plant and the cocaine episode. In 1880, when Freud took the exam in botany as part of his medical finals, he was again given a crucifer that he was unable to identify. He would have failed had the examiner not been his good friend Fleischl-Marxow, who later died an untimely death because of cocaine abuse.

What preconscious dream wish did the dream express? We have already implied that the dream could be perceived as a delayed reply to Königstein's reproaches. As in the dream about Irma, it was a question of academic competence and scientific career, but in this dream Freud seemed to be much more level headed in his reaction to criticism. He did not attack his critics (his father, the director, and Königstein) as he did Irma, Dr. M., and Otto. Instead, the dream wish contained this reply: "My scientific work is good enough; I have written an important paper on cocaine (despite the fact that another has reaped the glory); and I am capable of planning my work on my own." The dream work defined the cocaine paper with the help of two day residues: the monograph in the bookstore window and the letter from Fliess. The colored plate and the comparison with the herbarium revealed, meanwhile, how deeply lodged dream thoughts are in older memories. Königstein's reproaches had, after all, resurrected past embarrassing experiences even though they had appeared to be resolved.

The change between the two dreams was undoubtedly the result of Freud's self-analysis and his discovery of the Oedipus complex. Nevertheless, this did not mean that the repressed Oedipus complex was totally eradicated. It is striking that the many father figures are completely absent in the manifest dream. They had not been able to pass censorship because of the aggression and anxiety they released by their close relation to the father figure of the Oedipus complex, but had instead been repressed. We have outlined how Freud solved his Oedipus complex by uniting his conflicting feelings toward his parents in his passion for books: his father's demands were taken into account by a sublimation of sexuality, and sadistic impulses were expressed by the destructive treatment of books, much like Freud's destroying established scientific theories, in which he prided himself. The second component of the Oedipus complex, the sexual desire for his mother, was directly translated into a desire to penetrate books, appropriate their contents, and overcome their resistance. Freud was really a bookworm who ate books page by page, just as he ate artichokes. This solution to the oedipal conflict acquired another dimension in that Freud made his career by studying and treating female hysterical sexuality. Conversely, the Oedipus conflict reappeared every time his father, or authorities representing his father, reproached Freud for his monomanic interests, and this was apparently what happened in the dream of the botanical monograph. In the following section of psychic malfunctions, Freud's screen memory is an example of how to solve the Oedipus conflict, while forgetting the name Signorelli is an example of how to fail to solve it.

B.
PSYCHIC MALFUNCTIONS

After the work with dream analysis, Freud turned his attention to psychic malfunctions. They can be defined as more or less insignificant failures in psychic functions that an individual is otherwise able to perform correctly and, they can be immediately acknowledged and corrected upon discovery. This criterion is necessary in discussing "the psychopathology of everyday life" as distinguished from the psychopathology of neuroses and from more serious functional disturbances such as aphasia. Freud chose this field of study to prove once again that his psychological model was universally applicable and that there were unconscious processes in all human beings. Freud's book on the subject, *The Psychopathology of Everyday Life* (1901b), was published a year after *The Interpretation of Dreams* (1900a) and is much less pretentious in structure. It consists mainly of examples that all lead to the same conclusion: psychic malfunctions can be interpreted in the same way as neurotic symptoms and dreams. Freud's examples were mostly inoffensive; they did not threaten or violate important aspects of prevailing theories of man, and unlike *The Interpretation of Dreams*, Freud's new book quickly became very popular. Nevertheless, Freud's many examples pointed toward a new subject concept, in which the subject, in principle and in general, was reduced to an existence in the field of tension between preconscious and unconscious forces.

Everyone has experienced wanting to say something and accidentally saying something else by, for example, using a related word with an entirely different meaning. Such mistakes usually occur when we are tired or excited or thinking of something else. Normal psychic function has been disturbed and a mistake is made. Disturbed and disturbing intention can be located in the system *Pcs* and the system *Ucs* respectively, like day residues and repressed wish fantasies. The faulty function is like the preconscious dream wish, a compromise acceptable to both intentions. The disturbing intention has only to be disguised by displacement for it to pass censorship, and when it is merely displaced to a characteristic similar to the disturbed intention, it is able to substitute for it. According to this view, a slip of the tongue or lapse is not purely accidental but expresses an unconscious wish. Psychic malfunctions can be classified in different groups according to which function is disturbed. Aside from slips of the tongue, these groups include misreading, slips of the pen, mishearing, forgetfulness, profanity, and mislaying something. In addition, there are screen memories and jokes in which a repressed wish is expressed without its being a mistake. We will give two examples related to the memory function (screen memory and forgetfulness) and two related to the speech function (slips of the tongue and jokes). This division into functions is only for classification and does not describe the structure of the psyche in general.

1. THE MEMORY FUNCTION

It can be assumed that the husband who forgot to buy flowers for his wife on her birthday does not love her anymore. That kind of forgetfulness seems to be intentional. In most cases, however, the mechanism is more complex because the unconscious intention only expresses itself indirectly. If something repressed is regarded as truly forgotten, something temporarily forgotten is often related to that which is repressed, so that it itself is momentarily repressed. In a descriptive sense, the repressed memory can attract new memories. The opposite kind of memory disturbance is being unable to shake a relatively insignificant memory. We continue to think about something we have seen or heard without knowing why. In such cases, too, Freud assumes that repression plays a role by displacing cathexes to more distant memories in order to avoid censorship. The overcathected ideas are expressed as *idées fixes,* obsessions, or merely screen memories.

(a) The Screen Memory of Picking Dandelions

In 1899, Freud published a short article containing a part of his self-analysis (1899a). The text is structured as a dialogue between Freud and an erudite person interested in psychoanalysis, but there can be no doubt that Freud's interlocutor is Freud himself. The article takes as its point of departure the fact that most childhood memories focus on quite insignificant experiences, while important events are seldom remembered. Insignificant memories are called screen memories because they screen related repressed memories. Repressed memories may even stem from a later period than the screen memory.

The memory Freud analyzed occurred when he was two and still lived in Freiberg. The scene was a lush green field with many dandelions. In the background was a cottage where two women were standing and talking, apparently a farmer's wife and a nanny. Three children were playing in the field: Freud and his two cousins, a girl his age and a boy a little older. The children were picking dandelions. The girl had the prettiest bouquet but the boys ganged up on her and took her flowers. She ran up to the cottage crying and the farmer's wife gave her some homemade bread to console her. When the boys saw her with the bread, they dropped the flowers and ran up to the cottage and demanded a piece of the bread. The farmer's wife gave them each a piece and Freud recalled that the bread was delicious.

The memory did not appear until Freud's student years. For a time he could not get it out of his head. It bothered him but he did not know why. He did not find the answer until many years later when he discovered that this childhood memory had by association come to represent or screen memories of two intervening experiences. The first of these experiences occurred when the seventeen-year-old Freud visited the Fluss family in Freiberg during his summer vacation. He saw the city again for the first time, and this experience naturally united this memory with his childhood memory. He immediately fell in love with the two-year-younger Gisela Fluss, whose dark yellow dress he remembered vividly, but nothing transpired between them. The second experience was from another trip: when he was twenty, Freud visited his family in Manchester where he met his two cousins from his childhood memory. His female cousin was really his half brother's daughter, Pauline Freud. He did not fall in love with her because at the time he was only thinking of his books, but he had the distinct feeling that his father and half brother had secretly agreed to try to get him to abandon his uncertain medical studies and marry Pauline. In his later student years, when he had difficulty seeing any future in his work, he sometimes thought that his family's plans for him perhaps were not so bad after all. During this period he often went for walks in the Alps, and he assumed that the many dark yellow flowers he saw there reminded him of the field with dandelions in his childhood memory. And in fact, the memory only first appeared at this time.

The point of the analysis is that the unwelcome thoughts (his infatuation with Gisela, his uncertain future), associated with the memories of the trips to Freiberg and Manchester, gave their cathexes to the childhood memory which could become conscious without embarrassing affects. In spite of the chronological order, there was a connection between the infatuation with Gisela, her dark yellow dress, the dark yellow Alpine flowers, and the childhood memory of Pauline with the dandelions. The repressed wish for a sexual relationship with Gisela was expressed in the image of grabbing the flowers from Pauline: grabbing the flowers from = deflowering = taking her virginity. Moreover, there was a connection between the secret plans of Freud's family to get him to change the direction of his studies, his reflections during his walks in the Alps, and the delicious piece of bread in the childhood memory: he dropped the flowers to get some bread = he gave up his one-sided scientific interests in favor of earning his bread (livelihood) doing something more rewarding. The transformation of the childhood memory into a screen memory had thus been overdetermined by fulfilling two completely different repressed wishes at the same time. Freud regarded the fact that he appeared in visualized form on a par with Pauline and her brother as an external sign that the memory had been processed. He believed this was common to all screen memories.

This analysis further confirms the image of Freud's Oedipus complex we have formed in our discussion of the dream analyses. Woman was symbolized in Freud's unconscious by books as well as flowers. These were objects he appropriated violently and destructively, but which nevertheless provided him with a livelihood in keeping with the demands of his father and other male authorities. As bookworms live off the pages of books and Freud could eat the leaves of his favorite flower, the artichoke, he could provide a moderate income for his family without giving up his idealistic and one-sided research interests. The extremely artificial compromises on a symbolic level between the divergent impulses of the Oedipus complex had an organizing effect on Freud's life in reality. The two female symbols, books and flowers, were united in the attempt to establish a scientific career by studying the coca plant. In the two dreams focusing on the critique of Freud's theory of sexuality, the cocaine episode and the theory of sexuality were closely associated. One of the reasons that Freud so adamantly maintained his hypothesis of the sexual etiology of neuroses was thus that it via unconsciously symbolic links (penetrate the woman, study her sexuality) satisfied original Oedipal wishes in him, and he therefore reacted with such violent affects when anybody criticized his work.

(b) Forgetting the Name Signorelli

The following example is one of Freud's most famous. Like the previous example, it is taken from his self-analysis and treated three times (in a letter to Fliess from 22 September 1898, in a short article (Freud 1898b), and as the first chapter of *The Psychopathology of Everyday Life* [Freud 1901b]). This memory material is also similar to the previous example because it comes from Freud's travels. In September 1897 he traveled to central Italy and in Orvieto's cathedral saw the famous frescoes by Luca Signorelli, who vividly and in great detail had depicted the opposition between heaven and hell. This experience was the high point of the trip and the frescoes were "the greatest" Freud had seen. In the following year, in August and September 1898, Freud traveled again to Italy and to Dalmatia and Herzegovina. While traveling through Trafoi he received a message that a patient he had treated had committed suicide on account of an incurable sexual disturbance. Later during his trip he went on a little outing with Judge Freyhau from Berlin. The two tourists discussed the local populace, especially the Turks living in Bosnia and Herzegovina. Freud recalled an anecdote a doctor had told him about them. They were very fatalistic and if a doctor told a patient's relatives that the patient could not be saved, they usually answered him: *"Herr* (Sir), what is there to be said? If he could be saved, I know you would have saved him" (Freud 1901b, p. 3). Freud also knew another anecdote about the Turks, which would have thrown a particular light on the story due to its contrast to the first. The Turks value sexual pleasure above all else, and if a doctor discovers that a patient is impotent, the will to live vanishes. Thus a patient is supposed to have said: *"Herr* you must know that if *that* comes to an end then life is of no value" (Freud 1901b, p. 3). Freud refrained from relating this anecdote because he thought the subject unsuitable for conversation with a stranger. Instead, he turned the conversation to art and asked Freyhau if he had been to Orvieto and seen the famous frescoes of . . . hardly Botticelli and certainly not Boltraffio. The name had vanished, in spite of Freud's awe upon seeing the frescoes and the fact that he could remember the artist's face from one of them. Forgetting the name irked Freud. A few days later he heard the name Signorelli and recognized it immediately. He could now also recall the first name, Luca.

In his analysis, Freud concluded that his conscious attempt to suppress the story about the Turks had the unintentional effect of making him forget the name of the painter. He attempted to illustrate this substitution with a diagram:

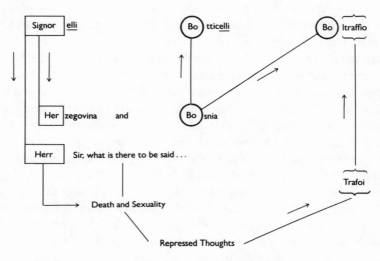

The arrows show the course of the associations, and how psychic energy was withdrawn from *Signorelli* and transferred to *Botticelli* and *Boltraffio*. Typical primary processes were at work, mixing pure sound associations with associations of content. *Signor* in Italian meant *Herr* in German, but was also present as *Her-* in Herzegovina. *Bo-* was found in Bosnia (which was always mentioned in connection with Herzegovina) and in the names of the two painters, while *-elli* was the only part of *Signorelli* that had remained conscious, in *Botticelli*. Death and sexuality were the common themes in the frescoes, the second story about the Turks, and the message in Trafoi concerning the patient's suicide because of sexual disturbances. Together with the *Bo-* in Bosnia, *Trafoi* produced another substitute name, *Boltraffio*. The analysis is based on the idea that the psychic energy removed from the story about the Turks momentarily reinforced the repressed thoughts, making them even more capable of attracting *Signor*. The conscious and probably intense attempt to produce the name Signorelli only obtained less anxiety-ridden derivatives from the repressed thoughts, *Bosnia* and *Trafoi,* which were then transformed into the two names of the wrong artists.

However, Freud's "repressed thoughts" are missing from this scheme.

He did assure the reader that they were related to death and sexuality, but he did not go into detail. From previous examples we can reasonably assume that the Oedipus complex comprised the repressed thoughts. We can add to this a part of the theory developed later: the unpleasurable affect that attends to the repression of the Oedipus complex is castration anxiety, the anxiety of being castrated by the father as punishment for the aggression against him and the sexual desire to possess the mother. In the normal development of a child, castration anxiety is integrated in the superego as guilt feelings and feelings of conscience. However, it is not unusual for part of it to contribute to the formation of a phobia, that is, anxiety for objects or sensations having only a peripheral relationship to castration. In part 4 we will discuss some animal phobias. During his self-analysis, Freud discovered that he suffered from a fear of traveling, especially on trains. The memories associated with forgetting the name Signorelli come from Freud's two vacations in 1897 and 1898, and it is therefore natural to investigate whether some of the elements of Freud's forgetfulness can be traced back to the genesis of his fear of traveling as a child. This fear developed during the family's long and difficult trip from Freiberg to Vienna in 1859 and 1860. Freud told Fliess about two memories from this trip. One evening or night, when the train came into the station in Breslau, Freud looked out the window and saw the city bathed in an unusual light from gaslights. He had never seen gaslights before and in his fantasy he connected them with souls burning in hell. He had already learned about heaven and hell and reward and punishment, from his former nanny, who had aroused violent affects in him. His concrete vision of hell thus made him associate his castration anxiety with traveling and traveling situations. The other memory was the time Freud saw his mother naked on the trip, which excited him sexually but also gave him guilt feelings.

Freud's trip to Orvieto in 1897 had several things in common with his childhood trip to Breslau. His fear of traveling doubtless plagued him. Because of his identification with Hannibal (see II.A.1), this fear intensified whenever he approached Rome. His fear was further intensified by the vivid portrayal of hell in the frescoes, which depicted monstrous devils attacking naked men and women in a way that had definite sexual associations. Freud also noticed Signorelli's self-portrait, which observed this scene with a stern eye. The hellish gaslight in Breslau can be associated with Signorelli's first name *Luca*, which means *light* in Italian. Furthermore, it can be assumed that the dark chapel adjacent to Orvieto's cathedral was lighted by somber gaslights during Freud's visit (the lighting is poor even today). The similarities between the two travel experiences were apparently not connected in Freud's mind until the trip to Herzegovina in 1898. Freud's traveling companion *Freyh-au* reminded him of the route from *Frei*berg to Bes*lau*. The story about the Turks and the message concerning his patient's suicide brought death and impotence together in a way that more than hinted at castration anxiety. When Signorelli's fresco was mentioned, the phobia struck like lightning, resulting in his forgetting the name. Signorelli, the stern gentleman, confronted Freud as the punishing and castrating father whose name was unbearable even to think of. Freud had an "authority phobia" alongside his fear of traveling, a need to rebel against all father figures and consequently suffered from horror, anxiety, and forgetfulness when he found himself a helpless victim of their revenge. In the dream of Irma's injection, he fearlessly attacked his critics, but in the dream of the botanical monograph they disappeared from the manifest dream in a way similar to a phobic reaction. Like Signorelli's, Königstein's name alone symbolized Freud's father: *König* = *King* = father symbol. Another father figure in the back of Freud's mind on his vacation trip, and who could also have contributed to the association *Freiberg-Freyhau,* was the minister who had just rejected Freud's application for a professorship: Freiherr von Härtel. His name was doubly frightening: it contained the word *Herr* (sir) twice *(-herr* and *Här-)* and his rejection touched a very sore point, Freud's ambition to become a "sir." An examination of *The Interpretation of Dreams* (1900a) also reveals that the many applications for a professorship played a large part in Freud's dreams even though the title did not have much practical significance for him. What mattered to Freud was its unconscious symbolic value and its help in overcoming castration anxiety.

2. THE SPEECH FUNCTION

In *The Psychopathology of Everyday Life,* Freud criticized a book by Meringer and Mayer on slips of the tongue and misreadings. The two writers were only interested in finding the formal rules of mistakes such as reversing the order of two words, combining two words into one, and choosing words that sound alike. According to Freud, their analyses were not incorrect, but incomplete. Slips of the tongue and misreadings are not caused by the speaking or reading subject's "making a mistake," but rather by a positive unconscious intention forcing consciousness to choose an expression that also satisfied it. In many cases Freud was able to use Meringer and Mayer's examples by inserting the correct unconscious intentions that seldom resulted in very complex analyses. Most of his examples of slips of the tongue and jokes unfortunately involved German expressions not easily translated into other languages. We will therefore only discuss a few of these.

(a) Slips of the Tongue

One day Freud decided to recite a couplet for his daughter that contained the words *Affe* (ape) and *Apfel* (apple). However, he began by saying *Apfe,* clearly a contamination of the two words. The reason for his mistake was apparently that his daughter was not interested in hearing the verse and Freud wanted to recite it quickly. A person who wanted to say something about *Schweinerei* (filthiness) but attempted to express himself more tactfully with a sentence containing the expression *zum Vorschein* (appear) ended up by saying *zum Vorschwein* instead. These mistakes attract special attention when they occur in official and supposedly well-rehearsed speeches. The President of the Austrian Chamber of Deputies opened a meeting with the following words: "Honored Sirs! I announce the presence of so and so many gentlemen, and declare the meeting closed." He should, of course, have declared the meeting open. His mistake can only be explained by his unconscious desire to close the meeting. A similar substitution resulted in the following: "Ich bin nicht *geneigt,* die Verdienste meines Vorgängers zu würdigen" (I am not *inclined* to appraise the service of my predecessor). The right word should have been *geeignet* (able) and despite the similarity in sound between the two words, there is of course a difference between not being inclined and not being able to appraise one's predecessor. A last example: Emil du Bois-Reymond was to give the main speech at a wedding of a child of his friend Hermann Helmholtz and a child of the tycoon Siemens. He had planned to finish his speech with the witticism "And so, three cheers for the new firm of Siemens and Helmholtz." Instead, he said the old name of the firm, Siemens and Halske. Freud refrained from guessing the motive of this mistake, but it is possible that du Bois-Reymond had reservations about an all-too intimate alliance between corporate industry and natural science.

(b) Jokes

After *The Interpretation of Dreams* (1900a) and *The Psychopathology of Every-day Life* (1901b), Freud wrote another book on a related subject, *Jokes and Their Relation to the Unconscious* (1905c). Fliess, among others, had criticized Freud for his analyses of neuroses and dreams, saying that they reminded him of jokes. Instead of rebuffing this criticism, Freud replied that jokes were a typical expression of the unconscious. A joke is formed by the agency of the primary process that disguises a given repressed or suppressed intention so it can pass censorship. The difference between a joke and neurotic symptoms or dreams is that the camouflage is immediately discovered.

Like dream work, jokes contain condensations, displacements, and sensory concretizations serving both as an expression of and a disguise for unconscious intentions. These primary processes neither adhere to logical rules nor consider external reality but establish a kind of pseudologic with abrupt short circuits and insane associations. Many of Freud's examples concern a person's trying to fool or defend himself against another person by using hidden primary processes in his speech. An especially subtle effect is achieved when a joke can embarrass someone without his noticing it while other listeners roar with laughter. The opposite effect is achieved when the joke is almost a slip of the tongue in which the use of primary processes causes most embarrassment for the narrator. Repeating an obvious slip of the tongue can be a joke in itself.

Freud demonstrated condensation in jokes by using a story told by the poet Heinrich Heine. An impoverished young man has just visited his rich noble family, who have treated him politely, but condescendingly. After his visit he relates that the Baron had treated him as an equal, quite *famillionaire*. The joke is that the aggression is expressed indirectly. The "famillionaire" treatment conceals the manner in which millionaires regard relatives with no money. There has been a condensation of *familiar* and *millionaire*.

Displacement can occur when a word has two meanings. One Jew asks another, "Did you take a bath?" and the other replies, "No, is one missing?" The suppressed meaning is the supposed aversion Jews have to taking baths. The witty answer is a defense against the naked thought but in this case reveals something about the person who asks the question. It is in this sense that the joke is told.

The absence of logic in the unconscious appears often in jokes. In the dream analysis of Irma's injection, Freud showed that the dream work did not register the opposition of the individual dream wishes. He compared this to the following joke: A man complains that a kettle his neighbor borrowed was returned to him with a hole in the bottom. His neighbor replies indignantly that he has returned the kettle undamaged, that there already was a hole in it when he borrowed it, and finally that he never borrowed it. These three arguments are mutually incompatible, although they would be good enough separately. It can reasonably be concluded that the neighbor was trying to cover up the truth. Another example of a correct defense (considered in isolation) that, however, is even more revealing, is this Jewish tale: A Jewish matrimonial agent has brought a young man to the home of his prospective bride. Her home is full of silverware and other riches. The young man observes skeptically that these objects are probably on loan. The matrimonial agent replies, "Of course not, do you think anyone would lend anything to these people?"

Freud observed that, unlike in dreams, there was no regression in jokes. However, it is clear that many jokes are made by taking a figurative expression literally, that is, the expression is broken up into its literal and figurative components. A priest tells the newly confirmed young man when he gives him a wafer, "This is the body of Jesus." The young man says to the priest, "Can I spit it out if there are bones in it?"

The effect of a joke on the listener occurs in two phases. The first things registered in a joke are the uninhibited primary processes. They provide the same word pleasure (or forepleasure) children love in meaningless rhymes and nonsense verse. Word pleasure is followed by genuine pleasure caused by unconscious or suppressed thoughts' passing censorship, appearing when it becomes manifest that there is "method in the madness." Laughter is the effect of released repressing energy. This energy is superfluous when censorship is circumvented. Laughter therefore expresses a momentary submission to the pleasure principle. However, many jokes are so bad that the surprise effect fails to appear. The intention is recognized before it passes censorship and instead of laughing we become irritated or embarrassed.

It goes without saying that analyses of slips of the tongue and jokes are not very profound. On the other hand, it can be useful as an introduction to the unconscious to try to analyze Laurel and Hardy films, Polish jokes, political cartoons, and the Donald Duck series created by Carl Barks. Many of the artistic effects employed in these media are to a great extent identical to processes in the unconscious. A partial dissolution of the opposition between fantasy and reality, means and ends, past and present, positive and negative, has taken place. "To sum up: *exemption from mutual contradiction, primary process* (mobility of cathexes), *timelessness*, and *replacement of external by psychical reality*—these are the characteristics which we may expect to find in processes belonging to the system *Ucs*" (Freud 1915e, p. 187).

C.

SOCIETY, RELIGION, AND ART

Freud's analytic work gradually expanded from the core of neurosis and dream theory to encompass broader fields of inquiry. This expansion is logical if the model of the psychic apparatus is taken into consideration. It was from the outset a general model containing neuroses and dreams as special cases. In order to prove its general application it was necessary to test it in totally different fields, which Freud attempted to do. The result of this work was a series of extremely controversial essays in which Freud selected subjects especially suited to demonstrate his theory. In many cases, the discussion became a question of accepting or rejecting psychoanalysis as a whole. For example, the relationship between psychoanalysis and Marxism developed into a serious dispute in the 1930s, with considerable inflexibility on both sides. Similar, though less vitriolic disputes arose within most humanistic and sociological fields.

We do not consider it our task to explain the fine points of these disputes. We are primarily interested in presenting Freud's analyses on their own premises. However, we will anticipate our conclusions by stating that we regard the sphere of intimacy as the primary field of study for psychoanalysis. The significance of psychoanalysis is thus proportional to the significance of the sphere of intimacy in society as a whole. Its validity depends partly on whether it is able to detect historical changes imposed on the sphere of intimacy by the sphere of production and the sphere of circulation. Conversely, as a theory of the sphere of circulation, Marxism should be able to analyze phenomena the sphere of circulation has received from the sphere of intimacy (for example, political leaders' consolidating power by posing as father figures). Freud's analyses of mass psychology seem to be able to fill some gaps in Marx, Engels, and Lenin on this score. Thus, psychoanalysis does not compete with sociology by studying social topics. In the last analysis, it provides sociology with an important supplement, which it is up to sociology to put to good use.

1. SOCIETY AND RELIGION

Freud had a twofold view of the relationship between the sphere of intimacy and the rest of society. First, he claimed that family life had been indistinguishable from the social and religious order in the distant past. Gradually, the gap widened but these social spheres continued to be influenced by the epoch in which every community was a family community. Second, he claimed that a child's original emotional ties to his parents were strong enough to be able to influence all other personal relationships and also more complex social relationships for a lifetime. In both cases, the Oedipus complex serves as the basic structure. Variations on this structure can be found outside the sphere of intimacy.

(a) The Historical Origins of the Oedipus Complex

Freud had discovered the Oedipus complex in 1897 during his self-analysis, and in the following years he realized the crucial importance of this complex in neuroses and dreams. The term derives from the well-known Greek myth of the king's son Oedipus, who as a boy was banished to the mountains on his father's orders because of a prophecy. He later returned and unknowingly killed his father and married his mother, thus fulfilling the prophecy. Freud saw a little child's most fervent wishes expressed in these two actions: like Oedipus, a child wants to get rid of his father in order to possess his mother alone. (The term *complex* is normally attributed to Jung. Freud used the term *Oedipus complex* for the first time in 1910. However, this does not change the fact that Freud had worked out the content of the concept long before meeting Jung. In Freud, *complex* means almost the same as *structure,* that is, a structure of ideas, fantasies, emotional ties, and so on).

In *Totem and Taboo* (1912–1913), Freud formulated a theory of how the Oedipus complex originated and developed. This theory was repeated and elaborated in several works, including *Group Psychology and the Analysis of the Ego* (1921c) and *Moses and Monotheism* (1939a). This theory was based on the major anthropological and ethnological works of the past (Darwin, Atkinson, Robertson Smith, Frazer, Wundt, and others) and united them in a monumental study of human development. Freud posited four successive phases in human development, characterized by four different relations to the father figure: (1) the primal horde, (2) the totemistic brotherhood, (3) the creation of myths, and (4) monotheism.

(1) The idea that the original structure of human society was a "primal horde" is pure hypothesis. Freud got the idea from Darwin's *The Descent of Man* (Darwin 1871) and attempted to define it. He imagined that the first society (or the first family) consisted of "a strong man" surrounded by many women, whom he used for procreation. The stability of the horde depended on whether the strong man could protect it from outside aggression. The father did not respect any incest taboos, and had sexual relations with mothers and daughters. On the other hand he enforced a rigid incest taboo on his sons. Violations of this taboo were punished by death or at least castration and expulsion from the community. Power was transferred to the youngest son of a woman who had been able to protect him against his father's oppression and punishment. He was thus well suited to take over the father's role after his death. Psychologically, the father figure was characterized by extreme narcissism. He did not have to give up any sexual gratification, and his sexuality therefore remained at a primitive stage. He did not establish any solid emotional ties to the others in the primal horde and was totally self-sufficient. However, forced sexual abstinence caused strong emotional ties in the sons. They learned to fear and admire their father intensely, and had homosexual relationships with each other that formed the basis for their mutual cooperation. When this love and feeling of cooperation were strong enough, they murdered the father, dismembered him, and ate him. At first, one of the sons tried to take the father's place, but the patricide was repeated until the primal father figure vanished altogether.

(2) The second social structure, which Freud called the totemistic brotherhood, can be examined in more detail, since nineteenth-century anthropologists and ethnologists had found totemistic societies in Australia, Africa, and South America. Their common characteristic was a close relationship between religious and social norms. Every tribe had a special totem animal (such as, a wolf, a kangaroo, or a rattlesnake) that was treated with special veneration. It was strictly forbidden to kill any members of the species of totem animals, and in some cases it was also forbidden even to touch or look at them. Furthermore, a number of other prohibitions

and restrictions applied to the worship of the totem animal. If a dead totem animal was found, the tribe performed a mourning ceremony, and if a tribesman was forced to eat a totem animal in an emergency, he had to perform a series of penitential acts. It was regarded as the progenitor and protector of the tribe, and tribesmen thought of themselves as wolves, kangaroos, rattlesnakes, and so on. During war with other tribes, special precautions were taken, since by eating a dead enemy a tribesman also consumed his characteristics and his totem, which could be either evil or good. The most important taboo in a tribe was usually incest. It was strictly forbidden to marry or have sexual relations with someone belonging to the same totem. A tribesman was forced to marry outside the totemistic community (exogamy). Women had a degree of power in these societies and the totem was inherited from the mother, not the father.

Freud did two things with this material. First, he chose to regard the totemistic society as the successor of the primal horde. Second, he used psychoanalytic concepts in an attempt to interpret the typical pattern of behavior in a totemistic society. In the latter instance, Freud found striking similarities between the taboos and ceremonies of primitive people and the phobias and compulsive actions of neurotics. Children often have animal phobias (see the case histories of Little Hans and the "Wolf Man" in IV.C.2,5), reacting to a particular animal species with exaggerated interest and anxiety. The phobia can be extended to include objects touched by these animals and places they have been. Similarly, obsessional neurotics have a set of difficult rules to which they must conform in order to avoid anxiety. In both cases, there is no rational reason for this behavior. Freud's analysis attempts to trace this behavior back to the Oedipus complex, in which the phobic object can be recognized as the symbol of the father and phobic anxiety as castration anxiety, while neurotic compulsion is a compromise between sexual desires for the mother and guilt feelings for the aggression toward the father. There is no difference in the unconscious between fantasy and reality, and castration anxiety is therefore as strong in a child today as it was for the male members of the primal horde, who actually witnessed castration as punishment. Guilt feelings for hating the father are likewise just as strong as guilt feelings for having murdered the father.

In this way, Freud established a logical relationship between the primal horde and the totemistic community which made it natural to suppose that the latter succeeded the former. If this is true, the totem animal simply functioned as a symbol of the dead father. The totem animal was the progenitor and protector of the tribe like the father, and inspired fear and admiration, hate and love. Whereas the sons or brothers refused to obey the living father, they later obeyed the dead father, respecting his incest taboo by observing exogamy. Religious ceremonies expressed guilt feelings over the parricide. It is especially interesting to note that a number of tribes killed and ate the totem animal while indulging in wild sexual orgies during their annual festivals. Freud saw in these ceremonies a ritual reenactment of the parricide. The totem feast was likewise a reenactment of the consumption of the dead father. These rituals actually served to maintain social order, which was reasserted after the festival. The similarity between the totem animal and the father was also seen in some tribes in which the chief met the same fate. Every year a new chief was appointed. He enjoyed all the privileges of his office, but was killed and eaten at the end of the year.

(3) Totemistic society was transgressed by the return of the father, which was the result of two developments. First, exogamy was replaced by the nuclear family which once again narrowed the limits of the incest taboo. The primal father was resurrected as the family father with strongly reduced powers, and mother right was replaced by father right. Unfortunately, Freud did not dwell on this issue. Second, the longing for a primal father led to the creation of myths. The image of perfection impressed upon the pleasure ego and the ego ideal was artistically expressed in heroic myths, legends, and fables. Freud believed that the first epic poet created the heroic myth as an expression of his longing for a father figure. The hero of the myth overcame the father who was still portrayed as a totemistic monster. The hero was often the youngest brother who had escaped his father's jealousy by acting like a fool. In the myth he alone performed the heroic deed that all the brothers had actually performed together. If the other brothers were described at all, they usually appeared as harmless helpers, such as small animals, who helped the hero find the monster. The epic poet who was able to enthrall his public with his tales could not take over the father's role. However, he created heroes that everyone could long for and identify with. In this sense, the epic poet could also become a hero to his public.

A constant motif in myths, legends, and fables is the opposition between the hero and the father (whether he be a monster, a king, or the real family father) and the erotic reward after the defeat of the father, a motif that resembles the structure of the Oedipus complex. A particular group of legends are similar to what Freud called "the family novel of neurotics." These legends recount a situation in which the hero is raised by strangers after he has been disowned by or has lost his real parents. Many neurotics attempt to solve their oedipal conflicts with their parents on their own by imagining that they have been substituted for another baby. They then long after their nonexistent ideal parents. Inspired by Rank, Freud listed a number of mythological and legendary heroes who conformed to this pattern, including Moses, Kyros, Romulus, Oedipus, Karna, Paris, Telephos, Perseus, Hercules, and Gilgamesch. Eighteenth- and nineteenth-century literature is replete with examples in which the reunion of a family is depicted as a more or less unattainable goal.

(4) Let us now repeat the number of father figures that followed in the wake of the primal father. First there was the totem animal, which became the object of ambivalent feelings. Totemistic society was based on mother right. The transition to a nuclear family structure eclipsed mother-right power, but the mother was for a time exalted as a goddess of life and fertility. However, the primal father did not merely return as the family father. The next stage of development was the mythological hero, who committed parricide in order to win the symbolic paternal dignity. From this figure, gods were created who were originally a combination of animals and man—animals with human heads, humans with animal heads, gods able to change into animals, and gods who fought dangerous monsters. The development of a social hierarchy coincided with the creation of a divine hierarchy as seen in Greek mythology. The highest form of development appeared with the creation of a spiritual, monotheistic god, the epitome of a primal father. He has created everything and he protects, judges, and decides everything. No one can escape his power; no one can hide from him. He even has access to man's innermost thoughts and desires. Guilt feelings for the parricide and the infantile aggression against the father has reached its zenith in the monotheistic demands for humility and penitence. As a psychic creation, the absolutist god is both a product of and supplement to the superego.

In his book on Moses (1939a), Freud attempted to show the concrete origins of the Judeo-Christian god. He believed that Egyptian society had contained faint signs of monotheism and that Moses had really been the son of an Egyptian king and held monotheistic views. Moses chose the enslaved Jewish people to cultivate his religion. After the exodus from Egypt, the Jews murdered Moses because he demanded unconditional obedience to his moral laws ("the ten commandments"). The memory of and guilt feelings arising from this murder compelled the Jews to compensate for the loss of Moses by creating a distant and immaterial god similar to Moses' monotheistic god and Moses himself. Judaism and Christianity both exhibit the preliminary stages of monotheism. Animal sacrifice and the totemistic feast are thus preserved in the killing of the oldest lamb whose blood was to be smeared on the doorposts of the community of Israel, and later in the killing of Jesus (the lamb of God) and in Holy Communion, during which believers eat the flesh and blood of Jesus. Similarly, the story of Moses, who was abandoned in the reeds and later taken out of the water (a symbol of birth) is a version of the heroic myth, since Moses—like certain neurotics—attempted to break out of his real family (the Egyptians) to find a better and more genuine one (the Jews). The transmitted myth therefore depicts Moses as if he originally were of Jewish ancestry.

(b) The Oedipus Complex in Industrial Society

It is evident from the previous section that Freud was acutely aware of the historical mutability of the Oedipus complex. He made an excellent analysis of the role the father figure played in many social functions. The power hierarchy of feudal society consisting of God, the Pope, kings, feudal overlords, and so on, can be effectively analyzed according to Freud's theories. However, the Oedipus complex is more difficult to trace in industrial, capitalist society. On the contrary, its significance as a socially organizing and regulatory structure has receded with the growing influence of economics. The Oedipus complex has thus been relegated primarily to the sphere of intimacy. Nevertheless, Freud's analysis of group psychology does show that father symbolism still plays an important social role. What Freud was unable to explain in society with the help of the Oedipus complex, he sought to clarify by means of drive theory. It was on this point especially that Freud encountered opposition from Marxist sociologists. We will in this section focus on (1) the psychology of normal love life, (2) analyses of group psychology, and (3) the use of drive theory to explain social dynamics.

(1) The modern nuclear family of father, mother, and children is not, according to Freud, identical to the Oedipus structure. The Oedipus structure is more comprehensive, the nuclear family being only one of its manifestations. For example, the Oedipus structure was also present in totemistic tribal communities, even though it was disguised. It would therefore be erroneous to conclude that it would disappear if the nuclear

family were to be temporarily or permanently dissolved. The crucial element is the presence of sexually conditioned emotional ties comprising the Oedipus complex, which can develop and flourish in many different forms.

We have already in part 1 described the opposition between the romantic family ideal of a positive haven for affectionate feelings and the misery of the father's uninhibited power, the sexual frustration and trivial work of the woman and the subjection of children to a harsh adaptation to social mores. Freud failed to understand that tensions within the family were inevitably augmented in capitalist society. However, he was acutely aware of the real problems of the family, as his case histories of female patients, the studies on hysteria (1895d), and Dora's case history (1905e) illustrate. Most of the women in his milieu probably exhibited an emotional life bordering on the neurotic, just as most children revealed compulsive acts and phobias in their behavior. Freud's great case studies of the "Rat Man," Schreber, and the "Wolf Man" showed that men were not immune to these problems either. We will examine these case histories in part 4.

Freud was not the first to point out the paradoxes of love life, but he was the first to analyze them using a scientific model. By paradoxes we mean ambivalence, the opposition between affectionate and sensual feelings, the opposition between forepleasure and end pleasure, and the malleability of sexuality (inhibition of aims, displacement of aim and object, sublimation, and so on). In his articles on "the psychology of love" (1910h, 1912d, 1918a), Freud illustrated the most obvious paradoxes. The "affectionate" sexuality of man became, through his loving mother's upbringing, opposed to sensual sexuality, which his mother could not accept. When he, as an adult, married a mother substitute, he was forced either to suppress his sensual desires or gratify them with women he really despised. In some cases, a man attempted to resolve this opposition by debasing the mother figure. He could then only give affectionate and sensual love to his wife by despising and debasing her. A woman was often just as poorly equipped as a man to cope in a nuclear family. In her frustration over not having found a gratifying sexual object in her childhood, she had a tendency to withdraw all her emotional ties back into her own ego and thus appeared to be selfish, narcissistic, and uninterested in her surroundings. If she nevertheless succeeded in establishing a positive father tie in her childhood, she might not be able to transfer it to her husband without the intrusion of deeper, more aggressive ties to a restrictive mother. Narcissism could also manifest itself by an exaggerated devotion to her children, whom she regarded as a part of her and therefore as her private property.

(2) Freud based his group psychology on a number of books on the subject, particularly Gustave le Bon's *Psychologie des foules* (le Bon 1895) and William McDougall's *The Group Mind* (McDougall 1920). According to le Bon, the influence of the group forced the individual to move several steps down the ladder of civilization. The intelligence and judgment of the individual was reduced in a group dominated by emotions. The individual became easy to influence, lost his critical sense, and became intolerant and orthodox in his beliefs. Individual inhibitions were discarded, and original animal instincts came to the fore. There was no doubt or insecurity within the group, no ability to synthesize contradictory ideas and no differentiation between fantasy and reality. The individual relinquished his own individuality, tended to imitate the others in the group and exhibited characteristics otherwise found only in children and in primitive societies. The historical context for le Bon's theory was obviously the many rebellions and revolutions in the wake of the French Revolution in 1789, and the increasing organization of the working class in the latter half of the nineteenth century. McDougall, writing twenty-five years later, agreed with several of le Bon's observations. However, unlike le Bon he offered a solution to the loss of individuality in the group by emphasizing that individual characteristics could be regained if the group developed under a system of law and order. The individual should know his place in the group, and its leadership should be stabile and just. In this sense, bourgeois or middle-class society was a positive group formation in which cooperation was for the benefit of all, and in which the individual did not lose his individuality and personal freedom.

Freud took these studies at face value and, as in his analysis of totemism, attempted to understand them by using the concepts of psychoanalysis. Le Bon's and McDougall's theories can be explained in the relationship between the unconscious, in which primary processes dominate, and the preconscious, in which secondary processes dominate. In the group an individual loses secondary acquisitions and succumbs to uninhibited primary processes. This distinction is also found in group psychology, which sets collectivity, affectivity, and primitive and determining reactions against individuality, reason, and highly developed, independent reactions. However, psychoanalysis and bourgeois group psychology explain these phenomena very differently. Without going into detail, we can summarize group psychological theories for these phenomena in the following points: (1) unconscious reactions are caused by a race soul, and every people has its own psychology (compare Wundt's folk psychology, which was very popular at the time Freud developed his group psychology), (2) characteristics developed in a group are caused by a special folk drive, and (3) suggestibility increases in the group, making the individual easy to influence.

Freud, on the other hand, focused on emotional ties among individuals in the group. He took a broad view of the concept of a group, which could encompass anything from a family to a nation. All emotional ties were based on an individual's ties to his father. A leader figure was thus an invaluable element of every group formation. The father loved all his subjects equally, which in turn promoted solidarity among individuals in the group. The group dissolved in the absence of this paternal love, which formed the basis for love between the individuals. The love of Jesus united the faithful as brothers of the church. To illustrate this point, Freud ironically chose a devotional novel about a group of swindlers who claimed to have found the place where Jesus was buried. They claimed therefore, that Jesus could not have risen from the dead and was thus not divine by nature. As a result, the Christians in the novel began to cheat and murder each other, doing everything they had once refrained from doing because they had belonged to the same community of religion. Unity in the army was based on the leader's love for his soldiers. If he was killed or if he treated his soldiers cruelly and unjustly the army dissolved. The prominent role of the leader made Freud consider whether leaderless groups had something that performed the same role as a leader figure, such as a "dominant" idea or abstraction, a common wish or common hate toward a person or institution.

Freud agreed that this factor was the ego ideal or superego, a psychic element representing the father and his power in an individual. The superego was always the umbilical cord connecting the individual with the group regardless of whether the external unifying factor was a specific leader, a totem figure, or a more or less abstract ideal, like the fatherland. The historical and individual genesis of the ego ideal pointed to the Oedipus complex as the actual foundation of social relations between subjects. Freud did not believe that there was anything primitive in this that humanity would one day transgress. Le Bon and others misled their readers in trying to defend the individual against primitivization in the group. It was the group that created and defined the individual. The ideal and the specific leader figure determined the character of the group. Terrible catastrophes could ensue if the superego was brought up to be strict and ruthless, and if the leader abused his power. Freud undoubtedly chose to examine two of the most respected institutions of bourgeois society, the church and the army, because he regarded them as just as dangerous as street mobs. There is no way to measure how high up "the ladder of civilization" a given group formation has climbed. The worship accorded sports heroes, film stars, and political and religious leaders in our time indicates that the longing for ideals has not diminished. The Oedipus complex thus retains its power despite a possible decline in the authority of the family fathers.

(3) In some of his writings, Freud attempted to give a general evaluation of modern civilization, using drive theory. In " 'Civilized' Sexual Morality and Modern Nervous Illness" (1908d), he maintained that social sexual morality was a direct cause of those nervous illnesses that were on the increase. Repressed sexuality was forced to find release in neurotic symptoms. In this case, Freud's views were intended as a critique of sexual morality, and his opinion on sexual drives does not therefore belong to drive theory in which there is no general opposition between sexuality and culture. It was only during the third metapsychological advance that Freud sometimes tended to explain culture *per se* as a conflict between biologically defined life drives and death drives. In *Civilization and Its Discontents* (1930a), Freud claimed that culture had resulted from life drives' having been able to make use of death drives as outwardly directed aggression. The death drives had thus indirectly provided humanity with the strength to overcome external obstacles to the upholding and perpetuation of life. Physical aggression had become increasingly unnecessary in modern culture, and the death drives were consequently not able to abreact, but remained in the organism where they—mediated by the superego—plagued the life of the individual. Modern civilized man had become hypermoral, but just around the corner loomed self-destruction in the form of neurotic disorders and masochism. The construction as well as the dissolution of culture were thus regarded as a result of drives. In addition, it can be noted that Freud also originated the famous theory of the anal character of capitalism. According to this theory, a child taught the virtues of cleanliness in the anal phase develops as an adult more or less neurotic characteristics of thrift, stubbornness, and love of order, which are regarded as positive characteristics in capitalist society. In part 5 we will examine Freud's drive theory more closely, which will give us occasion to evaluate the aforementioned hypotheses.

2. ART AND LITERATURE

Freud's analyses of works of art resembled his analyses of dreams and of neurotic patients. Artistic productivity was initially likened to dream work. Both involved unconscious wish fantasies that, in more or less recognizable form, achieved conscious and manifest expression. The artist was then compared to the neurotic. Freud reconstructed the life of the artist from available sources, emphasizing specific pathological features that were often present. As we have seen, repressed wish fantasies were almost always variations of the Oedipus complex, which put the childhood of the artist at the center of analysis. Freud believed that a work of art, like a joke or myth, had a liberating effect on its audience. A good work of art expressed unconscious impulses common to the artist and his public. If a reader or viewer was unable to find gratification for his repressed fantasies, the work of art allowed him to dream along, so to speak, with the artist's dream and thereby achieve gratification.

Freud never analyzed a work of art from all these perspectives, for obvious reasons. The available information on the artist is often so sparse that the analysis becomes no more than mere conjecture. In treating a patient, an analyst can ask questions, look the patient over and provoke significant transferences. In dealing with deceased artists, the psychoanalyst often lacks the answers to fundamental questions about the childhood and sexuality of the artist. Even if the analyst succeeds in formulating a hypothesis, he has no way of verifying it. The psychoanalyst rarely fares better with a living artist unless he can delve into and publish analyses of the artist's private life. It is tempting to conclude that psychoanalysis is not well suited to analysis of works of art. However, compared to the pre-Freudian biological method, psychoanalysis does quite well. Before Freud, it was very common to draw psychological portraits of great artists and relate them to their work. This method was employed by writers like Taine and Brandes. Their method suffered from the absence of a coherent psychological theory. Instead, they settled for a general psychological insight into the personality of the artist, supplemented by dubious observations on heredity and environment (in section I.B.6, we discussed the attempt by the naturalists to translate the concepts and methods of the natural sciences to literature).

(a) Leonardo da Vinci and
His Artistic and Scientific Work

In 1910, Freud published a monograph of about eighty pages on Leonardo da Vinci, the Italian Renaissance genius famous as both a painter and a scientist. This monograph was Freud's most ambitious examination of aesthetics, and showed the strengths and weaknesses of psychoanalysis as a method of analysis.

Leonardo (1452–1519) is commonly regarded as a divided and conflict-ridden personality. His work encompassed many fields. He was trained as a painter, but made scientific observations and constructed machines. He dissected corpses, built mechanical toys, played the lute, and drew plans for fortifications. He seldom completed any of his grandiose plans, and most of his paintings are only partly finished. He had no definite political views, serving the princes who paid him the most and leaving them if they got into any kind of trouble. His notes showed a scientific interest in reproduction, but at the same time a deep revulsion toward sex. He never married. His feelings ranged from profound compassion for all living things (he bought birds at the market and set them free) to the detached indiffer-ence of the scientist (he observed the physiognomy of condemned men before and after execution).

Freud took as his point of departure the only childhood memory re-corded in Leonardo's countless notes. While studying a kite (and using this study as a basis for the construction of an airplane), he wrote that he felt predestined to study just this species of bird because he remembered a kite's landing on his cradle when he was a baby, sitting on him, and sticking its tail between his lips. Freud did not think this was a real experience but more likely a fantasy or dream. In order to interpret the experience, Freud examined the sparse information on Leonardo's childhood. He was born out of wedlock. His mother was a poor peasant woman, his father a notary. At first, the child stayed with his mother, but he was later given to his father. His father was now married to a well-to-do woman who could not have children, so they brought Leonardo into their home when he was between three and five years old.

From this flimsy evidence, Freud attempted to reconstruct Leonardo's Oedipus complex. His sexual anxiety indicated intense repression. The fantasy about the kite made Freud assume that Leonardo's repression included passive experiences. His mother nursed him with an exaggerated love and expressed feelings for him that she could not give to the faithless father of her child. His mother was both mother and father, and the tail of the bird represented the breast and the penis. Leonardo only acquired the actual Oedipus complex after moving in with his father's family. This complex was not very pronounced since his stepmother could never be a very attractive object. The most important oedipal element was Leonardo's identification with his father, whose manifold activities were an example for emulation. The weak Oedipus complex was expressed in puberty when Leonardo was unable to make the "masculine" object choice of a passive "feminine" object. His stepmother was never important enough for him to have chosen her as a model for his object choice. However, his emotional ties to his mother were strong, but there was probably no possibility of a genuine passive object choice (subjection by a domineering woman or man). The maternal tie was therefore transformed regressively to an identification with the active mother. After this regression, Leonardo's psychosexual identity became permanently fixed to this attitude. He himself became like a mother with particular affection for boys.

Freud substantiated this analysis with information from Leonardo's later career as an artist. Even during his student days at art school, he was accused of homosexual advances toward some of the male models. He later recruited students for his workshop whose looks were more important than their talent. His notes contained meticulous accounts of expenses incurred for these students, their illnesses, their clothes, and general upkeep. Freud regarded Leonardo's almost compulsive meticulousness with these figures as an indication of his repressed wishes for anal sex with his students. On the whole, Leonardo's identity as an artist was associated with his identification with his mother. His other identity as a scientist and inventor, however, stemmed from his identification with his father. His tireless research of all kinds of subjects indicated intense sexual explorations as a child, that is, a constant return to the riddles of reproduction, birth, and gender differences. Throughout his career as an engineer and especially as the constructor of instruments of war (submarines, horse-driven tanks, and so on) Leonardo came into close contact with the nobility, and by doing so imitated his father's career in noble circles. Furthermore, he copied his father's infidelity toward his mother by his unscrupulous exploitation of his noble employers. However, Freud also detected an oedipal revolt against the father figure in Leonardo's unconscious opposition to scientific and religious authorities. He believed more in tangible nature than in spiritual nature and preferred observation to academic wisdom. His well-camouflaged notes, written in reverse script from right to left using code language and phonetic notation, contained the following controversial statement: The sun does not move. This was written about fifty years before Copernicus.

In Leonardo's life history, his identification with his mother and consequent latent homosexuality determined his first success as an artist, but from this position he gradually moved toward an identification with his father. He eventually gave up painting altogether because he was not satisfied with his pictures and therefore seldom finished them. His work as an inventor and scientist was also characterized by restlessness and it is likely that he wasted his talents by functioning as something of a jack-of-all-trades for his princely employers. According to Freud, his restlessness was caused by his unclarified relationship with his mother. Freud believed that a drastic change took place around the time of the death of Leonardo's mother in 1493. Leonardo had probably seen her again in this year and had only then been able to form a realistic impression of her. He understood how her character must have been influenced by her excessive love for him and her intense contempt for his father, who had failed her. Freud also postulated the hypothesis that Leonardo momentarily recognized the personality of his mother in a young noblewoman who several years later asked him to paint her portrait. Her resemblance to his mother made him accept the offer, although he had not painted for a long time. Leonardo worked on the famous portrait of Mona Lisa from 1503–1507 without ever considering it finished. For Freud, her ambivalent smile expressed Leonardo's view of his mother: her derision of and contempt for his father and her sensual and seductive invitation to a love affair. In looking at the portrait, both aspects are apparent by turns. Only by painting his mother's portrait was Leonardo able to free himself from his unhappy identification with her.

Leonardo's last great painting from 1508–1512, "Madonna, Child, and St. Anne," should be seen in this light. It hangs beside the "Mona Lisa" in the Louvre in Paris. The motif is the Virgin Mary sitting on the lap of her mother, St. Anne, and leaning forward toward the child Jesus who is holding a lamb. It is clear that Anne's facial expression resembles the Mona Lisa's and thus the mother of Leonardo, but the contemptuous and aggressive expression is replaced by a gentle and loving expression. The Virgin Mary therefore represents Leonardo's stepmother, and the strange union of the two mothers, who seem to be the same age, is the ideal wish situation for the child. The mother simply replaces the father, who by his absence is branded as a superfluous and unwanted figure. In the less well-known sketch of "Madonna, Child, and St. Anne" (which hangs in the National Gallery in London), Freud noticed that the two mothers appeared to have merged together. The sketch was more disquieting than the finished picture, and lacked the latter's somewhat vapid family idyll. The mother (St. Anne) was characterized by her demonic facial expression, and it was obvious that she was the masculine part of the foursome. The finger presumably pointing up to God was also a tangible symbol of phallus and power, and the child Jesus seemed to be leaning on it. The sketch indicated that Leonardo (the child Jesus in the painting) even at this stage identified with the active mother. His later homosexual affection for boys resembling him was emphasized by the fact that the lamb was not included in the sketch but had been replaced by John the Baptist as a child.

(b) E. T. A. Hoffmann: "The Sandman"

E. T. A. Hoffmann (1776–1822) belonged to the German Romantic school. We have already discussed him in Part 1 (see I.B.6.a), and he deserves our attention as one of the writers before Freud who best understood the strong forces found in the unconscious. In "The Uncanny" (Freud 1919h), Freud gave a short and concise analysis of Hoffmann's tale "The Sandman" (Hoffmann 1817). We have chosen to discuss this analysis here because it, despite its brevity, is more interesting than Freud's only extended literary analysis, that of W. Jensen's "Gradiva" (Freud 1907a).

The main protagonist in Hoffmann's tale was the young student Nathanael. In spite of a happy engagement to a girl, he was plagued by childhood memories associated with the mysterious death of his father, whom he loved dearly. As a child he had sometimes been sent to bed early with the warning that "the sandman" was coming. When he asked his mother who the sandman was, he was told that no such man existed. It was a figure of speech meaning that children were sleepy and felt as if they had sand in their eyes. However, his nurse told him another story that he found more plausible. The sandman was a wicked man who came when children would not go to bed. He threw sand in their eyes so that they jumped out of their heads. He took the eyes in a sack and gave them to his own children as toys.

Nathanael was often sent to bed early because a man came to visit his father. Nathanael supposed that the visitor was the sandman and one evening sneaked into his father's study and hid to find out who the sandman was. The visitor was the lawyer Coppelius, whom the children had never liked. Coppelius discovered Nathanael and threatened to take out his eyes, but his father interceded and prevented Coppelius from doing so. After this incident, Nathanael suffered a long illness. The year after, Coppelius again came to visit, and Nathanael's father was killed by a mysterious explosion in the study. Coppelius disappeared.

Even as an adult, Nathanael was unable to free himself from this horrible memory, and when he met an itinerant Italian optician named Giuseppe Coppola, he believed that he was the lawyer Coppelius who was following him. The optician wanted to sell him "beautiful eyes," spectacles, but he bought a pocket telescope instead. He used it to spy on Professor Spalanzani's house and saw his very beautiful, but silent and motionless daughter, Olympia. He immediately fell in love with her and forgot all about his fiancée, a good and sensible girl. Olympia, however, was a doll the professor had built whose eyes were provided by the optician Coppola. Nathanael entered the house as the two men were quarreling about the doll. Its bloody eyes lay on the floor. The professor took them and threw them to Nathanael, crying that they were his eyes, which Coppola had stolen from him. After this experience, Nathanael fell ill for a long time again. When he recovered, he decided to marry his fiancée. One day they went up to the tower of the town hall together. The girl saw something in the distance. Nathanael pulled out his telescope to see what it was, but suddenly fell into a fit of madness and tried to throw his fiancée from the tower. She escaped, but Nathanael saw the lawyer Coppelius on the street, threw himself from the tower, and was killed instantly. Coppelius disappeared in the crowd.

Without arguing the point, Freud believed that Nathanael might be Hoffmann himself, not down to the smallest detail, of course, but in the sense that Nathanael's psychic conflicts and ties were identical to Hoffmann's. The tale fluctuated between reality and fantasy. As in all his tales, Hoffmann described fantasy and the supernatural in such a way that they lent themselves to an interpretation as the expression of the madness of the protagonist. Naturally, Freud chose to interpret the tale psychologically. In other words, he regarded the fictive universe as an expression of Nathanael's (or Hoffmann's) more or less pathological fantasies. However, Hoffmann could not just be made into a patient, since his tales revealed an unusual self-knowledge and ability to formulate unconscious impulses in an artistically balanced form.

The only information on Hoffmann Freud used was the fact that his father left the family when Hoffmann was three years old. This experience increased his ambivalence toward his father whom he missed and hated for his faithlessness. This divided image of the father appeared in the two pairs of fathers: the evil Coppelius who disappeared and the good father who died, the evil Coppola who stole the doll, and the good professor who gave Nathanael his eyes back. The indelible childhood trauma was not the loss of the father, but the threat of having his eyes put out. This threat could only attain its central role because it represented castration anxiety. What had really happened was this: Nathanael could not or would not sleep during the night and had therefore had a chance surreptitiously to watch his parents having intercourse. He was discovered and consequently threatened with different forms of punishment if he did not immediately go to sleep again. However, his fear of being punished with castration was not sufficient to evoke a repression of the Oedipus complex, which had been inextricably associated with the experience of the primal scene (his parents' intercourse). As an adult Nathanael could neither free himself from nor come to an understanding of his traumatic childhood experiences. He continued to return to them and also retained his voyeuristic inclinations. Therefore the evil father (Coppelius, Coppola) continued to pursue him. His friends and his fiancée implored him to forget the past but in vain.

The Olympia episode provided short-lived happiness which Freud saw as an expression of a return to narcissism. Olympia was so unproblematically perfect because in reality she was only a product of Nathanael's narcissistic self-image. There was in her no opposition between life and death, between human or mechanical features, or between fantasy and reality. Even the castration had temporarily lost its significance since Olympia could have Nathanael's eyes without his losing them. The good father, Professor Spalanzani, attempted to protect this narcissistic happiness, but the evil father, Coppelius-Coppola, could not be held back. When Nathanael was about to realize a genuine heterosexual object relation (with the tower as a symbol of his sexual potency) his unresolved Oedipus and castration complex stood in his way again, which Hoffmann effectively emphasized in the drastic conclusion of the tale.

IV

THE THERAPEUTIC WORK

INTRODUCTION
TO PART IV

We will now consider the second of the three dimensions of psychoanalysis, namely, its therapeutic work. As a scientific, therapeutic discipline, psychoanalysis takes its place alongside psychiatry and neuropathology. Its primary object of study, which it took over from neuropathology, is the neuroses. It does, however, also include the psychoses and the perversions in its scope. Psychoanalysis bases its classification of diseases on a comprehensive metapsychological theory of the genesis and structure of the subject. It has its own method of treatment in which analysis and interpretation are prominent components.

In section A we will present an account of Freud's classification of diseases and compare it to efforts at classification made by psychiatry and neuropathology in the 1800s. In the subsection on psychiatry in part 1 (I.B.5) we only dealt briefly with this issue, and we will now address it in full. In section B we will consider Freud's therapeutic method including the special demands that treatment makes on the analyst as well as on the analysand. Therapeutic analysis differs from the other types of analytic work discussed in part 3 in that it treats a subject and not just a dream, a text, or a particular social behavioral pattern. The therapeutic effect is not inherent in the results of the analysis. It grows out of the analysand's reaction to the analysis. In section C we will discuss Freud's five most famous case histories, placing particular focus on the etiological aspect, that is, identifying the source of the disease in terms of the total social context of the subject.

A.

CLASSIFICATION
OF DISEASES

Within every scientific discipline great advances have followed in the wake of a successful classification system whether it was of animals, plants, chemical substances, societal organization, or works of art. There are in-numerable—more or less superficial—ways of making classifications. They can be made on the basis of color, shape, size, and structure, or on the basis of genetic or causal criteria. If we consider the classification of insanity over the past two hundred years, three classificatory criteria seem to predominate:

(1) The clinical descriptive method classifies diseases according to their symptoms and the overall clinical picture. One reason for using these criteria suggests itself: if the symptoms are considered to be the core of the disease, then causing their disappearance is synonymous with curing the disease. This is the predominating view among the moral therapists (see I.B.5), and it forms the basis of the extensive classification of the overall clinical picture that Pinel and his pupil, Esquirol, developed in the early 1800s. Later in that century, Kraepelin reinstated the clinical descriptive criterion, although for a different reason. Influenced by the rise of positivism, Kraepelin wanted to make psychiatry more scientifically consistent by ridding it of the speculative theories that had influenced psychiatry as well as neurophysiology and neuropathology for several decades. He wanted to rebuild psychiatry from the ground up. Therefore, as far as possible, he used only concrete clinical descriptions as the basis of his classification.

(2) The anatomical-physiological criterion classifies diseases according to which structures or functions of the nervous system are presumed to have been damaged. This criterion is very closely linked to the mechanistic subject concept. One of the earliest theories argued that the etiology of a

disease could be traced to the way in which the animal spirits circulated (circulation was too slow in melancholia and too fast in mania). Griesinger's hypothesis that all insanity was a brain disease was generally recognized from 1860–1885. During this period efforts to localize all of the brain's functions and functional disorders were at a peak. In the twentieth century research on the brain and its chemical processes has revived an interest in the anatomical-physiological criterion.

(3) Finally, the etiological criterion classifies diseases according to what causes them. This criterion is of relatively recent date, Griesinger being among the first to take a serious interest in the etiology of insanity. In the work of Morel, the creator of the degeneration theory, we have found what could almost be called an etiological classification of diseases. In addition to (a) inherited degenerative diseases, he listed the following: (b) insanity resulting from poisoning (for example, alcoholism or carbon monoxide poisoning), (c) general progressive paralysis (syphilis), (d) mental diseases caused by somatic illnesses (for example, delerium from fever), (e) dementia (defects in intelligence caused by the organic decay of brain tissue), and, finally, (f) insanity through transformation from the major neuroses (hysteria, hypochondria, and epilepsy). Whereas Griesinger tended to view insanity as stemming from the interaction between heredity and environment, Morel made a distinction between diseases whose causes were due to heredity and those whose causes were due to environment. Around the turn of the century this led Kraepelin to divide insanity into the endogenous and the exogenous. We will later return to how Freud also used the etiological criterion as a basis for classification.

In part 1 we mentioned how in the seventeenth and the eighteenth centuries the insane were locked up along with criminals, the destitute, and invalids. They were all treated as one class, which explains why long into the 1800s psychiatry still used a rudimentary classification system for deviants. A number of the diseases of the nervous system, such as aphasia and spastic paralysis, undoubtedly contributed to clouding the picture even more. Pinel, Esquirol, Zeller, and Griesinger were especially interested in melancholia, monomania, mania, dementia, and idiocy. It was noted that the same patient went through each of these stages successively. Zeller advanced the hypothesis that the developmental sequence represented a so-called unity psychosis. All forms of insanity were thus supposed to be various expressions of a single unity psychosis. Griesinger pointed out that melancholia, monomania, and mania were affective diseases that influenced mood, whereas dementia and idiocy directly attacked the intellect and broke down the personality.

Neuropathology (neurology) was established as an independent medical discipline around 1850. Its object of study was the diseases of the nervous system. In Griesinger's time a clear distinction was seldom drawn between psychiatry and neuropathology. The same methods and concepts were used by both disciplines. Gradually, however, neuropathology developed into the study of nervous diseases that did not attack the psychic functions, whether affective or intellectual. Initially, all nervous diseases were called neuroses, just as the psychic diseases were called psychoses. For instance, Romberg (1846) distinguished between sensibility neuroses (hypersensitivity and numbness in the sensory organs) and motility neuroses (convulsions and paralysis). During the 1850s and 1860s, the true diseases of the nervous system, such as polio, sclerosis, Parkinson's disease, and spastic paralysis, were identified. Charcot emerged as the leader in this field, and in 1882 he was appointed to a newly established professorship of neuropathology. Our previous mention of Charcot also concerned this period of his life (see I.B.5.b). It was then that he took an interest in the minor nervous diseases that still retained the name *neuroses*. The neuroses were a group of diseases left over after the neuropathological diseases had been defined. They included hysteria, hypochondria, epilepsy, and neurasthenia and had certain characteristics in common. They were expressed as "nervous" symptoms but did not significantly affect the true psychic functions, and their neurophysiological basis was unknown. Charcot was particularly interested in hysteria and described the sensory and motor disturbances that characterized it. Although he could not demonstrate that permanent neuroanatomical changes were the cause of hysteria, he did believe, in keeping with Morel's degeneration theory, that a hereditary neuropathic constitution was the basis of neurosis and that a traumatic experience could provoke a neurosis if the neuropathic constitution was present.

It must be mentioned that Krafft-Ebing was a forerunner in making a systematic description of the perversions and classified them as cerebral neuroses. This group consisted of sadism, masochism (both named by Krafft-Ebing), homosexuality, and fetishism. Krafft-Ebing probably decided to call them neuroses because he believed that they originated in the degenerative neuropathic constitution. (Morel himself had already characterized the perverse as degenerates.) Here we are walking the line between nervous diseases and psychic diseases, and there are a number of instances dealing with cases' crossing the line between the two, as when diseases start out as neuroses and then develop into psychoses (see point [f] in Morel's classification). *Neuropsychoses* and *psychoneuroses* were the terms reserved for such cases. In reality, these innovations were expressions of a delayed recognition of the fact that the neuroses were essentially psychic diseases.

Psychiatry of the 1880s agreed in general on the two main disease categories of the organic psychoses and the functional psychoses. This classification can be traced back to the distinction that Griesinger made between damage to the effective functions and to the intellectual functions. In organic psychoses, it was the intellect that had been impaired, and this was related to permanent anatomical changes in the brain. Whereas in dementia, intellectual functions were impaired due, for example, to arteriosclerosis, lesions, or tumors, in mental deficiency the intellect simply failed to develop. Permanent damage caused by poisoning (for example, alcohol, carbon monoxide, or morphine) were also classified under the organic psychoses. The criterion for the functional psychoses was that of emotional damage, but gradually more and more diseases outside its scope were added to melancholia and mania, for example, paranoia, delusions, hallucinations, and anxiety symptoms. The neuroses and the functional psychoses were classified in a similar way, the former as a residual group under the major neuropathological diseases, the latter as a residual group under the organic psychoses. In both cases no concrete anatomical, organic changes could be found. Instead, it was said that there had to be "functional" changes in the nervous system, changes that affected the magnitude, distribution, circulation, or perhaps the quality of neural energy.

From a historical perspective those who specialized had the greatest success, as did Charcot and Jackson in neuropathology and later Bleuler in psychiatry. Those, on the other hand, who tried to embrace neuropathology and psychiatry while at the same time endorsing neuroanatomical and neurophysiological tenets met with failure. Meynert is the best example. At the time of his death he was professor of neuropathology and psychiatry, but he failed to forge a bond between the two disciplines. He had the highly interesting theory that the functional psychoses might be related to changes in energy states in the cortex and the subcortex, but in general, he was hostile toward new ideas, such as those that Freud, among others, advanced about the neuroses.

The psychoanalytic classification of disease that Freud completed in the years after the turn of the century is noteworthy because it classifies types of diseases already known in an entirely different way. Freud's scientific background was in neuropathology and only to a limited degree in psychiatry. When he left for Paris to study under Charcot, he planned to continue his training as a neuropathologist. When Meynert started to expand his sphere of interest into psychiatry, he originally thought that Freud would succeed him as professor of neuropathology. After graduating, Freud sought work as a neuropathologist. By the 1890s he was widely recognized as the leading polio specialist of his day. Moreover, as a practitioner, he was most frequently confronted with the minor diseases, the neuroses. Nevertheless, he did succeed in fusing the two residual groups, the functional psychoses and the neuroses (the so-called minor groups) to create one scientific discipline. He was among the first to abandon the theory that a neuropathic constitution was the basis of the neuroses and instead to develop an independent theory on the etiology of the neuroses. We want to point out three successive achievements in Freud's work on classification:

(1) During the 1890s Freud grew increasingly convinced that the cause of functional psychoses and neuroses was a disturbance in the distribution and the flow of sexual energy. As is well known, this choice of sexuality as a delimiting principle proved to be highly productive even though there are functional disturbances that have no sexual etiology. Freud advanced the hypothesis of the existence of a general psychophysical sexual energy without, however, saying how it was related to ordinary neural energy. He thought that this sexual energy had two manifestations: one psychic and the other somatic. Based on this he divided his field into the psychic and the somatic disorders. In one sense it would have been more consistent to use the terms *psychosis* and *neurosis,* but Freud chose to align himself with the terms then in use. He called the functional psychoses and neuroses, which had psychic modes of expression, psychoneuroses (sometimes also called neuropsychoses) and the remaining somatic neuroses actual neuroses (Freud 1898a, pp. 21 and 29).

(2) In *Three Essays on the Theory of Sexuality* (Freud 1905d) Freud described the development of normal infantile sexuality (see V.B.2.a). With infantile sexuality as his point of departure, he listed three developmental possibilities: (a) the subordination of infantile partial drives to the primacy of genital sexuality, (b) a "positive" extension of infantile sexuality in the form of perversions, and (c) a "negative" extension of infantile sexuality as psychoneuroses. The terms *positive* and *negative* were used to indicate that perversions resembled infantile sexual modes of expression whereas psy-

choneurotic symptoms were the result of a defense against infantile sexual impulses. The (psycho)neuroses, Freud said, were the "negative" of the perversions.

(3) In the 1890s Freud used the concept of defense to describe two of the true functional neuroses (hallucinatory confusion and paranoia), but not until his association with Bleuler, Jung, and Abraham did he become seriously interested in the psychoses. In 1907 Jung suggested dividing the psychoneuroses into psychoses and transference neuroses, and in 1908 Abraham described the psychosis dementia praecox (schizophrenia), as a return to the autoerotic sexual overestimation of the ego. This inspired Freud to expand his ideas about the stages of the psychosexual development of the ego (see V.B.2.b), and in connection with this he attempted to understand the psychoses as narcissistic neuroses, and, adopting Jung's term, transference neuroses. The same two groups in present-day psychoanalytic terminology are simply called the psychoses and the neuroses.

To summarize, Freud used four groups, namely, the actual neuroses, the perversions, the transference neuroses, and the psychoses. We want to emphasize that Freud did not think of the perversions as true diseases in the way Krafft-Ebing and others had done. Our diagram attempts to illustrate how the relatively simple classification of disease in Romberg's early neuropathology and Griesinger's early neuropathological psychiatry were replaced by a bipartite division into functional and organic diseases and how the psychoanalytical classification of diseases was established by combining the two functional groups: the functional neuroses from neuropathology and the functional psychoses from psychiatry.

In this connection it should be mentioned that psychoanalysis incorporated Krafft-Ebing's cerebral neuroses as perversions without making any significant changes. The "major" neuroses, on the other hand, were totally split up: hysteria together with the compulsions (obsessions) from the functional psychoses became the transference neuroses; neurasthenia and hypochondria together with what Freud called the anxiety neuroses were classified as actual neuroses; and finally, epilepsy was transferred to the neuropathological diseases. Freud cannot be credited with this although it is true that he never recognized epilepsy as a neurosis. Where the psychoses are concerned, as mentioned, it was Jung and Abraham who described the groups with which psychoanalysis operates today.

In order to avoid repetition we have thus far not given a detailed account of each individual disease group. We will now, however, proceed to a

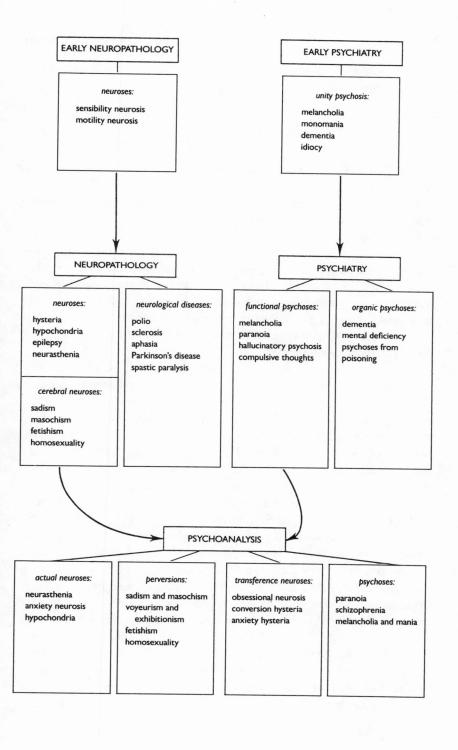

discussion of the four disease groups in psychoanalysis and the types that belong to each of them.

1. ACTUAL NEUROSES

As mentioned, Freud classified the neuroses as actual neuroses and psycho-neuroses, distinguishing between them on the basis of two criteria: the type of disease (the clinical-descriptive criterion), and the causes of the disease (the etiological criterion).

(1) In line with traditional practice, Freud distinguished between two kinds of symptoms: the somatic and the psychic. The actual neuroses were the "genuine" neuroses having only somatic symptoms while the psycho-neuroses had both psychic and somatic symptoms. In many cases, however, it was difficult to discern the psychic symptoms of the psychoneuroses since they could manifest themselves as imitations of somatic symptoms (for example, hysterical pains and paralyses). Freud, therefore, needed an additional classification criterion.

(2) Based on his clinical work, Freud reached the conclusion that hysterical patients always suffered from reminiscences or memories of the past. A past experience of some kind was always involved and was expressed in a veiled form. This regularity led Freud to present the more encompassing hypothesis that some earlier traumatic experience was always a part of the etiology of the psychoneuroses. However, an etiology of this kind could not be established for the actual neuroses. The etiology of the disease where these neuroses were concerned was always to be sought in the actual life conditions of the individual, primarily in excessive masturbation or excessive sexual abstinence. The term *actual neurosis,* therefore, indicated that the etiology was present behavior as opposed to an earlier experience.

(3) Freud did not employ the anatomical-physiological classification criterion directly, but it can be said that he used a hypothetical anatomical-physiological model to distinguish between the two categories of neurosis. What we have in mind here is the passage of sexual energy from the somatic neural pathways to the ideational structure. Freud viewed the purely somatic symptoms of the actual neuroses as a sign of the release of sexual energy before it reached the ideational structure. By contrast, a characteristic of the symptoms of the psychoneuroses was that they were organized by the ideational structure even when they were somatic. Thus, Freud noted that a true neuropathological paralysis of the arm had specific traits

that reflected the location of neural pathways whereas a hysterical paralysis of the arm simply began at the shoulder joint and was organized around a psychic idea of the arm (Freud 1893c). It has been said that Freud, with his concept of somatic sexual energy, anticipated the discovery of the sexual hormones. In our opinion, however, this is of secondary significance since he had already placed major emphasis on the erogenous zones as being the somatic sources of psychosexual energy, the libido, in his *Three Essays on the Theory of Sexuality* (1905d) (see V.A.2.b).

Freud included the actual neuroses as part of his classification for the rest of his life, although he hardly had anything new to say about them after the turn of the century. Sometimes he explicitly stated that they rightfully belonged to the research field of biochemistry. From a therapeutic viewpoint they cannot be treated within a psychoanalytic framework because psychic structures do not play a major role in their symptomatology. However, there are reasons for taking an interest in them within psychoanalysis. At the beginning of a new analysis, the psychoanalyst has to be able to decide whether the symptoms are psychoneurotic or actual neurotic, that is, if the disease is at all suited for psychoanalytic treatment. In addition, mixed types frequently occur either in instances where a developing psychoneurosis assumes the symptoms of an already existing actual neurosis, or when an especially massive repression of drives in a psychoneurosis forces sexual energy to find release in the form of actual neurotic symptoms. A similar reason underlies the requirement that a psychoanalyst have full medical training. Conversional hysterical symptoms, in particular, can be confused with ordinary somatic diseases that the hysterical patient is imitating. The scope of the problem is well illustrated in Freud's dream of Irma's injection (see III.A.2.a), where the question arises as to whether Freud overlooked a somatic factor and therefore followed a false lead in his treatment of Irma.

(a) Neurasthenia

The term *neurasthenia* originated with G. M. Beard, an American, who mentioned it for the first time in a short article in 1869 and who later wrote several books on the subject. *Asthenia* means fatigue and weakness, and *neurasthenia* therefore indicates fatigue or weakness with a neurological origin. In addition, Beard listed the following symptoms: physical and mental fatigue, difficulty in concentrating, headaches, lack of appetite, and low tolerance of noise, of light, and of other people. In a number of his articles he attempted to provide etiological explanations. First he suggested that the disease was caused by a lack of phosphorous in the nervous system; then he saw it as being caused by the stressful conditions of modern-day life; finally, he felt it was related to a deficiency of energy in the central nervous system. In a posthumously published work, Beard openly suggested a sexual etiology (Beard 1905).

In European medicine neurasthenia quickly took its place alongside hysteria, hypochondria, and epilepsy as a fourth type of neurosis. It was associated with a congenital neuropathic constitution and with the consumption of neural energy. For example, it was proposed that there was a connection between the neurasthenic's lack of appetite and the slow resurgence of neural energy. Krafft-Ebing mentioned a special type of neurasthenia that was sexual in nature, and that, among other things, could result from masturbation. However, we have not encountered any writers prior to Freud who maintained that the etiology was exclusively sexual.

Freud became interested in neurasthenia at an early stage, perhaps because he considered himself to be neurasthenic and used cocaine (see II.A.2) to treat the disease for a period around 1885. In an article written in 1894 (1895b) he distinguished between two different kinds of symptoms: one was fatigue and was classified as genuine neurasthenia and the other consisted of anxiety symptoms and was classified as anxiety neurosis (see below). Somatic sexual energy was involved in both cases, and neurasthenia was understood as indicating a deficiency of somatic sexual energy. Freud cited excessive masturbation and involuntary (nocturnal) emissions as reasons for this deficiency. The transfer of tension that was supposed to take place, in particular from the male seminal vesicle, failed to occur because the sperm was released too often or too early. Freud, however, did not reject the idea that hereditary constitution could be a significant factor. Nevertheless, he considered it a general condition that should not be confused with the specific cause.

(b) Anxiety Neurosis

Anxiety neurosis is a disease type of Freud's own invention. The symptoms he assigned to it correspond quite closely to what is generally termed "nervousness," that is, excessive apprehension and irritability. Somatic symptoms can manifest themselves as true anxiety attacks and consist of palpitation, difficulty in breathing, sweating spells, and muscle spasms. Moreover, there may also be insomnia, vertigo, and imagined bodily sensations. The typical anxiety neurotic is the apprehensive woman who lives in constant fear that her husband and children may have suffered some terrible misfortune.

Anxiety neurosis like neurasthenia arises because somatic sexual energy is not diverted through the psychic ideational structure. Freud did not include it among the defense neuroses, and therefore, it is not a defense process preventing sexual energy from being expressed physically. Whereas neurasthenia is caused by a deficiency of sexual energy in the nervous system, Freud believed that anxiety neurosis was due to an excess of it. The conditions for exceeding the threshold of consciousness are present in anxiety neurosis, and psychic anxiety indicates as well that part of the sexual energy has found psychic expression. There is, however, no processing at the psychic level. The existing channels for psychic discharge are not capable of carrying the entire load of sexual energy, and some of it is therefore relegated to subcortical and thus to somatic channels for psychic release (Freud 1895b). The cause of this is excessive sexual abstinence or an unsatisfactory sex life. Naturally, a general pattern of societal behavior is to be found behind these individual factors. Freud was aware of the connection between the neuroses and the sexual morality of a culture (see, for example, Freud 1908d). However, he was not the first to consider this issue, nor did he make an extensive study of it.

Freud carried out his work on anxiety neurosis during the 1890s at a time when he had not yet isolated the transference neurosis anxiety hysteria as an independent nosographic category. For instance, he named a number of phobias (fear of certain animals or situations) as examples of symptoms of anxiety neurosis that actually belonged to anxiety hysteria. Anxiety neurosis is only relevant as a category in cases where the anxiety is "free floating" and cannot be traced to an idea or fantasy about an earlier traumatic experience. As a theoretical consequence of his work on anxiety neurosis Freud maintained for many years that undischarged sexual energy was simply transformed directly into anxiety while it was being diverted through the somatic discharge channels as palpitations and breathing difficulty. He finally concluded, however, that the abnormal somatic discharge channels were also created as the result of a traumatic experience (perhaps at birth) such that all types of anxiety in one way or another were caused by the passage of psychic energy across the memory ideas. Notwithstanding, anxiety remains in principle different from transference neurosis and psychosis, although it can no longer have a place among the actual neuroses proper, that is, among neuroses solely related to present life conditions. (Reference is made, moreover, to the theoretical discussion of the concept of anxiety in V.C.2.b).

(c) Hypochondria

Hypochondria has been known throughout history, and it was once often considered to be the male counterpart of female hysteria. Toward the end of the nineteenth century it found its place within neuropathology as one of the four major neuroses. Freud might have been expected to classify it as an actual neurosis, but in reality he paid very little attention to it during the 1890s; the closest he came was to classify it as a special case of anxiety neurosis. Its symptoms were the patient's excessive apprehension about his health and a host of imagined illnesses. As in the case of anxiety neurosis, this indicates a nervous malfunctioning in which excess sexual energy finds expression as false sensory impulses that are registered as pain in the body organs.

It was not until he wrote his paper on narcissism (1914c, p. 97) that Freud identified hypochondria as the third actual neurosis. This was apparently because he needed it as a preliminary stage to the narcissistic neuroses, especially paranoia and schizophrenia, where the individual's interest in his body and his concern for it predominated. Hypochondria cannot be classified as a purely somatic neurosis because its symptoms stem from psychic ideational representations of the body organs. The organs, however, do not have the symbolic significance that they have in hysteria, paranoia, and schizophrenia. They seem to be chosen fairly haphazardly, eventually in extension of real organ sensations.

After having placed hypochondria among the actual neuroses, Freud later had nothing of any further significance to say about it.

2. PERVERSIONS

Perversions have been known and discussed ever since antiquity but were not dealt with on a truly scientific basis until the end of the nineteenth century. Most (such as Morel and Krafft-Ebing) mainly understood them as manifestations of a hereditary neuropathic constitution. There were others, however, (such as Binet and Schrenck-Notzing) who expressed the opinion that they could be acquired as a result of experiences in childhood. Toward the turn of the century another viewpoint appeared that asserted that constitution was a necessary prerequisite but that specific experiences were the determinants of whether a perversion would develop and, if it did, what type it would be (see, for example, Moll and Havelock Ellis). In each case, perversions were considered to be deviations from heterosexual genital sexuality, that is, they were caused by a prematurely developed sexual drive or one that developed abnormally. Only a very few writers suggested that there might be an unspecified or perverse sexuality in human development that preceded genital, phylogenetic, and ontogenetic development (see Fliess and Dessoir).

Krafft-Ebing and Havelock Ellis furnished the most extensive and uniform description of the perversions, and Freud accepted their classification as far as types were concerned without adding anything new. It may, therefore, seem as if he accepted their understanding of the perversions as deviations from a given norm. He thus tried to subdivide the perversions according to the types of deviation. Was it a deviation from the drive's normal object or from the drive's normal aim? Closer examination of what Freud actually said in the *Three Essays on the Theory of Sexuality* (1905d) leads to a different conclusion. A general characteristic of sexuality is that it originates simultaneously with the biological and psychic functions of the organism, but that it in itself has no immediate function. It has a biological function when the child breastfeeds, but has no function when the child later starts to suck its finger at will. A number of such nonfunctional activities occur during the child's development. Freud called them partial drives (or indications of partial drives), and these constitute infantile sexuality. It is now easy to understand that a baby sleeps better when it has sucked its finger and that it generally feels better when it is allowed to satisfy its sexuality. It can be said that satisfying the drives supports biological and psychic functions. It is along these lines of thought that Freud's use of the term *perversion* is to be understood. The child's pleasure-directed abandonment to sucking his finger and playing with his feces represents a perversion of basic biological functions that may disturb them, but the ensuing support given to the functions, on the other hand, produces a normalization of sexuality. From Freud's point of view, then, normal sexuality sustains certain known functions while perverse sexuality follows other routes. Freud's decision to adopt the traditional view of the perversions as deviations from heterosexual genital sexuality, despite his innovative ideas, stemmed from the fact that the genital drive sustains an important and well-defined biological function, reproduction, whereas partial drives when they appear in isolation tend to disturb and threaten this function. (A more detailed theoretical explanation of this complex of problems is an important theme in part 5 of this book.)

Freud originally understood the perversions as a positive extension of infantile sexual activities. All children had a penchant for sadism, voyeurism, and homosexuality, and it was such tendencies that developed into true perversions, whereas when repressed, they could only manifest themselves as neurotic symptoms. Freud gradually realized that perversions consisted not only of drives but of psychic structures as well, and this complicated the description of their etiology.

Freud assumed, for instance, that fetishism (see below) presupposed a defense against castration anxiety; therefore, it could not be considered a positive extension of infantile impulses. In many cases, the true character deviations (the psychopathies) can also be viewed as pathological defense mechanisms.

(a) Sadism and Masochism

Krafft-Ebing named sadism and masochism after the two writers, Sade and Masoch. The same syndrome is also known by other names, algolagnia, for example. Freud adopted Krafft-Ebing's clinical description of sadism and masochism, and made several attempts to explain their etiology. It is generally agreed that sadism and masochism are the active and passive variants of the same drive aim. Freud distinguished between three drive aims with regard to sado-masochism, namely, (1) destruction and annihilation, (2) mastery and domination, and (3) pain affliction. In Freud's first etiologically based explanatory attempt, sadism and masochism were related to the drive to master. In the second explanatory attempt it was taken back one more step, to the biologically defined destructive or death drive.

The drive to master, which is not one of Freud's most well-defined concepts, reflects the organism's ability to master an object through motor activity. This drive may have the character of the drive of self-preservation and the sexual drive, and as early as the oral phase indications of the urge to master sexually can be discerned in the way the child incorporates various objects. From the late anal phase on, the child enters into the active/passive polarity, and from then on its urge to master is clearly sadistic. It uses every means to control and dominate the individuals who are its love objects even using violence and force to attain its goal. When the object is not present or when a ban has been issued against threatening the object in that way, the child then learns to direct its sadism against itself. Typically, the sadistic impulses are isolated in the superego while the ego becomes the object of sadism. This relation is neither active nor passive, but reflexive (Freud 1915c, p. 131). Nevertheless, it provides a transition to the passive relation where the activity is placed in the object position, and it is only this relation that is termed masochistic. The ego finds sexual gratification in allowing itself to be controlled, humiliated, and maltreated by another person. The psychic and physical pain sets up a sexual coexcitation that is experienced as a "forepleasure" (actually a feeling of pleasure preceding the end pleasure of orgasm). It is a well-known fact that the greater the excitation that is built up prior to its discharge, the greater is the feeling of pleasure upon discharge. With the masochist, however, the forepleasure becomes a goal in itself, and it spreads to all other relations that either in fact or in fantasy place the ego in a passive position. The infantile sexual aims are transformed retroactively to masochistic aims as the genital sexual aims assume a masochistic quality (masochistic fantasies about being devoured, beaten, castrated by one's father, or of enforced passivity during a painful intercourse, or a painful delivery). It is one of Freud's important theoretical tenets that the sadistic pleasure of inflicting pain on others is not originally a part of the child but is developed after the masochistic enjoyment of pain has been discovered. According to this view true sadists have then been masochists for some period of time, and they are consequently also predisposed to regress to masochism (see further V.B.2.c, on gender-specific development).

After he introduced the concept of the death drive in 1920 (see II.C.2) Freud tried to create a clear drive theoretical foundation for sadism and masochism. A biological life and death drive was assumed to exist right from birth in all organisms, and Freud called the isolated death drive primal sadism. Its inherent drive aim was to return the organism to its inorganic state, that is, self-destruction, and primal sadism was therefore rather closer to "primal masochism." In the course of the development of the child, self-destruction was prevented by the fusion of drives. The life drive and the death drive were fused, thereby preventing the death drive from exercising its detrimental effects. The outer-directed portion of the fusion manifested itself as the urge to master, and its development into real sadism could be understood following the same guidelines set forth in the section above.

However, another part of the death drive still remained in the organism. It fused with the narcissistic libido and in so doing primary erogenous masochism was created. It subsequently linked up with secondary (erogenous) masochism which arose from the occasional withdrawal of outer-directed sadism into the organism.

We find it difficult to accept the theory of the death drives in its biological form (see our comments in V.A.2.b). Freud can have had valid reasons for introducing a primary erogenous masochism in the child's development insofar as the child at a very early stage embarks on a search for strong—and relatively painful—sensory impressions for the sake of sexual pleasure. However, this could be explained just as adequately within affect theory as within drive theory. The question is what the basic feelings of pleasure and pain actually are (see V.C.2.a on affects). Besides primary erogenous masochism, Freud also made use of two other types of erogenous masochism in his later theory referring to them as the moral and the feminine, but both can be placed within the framework of his early theory. Moral masochism is based on the sadistic superego's criticism of the masochistic ego, and this structure corresponds to the reflexive stage that is a transitional link between the active and the passive relation. It is characterized by the ego's unconscious guilt feeling and need for punishment and becomes especially apparent when the ego succeeds in provoking another person, the psychoanalyst, for instance, into making harsh and critical comments on behalf of the superego. Feminine masochism is true (secondary) masochism in which the ego in fact or in fantasy subjects and humiliates itself in relation to another person. *Feminine* refers to the fact that masochistic men, too, place themselves in roles that generally only belong to women.

(b) Voyeurism and Exhibitionism

Freud generally calls voyeurism and exhibitionism active and passive scoptophilic pleasures and assigned them to the "scoptophilic drive," which was one of the infantile partial drives. There is a certain measure of voyeurism and exhibitionism in all of us to the extent that these define the pleasure experienced when regarding the sexual object and being regarded in turn by it. The perverse modes arise only when the visual relationship becomes the sole desired means of contact with the sexual object and when interest is especially focused on the genitals. The true voyeur spies on others in order to see their genitals and eventually also to see them having sexual intercourse or when going to the toilet, while the true exhibitionist's aim is to show his erection, particularly to women and children.

In Freud's view the scoptophilic drive is a precursor to the "drive for knowledge." Both play a role in the child's sexual explorations, that is, in the child's efforts to acquire knowledge about the sexual life of its parents, about the appearance of their genitals, and—by extension—about his own origin. Freud assumed that the scoptophilic drive in its original state was autoerotic or narcissistic. In the same way that Narcissus admired his own image, the child experiences pleasure in looking at its own body, in a mirror, perhaps. This primary narcissism might be said to be analogous to the primary erogenous masochism mentioned in the section above. The subsequent development is different, however. Freud's idea was that the active as well as the passive scoptophilic pleasure developed directly from narcissism (see his diagram in 1915c, p. 133). Passive scoptophilic pleasure is therefore not the result of a reversal of active scoptophilic pleasure but a further development of narcissistic scoptophilic pleasure. Freud may have come to this conclusion because his observations led him to believe that very young children were particularly eager to exhibit themselves.

There are other of Freud's conclusions, however, that indicate that active and passive scoptophilic pleasure, etiologically speaking, correspond closely to sadism and masochism. In this case the active scoptophilic pleasure from the earliest stage is parallel with the urge to master. In the castration complex it is transformed into its reflexive form. Attention is focused, literally, on the individual's own genitals, which are compared with those of the opposite sex. Some children as the result of the castration complex place themselves in a passive position in relation to the love object. It is widely assumed that only men are exhibitionists and voyeurs and that they are so as a way of reacting to the castration complex. By showing his penis to women and children, the exhibitionist tries to reassure himself that he has *not* been castrated whereas the voyeur, by spying on women who are undressed wants to reassure himself that they *are* castrated. In both cases it is assumed that the castration complex has seriously damaged the male active identity and exposure and spying are meant to repair it.

When the scoptophilic drive is not isolated as a perversion, it is subsumed under the drive for knowledge. The drive for knowledge is seen primarily in its active and reflexive form as the urge for recognition from the world and for self-knowledge, but the passive form is not unknown (the urge to be explored by someone else). Genetically speaking the urge for self-reflection stems from the reflexive developmental stage that replaces the active stage, the prime motive being the problems having to do with overcoming the Oedipus complex. A pronounced case of narcissism will, however, also intensify self-reflection.

(c) Fetishism

A fetish is generally a small object that embodies the special power to be able to protect or to bring luck (such as an *amulet, talisman,* or *lucky coin*). Marx emphasized superstition in particular when he spoke of the fetish character of commodities, and in psychiatry the term *fetishism* is used to denote the bestowal of sexual significance onto objects or areas of the body that normally do not possess sexual content. The fetishist is generally sexually aroused by feet, hair, things made of leather or skin, shoes, and underwear.

In 1888 Binet became known for his theory stating that the object of a fetish was determined by a particular sexual experience in childhood, possibly with the first appearance of sexual impulses. Sexual excitement remained tied to objects that had played a relatively minor role in the given situation. Binet maintained also that fetishism was acquired and not inherited, and that it could be traced back to a traumatic childhood experience. Charcot, Breuer, and Freud had similar ideas with regard to the etiology of hysteria.

Initially Freud had some difficulty finding a place for fetishism within his general theory of perversions. Fetishism could not be understood as a fixation on a preliminary sexual aim and thus as the positive extension of an infantile sexual aim in the adult. An excessive sexual interest in, for example, feet and boots is not to be found in the child's normal sexual development. Freud therefore assumed that because the child was unable or had no possibility of reaching its infantile sexual aims, there was a displacement from the immediate object to a substitute object. The child's desire to play with its feces was thus displaced toward objects that smelled strongly, such as feet.

Gradually, however, Freud adopted another explanation. According to it, the fetish object is determined by the castration complex. Fetishism is a reaction on the part of the child when he discovers that his mother has no penis, and in the last analysis the fetish is a substitute for the mother's penis. The defense reaction against the mother's having no penis consists in a disavowal of that fact. The child refuses to believe that his mother has been castrated because, in the boy's case, this would result in the possibility of his own castration. Adult fetishists know perfectly well that women do not have penises. Freud said of this that their disavowal only concerned the psychosexual area while the disavowal on the part of psychotics also disturbed other areas of their understanding of the external world. The choice of a specific fetish to represent the mother's penis can be determined symbolically through complicated displacements in the unconscious, but there can also be a simpler explanation to the effect that the fetish is determined by the visual impressions the child has just before it discovers the missing penis. The choice of fur, for example, may be determined by the fact that the mother's pubic hair was the child's last visual impression before it discovered that she had no penis.

(d) Homosexuality

Homosexuality is the first topic discussed by Freud in *Three Essays on the Theory of Sexuality* (1905d), and it afforded him an opportunity to repudiate a number of scientific prejudices. He rejected the idea that homosexuality was the result of degeneration because most homosexuals were normally endowed both psychically and physically. Nor did he find any grounds for assuming that homosexuals in general were people who had the characteristics of the opposite sex (signs of hermaphroditism, changes in physique, or the development of a "masculine brain" in homosexual females and a "female brain" in homosexual males). Finally, he refused to consider homosexuality as a disease necessitating some kind of treatment. Psychoanalysis was thus only relevant if the homosexual himself expressed a wish to become heterosexual. In such a case it was possible to reintegrate already existing, but repressed heterosexual impulses into the ego.

For many years Freud had difficulty in designating the traits of infantile sexuality that further developed into homosexuality. In the case of male homosexuality he assumed that the erotic significance of the anal zone was maintained and was expressed by a preference for anal intercourse. Following the introduction of the concept of narcissism, the object choice of the homosexual was considered to be a narcissistic object choice. However, it was not until after the phallic phase was introduced in 1923 that the homosexual object choice for both sexes was genetically related to the heterosexual object choice. There are a number of branching points in the sexual development of boys as well as girls and one of the routes leads to homosexuality. We have discussed this in more detail in a later section on gender-specific development (see V.B.2.c). For the present, however, it may be stated that the gender-specific object choice, and consequently also the homosexual object choice, can at the earliest manifest itself as a reaction to the castration complex.

Around the turn of the century homosexuals were commonly thought of as individuals who had changed their gender. Their preference for individuals of their own sex as sexual objects was attributed to their image of themselves as belonging to the opposite sex. Freud had a more complex view, distinguishing between whether the homosexual played an active or a passive role in the relationship. These two groups merit in a sense two different names in line with sadist/masochist and voyeur/exhibitionist (and Ferenczi [1914] actually did distinguish between "object-homoerotics" and "subject-homoerotics"). The active homosexual male has kept his masculine identity choosing as his partner a male with a passive sexual aim. The same situation can, however, also conceal a more complicated mechanism: the active homosexual male can have identified with his active and dominating mother, and in his object choice he may prefer boys who resemble himself when younger, that is, boys whom his mother would have liked just as she liked him. Actively inclined homosexual women have often identified with their fathers whereas passively inclined types in childhood held on to the active mother as object after the castration complex instead of replacing her with the father.

3. TRANSFERENCE NEUROSES

The group of transference neuroses consists of obsessional neurosis, conversion hysteria, and anxiety hysteria, and today they are simply called neuroses whereas in the nineteenth century the term referred to a group consisting of hysteria, hypochondria, epilepsy, and neurasthenia (see the diagram in IV.A). Most of the credit for this reclassification goes to Freud. He formulated the concept of neurosis and neurosis therapy during the same period in which Kraepelin and Bleuler laid the foundation for modern psychiatry by describing the functional psychoses. As we will show in the following section, Freud also contributed to an understanding of the psychoses, and even the most stringently medically oriented psychiatrists must today acknowledge their indebtedness to Freud.

We distinguish in the foregoing between three successive achievements in Freud's classification work (IV.A) and will now discuss in greater detail elements that serve to delimit the (transference) neuroses. For brevity's sake we will use the term *neuroses* as meaning "transference neuroses."

(1) Neuroses always have a sexual etiology. Neurotic symptoms can be traced back to the frustration of sexual satisfaction. The neurotic has fled into his disease in order to avoid the anxiety that sexual satisfaction would cause. Sexual wishful ideas have been subjected to an affect transformation (from pleasure to unpleasure or anxiety), and it is anxiety that mobilizes the defense reaction against implementing the wishful ideas. The symptoms provide the individual with a substitute satisfaction and can relatively clearly be traced back to repressed sexual wishes. Moreover, the neurotic will achieve a secondary gain from illness by receiving attention and care on this account. Freud did not categorically maintain the theory that the etiology of the neuroses was exclusively sexual. After the introduction of late drive dualism, the etiological force of the death drives was also questioned. While Freud initially believed that the causes of disease were attributable to the fact that the sexual drives did not fit into the developmental framework he had created for the drives of self-preservation, he later held that in the final analysis the neuroses were caused by the disruptive influence of the death drives on the life drives.

(2) In relation to the actual neuroses, the psychoneuroses and thus also the (transference) neuroses are characterized by the fact that symptoms come from within, that is, from the memory ideas and not directly from present experiences. There is always a certain incubation period between the time of the experience that provokes the illness and its appearance. This is the same as saying that symptoms are mediated by psychic structures and are not the direct result of somatic conditions. In lecture 22–23 (Freud 1916–1917) Freud established a simple model of the etiology of the neuroses. In *this* model, however, he made use of several kinds of causes in a mutually supplementary relationship. For the neurosis to emerge,

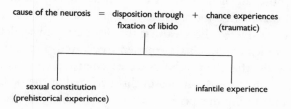

something other than an infantile traumatic experience is therefore necessary. The relative significance of such an experience will depend on the sexual constitution, a purely somatic factor consisting of nerve density, muscular strength, and the size of the organs forming the basis of the erogenous zones. An especially sensitive anus along with a traumatic experience will bring about anal fixation of the libido. This fixation will now exist as an inner disposition, and when the adult has a new traumatic experience, (a present frustration provoked by an external source) the libido will regress to its earlier fixation point out of which the neurotic symptoms will be formed. The relationship between trauma, fixation, and regression is considerably more complicated than we have been able to show thus far. For a more detailed explanation see the section on development and repetition compulsion (V.B.3).

(3) In comparison to the perversions, the neuroses are described as negative manifestations of infantile sexual wishes. Before neurotic symptoms are formed, a repression occurs, which prevents the wishes from manifesting themselves positively. The terms *positive* and *negative* can give the impression that perversions and neuroses are the direct opposites of each other, but this is not so. The positive sexual aims that are repressed are in fact built-in fantasies. They are ideas related in such a way that they can never be carried out in real life. Therefore, they cannot be negated either. As a rule, neurotic symptoms are best characterized in terms of their similarity to repressed fantasies rather than in terms of their difference, and this is also true where the perversions are concerned, except that in their case, disavowal and not repression is most probably their basis. So, the characteristic of the neuroses as the negative of the perversions cannot form the basis of a theoretically tenable definition of the neuroses. In some cases, however, it can make things clearer, for example, when anal drive aims are directly involved in perversions (touching the anal zone, playing with the feces), whereas the neurotic symptoms consist of cleanliness and an urge to hoard money (stack it, count it, hide it, and take it out again). In this case, it is called a reaction formation.

(4) Psychoses and neuroses are each characterized by the different points of psychosexual development where they are fixated. By the 1890s Freud had already considered the idea that the disease type was determined by the stage at which the traumatic experience occurred, and in the years after 1910 he asserted that the psychoses were fixated at the narcissistic stage of development while for the neuroses this occurred at the oedipal stage of development. During this period he even called the psychoses narcissistic neuroses because the symptoms could be interpreted as resulting from a regression to narcissism (see section IV.A.4 on psychoses). In order for

the terminology to be consistent, the neuroses would then have to have been called "oedipal neuroses" to signify that the symptoms always came from the repressed Oedipus complex. There are, however, problems associated with delimiting the neuroses in this way. There is never a total regression to a developmental stage. Return to an earlier point of development cannot occur as if all subsequent events had never occurred. Therefore, most psychoses will show definite signs of the Oedipus complex just as oral and narcissistic traits will intermingle with neurotic symptoms. One conclusion we can draw is that the time at which fixation occurs is not a watertight criterion for delimiting and defining a neurosis. The best delimiting criterion in relation to the psychoses, just as it was in relation to the perversions, is the defense mechanisms involved. In the psychoses such radical defense mechanisms as projection and disavowal are brought into play, which seriously upsets the conception of reality. People and things in the external real world are accorded the same status as the ego and the fantasies. The relationship between the ego and its objects is shaken to such an extent that Freud almost believed that it had ceased to exist, that the libido had been withdrawn from the objects to the ego. Repression is always the basic defense mechanism in the neuroses. Although certain ties between the ego and the object are repressed, new objects are always available as substitutes for them and, to a certain degree, they are treated on the same terms as the former ones. In this connection Freud spoke of transference just as he called obsessional neurosis conversion hysteria and anxiety hysteria transference neurosis. Clinically, the name *transference neurosis* denotes the palpable neurosis that develops when all transferences are concentrated on the person of the analyst, who is alternately given the role of the bad and the good mother, the punishing and the ideal father, and the helping and the rival brother. In this way the analyst is able to gather a major part of the material he needs for analyzing the neurosis.

(a) Obsessional Neurosis

In the psychiatry of the 1800s several authors were familiar with symptoms associated with obsessions. They spoke of compulsive thoughts or obsessions, that is, of being possessed by an idea. They related obsessional symptoms to both psychoses and neuroses but did not go so far as to establish them as a disease type. Accordingly, Griesinger said that they were one of the transitional stages between mania and dementia, and Krafft-

Ebing described them as phenomena that accompanied melancholia. Grie-senger's pupil, Westphal, was reputedly the first person to establish an independent disease type that he called the disease of obsessional ideas. The essence of his description is that morbid ideational processes can also exist in a normally functioning consciousness. The patient is subject to an obsessional preoccupation with the same ideas which he himself knows is a sign of morbid behavior. The disease attacks the ideational function selectively without leading to dementia.

In the 1890s Freud and Pierre Janet, Charcot's pupil, consistently as-sociated obsessional symptoms with the neuroses. Freud introduced the term *obsessional neurosis* while Janet, apparently with Beard's neurasthenia in mind, used the term *psychasthenia*. He maintained that the disease was due to hereditary factors. So, Freud was the first to uncover the psychic causes of the obsessional neuroses.

The obsessional neurotic personality is characterized by certain unmis-takable traits such as a tormented conscience, cultivation of suffering with others, a strict sense of reality, and an excessive urge for order and clean-liness. The actual symptoms of obsessional neurosis are obsessional ideas and obsessional acts. The obsessional neurotic will as a rule willingly expend his normally generous reservoir of energy in endless and exhausting spec-ulation that leads nowhere. The sight of such everyday things as a pair of scissors and some knives, for example, evoke thoughts about murder and mutilation that can lead to associations about hospitals and from there to wheelchairs and the difficulties an invalid must face in trying to get up and down stairways. This is not the living out of wishful fantasies. Although there are ideas about all sorts of crimes, the obsessional acts themselves are always quite harmless: a piece of clothing is put on and taken off repeatedly, and each time it is carefully inspected for dirt and holes. After any kind of direct or indirect contact with other people (handshakes, doorknobs, let-ters) the obsessional neurotic washes his hands again and again. When out walking, he carefully avoids cracks in the pavement and feels compelled to look back and make sure that he has not stepped on an insect. If he does not follow the rules completely in every case, he is assailed by anxiety and guilt. In fact, the obsessional neurotic thinks of his entire fate as being determined by each little movement he makes. Therefore, he is continu-ously plagued by doubts as to whether he is doing the right thing. Never-theless, when he finally does reach a decision, he is well aware that it is all a figment of his imagination. Yet, this does not prevent him from imme-diately having his obsessional ideas again.

Freud believed from the beginning (that is, from around 1894–1895) that the etiology of the obsessional neuroses was a traumatic experience. The ego repressed experiences and impulses that were unpleasant, and according to Freud's theory the memories of these caused the obsessional symptoms. A similar mechanism underlay hysteria. However, the study of the obsessional neurosis led Freud to realize that what was repressed was a pleasurable experience that had been associated with unpleasure during upbringing; an example is infantile masturbation. The transformation of affect of pleasure to unpleasure thus became the core of the process of repression. This insight came during the third phase of the inception of psychoanalysis (1895–1896; see II.B.3). At almost the same time Freud advanced his hypothesis that the choice of neurosis was determined by the time at which the trauma or fixation occurred. Hysteria was supposed to emerge in the period from zero to four years, obsessional neurosis from four to eight years, and paranoia from eight to fourteen years. After the theory of infantile sexuality had been formulated, all fixation points were thought to belong to the period zero to five years. When Freud discovered that the obsessional neurotic had many anal-sadistic traits, he quite naturally established the anal-sadistic phase as the period when the obsessional neurosis became fixated (Freud 1913i). Following the introduction of the concept of the anal phase (about two to four years of age), the oral phase (about zero to two years of age) was introduced in 1915, and the phallic phase (about four to five years of age) in 1923. (See further the section on psychosexual development, V.B.2).

However, anal-sadistic traits are seldom directly observable among the obsessional neurotic symptoms. The closest approximation to sadism is probably obsessional thoughts with violent themes, such as accidents, mutilations, and murder. There is also a correspondence between the child's retention of its feces and the stinginess and stubbornness of the adult. In other cases it is clear that repression of anal wishes can only succeed through a reaction formation (see IV.A.3), which means that the diametrically opposite side of the wish emerges as a dominant character trait. Obsessional cleanliness, cleaning mania, and excessive tidiness are all reaction formations against the wish to play uninhibitedly with one's feces. Gentleness, self-indulgence in pity, and oversensitivity to aggressiveness are reaction formations against the individual's own sadistic impulses. The obsession itself in the neurosis gets its strength from an inwardly directed sadism that originally was directed toward others. This aspect of the obsessional neurosis was first brought out in the 1920s when the superego was introduced as the successor to the repressed Oedipus complex (see V.B.2.b). It is the sadistic oedipal ego that continues in the form of the superego. The stronger the original oedipal sadism was, the harsher and more unrelenting the superego becomes. The superego punishes the ego for its earlier sadism, and the ego responds with anxiety and guilt. Many of the obsessional symptoms consist of actions that serve to undo previous acts or repair the damage resulting from them. The ego feels that it atones for its guilt by obeying the slightest signal from the superego, and anxiety immediately emerges again if the rules are not obeyed. The obsessional neurotic is generally plagued with doubts. Not only must the ego obey the superego, but it must also manage the impulses that emerge from repression. An ego controlled solely by the superego is not neurotic. The neurosis appears with the return of the repressed impulses. A special mechanism related to the formation of the obsessional neuroses is shown in the isolation of volatile memories from each other instead of repressing them. Individually, they do not represent a danger to the ego.

(b) Conversion Hysteria

The prehistory of the concept of hysteria has been discussed in three earlier sections namely, those on hysteria and hypnosis (see I.B.5.b), on hypnoid theory and splitting of consciousness (see II.B.1), and on the theory of defense and the psychic primary and secondary processes (see II.B.2). As these sections show, hysteria played a crucial role in the inception of psychoanalysis and in Freud's outdistancing Charcot and later Breuer. Charcot, Breuer, and Freud had different theories on the etiology of hysteria. They agreed that among the conditions was a trauma and that hysteria manifested itself as a psychic splitting (the name of Charcot's pupil, Janet, belongs here as well). Charcot, however, had the additional prerequisite of the neuropathic constitution, whereas Breuer introduced what he called a hypnoid state, a dream state in which the individual was particularly vulnerable to traumatic experiences. According to Freud a psychic defense against the traumatic memory was the most important etiological factor. During his cooperation with Breuer, Freud tried to avoid a break by distinguishing between different types of hysteria instead of confronting the various etiological models themselves. Breuer's theory was thus used to name "hypnoid hysteria," whereas Freud's own theory found expression in the name "defense hysteria." Freud also used "retention hysteria," something between the two, to indicate that a traumatic experience had not yet been abreacted so that its quota of affect disturbed the other psychic processes. After his break with Breuer, Freud considered all forms of hysteria to be defense hysteria so that the word *defense* was superfluous in the name. However, in 1909 he identified anxiety hysteria, a special type of hysteria (which we will discuss in the next section), and thereafter true hysteria was called conversion hysteria.

During the latter half of the 1800s at a time when hysteria was still placed among the neuropathological diseases—that is, as a disease of the nervous system—special attention was directed at symptoms that manifested themselves as sensory motor malfunctions. The sensory symptoms included temporary blindness, numb or hypersensitive areas of the skin, and hallucinations. There were also diverse bodily sensations that the hysteric often identified as signs of organic disorders. Among the motor symptoms there were cramps and paralyses. When actually having an attack, the hysteric could have violent affective reactions, exaggerated bodily movements, make miming gestures, and assume extraordinary theatrical poses including positions of the body accompanied by muscle cramps of such intensity that the positions would be impossible to assume under normal conditions. Freud regarded all such symptoms as conversion symptoms. He noted their psychic organization and always found an ideational structure as their basis. A hysterical paralysis of the arm is not a sign of malfunction in the nervous system. It reflects problems concerning the hysteric's idea about his or her arm, for example, a repressed wish to strike someone. It is the psychic energy of the ideational structuring, which converts to motor innervation, that in turn causes the paralysis.

Breuer was already aware of hysterical symptoms in addition to conversion symptoms when he treated Anna O. in 1882. There were, for example, her changing moods, her maliciousness, and her sudden ability to speak foreign languages. Beyond this, Freud pointed out the sexual themes in the hysteric's fantasies, which are often about seduction and sexual abuse. Furthermore, he also identified apprehensiveness and nervousness in anxiety hysteria. Many of the symptoms that were considered to be hysterical before the turn of the century would today certainly be classified as psychotic, for example, the depressions, persecution thoughts, fits of rage, hallucinations, and the splittings of consciousness. Therefore, the *Studies On Hysteria* (Freud [and Breuer] 1895d) must be read with certain reservations. Freud did not formulate a valid etiological explanation of hysteria until the fourth phase of the inception of psychoanalysis (1896–1897; see

II.B.4), and we will now follow his views on the etiology of hysteria from that date on.

In general, hysteria had the same etiology as obsessional neurosis which was (1) a traumatic experience, (2) repression of the memory about the experience, (3) a regression to and strengthening of the memory, and (4) the return of the repressed material as symptoms. However, Freud found it difficult to find a specific place for the traumatic experience within the development of the disease. Hysterics told very similar stories about seduction and sexual abuse, but these were built on fantasies, and from around 1897 Freud believed that seduction fantasies served to conceal infantile masturbation. Furthermore, he concluded, based on frequent oral symptoms such as coughing, difficulty in breathing and swallowing, anorexia and vomiting, that oral fixation had taken place. This composite of traits, seduction fantasies, active masturbation, and oral fixation were first unified theoretically within the framework of the Oedipus complex. Symptoms in obsessional neurosis stemmed from the repressed active Oedipus complex. This was the child's wish for active mastery of the mother and elimination of the father. In hysteria, on the other hand, the active Oedipus complex had often been transformed into a passive form before the repression or defense had taken place, that is, a partially active wish to eliminate the mother and a passive wish to belong to the father. The passive drive aim was regressively intensified by a subsequent traumatic experience, and expressed itself symptomatically through seduction fantasies. The hysteric actually wanted to become the passive partner in a sexual relationship with the father. The passive oedipal and the passive oral drive aim reinforced each other reciprocally, especially in hysterical women. Here the wish to incorporate the penis through the mouth and through the vagina were closely related. With this in mind it was easier to understand why it was primarily women who were conversion hysterics while men made up the majority of cases of obsessional neurosis.

(c) Anxiety Hysteria

The group of symptoms that Freud used to delimit anxiety hysteria was the phobias, that is, anxiety tied to specific things or situations. The most well known now, as they were also in the 1800s, are claustrophobia (dread of closed or narrow places), agoraphobia (fear of open spaces), and zoophobia (fear of spiders, snakes, mice, and so on). In the 1890s Freud pointed to the presence of phobias in anxiety neurosis, obsessional neurosis, and hysteria, but it was not until 1909 that he explicitly introduced the distinction between conversion hysteria and anxiety hysteria. (He had, however, announced the change the year before in the foreword he wrote in a book by Stekel (Freud 1908f).

Etiologically, anxiety hysteria bears a close resemblance to conversion hysteria. There is the same relationship between the oral and the phallic traits, and the repressed Oedipus complex contains both active and passive sexual wishes, although perhaps there are more active wishes in anxiety hysteria than in conversion hysteria. Symptom formation is the most characteristic trait of anxiety hysteria. The repressed wish impulses are not converted into bodily innervations but are tied psychically to substitutive ideas just as in obsessional neurosis. Furthermore, not all of the anxiety that has been tied to the repressing ideas is suppressed; some of it is displaced to other ideas. Freud's final opinion was that the repressing anxiety was identical with castration anxiety and that phobic anxiety therefore was a displaced castration anxiety. In animal phobias the fear of being bitten by an animal is displaced castration anxiety about the father. The defense against castration anxiety has partially succeeded in that it is easier to avoid dangerous animals than to avoid one's own father. All it requires is staying away from places where the animals in question are to be found. There are two distinctive differences between obsessional neurosis and anxiety hysteria: (1) In obsessional neurosis the obsessions have a positive content. There are certain actions that must be completed and certain thoughts that must be thought. In anxiety hysteria, on the other hand, the obsession is negative. There are actions and situations that have to be avoided at all costs. (2) In obsessional neurosis anxiety is generally avoided by obeying the obsessional impulses. Anxiety, when it finally appears, does so as conscience anxiety. In anxiety hysteria, anxiety has assumed the form of real anxiety. It is an ever-present potential but is kept at a minimum as long as situations associated with danger can be avoided.

Freud's clinical records show that anxiety hysteria is a common childhood neurosis. It is generally easily cured (see the case history of Little Hans, IV.C.2); but it can also herald an obsessional neurosis as in the case history of the "Wolf Man" (see IV.C.5). We have previously discussed a hysterical phobia, the case of Emma, described by Freud in 1895 (see II.B.2). Freud did not discuss Emma's infantile sexuality, her Oedipus complex, or her fantasies (these concepts did not exist at that time). One might supplement the analysis by adding that she had repressed her passive sexual wishes and that the grocer's advances were pure fantasy on her part conjured up to conceal those wishes. On the other hand, if one wants to maintain that phobic anxiety is displaced castration anxiety (in Emma's case the fear of entering shops), it has to be assumed that Emma has disavowed that she has no penis. In that case the significance attributable to the grocer's advances and his close scrutinization of her clothes is that if she were observed too intensely, it might be revealed that she had no penis. Finally it should be mentioned that Freud sometimes juxtaposed the boy's castration anxiety with the girl's anxiety of losing the love object. We are therefore unable to determine how he would have analyzed Emma if his theory had been fully developed.

4. PSYCHOSES

In the German psychiatry that influenced Freud, the distinction between the organic and the functional psychoses was generally acknowledged in the 1880s (see the diagram in IV.A.). The organic psychoses were known to be related to observable anatomical changes in the nervous system. As changes of this kind could not be found in the functional psychoses, it was believed that they were caused by irregularities in the distribution of neural energy. After the turn of the century, a new distinction was introduced, namely Kraepelin's distinction between endogenous and exogenous psychoses. The functional psychoses were generally thought of as endogenous or conditioned through heredity, but there was also some acknowledgment of the idea that traumatic experiences could be contributing or provoking factors, and from about 1910 the psychogenic psychoses (called by some the reactive psychoses) were simply made a separate category.

In the 1890s Freud combined the functional neuroses and the functional psychoses to create his own special field of study. As a joint designation for these groups he, together with others, used the term *psychoneuroses*. We have mentioned that he dealt mainly with neuroses, but he also studied two psychoses in detail, namely, hallucinatory confusion and paranoia (his letters to Fliess reflect his deliberations on melancholia and hysterical psychosis). With the psychoses, just as with the neuroses, he was concerned with three questions: (1) the traumatic experience causing the disease; (2) the defense against memory of it, and (3) the subsequent symptom formation. In the first years after the turn of the century, Freud showed little interest in the psychoses. It is therefore important to point out that he had already included them in the psychoanalytic system.

Freud's association with Jung, Abraham, and Bleuler renewed his interest in the psychoses. Freud's writings had proved a source of inspiration to them when formulating a psychologically based description of the psychoses, and it was Jung who, in 1907, introduced the distinction between transference neuroses and psychoses. In 1908 Abraham pointed out the autoerotic character of the psychosis dementia praecox, and in the years around his break with Jung (1910–1914) Freud created the concept of narcissism, which he used in his description of the psychoses as narcissistic neuroses. The distinction between the narcissistic neuroses and transference neuroses was that in the former the object relation, and thus also transference ability, was either lacking or unstable. Freud's new terminology never gained popular acceptance, which probably explains why in 1924 he reintroduced *psychosis* as the name for schizophrenia and paranoia. However, he continued to maintain that melancholia should be called a narcissistic neurosis although this never gained general acceptance either. The many changes in terminology are not really at issue here. What is important is that throughout his career, Freud was aware of the psychogenic origin of the psychoses and studied the mechanisms involved in their fixation, defense, and symptom formation. He did not take an explicit stand on the division of the functional psychoses as endogenous or psychogenic, but apparently he believed that they were two sides of the same coin as with the neuroses, that is, that the cases could be placed in a complementary series with endogenous causes predominating at one end and psychogenic causes at the other.

Later psychiatric textbooks contain comprehensive conceptual systems for classifying and characterizing the psychoses. They focus in particular on describing which psychic abilities and functions have been left intact and which have been damaged. This results in categories such as disturbances of consciousness (consciousness is weakened, becomes confused, or splits), perceptive disorders (illusions and hallucinations), disturbances of the ideational process (of a formal kind, unrealistic ideas, changes in the tempo of ideational activity), and emotional disturbances (changes in mood, disturbances in interpersonal relations). Instead of this purely descriptive approach to the psychoses, Freud placed them within his genetic-structural model of the subject. He found that most of the traits, that is, self-centeredness, lack of libidinous object cathexis, the loss of the sense of reality, and domination of primary processes, were related to their narcissistic mode. This is a workable idea only if the psychotic's regression to narcissism is not taken too literally. What in particular distinguishes the neuroses from the psychoses is their reliance on the defense mechanisms of projection and denial in contrast to repression. Freud tried to set up his own structural definition by establishing a pattern of correspondence according to which schizophrenia and paranoia are related to the conflict between the ego and the external world, melancholia to the conflict between the ego and the superego, and the neuroses to the conflict between the ego and the id (1924b, p. 336). We must reject this attempt for the simple reason that psychosis also has a defense against the drives in the id, namely, projection.

(a) Paranoia

The term *paranoia* can be traced far back to the time when it was used as a general designation for insanity. In the latter half of the 1800s its meaning was narrowed to cover persecution mania and megalomania in particular, in the third edition of Krafft-Ebing's textbook on psychiatry, published in 1889. After the turn of the century Kraepelin classified paranoia as an independent psychosis alongside dementia praecox, but at the same time he also used the special classification, paranoid dementia praecox (dementia paranoides). In 1911, Bleuler adopted the name schizophrenia as a substitute for dementia praecox (see IV.A.4b), keeping paranoid schizophrenia as one of its subclasses. At the same time, he ceased to regard paranoia as an independent psychosis. Today *paranoid schizophrenia* is the term generally used within psychiatry, but there are in addition other systems that classify paranoia as an independent psychogenic psychosis. This has led some writers to go one step further and introduce a distinction between the adjectives *paranoid* and *paranoic*.

Freud used the term *chronic paranoia* prior to the turn of the century, inspired perhaps by Krafft-Ebing. He distinguished it from hallucinatory confusion on the basis of different defense mechanisms. The (defense) mechanism in paranoia is projection whereas in hallucinatory psychosis it is detachment from some part of reality. In 1896 when Freud presented his theory on the specific points of fixation of the psychoneuroses, he placed paranoia as occurring later than both hysteria and obsessional neurosis, that is between the ages of eight and fourteen. Yet, in a letter to Fliess dated 9 December 1899, Freud stated just the opposite (Freud 1985b). Here he explained paranoia as the return to the original autoerotic stage and connected hysteria and obsessional neurosis with object eroticism, developing at a later stage. The next time Freud turned to consider paranoia was in his discussion of Schreber's case (1911c), where he used the term *dementia paranoides*. Freud's classification is somewhat unclear, however, since he rejected both the terms *dementia praecox* and *schizophrenia* and introduced instead *paraphrenia* which was given up after a few years. In the end he distinguished between the two distinct pathologies of schizophrenia and paranoia, the latter also including dementia paranoides. They were distinguished on the basis of three items: their symptoms, their defense mechanisms, and the time at which fixation occurred. The clinical picture in paranoia included many kinds of delusions, but a dissociation of the personality as in schizophrenia did not necessarily occur. More specifically it concerned persecution mania (including delusion of observation and delusion of interpretation), megalomania, delusion of jealousy, and erotomania. In the early stage of persecution mania, the paranoid individual felt that he was being watched and seen through. Later on he developed far-fetched fantasies about being spied on, poisoned, and irradiated by imaginary enemies. He was generally persecuted by important people or institutions (the Pope, God, the queen, the secret service, and so on). The paranoid individual could also assume foreign identities, believing he was Jesus or Napoleon, for example. Gradually he lost interest in the external real world and became permanently engrossed in himself and his own abilities. He felt that he was equipped with supernatural powers that made him capable of turning stones into bread, killing and resurrecting the earth's entire population, and changing the movements of celestial bodies. Jealousy and erotomania existed in many forms, but in paranoia they were combined with delusions. For example, the paranoid individual could insist that he knew with absolute certainty that his wife was being unfaithful when in fact there were no grounds for such a belief.

Freud's explanation was that the various symptoms were the results of a defense against the paranoid individual's own latent homosexuality. The homosexuality did not necessarily have to have been manifest before the onset of the disease but could have existed in a sublimated form as social relationships with other persons of the same sex. The defense set in when there were indications that a real homosexual love relationship was in the offing. The choice of defense mechanism, when a narcissistic fixation already existed, was the withdrawal of libido to the ego. Megalomania then arose, sometimes accompanied by fantasies of the end of the world. In the ensuing phase there was an attempt to return the libido to the object presentations. However, as this would constitute a homosexual object choice, a new defense mechanism was activated, namely, projection. Before they could be projected, the homosexual impulses had to be further distorted; the result was that the reconstructed world view of the paranoid individual was characterized by delusions. There was a transformation of affect in the persecuted paranoiac, so that homosexual love was transformed into hate. The projected hate made the paranoiac believe that he was being persecuted by the original object of his homosexual love. The jealous paranoiac projected his homosexual love onto his wife who was then suspected of heterosexual infidelity. There was least distortion in erotomania where rejected homosexuality was expressed as excessive heterosexual interest. Projection was not as clear-cut; it consisted only in that the erotomaniac felt that he was erotically interesting to all individuals of the opposite sex.

Freud achieved a deeper theoretical understanding of paranoia in his Schreber analysis by placing a narcissistic stage of development between the autoerotic and the object erotic stages (see the section on the development of the psychic structures, V.B.2.b). Paranoia was characterized by a narcissistic fixation and the paranoid mechanisms were the same as those that characterized narcissism: self-conceit, omnipotence of thought, projection and introjection, ambivalence toward the object that was initially considered to be an "extraneous remainder," and a disposition for a narcissistic (homosexual) object choice. However, paranoia was not exclusively narcissistic but also clearly comprised a negative (homosexual) Oedipus complex where the father was introduced as an ideal object for the male paranoiac and the mother for the female paranoiac. It was this ideal object with which the paranoiac identified in the early phases of his disease and that later assumed the role of persecutor.

(b) Schizophrenia

It was Kraepelin who in 1896 first identified and described the disease generally called schizophrenia. His name for it was dementia praecox, also popularly known as adolescent dementia. He identified the three pathological traits that are still used diagnostically today: (1) the hebephrenic (particularly changes in the emotions), (2) the catatonic (particularly motor disturbances, odd ceremonial gesturings, rigid positions of the body, and hallucinations), and (3) the paranoid (delusions of persecution, see IV.A.4.a). In 1911 Bleuler changed the name from dementia to schizophrenia, noting that the disease did not cause a general reduction of intellectual capacity (dementia) and that it did not necessarily begin in early youth (praecox). Schizophrenia means a split of the mind, and Bleuler's innovation was his attempt to create a more specific psychological description of the disease than Kraepelin had done. Bleuler associated schizophrenia with two successive processes. In the first one, there was a dissolution in which the psychic associations and functions broke apart, so to speak, and this was followed by the second process, in which they were erroneously reassembled to form new wholes, apparently organized more along emotional lines than along logical ones. This resulted in the characteristic schizophrenic symptoms that Bleuler called autism (emotional isolation from the surrounding world and absorption in one's own fantasies) and ambivalence (the simultaneous presence of opposed feelings concerning the same person and of opposed intentions).

During the 1890s Freud worked on a case of hysterical psychosis and on one of hallucinatory confusion both of which had traits in common with schizophrenia. He was familiar with the defense mechanism that consisted of suspending all contact with the surrounding world. After the turn of the century, he said nothing more about these psychoses. However, Bleuler's assistant Jung adopted Freud's ideas on neurosis and dreams and applied them with reasonable success. In 1908 another of Bleuler's assistants, Abraham, described dementia praecox in psychoanalytical terminology. Bleuler himself learned from his students and was also influenced by Freud. Thus it can be said that indirectly Freud was coresponsible for the development of the concept of schizophrenia, though he never liked the name itself. In the 1890s he described psychic splitting between the ego and what was repressed, and in the same connection he rejected the concepts of splitting that had come from Bleuler and Janet. Therefore, it undoubtedly piqued him to see Bleuler reintroduce a concept of splitting that was very similar to Janet's (dissociation, inability to make syntheses). During the 1920s Freud began to discuss splitting in an entirely new, third sense in connection with the psychoses and the neuroses. He found a splitting in the ego that caused two different attitudes to occur toward the object and reality, namely a concurrent acceptance and disavowal of gender difference (see IV.A.2.c, on fetishism).

Schizophrenia was one of the diseases to which Freud paid least attention. He did not believe it could be treated psychoanalytically because it was impossible for the analyst to establish transference relationships with the schizophrenic. He placed it at an even earlier phase of fixation than paranoia. In the analysis of Schreber (Freud 1911c), he found schizophrenia to be at the autoerotic stage of development, and in his later writings, he placed it at the narcissistic stage. Almost none of the organizational forms acquired are kept intact in the process of the schizophrenic's regression to narcissism, as is true for the paranoiac. The schizophrenic's own body is central in his fantasy world. Hypochondria is an initial state of schizophrenia, but gradually the organs of the body become embued with symbolic meaning indicating the existence of a psychic conflict. Freud said that the speech of schizophrenics was an organ language to emphasize that meaning was expressed within the very narrow alphabet of the body image. For example, a schizophrenic girl who said that "her eyes were not right but twisted" was actually only expressing a complaint about her fiancé. "She could not understand him at all, he looked different every time; he was a hypocrite, an eye-twister, he had twisted her eyes; now she had twisted eyes; they were not her eyes any more; now she saw the world with different eyes" (Freud 1915e, p. 198). Some schizophrenics astonish the people around them by speaking a totally incomprehensible jibberish. In Freud's view this indicates an attempt to get well, to break out of narcissism and regain contact with the surrounding world. The reason the attempt fails, however, is that the schizophrenic cannot grasp real things and people. He can only grasp words, which are then treated as things. This is a phenomenon also familiar from the dream work in which each word and expression is taken letter for letter, in schizophrenia, however, the entire vocabulary is treated this way.

The neurotic defense, repression, is directed toward what was originally pleasure giving but has become associated with unpleasure due to influences from the surrounding world; the ego sides with the surrounding world in the conflict with the id. In schizophrenia the direct opposite occurs. The schizophrenic defense, disavowal, is directed toward what originally was unpleasurable, especially the unpleasure coming from the surrounding world, and in this case the ego sides with the id in the conflict against the surrounding world.

(c) Melancholia and Mania

Melancholia and mania were among the first psychic diseases to be delimited and described. They figured prominently in the works of the well-known nineteenth-century psychiatrists Pinel, Esquirol, and Griesinger. They comprise the early stages of the unity psychosis in which only feelings and not the intellect have been affected. Many writers noted that the same patient could alternate between melancholia and mania, be depressed and excited, and Kraepelin combined the two clinical pictures and named the disease manic depressive psychosis (*melancholia* was translated as *depression*). However, the course the disease takes shows that there are considerable individual variations and that actual manic periods seldom occur. Freud considered melancholia to be a narcissistic neurosis in the same way as paranoia and schizophrenia were, and he kept this name even when he agreed to classify the latter two as psychoses. He distinguished explicitly between a psychogenic melancholia and a spontaneous melancholia (1912c), *spontaneous* probably referring to *endogenous,* and he was only interested in psychogenic melancholia. The etiology of the disease comprises the following aspects: fixation at the narcissistic stage of development (including prominent oral traits), object choice as in the narcissistic type, and marked ambivalence in the object relation. When this disposition is present, the loss of the love object is capable of provoking melancholia. Freud described the normal reaction to loss as mourning, which consisted of a withdrawal of interest from the external world. The mourner's spirits were at a very low ebb, and he lost his desire to do anything. The lost love object stayed locked in his memory and there was nothing else with qualities superior enough to be able to replace it. Although the mourner would hardly permit anyone to comfort him, he nevertheless generally recovered from the loss sooner or later.

Because melancholia resembles mourning in many respects, Freud meant that the disease was contingent upon object loss. The melancholic, however, is not aware of his object loss. Instead he traces all of his woes back to himself.

> In mourning it is the world which has become poor and empty; in melancholia it is the ego itself. The patient represents his ego to us as worthless, incapable of any achievement and morally despicable; he reproaches himself,

vilifies himself and expects to be cast out and punished. He abases himself before everyone and commiserates with his own relatives for being connected with anyone so unworthy. He is not of the opinion that a change has taken place in him, but extends his self-criticism back over the past; he declares that he was never any better (Freud 1917e, p. 246).

But, as Freud said, if one listens carefully to the self-accusations, it turns out that they do not apply to the melancholic himself. He is not criticizing himself but rather those individuals who are or have been close to him, and the self-accusations turn out to be accusations against them. This serves to explain why the melancholic speaks in an injured tone rather than in one of repentance or shame. He is not ridiculing himself but others. Perhaps he has been disappointed or jilted in love, and because of his predisposition, he adopts a narcissistic reaction pattern to deal with the suffering, not a total regression to narcissism but an identification with the lost object. The object does not stay in the memory as it does in mourning. It is introjected into the ego, and there it enters into a more or less perfect synthesis with the ego's other qualities (see V.C.3.a on identification). Once love has been disappointed, ambivalence causes hatred of the object to predominate. This too is known to be a normal reaction pattern, for example, when the feelings of the rejected lover change to hate. Thus, a pathological outcome presupposes narcissistic object choice as well as ambivalence.

In melancholia the ego and the superego are kept as separate elements. It is only the ego that is emptied of libido as a result of the introjected bad object. The superego continues to exercise its critical function over the ego, and the ego, now empty of libido, is a defenseless object for the sadism of the superego. The occasional change to mania occurs when the ego and the superego coalesce. Freud compared the manic patient to someone who was drunk and to the poor man who suddenly acquired wealth. When the pressures on the ego are suddenly lifted, it plunges, now free of restraint, into all sorts of projects—including new sexual relationships—makes grandiose plans, and ruthlessly brushes aside any hindrances in its path. Whereas the melancholic avenged himself on the introjected object, the manic individual, Freud said, avenged himself on the oppressing superego. These relations can only be understood within the context of the Oedipus complex. In both cases, however, the Oedipus complex stands on the ground of narcissism. Both self-effacement and self-conceit are characterized by delusions with a disturbing effect on the sense of reality, and none of the object relations are particularly stable.

B.

THERAPY

Freud's therapeutic method was especially created to treat transference neuroses. It is a form of psychotherapy that differs markedly from traditional somatic and medical therapies. Characteristically, it uses dialogue as its medium and deals with symptoms by analyzing and interpreting them. Freud's therapeutic approach can be compared with his method of interpretating dreams. Dreams are caused by repressed wishful fantasies that by some indirect means become conscious, and the process of interpretation retraces the dream work back to the wishful fantasies (see III.A). Similarly, neurotic symptoms are formed from repressed wishful fantasies, and by interpretating the symptom it becomes possible to reconstruct the etiological factors, particularly the traumatic experiences, around which the wishful fantasies have crystallized. Therapeutic analysis does not end simply with the uncovering of the repressed experience. A cure involves additionally a dissolution of the structures or constellations of ideas producing the symptoms. Furthermore, the analysand must work through the repressed experience so that he accepts it emotionally and intellectually, finally integrating it into his personality. This part of therapy is often far more demanding than uncovering what has been repressed.

We have structured this section around the relationship between the analysand and the analyst. One could say that each of them has a role to accept in order to achieve satisfactory results. Freud determined these roles by combining various sources (suggestion therapy, catharsis method) and from testing the combination in practice. During the inception of psychoanalysis (1886–1897) Freud's work exhibited a very fine alternation between theory and practice, in other words, between the general psychological model and the therapeutic method (see II.B). In the ensuing years these two dimensions were continuously attuned to each other. The most detailed account of the therapeutic method appeared in Freud's six papers from 1911–1915 on the techniques of analysis (1911e, 1912b, 1912e, 1913c, 1914g, 1915a). These are the sources that enable us to describe the demands he made on the analysand as well as on the analyst, the subject matter of sections IV.B.1 and IV.B.2. In section IV.B.3 we will discuss in broader terms the process of therapeutic analysis and its goals and also present a historical evaluation.

1. THE ANALYSAND

Freud mainly treated transference neurotics, that is, obsessional neurotics and hysterics. This group of patients consists of people who get along so well in daily life that there is no need for hospitalization and who come to a psychoanalyst of their own accord. This last point is important because the analyst has to rely on a good deal of cooperation to carry out the analysis. In the case of actual neuroses, the analyst may be able to indicate the factors causing the disease, but a formal analysis is unwarranted since the disease would automatically disappear on its own once these factors were eliminated. Similarly, in the perversions, pressures in the surrounding world are what make the perversions a problem. If the pervert were able to satisfy his sexual wishes with no limitations, he would feel no need to change himself. Freud realized that the perversions could not be thought of as psychic diseases. He therefore only treated them when specifically asked to do so. The result of treatment is seldom satisfactory because the pervert's personality is not dominated by the repressed impulses but by clear sexual impulses. However, there may be repressed genital and heterosexual impulses that can be strengthened. For example, some homosexuals might be "converted" back to heterosexuality if the latent heterosexual impulses were strengthened, but Freud did not specifically state that he ever succeeded in doing this.

The typical clinical picture of the transference neuroses can be understood in relation to the ego's dependence on the id, the superego, and the object (see the diagram in V.C.1.b). The ego becomes neurotic because it is unable to manage the impulses coming from the other three sources. The id demands satisfaction that is inconsistent with the ideals and anxiety preparedness of the superego. The ego therefore is also forced to relinquish the possibilities actually available for gaining satisfaction. Instead the demands of the id and the superego become synthesized into neurotic symptoms. For Freud, one of the goals of therapy was to strengthen the ego and he stated that the starting point of analysis was a pact between the patient's ego and the analyst, who had placed himself in the object's place. Their combined efforts were then used to resolve the conflict between the id and the superego, this conflict being the core of the neurosis. In effect this meant that the ego was able to defend itself against the oedipal wishes of the id by other means than repression. The choice of reaction would in principle be wiser when it was based on the total experiences of the id than when it was made solely on the basis of the idiosyncrasies of the superego. It was the task of the analyst to help the ego recognize instances where repression was used as a defense and to enable it to see the advantages in using self-reflection instead of this defense.

In the psychoses the relation between the ego and the object has itself been damaged. The ego does not distinguish between the internal and the external world according to ordinary criteria, but relies instead on its emotions. The internal world consists of pleasurable ideas while the external world is considered to be unimportant, foreign, or even cruel. Therefore, the analyst finds it difficult to establish any pact at all between himself and the psychotic ego or to establish meaningful conversation. Regardless of whether or not the analyst is able to analyze the symptoms, he still lacks the means of relaying his conclusions to the psychotic. The psychotic ego is under the direct influence of the id and even though it has some defense mechanisms available for use against the impulses of the id, it still does not have the necessary foothold in reality to enable it to make a pact with the analyst. Freud himself abstained from taking very many psychotics in analysis for this very reason, but it should be mentioned that many of his students and followers have tried to adapt the therapeutic technique to facilitate the treatment of psychotic patients. This forms a chapter of its own in the history of modern psychoanalysis.

The question of the analysis of children has also been raised. In 1909 Freud published an analysis of a horse phobia of a five-year-old boy (1909b; see IV.C.2). In his opinion this analysis was an exception only made possible by Hans's exceptional intelligence. In general he maintained that the analysis of children could not be sufficiently thorough for two reasons. Intellectually, children could not master the concepts that the analyst had to use to relay his ideas, and children were not able to give their thoughts and feelings linguistic expression. Very soon, however, therapeutic techniques were developed in this area as well, spoken language being supplemented by other significant forms of communication such as games, drawings, and arranging toy figures into patterns.

(a) Demands on the Analysand

Based on his experiences in therapy, Freud established a set of rules for both the analysand and the analyst. The intention behind these rules is clear enough: to avoid all the snares and pitfalls that appear in analysis. Freud was very careful to point out the adverse consequences of failing to follow the rules, in many cases having had to learn from his own mistakes. Freud's rules are still used by many analysts today and they can also have relevance outside the analytical situation because they reflect general laws that are valid for relations between subjects (intersubjectivity).

Before analysis can begin, the analysand must accept the formal framework of the analytical situation. Briefly, it is a question of time, place, and money. Freud found it most advantageous to carry out the analysis in one stretch, only interrupted by Sundays, holidays, and vacations. The analysis of one person could easily take from six months to several years. First there was a trial period of a few weeks to ascertain whether or not the therapy was suitable. An analytical session lasted one hour and was scheduled for the same time every day, for example between 3 and 4 P.M. This hour was at the total disposal of the analysand, but he also had to pay for it if he stayed away. As a rule Freud accepted neither illness nor family visits as excuses for not coming. He had discovered that many patients used such excuses when analysis reached a critical stage, and he therefore found that in the interest of the patients themselves, the fee could be used as a means of exerting pressure. The same reason led him to refuse to give free treatments. This took away the patients' incentive to get well and could, moreover, place the analyst in a difficult financial situation. Freud preferred a monthly settlement of the fee and was reluctant to give long-term credit. The analysand could terminate analysis at any time, but Freud naturally warned about the dangers involved in doing so.

Cartoons have made well known the fact that analysis takes place with the analysand lying on a couch. The analyst places himself out of the analysand's field of vision behind the head end of the couch. Freud's reasons for using this arrangement were that he could not stand being stared at eight hours a day and that patients were distracted in their train of thought when trying to search his face for signs of approval or disapproval. Once or twice Freud fell asleep during a session, but this was not the reason for this seating arrangement.

At the start of analysis the analysand and the analyst form a pact. The analyst promises full discretion similar to that sworn in a doctor's oath of confidentiality, and the analysand promises to hide nothing from the analyst. He must say everything that comes into his head even if it seems insignificant, meaningless, or embarrassing; this is the fundamental rule of analysis. The analysand can talk about whatever he wants as long as he does not come prepared or use too many abstract concepts. A prior knowledge of psychoanalysis can do more damage than good because it can cause the analysand to sort out thoughts and memories that might otherwise prove useful to the analyst. The purpose of the fundamental rule of analysis is to lift censorship, providing easier access to consciousness for the repressed. Sudden thoughts and impulses that have no clear connection with what has just been said stem in all probability from the unconscious; this is the principle behind free association. In the beginning Freud used hypnosis to gain access to the unconscious, but it had the drawback that the analysand often denied what he had said after he had been brought out of the hypnotic state (see II.B.1).

The fundamental rule of analysis must not be confused with the stipulation of complete candor. The analysand must remain on the couch and as far as possible he must express himself verbally. His position on the couch limits his field of vision. This proves effective in focusing attention on internal impulses. The cure presupposes an increase in self-understanding, and this cannot be achieved through spontaneous nonverbal expressions. In addition to the distinction drawn between verbal and nonverbal modes of unconscious expression, Freud made an even more subtle distinction between remembering and acting out. The ultimate demand made on the analysand is to have him consciously remember repressed experiences since otherwise they will return and be expressed as neurotic symptoms. Even the most distorted and twisted symptoms are repetitions of conflicts between repressed sexual wishes and the repressing anxiety. Freud spoke of acting out when distortion was at a minimum and symptoms were most clearly expressed. The neurotic expresses earlier emotional attitudes, ties, and conflicts in the present without any awareness of their past origins. This is most obvious in transference where the neurotic's childhood conflicts with parents and siblings are transferred to the neurotic's actual surroundings. Because the transferred feelings can both be hostile and loving, a distinction must be drawn between a negative and a positive transference. The clearest indication of transference is that the recipient of the transference has himself done nothing to provoke the respective feelings.

In *Beyond the Pleasure Principle* (1920g), Freud described very precisely how infantile experiences were repeated in the guise of transferences:

> The early efflorescence of infantile sexual life is doomed to extinction because its wishes are incompatible with reality and with the inadequate stage of development which the child has reached. The efflorescence comes to an end in the most distressing circumstances and to the accompaniment of the most painful feelings. Loss of love and failure leave behind them a permanent injury to self-regard in the form of a narcissistic scar, which contributes more than anything to the 'sense of inferiority' which is so common in neurotics. The child's sexual researches on which limits are imposed by his physical development, lead to no satisfactory conclusion; hence such later complaints as 'I can't accomplish anything; I can't succeed in anything'. The tie of affection, which binds the child as a rule to the parent of the opposite sex, succumbs to disappointment, to a vain expectation of satisfaction or to jealously over the birth of a new baby—unmistakable proof of the infidelity of the object of the child's affections. His own attempt to make a baby himself, carried out with tragic seriousness, fails shamefully. The lessening amount of affection he receives, the increasing demands of education, hard words and an occasional punishment—these show him at last the full extent to which he has been scorned. These are a few typical and constantly recurring instances of the ways in which the love characteristic of the age of childhood is brought to a conclusion.
>
> Patients repeat all of these unwanted situations and painful emotions in the transference and revive them with the greatest ingenuity. They seek to bring about the interruption of the treatment while it is still incomplete; they contrive once more to feel themselves scorned, to oblige the physician to speak severely to them and treat them coldly; they discover appropriate objects for their jealousy; instead of the passionately desired baby of their childhood, they produce a plan or a promise of some grant present—which turn out to be no less unreal (Freud 1920g, pp. 20–21).

In addition to the fundamental rule of analysis and the rule of verbalization and remembering, there is a third rule, the so-called rule of abstinence. The analysand is encouraged to avoid changes in his social situation, for instance, making new friendships, getting married or divorced, changing jobs, having a baby. Furthermore, he is advised not to discuss the analysis with his family. These requirements are the direct result of the fundamental rule of analysis. With the lifting of censorship in the initial phases of analyses, a good deal of libido is released and becomes available to the analysand. A natural reaction is to want to reinvest it immediately, for example, in a new love affair or to confide even more in a spouse, but this is inadvisable because the neurosis would not disappear but merely assume some other form (active participation in a religious movement, for example, can occasionally make symptoms disappear. Freud called this an indirect cure). The purpose of the rule of abstinence is to concentrate as much of the freed libido as possible in the analytical situation, generally as transferences to the analyst himself. The analysand is thus prevented from doing things he would come to regret later. Moreover, the analyst gets a privileged knowledge of the analysand's drives that is beneficial for the analysis as a whole.

(b) The Analysand's Resistance to Being Cured

Therapies of a romantic nature assume a drive that propels the patient toward getting cured. The doctor is not supposed to cure the patient, only help him to cure himself. Nor is he even supposed to eliminate the forces that work contrary to the cure. His function is only to help the patient remove them himself since resistance to the cure is part of the disease. It was probably ideas of this kind that led Freud to create "resistance" as a collective concept for all of the analysand's acts that impeded the arousal of consciousness and cure. Freud had already suspected the hindrances in the external environment, and he analyzed them according to the same pattern as parapraxis (see III.B). If a patient forgot his analytic session, broke a leg, or got pneumonia, Freud saw this as an unconscious intention, and resistance was made responsible for a brilliant strategy carried out behind a patient's back and his conscious self-understanding. In his more romantic formulations Freud almost turned resistance into an opponent, an internal double that was in opposition to the ego. He even personified resistance in the superego, which, as a pure state of the death drive, was in constant conflict with the rest of the individual.

Resistance manifests itself in analysis when the analysand fails to adhere to the rules. He tries to avoid saying everything that is on his mind, gives expression to his earlier experiences through transferences, and criticizes the analyst to his family and friends. Moreover, he refuses to accept the analyst's interpretations labeling them as improbable and refusing to admit things he has said previously. A major part of the work done in analysis is expended on overcoming resistance. If the analysand has difficulty in accepting that his symptoms are an expression of sexual wishful fantasies, perhaps instead he can be brought to see that his resistance actually pervades his entire personality and that progress can be made in analysis by searching for the causes of the resistance.

Resistance did not pose any theoretical problems for Freud as long as he could relate it to the pleasure principle. Originally, he thought of it as he had thought of defense (see II.B.2) that is, as an inappropriate way of reacting that was maintained in order to avoid an unpleasurable affect. The analysand's efforts to hide something from the analyst that he finds embarrassing are quite obvious, and this is equally true for the unconscious function of censorship and repression resistance. The inappropriate way of reacting is strengthened even further when it is the source of pleasure itself. The primary and secondary gain from illness can be so great that there is no motive for getting well. Freud says that the war veteran who begs for money from passers-by does not really want to regain the use of his limbs because doing so would deprive him of his income. The neurotic is similarly reluctant to give up his disease because it provides him with a certain continuous measure of attention, sympathy, and pity.

Freud also considered transference to be a form of resistance especially when in the extreme, positive or negative, form. In positive transference the analysand identifies the analyst either as the sexual ideal (particularly so for analysands of the opposite sex) or as the ego ideal (here by analysands of the same sex). Transference love and idealizations of the analyst cause such a degree of focusing on the analyst that the desire to get well abates considerably, and analysis can go on indefinitely. A similar situation arises in hypnosis and suggestion therapy when the patient obeys the doctor's orders to get well. Freud was critical of this method and tried to avoid intense transference by warning against it from the outset. Needless to say, intense negative transferences are detrimental to analysis. Hatred and mistrust of the analyst render cooperation and the pact, which are prerequisites for the analysis, impossible, and often result in the analysand's walking out of analysis. Freud had a number of such cases, but could do nothing about them because he was strongly opposed to any kind of coercion.

Freud had a very good conception of resistances of this kind insofar as they obeyed the pleasure principle. Yet, he was made uneasy by the increasing number of cases in which resistance seemed to be unrelated to any interest in attaining pleasure or avoiding unpleasure. It was as if some neurotics deliberately sought the unpleasure of the disease and refused to get well. He called this resistance the negative therapeutic reaction, and he introduced the death drive in 1920 (see II.C.2). The will to disease and to resistance against getting well were viewed as an indication of a drive in all people and all living organisms toward death and destruction. We will not discuss the concept of the death drive in any detail here, but we do want to point out that the negative therapeutic reaction actually includes two different mechanisms, or rather, the same mechanism can be explained in two different ways. First, the will to be ill can be related to a need for punishment or for an unconscious guilt feeling. The patient punishes himself with his disease without knowing what he has done to deserve the punishment. Perhaps primary masochism is involved (see IV.A.2.a) or perhaps it is an attempt to overcome castration anxiety. The patient may reason, "If I take my punishment now, then I will not be caught off guard by any unexpected punishment. Second, the negative therapeutic reaction always contains some element of repetition, a repetition compulsion. The mistreatment to which the neurotic subjects himself corresponds to some earlier traumatic experience. The repetition compulsion reflects one of the ways in which the unconscious functions in general, it maintains a certain inertness, and it is unaffected by the pleasure or unpleasure content of what is repeated. When a previously pleasurable experience is repeated, it goes unnoticed because it seems so natural, but when an unpleasurable experience is repeated, our normal ability to identify with it fails. We think of it, as Freud did, as a sinister, inhuman, mechanical, and almost supernatural compulsion. Freud could not find a therapeutic treatment for this kind of resistance.

2. THE ANALYST

We are used to dealing with other people exclusively in terms of the functions they have whether they are a cashier, doctor, taxi driver, or police officer. It is customary, however, in our conversations with such people to make informal or personal comments that blur the line between the official and the more personal aspects. We are, nonetheless, seldom in doubt as to where the line is: one of the functions is related to power and money, the other has to do with feelings. Even when feelings are a commodity, insofar as that is possible, there is very little confusion. There are, however, relationships in which the two overlap. A teacher can use the emotional dependence of his students to facilitate learning. An artist can get a following by publicly displaying his feelings, and a politician can get votes by letting himself be portrayed in a magazine as a family man and a trustworthy individual.

One need not be an expert in role playing to realize how difficult it can be to speak sociably with someone whose official or professional capacity already involves feelings, and the more feelings that are involved, the harder it becomes. These remarks should help to point out Freud's considerations of the double role of the psychoanalyst as business man and private individual. The analytical situation involves very intense feelings par excellence and it can prove difficult for the analysand and the analyst to deal with these feelings outside the analytical sessions. As mentioned, Freud had valid reasons for imposing abstinence on the analysand. Abstinence made the analysand invest the major portion of his feelings in the analyst thereby making analysis a more intense experience. This made another rule necessary, however. Private social interaction between analyst and analysand had to be avoided to prevent the analysand from quite naturally extending his transferences into the social sphere. The two thus had to avoid contact outside the analytical situation itself. Even the fact that the analyst knew the analysand's family could prove to be a burden, as was exemplified in Freud's discussion of his analysis of his dream about Irma's injection (see III.A.2.a). It is self-evident that the analyst and the analysand must not be related; however, Freud broke his own rule when he analyzed his daughter, Anna Freud, for a brief period.

(a) Demands on the Analyst

The psychoanalyst must, of course, be properly trained to do his job. During the first years after the turn of the century, when the psychoanalytic movement only consisted of Freud and a handful of supporters, Freud's only demand generally speaking was that his ideas be accepted. Moreover, he also recommended that each person analyze his own dreams as he himself had done, thereby becoming familiar with the unconscious. Freud probably considered the ability to analyze the most important qualification of a psychoanalyst, and this skill had to be acquired by working with patients. He lashed out at wild psychoanalysts, people who used the ideas of psychoanalysis without joining the movement, and he gradually realized that a formal training program was necessary for advancing psychoanalysis.

During the years around World War I an increasing number of analysts turned to colleagues for analysis, and in the 1920s it became a standing requirement that all new psychoanalysts had to undergo training analysis. This rule was not effected retroactively, and Freud, for example, never went into analysis with the exception of his self-analysis. We have mentioned how the American group succeeded in pushing through a proposal that would only allow medical doctors to enter psychoanalytic training (see II.C.2). Freud objected to this but could not get it reversed despite strenuous efforts on his part.

The most important methodological demand on the analyst is that of the even suspension of attention (*gleichschwebende Aufmerksamkeit*). Freud considered this to be the counterpart of the fundamental rule of analysis. In principle the analyst must be just as open-minded as the analysand. He must not try to analyze while the analysand is speaking, and he must refrain from making notes except in instances where he intends to publish his case histories. (Freud's journal of the analysis of the "Rat Man" still exists for this reason). The consciousness of the analyst must be free of any influence related to what the goals of his theory may be. The term *even suspension of attention* means that attention spans all the material offered by the analysand and that it must be kept in a state of suspension and not focus selectively on any one trait. A long period will often elapse before the myriad of details form a comprehensive pattern of ideas. Freud saw this crystallization as a result of the analyst's unconscious work. If the analyst tries to record everything the analysand does or says, he will from the outset force himself into making choices. He can avoid this by allowing his unconscious to register and then connect the details. The conclusions the analyst arrives at appear as sudden insights. Once this happens, however, he has to be able to reflect theoretically and formulate hypotheses about the traits that are still hidden, possibly as "constructions" (see the next section) and if necessary, expand or revise current theory.

The rule about letting the unconscious do the analysis carries with it the assumption that the analyst himself is not under the influence of repressed complexes. The purpose of training analysis is to ensure that this is the case and eventually resolve complexes that might exist. Every unresolved repression corresponds to a "blind spot" in the doctor's analytical perception, Freud said (1912e). It could be added that just as every retina has a blind spot, the analyst too has the repressed Oedipus complex in common with his neurotic patients. The analyst has managed to reduce its influence to a minimum and to make himself conscious of its influence. Freud also stated that the analyst had to analyze his countertransferences to the patient very carefully to prevent them from influencing the course of analysis.

The analyst must be neutral in many respects. He must not give the analysand's statements a moral, political, or social interpretation based on any such standards. He must not give the analysand advice within the analytical situation with the exception of the demands inherent in the fundamental rule of analysis and in the rule of abstinence. The analyst must avoid using his personality to dominate his patient. His own attitudes are irrelevant as are his feelings. Like a surgeon he must intervene without pity and use all of his psychic powers to address the task at hand. Freud felt, actually, that the analyst had to protect his own emotional life.

(b) Shortcomings and Weaknesses of the Analyst

The demands on the good analyst made by Freud can appear somewhat idealistic, and it is not difficult to indicate situations where one could not adhere to them strictly. They were probably formulated as an attempt to offset the errors Freud typically observed in his students and that he too perhaps had once committed.

The demand of the even suspension of attention paints a negative picture of the analyst as someone who immediately has to resort to theory in order to classify his patients and who schematically charts his patients' childhood, their case histories and their family relationships. Detailed protocols of analysis reminded Freud of the ostensible exactness he knew from psychiatry, and he did not feel that this was any way to remedy the lack of evidence in psychoanalysis (1912e).

The demands of neutrality and of avoiding countertransference are related. In Freud's view, at any rate, it was a serious mistake for the analyst to descend from his withdrawn position and behave like someone of "flesh and blood." The conscientious analyst, for example, should not try to create an atmosphere of confidentiality by revealing his personal secrets to the analysand, and needless to say he must not let his sympathies and antipathies become involved. He must only show that he is personally annoyed if it is relevant to the analysis, and it is a serious mistake to allow a positive transference of a patient to turn into a love affair.

As mentioned earlier (see II.C.2), Freud found it difficult to accept Ferenczi's "active analysis." Freud agreed that the analyst did not have to be passive, since the way he communicated his analysis to his patient was of paramount importance. Freud could also accept that in special cases the analyst might have to give advice and offer counsel. He could, for example, convince a patient not to commit suicide (the abstinence rule might well be applicable here). But he could not accept Ferenczi's idea of direct emotional involvement or even of bodily contact with patients and viewed it as a definite departure from the principles of psychoanalytic therapy.

The conflict between Freud and Ferenczi cannot be explained in terms of personality differences. The contrast in approaches still exists within modern psychotherapy, where there is a clear difference of opinion as to whether realization takes place through bodily and emotional expression or through an increase in self-understanding. This contrast can also be traced back to the relationship between a romantic and a rationalistic attitude toward therapy, Ferenczi leaning toward the romantic view and Freud toward the rationalistic.

3. THE PROCESS OF
THERAPEUTIC ANALYSIS AND ITS GOALS

Obviously, the demands for the analyst and the analysand do not contain all of the principles of analysis. The analyst must be prepared for and able to deal with a number of situations that typically occur in analysis. He must decide in what way he will give the analysand his interpretations, whether the patient should be allowed to play his transference to an end through him, and whether he will determine a definite period within which analysis must end in order to overcome the patient's resistance. It goes without saying that the goal of therapy is to restore the patient's health. However, this did not prevent Freud from having several points of view about the polarity of disease and health, each of which shapes the guidelines for the therapeutic process and its goals.

(a) The Therapeutic Process

The driving motivation in analysis is the analysand's request for help. A certain degree of awareness of the disease on the patient's part is thus a necessary condition for entering analysis. However, the analyst cannot promise to limit the analysis to the symptoms that are apparent at the beginning of analysis, for example, a nervous headache or a particular phobia. Once analysis starts, new and far more threatening symptoms may appear, and by then, it is too late to go back. Freud found that analysis could not be directed. The individual neurosis determined the course of analysis. Once a loose thread was chosen, it had to be followed to the end. Stopping midway would be the equivalent of letting the patient leave the operating table in the midst of the operation.

In the first sessions of analysis Freud's rule was that the analyst must say as little as possible and wait for the patient's transference. He pointed out that there would always be transference if only because of the rule of abstinence. The libido, which had been freed, had no other recourse than to turn to the analyst. The silence of the analyst served to sharpen the intensity of the analysand's expectations of the analyst. As long as the analyst did not reveal anything of his own personal life, then what emerged was the general attitude that the analysand already had toward other people. The analyst had to be as opaque as a mirror reflecting only what was actually enacted in front of it. Once the transfer relation had been established, the neurosis changed and became a true transference neurosis. The untreated neurosis also had elements of transference since all neurotics made the people around them bear the brunt of their Oedipus complex to some extent. However, these transferences were often so distorted that they could not be understood. A conversion hysteric who transferred the wish to kill her father to an innocent party did not attack that person; instead she got a muscle spasm in her arm. The undistorted oedipal wishes would be expressed in front of the analyst, which therefore meant that the transference would be directly apparent.

Since transference is a sort of acting out, and as such is in contrast to remembering (see IV.B.1.a), why did Freud not encourage his patients to remember their Oedipus complexes instead of sitting quietly and waiting for their transferences? Freud did not cease to think of transference as a danger in therapy. Yet he considered it necessary since very little progress was made using remembering alone. It is easier to analyze a present experience than some childhood memories that have been forced into consciousness and in which perhaps the patient takes no interest. The enemy must be confronted directly, not in absentia. In childhood the neurotic lost the struggle for the love object because he had to resort to the self-suppressing defense mechanism of repression. In the new struggle, the analyst is alternately object and opponent, and in this situation it becomes crucial for the neurotic to come through the struggle without any repressions. If he realizes that he can live through the Oedipus complex and master it without his ego's being totally disabled, then the previously repressed Oedipus complex will lose some of its force, and the ego can be convinced to give up its defense positions against the id. The transferences to the analyst will now also be dismantled. The importance of the analyst in the analysand's conscious will diminish because he, in fact, has only been an impersonal and abstract mirror for the patient's transferences.

The transferences affect almost every aspect of the material dealt with in analysis, and the analyst must make the patient aware of this. The transferences can manifest themselves as resistance when the patient does not come to a session or when he hesitates to tell the analyst what is on his mind. In addition, there are symptomatic actions directed toward the analyst, who also begins to appear frequently in the patient's fantasies. We have already mentioned that Freud saw no purpose in rattling off childhood memories during analysis; however, once the emotions associated with them were aroused, it was naturally vital to bring to light the traumatic experiences related to them. Freud even "constructed" childhood experiences for his patients when their memories failed, and these constructions could sometimes have the same effect on insight as real memories. Moreover, Freud defended the use of hypothetical constructions as being in principle a fully acceptable means of gaining access to the unconscious by stating that fantasies, which were fictive traumatic experiences, were the most important structures of the unconscious.

If you are afraid of the water and want to get over your fear, jumping in once is not enough; you have to do it several times to get used to it. The same is true of the neurotic who shrinks from giving up his resistance to getting well all at one time. Every experience that has ever undergone repression has some amount of resistance attached to it, and piece by piece these experiences must be retrieved from repression. During periods in analysis when no progress is being made, resistance is overcome step by step. Freud calls this process working through. The purpose of working through is to integrate the repressed experiences into the ego, thereby combining the qualitative aspects of emotional experiences with an intellectual understanding. Resistance to integration can be directed toward the emotional as well as the intellectual aspects. Some patients can achieve remarkable intellectual insight into their neurosis without reliving its causes, and they therefore fail to resolve the repressions. Others have no difficulty in experiencing traumatic scenes of major significance to their neurosis but fail to accept their consequences and give up their actual transferences.

In one of his last articles, "Analysis Terminable and Interminable" (1937c), Freud abandoned the idea of totally integrating the id and the ego, his idea of "where the id was, the ego must be" (Freud 1933a, p. 80; see V.B.1). No matter how long the analysis lasted, there would still be some neurotic traits left, and a successful analysis was no assurance that a new neurosis would not erupt. If this was so, analysis became a life task, a process of continued self-reflection and self-analysis even when the actual analysis itself had ended. Freud raised a delicate issue here by asking whether the analyst ought not to work actively to evoke all kinds of transferences, the positive as well as the negative, in order to be sure that all potential dispositions for future neuroses had been removed. In actual fact it was Ferenczi who had raised this problem in connection with his own active analysis. Ferenczi had personally reproached Freud for not including the negative transferences in his analysis of him in 1914 and 1916. Freud, nevertheless, was skeptical about this form of prevention, and he may have had more reasons than he stated explicitly. He had seen many analysts whose own analyses had only led to even greater psychic conflicts; several committed suicide. This led Freud to conceive of the death drive. He could, however, also have resorted to his favorite image of the analyst, the surgeon. The rule in surgery is not to excise as much as possible but rather only to do what is necessary for the survival of the patient. A psychoanalysis can lead to much more than integration and bringing repressed ideas into consciousness. As a by-product it can also provoke or even create unconscious fantasies that can prove to be even more of a burden to the patient than those he originally had. This is another reason why analysis can go on indefinitely.

(b) The Goals of Analysis

Infantile sexual experiences are always present in Freud's descriptions of the etiology of neurosis. In the end, symptoms are traced to repressed ideas related to such experiences. This does not, however, give a clear indication of how to cure a neurosis. What is it the neurotic actually has to experience in order to be cured? The strengthening of the ego, which we have mentioned, is an approximation to Freud's ideas. However, close examination shows that many other issues are involved. There is no immediate awareness of this because Freud uses numerous well-known and apparently universal principles about the psychic health of human beings. In part 1 of this book we made a distinction between three historical subject concepts that, within scientific, philosophical, and aesthetic disciplines, have influenced psychoanalysis. Using them as our focal point we have also been able to point to three different traditions, or modes of thought, that have contributed independently to Freud's view of therapy and its goal. Each influenced Freud successively during the inception of psychoanalysis from 1886–1897, but all of them retained a certain measure of influence in his therapeutic practice, and this in itself can explain some of the contradictions we have encountered thus far.

(1) According to the rationalistic disease concept, psychic illness is characterized by intense dominance of feeling. Development stops prematurely resulting in an inappropriate and maladjusted mode of functioning. The dominance of emotion makes the patient's behavior appear to be out of control and compulsive. The motto of the therapy is: *Enter reason!* The patient must learn self-control and how to take responsibility for his social actions. He must regain his freedom. This means not only his social freedom, being permitted to leave the mental hospital, but also his freedom of will, which according to liberalistic-rationalistic thought is related to reason. Tuke and other moral therapists stood as representatives for this type of therapy. Despite certain romantic ideas (such as that patients should leave the city and go to the country), they were basically good rationalists. They tried to resocialize the insane (see I.B.5) by giving them simple jobs and exerting moral pressure on them, including teaching them how to compete with each other. Freud approached this therapeutic technique by looking at Bernheim's suggestion therapy. Under hypnosis the patient was ordered to come to his senses and to give up his unreasonable and foolish symptoms. Both Tuke and Bernheim used their authority as doctors to facilitate the curative process. On later occasions Freud stated that he found Bernheim's method to be demeaning. As a precaution against this he instituted the principle that the analyst must not violate the individuality of the patient. If the patient were not given the opportunity to make decisions of his own free will, he would then hardly benefit from the cure. This difference of views between Freud and Bernheim shows Freud to be a liberalist in a truer sense of the word than Bernheim. Freud felt that it was not the doctor's function to impart reason because it would be tinged with the doctor's own moral and ideological attitudes. Instead, it should

come from the principle of reality and necessity (necessity of life, or *ananke*). The idea of therapy as a process of restoring reason can be found many places in Freud, for example, in the direction of development from the pleasure principle to the reality principle, in his use of the term *post education* about the theory, and in the effort to strengthen the patient's ego, as already mentioned.

(2) According to the romantic disease concept, the cause of a disease often turned out to be a foreign element that, coming from some external source, entered the soul and distorted and perverted natural emotions. In figurative terms (and in literature) it is expressed as demoniacal possession, as for example, in E. T. A. Hoffmann's *The Devil's Elixirs* (1813–1816) and in Hans Christian Andersen's *The Snow Queen* (1845), where a small piece of a troll's mirror gets lodged in little Kay's heart. In such tales, a good person can suddenly be transformed into an evil one. Sometimes the personality is split into a good and an evil part that alternately dominate, and sometimes the evil part is a double that tries to destroy its counterpart. Dramatizations of this sort are thinly veiled criticisms of contemporary societal reason: It is this compulsory form of reason with all of its egoism and calculation that contaminates feelings and changes them into dangerous and demonic forces. The motto of this therapy is: *Exit evil!* And translated into a broader program: Feelings must be allowed to develop naturally otherwise they will become demonic. Once they come under demonic influence, the conflict escalates and the patient must, as a rule, experience a serious crisis that either leads to his death or to his recovery.

If we are to give an example of romantic therapy it must be Mesmer's hypnotic therapy. The very provocation of an attack had a curative effect. Mesmer had witnessed so-called exorcisms himself, so the connection is undeniable (see I.B.5.b). Freud is also known to have studied a text from the Middle Ages on the subject in 1897 (*Malleus Maleficarum* from 1485 by Institoris and Sprenger). However, Freud's most important source for a therapeutic technique with romantic traits was Breuer's so-called catharsis method in which the patient obtained psychic purification through verbal expression (see II.A.2). For many years Freud thus considered the hysterical attack to be a delayed attempt to abreact a traumatic experience. Therapy, then, consisted of trying to release the suppressed affect while under a doctor's supervision. Only when this was successful would the symptoms disappear. Another romantic trait in Breuer's theory was his idea that the split-off ideas constituted an independent intelligence as significant as the conscious ego. Perhaps this is the wellspring from which Freud got his idea of personifying the psychic agencies (ego, superego, and id). For the sake of completeness it should be mentioned that the mechanical aspect of the catharsis method—the release of suppressed affects—had a correlate within medicine. This was the frequent use of bloodletting and clysters, the purpose of each, in its own way, being to release internal pressure.

Hypnosis creates a special tie between the hypnotist and the hypnotized person called rapport. Breuer's report on his treatment of Anna O. drew Freud's attention to an interesting aspect of this rapport, namely the sudden emergence in the patient of feelings of love for the analyst. Freud realized that the doctor was highly overestimated by his patient, but as mentioned above, Freud did not believe that a position of authority should be used to inculcate reason. The more he came to understand the nature of trans-ference, the greater was his conviction that the entire process took place inside the patient's own world of ideas. The doctor himself was an outsider whose role was almost that of an exorcist. He struggled with the inner demon in the patient in an attempt to replace the bad father (the devil) with himself in the role of the good father (God). In Freud's view, however, the good father was nothing other than the patient's recovered superego. The analyst's status is merely an abstraction that the analysand is free to give concrete form. The authority of the analyst is an artificiality, and Freud's decision to keep it distinct from the person of the analyst is a wise one. As a consequence the analytic dialogue cannot be an exchange between two equally competent subjects. This is not because the analyst is in any sense better than the patient, but because he as a person is in principle not actually present in the analytic situation.

(3) Although our intention now is to discuss the naturalistic disease concept as a source of inspiration for Freud, we do not have the psychiatrists who were oriented toward the natural sciences in mind. Their descriptions and nosologies were of vital significance to Freud, but their therapeutic method was somatic and mechanical and therefore only of minor signifi-cance in relation to psychotherapy. What we do have in mind are the ideas that were at the fore in the humanistic sciences and in literature that foreshadowed an entirely new source of human undoing: lying. A certain moralizing interest has of course always been focused on lying and the new aspect consisted only in looking upon lying as a defense mechanism that is used far too often by the ego, exerting an effect on rationality in general, and pervading the entire organizational fiber of society. When lying is used as a defense, whether done so consciously or not, the liar digs his own grave. The unpalatable truth will sooner or later demand its due. The more

it is concealed by new lies, the more serious the final breakdown will be. Therefore, the motto of the therapy is: *The truth must forth!* It is in this sense that Freud spoke of therapy as making conscious. He assumed that there would be an improvement in almost every case if the unconscious became conscious. If a patient can bear to hear the truth and will accept it, his life will be markedly improved. Yet the truth can be so brutal that it may totally disable him. In Scandinavian naturalism (Brandes, Jacobsen, and Ibsen), inspiration from the natural sciences led to a belief in an objective truth. Their declaration expressed the view that the elimination of hypocrisy in religion and in morality would result in sweeping improvements throughout society (see the discussion of Jacobsen and Ibsen, I.B.6.b).

We are aware that Freud was attracted by the idea of enlightenment, and perhaps this represents the reverse side of the theory of transference. As long as the analyst remains silent, he can only have the role of an abstract second party; however, once he begins to present his interpretations and helps in eliciting the truth, it becomes difficult to maintain his objectivity and neutrality even if his unconscious is doing the work. Freud's idea that the unconscious or the id is the abstract and impersonal aspect of the subject should not automatically lead us to ascribe a truth function to the unconscious so that the analyst is relieved of responsibility for his analyses. Freud sought to remedy this deficiency in his theory by placing more emphasis on countertransference, which in this connection is the sum total of all the concrete and individual traits in the analyst as a person. An epistomological evaluation of the problem *per se* lay beyond Freud's theoretical field of vision. Having said that, we hasten to add that the dimension of lie/truth is mainly relevant in connection with Freud's discovery of the defense. It was precisely in his conception of defense that Freud from 1892–1893 surpassed Breuer. Freud placed the major responsibility for the cause of neurosis on repression, which was originally understood as a conscious attempt to forget embarrassing experiences. Without being aware of it, the neurotic is controlled by his earlier lies, his earlier forgetting of what was embarrassing. Therefore Freud also characterized the hysteric's repression as a "proton pseudos," an early, original lie that turned the rest of the person's life into a web of new lies. The patient's scope of activity was drastically reduced, and he used most of his energy trying to avoid, evade, cover up, and rationalize events in his life. For many years Freud considered his primary therapeutic task to be *finding* the truth that the lie had repressed. His failure in therapy, as already mentioned, led him to create an additional analysis of resistance, and this analysis of "the lie about the lie" lengthened the therapeutic process, making it more difficult without changing its principles.

We have now reviewed three aspects of analytic therapy, tracing them back to the three subject concepts. We have shown how they existed concurrently in Freud's mind as three different routes to therapeutic integration: (1) an adaptation between the individual and his environment by inculcating the ability to reason; (2) a reincorporation of the split-off parts of the personality by exorcising evil, and (3) a reconciliation between the past and the present by uncovering the truth about the past. In our opinion, however, the synthesis of these points raises certain issues, since they modify each other reciprocally and in the end Freud had additions to make to all of them. Those theoretical issues, as we see them, are: (1) the reality principle, which is not directly applicable to sexuality as it stands, and is therefore not applicable to the psychology of the neuroses either; (2) the unconscious, or the id, which will always contain non-integrated elements no matter how long or how conscientiously analysis is carried out; and (3) truth, which is not an objective criterion because the lie/truth dimension within as well as outside neurosis is determined by the psychic reality of the fantasies. With these few theoretical comments, we have introduced the issues to be dealt with in part 5. We will return to them again in section V.C, on the structure of the subject.

C.
CASE HISTORIES

Between 1905 and 1918 Freud published five comprehensive case histories, each about one hundred pages long (Freud 1905e, 1909b, 1909d, 1911c, and 1918b). These case histories mark the pinnacle of his production and consist of concrete examples that show how Freud analyzed the disease symptoms of individual patients and in four cases how he treated them. The cases are vividly elaborated, arousing the reader's empathies as the pathogenic structures are gradually revealed. Moreover, a chronological reading of them furnishes a closer understanding of how Freud, starting with concrete problems, developed his nosography, his therapeutic technique, and his general theory of the genesis and structure of the subject. Finally, the case histories can easily be read as examples of how family relations in the upper social echelons created the best possible conditions for the development of neurosis. The spheres of production and circulation exerted pressure on the sphere of intimacy, which affected child rearing by making it an increasingly complicated and convoluted process, causing friction, tension, and conflict. The child's ideational world became correspondingly complicated and contradictory, and conflicts that had been inadequately solved in childhood left their undeniable traces on the entire life history of the individual as a typical neurosis.

If every perspective were to be discussed, a book could easily be written on each of these case histories. Our discussion places emphasis on two issues: the etiology of the diseases and the mechanisms involved in the system formation. For clarity's sake we will depart from our usual procedure, which has been to follow closely Freud's own development chronologically. Instead we will use Freud's theory from the 1920s about the relation among the phallic phase, the Oedipus complex, and the superego as our point of departure and give a reading of the case histories with these concepts in mind. In fact, the case histories helped pave the way for the new concepts.

The development of infantile drives is generally divided into three successive phases (oral, anal, and phallic), which lead to the organization of the genital drive in the adult (see V.B.2.a). The phallic phase, in which the sensitivity of the boy's penis and the girl's clitoris predominate, can be subdivided into four phases, or factors, that are based on the relationship between the ego and the object. (1) In what may be called the active phallic phase, the ego is intent on dominating and controlling the object. The activity cannot be adduced from any of the physiological functions of the phallic organ. The connection between the active and the phallic is created through the active masturbation of the boy and the girl, and is often accompanied by fantasies about the object. (2) The first repression occurs with the awareness of the anatomical sexual difference. Masturbation ceases abruptly, as do the fantasies that accompanied it because of castration anxiety in the boy and a feeling of inferiority, among other things, in the girl. Freud believed that in numerous cases infantile sexual development stopped at this point and was supplanted by the formation of the superego. (See also the discussion on primal repression in V.C.2.b.) (3) However, there are factors that indicate that there is another defense mechanism that can appear either instead of or as a supplement to repression. This is the reversal of the active aim to a passive one. This leads to passive wishes to have the sexual organs stimulated by someone else, and as a consequence of the castration complex, to receive gifts from others. Freud saw this as a typically feminine attitude. (4) In many cases even the passive wishes will be repressed, but this other repression will be less apparent than the first one. According to Freud, the passive sexual attitude is relinquished not so much because of its threatening nature, but because of a disappointment. The girl gets neither the satisfaction nor the presents she has anticipated, and if the boy is to live up to the expectations from the people around him, he is forced to adopt a defense against his own passivity.

Freud believed that some sign of a complete Oedipus complex, that is, a positive (heterosexual) and a negative (homosexual) element, could be found in everyone. Thus, the positive Oedipus complex of the boy (love for his mother and hatred toward his father) is identical to the girl's negative Oedipus complex while her positive Oedipus complex (love for her father and hatred toward her mother) is identical to that of the boy's negative one. This symmetry is actually the sign of a more fundamental parallelism between the development of the boy and the girl. Both first reach the stage where they love the mother and hate the father. This occurs at the end of the anal phase and in the active-phallic phase. These two sexual organizations mutually reinforce each other, which is quite apparent in the clinical picture of the obsessional neuroses. The Oedipus complex in this case can, where both sexes are concerned, be called the active Oedipus complex. Oral traits will often reappear in the passive phallic phase due to the preponderance of passive impressions in the oral phase, and it is now these two sexual organizations that mutually reinforce each other as is shown in the clinical picture of hysteria. The Oedipus complex for both sexes in this case is called the passive Oedipus complex. This is illustrated by the following diagram:

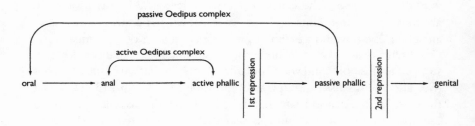

In each of the five case histories Freud tried to show how one of the configurations of oedipal wishes had been frozen fast because either excessive or inadequate defense mechanisms were used to overcome them. The symptoms were a compromise formation between the oedipal wishes and the defense. The most straightforward way to interpret symptoms is to relate the oedipal wishes and the anxiety motivating the defense to specific traumatic experiences, for example, a scene where the little boy masturbates, is caught, and is threatened with castration. Freud, however, could not always find traumatic experiences of this kind, and even when he did, he found it difficult to understand why the effect was so severe. He came to the conclusion that the structures involved were a combination of real experiences and invented fantasies. Infants, of course, do not understand all that they experience, sexual matters in particular represent an inexplicable riddle causing endless speculations. In lieu of satisfactory explanations they use their fantasies to create a number of false explanations that become psychic reality but in an unconscious and repressed form. The result is that the children then resist all subsequent attempts to give them adequate sexual information. These are the unconscious fantasies that essentially are part of the symptom formation in neuroses, psychoses, and perversions.

A few typical infantile fantasies follow. In terms of the Oedipus complex, the child shows an interest in its parents' sexual relationship. It thinks of coitus as an act of violence in which the father attacks the mother. The mother gets pregnant because she took the father's spit into her mouth, and the baby is born through the anus. To the boy, sexual differences exist because the girl has been castrated and castration is thought of as a punishment. The girl blames her mother for not giving her a penis. During this period both sexes take it for granted that the mother has kept her penis although other women have lost theirs. A penis-lacking creature is the object of scorn. Thus, the girl becomes the object of her own self-hate. Some children explain their own sexuality by describing a scene in which they were seduced, an older sibling or a parent having misused them sexually. They have been forcibly introduced to sexuality.

The model above is to be used as a guide in understanding the sexual development of the five patients. They all progress from oral to genital development. They differ, however, in terms of the intensity with which they live through each of the phases, which in connection with the defense mechanisms result in different fixations. These are later intensified by regression and are the determinants of the symptom formation. Sexual attitudes stemming from two contiguous developmental phases will always interrelate. For example, oral fantasies about assimilating objects through the mouth will be connected with anal fantasies about assimilation through the anus, and similarly anal fantasies about defecating will correspondingly be associated with phallic fantasies about losing the penis. A further connection is that between fantasies with active content (particularly between the anal and the active phallic attitude) and between fantasies with passive content (that is, between the oral and the passive phallic attitude). These are the typical relations, but the picture becomes even more complex because the oral and the anal phases can be subdivided into an active and a passive using purely physiological criteria (see the section on the genesis and development of the sexual drives, V.B.2.a). As the respective case histories show, Freud always attempted to reconstruct the development of infantile sexuality although in his analysis of Schreber, he did this on the basis of pure guesswork. In our account, which is highly summarized, we must place main emphasis on these reconstructions. Anyone wishing to follow Freud in his process of gradually uncovering the infantile material, is referred to the original texts.

1. DORA (Conversion Hysteria)

Dora was the pseudonym of an eighteen-year-old girl who started an analysis with Freud during the fall of 1900. She suffered from various hysterical symptoms, primarily a bothersome cough that led to hoarseness and periodic loss of voice. She had furthermore become unreasonable and uncooperative, reserved, and dispirited. After a feigned suicide attempt and a fainting fit, her father sent her to Freud for treatment. The analysis only lasted three months and Dora interrupted the treatment because she was dissatisfied with Freud's effort. At the end of the three months, some of the symptoms had been removed, but not all of them. Freud wrote the case history in 1901, but first published it in 1905 as a "Fragment of an Analysis of a Case of Hysteria" (1905e).

Dora's family was Jewish and came from Bohemia. The father, Philip Bauer, was a wealthy manufacturer who owned two textile mills. He was described as the dynamic figure in the family, charming, intelligent, and affable. Freud described the mother, Käthe Bauer, as uneducated and unintelligent, yet with enough authority to torment the rest of the family with her cleaning mania. Freud had very little to say about Otto Bauer, the older brother (born in September 1881). He avoided the family fights as far as possible although in critical situations he sided with his mother. After he grew up, he became a leading figure in the Austrian Socialist party and was the minister of foreign affairs from 1918–1919. The last member of the family was "Dora," or to use her real name, Ida Bauer (born 1 November 1882).

The effect that the tensions in the home had on the children at a very early age is not difficult to imagine. The relationship between the parents was only tolerable because the two managed to avoid each other. The father's failing health can only have served to intensify the emotional pressure felt by the children. In 1888 he contracted tuberculosis, and they moved south to a milder climate. Freud referred to their new town as B. In 1892 Bauer suffered from a detached retina. The treatment was difficult, and in 1894 he consulted Freud with a complaint of "confusion." Freud associated this symptom with a syphilis the father had gotten prior to his marriage, and Freud started treatment. Apparently it was successful. Several years later Freud was chosen to treat Dora.

Dora had an extremely poor relationship with her mother, whom she despised and ignored. From the time she was very young she felt a great affinity for her father, and when he fell ill, she was the one he preferred to nurse him. The mother never went near his sick bed. In B. the family made friends with the Ks, a younger couple with two small children. Dora's functions were taken over by Mrs. K., and there is every reason to believe that she soon became the father's mistress. In the beginning Dora approved of this relationship, and she found compensation by taking loving care of the Ks' children just as she did what she could to see to it that her father and Mrs. K. could be alone. Later, she became a bitter critic of this unseemly relationship.

In adolescence Dora fell in love with Mr. K., wrote to him when he was traveling and received small presents and acknowledgments in return. Once when they were alone in his shop, he suddenly embraced and kissed her, but she broke loose and ran away. A few years afterward during a vacation at an alpine lake (called L. by Freud), he tried once more to approach her. Again Dora reacted promptly; she slapped his face and ran away. Later she told her parents of the episode but it was hushed up. No one wanted a scandal, and the whole thing was explained away as the lively imagination of a young girl. Even her former "friend," Mrs. K., failed to support her on this occasion. Dora got the impression that her father, without telling her, had wanted to give her to Mr. K. in exchange for Mrs. K. This suspicion intensified her symptoms and brought her to Freud for treatment.

From the information gathered in analysis Freud was more or less able to reconstruct Dora's psychosexual development. She was very fixated at the oral stage. She sucked her thumb until she was four, and her father told Freud that he had to make her stop. There is nothing that indicates how he did so. Dora remembered as a child sitting on the floor in a corner sucking her left thumb while "pinching" her brother's earlobe with her right hand. There is no corresponding sign to indicate the importance of the anal phase, so it must be assumed that it only played a minor role in Dora's development. At the same time, Freud found clear signs of what we have called the active phallic phase. Dora continued to wet her bed until the age of seven or eight, and Freud took it for granted that this was related to her active masturbation. Masturbation had simply replaced thumbsucking as a source of pleasure, children having no other means for finding release from sexual tension than to urinate. Dora did not remember ever having masturbated, but according to Freud, this was due to the defense against remembering. She did remember, however, being awakened by her father at night to urinate so that she would not wet her bed.

It is likely that being awakened this way was a crucial event in Dora's psychosexual development. On the face of things, her father spared her the unpleasantness associated with bedwetting, but being awakened in this way can be interpreted as being watched over, which in itself can be a means of enforcing the ban against masturbation. Whether or not her father actually mentioned her touching herself under the covers, his sudden appearances at night reminded Dora of situations where he had caught her sucking her thumb. If Freud had been cognizant of the castration complex at the time, it would certainly have occurred to him that Dora had seen her father's penis during these nocturnal visits. According to Freud's later theory, the awareness of sexual difference is the girl's primary motive for ceasing to masturbate. In the normal psychosexual development of the boy, castration anxiety is the driving force behind the repression of the Oedipus complex. In the development of the girl, there is a reversal from active to passive sexual aims, that is from active phallic to the aims of the passive phallic phase, and thus from the active to the passive Oedipus complex. Dora's understanding of the situation could have been that she either could not or must not masturbate. Instead she was to wait for a penis and for sexual stimulation from someone else. Passive expectations of this kind can be a rather unstable reaction formation against the earlier active wishes that have had to be repressed. In Dora's case, her passive Oedipus complex was intensified by a memory of an earlier passive oral satisfaction from her mother's breast. Dora's hope was that she might get a similar satisfaction from her father and his penis. She had lain awake at night, waiting for him to come, and she had been slightly anxious thinking about the presents he had brought back for her from his trips. From about eight years of age, when she stopped wetting her bed (and masturbating), there was an obvious change in her behavior. She changed from boy to girl, from tomboy to a polite and quiet child. If it were not for the onset of the neurosis, this development would have been a very normal one. It does seem to indicate however, that the role provided for the girl and the adult female in the middle class family pattern is itself conducive to neurosis.

Freud explained the difference between normal and neurotic development in the following way: In normal development of the girl the passive Oedipus complex gradually disappeared because she realized that it was futile to wait. Somewhat delayed in relation to the boy, she passed into latency. In Dora's case, however, there must have been a pathogenic repression of the passive wishes. The condition for the repression was a transformation of affect, that is, a change from the pleasure associated with wish fantasies to unpleasure. After the transformation of affect, Dora gave up her wish to have her father stimulate her clitoris, and she only felt unpleasure and anxiety if anyone tried to make sexual advances. Several causes for the transformation of affect can be mentioned: she could have had such an intense feeling of expectation toward her father that frustration alone could produce a reaction. Furthermore, the anxiety preparedness that her father's earlier efforts to stop her thumbsucking had aroused could have become associated with the new wish. Freud himself mentioned that Dora's vaginal discharge (fluor albus) could have had the overall effect of making her react with disgust toward anything sexual.

Dora exhibited decidedly hysterical symptoms from the age of eight. In a later section (see V.C.2.b) these symptoms are described as a compromise formation to denote that a single symptom has to be analyzed into three component parts. These are the three impulses for action stemming from the id, the ego, and the superego. The id attempts to use the symptom to obtain substitute satisfaction. The choice of symptoms tends to resemble the wishful fantasy as closely as possible. The aim might be achieved through the secondary gain from illness, which is one way of getting attention and support otherwise not forthcoming gratuitously from the environment. The superego causes the ego to have guilt feelings about repressed wishes as if they still were a part of the ego. The ego tries to reduce the guilt feelings and reestablish a balance by punishing itself with symptoms that often prove quite painful to the individual. The ego assigns its special characteristics to the symptoms through reaction formation which conceals the original wishes either through reversal or by strengthening of the opposite.

The most pronounced symptoms of conversion hysteria resemble identifications. They are difficult to analyze because they can resemble ordinary somatic symptoms completely, and they can be traits borrowed from other hysterics. The same hysterical cough can have existed in a family for generations and be handed down from mother to daughter. Hysterics are quite ingenious when it comes to acquiring each other's traits, often without being aware of this themselves. Dora's first hysterical symptoms took the form of an asthma attack when she was eight years old. She had the attack during a walk in the mountains while her father was away on a trip. The father had himself been forbidden by his doctor to take walks in the mountains because of his tuberculosis, and then Dora managed to get a

similar order. There is no doubt that this symptom represented an identification with the father. It came while he was away and arose through the
mechanism Freud called identification with the lost or absent object. The
identification was only related to "a single trait" of the father's (see Freud
1921c, p. 107), and the symptom did not indicate a general regression to
the active Oedipus complex where Dora's father was still her favorite object.
The condition did, however, allow the active wishes room for expression,
as Dora prided herself on taking good care of her father and the K.s'
children, just as she took a "fatherly" interest in seeing to it that hindrances
to her father's affair with Mrs. K. were removed. The eighteen-year-old
Dora's feigned suicide note resembled a previous incident in which her
father invented a suicide story to explain his relationship to Mrs. K. (It
was supposedly Mrs. K. who succeeded in talking him out of it.)

Another series of identifications were directly associated with the passive
Oedipus complex. Dora identified with several of her rivals by borrowing
their most common traits. These women were her mother, Mrs. K., a few
nurses, and a cousin who was jealous of her younger sister. This female
universe was subject to paradoxical rules which Dora tried unsuccessfully
to understand: Men were desirable because they had financial means; they
could give women presents and take care of them, but their sexual "presents" had no value. Indeed, they were more akin to something dirty.
Women only gave themselves to men in return for material compensation.
This attitude was not at all consistent with Dora's original sexual wishes,
neither the active nor the passive, but it was readily assimilated into her
hysterical symptoms. For example, from her mother and Mrs. K. she
learned how hysterical symptoms could be planned so as to coincide with
the travel schedule of the two husbands: When they were away, the women
had no symptoms; when they returned, the health of both women suddenly
declined in order to avoid having marital relations. Dora used this ploy for
the opposite reason; when Mr. K., to whom she had transferred her love,
traveled, she lost her voice. She was thus completely free to concentrate on
her letters to him, and when he returned, she got her voice back and could
speak to him. Gradually, however, she was forced to change her attitude.
When she started having vaginal discharge and her "catarrh," she realized
that her mother had many real somatic symptoms caused by her father's
venereal disease. Her father had had other women before his marriage, and
his disease was the reason the mother and the daughter were suffering
now. This knowledge provided the material for Dora's hysterical fantasy
about seduction and defilement. She had a reaction formation against her

own sexual wishes and was dominated by the idea that all men were out to misuse her sexually. This affected her relation with Mr. K.

At the age of twelve Dora developed a nervous cough with a characteristic spasmodic rhythm that did not disappear until after analysis. Freud said the cough was a symptom of Dora's identification with Mrs. K.; Mrs. K. had no cough, but Freud found another connection. By questioning Dora he learned that she was aware of her father's declining potency. He was scarcely capable of having intercourse in a normal way, and Mrs. K. therefore had to help by using her mouth. Whether this actually was the case or not, Freud said that Dora's desire was determined by the fantasy image of Mrs. K. with the father's penis in her mouth. The pleasant childhood memory of herself with her finger in her mouth and a soft earlobe in her hand is perhaps only a screen memory for this fantasy. The fellatio fantasy could be conscious for several reasons. Dora had repressed her active as well as her passive sexual wishes, and her jealousy of Mrs. K. made the idea unbearable. The fantasy picture could only find expression as a symptom and Dora's spasmodic cough was a recasting of the thrusting movement the penis made in the mouth and throat. The cough also served to punish Dora for her sexual desire and her wish to be in Mrs. K.'s place with her father. Dora's hysterical rejection of Mr. K.'s advances later on also had oral traits associated with it. After being kissed by Mr. K. when she was fourteen, she had a loathing for food for a long time afterward in addition to her other symptoms. Again, at the age of sixteen when she responded to his remarks by slapping his face, she had just finished smoking a cigarette that he had given her.

Freud wanted to publicize his analysis of Dora to show how his interpretation of dreams could be used in actual practice. It was, in fact, his interpretation of two of Dora's dreams that led him to uncover the pathogenic material. Dora had the first dream several times. The first time was during the summer vacation when she slapped Mr. K. The dream was told as follows:

> A house was on fire. My father was standing beside my bed and woke me up. I dressed quickly. Mother wanted to stop and save her jewel-case; but Father said: 'I refuse to let myself and my two children be burnt for the sake of your jewel-case.' We hurried downstairs, and as soon as I was outside I woke up (Freud 1905e, p. 64).

For the sake of comprehensiveness the relevant day and memory residues have been divided into four groups.

(1) During the previously mentioned summer vacation Dora and her father were visiting the K.s in a summer chalet situated near an alpine lake. They arrived the evening of a terrible storm. The wooden house had no lightning rod, and they discussed the danger of a fire ("A house was on fire . . ."). The father planned to stay several days after which Dora would stay on alone with the K.s. After the unfortunate episode on the walk with Mr. K., Dora took a nap but was awakened by his presence at her bedside ("My father was standing beside my bed and woke me up."). Dora wanted Mr. K. to leave, but he replied that it was his bedroom and he had a right to be there. She tried to find the key the next afternoon, but it was missing, and she suspected Mr. K. of having taken it. In the morning she dressed quickly in order to avoid being taken by surprise by Mr. K. ("I dressed quickly."). She decided, furthermore, to leave with her father, feeling that she could have no privacy as long as she stayed with the K.s (in the reversal of the dream: ". . . as soon as I was outside I woke up").

(2) Just before this vacation Dora had overheard an argument between her parents. Her mother wanted to lock the dining room at night. Dora's father opposed this because Dora's brother slept in a room to which there was only access through the dining room. He warned that something could happen at night so that Dora's brother would need to leave the room. Dora interpreted this as meaning the danger of fire (". . . Father said: 'I refuse to let myself and my two children be burnt for the sake of your jewel-case.").

(3) The jewel case is significant in another context. It had become the custom in the family's social circle to give each other presents. This had developed most likely because the father bought expensive presents for Mrs. K. and in order to try to conceal this, he began to give presents to his wife and Dora. Once when the mother had wanted a pair of pearl droplet earrings, she got a bracelet with the same pearls as those on the earrings instead, and she became angry. Dora would have liked the bracelet. Mr. K. had given her a jewel box, creating for her the problem of whether she, like Mrs. K. in relation to her father must make herself sexually available in return.

(4) Finally, one of Dora's childhood memories was involved in the dream. The fact that Dora wet her bed and that her father used to wake her to prevent the bedwetting has been mentioned ("My father was standing beside my bed and woke me up."). There is a symbolic similarity between "danger of water" and danger from fire. There is a saying that

children who play with matches wet their beds, and apparently Freud believed that masturbation led to the same result. Thus, the dangers of water and of fire betoken sexuality. The association is strengthened even further by the connection Dora made, from what her mother had told her, between her vaginal discharge and her father's venereal disease.

Dream formation starts when an unconscious and repressed dream fantasy occupies the preconscious day residues, producing a preconscious dream wish (see III.A.1.a,b). Normally, there is a certain degree of similarity between the unconscious and the preconscious dream wish (the "capitalist" and the "contractor" of the dream) such that interpretation of the latter is confirmed by interpretation of the former. The relationship may turn out to be a different one in the dreams of neurotics because the defense mechanisms and repression, in particular, are more pronounced. The two dream wishes may very well be contrary to each other, and this was the case in Dora's dream where the repressed wishful fantasy consisted of Dora's passive Oedipus complex while the preconscious dream wish was made up of the hysterical reaction formation against this Oedipus complex.

The preconscious dream wish is not difficult to analyze. Dora was afraid that she would be sexually molested by Mr. K. and wanted to escape. Freud recounted it as follows: " 'I must fly from this house, for I see that my virginity is threatened here' "; " 'I shall go away with my father, and I shall take precautions not to be surprised while I am dressing in the morning' " (Freud 1905e, p. 85). The dream wish was fulfilled in the manifest dream, but at the same time it was also displaced to other thematic areas because it could not be presented plainly. The danger of being raped became instead the danger of burning to death. Nevertheless it was only with her father's help that Dora managed to get out of the house. Another suggested danger was that of wetting her bed. Here, her father had the role of helper while it was her mother who appeared as her adversary. There was, however, a reversal because it had, in fact, been Dora's mother who warned her about the sexual "pollution" from men. In the dream the father took over the role of the mother because it was he who actually was going to help Dora against Mr. K. and because he really was right in his argument with the mother about locking the dining room door. In her waking state, Dora confided in her mother about Mr. K., and her mother was probably the only person who did not think she was making it up.

The repressed passive Oedipus complex also left a positive impression on the dream, interpreted in the following way. The father and daughter belonged together but the mother was trying to kill them. Dora would have liked the presents the father gave to the mother, but that the mother criticized. "The drops" (the pearls) had a negative significance for the mother (defilement, discharge, and infection) but a positive significance for Dora (at first mother's milk and then semen that the woman received during intercourse). The father who stood by her bed and awakened her was the good father who satisfied her desire, something that Mr. K. did in the day residues. Dora wanted to repay him sexually for the present of the jewel box. The most significant paradox in the dream also confirmed the passive Oedipus complex, and it can perhaps be interpreted as Dora's dawning awareness of the causes of the neurosis: the mother pointed in two different directions in the dream. On the one hand she wanted to protect the sexual organs from being defiled by the male (she saw to it that the jewel box, a symbol of the female sexual organ, was saved from the fire). However, in so doing, she exposed Dora to the fire. The avoidance of one of the dangers increased the chances of the other. This defense against sexuality was the cause of the neurotic disease.

Toward the end of treatment Dora had another dream of which we will only give the major points. Dora was walking in a strange town. In the house where she lived there was a letter from her mother with news of her father's death. Dora went to the railway station, asked for directions but refused a man's offer to accompany her. When she returned home, her mother and the others had already gone to the cemetery. She felt no sorrow but went up to her room to read a thick book. In this dream Dora's active (homosexual) Oedipus complex found expression. She was now her own "master" and her father's death removed her aggressions. She could now read whatever she wanted (books on sexual education, for example), and she did not need help from strangers. The homosexual wish was not openly expressed but its contours were suggested by her decision to read. Mrs. K., with whom Dora was in love, disappointed Dora by telling the men about her reading. The father was the one who stood between her and her access to Mrs. K. and her mother, and he was put out of the way because he was an adversary. He helped Dora to stop sucking her finger and later to stop masturbating, but it was he who gave her his disease. His prohibitions made him a new object for Dora's passive sexual wishes, but he was unable to fulfill them.

When the two dreams are combined, three competing levels in Dora's personality emerge:

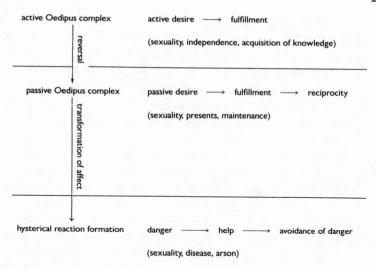

active Oedipus complex   active desire ⟶ fulfillment

          reversal   (sexuality, independence, acquisition of knowledge)

passive Oedipus complex   passive desire ⟶ fulfillment ⟶ reciprocity

      transformation of affect   (sexuality, presents, maintenance)

hysterical reaction formation   danger ⟶ help ⟶ avoidance of danger

          (sexuality, disease, arson)

Dora broke off her analysis not only because she was dissatisfied with Freud but also because through her transference she identified him with her father and Mr. K. Freud did not become aware of her homosexual love for Mrs. K. until it was too late. Nor was his attitude neutral enough for him to serve as an object for her transferences in this respect. He probably thought that regression to the passive Oedipus complex was a satisfactory outcome of Dora's treatment. Once she gave up her hysterical formation, she would again learn to enjoy passive sexuality. Freud found that her actual future prospects were quite good: both couples were to get a divorce, and the father was to marry Mrs. K., and Dora Mr. K. It is almost superfluous to add that Freud should have gone on with the analysis. Dora's passive Oedipus complex was clearly not a stable formation. It was rather a reaction formation against the active Oedipus complex. The only reasonable basis for the treatment of Dora was the active Oedipus complex, especially since her need for knowledge stemmed from there. Through a process of systematic self-reflection Dora might have been able to deal with the social rules that reduced her to a sexual barter item. Yet, on Freud's behalf it can be argued that anyone in puberty will be difficult to analyze because of the existing inconclusive and experimental relations toward the sexual role. Moreover, judging from the available material, Dora did not have good models to choose from among the two families comprising her sphere of intimacy in order to establish her sexual identity.

Dora remained hysterical for the rest of her life but she was still able to lead a relatively normal existence. In 1903 she married one of the employees in her father's mill, a quiet, retiring type who wanted to become a composer. It is said that on at least one occasion, Philip Bauer hired an orchestra to play one of his son-in-law's pieces. As could be expected, the marriage was not a happy one. Dora had a son to whom she was very devoted, but she refused to have any more children, because of the delivery pains, among other things. Her husband was injured during World War I and never regained his health.

In 1923 Freud was able to add something to Dora's case history. He had heard that she had been ill again and had been treated by a doctor who had no difficulty in recognizing her as the Dora in Freud's publication. The doctor was Felix Deutsch who himself reported the episode. In an ambulatory psychoanalysis he cured some of her symptoms by identifying them as the anxiety she felt while waiting for her son to return. This was in 1922. Later he heard more about her. An "informant" told him that her husband had died, tormented by her paranoid behavior. In the 1930s Dora went to the United States with her son whom she also tormented with her endless demands and reproaches. She died in New York in 1945 and Deutsch's informant epitomized her as follows: She was one of the most repellent hysterics he had ever known.

2. LITTLE HANS (Anxiety Hysteria)

The central figure in this case history, whom Freud called little Hans, was born in 1903. Freud had treated the mother of the boy in her youth for a neurotic disorder and the father, Max Graf, was an old member of Freud's Wednesday club (see II.C.1). He was an assistant professor at the music conservatory and his interest in psychoanalysis was that of a nonprofessional. After Freud's publication of *Three Essays on the Theory of Sexuality* (1905d), Graf started to make notes on his son's development, and Freud used some of this material in 1907 for his paper on the sexual education of children (1907c). Early in 1908 Hans developed phobic symptoms. His anxiety was related to horses and for four months he would hardly leave the house. The father immediately went to Freud with the problem, and it was decided that Graf should try to psychoanalyze his son according to Freud's instructions. From then on he carefully wrote everything down. Little Hans only visited Freud's office once, toward the end of March 1908, and his symptoms disappeared completely during the month of May. After this, Freud compiled a case history consisting partly of the father's notes and partly of his own comments and theoretical conclusions. The case history was published in 1909 as "Analysis of a Phobia in a Five-Year-Old Boy" (Freud 1909b).

This case history is a classic example of how repression of the Oedipus complex leads to the formation of neurotic symptoms. The active Oedipus complex emerged clearly in October 1906 when Hans's little sister was born, and Hans was then three and a half years old. He now ceased to be his mother's favorite and was banished from his parents' bedroom and sent to sleep by himself. The sight of the poor, helpless creature made him reflect on his own identity, and for more than a year he took the active role in his fantasies and staged these for anyone who was willing to accept the passive role. In his fantasy, during summer vacation, his playmates became his children, whom he could master and dominate (" 'My children Berta and Olga were brought by the stork too.' " [Freud 1909b, p. 13]). That same winter he met a couple of ten-year-old girls who ignored him, but whom he immediately thought of as his conquests (" 'When am I going to the rink again to see my little girls?' " [1909b, p. 15]). He made sexual advances to both boys and girls. While on vacation the following summer he left home one evening to visit a fourteen-year-old girl with whom he wanted to spend the night. His mother's taunts affected him not in the least (" 'Well, if you really want to go away from Daddy and Mummy, then take your coat and knickers and—good-bye!' " [1909b, p. 17]) and they had to bring him back from the stairs. He was not faithful to his conquests, finding comfort with one in the absence of another. He also liked to have them see him urinate and to see them do so, but the grown-ups had forbidden this. But when he troubled his mother long enough, she let him come out to the toilet with her.

Freud believed it was normal for children to begin to be reticent about anything sexual or anything related to defecation around the age of five. They also start to wage a battle against their own masturbation. The repression is due to transformation of affect where the previously pleasurable becomes associated with unpleasure. Naturally it is those who rear the child who are responsible for how violent and dramatic the transformation of affect will be, but the outcome is not always predictable. This is because the defense against remembering things that have already been done is in any case difficult for the child. It was Hans's case history that first made Freud aware of the castration complex. The father's notes enabled Freud to follow the development of Hans's interest in his penis (which he called "widdler," compare German: *Wiwimacher*). When only three years old he asked his mother if she had a penis and she told him that of course she did. After that he saw penises everywhere: on cows' udders, on lions in the zoo, and on locomotives releasing water. However, he did learn to distinguish between dead and living things (" 'a dog and a horse have widdlers; a table and a chair haven't.' " [1909b, p. 9]). When he was three and a half, his mother caught him playing with his penis and said that if he didn't stop, she would have the doctor cut it off, and what would he urinate with then? " 'With my bottom' " was Hans's reply (1909b, p. 8). There may have been other episodes of this kind, but they made no lasting impression on Hans. When he was four and a quarter years old, his mother once powdered him after his bath but carefully avoided touching his penis, which led to the following exchange between them. "Hans said: 'Why don't you put your finger there?' *Mother:* 'Because that'd be piggish.' *Hans:* 'What's that? Piggish? Why?' *Mother:* 'Because it's not proper.' *Hans* (laughing): 'But it's great fun.' (1909b, p. 19). When Hans saw his little sister being bathed, he commented on how small her penis was but found comfort in the thought that one day it would get bigger. During their last vacation before the phobia appeared his father noticed that Hans was beginning to become shy. He would not urinate in the presence of strangers.

The age of four and three-quarters marked the appearance of Hans's first phobic symptoms. First, he had an anxiety dream in which his mother had died. A few days later when out for a walk with his nurse, he began to cry and insisted on going home to "cuddle" with his mother. The next day he said he was afraid a horse would bite him or that a horse would get into the house. The family had moved to a house opposite a warehouse which had a ramp where horse-drawn wagons were loaded and unloaded all day. Therefore, Hans was afraid to go out at all. Even when indoors he was often depressed and his mother had to give him more of her attention than usual. He was once again allowed to sleep in his parents' bed occasionally, but his father pointedly told him not to touch his penis while he was sleeping. Hans learned to think of his phobia as a problem and talked about his "nonsense" (1909b, p. 30). Hans's father had long talks with him and succeeded in getting Hans to say specifically what it was about white horses that frightened him. Hans was afraid that white horses would bite him. He was afraid that horses would fall and lie with their legs kicking in the air. Large heavy horses scared him more than small ones. He was afraid of horses with black nosebags; he was frightened when a horse started to move; and he was afraid of wagons with heavy loads (mail wagons and coal wagons); and that they might tip over when entering the warehouse driveway. These details made it possible to continue work on Hans's associations. Each of the menacing situations can be traced back to memories that turn out to be related to the Oedipus and the castration complexes. These memories were the determinants of the symptoms because they had been repressed instead of being worked through in the mind.

One set of Oedipus fantasies was about Hans's relationship to his father. His father was the one person preventing him from having free access to his mother and who chided her for spoiling Hans. Hans would therefore actually have liked to get rid of his father. During their summer vacation, Hans was again allowed to sleep with his mother when his father was in Vienna. In departure and leave-taking situations Hans probably wished that his father would stay away forever. He could remember the following episodes from his summer vacation: A girl from the neighborhood was going away, and a carriage with a white horse was standing in front of the house. Her father told her not to stick her fingers near the horse's mouth because it bit. Moreover, Hans played horses with his friends on one occasion when one of them happened to strike his foot against a stone, causing the foot to bleed. Shortly before the phobia broke out, Hans was shopping with his mother. They saw a mail wagon that had turned over and the horse was on the ground, its feet kicking in the air. In Hans's fantasy the father was both the horse that bit and the horse that had fallen. The aggressive attitude that Hans had toward his father gave substance to the wish to see him fall down just like the horse. Nevertheless, this wish could become conscious because Hans loved his father too. His father, moreover, was capable of punishing him: Having a finger bitten off was a metaphorical image of castration. Castration was the punishment for all his oedipal wishes of putting his fingers near his penis, of wanting to be alone with his mother, and of wanting his father dead. Although it was the mother who introduced the idea of castration, it would be done by the doctor, whose status was the same as the father's.

The first preliminary goal of the therapy was reached at the end of March 1908, just before Hans visited Freud. His tendency to try to compensate for his limited freedom of movement by clinging to his mother's skirts had been checked, thus eliminating the possibility of his ending in a passive and perhaps homosexual Oedipus complex. His fantasies and dreams clearly showed that he had begun to deal with the active Oedipus complex once more and to understand its consequences. Hans had a dream with anxietal aspects in which his father was a large giraffe and his mother was a small "crumpled" one (1909b, p. 37). Hans got hold of the little giraffe and sat up on it (mastered it). The big giraffe started to scream. At another time, after a stroll in the zoo, Hans fantasized that he went into a forbidden area and also that he felt like smashing a window in the train. In his play he showed aggressive behavior toward his father and readily admitted that he would prefer to have his mother to himself. All that Freud did was to tell Hans that his father and the dangerous horses were identical and that many years before Hans was born he (Freud) had known that a little boy would be born who would love his mother so much that he would be afraid of his father, but that Hans mustn't be afraid of him because his father only wanted what was best for him. On the way home Hans suddenly said: " 'Does the Professor talk to God, as he can tell all that beforehand?' " (1909b, p. 42–43).

During the next month the anxiety for horses decreased, but Hans developed a new symptom instead. At first it appeared to be an exaggerated loathing for excrement, but it actually proved to have something further to do with horses. The processes of conceiving and giving birth were still an unexplained part of Hans's active Oedipus complex. His parents had explained that the stork had brought baby sister, but he did not really believe that. Naturally he had noted that his mother's belly was smaller since the arrival of the baby. More than a year later, while with his mother, he saw a turned-over mail wagon and the horse was kicking its legs in the air. An associative connection was suddenly established between the two memories and repression set in. The pregnant mother with her swollen belly was associated with the wagon's turning over. (Freud seemed to find a generalized symbolic relation between "fall" and "deliver.") For Hans everything changed after that disturbing event (the birth of his sister) because he was no longer his mother's favorite. He feared, therefore, that the heavy wagon would tip over and result in a new "delivery." Freud wanted to associate the horse's kicking its legs with Hans's having seen his parents having sexual intercourse, but the father was unable to confirm that this was so. He did, however, have an entry showing that the only thing Hans really noticed when he came into his mother's room was a basin with bloody water in it which prompted him to say: " 'But blood doesn't come out of *my* widdler.' " (1909b, p. 10). What he did have a very clear recollection of was the episode when he had played horses and the foot that had bled. He may also at some time have seen his mother's menstrual blood. There was one more connection to the kicking legs of the horses.

Hans used to stamp his feet when forced to stop playing and go to the bathroom. It was by such pathways of association that Hans's wish to make children became focused on feces: he called excrement "lumf" (compare German: *Lumpf*), a word that resembled those for *stocking* (in German: *strumpf*) and *sausage* (in German: *Soffilodi*). Hans said that he could lay eggs and that he had fantasized a child he called "Lodi." At Freud's suggestion, Hans was given the sexual education he needed. For a short while he was very preoccupied with babies. Then his phobic symptoms disappeared. The Oedipus complex had been overcome.

Childhood phobias, like Hans's, generally disappear by themselves. They can, however, develop into compulsion neuroses as in the case of the "Wolf Man." Hans's positive transference to Freud accounted for one of the reasons behind the success of the analysis and the treatment. His feelings toward his father oscillated between love and hostility. Freud ("the Professor") as he was called in the letters Hans dictated to him was totally good and omniscient and did not misuse the boy's confidence. Something that neurotic parents are prone to do. "The Professor" was Hans's abstract ideal of the good father. In this regard, the story has an interesting epilogue. Max Graf, the father, became a professor in 1909 and a few years later he broke off with Freud. He could not accept what he thought of as Freud's authoritarian behavior toward, among others, Adler. Having to share his parental authority with Freud was also a problem and some of Freud's comments on the treatment also show signs of his irritation toward Graf. Freud wrote in an afterword from 1922 to the case history that Hans had visited him and that he was doing well despite his parents' divorce (Freud 1922c)! The adult Hans, Herbert Graf, later became an opera instructor and worked at the Metropolitan Opera in New York.

3. THE "RAT MAN" (Obsessional Neurosis)

We now turn to a patient whom Freud called Paul. His real name according to Freud's journal was Ernst but his full identity has not been made public to date. Because his most significant symptoms were related to the idea of rats he is in modern literature spoken of generally as the "Rat Man."

The Rat Man was born in 1878. His mother came from the poorer side of a large Jewish industrial dynasty but did have some means of her own. The father was a low-ranking military officer. After their marriage, the wealthy side of the family gave him a good job. The father died in 1899 when the Rat Man was twenty-one years old. The Rat Man had manifested some neurotic symptoms in childhood and after his father's death, they worsened. He did manage, however, to get a degree in law, although with some delay. His obsessional neurosis worsened during a military exercise he took part in as officer of the reserve. Shortly thereafter, in October 1907, at the age of twenty-nine, he entered analysis with Freud. Treatment lasted eleven months and after that he was completely cured. No post-analytic investigation of the Rat Man, who died in World War I, was ever made. Freud published the case history in 1909 under the title, "Notes upon a Case of Obsessional Neurosis" (1909d). Contrary to his general practice, Freud did not destroy the notes he made on this analysis. The notes from the first two months exist and have been published (Freud 1974a). We have drawn on both sources for our discussion.

In the second and third hours of analysis the Rat Man talked about the military exercise that had intensified his symptoms. He was on a march and wanted to gain the respect of the enlisted men not only because he was educated but also for his stamina. During a halt he happened to sit next to a captain who advocated reinstating corporal punishment in the army. To illustrate his point he told about an extremely harsh punishment practiced in the Orient, in which the prisoner was tied to a pot in which rats had been placed. The rats ate their way up his intestines, and he was helpless to prevent it. The march continued, but the Rat Man lost his lorgnette. Although he could easily have found it, he did not want to be responsible for delaying the exercise. Instead he telegraphed to his optician in Vienna for a new one. It arrived the next evening and was handed to him by the "cruel" captain, who asked him to settle the amount with Officer A who had outlaid the money for him. The Rat Man's first impulse was not to pay. (It later turned out that he had already known that it had not been A who had made the payment for him.) His next impulse was that he *must* pay otherwise the woman he loved and his deceased father would be put through the rat punishment. This purpose became a holy oath. Its obsessional nature was confirmed by the fact that he was told unequivocally that it was not to A that he owed the money. Nevertheless, in order not to break his oath, he found A, gave him the money, and had him hand it over to Officer B, the real creditor. Carrying out his plan delayed him in getting home. He took the train to Vienna as planned, but at each station he was ready to get off and go back. Once in Vienna, he went to a friend to discuss the matter, having assured himself first that there was a night train to the town where A lived. Something delayed him, and when his friend succeeded in getting the truth out of him, he gave up his plan for the time being. He had known all along, even before the "cruel" captain delivered the package, that the woman employed at the post office had outlaid the money, believing in the integrity of the unknown soldier. His friend saw to it that he sent her the money. However, this did not stop the Rat Man from speculating about how he could get the money to A. A month later he visited Freud, who, as a doctor, could write a statement explaining the necessity of such a curious arrangement.

In the beginning Freud could not understand the meaning of the story. Compulsive thoughts were quite obviously involved and therefore he had to try to uncover the unconscious fantasies which the compulsive thoughts represented. The strongest affects seemed to be linked with the idea about the rat torture and when subjected to closer analysis, this turned out to be the focal point for a very large number of chains of association that collectively spanned the major part of the Rat Man's early life. The connection between the anal and the phallic phase is particularly obvious. The story of the rat torture provides at least four thematic relationships.

(1) Rats are like the excrement that is passed from the intestines. Stinginess is a typical anal trait. The feces are held back just as money is. Rats and money thereby also became associated. Partly in jest, the Rat Man used *rat* as a unit of money and pointed out that there was a certain degree of homonymity between *rats* (German: *Ratten*) and *rates* (German: *Raten*). Having to settle his own debt reminded him of a story about his father when he was in the army. He was a born gambler (in literal translation *Spielratte* in German means *gambling rat*). He had run up a big debt, which a friend had settled for him, but later he was unable to find his friend and repay him.

(2) Corporal punishment and the rat punishment can be related to a specific episode. The Rat Man's father had once given him a beating for biting one of his nurses (biting is an aggressive trait in rats). Therefore, he deserved to be punished. At a deeper level the punishment is related to forbidden sexual activity.

(3) There are several lines of association leading from rats to children. In Ibsen's *Little Eyolf* (Ibsen 1894), the rat maiden acts as a rat catcher, attracting the children to her. The Rat Man wanted very much to have children, but he had great reservations about marrying a certain woman who, after an operation, was no longer able to have any (there is an association between *rats* and *heiraten*, (to get married).

(4) Finally, rats transmit diseases. The symbolic interpretation is that the

penis can be the carrier of syphilis. In the army, nothing is more feared than syphilis. The woman's father had died from it (paralysis), and the Rat Man suspected that his own father had a venereal disease.

These four points are merely a very compressed account of how in analysis more and more material emerges. From this material Freud uncovered the most important etiological aspects in the Rat Man's development. They might concern incidents that the Rat Man did not even remember and that Freud therefore had to reconstruct. This was especially true for the earliest stages of development. With this reservation in mind we will now discuss the development and formation of the structures that underlie symptom formation in obsessional neurosis.

Apparently, there are very strong pleasurable experiences related to the active Oedipus complex (that is, the anal and active phallic phase). The Rat Man had very few memories from this period in his life, but his subsequent development was unmistakably evident, in particular, in his anal interests. The family consisted of three older sisters, a younger brother, and two younger sisters. Freud believed that the Rat Man had displayed sexual activity with his siblings. His oldest sister died when he was between the ages of three and four, and this event proved to be a turning point in his life. He only remembered seeing her once sitting on the potty and this made him aware of the sexual anatomical differences. There was a story in the family, that he himself did not remember, about this incident, which had taken place just before his sister died. The story was that his father was giving him a beating because he had supposedly bitten one of his nurses. Quite unexpectedly he flew into a rage right while the blows were falling, and not knowing any swear words, he called his father names like, "you lamp," "you towel," "you plate." The father was astonished by this outburst, stopped, and exclaimed: "The child will be either a great man or a great criminal."

Freud concluded from later symptomatic actions that the punishment was somehow related to the boy's sexual activities. Perhaps he had masturbated, been fooling around with his sisters, or tried to make sexual advances toward his mother or his nurse. Perhaps someone had told him that he could die from touching his sexual organs and this might have led him to believe that that was the cause of his sister's death. He might also have been subjected to the threat of castration. What was exceptional in the case of the Rat Man was that the active Oedipus complex was not simply repressed and replaced by a strong superego. Instead there was a partial reversal of the active drive aim to passive ones together with the foundation of a passive Oedipus complex. This structure functioned as a reaction formation against the active Oedipus complex, which then could be held partly repressed. One effect of reaction formation is that aggression and sadism are transformed to compassion. The predominating emotional tie to the father is neither hate nor anxiety but compassion and solicitude, an ever-present concern that some harm may come to him.

According to Freud, the Rat Man's personality consisted of three separate structures, which could be traced back to an imperfect accomplishment of the active Oedipus complex. (1) The active oedipal wishes were in the unconscious, or the id, where they were kept repressed by reaction formation. These wishes were concerned with the active mastery of the mother or her substitute as well as hate and aggression toward the father. In this instance, hate was expressed as the wish for revenge, that is, the Rat Man had a strong wish for revenge on his father for having punished him as a child. (2) The preconscious, or ego, contained a number of traits related to reaction formation. Initially they appeared to be homosexual in nature, but this homosexuality had been modified due to the distance to the father. Being forced to submit to his father turned him into a fervently religious person in the years after puberty. He experienced a feeling of self-esteem when, for a while, an older friend treated him as though he had exceptional gifts, only to discover that his friend was using him to get to know his sisters. He described this as the most shattering experience of his life. The passive traits in his personality found expression later in moral and aesthetic attitudes, albeit shallow ones. His manner was servile and ingratiating, and he made himself especially conspicuous at funerals with his excessive grieving, (his sisters mockingly called him a "corpse vulture.") His father spoke of him as his best friend, and he did his utmost not to disappoint his father by attending to his studies and creating a career for himself. (3) However, the preconscious had another structure that was organized around the derivations from the repressed active Oedipus complex. Freud evidently sympathized with this structure in the Rat Man's personality and tried to rehabilitate it therapeutically. It found its most consistent expression in the Rat Man's long and persevering love for a certain woman (who, it turned out, was his cousin). He would have liked to marry her but was unable to do so for financial reasons. His parents were violently opposed to the idea, and his mother had gone so far as to make arrangements for him to marry into the wealthy part of the family once he got his law degree, thus ensuring him financially. His real reason for insisting on marrying the woman was an inveterate attempt to taunt his father and take revenge. He rejected his father as an ideal worthy of emulation. His father, in his own youth, had also broken off with a girl of poor means, and by not following his example, the Rat Man was able to demonstrate his contempt.

In the obsessional neurotic the obsession generally comes from unfulfilled wishes in the id. Displacement makes these wishes acceptable to the superego so that the compulsive act is actually a compromise formation between the id and the superego. The superego is severe and detached and does its best to make the compulsive action an unpleasant experience with the result that it instills in the neurotic a vague but intense feeling of anxiety or conscience if he fails to obey the impulse for the action in every detail. Excessively moral individuals also exhibit this type of compulsion. The obsessional neurosis of the Rat Man was more serious, at times almost psychotic in nature. Individual compulsive acts were not compromise formations. On the contrary, their force came from an affective preparedness attached to traumatic memories and fantasies that were related to the person of the father. The Rat Man carried out his compulsive actions by convincing himself that something terrible would befall his father or the woman if he did not do so. Each intention for each action manifested itself through many different kinds of affective preparedness whose traumatic source, however, was well hidden.

The neurotic compulsion, just like the repetition compulsion in general, serves to correct a fundamental imbalance. In the case of the Rat Man, this imbalance was locked into the unconscious. Therefore, consciously motivated actions were doomed to fail at the outset. Even when actually carried out, they would never be able to fulfill the unconscious wish. The Rat Man's compulsive actions were symbolic attempts to repay old debts. Schematically, three "financial accounts" and three types of "debts" could be distinguished.

(1) His vengefulness was his way of repaying his father for what he had had to suffer in the past. The intensity of the affect stemmed from specific punishment situations in childhood when he swore to avenge himself. It is possible to assert a "normal" and preconscious revenge where the avenger knows *what* is to be revenged and on *whom* revenge is to be taken. (There are numerous films and novels that illustrate how sweet revenge is.) It was difficult for the Rat Man to take revenge since he felt no resentment toward his father.

(2) Another balance of payment concerned paying off his positive debt. Basically, the Rat Man felt that the only way he could repay his father for

his life was by committing suicide. He would have liked to have children but was unable to do so because the woman he wanted to marry was infertile. Following the same pattern he was plagued by the thought that a friend from the army had once been kind enough to settle a debt for his father and that his father had not been able to find the friend later when he had wanted to give him a generous repayment as thanks. The Rat Man's urge to pay A for the lorgnette was in part related to this theme.

(3) Finally, the Rat Man had a so-called reparation compulsion, the compulsion to make up for wrongdoings. It stemmed directly from the reaction formation. His aggression and his wish for his father's death were balanced by his intense feeling of compassion for him. Many of the Rat Man's compulsive actions, especially those after his father had died were his way of atoning for his guilty feelings. Two actions that illustrate this were his participation in funeral ceremonies and his avoidance of sensual pleasure.

The Rat Man might have been able to lead a normal life if his compulsive impulses had not conflicted with each other. Instead he found himself in a dilemma. Obeying one of his impulses immediately forced him to obey the other, and so on indefinitely. In the last analysis the conflicting impulses belonged to the active and the passive Oedipus complexes. The most effective obsessional neurotic defense mechanism consists of isolating these impulses from each other and from their unconscious sources. If the neurotic succeeds in isolating them, he is not directly troubled by his neurosis. Rationalizations are used to dampen the conflict. If he does not succeed, the impulses are first expressed as indecision and doubt. It is typical that the Rat Man accomplished very little while studying because he constantly worried about trivial matters. Freud believed that the Rat Man's ineffective study habits were a means of postponing the choice of a wife, since the agreement was that the marriage would not take place until after he had his degree. In very crucial situations there is a so-called shortcut between the conflicting impulses. This occurs when, via unconscious associations, they both become linked to the same current theme and as a result are expressed in the same paradoxical action sequence. In closing, a few examples can be mentioned.

(1) One day, shortly before the woman he wanted to marry was to go away on vacation, the Rat Man struck his foot against a stone lying in the street. He got the idea that he had better move the stone so that the carriage in which the lady would be traveling would not turn over (urge to protect).

Twenty minutes later he got another thought: he must go back, find the stone, and put it in its original place (reparation compulsion, vindictiveness toward the lady for rejecting his marriage proposal).

(2) On another occasion, he got the idea that he was overweight and went on an agonizing diet. The explanation for this was that he wanted to murder the lady's English cousin, Dick, and therefore he had to punish himself. The process of unconscious displacement resulted in the punishment of getting thinner, *dick* being the German word for *thick*.

(3) In his childhood the Rat Man was an avid voyeur and occasionally an exhibitionist as well. He studied his nurse's naked body intently and showed his mother, although hesitantly, his erection. This signified a rejection of the castration threat (see V.C.2.b). After puberty a distinct conflict relation was established between asceticism (obeying the father) and sexual activity (disobeying the father). For a while, after his father's death, he masturbated and was especially aroused by situations in which he could defy some prohibition or other. He had sexual intercourse for the first time at the age of twenty-six and realized that he could have killed his own father in order to have such an experience. A few years later, after his father's death, he started staying up late to study for his exam. He used to open the door between midnight and 1 A.M. so that his father's spirit could enter the room. He then undressed and looked at his erection in the mirror. There were two reasons for his doing this. While his father was ill, the Rat Man had once asked the doctor when the crisis would pass. Then he had lain down again but been awakened at 1 A.M. by the nurse who had told him that his father had just died. She had also told him that his father had called for the Rat Man from his deathbed. The Rat Man blamed himself for having failed in his duty and opened the door for his father's spirit at the hour of his death (between midnight and 1 A.M.) and showed him that he was doing what was expected of him, that is, studying for his exam. However, his voyeurism and his exhibitionism were his way of avenging himself on his father, demonstrably rejecting the castration threat and insisting on his right to manage his sexuality himself.

(4) Without going into all the details of the analysis we can in conclusion point out that the compulsive actions related to the military exercise were caused by the same split. Paying money to the wrong person was a symbolic way of settling his father's debt. It was also a capitulation to the delusions of reaction formation. On the other hand, failure to pay was the same as defying the father's (the "cruel" captain's) orders, thereby insisting on the independence of his own reason. (The Rat Man knew very well to whom

he owed the money.) The train headed for Vienna that the Rat Man finally took and the other train headed for the military camp were striking symbols of his choices: flight into disease or return to reality.

4. SCHREBER (Paranoia)

The next case history differs from the other four in two important respects. First, Freud never had direct contact with the patient; he based his analysis solely on Schreber's autobiographical account of his life and his disease. Second, the disease was a psychosis, which in Freud's view excluded the possibility of a therapeutic analysis. Freud made no claim that he could have given Schreber a better treatment than he had gotten through the traditional psychiatrists who had been responsible for him. Freud's intention was merely to demonstrate that the course of the disease and symptom formation could be understood psychologically using a psychoanalytical conceptual framework. Before he published his analysis, Freud did some research on Schreber's family. Later, additional information was brought to light that in the main substantiated Freud's hypothesis. We will therefore use both sources in the following discussion.

Daniel Paul Schreber was born in Leipzig in 1842. He had one older and two younger sisters and an older brother who committed suicide in 1877. The family was wealthy with income from, among other sources, an estate. His father was well known as a doctor for two reasons in particular: he introduced the idea of colony gardens for the workers and was the originator of a special system of health gymnastic exercises (one of his books on the subject sold several hundred thousand copies). He died in 1861 when Schreber was nineteen years old. Schreber studied law and advanced rapidly in his career. He was hospitalized at psychiatric institutions three times in his life. The first time was from 1884 to 1885 and followed his failure to be elected to parliament. The disease was diagnosed as hypochondria. The second time was from 1893 to 1902. Shortly before this hospitalization Schreber had been appointed president of the supreme court in Dresden. This time the disease was diagnosed as paranoia. While he was hospitalized he worked out a comprehensive teleological system that showed distinctly paranoid traits. He thought of his disease as a nervous disorder (as opposed to a mental disorder). From 1900 to 1902 he wrote a complete account of his teleological system which revealed all of his delusions, although he did not view them as such. He also leveled clear accusations against the psychiatric system for using force in its treatment methods. He filed a suit to have the right to manage his property restored to him, which, after a lengthy legal battle and despite his doctors' strong protests, was granted in 1902. The court (the same one on which he had sat as president) found him not to be dangerous and to be in full possession of his juridical faculties. His autobiography was published in 1903 (after a number of passages about his family had been censored by the authorities) and was entitled *Memoirs of My Nervous Illness* (Schreber 1903). Freud's analysis was based on this work. The third time Schreber was hospitalized was in 1907 after his wife had a stroke. He died in the hospital in 1911, broken in mind and in body. Freud worked on the analysis of Schreber's autobiography during the summer and fall of 1910 but did not publish the paper "Psycho-Analytic Notes on an Autobiographical Account of a Case of Paranoia (Dementia Paranoides)" (1911c), until several months after Schreber's death in 1911.

Freud described Schreber's book as a strange mixture of nonsense and brilliance and of borrowed and original elements. He found a third contrast as well, that between Schreber's attempt to find a sensible and scientific explanation for his disease and his tenacious adherence to the most incredible delusions. The description of the action that made up the work was a piece of teleological science fiction, in which the dead and the living, split souls and whole ones, gods and humans, all fought a tremendous battle. In keeping with the nature of psychosis, Schreber heard voices, was goaded by impulses to act that he could not control, and saw his world transformed beyond recognition. These were real events as Schreber experienced them and he tried to give them verbal form. He emphasized throughout the work that the details might not be fully correct and therefore he appealed to science to help him. Freud was probably the first to take Schreber's book seriously, and it is naturally to be regretted that he never had the opportunity to analyze Schreber in person.

According to Schreber's view of the world God was made up of nerves, and when he created the universe, he sent forth some of his nerves as rays (God's rays were considered to be life giving just as the sun's rays were). Thus, every human soul consisted of some of God's rays. Normally, God did not interfere in the course of human events; he was only interested in dead souls. When a person died, the nerve substance was gradually withdrawn back to God. Each soul gradually lost its independent consciousness, entering into more sublime systems of souls (in heaven's courtyard), until it attained salvation by once again becoming one with God.

Schreber went on to tell about a crisis in the kingdom of God caused by a combination of many unfortunate events: In more recent times there had been a general increase in nervousness among people, which was actually an excessive sexual excitement. The psychiatrist who was to treat him at the hospital, Paul Flechsig, was tempted to experiment with his soul. Perhaps it all started with hypnosis, but then Flechsig or unconscious parts of his soul, hit upon the idea of assassinating Schreber, that is of murdering his soul. Flechsig's motive was to get something he wanted, for example, to change Schreber into a woman and take advantage of his body sexually. Schreber believed that Flechsig had, by means of force, seized heavenly powers and was able to direct the rays for God by convincing him that Schreber's soul had gone insane.

From this point on the crisis worsened. The more Schreber was tormented by God and Flechsig, the greater were the excitations of unpleasure that were produced in his nervous system, until finally he became such a center of energy that he threatened God's very existence by attracting and pinioning God's nerve energy. In the heat of the battle the world was destroyed and to Schreber the people around him were unreal ghosts whom God had created for the purpose of winning the battle. After his many trials and tribulations, Schreber came to the conclusion that he could save the world if the irradiation to which he was subjected could create pleasure instead of unpleasure. He had to be transformed into a woman and become God's wife. This would remove the obstacles preventing him from being drawn back to God and would make it possible for other souls to attain salvation. Schreber did not really want to become a woman but recognized the necessity of it if world order were to be restored.

The main thesis in Freud's analysis was that Schreber's relations to Flechsig and God reflected his earlier relation to his father. Freud had no proof of this. He knew nothing more about the father than what has already been stated, that is, that he was a well-known doctor who was a specialist in health gymnastics. It is therefore worth noting that later information fully corroborated Freud's assumptions. Schreber's own case record indicated that his father suffered from compulsive thoughts and had murderous impulses. Viewed as a whole the father's books reflect an entire philosophy of life. Schreber senior wanted to revitalize the German people. They had become soft and weak through an excessive devotion to purely intellectualized cultural activities. The soul and the will were formed in accordance with the body. Therefore, the body had to be strengthened. Body culture was very important and gymnastic exercises were one way of promoting it. Attention had to be focused on the very young. All deviations from the norm were to be treated before it was too late. Schreber senior recommended that infants should be subjected to corporal punishment before the age of one. After this, as he put it, the child would always obey. The child could be controlled by a look, a word, or just one threatening gesture. Most bodily ailments were to be treated with laxatives, and the child was to acquire good posture with the help of certain stands and belts. The sexual activity of adults should be kept at a minimum. Married couples should have separate bedrooms and sex should only be indulged in for the purpose of procreation. Finally, it should be mentioned that the philosophy expounded by Schreber senior had a short resurgence in our century under the Nazis.

It does not require much effort to imagine what effect this domineering, fanatically reformatory, and emotionally ambivalent father had on Schreber. Constant supervision did not produce the desired result. It led instead to an early hypersexuality that in turn provoked new disciplinary measures. Freud said that there had been a narcissistic fixation; however, this did not mean that Schreber had stayed at the same stage of development, only that in a crisis he was likely to revert to the primitive narcissistic defense mechanisms as his only effective options. Schreber's delusions evinced very few traces of the active Oedipus complex. His mother was described as being a weak and insignificant person given to depression. Undoubtedly then it was Schreber's father who was responsible for suppressing the active oedipal tendencies, especially masturbation. Schreber did not react to the castration threat using repression. He used the more primitive mechanism of a reversal of the active sexual aims to passive supplemented by a direct masochistic tie to his father. This would be a normal development for the sisters, and they at least led reasonably normal lives as adults. Schreber (and his brother) on the other hand had difficulty in following in their father's footsteps. The passive homosexual attitude was pushed into the background in puberty probably because the father had emphasized masculine behavior. Freud suggested that Schreber's strong homosexual libido had been effectively sublimated and had formed the basis for his exceptionally rapidly advancing legal career. He did not marry until the year after his brother's suicide (in 1878, at age thirty-six). He may have done so because he was then the only one able to produce an heir or, at any rate, to carry on the family name. His autobiography showed that he had neither a high regard nor warm feelings for his wife. She had six miscarriages and never gave him a son.

The first two bouts of illness closely followed periods in which Schreber had been working under a heavy strain. Moreover, his position in society was threatened by certain competitive situations. First, he lost an election and then at a relatively young age he was appointed to the position of supreme-court president, which he could scarcely be expected to be fully qualified to assume. There he probably received little or no support from his subordinates who in general were a good deal older than he was. As in childhood, he reacted with a reversal of the active aims to passive ones, first a suicide attempt and a demand to receive the deserved punishment, later desublimation of the homosexual libido in relation to Flechsig. The paranoia developed in connection with the passive homosexual attitude toward Flechsig. Flechsig was a successful neuropathologist and psychiatrist, and he clearly rekindled the emotional ties Schreber had had to his father and his brother. It was therefore very difficult for Schreber to return to the active emotional position. Moreover, as a doctor, Flechsig had unlimited power over Schreber who while hospitalized was subjected to many forms of violent treatment. Situations of this kind forced Schreber to resort to the partial regression to the narcissistic stage of development as a defense mechanism. It was the easiest way to escape from the passive homosexual attitude (see diagram in IV.C).

Schreber's paranoia had two phases. The first was his delusions of persecution. He projected his own homosexual wishes on to Flechsig while still maintaining the passive position. His persecution ideas were the result partly of transformation of affect, that is, an attempt to veil the homosexuality, and partly of having had to experience his father's training methods once again. The use of laxatives, belts, and body stands had destroyed the integrity of his body and had forced him to withdraw to an unassailable psychic region. Schreber's delusion of persecution forced him to admit that here, too, Flechsig and God were getting control of him. Moreover, the plan to murder his soul did not succeed. On the contrary, Schreber now threatened the very existence of God. His characterizations of God's shortcomings and failings were clearly posthumously formulated criticisms and bribes intended for his father. God was only interested in the dead and not in living things (an unfortunate trait in a doctor); he was unable to learn from experience (an unfortunate trait in a teacher); and finally, his "miracles" were of a very strange nature indeed, for example, when he suddenly gave Schreber the uncontrollable urge to defecate. (In his books, Schreber senior preferred the expression *miracle* (German: *Wunder*) and he had probably also used it when he was able to cure his son's stomach ache with a laxative. The second phase of his paranoia was his megalomania which was also mixed with some traits of erotomania. Metapsychologically speaking, megalomania is a condition in which all libido has been withdrawn from the ideational object to the ego which means a return to narcissism. That the ideational object was emptied was demonstrated by Schreber's belief that the world had ended and that the people around him were unreal. His totally insane project of saving the world had apparently enabled him to get rid of his tormenters, and he had now accepted the order of the world. He could put an end to the conflict by making sensual pleasure a duty instead of a sin. As God's wife he would not only feel better, but would also come through the crisis alive. Schreber's megalomania allowed him to express in a distorted way his passive homosexual attitude. He accepted castration instead of repressing the castration complex and for a while he spent hours in front of the mirror studying his feminine qualities. Moreover, he also felt that his body was replete with feminine "carnal nerves."

5. THE "WOLF MAN"
(Anxiety Hysteria and Obsessional Neurosis)

We have now come to the last and perhaps the most famous of Freud's case histories. Freud named the patient the "Wolf Man," and the name has been kept ever since. The Wolf Man was a Russian with a very unusual background. His family was among the wealthiest landowners and the father was active in "liberal politics." The Wolf Man's real name was Sergej—or Sergesius—Pankejeff. He was born on 6 January 1887, or, according to the Russian Julian calendar, on 25 December 1866. The significance of this coincidence of Christmas and birthday for him will be discussed further on. His only sibling was a sister, two and a half years older. His psychic problems began early in childhood. At the age of three and a half he suddenly became irritable and unmanageable and showed clear sadistic tendencies. At four the symptoms changed to phobic anxiety of different animals, including wolves, and from the age of four and a half his obsessional anxiety was replaced by obsessional symptoms of a religious nature. The obsessional symptoms abated after the tenth year. At the age of seventeen he got gonorrhea and had a nervous breakdown that led to an impairment in his ability to work. In the ensuing years he underwent various psychiatric treatments, consulting, among others, Kraepelin, who diagnosed him as a manic-depressive. A Russian doctor happened to suggest that he try an analysis with Freud. The analysis started in February 1910 and continued until the summer of 1914. Freud wrote the case history the same year but did not publish it until 1918. Its official title was "From the History of an Infantile Neurosis" (Freud 1918b). The title indicates that Freud was more interested in the symptoms that pertained to childhood than in the symptoms of the Wolf Man. Thus, in childhood it was possible to differentiate between one phase dominated by anxiety hysteria and one dominated by obsessional neurosis, while the symptoms Freud found himself confronted with could be grouped together as "a condition following on an obsessional neurosis which has come to an end spontaneously, but has left a defect behind it after recovery" (Freud 1918b, p. 8). It is self-evident that in order to cure the adult neurosis Freud had to go back to the infantile one, and this too will be our approach.

In order to give a comprehensive view we have indicated the most important points in the infantile sexual development of the Wolf Man on a time axis:

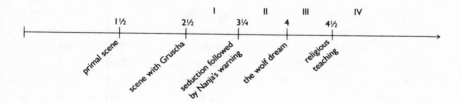

The Wolf Man remembered the last four events, but not the primal scene, which Freud constructed in order to create an intelligible picture. Freud stated that there was a specific unconscious ideational structure that marked each of the subsequent stages of development, and had its origin in the primal scene. Freud devoted lengthy theoretical passages to a discussion of whether the primal scene was a real event or a fantasy. Our discussion of this point has been postponed until part 5 (see in particular sections V.B.3 and V.C.3.b), and with this qualification in mind, we will consider the primary scene as a real event.

During the Wolf Man's childhood, he and his sister were raised by servants. His parents often traveled abroad, and when they were home his father was very preoccupied with business matters and his mother with her illnesses. His nurse, Nanja, who was described as a woman of the people, was the most important person in his life. She regarded him as a substitute for her own son who had died. She defended him against others like a lioness, and was indulgent and permissive toward him. His upbringing was left to governesses and tutors, apart from her.

The reconstructed primal scene had the following content: At the age of one and a half the Wolf Man had malaria and was in bed in his parents' bedroom. Around five o'clock one hot summer afternoon he woke up and saw his parents having intercourse. He registered the scene without understanding it. His mother was on her knees and his father had inserted his penis from behind. Only a special position of this kind could explain the symptoms that the Wolf Man later developed. Each of the four intervals, or phases (I, II, III, and IV), was precipitated by its own event, and each of these shared certain traits through their relationship to the primal scene.

I. This phase was characterized by the beginnings of active sexual aims that were neither clearly anal nor phallic but urethral. One of his earliest memories (around two and a half years) concerned his nurse, Gruscha. She was on all fours scrubbing the floor. The Wolf Man was standing beside her and the sight of her aroused him sexually, and he reacted by urinating on the floor. She responded jokingly by threatening him with castration, saying something to the effect that little boys who urinate on floors should have their penises cut off. The connection between Gruscha's position and that of the mother in the primal scene was clear and Freud explained that the Wolf Man already had identified with his father. This phase had no other memory that could be singled out as the origin of the active sexual aim. On the other hand, the adult sexual life of the Wolf Man was affected by the scene with Gruscha: He preferred servant girls whom he could debase and had a special preference for their buttocks using only the position of intercourse from the primal scene. He had a special interest in anal intercourse.

II. The actual phallic phase was brought about by a seduction scene (at the age of three and a quarter) in which his sister was the seducer. The children were playing on the floor when his sister took his penis and played with it. She explained her behavior by saying that Nanja did the same with everybody, for example, with the gardener: The sister made him stand on his head and tried to get hold of his genitals. The Wolf Man rejected her advances and tried instead to make advances toward Nanja. He started to play with his penis in front of her, the equivalent of trying to seduce her. Nanja, who was otherwise very compliant toward him, assumed a serious mien and explained that children who did such things got a "sore" there. The Wolf Man took this as a clear threat of castration. The pleasure feeling he had just discovered by masturbating was ruined even before he had learned to relate the active sexual aim (mastery, control) to the phallic feelings of pleasure. Therefore, the "premature" castration threat did not have its usual effect of the repression of the active Oedipus complex. Instead, a more primitive defense mechanism was used; Freud called it repudiation. The wolf man repudiated the castration threat and acted as if sexual differences did not exist. He regressed from the phallic to the anal phase without actually being able to erase the impressions he had gotten during his attenuated passage through the phallic phase.

The first indication of aggression was an abrupt change in his character. While previously he had been a fairly quiet child, he now turned into a veritable monster. He was aggressive and cruel toward both animals and people. He had fits of rage for no apparent reason and tormented his dear Nanja to distraction. His character change occurred during a summer vacation while his parents were away on a trip. On their return they blamed the governess who had been hired that summer. Freud, however, rejected this explanation because the governess had not been hired until after the scenes with the sister and Nanja. Regression to the sadistic anal phase was a reaction against the castration threat, Freud said, but added one further element to this solution: the unreasonable and cruel behavior was not primarily controlled by sadistic sexual aims but by masochistic ones. It served to provoke punishment and pave the way for him to be spanked on his bottom. The change in the direction of the aim from active to passive was started by his sister's seductive behavior and it brought a number of other changes in its wake. Regression to the anal phase opened the way for the replacement of the object. The masochistic impulses were transferred from Nanja and the mother to the father because he was the embodiment of authority in administering punishment.

During that long summer vacation when the traumatic events were taking place, the Wolf Man found himself in an impossible situation. On the one hand he was the smallest and the weakest person in this female universe, and on the other he could not accept these women and their power as valid objects of identification. His unacceptable choices were an irresolute grandmother, who was supposed to keep an eye on the children's upbringing but who failed to intervene; the impossible English governess; Nanja, whom he usually could order about; and his sister and her friend whom he despised. Being unable to assume his father's position, he expressed his yearning for his father through his provocations and the roles of the primal scene now settled into a new pattern. The Wolf Man identified with his mother. He wanted his father's violent power manifested and felt sexually aroused when he imagined his father's penis in his anus, like his mother in the primal scene as he now understood it. There had thus been a transformation of the active but weak heterosexual object choice of Gruscha to the passive homosexual object choice of the father.

III. Despite all this, repression of the Oedipus complex still took place in the Wolf Man. The special feature in this case, however, was that it was the passive Oedipus complex that was repressed. Freud's explanation was that once the Wolf Man had made the object choice of the father with main emphasis on anal satisfaction, he again progressed to the phallic phase. Unconsciously he realized that if he identified with the mother, he could not also expect to have his penis sexually stimulated. His mother had previously suffered from abdominal bleeding, and the Wolf Man associated this with the sore that Nanja spoke about. If he wanted to take over his mother's position, he would in effect have to accept losing his penis, something that he rejected in the end. Castration anxiety was thus the driving force behind repression of the passive Oedipus complex and in the resulting animal phobia it was the passive wishes, the oral, the anal, and the phallic, which along with castration anxiety, were the determinants of symptom formation.

Freud set the age of four as the dividing line between phase II (masochism) and phase III (animal phobia), more precisely, 24 December, the night before the Wolf Man's birthday. The turning point was an anxiety dream that the Wolf Man still remembered as an adult and retold as follows:

> I dreamt that it was night and that I was lying in my bed. (My bed stood with its foot towards the window; in front of the window there was a row of old walnut trees. I know it was winter when I had the dream, and nighttime.) Suddenly the window opened of its own accord, and I was terrified to see that some white wolves were sitting on the big walnut tree in front of the window. There were six or seven of them. The wolves were quite white, and looked more like foxes or sheep-dogs, for they had big tails like foxes, and they had their ears pricked like dogs when they pay attention to something. In great terror, evidently of being eaten up by the wolves, I screamed and woke up (Freud 1918b, p. 29).

It was the wolves in this dream that gave the Wolf Man his name. Freud heard the dream at an early stage in the analysis and the process of interpreting it lasted for several years and took place in many contexts that we are not able to discuss here. Briefly, the dream formation began with the dawning passive phallic wish for the father as sexual object. This wish correlated quite naturally with the wish for the Christmas and birthday presents anticipated the next day. (Most children think about presents when they go to bed the night before Christmas.) Both cases involved *receiving* something from the father. The preconscious dream wish manifested itself as the wish to *see* the presents especially those given by the father to the mother (in the sexual sphere), which the Wolf Man envied her. The dream fulfilled this wish by calling forth the primal scene from memory (and we must at this point mention one of Freud's qualifications: a primal fantasy may be put in the place of the primal scene retroactively as a combination of the wish and real experiences from other areas). However, the primal scene did not get the opportunity to become conscious because it immediately triggered castration anxiety, which did the work of dream censorship. The manifest dream was the result of considerable dream work, which transformed the primal scene into a more acceptable form. The dream picture of the wolves in the walnut trees showed the presents hanging on the Christmas tree but indicated also through anxiety that it was associated with danger in receiving presents.

The dream work can only be understood if the memory material that associates the primal scene to the manifest dream is known. Initially it is difficult to see any resemblance. We will therefore point to the three most important connecting points. (1) The Wolf Man's grandfather had told him a story about a tailor and a wolf. The tailor was at work when a wolf suddenly jumped in through the window. The tailor managed to cut its tail off, and the wolf fled. Later, the tailor was walking through the forest and was surprised by a pack of wolves. The tailless wolf was among them and wanted revenge. The tailor ran and climbed a tree to escape but the tailless wolf suggested that the wolves stand on each other's backs so the wolf at the top could reach the tailor. The tailless one was at the bottom. When the pyramid formed by the wolves was almost complete, the tailor suddenly shouted: "Grab the grey one by the tail." The tailless wolf became so frightened that he turned and ran away once again and the pyramid collapsed. (2) The Wolf Man had heard the fairy tales involving wolves, for example, "Little Red Riding Hood" and "The Wolf and the Seven Kids." In the latter tale the wolf succeeded in eating six of the kids. It got the kids to open the door by powdering its paws white and pretending to be their mother. The Wolf Man's book of fairy tales had a picture of a wolf standing on its hind legs like a human being. (3) Finally, Freud believed that the father had played wolf with the Wolf Man and jokingly said: "I'm coming to eat you." Moreover, the Wolf Man clearly remembered his father's taking him out to see the sheep at a time when they were suffering from some serious disease and most of them had died. Freud suggested another aspect relevant to the primal scene: Perhaps the Wolf Man had seen sheep or herd dogs (German shepherds) mating. He might have heard that wolves attack flocks.

We can now sketch a rough outline of the process of dream formation and dream distortion. In the primal scene the father is copulating with the mother from the rear (as dogs do, said Freud, allowing for the possibility that the Wolf Man had seen dogs or sheep copulating and imagined that his parents had intercourse in the same way). The manifest primal scene suggested other things to the Wolf Man: If he were to take his mother's place, his penis would have to be removed, and he would instead have an open "sore." This idea resulted in an overpowering castration anxiety. Castration was depicted in the story of the wolf that lost its tail. The tailless wolf that the other wolves crawled up on thus represented the mother and, correspondingly, the wolf standing on its hind legs (in the book of fairy tales) represented the father. The idea of being eaten by the wolf represented the copulation except that the relation had been displaced from the phallic to the oral zone. In the manifest dream, the primal scene was now evinced through other parts of the wolf stories, and Freud was especially conscious of the reversals (special cases of distortion) that had occurred. The window opened by itself in the same way that the Wolf Man's eyes did when he glimpsed the primal scene. The wolves stared at him, as in the primal scene he had stared at his parents. It was the pursuing wolves and not the pursued tailor who sat in the tree. The wolves were white (like sheep and like the wolf's paw that had been whitened with flour and perhaps like the naked parents in the primal scene). They were motionless (in contrast to the parents' strenuous movements) and had large foxtails (attempt to deny castration).

The wolf dream, as already mentioned, introduced a phase in which the phobic symptoms were predominant. The Wolf Man was not only afraid of wolves but also of the smaller animals he generally mistreated. He remembered once having followed a large butterfly. It lighted on a flower (and would have been easy prey for his sadistic impulses), but suddenly he was seized with anxiety and ran off crying. In Freud's view each instance of anxiety was actually displaced castration anxiety. However, in contrast to the phobia of little Hans, the repressed impulses directed toward the father were not the active sadistic but the passive phallic and homosexual instead. The Wolf Man's phobia was by far the more serious because overcoming the repression only created a new problem for him, that of managing and further developing his homosexuality. Freud said that the Wolf Man's intestinal troubles, which developed later (constipation, diarrhea, and intestinal pains), were true hysterical symptoms. They were signs in distorted form of a wish to achieve the homosexual object choice through anal intercourse. Freud ran into some theoretical difficulties in this regard when he maintained that the Wolf Man simultaneously repressed and rejected the homosexual attitude (in repression, the idea that the penis must replace the vagina was maintained; in repudiation, the alternative was avoided by regression to the anal phase). In reality it is very unlikely that the Wolf Man at this point had an idea of the vagina. Only a few years after publishing the case history Freud declared in a discussion with, among others, Karen Horney and Melanie Klein that neither boys nor girls knew anything about the vagina before puberty (see V.B.2.a). Thus, it was the idea of anal intercourse with the father that was repressed and was the cause of the phobic symptoms. In our view the concept of repudiation only seems relevant in connection with the Wolf Man's reaction to Nanja's castration threat.

IV. After his fourth birthday the Wolf Man started to become a problem child. He had retained his sadistic and especially his masochistic attitudes shown by his irritability, blatant disobedience, and cruelty toward animals. Moreover, he was also hysterically fearful. When he was four and a half years old, his mother and Nanja started his religious education. This caused the disobedience stemming from his masochism to abate along with his sadism, and his phobic anxiety disappeared. Instead, the Wolf Man developed a remarkable compulsive piety, said the Lord's Prayer, crossed himself continuously, and kissed all the images of the saints in his room before going to bed at night. It is to be assumed that religion combined the ideal formations and the anxiety preparedness of the castration threat with an integrated and stabilized superego. The superego was an impersonal and abstract structure originally formed in the parents' image, but gradually it separated from it and established a psychic position in which different concrete ideals (father, God, the tutor, and Freud) could reside in turn. The superego of the Wolf Man contained an abstract concept of justice that the concrete ideals also had to attain. This explains why with such relative ease he could exchange one ideal for another without his personality's breaking down.

The Wolf Man's religiosity, as already indicated, was directly obsessional neurotic in periods and when so, it reflected basic psychic conflicts. In Freud's view, the religious instruction was so effective because the Wolf Man identified with Jesus. They had the same birth date and the Passion of Jesus appealed in particular to his masochistic feelings, which were a part of his piety but in sublimated form. The repressed homosexual wishes were, however, able to gain access to the religious world of ideas. The Wolf Man wondered if Jesus had a bottom and if he had bowel movements just like everyone else. He repressed these thoughts and explained them away so that only the masculine and active side of Jesus was in evidence. At the same time the Christian morality was also responsible for the repression of sadistic impulses in their external form. They became part of the repressed, which was then reorganized and started to produce new symptoms. The initial purpose of the many prayers was to veil the repressed sadism, but the compromise formation gradually began to weaken. The "good" impulses from the superego and the "bad" impulses from the repressed combined openly with each other. The Wolf Man had compulsive associations, for example God-pig-shit. There was, in fact, a period when the Wolf Man could not see three piles of horse droppings without thinking of the Trinity. This developed into pure blasphemy and a clearly formulated clash with God: God was bad and unjust because he did not take all evil out of the world even though it was in his power to do so. Later when the Wolf Man got an irreligious tutor, he definitively gave up his faith.

There were traits in the Wolf Man's compulsive piety that we have not yet mentioned. A deep inhalation signaled the intake of the Holy Ghost and a strong exhalation the expulsion of evil spirits. The sight of sick and handicapped people, for whom he had great compassion, caused an intense exhalation and, one time, when visiting his father in the hospital, the sight led him automatically to see his father in the same light. This contained a new association back to the primal scene. The intense breathing with its in- and outgoing movements reminded him of the parents' intercourse, and the compassion he felt for his father was represented in the idea of his losing his penis when it disappeared into his mother. The primal scene (at around age one and a half) was thus a bridge between narcissism and the Oedipus complex (between the narcissistic pleasure ego's introjection and projection and the oedipal ego's interest in disappearance and reappearance). Later Freud had occasion to make the same observation when he saw his one-and-a-half-year-old grandchild play the game of peek-a-boo with a wooden spool (see mention of the "*Fort-Da*" game in V.B.2.b).

The Wolf Man's obsessional neurotic symptoms disappeared when he was around ten years of age. The explanation for this is that he succeeded in finding a sphere of interest where his active and masculine attitude could find expression. This sphere was in the military, and Freud was aware of its similarity to the church. After puberty the Wolf Man developed heterosexually, and his interest centered on broad-bottomed servant girls. However, the weaknesses in his psychic structure emerged when he got gonorrhea at the age of seventeen. He felt his narcissism wounded and his masculinity threatened, and his repressed homosexuality became apparent again as hysterical intestinal troubles. Moreover, he acquired such a morbid relation to money that he thought first and foremost of his inheritance when his sister committed suicide and his father died. He oscillated between stinginess and extravagance on a parallel with this constipation and diarrhea. While at a sanatorium he fell violently in love with a nurse, but his relationship with her was no less ambivalent than the Rat Man's was with his woman.

The Wolf Man's analysis with Freud had two results. It removed some of the ambivalence from his manifest heterosexual love for the nurse so that after a while Freud found that marriage was acceptable. Furthermore, it freed the latent homosexual impulses that all along had been sublimated and bound to aesthetic interests. An epilogue to this story is that the Wolf Man lost his entire fortune during the Russian Revolution. After the war he returned to Vienna and had to manage as an office clerk in an insurance company. Despite his difficult position, he only had minor relapses. Freud treated him free of charge from 1919 to 1920 and collected some money for him. Ruth Mack Brunswick treated him from 1926 to 1929 for symptoms initially resembling hypochondria but that developed into a mild case of paranoia, including megalomania in that he thought of himself as Freud's closest associate, and a persecution mania focused on a professor who had operated on his nose (see Brunswick 1928). After his wife committed suicide in 1938 he suffered from depression. When he retired from the insurance company in 1950, he wrote his autobiography, which was published by Muriel Gardiner (Gardiner 1971).

In the 1970s the Wolf Man was interviewed by the journalist Karin Obholzer. In the interview he made some critical comments about Freud and psychoanalysis. These interviews were published in 1980 (Obholzer 1980), the year after his death, and were critically commented on by Muriel Gardiner. Other interviews, among them one by Kurt Eissler, reside in the Sigmund Freud Archives and have not yet been made available to the public.

V

THE THEORETICAL WORK

INTRODUCTION
TO PART V

Having reviewed Freud's analytic and therapeutic work in parts 3 and 4 respectively, we now turn to his theoretical production. Freud used the term *metapsychology* to denote psychoanalytic theory. He originally intended to create a counterpart to metaphysics, which he believed had put the cart before the horse. Through the ages idealistic philosophers had seen the material world as based on the world of ideas. Freud now wanted to strike back by positing the central nervous system as the basis of all psychological phenomena. This move was naturally inspired by the materialistic mechanism that had become popular in the natural sciences during the middle of the 1800s, but it did not represent Freud's definitive stand on the relationship between the soul and the body. He nevertheless continued to refer to psychoanalytic theory as metapsychology long after he had given up translating psychological phenomena into neurophysiological terms.

Freud made changes in metapsychology at regular intervals. It is possible to isolate three periods in which he worked on theoretical problems with particular intensity. We call these periods metapsychological thrusts. Though its results were first published in chapter 7 of *The Interpretation of Dreams* (1900a), the first metapsychological thrust occurred during the 1890s and coincided roughly with the birth of psychoanalysis. The next metapsychological thrust followed in the years 1910 to 1915. Divisions within the psychoanalytic movement were particularly instrumental in motivating Freud to make his theoretical position more explicit. In specific response to Jung, he clarified his theory of drives defining their genesis in a fundamental duality between sexual drives and drives of self-preservation. Furthermore, he reintroduced the concept of the ego, which he had abandoned in 1896 when he introduced the concepts of the unconscious and of the preconscious. His theory of drives once again underwent changes during the third metapsychological thrust of 1920 to 1925. The duality of sexual drives and drives of self-preservation was replaced by a new duality of life drives and death drives, which Freud found more consonant with his experience. The theory of the ego was completed by the formulation of the tripartite concept comprised of the id, the ego, and the superego.

It would be misleading to present Freud's theoretical work in such a way as to suggest that he finally succeeded in finding definitive solutions to all the theoretical difficulties he faced up to the time of his last theoretical thrust. Each metapsychological thrust had its own attributes and included points that could not be, and have not since been, integrated into the conceptual framework of the other thrusts. Thus, they all three deserve equal attention. Unable and unwilling as we are to abolish the contradictions and paradoxes inherent in Freud's theories, the reader would be mistaken in expecting to find a coherent conceptual edifice presented in the pages that follow. On the other hand, we would not be content to give a kaleidoscopic presentation of Freud's various theories without taking a stand on their value. Consequently, in section A we have chosen to examine Freud's three metapsychological viewpoints (topographic, economic, and dynamic) on the subject in a historical context and to appraise them. This appraisal guided our choice of relevant material for sections B and C on the subject's genesis and structure so that what is novel in Freud's theories is stressed at the expense of his more conventional psychological views, more often than not derived without change from the philosophy, psychology, and natural science of the 1800s. Referring to sections in the first part of the book enables us to show fairly accurately when Freud followed the views of his predecessors and when he took a step beyond them. This does not mean, of course, that these predecessors were insignificant, because without them and the experience that came with changed historical circumstances, Freud would not have been able to accomplish anything.

A.

THE CONCEPTUAL APPARATUS
OF METAPSYCHOLOGY

In order to understand the conceptual apparatus of metapsychology, we have to understand how Freud succeeded in transcending the traditional antithesis between mind and body by positing the unconscious as a link between them. We are dealing with a continuous epistemological process in Freud and it is not possible to say with certainty at what point in his theoretical evolution the idea of the unconscious came to him. This is in part because he never bothered to express his thoughts in traditional philosophical terms. Sometimes, he simply resorted to the purely natural-scientific explanations of the human subject from his student days; as a rule, however, he maintained his point of view that the unconscious was in principle different from both the realm of consciousness and the realm of neurophysiology.

There can be no doubt of the source of Freud's neurophysiological materialism and reductionism. These viewpoints had permeated the works of the Helmholtz school, taking a quasi-religious turn, and had spread to most European universities before being driven back by positivism and empiriocriticism (see I.B.2.a). Freud had already become acquainted with these ideas during his first years at the university and was later to get a first-hand presentation of them when he worked in Brücke's laboratory. Even Meynert who, as a psychiatrist, came from the Griesinger tradition, did not question the mechanistic and materialistic subject concept. Charcot, despite his work with hypnosis, was at bottom also a materialist, and Freud's two personal colleagues, Breuer and Fliess, believed in the fundamental principles of materialism and mechanism. Certainly no one denied the existence of consciousness or repudiated sense perception as a basis for cognition. A good empiricist did not need to succumb to positivist idealism.

Scientists were therefore careful not to overestimate the importance of consciousness. Consciousness was considered an appendage to neurophysiological processes, a dependent variable that could not by itself add or subtract anything to or from these processes. In philosophy, this concept of the relationship between mind and body is called epiphenomenalism, which implies that consciousness is a superficial phenomenon, an epiphenomenon.

Freud did not maintain the epiphenomenalistic point of view, but his rejection of positivism as an alternative may be attributed to his admiration for Fechner (see I.B.4), one of the first who took the manifestations of consciousness so seriously that he set out to find the precise relationship between mind and body using methods derived from the natural sciences. Freud learned from Fechner's psychophysics that it was possible to explore consciousness as a parallel to the physiological processes of the brain (inner psychophysics) and as part of the sensorimotor reflex (outer psychophysics).

Fechner did not get very far in his study of inner psychophysics. He discussed various conceptions of localization and consciousness and finally reached a compromise, saying in effect that processes taking place in various parts of the brain could be conscious at different times (this is what we have previously referred to as his theory of sleep). With Fechner, Freud rejected the narrow localization theories of scientists like Meynert. It was unthinkable that each sensory impression, each word, and each idea were specifically localized in one or several nerve cells. Instead, a complex neurophysiological process impossible to study directly was thought to correspond to each idea.

Fechner thus created the outer psychophysics to replace the inner psychophysics. We believe that Freud learned from this that it was possible to combine a psychological with a physical analysis without resorting to the old theory of psychophysical interaction. With the help of a complicated experimental apparatus it is possible to study how consciousness perceives a given, physically definable, stimulus. It then becomes meaningful to view consciousness as a serial connection between stimulus and response.

Freud's clinical work with nervous patients prompted him to abandon epiphenomenalism. Available data was collected from the associations and thoughts of patients, the exploration of processes in the nervous system being excluded from the beginning. For lack of anything better, Freud therefore accepted the necessity of working with phenomena of consciousness. This was his attitude when he introduced the works of Charcot and

Bernheim in Vienna around 1890. The argument was blatantly obvious and did not at first pose a threat to either materialism or mechanism. In his studies of hysteria, Breuer too made use of psychological concepts instead of using neurophysiological ones, which he defended in the following quick-witted manner:

> In what follows little mention will be made of the brain and none whatever of molecules. Psychical processes will be dealt with in the language of psychology; and indeed, it cannot possibly be otherwise. If instead of "idea" we chose to speak of "excitation of the cortex," the latter term would only have any meaning for us in so far as we recognized an old friend under that cloak and tacitly reinstated the "idea." For while ideas are constant objects of our experience and are familiar to us in all their shades of meaning "cortical excitations" are on the contrary rather in the nature of a postulate, objects which we hope to be able to identify in the future. The substitution of one term for another would seem to be no more than a pointless disguise" (Freud [and Breuer] 1895d, p. 185).

Freud was no stranger to psychological terminology, as evidenced by his great interest in fiction, poetry, and drama, his attendance at Brentano's lectures on the history of philosophy and his encounter with Bernheim's suggestion therapy, which continued the tradition of humanistic and moral therapies. As we saw in our discussion of the inception of psychoanalysis, Freud's work with nervous patients quickly led him beyond a psychology solely based on consciousness. Hypnosis and particularly posthypnotic suggestion were probably experiences that marked a watershed in Freud's development, since these phenomena demonstrated that a psychologically well-formulated motivation for an action could be both unconscious and lead to concrete action at the same time. Further evidence of this were the patients' "forgotten" experiences, their strangely structured symptoms, and the therapeutic effect of bringing repressed material to consciousness, all of which made Freud aware of the relationship between the conscious and the unconscious.

The idea of the unconscious had a long history with which Freud was somewhat acquainted. At the end of the 1800s, a voluminous thesis on the unconscious by E. von Hartmann (see I.B.1.b) attracted tremendous attention. Von Hartmann's thesis showed, if nothing else, that the concept was exceedingly complex. Since the term *unconscious* could be used about whatever was not conscious or whatever lay outside of consciousness, it could be used to mean anything. The realization alone that thoughts and perceptions in memory could be for the most part not clearly conscious suggests that the unconscious was part of any psychology. At least three fairly precise definitions of the unconscious (with or without explicit use of the term) can be discerned in the history of philosophy. They are as follows: (1) the unconscious as the misconceived or vaguely comprehended (Descartes, Leibniz), (2) the unconscious as the first cause of volition (Hobbes, Spinoza), and (3) the unconscious as what has not yet manifested itself and as the unrealized (Rousseau, Hegel). Herbart elaborated on the concept by introducing a threshold of consciousness between the conscious and the unconscious, and by furthermore placing both the unrealized in the outside world and the unrealized in the subject in the unconscious (see I.B.1 on philosophy).

We gave concrete examples of the unconscious in psychiatry and literature in the corresponding sections in part 1. According to the rationalistic point of view, the unconscious was that which lay outside the control of consciousness, such as passions that from time to time overpower reason like unconscious reflexes. Conversely, the romantics did much to explore the true nature of the processes outside of consciousness. It is from their work that the idea arose of an almost divine intelligence, on all counts superior to conscious intelligence. The belief in such an unknown agency was interpreted psychologically as a deeper layer in the subject, a layer containing memories of a distant past, particularly close both to feelings and to nature. According to many naturalistic authors the unconscious was, for better or worse, identical with the psychological universe of childhood, and the course of life could be measured by success in integrating the longings and traumatic experiences of childhood in the adult personality.

In neurophysiology, there were several rudimentary conceptions of the unconscious. The most primitive one defined the unconscious as the neurophysiological correlate of consciousness. The conscious and the unconscious were regarded as parallels, consciousness being the dependent variable. Johannes Müller's ramified reflex model (see I.B.3) was a slightly more complex proposition. Here, the spinal reflexes not involving the medulla oblongata were clearly defined as unconscious. Finally, Jackson's and Meynert's genetic-hierarchic models made it possible to place the unconscious in lower and, genetically speaking, more primitive reflex centers, that could occasionally become conscious and control the behavior of the individual when higher and more recently developed centers were damaged.

Freud attempted to give the unconscious a neurophysiological definition several times. Had he succeeded, he would have been able to reconcile both his theoretical epiphenomenalism and his clinical experience. None of the three above-mentioned possibilities satisfied him, however, in part because they left no room for the concepts of splitting and defense discovered in his clinical work. He therefore proposed a fourth possibility, the retranscription model of December 1896. This has already been mentioned in the section on the inception of psychoanalysis (see II.B.3), and we will deal with it again later (see V.A.1a). For now, it will suffice to point out that its objective was to place both the conscious and the unconscious in the same reflex path. Sensory impulses were invariably supposed to pass through a series of systems including the unconscious before reaching consciousness. The systems were ordered in the same sequence as that in which they had been formed, and each system represented a specific phase of development. Unlike Meynert's and Jackson's theories this model held that the lower systems were able to organize and carry out their processes without putting higher systems out of function, and that boundaries between systems were not fixed. The elements of one system could, through defense mechanisms, be split off from it and join another system.

Even if Freud's hypothesis did not explicitly separate the unconscious from its neurophysiological definition, he certainly had great difficulty imagining that the series of psychological systems could be located in the cerebral cortex. Such a view would, for example, imply that neurons (nerve cells) were "written on" like a sheet of paper, from top to bottom, and that the memory traces of a two-year-old child were only to be found in one corner of his cerebral cortex, while the rest remained blank. Hence, we may affirm that it was the untraditional place of the topographical model in relation to the reflex arc that compelled Freud to separate the unconscious from neurophysiology. Had he not realized the necessity of taking this step, he would have exposed himself to the same criticism he had so mercilessly directed at Meynert's localization theory a few years earlier. Freud, however, first made his new point of view known when he introduced the fictitious topographical model in *The Interpretation of Dreams* (this model is discussed below; see V.A.1.a):

> What is presented to us in these words is the idea of *psychical locality*. I shall entirely disregard the fact that the mental apparatus with which we are here concerned is also known to us in the form of an anatomical preparation, and I shall carefully avoid the temptation to determine psychical locality in any anatomical fashion. I shall remain upon psychological ground, and I propose simply to follow the suggestion that we should picture the instrument which

carries out our mental functions as resembling a compound microscope or a photographic apparatus, or something of the kind. On that basis, psychical locality will correspond to a point inside the apparatus at which one of the preliminary stages of an image comes into being. In the microscope and telescope, as we know, these occur in part at ideal points, regions in which no tangible component of the apparatus is situated. I see no necessity to apologize for the imperfections of this or of any similar imagery. Analogies of this kind are only intended to assist us in our attempt to make the complications of mental functioning intelligible by dissecting the function and assigning its different constituents to different component parts of the apparatuses. So far as I know, the experiment has not hitherto been made of using this method of dissection in order to investigate the way in which the mental instrument is put together, and I can see no harm in it. We are justified, in my view, in giving free rein to our speculations so long as we retain the coolness of our judgement and do not mistake the scaffolding for the building. And since at our first approach to something unknown all that we need is the assistance of provisional ideas, I shall give preference in the first instance to hypotheses of the crudest and most concrete description (Freud 1900a, p. 536).

The result of Freud's constructions are some psychological systems that are neither conscious nor neurophysiological. They are, in the broad sense of the word, unconscious. The unconscious is the intermediary link between the psychological and the physical. In a 1917 letter to Georg Groddeck, Freud frankly called it "the missing link." It has been noted that in his metapsychology Freud described the unconscious with concepts similar to those employed in neurophysiology (memory trace, psychic energies, energy displacements, and pathways), but this must not be misconstrued to indicate that metapsychology is merely neurophysiology in disguise. In fact, just as many Freudian concepts are derived from the humanities, for example, the Oedipus complex, the castration complex, and unconscious fantasies. Freud sometimes said that the (descriptive) unconscious had the same characteristics as the conscious, but simply lacked the quality of consciousness, thus implying that the unconscious was located at the level of psychic quantities. So, all in all, then, he operated with the following three descriptive levels: (I) the physical-biological level and, within the psychic level, (II) the level of psychic quantities (or the level of the descriptive unconscious) and (III) the level of psychic qualities (or the level of consciousness).

Using the three levels, we can now illustrate Freud's basic reflex model, which differs from Müller's and Fechner's reflex model:

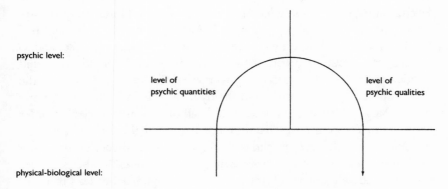

The three levels are not parallel, but have relative autonomy. A given impulse is processed in three principally different ways at the three levels, and this corresponds to Freud's three principally different ways of looking at the subject. When speaking of the human organism at the physical-biological level, he still used the language of mechanism, though now and then he was also inclined to use vitalistic language, and seemed to use mechanistic and humanistic conceptual contexts when describing phenomena at the level of psychic quantities. This duality, however, covers what we will call a structural understanding of the unconscious (see V.C). Finally, to characterize thoughts and feelings on the level of psychic qualities, Freud used terms from the traditional psychology of consciousness.

We can immediately affirm that Freud did not "solve" the psychophysical problem by positing these levels. Rather, he created three problems instead of one, that is, one problem related to each of the transitions between levels. Why did he complicate matters? For the simple reason that his goal was to give a thorough and practically useful picture of the forces that governed the human subject rather than to present a logically consistent and philosophically unassailable theory. We are used to accepting that processes take place within the human body that do not manifest themselves in consciousness even if they are essential to life. Conscious somatic sensations do not tell us the whole story. Likewise, Freud claimed, many psychic processes take place without ever becoming conscious, or maybe by becoming only partially conscious.

In the following section, we will occasionally make use of the three-level model in order to clarify some of Freud's points. This will afford us the opportunity to discuss the decisive question of the relationship between levels, that is, the ways in which processes at one level influence processes at the other levels. Freud's metapsychology is primarily at the level of psychic quantities, but it must be related both to organic processes and to feelings and thoughts before it can reveal its fullest implications. Freud divided metapsychology according to three different points of view, the topographical, the economic, and the dynamic. He insisted that any metapsychological explanation must include all three points of view in order to be complete. We have already made use of all three to describe the inception of psychoanalysis, and in doing so obtained an idea of the nature of their mutual relationship. At best they complement each other, at worst they are mutually exclusive, since using them together can lead to unresolvable contradictions. However, we will again make use of them in this section, because they furnish us with an excellent overview of the conceptual apparatus of metapsychology. The topographical aspect concerns psychic systems and their mutual relationships. The economic aspect concerns the theory of drives and affects, while the dynamic aspect concerns psychological processes and their regulatory principles.

1. THE TOPOGRAPHICAL VIEWPOINT

Two related sources served as inspiration for Freud's topographical or spacial model of the psyche. The first source was the association psychology of the 1600s and 1700s (see I.B.1.a) and the second the neurophysiological localization theories of the 1800s (see I.B.3.a). The basic building blocks of association psychology were thoughts and ideas connected by association paths of varying strength. A "train of thought" was hence a movement of thought from idea to idea; a concept was a group of ideas associatively linked by a common trait. Herbart's theory of a threshold between conscious and unconscious ideas in particular suggested that they had a topographical localization. Many neurophysiologists became adherents of associationism, thinking it gave them a true picture of the way the brain was organized. The function of the brain was interpreted in terms of ideas placed in different parts of the cerebral cortex and connected by a complicated network of neural paths.

Freud became acquainted with these problems at a time when the extreme localization theory was falling out of favor, and he contributed to the criticism leveled at it by attacking Meynert and others. Nevertheless, he continued to invent topographical models, although they were neither neuroanatomic nor neurophysiological, but rather fictitious. In doing so he returned in a sense to philosophical association psychology. The difference was that he divided ideas into new groups and defined new types of associations between them.

(a) Freud's Models of the Psychic Apparatus

Freud's 1891 monograph on aphasia contained a critical review of a number of works on the subject (Freud 1891b). Most authors pursued a line of reasoning in direct continuation of Broca (see I.B.3.a), and in order to explain various types of speech disturbances they attempted to place the function of speech in relation to a sensorimotor reflex model. Along the ramifications of the reflex through the brain they placed sensory and motor centers that were connected among themselves by various neural paths. The model was then used to explain different types of aphasia. In his exposition Freud made direct use of the graphic models found in Werniche's, Lichtheim's, and Grashey's monographs. In order to illustrate his own conception he added a diagram of the elements comprising a word presentation (the idea of a word) and the elements that constituted the object idea. The model is Freud's first draft of a model of the psychic apparatus (1891b).

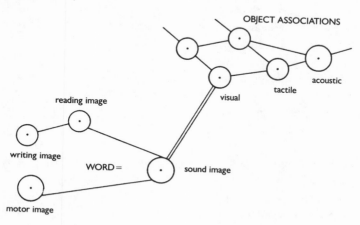

What was new in the model was that the elements of the word presentation comprised a coherent group separate from the elements of the object presentation. Taking the word *horse* as an example, the object presentation would be comprised of elements derived from sense perception, for example, the horse's appearance (visual), how the horse feels (tactile), and what sounds the horse makes (acoustic). This group of elements is open, which probably means that the object (in this case, the horse) has an unspecified number of characteristics. The word presentation on the other hand, is closed, since it is only composed of the following four elements: the sound image (the sound of the word), the motor image (the idea that allows the word to be uttered), the reading image (the way the word appears on paper), and the writing image (the idea that allows the word to be written). It is implied that the main direction of the reflex goes from the object presentation to the word presentation and that linkage (association proper) takes place between the visual image of the object (which represents the entire object presentation) and the sound image (which thence represents the entire word presentation). The only part of the model Freud kept in his subsequent work was the emplacement of the object or thing presentation and the word presentation into two separate systems.

Freud's work with hysterical patients made it possible for him to see the organization of the psyche in an entirely new light. The stimulating though often somewhat vaguely formulated idea of split consciousness invited a topographical description, and when Freud shaped his conception of defense during the period from 1892 to 1895, the model of the psychic apparatus took form. There were two mutually incompatible groups of presentations each with its own content. The one included normal and generally accepted ideas, while the other included ideas that in one way or another were unpleasant, secret, or objectionable (see II.B.2).

In the "Project for a Scientific Psychology" (Freud 1950a) from the fall of 1895, Freud temporarily returned to his neuroanatomic and neurophysiological point of departure. In the "Project," he no longer expressed himself in terms of groups of ideas, but in terms of groups of neurons (nerve cells). Despite this, it was later possible for him to transfer many aspects of the "Project" to a purely psychological theory. This was, for example, the case for his conception of the psychic apparatus as a reflex apparatus. In the "Project" the nervous system was susceptible to two different types of impulses, namely, external stimuli (sensory impulses) and internal stimuli (normally called impulses of need). The nervous system coordinated the two types of impulses in its choice of motor reactions. This led to the following general model, the prototype of all of Freud's later models:

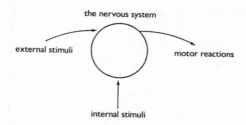

The model contained nothing new or original. Countless authors before Freud had already made use of it (see I.B.1.D, I.B.3.b). In this context, Freud's merit lay only in having worked out the theory of bodily stimuli of a sexual nature (the sexual drives).

External stimuli are picked up at the outer periphery of the nervous system by the sensory organs and are led from there to a so-called perception system Freud called φ (phi). From there, two paths lead to the system of consciousness ω (omega), both a direct one and an indirect one that first passes through the memory system ψ (psi). The direct path can be interpreted to mean either that all sensory impressions become immediately conscious, or that any cathexis of the system φ influences the system ω in such a way that it becomes receptive to impulses from the system ψ (we have briefly discussed this problem in connection with dream formation; see III.A.1). Characteristic of φ and ω is that neither holds back or inhibits impulses and consequently does not involve memory. Freud said that consciousness and memory excluded each other. The system ω is able to transform quantities of energy into qualities (corresponding to the transition from the quantitative to the qualitative level) because specific oscillations take place in it. It is furthermore the last neuronic system that energy impulses pass through before they are transformed into motor innervation and thus into external muscle reactions.

In the system ψ, there are initial contact barriers between all the neurons, but these contact barriers are broken down by the impulses that pass through the system. This phenomenon is called facilitation, and it is a condition of memory. Facilitations are so conceived as to be able to sort out impulses. Large impulses go one way, while small impulses go another, and when an impulse of the same wave length or of the same amplitude comes along, it will follow the same channel as its predecessor, and subsequently trigger the same impression in consciousness.

The body's own stimuli (stimuli of need) reach the nervous system elsewhere, that is, along the inner periphery corresponding to receptors inside the body. They do not directly activate consciousness, but are stored in that part of system ψ Freud called nuclear neurons. From there they are transferred to the true ψ neurons, also called mantle neurons, and it is here they in a manner of speaking mingle with sensory impulses.

In general, it can be said that the partitioning of the memory system into object presentation and word presentation or into two incompatible ideational groups is not integrated into this model. Freud, incidentally, did not make a drawing of his model. This has led to many proposals through the years. We suggest the following graphic description, corresponding to the systems and relations we have mentioned:

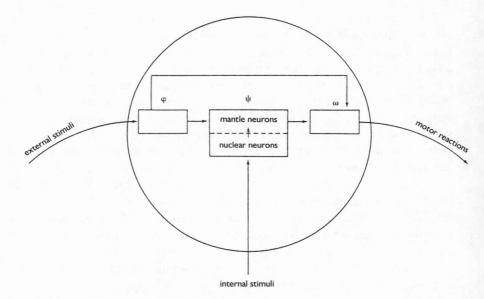

We will discuss more thoroughly how these systems function in the section below on adaptive development (see V.B.1).

In a letter to Fliess dated 1 January 1896 Freud expressed doubt as to the reciprocal order of the systems, but it was first in the letter dated 6 December 1896 that he integrated the distinction between different types of memory ideas. Freud did so in the retranscription model that we have already mentioned (see quotes in II.B.3) and that Freud diagramed as follows:

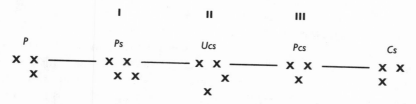

The internal stimuli have clearly been left out. Only the true sensorimotor reflex is left. As above the outer systems are a perception system *(P)* corresponding to φ and a system of consciousness *(Cs)* corresponding to ω. In between, as Freud stated, lie at least three memory systems corresponding to ψ, that is: I, a system of perceptual signs; II, the unconscious; and III, the preconscious. The difference between the systems lies in (1) the various times at which the facilitations of memories are established (first *Ps*, then *Ucs*, and finally *Pcs*), (2) the types of memory ideas (*Ps* contains pure sensations, *Ucs* contains conceptual presentations, and *Pcs* word presentations), and (3) the types of associations characteristic of each (from relations of similarity and contiguity in *Ps* to complex connections in *Pcs*), and finally, (4) pathological splitting is now made consistent with the general model to the degree that whatever is split off (unpleasant, objectionable, and secret ideas) is held back in the system *Ucs*. Thus, pathological repression consists in thing and conceptual presentations in *Ucs*'s not being translated into word presentations in *Pcs*.

The model evoked in this letter of 1896 is quite similar to the following model completed in 1899 and elaborated in *The Interpretation of Dreams* (1900a, p. 541):

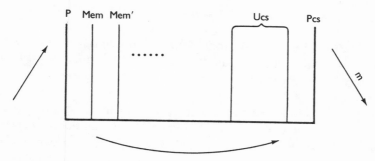

There are, however, some differences; the system of perceptual signs is changed to an undefined number of memory systems (Mem, Mem', and so on), and the system *Cs* is entirely left out. In our examination of the phases of dream formation (see III.A.1.a) we suggested another version of the model, one where the memory systems preceding the system *Ucs* are left out while the system *Cs* is put in after the system *Pcs* in agreement with the 1896 letter. Judging from the text, Freud still believed that the impulse became conscious between *Pcs* and the motor reaction (m). It is therefore difficult to guess what made him leave out the system *Cs*.

After *The Interpretation of Dreams,* Freud ceased inventing new models for some time. Until the essays of the second metapsychological thrust (1910–1915) nothing new happened, and even in them Freud still referred to the reflex model of *The Interpretation of Dreams*. It is evident, however, that he relied more and more on a simplified version of the model, where only *Ucs, Pcs,* and *Cs* remained, and where *Ucs* received drive impulses coming from the inner periphery while *Cs* received sensory impulses from the outer periphery. This corresponded to the following model:

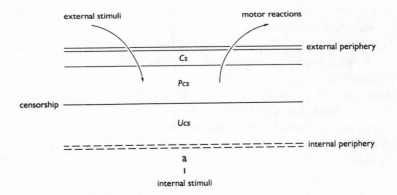

In the pedagogic introductory lectures on psychoanalysis from 1916 to 1917, Freud described the model using figurative language that left no doubt as to the place of the system *Cs*. A guest is in the entrance hall *(Ucs)* and wishes to enter the drawing room *(Pcs),* but a watchman (censorship) stands at the door and inspects the guests to make sure that they are presentable (drawing room qualifications). If a guest is not presentable, he is turned away. If, on the other hand, he is let in, the last step consists in being noticed by consciousness, standing at the back of the drawing room. Perhaps Freud imagined that the host of the party hadn't had time to speak to all of his guests and therefore had been forced to focus his attention on the most noteworthy ones. This relates to the metapsychological idea that ideas in *Pcs* are not conscious but easily can become so, whereas ideas in *Ucs* first must obtain access to *Pcs* before they can become conscious (see 1916–1917, lecture 19).

The model was altered once again during the third metapsychological thrust (1920–1925). In *Beyond the Pleasure Principle* (1920g) the psychic apparatus was compared to a simple unicellular organism made up of protoplasm. It was influenced by various stimuli coming from the external world, forming a protective layer around itself (a stimulation barrier). The now unified systems of perception and consciousness *(P-Cs)* arose from this layer. Consciousness also received impulses from within, but it had no other protection against them than the defense mechanisms it progressively deployed. The undifferentiated protoplasmic vesicle became the prototype of the id, that is, the new concept Freud introduced to replace the system *Ucs*. The part of the protoplasmic vesicle that differentiated as a result of the influence of the external world became the prototype of the ego. The ego arose on the vesicle's surface from the system *P-Cs,* replacing the latter concept.

Freud had several reasons for changing his concepts. For example, it was unfortunate that the relationship to consciousness alone determined the dividing line between the system *Pcs* and the system *Ucs*. In principle, many other criteria could be as valid, for example, the distinction between word and thing presentations, between primary and secondary processes, and between memory ideas of childhood and memories acquired later. As long as the divisions were congruent, there was no problem, but Freud had discovered that they were not so on at least one count. It was striking that in many patients not only were repressed ideas unconscious, but so were repressing ideas. The perhaps traumatic memories inducing repression are themselves unpleasurable and thus lack the ability to become conscious. Still, they logically belong to the secondary system that, in a manner of speaking, defends itself against sexuality. The repressing ideas are not themselves repressed, since they do not attempt to become conscious. The topographical model must be modified for them to be integrated. Whereas earlier Freud tentatively described the repressing agencies as censorship between *Ucs* and *Pcs,* though belonging more to *Pcs,* he now called the entire secondary system the ego, where the repressing ideas were on a par with all other ideas. Freud sometimes even went so far as to call them the core of the ego.

Freud had often used the term *ego* before he introduced the preconscious in 1896. Also the concept of the ego appeared in several papers during the second metapsychological thrust, and it was natural to select it when the preconscious had to be replaced. Freud, on the other hand, did not have any useful concept at his disposal with which to replace the unconscious. His choice of the id *(das Es)* was inspired by the German physician Georg Groddeck, with whom he corresponded extensively around 1920. Groddeck had borrowed the concept from Nietzsche, for whom the term covered "whatever in our nature is impersonal and, so to speak, subject to natural law" (Freud 1923b, p. 23). Freud did not agree with Groddeck's almost romantic definition of the id as a supreme psychosomatic intelligence, although he did recognize that the id had its roots in biology and consequently integrated all (supposed) innate biological forces in the id.

The first diagram of the new topographical model is to be found in a letter from Freud to Groddeck dated 17 April 1921. In it, the repressing ego and the repressed ideas face each other on the horizontal axis, while the relation between *Ucs, Pcs,* and *Cs* is retained on the vertical axis (on the condition that the repressed, the id, and the repressing part of the ego are synonymous with *Ucs*). The following model is drawn on the basis of Freud's diagram:

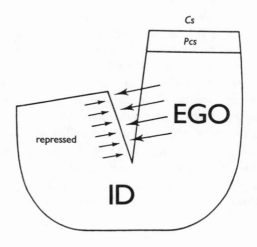

A distinction between a conflictual dimension (horizontal) and a genetic one (vertical) permits two conceptions of the ego. It is possible for the ego both to be in conflict with the repressed and to merge with the id. It can be both unconscious and preconscious and contain both primary and secondary processes. Missing from the model is the concept of the ego ideal Freud had been using sporadically for a number of years, and which he had analyzed in depth in *Group Psychology and Analysis of the Ego* (1921c).

In *The Ego and the Id* (1923b) the analysis of the ego ideal was pursued, only the agency was renamed superego and defined as an independent psychical system. It was largely unconscious, implying that it contained the repressing ideas. Freud doubted whether he should consider the superego as part of the ego or not, and consequently did not include it in his first official model of the new topography. In the new model, however, P and Cs were explicitly joined together (with the curious exception of hearing, that is, "acoust.") Finally, it is notable that the repressed was no longer so sharply demarcated from the rest of the apparatus. The model is as follows (1923b, p. 24):

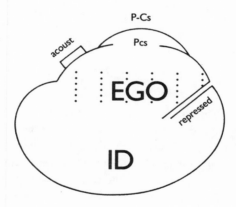

In Freud's last version of the model as it appeared in *The New Lectures* (1933a), the superego was drawn in and the proportions somewhat modified. The id became relatively larger and was drawn with an opening at the bottom to suggest that it merged with the somatic. The repressed was moved to the upper side of the barrier, unlike in the first model, although this was probably due to an error. Finally, the apparatus was split in two by a dividing line placed between the preconscious and the unconscious. This showed that the kinship between the old and the new terms was not simple. The old terms *(unconscious, preconscious,* and *P-Cs)* were to be read horizontally, whereas the new terms *(id, ego,* and *superego)* were to be read vertically. Incidentally, the whole model was placed horizontally in the first edition of *The New Lectures.* Furthermore, it is often somewhat cramped and we have enlarged it below.

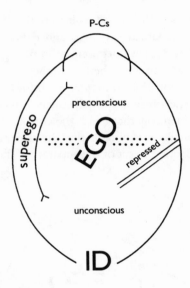

In the text that accompanied the model (1933a, lecture 31), the same characteristics were ascribed to the id as had been ascribed to the system *Ucs* earlier, which again showed that the relation between repressed and repressing was the major hinderance in maintaining the old terms. Incidentally, the idea that repression is the work of the superego and thus that the repressing ideas are to be found in the superego was most clearly stated in lecture 31.

(b) Comparison and Appraisal of the Topographical Models

The best way to compare the topographical models is to place them in relation to the three levels we presented at the beginning of this section and to introduce the distinction between the repressed and the repressing as a basis of comparison at the level of psychic quantities. By doing so, we obtain the following relations:

PHYSICAL-BIOLOGICAL LEVEL	somatic				
LEVEL OF PSYCHIC QUANTITIES	thing presentations / the repressed	Ucs	id		topographic unconscious
	the repressing / word presentations	Pcs	superego / ego	dynamic unconscious	descriptive unconscious
LEVEL OF PSYCHIC QUALITIES	the conscious	Cs			

The second topography disregards the dividing line between levels inasmuch as the id includes somatic components, whereas the ego contains memories and is also the conscious subject. While the repressed may be both thing and word presentations the repressing is in principle always made up of word presentations. In connection with the transition from the first to the second topography, Freud pointed out that he used the term *unconscious* in three different ways: (1) The topographical unconscious was the same as the system *Ucs*, a definition that is only relevant to the first topography. (2) the dynamic unconscious included all the ideas that for one reason or another could not immediately become conscious, that is, both the original thing presentations and the repressed and repressing ideas. In the somewhat simplified diagram above, we have equated the superego with the repressing (and thus dynamic) unconscious ideas, even if the superego also contains ideas that have direct access to consciousness. The confusion, however, also stems from the fact that Freud never clearly indicated the line of demarcation between ego and superego. (3) The descriptive unconscious included all the ideas that were not conscious, regardless whether they might become so or not. The descriptive unconscious thus covers the level of psychic quantities as a whole, and it is in this sense that we used the term in the introduction of this chapter.

A recurring problem in all the models is how to understand the relationship between perception and conscious systems. Freud may have had several things in mind when referring to a perception system, for example, the peripheral sensory receptors, the medulla oblongata, the sensory centers of the cortex, or perhaps all three localities at once. In any case, he seems to have used the term *perception (Wahrnehmung)* in the sense we usually use the word *sensation*. In contrast, the system *Cs* is the locality where true sensory perceptions and thinking become conscious. Impulses are processed as they pass through existing memory traces and are sorted out and analyzed in this way. This form of consciousness arises in the neurophysiological model where impulses are transformed into motor reactions, that is, at the motor (as opposed to the sensory) end of the reflex arc. This is consistent with Freud's statement that consciousness "controls the access" to the motor apparatus.

We do not wish to take a stand on the question of whether there exist a primary sensory consciousness and a secondary motor consciousness. Nevertheless, we do wish to point out fundamental problems that arose when Freud finally united the system *P* with the system *Cs* and placed them at the outer periphery. One gets the impression that impulses coming from the outside immediately become conscious as they are sensed, which is contrary to the common experience that they are processed before becoming conscious. Two people never perceive the same thing in the same way because each relates its characteristics to memories of his own. This supports Freud's statement that memory ideas prepare consciousness from the inside so that perception is the result of the crossing of outer and inner impulses in consciousness.

Even if one accepts this explanation, a problem still remains, namely, understanding the meaning of regression and its connection with dream formation (see III.A.1.a). In the first topography (and in particular in the model shown on page 158) the dream is perceived in the system *P,* to which it arrives by way of regression through *Pcs* and *Ucs.* This regression explains why dreams express themselves with, or are formed with the help of, simple sensory impressions. In the second topography (in particular in the completed model shown on page 336) there is no perception system below the id, since *P* has been joined with *Cs.* Freud might have been expected to revise the theory of dreams after the introduction of the new topography, but he did so only partially. Although it is true that the first lecture (no. 29) of *The New Lectures* (1933a) is entitled "Revision of the Dream Theory," Freud nevertheless spoke of regression as if the first topography had still been valid, which may have been true considering that the new topography was first introduced in lecture 31 (1933a), re-gardless of the fact that it had already existed for ten years. In *An Outline of Psycho-Analysis* (1940a), the order was reversed. Topography was dis-cussed in the first chapter and dream theory in the fifth, whereas regression was not mentioned at all. Dream theory was presented as if the id had carried its operational modes unchanged to the ego, whose ideas were subject to the rules of primary processes. We insist, however, that the three-phase explanation of dream formation is the most illuminating, since each of the three phases leaves its imprint on the manifest dream. It is an important factor in our inability to view the second topographical model as the best.

It would be fairly easy to build a model including both the inner and outer periphery, as well as regression and the agencies of the second topography. Deeper causes, however, explain why such a model would never be entirely satisfactory. In his work, Freud always assumed that no perception or thought could ever be forgotten. All impressions were in-scribed in the psyche as if on a slate where once inscribed they remained forever. With this hypothesis, Freud indirectly dissociated himself from Herbart's dynamic model, where ideas themselves were mobile, that is, able to move back and forth across the threshold of consciousness. Freud maintained (probably inspired by neurophysiological thought) that ideas were immobile (like neurons) and that psychic energy (corresponding to the electrical activity of nerves) gave the system motility. He elaborated the supposition that impressions from the same period of life were stored side by side and that later impressions were stored in layers above these, in such a way that the memory system taken as a whole was reminiscent of piles of slates where each new slate contained a revised reformulation of the memories that were inscribed on the slates below plus new memories. In doing so, Freud could explain how the original thing presentation on the first slate was transmitted to the next slate as word presentation and how some ideas were repressed by not being transferred to the new slates at all (see V.A.1.a).

The central position of ideational elements is the model's weakness. In the spirit of association psychology, memories are presented as subjects/ objects having specific characteristics or performing specific actions. Mem-ories recorded once and for all, for example, childhood memories, form a closed system of ideas that can no longer be altered once they have been covered by another system. One might add that it is rather the associations

that form the content of ideas, and that a given childhood memory continues to change character throughout life because it is constantly being put
in relation to new ideas. A textbook example of this is the Emma case (see
II.B.2) where the grocer's advances meant "incomprehensible behavior"
to the eight-year-old Emma, whereas they meant "forbidden sexual relations" to the twelve-year-old Emma. Other examples cited by Freud show
that repressed unconscious ideas do not originate from real experiences,
but are fantasies that have arisen by deferred action when a *later* knowledge
or drive attitude has crystallized around an *earlier* experience (see V.B.3).
This delayed formation of active unconscious fantasies is difficult to understand within the framework of a topographical model based on the
elemental psychology of associationism. The same is true for most primary
processes where an element first acquires meaning and structural value
through the relationship it establishes to other elements.

We may conclude that Freud's analytic experience was not entirely integrated into his topographical models. In order to bring the models into
agreement with experience, we must revise Freud's concept of the idea.
Ideas are not closed elements, but rather nodal points in a constantly
changing structure that induces change in the character of ideas. We must
add to this that ideas must not be thought of as meaning or content. What
is stored in memory is not stored as meaning or as perceived objects, but
as elements of form or expression able to induce meanings in consciousness.
Freud said that it was really more correct to speak of memory traces than
of ideas in memory. It is in consequence of this that we have drawn a line
between the level of psychic quantities and the level of psychic qualities.
In practice, however, it is often still necessary to speak of the structures on
the level of psychic quantities as if they were conscious ideas, which is what
we have done up to now. Given that this is so one could of course argue
that radicalizing the concept of the unconscious was a futile gesture (analogous to issuing inconvertible bank notes drawn on neurophysiology's
account). This would be the case were it not that some of the most exciting
aspects of Freud's work have to do with fantasy structures, symbolic sliding,
overdetermined elements, and the like. To this must be added that newer
attempts to describe the unconscious from a structural point of view have
led to encouraging results.

2. THE ECONOMIC VIEWPOINT

Freud's drive theory is his theory of the "internal stimuli" of the topographical models. Internal and external stimuli are comparable quantities of energy seen from the economic viewpoint. The internal stimuli, however, play the major role because they come to the psyche in a constant flow, whereas the external stimuli arrive as "momentary impact." The internal stimuli put the psychic apparatus to work while the external stimuli provide information about the world that makes work easier (however, external stimuli may have some independent economic importance in traumas, see V.C.2, below). In the next section we will therefore be concerned almost exclusively with internal stimuli. By way of introduction we will summarize the most important historical sources of the drive concept presented in part 1.

(1) *The vitalistic teaching concerning animal spirits.* The animal spirits were originally perceived to be animate beings circulating in the organism with movements determined by their own volition. Later, they were conceptualized as gases connected to the nervous system, filling all cavities and circulating in nerves thought to be hollow. Mental traits were metaphorically or literally connected with the movements of the animal spirits. Sluggish spirits corresponded to a phlegmatic or melancholic temperament, whereas swift spirits expressed themselves as liveliness. For a period, these descriptions were taken quite literally by psychiatrists and treatments were instigated on the basis of them.

(2) *The philosophical and literary teachings concerning affects.* We have mentioned Spinoza as an example of a philosopher who for all practical purposes considered affects and feelings as forces, and who was prepared to calculate the result of conflicting feelings much as one might calculate the resultant force vectors in a parallelogram: Philosophical, literary, and pedagogical teachings on feelings centered on descriptions of how wild and violent passions could best be tamed and harnessed. If a passion could not simply be suppressed, the next best thing would be to think of something else, that is, to transfer the affect to a new idea that was already cathected by other affects. In this way the latter affects were intensified while the former passion was harnessed.

(3) *The concepts of force and energy in physics.* The theory of thermo-dynamics stating that all forces could be measured by applying the same standards revolutionized physics. The only true difference between forces was whether the energy was available (free energy) or not (bound energy, that is, energy bound in the form of heat; see I.B.2.a). Similarly, Freud was of the opinion that all psychic energies could be appraised by the same standard, and like Helmholtz he distinguished between free and bound energies, though in a sense quite different from Helmholtz's (see below). Neurophysiologists generally used the science of electricity as a model in describing processes taking place in the nervous system, since the relation-ship between potential difference, resistance, and current intensity was equally valid for nerve electricity. The neurophysiological theory outlined by Breuer in the studies on hysteria held that a certain excitation (tonus) had to exist in the nervous system for electric impulses to pass. In sharp contrast to Breuer, Freud chose a more primitive energy theory as a model for his neurophysiology in the "Project," also written in 1895 (Freud 1950a). In Freud's eyes, the energy of the nervous system behaved much like steam in a steam engine. It sought release by applying force and pressure and set the system in motion doing so. One might say that Freud combined the animal spirit theories of earlier times with a veritable mechanical model, but refrained from using the science of electricity as a model for his psychology.

(4) *Instincts and needs in a neurophysiological context.* During the 1800s there were two competing theories of the internal biological moti-vating forces. While instinct theories focused on the inherited and species-specific reflex paths that determined behavior, the need and drive theories concerned themselves with individually acquired reflexes, created to elim-inate the unpleasure associated with hunger, thirst, and so on. Freud's elder colleague Exner combined these two theories by placing instincts in the lower centers of the nervous system and needs in the cerebral cortex. It was common to divide both needs and instincts into groups, and Exner thus operated with (1) instincts of self-preservation (nourishment and protection of the individual), (2) sexual instincts (procreation and parental care), and (3) social and moral instincts (see I.B.3.b).

Like his topographical models, Freud's conception of drives changed a number of times. A number of general traits did, however, remain un-changed. We will attempt to outline them by way of introducing the subject. We use the three descriptive levels we presented in the introduction to this chapter, since the definition of drive involves all three.

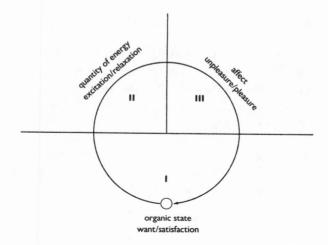

I. *The physical-biological level.* A drive arises as a stimulus or an excitation in an organ. This is true for hunger and thirst, for example, though we will not attempt to localize the organs involved more specifically. The stimulation sets a process in motion that is first completed when the stimulus ceases, that is, when hunger or thirst is satisfied.

II. *The level of psychic quantities.* The drive itself is generally defined as the psychic representation of the organic stimulus. It is imagined as a quantity of energy or quota of affect spread out over the memory traces. For the sake of simplification, Freud sometimes called memory traces ideas. Similarly, he often called quantity of energy and quota of affect affect, pure and simple, as if it were conscious. The energy creates excitation in the psychic apparatus, and the various energy displacements it causes aim at relaxation.

III. *The level of psychic qualities.* The energy quantum first becomes an affect when it is completely or partially discharged through consciousness. If excitation is maintained with almost no discharge, it will be experienced as unpleasure, whereas total discharge is experienced as pleasure. Discharging psychic energy through consciousness leads to a motor reaction of some kind; when this reaction consists in eradicating the organic stimulation the circle is closed (for example, by drinking a glass of water). In spite of the difference between them, both the affect and the reaction are part of the conscious registration of the drive. If we pursue our comparison of the psychic apparatus with the steam engine, the motor reaction corresponds to the movement of the piston, whereas the affect corresponds more to the sound emitted by the steam whistle, or for that matter, to the music played on a steam organ.

In order to reap benefit from this outline, we will probably have to imagine that, as in a spiral, several circular movements are necessary to close the original circle. A lengthier thought process will necessitate making each idea conscious and eventually carrying out test actions before finding the right way to react. We describe such complex processes in a later section (see V.B.1).

It must be pointed out that the outline best fits physiologically well-defined needs, and that the problem becomes significantly more complex where the sexual drives are concerned. They are, it will be recalled, the main subject of psychoanalysis (see V.C.2., on pleasure and unpleasure).

(a) The Development of the Drive Theory

During the first metapsychological thrust, Freud did not yet use the term *drive,* but generally spoke of internal stimuli instead. These stimuli were tied to nutritive functions as well as to sexuality, and Freud was not particularly preoccupied with making the distinction. It was first around 1897 that he began to take serious interest in infantile sexuality (see II.B.4), and in 1905 he published a complete sexual theory in *Three Essays on the Theory of Sexuality* (1905d). The theory made room for the four main forms of sexuality, that is, the infantile, the genital, the perverse, and the neurotic. It is there that the term *drive* appeared for the first time. All the drives were systematically studied with regard to their (1) source, (2) goal, and (3) object. The fourth determination of a drive, its pressure, in a sense less important than the others, was first added in 1915. We will review these terms one at a time, referring to Freud's later comments on them for the sake of completeness, although we wish to stress that they were in the main already defined in the first edition of *Three Essays on the Theory of Sexuality* (1905d).

(1) *The source of a drive.* The source of a drive is almost always placed at the physical-biological level. It is a stimulus applied to a specific organ by, for example mechanical or chemical means, that then reaches the psyche. Drive stimuli originate within the organism itself, which might lead one to think that they result from a gland function of some kind. Freud himself from time to time stated that the source of a drive might in some way be connected with the production of sperm cells, for example, but this was

refuted by the sexual life of children. On the contrary, the study of the sexual life of children shows that sexual stimulation arises preferentially from the surface of the body. A classical example is the analysis of the oral drive. One may observe that breast feeding does not simply serve the function of giving children nourishment. Contact between the breast (eventually, the pacifier) and the oral zone of the child is itself a source of stimulation and a pleasure experience of a sexual nature. This is supported by the fact that children often stimulate their oral zones even at times when they are not ingesting food. The child sucks its thumb or other appropriate objects it can get its hands on, and achieves obvious satisfaction doing so. It is conversely dissatisfied when prevented from sucking.

The above example confirms that sexual stimuli arise anaclitically from the processes of nutritive functions, particularly suction, the first prerequisite for ingesting food. The sexual stimulus is seen as a coexcitation emerging as a byproduct of the function of nutrition, but which has freed itself from the latter and become able to organize its own mode of satisfaction (sucking rather than suction). Freud said the area of the mouth had become an erogenous zone, and that the stimulation that had appeared really formed the basis of the oral partial drive. Further analysis suggests the existence of several such partial drives. First of all the anal, tied to processes located around the anus, and the phallic, tied to processes centered on the penis and the clitoris. Both these zones play a central role in carrying out bodily functions, from eating to defecation and urination. In principle, the entire surface of the body is a potential source of sexual excitation and the same is even true of the inside of the organism. We may compare coexcitation with the frictional heat generated in a machine with movable parts in operation. The parts of the machine that are most exposed will generate the greatest amount of frictional heat, even though all moving parts will in principle contribute. Similarly, Freud saw any movement made by an individual, from fist fights to train trips, as generating sexual excitement. He was also of the opinion that psychic processes generated sexual coexcitation, in particular exhausting intellectual work and strong emotions. In general, all the activities in which an individual may engage can be seen as sources of sexual excitation where even sexual activities themselves generate new sexual excitation. In a narrow understanding of the term, however, the sources of sexual drives are located in the erogenous zones of the body. Because of their anatomical locations and their physiological functions, these zones are particularly apt to attract and accumulate sexual excitation.

(2) *The aim of a drive.* According to the general definition of a drive, its aim is to eliminate the state of tension that is its source. It may be said that the drive finds satisfaction and induces a feeling of pleasure in doing so. However, it must be added that the aim of a drive also includes the activity necessary to remove the drive stimulus, for example, the activity of sucking. Although these aspects are all part of the definition, focusing on activity leads to the most thorough understanding of the concept, because partial drives may be distinguished from each other by virtue of the various activities that satisfy them, whereas it is not possible to do so on the basis of types of satisfaction or pleasurable affects. The oral partial drive is thus satisfied by sucking, biting, and incorporating, the anal by expulsing and retaining, the phallic by fondling and rubbing against other objects. There are partial drives less evidently associated with specific regions of the body, such as the partial drives of sadism/masochism and voyeurism/exhibition-ism. As far as the first are concerned, Freud assumed that they were related to motor and sensory organs respectively, such that the sadistic drive preferentially found satisfaction through activation of the arms and hands, whereas the masochistic drive found satisfaction in being exposed to strong sensory stimuli, for example, on the buttocks (see IV.A.2, on perversions). It follows from the above that some of the partial drives are ordered in pairs with regard to their aim, one of the pair being active and the other passive. We will return to this polarization in section V.C.1.

The importance of the activity leading to satisfaction is much more fateful for the sexual drives than it is for the nutritional drives. The sexual aim of orality (sucking) may be displaced to areas other than the oral part of the body. One may, for example, swallow the world with one's eyes or be particularly open to new ideas, and so on. In this way, the original sexual aim may remain as a character trait throughout life. The drive aims of the nutritional drives are organically determined. As long as the need for food is satisfied, it has no importance whether one sucks for food or eats it with one's fingers or with a knife and fork.

(3) *The object of a drive.* The sexual object is, according to Freud's definition, the person who exerts attraction or the person with whom or through whom the drive can attain its goal. If we compare sexual with nutritional drives, it is clear that the object of the latter is simply food, though granted, food that must contain proteins, carbohydrates, fats, and so on in a judicious ratio. The first food and the first object of the drive of nutrition is thus mother's milk. The oral partial drive that arises in anaclisis to the drive of nutrition does not have mother's milk as its original object,

but rather the mother's breast. It is not, as previously mentioned, dependent on this object, but may find satisfaction autoerotically, that is, without the support of an external object. The child may put his thumb in his mouth and suck on it, or perhaps rub his tongue against his lips and find satisfaction in doing so.

Based on the partial drives, the child gradually forms a group of ideas covering everything related to drive satisfaction, including ideas of good objects such as the mother's breast as well as other ideas concerning the zones and characteristics of the body. Freud called this group of ideas the pleasure ego. It is distinguished from later ego formations by disregarding the dividing line between the individual and the outside world. Such a line does not yet exist in the child's ideational world. One could go so far as to say that the world does not exist for the child and that his ideational world is one big pleasure ego. The child does not love any object, but only himself, which is why Freud called this developmental stage the narcissistic developmental stage. In this stage, the sensual stimuli tied to the erogenous zones are still satisfied autoerotically.

Narcissistic love is replaced during development by true object love. When the ego learns to distinguish between itself and the world, it generally learns to love an object in the world. The question now is what determines object choice. We will deal thoroughly with this question in section V.B on the subject's genesis, but we can already say that there are really two choices to be made: (1) In object choice of the narcissistic type the ego chooses an object that in some way resembles the ego itself (for example, in homosexual object choice). In object choice of the anaclitic type the ego chooses an object, much as the drive originally did, that is related to the satisfaction of the nutritional drives. Since the mother originally attended to feeding and care (and thus created sexual coexcitation), she is the most obvious choice, just as persons resembling the mother are preferred later. (2) The second choice has to do with the drive's having been split. One part has its basis in the erogenous zone and its stimuli, whereas the other has its basis in the pleasure ego. These two parts are the sensual and affectionate components of the drive, which according to Freud merge in such a way that the person one loves affectionately is also the one able to give sensual satisfaction. When this does not succeed, a typical pattern arises in which the male in particular must have two objects: a mother substitute to satisfy the affectionate impulses and a prostitute to satisfy the sensual ones.

(4) *The pressure of a drive.* Freud first added this determination of

drive in "Instincts and Their Vicissitudes" (1915c), in which he also gave a more systematic presentation of the three earlier determinations. The pressure of a drive is the amount of work demanded of the mind by drive stimuli and eventually manifested as a motor action. There is no exact measure with which to quantify such demands and Freud was unwilling to formulate a psychophysics similar to Fechner's in an attempt to do so. The concept of drive pressure can thus only be used to compare the various drives. It might for example be said that the anal partial drive of a given person is greater than the oral, and thus that its pressure is greater.

The modification undergone by drive theory during the second meta-psychological thrust (1910–1915) was probably directly caused by Jung's idea of a unified energy he called libido. Jung did not wish to give sexuality a place apart, and he accused Freud of letting sexuality become the all-dominating factor in his psychological theory (see II.C.1). Provoked by this, Freud attempted to clarify his conception of sexuality by distinguishing between sexual drives and ego drives (or drives of self-preservation, as he also sometimes called them). This distinction had already been implicit for several years, but was now put into sharper focus and explained in more traditional biological terms.

I. *The physical-biological level.* The fundamental biological contradiction in the individual is between preservation of the species and self-preservation. Biologically speaking, the sexual drives serve the species because they assure procreation, whereas the ego drives serve self-preservation because they are made up of the organism's biological needs (self-preservation is assured by eating, drinking, and so on). In principle, the two drives are in conflict with each other. This is particularly obvious when it comes to primitive organisms that die after procreation. In human beings, a degree of collaboration has been established; procreation affords the individual a certain amount of pleasure without endangering his existence.

II. *The level of psychic quantities.* In the "Project" (1950a) Freud had already distinguished between free and bound energies. This conceptual pair gains a new dimension when sexual drives are seen as free energies, while ego drives are seen as bound energies. Sexual drives, whose mental energy is called libido, aim at quick discharge by the shortest path without regard to consequences; it is difficult to teach them more complex patterns of thinking. Ego drives express themselves in the interests of the ego and move more slowly and more cautiously. They keep certain ideas constantly cathected, namely those comprising the ego, and serve the ego through their ability to think logically, to postpone satisfaction, and to inhibit other processes. Freud incorporated significant traits from vitalism and philo-sophical teachings on emotions (see the introduction of this section), even while using Helmholtz's concepts of free and bound energies. His idea that the ego drives were able to bind and inhibit the sexual drives had similar origins, as did the idea that the sexual drives might in some cases even be sublimated, that is, their energies put at the disposal of cultural and spiritual tasks far removed from the aims of the original sexual drives. The part of libido that follows the ego drives and cathects an object is called object libido, and the part remaining in the pleasure ego is called narcissistic libido or ego libido. The one form can automatically be trans-formed into the other, so the distinction has no drive-theoretical consequence.

III. *The level of psychic qualities.* Finally, Freud examined the ways the two types of drives found expression in consciousness, and claimed that the sexual drives expressed themselves as "love," whereas the ego drives found expression as "hunger." Love and hunger are, in other words, the typically unpleasurable forms of the drives, which when satisfied give rise to two different types of pleasure.

2d thrust (1910–15)	sexual drives	ego drives
THE PHYSICAL-BIOLOGICAL LEVEL	preservation of the species	self-preservation
THE LEVEL OF PSYCHIC QUANTITIES	free energy libido object libido ego libido	bound energy ego interest
THE LEVEL OF PSYCHIC QUALITIES	"love"	"hunger"

The transition from the second to the third metapsychological thrust is somewhat complicated with regard to drive theory, and we will therefore postpone the discussion of this transition until section V.A.2.b. For the moment, we will restrict ourselves to the unproblematic form of the drive theory of the third metapsychological thrust. The two basic categories are life drives and death drives, or Eros and Thanatos, as it later became customary to call them. We again obtain the most accessible overview by exploring the drive duality on each of the three descriptive levels separately.

I. *The physical-biological level.* The new drive categories are also defined biologically. Apparently, they are still to be understood as psychically represented stimuli making demands for work on the mind, but we are now dealing with new and fairly uncommon demands. The general aim of drives is to reestablish an earlier state, which assumes that a state exists that has been altered. Because all life comes from inorganic matter, the aim of the death drive is to lead life back to death, that is, to extinguish all trace of organic life. After the death drive, however, a life drive developed whose goal was to reestablish life. This drive assured in part procreation and in part the survival of the organism. The existence of two fundamental drives leads to a perpetual conflict where no state is permanent. Freud apparently believed that life drives had the upper hand at the beginning. The course leading from life to death lengthened as organisms of increasing complexity developed with ever more numerous survival mechanisms at their disposal, even when it did not take them longer to die. Furthermore, it became more difficult to distinguish the activities of an organism controlled by life drives from those controlled by death drives. In some cases, death drives served survival as externalized aggression, their aim being the natural death of the organism from old age and not its death as a consequence of chance attack coming from the outside.

II. *The level of psychic quantities.* Since Freud persisted in distinguishing between free and bound energies, the changes at this level were not very significant. Death drives are represented by free energies, confirming the assumption that they break down, split, and dissolve living matter. Life drives are represented by bound energies in consonance with the idea of them as general builders and creators of increasingly complex relations. In the psychic apparatus, death drives produce forces for aggression, whereas the energy of the life drives comes under the single heading of libido. Freud was still dividing libido into ego libido and object libido or more generally into ego drives and object drives. It was at this point that terminological difficulties developed as a result of the changes made in the theory of drives.

III. *The level of psychic qualities.* The purest affect of life drives is love, meaning love for life. Death drives find expression in consciousness as hate, in its purest form as self-hate. Freud also said, however, that death drives were silent, that is, they exerted their influence entirely outside of consciousness (Freud had the appearance of cancer cells in the organism in mind). In general, life and death drives manifest themselves together, enabling life drives to get the upper hand in the conflict. If life drives can bind a certain amount of the energy of death drives, they may use it to deploy the aggression necessary for self-preservation and procreation. In order to clarify the concept of sublimation of sexual drives, Freud advanced the concept of desexualization of life drives, meaning that their original aim was abolished and their energy put at the service of new aims.

All in all, a number of changes have taken place since the last diagram.

3d thrust (1920–25)	death drives (Thanatos)	life drives (Eros)
PHYSICAL-BIOLOGICAL LEVEL	return to the inorganic	preservation of life
LEVEL OF PSYCHIC QUANTITIES	free energy aggression	bound energy libido object libido ego libido object drive ego drive
LEVEL OF PSYCHIC QUANTITIES	"hate"	"love"

(b) A General Appraisal
of the Drive Theory

Freud did not believe the different steps taken during the development of the theory of drives were inconsistent with each other. For the most part, several additions made the complete drive theory more comprehensive. We do not agree unconditionally with this point of view and will therefore emphasize a number of points where Freud contradicted himself.

In *Three Essays on the Theory of Sexuality*, (1905d) sexual drives were described as partial drives arising through stimulation of the erogenous zones of the body. The stimulation may be called drives because they are able to set an activity in motion whose aim is to alleviate the stimulation, but also because the stimulation returns repeatedly after having been alleviated. Alongside them, we find the nutritional drives that were united under the term *ego drives* or *drives of self-preservation* during the second metapsychological thrust. They can be distinguished from sexual drives as follows: the body's need for food substances furnishes psychic stimuli that necessarily lead to an action by which food substances will be obtained; only when food has been ingested do the involved organs send a message back (feedback) to the mind temporarily interrupting the flow of stimuli. This closed circuit is so wisely conceived that the individual is forced to search for food; one may then justifiably speak of drives of self-preservation. But it is a different matter with sexual drives. Their source is stimuli in the erogenous zones and these stimuli do not have the same compelling influence on the mind as do the drives of self-preservation. The individual does not die if they are not removed, and their removal does not in itself serve any biological function. When a child has sucked his thumb long enough, he ceases doing so. It is therefore misleading to attribute to sexual drives superior biological aims such as the preservation of the species through the procreation of the individual. Most sexual drives have nothing to do with procreation and are quite able to unfold their activities without leading to acts resulting in procreation. This is in essence what Freud himself said when he criticized traditional sexual theories.

The next point concerns the relationship between the two drive dualisms. In *Beyond the Pleasure Principle* (1920g) Freud first attempted to equate ego drives with death drives and sexual drives with life drives, but soon abandoned this and then adopted the following formulation: ego drives and sexual drives might together be called the life drives, whereas the death drives comprised an entirely new category of drives.

death drives	life drives	
	sexual drives	ego drives

This understanding is only possible when the biological level is considered to be the fundamental one insofar as self-preservation and the preservation of the species both may be said to be ways of sustaining life. At the level of psychic quantities, on the other hand, it was necessary for Freud to abandon the earlier sharp line of demarcation between ego drives and sexual drives in that the single term libido designated the energy of the life drives since the energy of life drives and sexual drives could be transformed into one another like ego libido and object libido. When object libido was withdrawn to the ego it was desexualized (or sublimated) making its energy available for self-preservation. The concept of narcissism that had been so important earlier now faded into the background.

If we forget for a moment that the general aim of death drives is to bring organic life back to inorganic, dead matter, then their other characteristics are not new. They are already part of the sexual and ego drives, though less clearly formulated. We must therefore reject the idea that the introduction of the death-drive concept is a pure addition to the earlier drive dualism. If we follow the development of the theory of drives chronologically, another explanation develops. In his introductory lectures on psychoanalysis (1916–1917), Freud had already abandoned the dualism between ego drives and sexual drives, without yet having reached the dualism between life drives and death drives. In lecture 26 (1916–1917), Freud suspected that the opposition between the preservation of the individual and the preservation of the species was perhaps not so important after all, in any case not so decisive as to justify a drastic psychic conflict. Sexual drives (the representatives of the species in the individual) had heretofore been looked upon as ill-mannered, asocial, and the cause of disease, whereas ego drives, apart from representing the individual himself, had been looked upon as the representatives of reality and rationality. Freud now created a new group of drives called "egoistic drives," that is, drives that catered to the welfare of the individual. In doing so he discovered that many of the sexual drives fit this category, since it might very well be to an individual's advantage to love others. Logical antitheses to egoistic drives were drives that caused the individual harm. This group included the remaining sexual drives as well as—and this was new—a number of ego drives. Ego drives could under certain circumstances suffer illness, as when they were the cause of excessive repression of sexual drive, for example, or in certain psychoses where the individual's desire to continue living had suffered damage. After introducing the polarity between usefulness and harm, it was not a great step to introduce the new dualistic opposition between preservation of life and restoration of the inorganic state in death, that is, between life drives and death drives.

The change in drive categories makes it possible to observe the following: the free energy of the sexual drives was transferred to the death drives, whereas the bound energy of the ego drives became part of the life drives. This also means that libido and sexuality completely changed character from free energy to bound energy. Furthermore, life drives acquired a number of other characteristics, such as the drive aim of procreation and the affect of love from the sexual drives and egoism and the tendency to self-preservation from the ego drives. The tendency to relaxation was a trait death drives had in common with sexual drives, and also the basis for certain perversions, such as masochism. From the former ego drives, the death drives assumed the task of inhibiting sexuality and the ability for outwardly directed motor activity, destructiveness, and hate. These complicated transformations can be illustrated as follows:

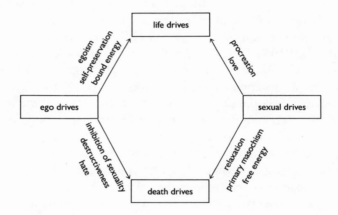

Our intention has not been to affirm that the last drive dualism is superfluous. Death drives in particular contain elements other than those derived from sexual drives and ego drives. In *Beyond the Pleasure Principle* (1920g), Freud presented a number of cases of repetition compulsion, where patients repeated the most painful experiences from the past without good reason, even when they did not either directly or indirectly lead to the attainment of pleasure. In some cases Freud could discern the precursor of a security measure, the rationale of which was that it was better to take unpleasant experiences in advance than to wait for them to come unexpectedly, as had happened at the time of the traumatic experience. But it was generally so difficult to get patients to perceive this relationship, and thence to give up their symptoms, that Freud thought that a true death drive must be involved. One example of this is the negative transference in which the patient would rather destroy his relationship to the analyst, and in doing so the possibility of being cured, than to establish a positive relationship of trust. Even if Freud could see an old hate for the parents in this behavior, he could not see any reason other than biological ones for its expressing itself so uninhibitedly. The common compulsion of death drives to return to death manifested itself here as a concrete repetition compulsion, a returning to situations that smacked of self-destruction and death. In this scheme masochism and melancholia also fell into place.

It has probably become apparent through this section that we have not been able to see the connection between the often far-ranging aims of drives on the physical-biological level and their psychological meaning. We believe that it is practically irrelevant to postulate that death drives have death as their final aim when at the same time they exert influence on the most various psychic processes. Where is the biological intelligence located developing the strategy to be followed and in each single case determining whether an action serves life or death? With his generalized death drive concept Freud probably gave in to the intellectual tendency of the time, not only to the widespread sense of pessimism among philosophers in the West, from Schopenhauer and Nietzsche to Spengler, but also to the demands of philosophy for a general view encompassing biology, psychology, and sociology.

It is our opinion that the best part of the drive theory is the theory of partial drives' arising in anaclisis to the life-preserving functions. We find many of the considerations related to the death drives important only because they reveal new aspects of sexual drives. *Thus, the psychological characteristics of the death drives should rightfully be attributed to the sexual drives.* We do not deny that highly complex biological mechanisms, perhaps even instincts, exist in man. They are only meaningful to psychoanalysis, however, to the extent that they are points of anaclisis for sexual drives. Regardless of whether they are called drives of self-preservation, life drives, or needs, they do not comprise a symmetric pair with sexual drives since these are specifically characterized by having no compelling biological aim. Nor may one speak of a conflict between the two drive groups if one thereby means a sort of trench warfare in the psychic apparatus. We will study this question in more detail in the next section.

3. THE DYNAMIC VIEWPOINT

The dynamic viewpoint of metapsychology is a logical consequence of the topographical and economic viewpoints. It deals with psychic processes in the broadest sense, that is, the displacement of affects, or psychic energies (the economic viewpoint), between ideas or memory traces in the psychic apparatus (the topographical viewpoint). The processes are determined by a combination of psychic energies and facilitations between memory traces present in the mental apparatus. They are two mutually heterogenous factors whose relative influence on mental processes is difficult to assess.

Energies represent the demands made by the drives, whereas facilitations represent the reality of the world; mental processes are therefore a compromise between them. Overemphasis of either one of the factors will inevitably lead to a distorted understanding of the dynamics involved.

Freud divided psychic processes into types (primary processes and secondary processes), each ideally characterized by its own type of energy, and its own type of facilitation. In order to characterize these processes further Freud also referred to particular regulating principles, for example, the pleasure principle. These principles do not, however, comprise a third determining factor besides energies and facilitations. Rather, the explanatory power attributed to them is similar to that of the laws of nature. The laws of nature are the sum of all the processes in the universe, but they do not have special forces at their disposal and there are no reprisals if they are violated, in which case they simply must be changed. Freud's regulation principles are likewise the sum of the processes they are said to regulate and they are unable to add anything to or take anything away from these processes.

Finally, conflicts in the psychic apparatus belong to the dynamic viewpoint. A conflict develops when processes compete for access to consciousness and motor reaction. Defenses, symptoms and compromises, static cathexes, and other very complex processes result from these conflicts. They have a dynamic aspect by virtue of their being potential processes or exerting influence on the real processes. Conflicts between, for example, the ego and the id (the topographical viewpoint) or between life drives and death drives (the economic viewpoint) are typical, but only indicate that one or the other aspect is emphasized, since all conflicts in principle belong to the dynamic viewpoint.

The sources that influenced Freud's description of mental processes are found in every field discussed in part 1. In general, Freud attempted to circumscribe the relationship between an inborn or primitive and an acquired operational mode in the subject (see our diagram of the three subject concepts, I.A.4). It was common to oppose feelings and reason, and to have them lead to conflict. Freud's conceptual pairs (for example, primary versus secondary and pleasure versus reality) dovetail very well with this opposition; where these conceptual pairs are concerned, Freud stayed within the bounds of the traditional polarity between feelings and reason. We will argue this point more thoroughly in section V.A.3.a. It is not possible, however, to have the *whole* of Freud's metapsychology fit satisfactorily into such a scheme. A number of fundamental concepts and statements conflict with it, and if they are studied more closely, the contours of an entirely new conceptual polarity develop, which replaces the polarity between feelings and reason. The importance of this undercurrent in the writings of Freud cannot be emphasized enough, for without it psychoanalysis could not be said to go beyond elementary conceptions of the subject, as we maintain it does. In section V.A.3.b we will briefly sketch our understanding of the new conceptual polarity, and in the rest of the book we will attempt to make use of it and to discuss its scope.

Fechner is probably the person who inspired Freud to formulate the rules of processes in terms of principles. In the 1840s, Fechner operated with a pleasure principle and in the 1870s it was subsumed under the principle of stability, the tendency toward the latter being universal and not just psychological (see I.B.4.b). As we shall see, Freud's development followed a similar path, but unlike Fechner, he ordered principles in pairs originally corresponding to the polarity between feelings and reason.

(a) Types of Processes and
Their Corresponding Principles

In his 1895 "Project for a Scientific Psychology" (Freud 1950a), Freud introduced the terms *primary processes* and *secondary processes* to denote processes resulting from the two fundamental operational modes of the nervous system, the primary function and the secondary function (see II.B.2). Primary processes are processes occurring in an uninhibited manner, following the closest and most accessible paths leading to the elimination of the adduced quantity of stimulation. The corresponding principle is called the principle of inertia. In the beginning, Freud was particularly interested in showing how these processes were biologically harmful. They did not respect reality; they promoted the free energies instead of inhibiting and binding them; they always looked for the easiest and fastest way to discharge, without regard for consequences. In his writings on psychopathology and general psychology, Freud presented a thorough analysis of the different associations comprising primary processes (different types of condensations and displacements; see the examples in parts 3 and 4). Furthermore, he defined their metapsychological status by placing them in the system *Ucs,* and in *The Interpretation of Dreams* (1900a) he replaced the term *principle of inertia* with that of *unpleasure principle,* identical to what would later be known as the pleasure principle. The change was a consequence of the general replacement of neurophysiological terminology with psychological terminology. Therefore, at first it did not bother Freud that there was a difference between the tendency toward energy leveling (the principle of inertia) and the tendency to seek pleasure and avoid unpleasure (the pleasure principle).

It could be said of the secondary processes, that is, the counterpart of the primary processes, that Freud created a concept to characterize normal, reality-oriented thinking able both to make logical calculations and to inhibit primitive reaction patterns causing harm to the individual. Freud originally called the corresponding principle the principle of constancy, assuming that secondary processes necessitated a constant energy supply consisting of bound energies. In the "Project" he placed this energy supply in the group of neurons he called the ego, although he had no term for the remaining neurons. After December 1896, at which time the retranscription model was formulated, the secondary processes were topographically located in the system *Pcs*, but it was first in a little article in 1911 (Freud 1911b) that the reality principle was posited to characterize the secondary processes. Both the pleasure and reality principles aimed to achieve pleasure and avoid unpleasure, the difference being that the pleasure principle sought to achieve pleasure and avoid unpleasure in the here and now, whereas the reality principle concentrated on long-term pleasure and unpleasure, regardless of present affects.

In *Beyond the Pleasure Principle* (1920g), Freud again discussed the pleasure and reality principles, now from a new vantage point. If these two principles, which both aimed at achieving pleasure, reigned supreme how was it that human beings often used so much energy inflicting pain and unpleasure upon themselves? The question gave Freud the opportunity to introduce death drives and the so-called Nirvana principle, the gist of which is that the processes determined by death drives aim at total relaxation regardless of whether this leads to pleasure, unpleasure, or no affect at all. Freud's more detailed explanations touching upon these matters were in many ways confusing because he mixed psychology and biology. In one moment, he would be speaking of unicellular organisms, in the next of neuroses, and in the next again of the relationship between the feeling of pleasure on the one hand and excitation and relaxation on the other. Notwithstanding, he succeeded in standing firm on the question concerning processes that do not obey the pleasure and reality principles. We will examine his answer by arranging his statements in the light of the three descriptive levels we introduced at the beginning of part 5. His answer in essence stated that *what lies beyond regulatory principles on one level will obey the same principles on another.* Interferences between levels now come to light.

I. *The physical-biological level.* As mentioned earlier (see V.A.2.a), Freud put order in his drive theory at the biological level by opposing death drives and life drives, and by placing both sexual drives and drives of self-preservation under the life drives. The Nirvana principle is the term identifying the general trend of the death drives and thus characterizes the biological processes leading the organism back to inorganic matter (relaxation, dissolution, and extinction). Freud was apparently thinking of what happened when one died of old age. The life drives activate reverse processes to maintain the individual (intake of food) and the species (reproduction). Everything preventing immediate drive discharge serves life, since it forces drives to find new channels. Freud sometimes spoke of *"ananke"* or *"Not des Lebens"* (necessity of life) as the principle of these processes. In more contemporary works of biology, for example, Cannon (Cannon 1929), one may speak of a homeostatic principle (a principle regulating the organism's fluid balance, acid/base balance, and so on), but since Freud's concrete references to biology mostly concerned unicellular organisms direct comparison is impossible. What he seems to have had in mind is Fechner's principle of the tendency toward stability, since the reproductive cycles of the organism constitute a stability at a lower level than the absolute stability of the state without excitation.

II. *The level of psychic quantities.* We have shown that true psychic processes are determined by two factors, energies and facilitations. The quantitative distribution of the energies is directly related to the extent of facilitations, and free energies move differently in the apparatus from the way bound energies move. If other levels did not interfere, the free energies would flow unhindered out of the apparatus, whereby excitation would fall to zero. This flow (or outflow) is the true primary process. It is exclusively regulated by mechanical factors. This principle can be called by the term originally used by Freud, *the principle of inertia.* Similarly, bound energies are first set in motion when a certain level of excitation has been reached; their processes, the secondary processes, flow more calmly. In the mechanical description the constant level of excitation is determinant for the processes, and the corresponding principle is accordingly called the principle of constancy. It can safely be said that the processes on the two levels are not identical. There is a difference between an organism's death and energy discharge in the psychic apparatus, just as there is a difference between an organism's reproduction and the maintenance of a constant level of excitation in the psychic apparatus.

III. *The level of psychic qualities.* The decisive question now is what is the difference between the processes on the two psychic levels (the quantitative and qualitative). On first thought, one might believe that because the energy impulse becomes conscious at the moment of discharge, the process of discharge itself does not have to be altered. Freud said somewhat vaguely that consciousness was able to make fine adjustments in the process. In other words, there is feedback from the motor reactions that always accompany conscious impressions. The reaction, whatever it might consist of is perceived again and the perception then contributes either to promote or to inhibit the discharge process already set in motion. Freud added that conscious affects in particular had the ability to modify discharge processes. Pleasure promotes and unpleasure inhibits discharge. The quality of the affect thus seems to have an independent function in the reflex arc in relationship to the quantitative processes.

Another objection to separating the two levels could be that the quality of affect is part of the quantitative process insofar as pleasure corresponds to relaxation and unpleasure to an increase in excitation. In this case, the principle of inertia could be equated to the pleasure principle and the principle of constancy to the reality principle. Freud, however, excluded this possibility by pointing out that certain forms of pleasure presupposed a high level of excitation. This is particularly true of forepleasure. Forepleasure arises from stimulation of the erogenous zones, as opposed to end pleasure, which accompanies the cessation of stimulation, that is, orgasm. In the adult these two forms of pleasure are bound together inasmuch as stimulation of the erogenous zones creates a state of excitement that serves as preparation for orgasm. For physiological reasons, the child cannot achieve true orgasm and must make do with the pleasure he can derive from stimulating his erogenous zones. Masochistic perversion is somewhat similar to infantile forepleasure because it does not aim at relaxation, but at ever increasing excitement, to the point where pain and excitation are its regular companions. It follows that it is impossible to identify pleasure with relaxation, and that therefore two different types of processes leading to pleasure and relaxation respectively must exist.

Finally, the objection to the separation of levels might be that the entire psychic apparatus might obey either the pleasure principle or the reality principle, whereby the principle of inertia and the principle of constancy would become superfluous. However, it is necessary to suppose that the pleasure/unpleasure criterion of consciousness is only directly valid for those processes that become conscious because they are the only ones giving inhibiting or accelerating feedback to consciousness. It means, furthermore, that only the topographical systems bordering on consciousness (system *P-Cs*) are subject to the influence of the pleasure and reality principles. The processes implicated are then processes in the system *Pcs* or in the ego (depending on which topographical model is used). Contrariwise, processes in the (dynamic understanding of) unconscious systems should be characterized through mechanistic principles, that is, the principle of inertia and the principle of constancy. However, Freud did generally say that precisely unconscious primary processes obeyed the pleasure principle. This is true to the extent that at the time it was formed, the system *Ucs* (in the first topographical model) was open to the influence of consciousness. At that time the pleasure principle reigned supreme and determined the formation of facilitations in the system. After new systems were superposed on the system *Ucs* it no longer had direct access to consciousness, and from then on its processes only *appeared* to obey the pleasure principle because of the facilitations. We have already discussed the problems related to the topographical systems (see V.A.1.b), and we reached the conclusion that the system laid down first could continue changing character after having other systems were superposed on them. In *Beyond the Pleasure Principle* (1920g), Freud gave an almost tangible description of how violent traumatic experiences were able to break through the stimulation barrier protecting the psychic apparatus, and wreak such havoc that the pleasure principle was abolished. It is natural to conceive of this havoc as damage done to the original facilitations in the unconscious and thus as the cause of changes in the flow of processes that still seek discharge through the widest channels but no longer obey the pleasure principle. In our opinion, a similar *delayed* change in unconscious memory traces takes place through the formation of repressed wishful fantasies (see V.B.3), and the processes and the repetition compulsion that lie "beyond the pleasure principle" emanate from just such unconscious structures.

In view of the relative lack of clarity surrounding the pleasure principle and the repetition compulsion in Freud's writings, placing the concepts in the context of a separation of levels as we have done puts some order in his terminology. The critical point here is undoubtedly the description of the processes at the level of psychic quantities standing outside the influence of consciousness. We suggest that the principles of inertia and constancy treated in the "Project" are valid for the aforementioned processes only because Freud persistently referred to free and bound energies. The free processes in the id could be placed under the principle of inertia, and the bound processes in the ego and the superego under the principle of constancy.

The diagram below does not present a general view of Freud's dynamics theory. We will therefore make no further effort to place it in relation to topographical models of drive theories. It is only useful when sorting out Freud's statements on psychic and biological processes. It serves no purpose to let oneself be fascinated by Freud' paradoxes and ambiguities if one does not look for their true basis. Thus, when Freud described a process that was apparently both biological and psychological, whether this process corresponded to something that took place one level or another must be examined. Doing so permits making significant headway in understanding a text as difficult as *Beyond the Pleasure Principle*.

	free processes	bound processes
THE PHYSICAL-BIOLOGICAL LEVEL	NIRVANA PRINCIPLE: relaxation dissolution	THE PRINCIPLE OF THE TENDENCY TOWARD STABILITY: processes which reproduce the individual and the species
THE LEVEL OF PSYCHIC QUANTITIES	PRINCIPLE OF INERTIA: primary processes discharge to point o	PRINCIPLE OF CONSTANCY: secondary processes constant level of excitation
THE LEVEL OF PSYCHIC QUALITIES	PLEASURE PRINCIPLE: discharge processes that immediately lead to the attainment of pleasure and the avoidance of unpleasure	REALITY PRINCIPLE: discharge processes that in the longer run lead to the attainment of pleasure and the avoidance of unpleasure

(b) The Adaptive and
the Psychosexual Registers

In metapsychology, there is a striking homology among the conceptual polarities of the three viewpoints. The topographical polarity unconscious/preconscious corresponds to the economic polarity sexual drives/drives of self-preservation, which in turn corresponds to the dynamic polarity primary processes/secondary processes. Furthermore, the polarity is also genetic, in the sense that feelings are dominant in the child the way reason is dominant in the adult. Finally, one may apply a superior adaptive viewpoint in summarizing the others. In the adaptive viewpoint, the focus of attention is on the individual's adaptation to his environment. The unconscious, sexual drives, and primary processes express a small degree of adaptation, whereas the preconscious, the drives of self-preservation, and the secondary processes adapt more. All in all, we obtain the following diagrammatic relationships:

genetic-adaptive viewpoint	topographical viewpoint	economic viewpoint	dynamic viewpoint
child	the unconscious	sexual drives	primary processes
unadapted	thing presentations	free energies	principle of inertia
adult	the preconscious	drives of self-preservation	secondary processes
adapted	word presentations	bound energies	principle of constancy

One need not have read much Freud to notice these homologies. It is therefore possible to get the impression that we are facing most fundamental truths of psychoanalytic theory, a logical nucleus to which may be added details, but which is itself unshakable. A picture begins to emerge of a hierarchic structure, where the lower echelons form the basis of primitive and affective reactional odes, whereas the upper echelons accomplish the most complicated intellectual performances. The lower echelons consist of mutually unrelated associational paths, which are all gathered and coordinated at the top of the hierarchy. It is not our opinion, however, that we have here the logical nucleus of the theory, which might form the basis of all later theoretization as it stands. Freud originally developed the idea in the "Project" (Freud 1950a) at a time when he wished to described the generic-adaptive processes related to simple needs (see V.B.1). It gave him a standard of reference for his description of specifically sexual processes and a basic tool with which to understand their specificities. When he later further developed the theory of sexuality he still sometimes used the genetic-adaptive and hierarchic model as a standard of reference. This led to the formulation of a number of negative statements concerning sexual processes, of which the following are some: they are *not* adapted to the world, *not* subjected to reality testing, and *not* prepared to submit to the demands of reality. The negative definition exerted some influence on the concept of normality, insofar as normal sexuality should preferably be on par with the other physical needs. Let us take a closer look at what this implies.

Freud used a fairly simple criterion to determine whether a given process was adapted to reality or not. If a process stemmed from an impulse of need, then it was unadapted if it only deflected the energy quantum (for example, by abreaction), but adapted if it led to satisfaction of the need (by removing the stimulus at its source). The process adapted to reality obtains its effect by thinking its way to an adequate reaction. From a genetic point of view, it is forced to do so through regulation of affect, that is, unpleasure remains until the need is satisfied. It is true that it takes a certain amount of time for a person to be able to take care of himself (he has to go through a learning process), but in principle it is impossible for needs to be deflected from their true and original aims. They do not give up until the circle is closed (see the model in V.A.2).

If sexual drives are now inserted in the same model, we notice that they are, using Freud's own expression, less teachable than the needs or drives of self-preservation. If the biological aim of the sexual drives is defined as procreation, or at least the attainment of orgasm, then it is clear that the first dispersed partial drives have a long and complicated development ahead of them. Furthermore, it is characteristic of sexual drives, as opposed to drives of self-preservation, that they can more easily be deflected off course, since their biological aim is not compelling. The absence of orgasm or procreation does not necessarily lead to a feeling of continuous unpleasure. In the meantime, sexual drives may have formed entirely new and more compelling aims, perhaps never reaching the unity called genital sexuality (see section V.B.2). In fact, according to Freud, certain sexual drives always remain at a lower developmental stage, which means that the personality contains both primary processes and secondary processes.

In summary, sexual drives are so different from the drives of self-preservation that it is almost misleading to maintain the genetic-adaptive model as a frame of reference. In characterizing the processes from an adaptive viewpoint, a stable and unequivocal biological mooring must be found for them (a function is either fulfilled or not, which is not the case for the psychosexual processes). In the section on the economic viewpoint (V.A.2), we have argued that the procreative function could not determine sexual drives, and thus the entire adaptive description of sexuality falls apart. Instead, we stressed the concept of anaclisis as a general premise for understanding sexual drives. Compared to the need reflex, in principle a closed circuit, the anaclitical points are placed as independent satellites, ultimately perhaps following the same paths, but nonetheless able to function detached from each other.

On the physical-biological level, sexual drives prefer to be attached to the motor end of the need reflex. The suction movement of the mouth necessary to ingest food, is the motor reaction to which the oral partial drive has attached itself. In general, partial drives appear from the coexcitations that develop in the erogenous zones and that from there are able to influence the psyche. Stimuli or excitations are best removed by further stimulation of the erogenous zones (for example, by continuing the movement of suction in the act of sucking), although we cannot speak of clear and unequivocal satisfaction concerning partial drives. Such satisfaction is only physiologically possible during genital orgasm, where a series of muscle contractions can cause a marked decrease in the level of stimulation and tension/excitation.

On the level of psychic quantities, special ideas are formed that are cathected by the sexual drives, and especially concern their goal and object. The aim of a drive develops anaclitically from the aim of the need reflex, for example, sucking as a pleasure-giving movement (*"Lutschen"* in German) develops in attachment to suction (*"Saugen"* in German). This goal is not permanent however, but may be displaced to other activities similar to suction or to the absorption of food. We have also mentioned that the oral partial drive may ultimately have "absorption of knowledge" as its aim. The sexual object is also determined in anaclisis to the object of the need reflex, in such a way, however, that a displacement takes place from the beginning. Not milk, but rather the breast is the first object of the oral drive, and other displacements develop from there, for example, from the breast to the mother as a whole, or from the breast through the penis to the father as a person. Aim and object presentation coalesce in decisive ways to form the repressed wish fantasies outside the reach of the pleasure principle, which continue to organize sexuality throughout life. They are as important for sexuality in its final form as the erogenous zones are.

At the level of psychic qualities, it is finally possible to establish that sexual pleasure is different from the pleasure of the need reflex. Sensual pleasure is localized to the erogenous zones (mouth, anus, penis, and clitoris), and Freud called it organ pleasure, as opposed to the functional pleasure arising from the satisfaction of a need. Even more important is the idea that sexual excitation or sexual excitement themselves comprise the true feeling of pleasure, whereas discharge and relaxation characterize the cessation of pleasure (see the terms *forepleasure* and *end pleasure* in V.A.3.a). In sexuality, orgasm is obviously not an aim in itself, since premature ejaculation (ejaculation precox) is considered to be pathological. Hence, abstaining from immediate sexual gratification may under certain circumstances be a means of intensifying pleasurable sexual excitement, and pleasure and pain then have a tendency to intertwine. If one were to attempt to define a reality principle of sexual pleasure, it would sound quite different from the customary reality principle. The specific sexual unpleasure affect is anxiety, and it is part of all defense mechanisms (see our more thorough analysis in V.C.2.b).

This outline illustrates that sexual drives have their specific base on all three levels. Although they have arisen in anaclisis to the closed need reflex, they are not more bound to the one level than to the other. Sexual drives deploy forces seeking repetition and satisfaction of the erogenous sensual stimuli, of the specific unconscious fantasy constellations, and of sexual excitement and sexual desire. The three bases of sexuality may unite into a whole and further each other in accordance with the pattern of the need reflex, but they need not do so in order to exist. It can even be said that obtaining maximal sexual pleasure seems to presuppose some anarchy, a certain degree of "polymorphous perversity."

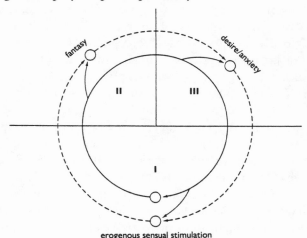

erogenous sensual stimulation

The above model shows how sexual drives are related to needs or to drives of self-preservation. Three points of anaclisis are included. They are only intended to show that anaclisis takes place on all three levels.

We have now outlined our positive understanding of sexuality. We do not believe that sexuality can simply be characterized in relation to biology through a number of deficiencies. Sexuality can easily be organized into complex structures, for example, the Oedipus complex and the superego, but can also form stable ties without following in the footsteps of the drives of self-preservation. We will therefore place conditions of the organizational forms of sexuality in the psychosexual register, as opposed to the adaptive register, which exclusively concerns organizational forms aiming for the satisfaction of biological needs and the carrying out of biological functions. It is not possible, of course, to keep the two registers completely separate. The psychosexual register is the primary object of psychoanalysis, but just to describe the process of anaclisis some consideration must be given to the adaptive register. Conversely, it would be erroneous to describe the adaptive register as if it were autonomous. In the hierarchic adaptive model, optimal adaptation between the individual and surrounding world is embodied by the reality principle, and supporters of the reality principle (whether as theoretical concept or pedagogical principle) apparently believe it is possible to reach such a degree of adaptation by the help of reason. The objection to this view is that optimal adaptation does not exist. Even if it may be compatible with reason to postpone the attainment of pleasure in order to assure it, this postponement may also be exaggerated to an extent where unpleasure becomes an aim and source of pleasure in itself. Many will accept this as being pathological, but objective criteria with which to determine where the dividing line goes do not exist. It is impossible to say which is better, immediate pleasure and unpleasure in five years, or immediate unpleasure and pleasure in five years. First, pleasure and unpleasure cannot be quantified (trying to calculate the interest that could be earned saving pleasure and unpleasure is a senseless undertaking), and second the concept of reality's dictating choice is influenced both by the subject's own (psychosexual) character type and by the dominant ideological norms of society.

In the historical perspective presented in part 1 (in I.A and I.C in particular), we outlined the views of several previous epochs on the question of feeling and reason. Freud's historical contribution consists in his proposing a new basis for the understanding of sexuality. He borrowed many themes directly from the romantic conception of feelings and passions (such as that emotional life had its wellspring in the unconscious and that the feelings had the ability to organize themselves alone), but corrected many others in the course of his own analyses. Foremost among these corrections was the idea that feelings were produced and structured within the framework of the family. In doing so, he burst the traditional polarity between nature and culture that had lain at the basis of the understanding of feelings and reason. The separation between psychosexual and adaptive registers does not correspond to the polarity between nature and culture. Both registers include elements of nature and culture, or, stated differently, both are determined by biological as well as social factors.

B.

THE SUBJECT'S GENESIS

The word *genesis* refers to the idea of origins, of creation, and of becoming; and the origin and creation of the human subject is precisely what we are going to examine in this chapter. Though not precluding the invocation of certain facts from the physical-biological level, psychoanalysis sees this process as largely synonymous with childhood development from birth through puberty.

Although Freud seldom had children in therapy, he was forced to recognize the importance of childhood by cases of perversion and psychoneurosis in the adult, and by the fact that either covert or undisguised childhood memories were invariably related to him by his patients. These memories were often psychically active and left obvious traces on the personality of the adult. In order to understand their role better, Freud himself reconstructed the development of the child. He did so first by trying to pinpoint the personality traits that played a central role in the life of the adult, and thereafter by attempting to elucidate the conditions in childhood under which they could have been formed. Finally, he sought to place the successive and simultaneous formation of these various personality traits in a linear time continuum. We again wish to emphasize that Freud seldom actually worked with children, and that apart from his short stay at the Kassowitz Hospital, he never undertook any systematic study of children and childhood. However, he certainly drew from both the body of knowledge concerning children available at the time, and personal observations of children in his immediate surroundings. It can thus be concluded that it was not so much children and childhood that interested Freud, as the way childhood manifested itself in the adult. Consequently, the importance of childhood in psychoanalysis pertains mostly to the place it holds in the life history of the adult.

Freud was well versed in the genetic theories of his time. Here, we will discuss three essentially different models, one corresponding to each of the three subject concepts presented in part 1. Each of these models embraces developmental ideals, pedagogical practices, and measures concerning sexual education. Within each of these models, it often occurs that the boundaries between completely different fields of inquiry are obscured; for example, child development will be paralleled by the development of all of humanity, the development of the species, and the development of the entire universe, sometimes all in the same breath.

(1) The liberalistic-rationalistic developmental model, derived from Hobbes, among others, states in essence that a child's spontaneous behavior is determined by his selfish search for pleasure, and that this must be changed by promoting self-restraint at the expense of selfishness. We can already easily recognize the duality—if not outright opposition—between the pleasure and reality principles later formulated by Freud.

(2) The humanistic-romantic developmental model is characterized by a positive interest in childhood and a belief in the idea that impetus for development comes from inside and not from outside (Rousseau as well as the true romantics shared this point of view). Romantic ideology is founded on the belief that the vast majority of normal adults are devoid of positive human traits because they have been stifled by the oppressive forces of modern civilization. For the romantics, the awareness that these traits have been lost is a reminder to us that they once existed, and that they can still be found in those not yet contaminated by the pestilence of culture, namely children. Thus one important similarity between Freud and his romantic predecessors is the idea that the emotional life of human beings cannot be subordinated to the stringent laws of reason. Such similarities, however, should not lessen the importance of the incompatibility of these two concepts in their subsequent development. Whereas the romantics imagined that the longings and dreams of adults could find satisfaction in childhood, Freud focused on childhood as psychological structure in adults. Furthermore, the romantics saw feelings as divine forces of nature beyond the grasp of understanding, while Freud subjected them to analysis.

(3) The development of the mechanistic subject concept in the middle of the nineteenth century marked a return to some degree to the liberalistic-rationalistic developmental model's heavy-handed pedagogical principles. This time, however, feelings and instincts were not seen in a psychological light, but rather as objective factors closely associated with innate reflexes. In addition, the idea that developmental grand designs were an inherent

part of nature was abandoned, and instead new criteria were proposed to determine whether development was moving forward or backward. We have already mentioned the contradiction existing between Morel's theory of degeneration and Darwin's evolutionary theory (see I.B.2.b). One of these contradictions concerns the interpretation of the propensity for unforseeable change attributed to genetic material. Darwin opposed the degeneration theory because he found in this propensity an explanation for the ever-more-effective adaptation of individuals to their surroundings (natural selection). This adaptive point of view also dominated Jackson's and Meynert's genetic-neurophysiological theories (see I.B.3.a,b). True theories of the psychological development of children did not exist before Freud, however; there were only generally meticulous records of the acquisition of various skills during childhood. In the field of psychiatry, there were no special developmental theories either, even though Griesinger and Charcot, each in his own way, had begun to look for etiological factors in the previous history of their patients. No one came closer to Freud in thoroughly and carefully examining the earlier life history of people in order to find causes for the difficulties that later befell them than the naturalistic writers of his day.

In dealing with Freud's developmental theories, the question of how the various facets of development are interrelated comes to mind. These facets include the development of partial drives (oral, anal, phallic, and genital), the development of sexual organization (autoeroticism, narcissism, Oedipus complex, and castration complex), the development of the ego (original reality ego, pleasure ego, and definitive reality ego), as well as the development of thought, language, and adaptation to reality (primary processes, secondary processes, and so on). The truth is that Freud himself did not do much to make this interrelationship explicit. He worked with these partial developments separately and was careful not to compare them. It seems to us that this was the case for one main reason: the development of the subject consists of two interrelated but heterogeneous developmental paths, one dominated by drives of self-preservation, which we have placed in the adaptive register, and the other dominated by the sexual drives, which we have placed in the psychosexual register. One section of this chapter will be devoted to each of the two developmental models. We will first review them separately, risking the simplification this procedure entails. In section V.B.3, we will discuss how these paths are interrelated and how the chronological developmental description is useful in describing the subject's structure.

1. ADAPTIVE DEVELOPMENT

It should come as no surprise that the adaptive way of thinking, primarily based on the theories of Darwin, Jackson, and Meynert, held a prominent place in Freud's writings, particularly the early ones. Freud's adaptive psychology was only to a small extent based on experience from his psychoanalytic practice; it initially provided a framework for his sexual hypotheses. After making his drive theory more explicit, Freud usually formulated adaptive problems in biological terms, which did not mean, however, that his psychology became biologically oriented. It would be more appropriate to say that the adaptive psychology described in such detail during the earlier years was gradually reduced to biological clichés lacking true analytic punch. It was as if the subject matter no longer interested Freud, as if he wished to hand it over to biologically oriented psychologists.

Passages in Freud's writings where adaptive development is treated can be found by asking two questions: (1) Are we dealing with genuine bodily needs such as hunger and thirst? (2) Is the overall relationship between the organism and its environment involved? Posing these questions takes us to a number of passages from Freud's official writings. We will examine these by way of introduction before going back to "A Project for a Scientific Psychology" (1950a), by far Freud's most important contribution to adaptive psychology.

In the first metapsychological thrust, two passages in particular from *The Interpretation of Dreams* related explicitly to the subject's genesis (1900a, pp. 565–68 and 596–97). They presented three (logical rather than temporal) features of development, and sought an explanation for the principles governing development. Let us briefly outline these three features of development.

(1) The psychic apparatus is looked upon as a reflex apparatus (see V.A) that originally simply attempted to avoid excitation or stimulation. The psychic apparatus does well for external stimuli that a child may flee with the help of his reflexes. The same does not apply for internal stimuli of need. There, the reflexes are relatively ineffective inasmuch as the stimuli cannot be removed by motor action. The little child screams and kicks (Freud called this an internal change or an expression of emotion), but even if such reactions can give some relief, the basic situation remains

unchanged; the apparatus is exposed to ever-more-intense need stimuli coming from within the organism.

(2) The next developmental stage takes place when the stimulus is ended by the experience of satisfaction, which the child achieves with outside help. Hence, it is not merely a matter of having a need satisfied, but also of *experiencing* satisfaction. The experience is made up in part of a perception of, or a presentation of, the satisfying object (typical examples being the mother's breast and the mother's milk) and in part of a pleasurable experience, whereby a more complicated reflex is introduced leading from the need stimulation (hunger), through memory ideas (the breast and the pleasurable experience) to motor discharge (suction activity). On the basis of this primary association, a wish is defined as a psychic impulse to recathect the idea of satisfaction: "A current of this kind in the apparatus, starting from unpleasure and aiming at pleasure, we have termed a 'wish' " (Freud 1900a, p. 598). Thereafter, wishing is the only independent mental activity of the apparatus, even in the absence of the object. The result is either a hallucination, since cathexis gains access to that part of the apparatus where sense perceptions arise, or else the initiation of futile motor reaction, such as suction. While able to imagine satisfaction, the child remains unable to attain it in this way.

(3) The third developmental stage bears the mark of the postulate that the bitter experience of life must have changed this primitive thought activity into a more expedient secondary one. The reason is that the apparatus learns to inhibit primary thought processes in such a way as to avoid hallucinations or motor discharge at the wrong moment. Instead, it becomes able to send explorative cathexes in many directions to discover how the wish cathexis can most effectively lead to true satisfaction. Thus, the apparatus should be able to hinder direct discharge, find the necessary detours to wish fulfillment (namely by finding the motor action procuring the object of satisfaction), and finally remove the inhibition precisely while the object is present. Development takes place when a secondary system overlays a primary system; but Freud did not say much about how this took place in *The Interpretation of Dreams*.

The presentation of adaptive development was repeated in two articles from the second metapsychological thrust, that is, "Formulations on the Two Principles in Mental Functioning" (1911b), and "Instincts and Their Vicissitudes" (1915c). On the basis of these articles, it is possible to add one ego formation to each of the three successive developmental stages: the original reality ego to the first, the purified pleasure ego to the second, and the definitive reality ego to the third. The psychic apparatus is replaced by the nervous system in the theoretical considerations (1915c, pp. 118–20), when Freud asked the reader to imagine "an almost entirely helpless living organism, as yet unorientated in the world, which is receiving stimuli in its nervous substance" (1915c, p. 119). After having considered the relative influence of internal and external stimuli, Freud concluded that "Instincts and not external stimuli are the true motive forces behind the advances that have led the nervous system, with its unlimited capacities, to its present high level of development" (1915c, p. 120).

In the third metapsychological thrust, adaptation between organism and environment is seen from a purely biological and often phylogenetic perspective. In *Beyond the Pleasure Principle* (1920g), Freud imagined the prototype of a living organism as "an undifferentiated vesicle of a substance that is susceptible to stimulation" (1920g, p. 26). As the vesicle encounters the world, differentiation takes place on its surface, which turns into a sort of bark protecting the viscera and serving as an organ for the reception of stimuli. The altered part of the vesicle is identical to the perception system and to the ego built upon it. The ego is molded by its environment and regulates internal processes according to the means offered by the environment. It also attempts to change the environment in order to satisfy the internal needs. In later texts, the id replaced the internal soft tissues, which were gradually transformed into ego structures as a result of the environmental influence. It will be recalled that Freud ended his thirty-first lecture with the solemn statement that "*Wo Es war, soll ich werden* " ("Where the id was, the ego must be," or literally "Where it was, must I be" [Freud 1933a, p. 80]).

As already noted, the unofficial and posthumously published manuscript entitled "A Project for a Scientific Psychology" from 1895 (Freud 1950a) contained the most complete descriptions of the child's adaptive development. The same developmental stages used in *The Interpretation of Dreams* formed the skeleton of development in the "Project," but in the latter more effort was made to explain their logical and mechanistic causal relationship, and Freud was quite successful in his attempt to give credibility to the idea that all cognitive functions (perception, memory, thought, and so on) fit within the framework of the model.

According to Freud, the nervous system is comprised of different systems of neurons (see V.A.1.a). The nervous system functions like a reflex apparatus, receiving internal and external stimuli and discharging these in the form of motor actions. It does its best to avoid stimuli (quantity) and this task is taken care of in two principally different ways. In accordance with the primary function, a quantity of excitation is discharged through motor actions, thus removing it from the nervous system. In accordance with the secondary function, discharge also occurs but here with the result that the stimulus source temporarily ceases to influence the nervous system. It is fairly easy to picture the transition from primary function to secondary function where external stimuli are concerned. It is common experience that a pain impulse triggers motor reflexes or reactions. Pain is abreacted, for example, by shaking the injured hand. Some external sources of pain, however, continue to exert their effect until they are removed (such as a thumbtack one sits on). The infant, Freud believed, quickly learned that some reactions were more expedient in removing pain than others. Such learning results from the genesis of the secondary function concerning external stimuli; flight from stimulus is added to simple abreaction. Naturally, this is too weak a basis upon which to build a genetic theory. The nature of the external stimuli will determine whether they can be removed at all. For example, if there is a fly on a child's nose, a reaction of almost any kind will remove it. On the other hand, if a child is too warmly dressed, none of the means he has at his disposal to change the situation are sufficiently effective. Hence, external stimuli are not themselves part of the genetic scheme, but only models for the functional development of internal stimuli.

Internal stimuli (needs or drives) are the genetically active ones. They force the nervous system to develop and adapt to the environment, and it is therefore the stages through which they pass that leave their mark on development. External stimuli only have meaning in relation to internal stimuli, insofar as the former permit or hinder the satisfaction of the latter. As already mentioned, the main axis of development is comprised of the same three developmental stages Freud described in *The Interpretation of Dreams*. The key terms of genesis are indicated in the following diagram, and we wish to bring to the attention of the reader the diagram's terminological inconsistencies. The reflexive defense is not a reflex process, but

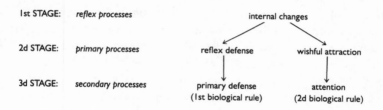

1st STAGE:	*reflex processes*		internal changes
2d STAGE:	*primary processes*	reflex defense	wishful attraction
3d STAGE:	*secondary processes*	primary defense (1st biological rule)	attention (2d biological rule)

a primary process, and the primary defense is not a primary process, but a secondary process.

Reflex and primary processes perform the primary function in two different ways, while secondary processes carry out the secondary function. Discharges in accordance with the primary function occur as internal changes on the first stage. The child reacts to hunger by crying, screaming, kicking, and reaching out (what Freud later called "expression of emotion"). However, even at this stage, a total release of excitation is inhibited by the contact barriers between neurons; causing an accumulation of excitation or energy to begin to take place in the nuclear neurons (see the diagram below). Internal stimuli, unlike external stimuli, do not have great ability to establish facilitations, that is, to force contact barriers in order to permit motor discharge. The contact barriers thus cause the first accumulation of stores and consequently also the first ego formation.

During the second developmental stage, the reflex processes called internal changes are transformed into primary processes. The transformation is based on the implantation of two types of memory ideas in the mantle neurons, pleasurable memories of gratifying experiences and unpleasurable memories of painful experiences. The further course followed by the processes is now determined by the polarization of affects into pleasure and unpleasure.

The memory image of the experience of satisfaction is analyzed in accordance with its three components: (1) the idea of the satisfying object, (2) the experience of pleasure, and (3) the motor image of the specific action the child executes in connection with satisfaction. The motor image has a double function since it develops by way of the so-called information of discharge (the child's perception of his own movement), but may later be cathected and hence again elicit the action in question. It must be emphasized that the child may perform a specific action without finding satisfaction, for example, as when he sucks in the absence of an object. To the extent that the experience of satisfaction leads to facilitations between the three components of the memory image, cathexis of one will cause cathexis of the others. Facilitation established at the time of the first experience of satisfaction will compel the accumulated and continually increasing excitation of the nuclear neurons to recathect the memory image, leading to intensified energy cathexis of the given ideational complex. This tendency of the apparatus to recathect ideas tied to the experience of satisfaction is called wishful attraction. At first the wishful attraction only leads to the memory image's being so strongly cathected that a hallucinatory wish satisfaction results, sometimes accompanied by a futile motor action (suction). The child remains as helpless as ever.

Like the experience of satisfaction, the experience of pain is divided into the following three components: (1) an increase of the level of excitation in the ψ system that is felt as unpleasure in the ω system, (2) a tendency toward discharge, and (3) a memory image of the object causing the pain. Freud imagined that the quality of unpleasure was a result of a facilitation between the memory image of the object and special secretory "key neurons" strengthening cathexis and thus creating the economic conditions for unpleasure in the ω system. An increase in excitation and pain leads to an increase in the tendency toward discharge. Consequently, energy tends to be displaced reflexively from the idea of pain to any other idea associated with it; the other idea then signifies the cessation of pain. Freud called this process reflexive defense. Reflexive defense follows the general tendency of the nervous system to divert any excitation as quickly as possible, while at the same time, because of the key neurons, even small amounts of unpleasure are intensified, provoking premature discharge or decathexis.

It is in connection with these two mechanisms, the wishful attraction and the reflex defense that Freud first spoke of primary processes: "Wishful cathexis to the point of hallucination and complete generation of unpleasure which involves a complete expenditure of defense are described by us as *psychical primary processes*" (Freud 1950a, pp. 326–27). From the adaptive point of view, these processes are deemed to be biologically harmful, and their field of action is quite narrow since the energies determined by needs (later drives of self-preservation) only in small degree let themselves be subordinated to the primary processes. The tendency, however, to think about one's wishes and to avoid thinking about anything unpleasurable is a common behavioral pattern.

We will now examine how the two basic primary processes develop into secondary processes, and consequently how the primary function (removal of excitation from the nervous system) develops into the secondary function (influencing the source of stimulation in such a way that it temporarily ceases sending stimuli). In the "Project," Freud often regretted being unable to give a mechanical explanation for development, and was therefore led to posit that there had to be a biological explanation. He said that the individual was "taught biologically" and called the two secondary processes (primary defense and attention) the first and second biological rules. However, we are interested in the mechanistic explanation to the extent that it corresponds to the psychological one, and will therefore attempt to make a synthesis of the fragments to be found in the "Project." More simply, we will attempt to find out how the child, according to Freud, stops hallucinating his satisfaction and deploying intense defense reactions. In section V.A, we attempted to show how comprehending the psychic processes (the dynamic viewpoint) presupposed an analysis of psychic systems (the topographical viewpoint) and psychic energies (the economic viewpoint), and we will therefore first look at the basis of the secondary processes from the two latter viewpoints.

Although Freud did employ an ego when adopting the topographical viewpoint, he had no unified system outside the ego. The ego is the seat of structures rooted in reason and determined by experience, and consists of a group of neurons between which there is an extended system of facilitations. These facilitations transmit an image of the outside world and help the individual orient himself in it. Ego structures are linguistic, inasmuch as only linguistic structures permit the abstraction, classification, and logical thinking necessary to understand the world. Nevertheless, Freud did not succeed in reaping the full benefit from the topographical viewpoint in the "Project," since he did not employ clearly separated memory systems at the time (see V.A.1.a).

From the economic viewpoint, the ego is a reservoir of energy, that is, the energetic condition necessary to perform secondary processes. The ego regulates psychic processes with its constant energy cathexis, it inhibits the needless and harmful primary processes and promotes logical thinking, including weighing ends and means in such a way that a specific action can be prepared by carrying out other necessary actions. As mentioned earlier, the influence of the ego depends on its access to a certain amount of energy, as well as on the ability of a cathected neuron to use its cathexis to attract the cathexes of other neurons. This may seem illogical and in direct contradiction to the general tendency of the nervous system to relinquish its cathexes; consequently there must be particular reasons for the accumulation. We have already mentioned that the contact barriers between neurons can prevent energy from escaping and hence cause accumulation. There are, furthermore, special conditions concerning facilitation related to pleasurable ideas. They are provided with energy from several sources, but only discharge this energy in small quantities. Finally, with regard to the ego's ability to attract new cathexes, the energy in a cathected neuron might momentarily exert pressure on existing facilitations, facilitating access through them. Incoming energy would prefer such facilitations to less negotiable ones. This also presupposes, however, that a channel may only be traversed in one direction and that regression cannot take place.

We will now describe the genesis of the two fundamental secondary processes from the dynamic viewpoint. By *primary defense,* Freud meant first of all the nervous system's ability to inhibit and prevent undesirable and harmful processes from taking place. Freud said that a side cathexis came from the ego and that it attracted the free cathexes that had a potential of eliciting unpleasure, that it deflected them from their path and thereby prevents unpleasure. Freud illustrated this as follows (Freud 1950a, p. 324). Inspired by Jean Laplanche (Laplanche 1970, p. 99), we have added a dotted line to delimit the ego.

The small circles are neurons and the lines connecting them are interrupted by contact barriers. The idea of the model is to show that the cathexis of the unpleasurable idea (that is, neuron) *a,* following the facilitations would lead to key neuron *b,* in turn release unpleasure and cause a defense reaction in the form of a reflex decathexis of neuron *a.* The ego, however, attracts the cathexis of neuron *a* through neuron α, whereby both unpleasure and reflex defense are avoided. Genetically, one must suppose that the first decathexis to take place consisted of the transfer of cathexis energy from neuron *a* to neuron α. The greater the unpleasure, the greater the cathexis transferred to neuron α, the greater the neuron's ability to inhibit subsequent processes. In other words, once bitten, twice shy and the more bitten, the more shy. This reaction pattern would easily be able to block all thought processes containing unpleasurable ideas if it operated in isolation, but the mechanism of attention prevents it from doing so.

Attention generally implies not only the passive registration of external impressions, but also deeper reflection upon them. According to Freud, attention suggests that ideas cathected by perceptions are further cathected by the ego to put them into sharper focus. In economic terms, one will speak of the overcathexis of perceived ideas. The mechanism is a further development of wishful attraction where all pleasurable ideas are overcathected. After the formation of the primary defense, however, barriers have been formed to oppose all harmful overcathexes, particularly those that lead to unpleasure in the long term. Why the mechanism of attention is not blocked by primary defense was explained by Freud as follows. If one supposes that the desired object is in fact present, then it must be cathected both from inside (wish cathexis) and from outside (perception cathexis). Even in such cases, primary defense will generally cause a specific action *not* to be set in motion (for example, sucking if the object is the breast). The ego is unable to tell on first sight whether an idea is hallucinated or perceived. Perception, however, implies not only cathexis of the given ideas, but also an almost imperceptible motor reflex. This is not true movement, but rather slight adjustments of the sense apparatuses, for example, spontaneous eye, head, and hand movements in response to external contact. Such slight movements are in turn perceived as ideas of discharge, which act as signs of reality for the ego (and as the basis for what Freud later called reality testing). When both the wish presentation and the idea of reflex discharge are cathected, primary defense is canceled, leading to the overcathexis of the wish idea and the performance of a specific action. In order for this specific action to fulfill the demands of the secondary function, it has to result in an external change satisfying the need, as opposed to the internal change that only satisfies primary function by removing the excitation from the nervous system.

Given these elementary aspects of the genesis of the ego and secondary processes, it is now easier to understand how other aspects of the secondary processes developed. What we have in mind in particular are (1) language, (2) thought, and (3) the function of judgment.

(1) *Language.* A significant part of the subject "psychoanalysis and language" belongs to the psychosexual register, where its theory is still in its initial stages. This does not preclude, however, the adaptive register from employing language functions, insofar as language is an important part of the individual's adaptation to the world. What we would first of all

like to discuss here is the meaning of word presentations for the development of the ego, a question that Freud examined in the 1890s. As mentioned, primary defense only allows the ego to overcathect ideas whose reality signs are already cathected in perception. Therefore the internal stimuli lack independent motor expression, which they lost by excluding internal change (crying and kicking) and primary process discharges (for example, spontaneous sucking motions). They have, however, acquired a new possibility of discharge, whose motor basis is not the muscles of sense organs (eyes, fingers), but those of the speech organs. Accordingly, cathexis of the motion images of the speech organs (the motor ideas corresponding to the articulation of definite sounds) are not signs of outer reality, but of psychic reality. In short, language makes conscious self-reflection possible for a child, without the child thereby falling prey to fantasizing without any basis in reality.

Freud imagined that facilitations were established between specific object presentations and specific word presentations during the process of language learning. The relation was already illustrated in a characteristic manner in the monograph on aphasia from 1891 (1891b; see V.A.1.a). As opposed to contemporary theoreticians of aphasia, Freud believed that word presentations should not be too sharply divided into sensory and motor parts (for example, a sound image and a motor image). These parts are as closely related as the presentation of perception and the reality sign; only seldom are they separated in aphasia. In the "Project" Freud practically ignored the distinction between sensory and motor word presentations. The most important in linguistic associations consist of facilitations between the object or thing presentation on one hand, and word presentation on the other. Linguistic associations are, according to Freud, few in number and exclusive, by which he probably meant that one object presentation corresponded to one word presentation only. This atomistic and associationistic theory has its obvious limitations (see our critical comments in V.A.1.b) and does not include those cases where word presentations are part of psychic primary processes (for example, in dreams and psychoses).

In the "Project," language is ascribed a genesis of its own. Although it does follow the schematized developmental stages, it skips stage 2 at first (the primary processes). Internal changes (screaming) comprises a security outlet for the internal stimuli, but already the first unarticulated scream fulfills not only a primary function, but also a secondary one, insofar as it generally succeeds in getting the required help. Language, however, is primarily a product of external stimuli, which become linguistic under two circumstances: (1) when a pain-provoking object makes a child cry, whereby the crying by association becomes a characteristic of the object, and (2) when the object itself makes a noise the child is able to imitate (a train's choo-choo or a cat's meow). Learning also takes place, of course, when a word is heard at the same time as the object it designates is seen. However, word presentations are, regardless of their origin, particularly closely related to internal processes by making thinking possible. Freud, like later behaviorists, considered thought to be suppressed speech.

(2) *Thinking.* In principle, Freud regarded all psychic processes where cathexis was displaced from one presentation to another as thought processes. This made it possible to distinguish between primary process thinking and secondary process thinking. The latter implies the participation of word presentations (indications of thought reality or indications of speech) and is the one corresponding to our usual conception of thinking. In this section, we will examine reproductive thinking, whose task it is to lead wish cathexis by the shortest path to need satisfaction.

Reproductive thinking is generated by lack of identity between wish cathexis and perception cathexis. If wish cathexis includes neurons $a + b$, and perception cathexis neuron $a + c$, experience teaches the child that it is risky to implement a specific action. It must therefore attempt to obtain a perception complex comprised of neuron $a + b$, that is, to replace neuron c with neuron b, which may be done by placing a mediating motor reaction via a motor image between c and b to change the actual perception of $a + c$ (perception cathexis) into perception of $a + b$ (wish cathexis). When identity between the two cathexes is thus obtained, the reality sign will confirm the real presence of the object, and then the specific (need satisfying) action can be performed.

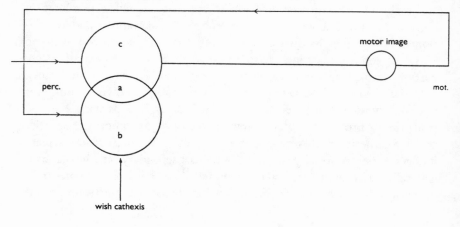

We may apply Freud's own example to the model (1950a, pp. 327–30). The child's wish cathexis *a* + *b* stands for the mother's breast plus the nipple, but perception only permits him to cathect *a* + *c,* that is, the breast seen from another angle, from an angle where the nipple is missing. Ego work teaches the child that making a certain movement gives access to the perception of *a* + *b*. This movement is stored in the memory system, as a motor image of a certain movement of the head, for example. The current of reproduction goes from perception cathexis to wish cathexis, and neuron *b* directs the current. Freud says that the ego makes small tentative displacements in all directions away from neuron *c* until it finally finds a connection. The combination of primary defense and attention assures that unpleasurable ideas also can be cathected if need be in thinking processes, without unpleasure's becoming too great.

(3) *The function of judgment.* In the "Project," along with reproductive thought, Freud made use of another form of thought, cognitive thought, or judging thought, consisting of assigning attributes to things, for example, the house is red or the breast has a nipple. Originally, things and their attributes are not separated in a child's perception; the separation first takes place when the child is able to distinguish the stable element of what is perceived (the thing) from the variable ones (attributes or predicates). Freud further developed this theme during the second and third metapsychological thrusts, when he spoke of the judgment function in the same sense as judging thought. We will therefore complete our presentation of the "Project" by adding these later formulations. The jump is not great, since Freud maintained the three developmental stages of the "Project." The function of judgment is related at each step to a specific ego formation able to distinguish between two choices, an affirmation and a negation. What is affirmed or negated, on the other hand, varies from stage to stage.

The original reality ego only appears in a single text, "Instincts and Their Vicissitudes" (1915c), understood as the perceiving nerve substance or simply the nervous system. Freud attributed to the reality ego the ability to distinguish between external and internal stimuli, insofar as its function permits it to escape external stimuli, but not internal ones. From the point of view of the reality ego, stimuli that can be silenced by a muscle action distinguish themselves from stimuli that continue to have their effect regardless of the organism's reactions. Hence, judgment concerning the stimuli distinguishes stimuli that can disappear from those that cannot. The reality ego does not have any true knowledge of what is internal and what is external, and when Freud called the first group of stimuli external and the second group internal, he did so on the basis of knowledge that was first acquired by the ego at a later stage. The same was true of external stimuli characterized as real and internal ones as not real (1917d). The reality ego can only determine whether it can escape stimuli or not and if it is at all possible to speak of a judgment function in this context, it must be called reflexive.

The purified pleasure ego is formed at the second developmental stage. Unlike the original reality ego, it is comprised of a delimited group of ideas, namely pleasurable, or good, ideas. The metapsychological explanation of the purified pleasure ego lies in the two primary processes we mentioned above, wish attraction and reflex defense. The pleasure ego is simply defined as constantly cathected ideas, which because of wish attraction means the pleasurable ones. They may originate from the body itself or from foreign objects. So, the idea of the mother's breast is an important part of the pleasure ego. The unpleasurable ideas decathected by reflex defense lie outside of the pleasure ego. Such ideas may represent objects causing pain, but also, for that matter, stimuli related to hunger or to pain caused by constipation or stomach ache. It follows that the identity of the pleasure ego is not closely related to the body. Freud completed his picture by describing the world as it was seen by the pleasure ego. The pleasure ego makes all that it likes well part of itself and because of the child's predominantly oral contact with the world, the pleasure ego continuously has fantasies of swallowing, incorporating, and introjecting good objects, but also of spitting out what tastes bad, that is to say expelling or projecting it. The judgment function of the pleasure ego is affective. The ideas in the pleasure ego are given the attribute good. This judgment expresses the pleasure ego's love for the objects concerned and is an affective affirmation of them. Conversely, ideas the pleasure ego does not want to acknowledge are given the attribute bad, which is a negation, because hate of the world is related to the wish to annihilate it, deny it. The judgment is an affective negation of the outside world. What is annihilated and brought to an end for both the original reality ego and the pleasure ego is the outside world, whereas the inside remains constant and lasting.

At the third developmental stage, the definitive reality ego is formed. Its judgment functions reestablish the realistic limits between the body and its surroundings. The definitive reality ego corresponds to our normal conception of an ego. Its identity is tied to the body and its attributes and it furthermore has access to a certain amount of knowledge about the world. Its judgment function is truly intellectual. Reality testing permits it to determine whether an object exists in reality or only in fantasy, that is, whether or not it is real. Freud believed, as mentioned, that the original reality ego possessed some degree of the same function. But the definitive reality ego is furthermore able to pass judgment on the attributes of objects or things. It is able to determine whether an object has a specific attribute or not. To negate an attribute is not the same as to destroy it. The negated attribute may be maintained as a contrast to other attributes insofar as an idea that comes to mind first takes on its full meaning when juxtaposed to its absent antithesis. In some cases, affective judgment is able to disturb intellectual judgment in such a way that negation is used as a defense mechanism or as a substitute for other defense mechanisms (see Freud 1925h). It may therefore be useful to remind ourselves that the genetic precursors of negation consist in calling something bad, denying its existence, or destroying it.

The three types of judgment functions can be schematized as follows:

JUDGMENT FUNCTION	affirmation	negation
reflective judgment function (original reality ego)	flight (removable stimulus) external (stimuli) real	flight impossible (obimulus cannot be removed) internal (stimuli) not real
affective judgment function (purified pleasure ego)	good (idea) internal introjection	bad (idea) external projection
intellectual judgment function (definitive reality ego)	idea + object exists (external) S is P	fantasy does not exist (internal) S is not P

S stands for subject. P stands for predicate.

This genetic scheme shows that the genesis of the recognition of reality follows a crooked path. From the incipient recognition of reality in the first stage, development leads to the destruction of this recognition in the second. Here, the judgment function is neither objective nor unpartial, and the child only has his own fantasies and sensations upon which to base his judgment. This genetic sidestep is fateful, for even if in the third stage the reality ego more or less reestablishes the lost balance and thereby an objective and unpartial recognition of reality, it can never entirely free itself from the affective judgment function. Recognition of reality retains its character of acquisition and assimilation just as negation retains its character of hate and expulsion. This is particularly evident in psychopathology where repression and verbal negation are defense mechanisms against something unpleasant and threatening, as were the projections of the pleasure ego.

In summary, it can be said that Freud gave us the rudiments of a genetic epistemology, which not only included the subjective factor in general, but also specified the nature of its influence on knowledge.

2. PSYCHOSEXUAL DEVELOPMENT

Freud's views on psychosexual development differed markedly from his views on adaptive development. His line of reasoning concerning the former was derived from the humanistic-romantic developmental model (see V.B), which did not keep him from criticizing and reformulating it. He stood close to the romantics as far as his way of looking at feelings and drives was concerned: they were great beings, containing violent forces, but also very brittle and vulnerable. If ignored, suppressed, or outright mishandled, they could take cruel revenge by inflicting painful psychological sufferings on the subject or by destroying it from within. Freud, however, did not fully agree with the romantics. He did not consider sexual drives to be exclusively forces of nature, and he was far from viewing their unbridled expression as a worthy ideal, just as he did not believe that they alone could point in the direction of a better life or a better society.

For the sake of clarity, we have chosen to present drive development and ego development separately, devoting one of the two first sections to each. We have given our survey a somewhat rarefied turn, and laid particular stress on what is typical for each. In the third section, we will examine the different features of development for boys and girls, and this will give us an opportunity to discuss how drive development and ego development are interwoven. Individual variations in this development have already been discussed in part 4 on Freud's therapeutic work, both in relation to our survey of various mental afflictions and in relation to the case histories.

(a) The Genesis and Development
of the Sexual Drives

Until 1897 Freud's view of sexuality was fairly conventional; he saw it as a phenomenon that first developed at puberty and was limited to the sexual organs (genitals). In 1897, for the first time he expressed the opinion (he might have been inspired to do so by Fliess) that sexuality was also found in children, and that theirs was less concentrated in the genitals than was adult's. In *Three Essays on the Theory of Sexuality* (1905d), infantile sexuality was defined on the basis of a number of partial drives related to different zones of the body (the mouth, the bowels, and the genitals all played a sexual role in children). The partial drives existed independently of each other, and the subsequent anarchy was called polymorphous perversity. In the following years, Freud discovered connections between some partial drives and some forms of neurosis, especially between the anal partial drive and the obsessional neurosis, as presented in the analysis of the Rat Man (see IV.C.3). Since he already had a theory stating that the neuroses were fixated in various developmental stages, it was natural for him to place the partial drives in successive phases. Thus, in the third edition of the *Three Essays* from 1915 he distinguished between two pregenital organizational phases of sexuality, the oral or canibalistic phase and the sadistic anal phase, and in an article from 1923 (1923e), he added yet another phase, one dominated by "the infantile genital organization," the phallic phase. The year after, Karl Abraham published a unified presentation of the three phases (Abraham 1924), which became the starting point of all later discussions of the phase theory, including Freud's own.

It is quite late in Freud's career that the definitive sequence of sexual organizational phases appears (oral, anal, phallic, and genital). The phases do not form a logical sequence, and it would be quite erroneous to think that the sexual drive (singular) developed by passing through them. All the partial drives are in principle present simultaneously, only they take turn dominating, and it is in this way the successive phases develop. The succession is to some degree determined by the organic functions with which partial drives are attached. Oral sexuality dominates first because food intake and the passive sensing of the world predominate in the newborn baby. The zone of the bowels first becomes important when feces are solid and when the child has sufficient mastery of his sphincter that defecation can be regulated, thus making sexual sensations possible. It may seem less well founded to maintain that the genital zone first dominates later, when the zone is stimulated already immediately after birth, when the child urinates, and in fact Freud did assume infant masturbation immediately after birth, alongside the masturbation of the phallic phase. Furthermore, he distinguished a urethral ("pee") sexuality from phallic sexuality.

The value of the phase theory lies in its contribution to the understanding of neuroses, psychoses, and perversions, as well as fantasies and character types in general. The partial drives play an important role because their ideational representatives are able to exert influence on all psychic processes. One should scarcely seek the logical roots of these developmental phases on a deeper biological plane as Abraham and Ferenczi, for example, did in their embryological and phylogenetic theories. The essential point of the partial drives is that they develop in attachment (anaclisis) to organic and psychic processes, and that social behavioral patterns from the surveillance of sexual activities to toilet training contributes in determining their strength as well as their character.

(1) *The oral phase* (0–2 years). The source of the oral partial drive is, simply stated, the function of nutrition, or more precisely, the stimulation of the zone around the mouth and lips generated by the process of nutrition. This stimulation creates a pressure to repeat that is independent of nutrition. The pressure is expressed as a psychic sensation of tension and a sensory stimuli sensation around the mouth. These sensations can only be removed by further stimulation of the oral zone. A child quickly learns that he can find satisfaction by sucking on a finger or other object when the breast is not at his disposal. Hence, the aim of the drive: the sucking activity that provides satisfaction.

Elaborating on Freud's analysis Abraham distinguished between an early and a late oral phase. During the early oral phase, sucking alone is the aim, regardless of what is sucked upon. Were the mouth to be stimulated mechanically, the child would not even need to suck. We suggest that only the pure sensory experience matters to the child. When a drive becomes associated with a psychic ideational representative, the concrete situation of satisfaction however becomes part of the idea, and the aim of the drive is thereby altered. Although it is impossible to know how the aim of a drive is experienced by an infant, analyses of patients indicate that the original drive aim seems to consist in passive incorporation, a wish to *get* and *receive* without further specification as to the object. This means that the drive is not yet psychically associated with an object. In this sense, the early oral phase is objectless and autoerotic.

The late oral phase is characterized by teething. It is a source of pain and the child learns to abreact the pain by biting certain things. The corresponding partial drive arises in anaclisis to the biting, and the drive aim now has a clearly motor component, to the extent that an external stimulus will no longer be able to satisfy the drive. Psychically, the drive aim is expressed in the late oral phase as active incorporation, a tendency to *take* and *take in*. Ideas of the object of the drive are formed, although they are not separated from the ego. For Abraham, the late oral phase was contemporaneous with narcissism, and hence the narcissistic pleasure ego's wish to take in all good objects was based on the oral partial drive. However, there is also an opposed tendency in the drive aim, in which internal experiences of pain related to teething combined with experiences of frustration attendant on the absence of the breast lead to rage and aggression against the breast and to a sadistic wish to destroy it (oral sadism). The object is then experienced psychically as being both satisfying and frustrating, both good and bad. This double tie, causing the child great difficulties throughout most of childhood is generally called ambivalent.

(2) *The anal phase* (2–4 years). The anal phase can be analyzed along the same lines used to analyze the oral phase. The anal partial drive is related to the function of defecation, and its source is closely related to the stimulation generated in the rectal mucosa during defecation. Not before the feces become solid does the intensity of the stimulation reach a level sufficient to make it erogenous, which is why the anal phase follows the oral. Anal sexuality does not manifest itself as openly as oral sexuality (there seems to be no anal instrument comparable to the pacifier), and satisfaction must therefore be obtained in direct conjunction with the emptying of the bowels. If the child is exposed to excessive toilet training or if enema syringes are used, the anal drive will naturally be increased and its further fate influenced accordingly. In connection with anal sexuality, a special olfactory or acoustic eroticism may develop into independent partial drives. Anal drive aims are predominantly sadistic, that is, they aim at destroying and dominating the object. Oral and anal sadism cannot, however, be understood solely on the basis of drives, because they are also connected to ego development. During the third metapsychological thrust Freud attempted to explain both sadism and masochism as a result of innate

biological death drives, but as we have stated earlier (see V.A.2.b), we have chosen to consider all the sexual partial drives from the perspective of the theory of anaclisis and coexcitation.

Abraham divided the anal phase the same way he had divided the oral. In the early anal phase, the child does not yet have mastery of the anal sphincter, and his satisfaction therefore consists exclusively in stimulation of the rectal mucosa. The sensory aspect is decisive. At the psychic level, the drive aim is modeled on defecation; the aim is to eject and destroy the object. This aim may influence the oral drive aim in such a way that the tendency to spit out and throw up dominates. The object of the anal partial drive is the feces, not just the real ones, but also their psychic representatives. The child takes interest in feces as much as he is allowed, and excrement holds a primary place in the child's relations to other persons. The child gives it away as gifts, expects special attention to be given to it, and wants to be present when others relieve themselves. The sexual object of this phase may be characterized as a partial object. The sexual wishes of the child are not aimed at a whole person, but at the feces, or perhaps the buttocks of the person. If he is prevented from carrying out these wishes, he must continue to unfold his sexuality autoerotically.

The late anal phase is characterized by the use of the anal sphincter. The child learns that he is able to regulate defecation, just as he discovers that he can increase and intensify pleasure by holding back feces. The psychic representation of this drive aim leads to a decisive change in the child's entire character. The child experiences everywhere what it means to "hold back." Suddenly, he doesn't want to sit on the pot when the parents wish it, and if he is forced to, he does not defecate. A fixation to this phase is expressed by the following well-known behavioral and character traits: orderliness, cleanliness, stinginess, and stubbornness. The sadistic drive aims are formed according to the same pattern. The child not only wishes to decide for himself, but also for others. He wants to own others, dominate them, strike and punish them if they do not obey his orders; true to the anal origin of the drive aim, he wants to "shit on them." Objects have now become total objects or persons, since the entire person and not just a bodily part is the object of the drive. In "Instincts and Their Vicissitudes" (1915c), Freud discussed the fate (vicissitude) of the sadistic drive when satisfaction by the object was prevented. First, the object is replaced by the individual's own person. The wish to dominate and punish others is transformed into self-torture and self-punishment, as is known from obsessional neurosis. If an object is then found to take over the subject's earlier role, true masochism results, where sexual pleasure consists in letting oneself be tormented and dominated by another. See our treatment of sadism and masochism in part 4 (IV.A.2.a) as well as our treatment of the active/passive polarity below (V.B.2.b).

(3) *The phallic phase* (4–5 years). Contrary to the oral and anal partial drives, the phallic partial drive has no obvious source. It might be said, of course, that the sexual organs are stimulated in connection with urination and hygiene, but this is true throughout childhood. One must therefore fall back on the common observation that the interest of children in their sexual organs culminates at about four to five years of age. There is no doubt, however, concerning the erogenous importance of the penis to boys and of the clitoris to girls (regardless of the many disputes between Freud's followers). Physiologically equipped with a high degree of sensitivity, these organs afford children a certain measure of sexual satisfaction through masturbation, even if they are usually unable to achieve orgasm.

Although at first glance, both the girl's stimulation of her clitoris and the boy's stimulation of his penis might be equally considered the dominant drive aims of the phallic phase, the parallel ends here. A common psychic representation of the drive goal does not exist (corresponding to incorporation, expulsion, and retention). According to Freud, both the boy and the girl consider the penis to be the more desirable organ, since it is bigger, more fit to urinate with, and (or so the children think) more sexually sensitive than the girl's organ. A boy's psychic drive aim is at first derived from the urethral function; his ability to urinate at a distance becomes a measure of his power. A girl, on the other hand, sets her sights on the utopian goal of one day acquiring her own penis. At this point, she has no idea what the vagina is or what its functions later will be. Gender differences play an important role in the mental life of both boys and girls. We will not anticipate our examination of the castration complex, but it is noteworthy that interest in gender differences is a source of new partial drives. One is the scoptophilic drive, found in an active and a passive version (voyeurism and exhibitionism), another the drive for knowledge, which arises from the child's speculations concerning how children are conceived, gender differences, and other questions, and is based on the principle that sexual pleasure is achieved by acquiring knowledge.

The object of the phallic drive is a total object, that is, a person, and at first it is the mother for both boy and girl. If the drive aim is to exercise sadistic mastery over the mother, perhaps with the help of the penis, a boy and a girl still do not have a more definite idea of the object relation they wish to have with her. Consequently, their fantasies often bear the mark of oral and anal traits. We will save our more thorough discussion of the Oedipus complex for the following sections.

(4) *The genital phase* (from puberty onward). The phallic phase generally ends with a process of repression's ushering in the period of latency. According to Freud, in the latency period, sexuality has not disappeared but remains repressed, even split in such a way that one part (the superego) keeps the other (the sensual and oedipal) in check. Some components, however, have other fates; they are transformed into affectionate feelings for the parents. Lastly, extensive sublimation occurs, which means that the sexual drives support the development of the ego drives. Under the impetus of hormonal and physiological changes (the boy's erections and ejaculations, the girl's mentruations, and so on), new sexual currents arise during puberty. Phallic sexuality is now further developed, until it takes on its definitive form as genital sexuality. Abraham even called the two phases the early and the definitive genital phase. Their relationship resembles the relationship between the early and the late oral and anal phases. The phallic (or early genital) phase is dominated by the sensory organ stimulation of the penis and clitoris, whereas the definitive genital phase is dominated by the motor abreaction of this stimulus through orgasm. Orgasm consists of muscle contractions in the penis during ejaculation in boys, and muscle contractions in the vagina in girls.

Drive aims are psychologically specified or altered during the genital phase. The drive aim of the male is to penetrate the vagina, that of the female to be penetrated by the penis; sexual excitement is now coupled with these aims. According to Freud, neither boys nor girls know anything about the vagina until puberty, at least not about the function of the vagina. As for the sexual object, the boy extends his object choice of the mother from the phallic phase, to another female object. At the end of the phallic phase, girls have already gone through changes that prepare them for the heterosexual choice of a male object.

Freud believed that the pregenital partial drives coalesced during the formation of the genital drive, which might then be called the sexual drive (in the singular). The image is reminiscent of the way streams flow together to form a river. Although the erogenous zones retain some of their sensitivity, stimulation of them is automatically transferred to the genital zone (a kiss, for example, can cause genital excitement). Freud said that the erogenous zones were subjected to the primacy of the genital zone. The original aims and objects of the partial drives were to some extent abolished, because their ideational representatives were associated with the aim and object ideas of the genital drive.

One must naturally add that genital sexuality very seldom succeeds in exercising complete domination over the partial drives. If the latter fail to manifest themselves directly (or positively) as perversions, they may find indirect (or negative) outlets in neuroses and psychoses. In addition, there is the possibility of their emphasizing and reinforcing certain character traits that provide a certain amount of satisfaction. The oral drive aim can, for instance, express itself as openness and receptivity, the anal as thrift and defiance, and the urethral as ambition. Freud sometimes used the concept of sublimation to explain how drives originally difficult to control could make significant contributions to long-term cultural and religious goals. The concept implies that freely displaceable energies become less fluid and consequently less mobile. During the third metapsychological thrust, Freud used the concept of desexualization as synonymous with sublimation (see V.A.2.a).

We have attempted to summarize our remarks in this section in the scheme on page 394. For the sake of clarity, we distinguish between the character of the aim and the object on the physical-biological level and on the psychic level. Thus, the aim of the drive may be considered as either the immediately observable activity, or as a more abstract and psychically mediated aim activity that can be carried out on several different planes. Where the drive's object is concerned, the real object must be distinguished from the ideational object. The latter is the true object of the drive, and it is only when the ideational object determines object choice that the real object also becomes part of the aim of the drive. Thus, it is reasonable to say that the early oral drive has no object, even if the child sucks on the breast, on the thumb, as well as on a number of other objects. Separations between physiological and psychic aims and between real and ideational objects are not surmounted before the genital phase in such a way that a stable synthesis is formed.

(b) The Genesis and Development of Psychological Structures

In the preceding section on the development of drives, we dealt only briefly with the psychological structures representing them. In this section, we

THE DEVELOPMENTAL PHASES OF THE PARTIAL DRIVES	SOURCE	AIM (satisfying activity)		OBJECT	
		physiological	psychic	real object	ideational object
ORAL — EARLY ORAL PHASE (sensory dominance)	nutrition stimulation of lips, mouth, and tongue	sucking	passive incorporation (get, receive)	breast finger	no object
LATE ORAL PHASE (motor dominance)	teething	biting	active incorporation (take in, take) destroy	pacifier etc.	part object (no separation between ego and object)
ANAL — EARLY ANAL PHASE (sensory dominance)	defecation	defecation	ejection destruction	feces enema syringe	part object
LATE ANAL PHASE (motor dominance)	mastery of sphincter	retention of feces	control domination	finger etc.	incipient totalization of the object
PHALLIC (sensory dominance)	emptying the bladder stimulation of the penis and clitoris	masturbation	mastery possession	hand other person	total object "mother"
GENITAL (motor dominance)	physiological possibility of orgasm subsumption of other drive sources	orgasm	penetration/perception	partner of opposite sex	total object

intercourse

"the loved one"

will focus on the genesis and development of these structures. We have seen that treating the object of a drive presents some difficulty. We do not usually say that a drive loves its object, but rather that the ego loves the object. To describe more precisely how the ego's object relations are established, we must again take a look at the developmental path going from objectless state to the acquisition of a total object. But even when seeing things from this vantage point we must not forget that partial drives still supply the energy of drives, even if they already can be inhibited and bound to such an extent during the pregenital phases of development that they no longer divulge their source. Freud then spoke of affectionate drive impulses, as opposed to sensual drive impulses. Affectionate impulses constitute the subject's emotional ties as well as being the reason it can love others intensely in the absence of physical contact. The exalted and perennial feelings described by the romantics are typical manifestations of aim-inhibited drive impulses.

The three developmental stages named by Freud, (1) autoerotism, (2) narcissism, and (3) object love, as well as the psychological structures that correspond to them, can be illustrated as follows, noting that object love is composed of an oedipal and a postoedipal part, corresponding to the manifestation and overcoming, respectively, of the active/passive polarity:

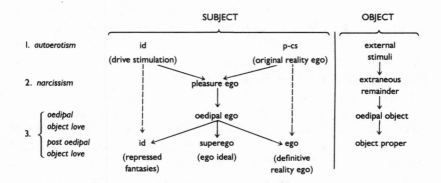

There is a parallel between these three developmental stages and the stages of adaptive development (see V.B.1), even if they are not contemporaneous. It was a recurring problem for Freud that he sometimes worked with the id, superego, and ego as all-encompassing agencies of the psychic apparatus, and other times suggested that alongside the ego there was a group of object presentations that the ego could cathect, but that did not itself belong to it. In the psychosexual register, this latter possibility must be preferred as it is necessary here to be able to distinguish when the ego loves itself from when it loves another, that is, whether cathexis is bound to the group of presentations that make up the ego or to that which makes up the object. *Subject* in this context does not refer to the individual, but denotes the psychic structure that represents the individual. Likewise, *object* does not stand for the real object, but for the representation of the object (or for the genetic preconditions for that representation). In our review of the three stages of development, we have emphasized the general traits that lead to object choice while leaving other central questions for discussion in the next section (gender-specific development, deferred action, modes of identification, and mechanisms of defense and fantasies).

(1) *Autoerotism.* Autoerotism is obtaining satisfaction without recourse to an outer sexual object. Autoerotism can manifest itself at all levels of psychosexual development, but Freud also thought that it was, genetically speaking, the earliest and, for a time, only form of sexual satisfaction known to the child. Whether a child sucks at its mother's breast or sucks its own thumb makes no difference; both activities are equally autoerotic. Autoerotic activity is certainly conditioned by the memory of a satisfying experience and not by the presentation of an object, where sucking primarily suggests a reflex process. The first oral partial drive already contributes to the disruption of the earliest function of the reality ego, since autoerotic sucking in fact allows the child to cope with drive excitation alone. It is precisely this relative success that makes narcissism such an important step in the sexual development of the child, whereas it does not play a significant role in adaptive development.

Autoerotism appears in anaclisis to life-supporting functions, and thus does not exist from birth, but first emerges after a presexual period when suckling becomes routine in the child's life. Freud did not attempt to delimit this period because it started with the gradual emergence of tendencies already detectable after the first suckling.

(2) *Narcissism.* Narcissism denotes the transition to the first true ego formation, insofar as the original reality ego simply was the nervous system, and in particular, the perception-consciousness *(P-Cs)* system. Earlier, we discussed the ego's status as a topographical system within the psychic apparatus (see V.A.1) and in relation to the judgment functions in the adaptive register (see V.B.1). If we are now to give a definition of the ego that specifically takes into account its status within the psychosexual reg-

ister, we arrive at the statement: The ego is the individual's image of itself. With this definition, we account for the notion that the ego is a mental agency susceptible to change. The ego is not necessarily a true or complete image of the individual, as attested by the fact that it is possible by way of projection, identification, and repression to create a sexual identity within the ego that does not correspond to the individual's biological gender.

The earliest ego formations are comprised of the images of body presentations. A child has different ways of perceiving its own body. Some parts of the body it can see, others it perceives through different modalities of sensation, including proprioception. When these images associatively begin to fit together, we can speak of a body ego; narcissistic love is actually the body ego's love of itself, that is, of the image of the body.

Meanwhile, Freud maintained that the body image was not objective, and that perpetually cathected ideas in the ego were not necessarily identical to body presentations. At the narcissistic stage, pleasure and unpleasure form a radical psychic polarity insofar as the affects of pleasure and unpleasure have accelerating and inhibiting effects, respectively, on the course of psychic processes. Psychic memory traces are grouped in accordance with this affective polarity, so that the pleasurable representations form a coherent group. This is the group Freud called the pleasure ego, while the other group, of unpleasure presentations was called the extraneous remainder. The pleasure ego is not identical to the hypothetical body ego, but must presumably consist of pleasurable presentations of external objects, first of all the mother's breast. Likewise, the extraneous remainder is made up not only of presentations of external pain-provoking objects, but also of presentations of inner bodily sensation of unpleasure, for example, stomach pains or constipation. The entire structure bears the stamp of the pleasure principle, as pleasurable presentations are uninhibitedly cathected while unpleasurable presentations are just as uninhibitedly decathected. On the diagram, there should really be an arrow between the first and second stages from the id to the extraneous remainder and from the external stimuli to the pleasure ego, just as there should be one between the second and third stages from the pleasure ego to the object and from the extraneous remainder to both the id, and the superego, and the ego.

In adaptive development, the child does not remain long in the narcissistic stage. Even if he is able to satisfy his needs through hallucinatory satisfaction of wishes, he will quickly find that the need remains with undiminished force and makes demands for real satisfaction. Still the child is able to satisfy his sexual drives autoerotically, and this is a precondition for his psychic representations' seldom reaching frankly unpleasurable levels of tension. When a child is allowed to suck his thumb and abandon himself to an inner fantasy universe, he is in a sense in a state of bliss. Not needing others, he is absolutely narcissistic. Fantasies meet no resistance, leaving a memory of boundless self-sufficiency that never again will be reestablished. Here, Freud spoke of omnipotence of thought, underscoring the contrast between these inner ideas of grandeur and the child's actual helplessness and dependency.

Freud distinguished between primary and secondary narcissism. Primary narcissism is the narcissism of the stage we are discussing, while secondary narcissism arises by regression to this narcissistic state; it is a libidinal withdrawal of object presentations and corresponding recathexis of the ego. Secondary narcissism is known from psychosis and sleep. Though Freud does occasionally state that the fetal state is the original narcissistic state, this does not mean that we must move the narcissistic stage to a time before birth. If fetal life leaves memory traces, they are first activated when joined together with, eventually supplementing, the child's other narcissistic notions. Abraham (1924) imagined a simultaneity of the early oral phase and autoerotism and a simultaneity of the late oral phase and narcissism, though this must be said to be a very rough approximation. Finally, if one must give a timetable for the development of primary narcissism then it must be the time when a child is able to recognize his own image, eventually in a mirror, like Narcissus, without, however, being able to distinguish clearly between the ego and objects in the world around him, that is, between the ages of six and eighteen months.

(3) *Object love.* Variants in common usage of the phrases "the ego loves an object" generally leave no doubt as to their meaning. The loving one wishes to be near the loved one and takes perpetual interest in the loved one, to whom all sorts of real or imagined qualities are attributed. We have already seen how Freud analyzed object love from the point of view of drives. The object was a necessary prerequisite for the satisfaction of the drive, that is, for the release of drive energy. Without this release, a high and unpleasurable level of tension would result. The same line of thought lay behind Freud's analysis of the ego's object love. The ego was conceived of as a large reservoir of libido; if the ego only loved itself, the level of tension would rise, resulting in a more or less pathological state, megalomania for example. Thus for Freud, it was an economic necessity

that the ego sooner or later begin loving an object. However, the ego might also love an object so intensely that it lost all libido, which led to the object's being overvalued, while the ego held itself in contempt. In a declaration of love, the lover preferably had to annihilate himself in the sight of his loved one. Metapsychologically speaking, the ego and the object were two intimately associated ideational groups, and it was from this idea that Freud set out when seeking to explain the vicissitudes of love life.

In the narcissistic state, the pleasure ego loves itself, but the reason for this is primarily that all pleasurable presentations automatically become part of it. As the child's awareness of the world around him increases, he becomes increasingly able to distinguish those pleasure ego ideas originating in this external world from others originating in his own body. This transcendence of narcissism manifests itself by a more systematic interest in the external objects. At the beginning, it is a question of part objects. These may be greatly cherished toys (a pacifier, a teddy bear, and so on) or specific parts of the body of the nursing person (breasts, hands, posterior, or even excrement). If at this developmental stage the mother is considered an object, it is not as a person, but as a conglomerate of part objects that she is sexually desirable. The child has not yet reached the stage of the Oedipus complex; if one wishes to characterize this transitional stage between narcissism and Oedipus complex, then it must be through the ego's relation to part objects.

The Oedipus complex played a key role in almost all the analyses discussed in parts 3 and 4. The concept has been traced as far back as 1897 and constantly changed character during the long span of time Freud used it. Until 1924, discussion was almost exclusively centered around the Oedipus complex in boys, since that of girls was simply considered to be analogous to that of boys. During the years 1924 to 1933, however, Freud wrote a series of articles in which he explained his views on gender-specific development. We will treat this problem in the next section, limiting ourselves here to comments primarily concerning the Oedipus complex in boys.

Superficially, in the Oedipus complex, the boy loves his mother and hates his father, who is considered a rival. The boy's love and hate are, however, of a kind that does not correspond to our common understanding of the terms. The boy shows his love for his mother by trying to possess and dominate her. He wishes to decide all her actions and gives orders and instructions that he expects her to follow to the letter. The feeling of sexual pleasure is associated with this often-sadistic display of strength, which does not bar the boy from seeking to turn his strength to account to obtain sensual sexual contact with his mother. The boy follows his mother everywhere and tries every trick in the book to see her in the nude. In addition, he clearly expresses the wish to have a child with his mother, and willingly takes possession of and deploys his hardly masked sadism on any newborn or smaller child that might be at hand. The suffering and punishing of others have an enormously exciting effect on him, and punishment and humiliation are part of his fantasies. During the phallic stage, the child learns to masturbate by stimulating his or her own genital organs, and this activity then replaces the oral and anal autoerotic activities of the earlier stages.

It goes without saying that the child does not cope with all of these ventures with equal success. In the long run, the mother refuses the child's demands, and the child feels deeply wounded and offended when reprimanded and forced to face his own powerlessness. Considering himself to be the center of the universe, he cannot understand how his mother can take interest in anything else. As the boy puts these facts together, they increasingly seem to point in the same direction, namely to the important role played by his father in all these matters. After all, the father is the one the mother is interested in, and it is the father who has the power to decide over the child, and it is the father who punishes the child if he masturbates in spite of explicit injunctions against doing so. Hence, the child must compete with his father for the attention of his mother, and the hateful feelings he entertains for him are an expression of his wish to accede to the power and attributes of his father.

We have just presented some of the most striking aspects of the Oedipus complex, but we have not as yet given a theoretical explanation for it, and in fact this explanation is not easy to find in Freud's writings. Freud stated that the Oedipus complex was universal, and thus was to be found in all human societies at all times. In an earlier section, we reviewed Freud's theories concerning the historical roots of the Oedipus complex (see III.C.1.a). We saw how he imagined that patricide was perpetrated in the primitive horde, imprinted in the id as a lasting memory trace, and transmitted biologically from generation to generation, inducing in each individual a compulsion to repeat patricide in fantasy. It is natural to reject this explanation and conclude that if the explanation is wrong then the Oedipus complex cannot be universal. If we pursue this line of thought, we are led to another conclusion, namely that the Oedipus complex first appears in history with the advent of the nuclear family, itself closely bound to the rise of petit-bourgeois social classes. Be that as it may, the analysis of the Oedipus complex of the nuclear family was a precondition for discovering other variants of the Oedipus complex. It would also be tempting to say that before the rise of the nuclear family the Oedipus complex itself existed only in germinal form, and that conflicts under these conditions were short-lived and incomplete. Yet this did not necessarily mean that the castration complex is the definitive end result of the dissolution of the Oedipus complex. Here again, we are dealing with an abrupt curtailment of the conflict, resulting in an Oedipus complex that continues its existence in a repressed form.

If we reject both the biological and social-historical explanation of the Oedipus complex, what other theoretical explanation can there be? We believe that Freud himself suggested an answer in his analysis of children's games in *Beyond the Pleasure Principle* (1920g). The first example is that of Freud's own grandchild, and eighteen-month-old boy, very well behaved, who had the unfortunate habit of throwing all small objects within his reach away from himself as he exulted with a lengthy, satisfied "o-o-o," meaning *"Fort"* ("away"). Once, Freud saw a more complete version of his game. The boy had a wooden reel around which he had tied a piece of string, throwing it with great dexterity over the edge of, and into, his little, curtained cot, while making his expressive "o-o-o" sound. Afterwards, he removed the reel from the bed by pulling the string and welcomed its reappearance by sounding an enthusiastic *"Da"* ("here"). Freud associated this *"Fort-Da"* game to the boy's relationship to his mother (Freud's daughter). In spite of his great attachment to his mother, the boy never expressed sorrow when she was away, and Freud suggested that his game was his way of making himself master of her departure. With the *"Fort,"* it was as if he wanted to say that if his mother didn't need him, then he didn't need her either.

In a succeeding example, Freud told us how children were in the habit of repeating in their games experiences that had made particular impressions on them, even unpleasurable ones:

> If the doctor looks down a child's throat or carries out some small operation on him, we may be quite sure that these frightening experiences will be the subject of the next game; but we must not in that connection overlook the

fact that there is a yield of pleasure from another source. As the child passes over from passivity of the experience to the activity of the game, he hands on the disagreeable experience to one of his playmates and in this way revenges himself on a substitute" (Freud 1920g, p. 17).

One should not interpret these games merely as examples of unpleasure mastery. Children simply do not act in accordance with the reality principle by mastering unpleasure in order to obtain more certain satisfaction in the long run. Freud's grandchild was not trying to return to the pleasurable experience that his intimate relationship to his mother during his first months of life certainly must have been. In fact, through a symbolic act of revenge, the boy became acquainted with an entirely new form of pleasure, one stronger than the first, namely the pleasure of being active, with all that that entailed. Moreover, the continuation of the story showed that the boy had in fact become independent of his mother. When she died a few years later, and thus truly was *"Fort,"* he showed no sorrow. In the second example, the child took revenge on the physician by using a playmate as a substitute, and here Freud stated outright that it was taking the active position that gave pleasure. He made this point in another way, saying that "it is obvious that all their play is influenced by a wish that dominates them the whole time—the wish to be grown-up and to be able to do what grown-up people do" (1920g, p. 17).

In these two examples, we recognize typical traits of the Oedipus complex: The child's pleasure is associated with sadistic domination of the mother. In the Oedipus complex as it was originally formulated, the child became active by identification with his father, but the above examples seem to show that the casting of parents in such specific roles is not necessary. Before the child begins to divide people into two groups, those who have a penis and those who do not, he enters the activity/passivity polarity, and it is in accordance with this polarity that we view the Oedipus complex, on a deeper level, to be an activity/passivity complex. In the *"Fort-Da"* game, the activity of the boy did not come via the father, but via the mother. By identifying himself with his mother, the boy could throw the little child (the reel) in bed and pull him out again, as often as he pleased. Playing doctor, he identified himself with the physician, who naturally could represent the father, the activity now being deployed not in relation to the mother, but in relation to a playmate. This corresponds to the fact that the oedipal wish to possess the mother can give way to the desire to have a child. These examples show us the continuity from narcissism to the Oedipus complex. The Oedipus complex is an acceptable alternative to narcissism because, by identifying himself with persons around him, the child attains the power and importance he fantasized in the narcissistic state.

The formation of the Oedipus complex takes place during the anal stage and is modified during the phallic stage to produce the castration complex, an untenable and, for the child, intolerable structure. Genital masturbation is the dominant trait of the phallic stage, and the castration complex is marked by an interest in genital organs and gender differences in particular. The child imagines being or having been castrated. The aggravation of the Oedipus complex is related to the fact that parents not only keep their children from being active in their relationship to objects, but also forbid masturbation. Whereas they frankly encouraged the child to suck by giving him a pacifier, and to a certain extent tolerated his anal eroticism, they usually strongly prohibit masturbation. It may be difficult to see what the child's oedipal love for his mother and other passive love objects has to do with masturbation, which is specifically autoerotic. Apparently, Freud believed that the child masturbated to fantasies involving the mother. Another theoretical difficulty is that prohibition of masturbation is not necessarily universal, which amounts to saying that the theory of castration in its present form is not universal either. This difficulty underlies our assumption that the castration complex is less universal than the Oedipus complex. Or, put differently, historically speaking, we may imagine paths leading to the dissolution of the Oedipus complex other than the one that leads to the castration complex.

Before we continue our discussion of the castration complex, we wish to stress some of the physiological traits that distinguish phallic from oral and anal sexuality. In the beginning, sensory stimulation of the oral and anal zones is pleasurable and generates an urge to repeat. However, in the slightly longer run, this stimulation also creates excitation that must, at the end of the two respective stages, be transformed into motor activity in order to be abreacted. In this way, motor activity becomes part of the aim of the drive and at the same time hinders unpleasure from arising as a consequence of accumulated excitation. In both cases, the mechanism succeeds owing to a voluntary motor action (biting, contracting the sphincter, and so on). As for the phallic zones (penis and clitoris), there is no voluntary action or orgasmic reflex that can eliminate the excitation. Though the child can masturbate, this does not lead to orgasm. This might be even more true for girls than it is for boys, since girls are not aware of having a vagina or vaginal musculature. Thus, the sensory stimulation at first leading directly to pleasure turns out to be a source of problems. The child doesn't know what to do with his sexuality as long as he neither has a clear idea of object relations (it is questionable whether a phallic drive with penetration as its aim is to be found in the boy), nor is able to obtain any kind of unambiguous satisfying pleasure from it. This state of affairs may be the economic precondition for castration anxiety.

Freud's line of reasoning concerning the genesis and dissolution of the castration complex is as follows: The child's preoccupation with the phallic zone leads to an interest in the anatomical sex difference. The child experiences (or remembers an earlier experience indicating) that other persons exist—siblings, playmates, parents, or others—with an anatomy unlike his own. The boy, seeking a logical explanation for the anatomy of the girl, is led to imagine that it is the result of a castration, a severing of the penis. From there, he goes on to fantasize that he too could lose his penis as a consequence of similar castration. This possibility makes him react with anxiety precisely because the penis is such an important source of pleasure, and because he is seriously falling into discredit with his parents when fingering his penis. Naturally, the boy's anxiety will not diminish if he is outright threatened with having his penis cut off if he doesn't keep his hands away from it.

Castration anxiety gives the Oedipus complex a special turn. The boy now discovers the danger associated with wanting to replace the father as the one who actively possesses the mother. In the boy's fantasy the father is the one who carries out castration and, faced with the choice of being castrated or giving up his sexuality, the boy opts for the latter since he is unable to maintain an active sexual position anyway. Masturbation is suppressed and the wish to possess the mother actively is weakened. The original positive identification with the father resurfaces under a new guise, this time reconciled with the father's real existence. Admiration for the father does not now lead to emulation and substitution but to a wish to obey him. This tie to the father is something between an identification and an object tie. The idea of the father is split off from the ego and isolated in the ego ideal or superego as the voice of conscience. Repression of the Oedipus complex has now taken place, and the superego thereafter becomes its successor in the psyche as well as the repressing agency.

We defined the ego as the individual's self-image, and it is with this definition in mind that we will attempt to look more closely at the actual fate of the pleasure ego. It is safe to say that the pleasure ego is a somewhat one-sided and unrealistic idea of the individual. It contains only pleasurable images and does not account for whence they come. The first differentiation consists in outside reality's arising as a psychic group of ideas. Henceforth, some of the pleasure ego ideas are acknowledged to be part of this group (the feeding breasts, pacifier, and so on), while some of the unpleasure ideas, until now assigned to the extraneous remainder, are gradually recognized as belonging to the body and thus to the ego. With the advent of the Oedipus complex, objects take on the character of persons, and persons are divided into active and passive ones. The ego identifies with the active, regardless of the fact that this isn't very realistic either. Both the narcissistic and the oedipal egos suffer from having too high an opinion of themselves, and the three- to four-year-old child who takes possession of the world with the same nonchalance as the adult cannot avoid provoking a certain mirth. The next change consists of the oedipal ego's being split, under the influence of castration anxiety, into three different psychic agencies: (1) The presentations of the parents' active traits, in particular those of the father, are isolated in the superego, where they block the expression of the original oedipal impulses. Of Freud's formulations concerning the dissolution of the Oedipus complex, we prefer the one stating that the Oedipus complex is repressed and that the structures that supply countercathexis in repression coalesce in the superego. (2) The wish actively to possess the mother and to kill the father continues to exist in the id as repressed oedipal fantasies, and it is in this form that the Oedipus complex exerts its greatest influence (see the analyses in parts 3 and 4). (3) Finally remaining alone in the true ego (the definitive reality ego) is the individual's realistic and socially acceptable self-image. This ego will remain perpetually dependent on the surrounding psychic structures. It must adjust to the love objects that it encounters in the world; it must learn to deal with wishful impulses coming from the id; and it must obey the ideals and moral precepts encoded in the superego if it is to avoid feeling anxiety and guilt.

(c) Gender-Specific Development

In his analysis of gender-specific development, Freud distinguished three approaches to sexual differences; biological, sociological, and psychological.

(1) Biologically speaking, the differences between the sexes are fairly well defined. Men and women each have their tasks to perform in procreation. They are equipped with different genital organs and different builds and are otherwise different in numerous ways that it is unnecessary to detail here. It should be sufficient to repeat that Fliess and Freud were among the first to make manifest use of the concept of constitutional bisexuality, that is, the presence of varying degrees of both male and female traits in men and women. This later stood Freud in good stead.

(2) Sociologically, sex differences have to do with sexual roles, and these vary greatly from one period of history and from one culture to another. During his research on the historical origin of the Oedipus complex (see III.C.1.a), Freud became acquainted with the theories of both matriarchal and patriarchal societies and he was perfectly aware of the fact that the social positions of men and women were not biologically determined, even if politically, he was an opponent of women's emancipation.

(3) From a psychological point of view, various character traits may be related to sex differences, in any case, writers who have done so are legion. Before Freud, almost everyone built on changing, but nonetheless standard, notions of what was thought to be typical of men (for example, the "he-man") and typical of women (for example, the "feminine mystique"). Among the various attempts made to explain characterological differences between men and women were theories on the differences between the male and the female brain, although theories concerning the influence of environmental factors on character formation were also known in the 1800s.

Of the three approaches to sex differences, it was the third, the psychological, that engaged Freud, and he employed the two others only to the extent that they were able to shed light on the third. Merely by glancing through Freud's writings, it is easy to get an understanding which psychological traits he considered to be prominent in men and which in women. The male was aggressive and impetuous, independent and self-willed, able to show great strength of character, and often in possesssion of outstanding intellectual and moral traits. The female was passive and dependent, narcissistic and self-centered; she let herself be dominated by her feelings and lacked moral rectitude. These opinions of Freud's never changed, and it is even possible that they were an accurate appraisal of the people in the milieu he and his clients came from and lived in. On the other hand, he wondered more and more about the origin of these traits, and during the years 1924 to 1933, he elaborated a coherent theory of the Oedipus and castration complexes of both boys and girls, all the while exchanging views with writers such as Abraham, Horney, Deutsch, Lampl-de Groot, Jones, Klein, Brunswick, and Fenichel.

In our examination of Freud's theory we will once again trace the psychosexual development of the child, concentrating this time on how sex differences become part of the psychic apparatus and what consequences this process has for character formation. Stated more succinctly, the question is: How and when does sexual identity become part of the ego (the individual's self-image) and the idea of the object? With regard to the chronology of events, Freud's answer to the question is quite surprising; he was of the opinion that in psychosexual development sexual identity played no appreciable role before the phallic phase and thus before the castration complex. What is surprising about this is that the Oedipus complex, the drift of which is, in the case of boys, loving the mother and hating the father, precedes the castration complex. In this object choice sexual identity apparently plays an important role. In review of the Oedipus complex, however, we specifically stressed that the child does not take particular interest in the object's sex, but instead greatly emphasizes its passivity in allowing itself to be led, dominated and possessed by the child. The reason that the mother turns out to be the preferential passive object is solely due to the fact that, because as the nursing person, she is the one with whom the child has had the most intense and intimate relationship. If Freud had had patients in analysis who during the first years of life had been nursed and looked after by their fathers, he would have observed an Oedipus complex with the father as the primary object. Even though psychoanalytic theory easily could have accommodated this eventuality, the idea of a nursing father seemed so far-fetched at Freud's time that it was never explicitly incorporated in the theory.

Before going any further, let us first repeat the normal development of boys in order to keep it in mind as a standard of comparison. The Oedipus complex is, as it manifests itself during the anal stage, marked by the active/passive polarity. The ego is active and has become so by identifying with the mother; it accordingly has as its object a passive person willing to take on the role the child himself had before the Oedipus complex. Originally, Freud was of the opinion that the boy's active ego was the result of identification with the father, but he realized as time went on that it was more with the mother, who, on all counts, was the most important person in the boy's life. The oedipal relationship between mother and son breaks down because of inner tension. The boy's difficulties in getting the mother to accede to his wishes cause him to look for an explanation of them. In doing so, he discovers that his father makes demands on his mother similar to his own. This leads the boy to imagine that the greater his failings, the greater his father's success must have been, a success he at first attributes to his father's greater size and experience. At this point, the boy therefore tends to emulate his father. Meanwhile, in transition to the castration complex, he has become acquainted with a new polarity, the polarity phallic/castrated. Hereafter, the father's penis symbolizes his activity and power, and the boy feels that the power play with his father must result in one of them losing his penis. In order to avoid castration, he deposits, so to speak, his activity/power/penis in the superego. He temporarily gives up the power play with his father and instead increases his self-discipline under the surveillance of the superego, at the same time finding it easier to give up his mother as a sexual object as he begins to hold her in contempt for her lack of a penis. During the latency period, initiated by the repression of the Oedipus complex, he uses his drive energy in part to maintain repression and in part to conquer his surroundings physically and intellectually.

In puberty, oedipal drive impulses once again come to the fore and the boy's (or the young man's) problem then is to integrate them into the personality. It is now for the first time that the sexual polarity male/female takes on its real meaning insofar as the woman, after having been devalued because of her lack of penis, is now revalued because of her vagina. The ideal solution for Freud is when the choice of the mother as an oedipal (at first sadistic, and later aim-inhibited and affectionate) object is able to coalesce with the newly formed sensual genital drive aim of penetrating the vagina with the penis. This is what Freud compared to digging a tunnel from both ends. Either the affectionate and sensual currents join at some point of their respective trajectories, or they don't. If they don't, their coalescence is missed and each pursues its own path. A common example of this second possibility is the man who marries a woman just like his mother. He shows his affectionate feelings by protecting and worshipping her, eventually by holding her down, but does not feel sensually excited by her. On the other hand, he does not love the women who awaken and satisfy his sensual passions, and who can only be chosen as sexual objects because of their vagina.

Naturally, drives may have many vicissitudes. The sensual drive impulses do not necessarily coalesce in the genital drive, but may instead continue to exist in the form of partial drives (oral and anal sexuality play an important role in several perversions). Affectionate drive impulses can eventually be bound to an ideational object other than the mother and, in the case of boys, there are several paths to homosexual object choice: (1) narcissistic object choice of a male object; (2) projection of the oedipal identification with the father onto the ideational object; (3) identification with the mother and the choice of a male object to her taste. In other cases, the superego's repression of the Oedipus complex continues with unabated intensity such that affectionate and sensual drive impulses are only permitted to manifest themselves as neurotic symptoms. The typical transference neurosis of men is the obsessional neurosis conditioned by a strong repression of drive organization in the late anal phase.

The girl's path to heterosexual object choice is more complicated than the boy's. At first she runs into the same Oedipus complex as the boy, namely, the attempt actively and sadistically to possess the mother. Freud spoke alternately of a negative, that is, homosexual, Oedipus complex and of a preoedipal mother tie but we prefer the first possibility as being the more correct one, since the emotional ties of girls and boys at this developmental stage are still identical (see the terminological discussion below). When the ego has incorporated the active drive aims in its identity, its object choice can be diagrammed as follows:

During the phallic stage, the girl begins intense clitoral masturbation, and the subsequent recognition of the anatomic sex differences is just as disturbing to her as it was to the boy. She is forced to see herself as castrated, and through the symbolic equation of activity, power, and possession of a penis she loses the base of activity and power in her ego identity. At first, her reaction to the absence of a penis is the same as the boy's reaction to the threat of castration: the sadistic object relation to the mother is brought to a halt and the sadism redirected against the ego itself, where it serves to repress the tendency to masturbate:

Even though the girl is not pressed by the threat of castration to execute this maneuver, she executes it as effectively as the boy, and Freud was at some loss to explain this. It is true of both sexes, however, that the oedipal tie to the mother must of necessity be modified, as it is otherwise impossible to bring it to its logical conclusion. Whereas the boy carries this modification through in reaction to a fantasized threat of castration, the girl does so either from anxiety concerning the loss of love or from feelings of direct hate or resentment for the mother: she considers it to be the mother's fault that she has no penis. Regarding masturbation, her thoughts turn elsewhere. Since she can't compete with boys, she prefers forgetting everything about masturbation and genitals. If she succeeds in repressing sexuality, frigidity may be the result; on the other hand, if she only succeeds in repressing the involved ideas, complicated hysterical fantasies may result where her desire to masturbate takes the form of an imaginary seduction or rape, or where her body sensations indicate the presence of symbolic genitals.

The boy achieves a relatively stable personality structure during the latency period, where active sadistic impulses are isolated in the superego and from there direct the ego. Freud called this tie reflexive and considered it a cross between an active and a passive object relation (1915c, p. 127f.). The structure is stable because the idea of the powerful penis in the superego makes the entire superego a secure point of reference for the ego. The girl, on the other hand, must suffer all the qualms of penis envy if she accepts her identity as someone castrated. Not only does she lack a penis, but she has never had one, and this now retrospectively wounds her oedipal as well as her narcissistic ego identity. The missing penis threatens to disrupt previously negotiated developmental stages, and what is introduced through deferred action as an absence in her pleasure ego continues as an absence in her superego. In this difficult situation, Freud saw two fundamentally different developmental possibilities for her. Either she had to acquire a penis on her own, or else she had to hope to get one from someone else.

In the first case, the girl must place hope in the future, maybe the penis will grow out again, or else she must, figuratively speaking, go out into the world to find it. If her will and belief in her own strength are strong enough, she will be able to anticipate the acquisition of a penis by installing an imaginary penis in her identity. Freud then spoke of a masculinity complex, and so characterized the group of women who have superegos as strong as men's, who are often homosexual and who in practice obtain their substitutes for the missing penis by equipping themselves with phallic attributes, for example, cigars, riding whips, and tall boots. Indeed, it seems Freud thought the greatest advocates of women's liberation came from this group, and this is why he did not accept their viewpoints as valid for all women.

In the other case, where the girl hopes to get a penis from someone else, she must prolong her psychosexual development with another stage, namely the positive (heterosexual) Oedipus complex, where she loves her father and hates her mother. This stage arises from a symbolic displacement from penis to child. If she can't get a penis, she can at least get a child to fill the lack in her identity, and furthermore, the child has the advantage of being a passive object allowing her a certain measure of activity. Still, she has no child, and so she turns to her father with the wish to have one by him. Her love for him is not active or dominating but passive and receptive, and this is a sign that a decisive change has taken place in her relation to the sexual object. The penis missing in her ego identity and in her superego is refound in the father's possession; at the same time, the active and dominating traits of her oedipal identity are transferred to the object. The positive Oedipus complex lasts several years, since the rivalry with the mother is not strong enough to provoke its repression. When the girl finally abandons the positive Oedipus complex, she does so out of frustration over not having received the wished for present from her father, eventually also out of fear of losing his love if she maintains her wish.

The three models show how an active sexual aim (in the girl's negative Oedipus complex) is transformed into a passive one (in the positive Oedipus complex), and how initial sadism is turned into masochism. An adult woman often only feels sexual excitement and satisfaction during intercourse when experiencing it masochistically; the man mistreats and humiliates her by penetrating her with his penis. Conversely, there is the positive (but likewise passive) experience of the penis's being received by the woman as a present given to her by the man during intercourse.

Here, we would like to refer the reader to the model of infantile sexual development we used in connection with case histories in part 4. The boy's positive and the girl's negative Oedipus complexes were joined under the heading *the active Oedipus complex* and correspondingly the boy's negative and the girl's positive Oedipus complexes were joined under the heading *the passive Oedipus complex*. The reason for this was and is that there need not be anatomic grounds for differences between the development of boys and that of girls. The two Oedipus complexes together comprise the complete Oedipus complex that Freud introduced in *The Ego and the Id* (1923b), and it is precisely the complete Oedipus complex he maintained he always was able to find in neurotic patients of both sexes. In other words, the girl never entirely surmounts the active Oedipus complex to settle in the passive, nor does the boy succeed in completely repressing the active Oedipus complex, and he is thus left to execute the, for girls, typical reversal of activity into passivity. The much-talked-about bisexuality (see below) simply means that neither boys nor girls assume their "natural" identity without difficulty, but keep a mixture of active and passive drive aims throughout life.

Let us again take a look at some of the character traits Freud considered typically female. What is decisive in the "normal" development of the woman is that the power center of her personality is transferred from the ego to the object, whereby she is in fact led to put her psychic strength at the disposal of her husband. On the other hand, she cannot derive self-confidence from her superego, for it is less developed than the male's and because of her propensity for self-sacrifice, she has to bear the burden of Freud's characterization of her as lacking independence, deficient in her sense of reality and in her sense of justice, and lower in morals, and not only that, the passive sexual aim is considered a need to be loved instead of to love. Women really only love themselves and are at bottom narcissists. The passive Oedipus complex builds on psychological structures preceding the active Oedipus complex insofar as the majority of all passive experiences stem from early childhood, when they simply were not felt as being passive.

Incorporation of the penis as the genital drive aim is a continuation of the oral incorporation of the breast. For these reasons, women will easily manifest infantile character traits in their lives with their husbands, including old feelings of resentment to their mothers, wounded narcissism, and penis envy.

It is not our opinion that Freud's analysis of female development should be rejected as a manifestation of antifeminism. The absolutely unflattering description of typical female character traits must be seen in its historical context. It is a description of the housewife in a specific class in a specific period of history, and the analysis of her psychosexual life is the best starting point from which both to criticize and change her situation. Even if the castration complex and penis envy theories are correct, it does not follow that the male sexual organ for all time will symbolize activity and power, and perhaps it is already true in our day that the gender-specific castration complex (castration anxiety and penis envy) is a less common psychological formation than it was at the time of Freud.

We have discussed the part of Freud's developmental theory we consider most tenable, purposely leaving out a couple of his biological and physiological points. One of these treats the constitutional bisexuality of human beings. For bisexuality as a psychological concept, it is useful to stress that, in a given personality structure, both homosexual and heterosexual object choice may be found. As a biological concept, bisexuality tells us that masculinity and femininity deal with the relative dominance of a series of gender characteristics. But it is not thus proven that a mechanism as complicated as that of the choice of a sexual object based on gender can have directly biological causes. On the contrary, it seems that Freud's analyses confirm that object choice, by all accounts, is determined by concrete experiences during the child's development. Constitutional factors always have *indirect* bearing on the matter: greater muscular strength makes possible the acquisition of more experience based on activity, and thus the consolidation of the active sexual aim; greater nerve density in one part of the body can result in more intense sensory experiences there, and thus further its importance as an erogenous zone; finally, of course, one can say that the male and female genital organs fit together, if only they meet. This is probably what induced Freud to consider the clitoris and the vagina as two competing erogenous zones, in spite of the fact that together they constitute the sensory and motor halves of the same genital organ.

3. DEVELOPMENT AND
REPETITION COMPULSON

In the last two sections, we dealt with the adaptive and psychosexual registers separately, in part to show that Freud, throughout his writings, alternately looked at development from completely different points of view. This does not mean that the tendencies of adaptive and psychosexual development are allowed to manifest themselves in their pure forms. They always appear as different mixtures of the two. To our minds the fundamental relationship between the adaptive and the psychosexual registers cannot be seen as a conflictual one. It is more like teamwork in which the registers support each other and exert mutual influence. We can make the following rough description of the subject's development. The first reflexive discharges of the drives of self-preservation make possible, through the mechanism of anaclisis, the formation of autoerotic partial drives. Satisfaction obtained in this manner induces the development of a primitive wish to repeat. As this wish is elaborated, the pleasure ego of the sexual drives is formed. The presence of the pleasure ego then eases the acquisition of the secondary function by drives of self-preservation, and likewise permits the development of the first rudiments of the reality ego. Sexual drives are once again attached to drives of self-preservation, and both groups choose the same object, the mother. On the other hand, the sexual drives lead the ego throught the Oedipus complex and bring about the division into ego and superego. The superego gets its strength from the sexual drives, and it is the superego that eases the ego's extensive adaptive development during the period of latency.

Because of this constant interplay, disturbance of either adaptive or psychosexual development disrupts the *entire* development. Children who get too little love seldom have the necessary psychological energy to carry through normal adaptive and cognitive development. The ongoing interplay between the two registers raises the question of where development as a whole leads. Does it lead to an increasingly better adaptation between the individual and the environment, or does it aim at the fulfillment of sexual desire? Freud did not think he could trace any general tendency in development toward a higher goal or better adaptation, because sexual desire constantly sought to repeat earlier experiences of pleasure. This, however, does not mean that sexuality takes the same path backward it took forward. Rather, it forces development into a gigantic circular movement, leading to the discouraging discovery that instead of moving further and further away from the point of departure, one has simply gone in circles. As mentioned earlier, Freud considered biological death drives to be the expression of a superior repetition compulsion, whose goal was to lead all living things back to the dead inorganic matter from which life sprang.

To some, this is a sign that Freud had forseen the development of the bomb. We believe, however, that Freud's ideas on death drives and repetition compulsion should rightly be applied to the sexual drives as Freud suggested in the following passage from *Beyond the Pleasure Principle* (1920g):

> It may be difficult, too, for many of us, to abandon the belief that there is an instinct towards perfection at work in human beings, which has brought them to their present high level of intellectual achievement and ethical sublimation and which may be expected to watch over their development into supermen. I have no faith, however, in the existence of any such internal instinct and I cannot see how this benevolent illusion is to be preserved. The present development of human beings requires, as it seems to me, no different explanation from that of animals. What appears in a minority of individuals as an untiring impulsion towards further perfection can easily be understood as a result of the instinctual repression upon which is based all that is most precious in human civilization. The repressed instinct never ceases to strive for complete satisfaction, which would consist in the repetition of a primary experience of satisfaction. No substitutive or reactive formations and no sublimations will suffice to remove the repressed instinct's persisting tension; and it is the difference in amount between the pleasure of satisfaction which is *demanded* and that which is actually *achieved* that provides the driving factor which will permit of no halting at any position attained, but, in the poet's words, *ungebändigt immer vorwärts dringt* (presses ever forward unsubdued) (Mephistopheles in Goethe's "Faust," Part I [Scene 4]). The backward path that leads to complete satisfaction is as a rule obstructed by the resistances which maintain the repressions. So there is no alternative but to advance in the direction in which growth is still free—though with no prospect of bringing the process to a conclusion or of being able to reach the goal. The processes involved in the formation of a neurotic phobia, which is nothing else than an attempt at flight from the satisfaction of an instinct, present us with a model of the manner of origin of the suppositious 'instinct toward perfection'—an instinct which cannot possibly be attributed to every human being. The dynamic conditions for its development are, indeed, universally present; but it is only in rare cases that the economic situation appears to favour the production of the phenomenon (1920g, p. 42).

Even if Freud first explicitly referred to the compulsion to repeat in "Remembering, Repeating and Working-Through" (Freud 1914g) the concept was in a way part of his developmental theory from the beginning. Freud showed us several ways in which we were bound to the past and whereby the past influenced the present. The past gains its greatest influence when it makes its action felt from a position in the unconscious. It typically takes the form of a traumatic memory, which the ego is an unsuccessful in its repeated attempts to flee as it is unable to avoid moving back toward it making the life history of the subject a complete whole. We have put the manifestations of the repetition compulsion under three headings: (1) fixation and regression, (2) trauma formation with retroactive effect, and (3) trauma as fantasy. These three headings are in fact but three aspects of the same matter.

(1) *Fixation and regression.* If one imagines development as a temporal sequence to be seen from the three metapsychological points of view, then a topographical structure, a specific energy distribution, and a specific type of psychological process will correspond to each developmental stage. As development progresses, one topographical system will be superposed on another. In the first metapsychological thrust, Freud imagined this superposition as the translation of older memory traces into new ones, for example, the translation of thing presentation into word presentation (see V.A.1.a). For energy to be able to flow from one system to another, there must be points in common between the implicated ideas. Even so, some of the psychic energy will remain in the original system, that is, specific memories, identification, and object ties are maintained.

When Freud spoke of fixation, he meant that certain traits of a given developmental phase were particularly well preserved. Since no memory trace is effaced, it is their relative strength that determines their fixation. For example, during the narcissistic developmental stage certain pleasurable experiences may come to the fore that are only abandoned on the condition that the following stages are able to bring comparable satisfaction. If this is so, the fixation is modified, even if, in a certain sense, repetition takes place. This is the case when narcissistic ideas of omnipotence and perfection are transferred to the oedipal ego's ideas of power and possession, leading ultimately to the ego ideal or to the superego. Without the compensating ego ideal, a narcissistic fixation would perhaps have taken place. Similar mechanisms are valid concerning the formation of perversions, where even with the superposition of new systems, perverse sexual aims are transferred relatively unchanged. In some cases, an earlier means of satisfaction may be abandoned for the benefit of a later one, but if the first satisfaction was greater than the second, or if the second is exposed to threats, a return to the first takes place. One can then speak of regression.

The most tangible cause of fixation is repression, where translation is positively hindered and damming up of the libido results. Repression is caused by the original satisfaction's having been associated with unpleasure (the transformation of affect) during development. There are, however, other types of defenses that can cause fixation, for example, the psychotic defenses of repudiation, disavowal, and projection. In such cases, as a rule it is a negative experience that is sought to be avoided; the insufficient elaboration of the problem develops into a fixation and is the reason subsequent psychological acquisitions are easily abandoned again.

Fixation is open to direct observation when it provokes a regression, that is, when the structures to which ties have been established are in one way or another repeated after having been repressed (the return of the repressed). Metapsychologically speaking, the underlying systems obtain new and easier access to consciousness, however without ever becoming conscious in their original form. The superposed systems always retain some influence, and this is why Freudian regression is different from comparable concepts in Jackson and Meynert (see I.B.3.a,b). According to them, a dissolution of the higher center is required in order for the lower ones to function uninhibitedly. There is no middle ground. In Freud, on the other hand, defense continues with the strength and means it has at its disposal at any given time. Like unconscious impulses, it never entirely capitulates.

In *The Interpretation of Dreams* (1900a, p. 548), Freud distinguished between three types of regressions, or rather three aspects of regression, being the topographical (withdrawal of energy to an underlying system), the temporal (the increased dominance of memories from earlier phases of development), and the formal (the fragmentation of the superposed ideas in their component parts: word presentation into thing presentation, concepts into isolated sensory experiences, and so on). Freud categorized psychopathology according to the developmental stage to which each type of disease was fixated and which again appeared when regression recurred. Thus the psychoses are dominated by narcissistic traits, whereas the transference neuroses are dominated by oedipal traits.

We can sum up the content of this section by stressing the fact that the repetition compulsion can manifest itself in both progressive and regressive manners. In normal development, it always manifests itself progressively, as when a specific structure is given up only for the benefit of another structure resembling the first on a sufficient number of points and procuring the pleasure desired to warrant taking a step forward. In pathological development, the repetition compulsion also manifests itself regressively, as when underlying ideational structures once again force their way into consciousness after having been suppressed.

(2) *The formation of the trauma with retroactive effect.* In part 2, we accounted for what makes the ego choose a pathological defense (repression) against unpleasurable experience instead of a normal one (see II.B.2). In Emma's case, the correct reaction to the grocer's offense would have been for her to run out of the store and never go back. This reaction, meanwhile, was not possible since the experience had not yet taken on its traumatic character. This first happened with retroactive effect when the twelve-year-old Emma, standing in a store four years later, was reminded of her earlier experience, and could now assess it in the light of her newly acquired knowledge of sexual matters. In a desperate attempt to shield herself from the memory of the event, with four years' delay, she rushed out of the store and subsequently avoided all stores. This symptomatic act permitted her to repress the memory of the grocer's act, but was otherwise in its primary process displacement just as ineffective and pointless as counting grains of sand at the beach.

The structure of this mechanism can be illustrated as follows:

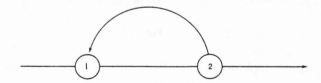

Experience 1 and experience 2 take place on two successive developmental stages and are thus embedded, each in its own memory system, each with its own set of rules and norms. Experience 2 is the spark that reactivates the memory of experience 1, and the cathexis of experience 1 forces the secondary system to repress this memory. In return symptoms must be allowed to manifest themselves.

Although Freud gradually came to believe that retroactivity was a necessary condition for choosing a pathological defense, it must be added that the effect is part of any development. Perhaps an ethical problem will illustrate this best. You can, roughly speaking, be forced to choose between good and evil, between what is in accordance with your moral precepts and what is not. If you choose to break with morality for the sake of greater personal gain, the consequences are known in advance. Maybe the plan will succeed, maybe it won't, but whatever the outcome, the action taken leads to the loss of some self-respect. For the child, however, the order of events is different. Already from birth, he is involved in actions and ideas that have consequences of which he is not aware. When he later learns to master his drive impulses and is taught the moral precepts he is expected to follow, it is unfortunately too late. By that time the precepts have been transgressed many times and his entire being has become accustomed to doing so. The child then begins to entangle himself in a mesh of attempts to cover up his deeds, which only makes matters worse. It is the meeting of memory and newly acquired morals that bring about the formation of a primitive and insufficient defense. The child can defend himself against something coming from the outside, or avoid doing something that is forbidden, but only with great difficulty can he protect himself from the consequences of something he has already done. Hence, he inherits his sin and his guilt from his parents.

This problem is often brilliantly related in literature. In attempting to realize its potentials, the subject is forced to come to terms with itself, and thus with its own past and origins. It is not by chance that Freud named what is perhaps his most important concept, the Oedipus complex, after king Oedipus. Trivial events of childhood take on dramatic proportions, comparable both to Oedipus's patricide and to his incestuous relationship to his mother, in the unconscious fantasies of the adult. Oedipus remains unaware of the content and implications of his actions until it is too late, and therefore becomes the victim of a fate apparently as unavoidable as it is cruel. We have shown how this theme recurs again and again in Ibsen's dramas. In at least one play (Ibsen 1886) the past sin is a sexual relationship which, turns out to have been unwittingly incestuous (see I.B.6.b) as well as Freud's own analysis of *Rosmersholm* [Freud 1916d, pp. 324–31]).

   (3) *The trauma as fantasy.* Freud goes one step further by pointing out that repetition compulsion does not even have to originate in actual traumatic experiences. A fantasy in the unconscious may be sufficient. Unconscious fantasies, just like traumas themselves, are formed retroactively, illustrated as follows:

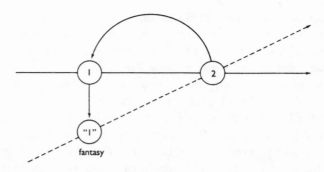

Let us take an example from the psychosexual development of girls (see V.B.2.c). Experience 2 is a girl's discovery of the difference between the sexes as well as the thoughts related to this discovery. Experience 1 is the experience of oral frustration at the autoerotic and narcissistic developmental stages. The girl can then have reminiscences related to the fact that she didn't get the breast when she wanted it, that the breast did not contain enough milk, or that it was withdrawn too early. As we have heard, the idea of the breast is an important part of the pleasure ego, and the developmental stage of the pleasure ego is only abandoned when the oedipal ego and later the ego ideal contain the same qualities. The discovery of sex differences threatens the girl's oedipal ego identity and invariably causes a retreat to the pleasure ego's more secure identity. This, however, has the completely unintentional effect of reactivating memories of the mother's withdrawal of the breast, and because of the castration complex this memory is retroactively transformed into a fictive traumatic experience (experience "1"): either the mother has taken her penis, or she has failed to give her one. Thus, the girl becomes deeply wounded in her narcissistic self-esteem. She discovers too late that castration has already occurred, and she doesn't have the same opportunities to defend herself against the treat of castration as the boy, but instead she must be content with defending herself against the discovery. The fantasized past trauma becomes a psychic reality for her and is able to cause a repetition compulsion, just as other unconscious memories do. The repetition compulsion is, in this case, a double mortification, because it forces the subject to repeat an event that has never taken place. The girl has never been castrated, and her fantasy of castration has never been conscious. She has, then, very little chance of understanding what it really is she is reacting against, repeats under new guises, and harbors within herself as a fundamental attitude at the core of her being. All this testifies amply to the importance of fantasy, that the delayed installation of a fictive trauma in the unconscious can change the course of the entire development as it happens for some. It shows to what extent Freud, in his developmental theories, placed himself beyond the elementary oppositions (like before/after, and lower/higher) that were crucial to most of the developmental theories existing in his time.

C.

THE SUBJECT'S STRUCTURE

We now return to the question that has preoccupied us throughout this book: What was Freud's actual conception of the human subject? It is obvious that he was dissatisfied with the previous subject concepts outlined in part 1, even though he never criticized them systematically. On the basis of the earlier sections, however, we can to some degree assume what his criticism of these subject concepts would have been.

(1) The liberalistic subject concept may be found in isolated form in Freud's adaptive psychology, a psychology subordinate to the reality principle, but without universal application, since it does not deal with the psychosexual register and hence the subject as a whole. The basic bodily needs force the subject to adapt to the world, that is, to understand how the world functions, to find the easiest detour to the goal when the shortest route is obstructed, to delay immediate satisfaction when it involves certain dangers, and to stock up when necessary. Freud discovered, however, that this general program of the reality principle was never realized because sexuality prevented it, and Freud did not analyze the role of sexuality the same way the liberal philosophers did. Passion and reason are not constantly opposed in Freud; passion is not a rung to be passed on the ladder of civilization; and above all, one must not think that sexuality can be made to follow in the footsteps of reason by extended and persistent castigation. Since the goal of sexuality is constantly changing, the subject must revise its life goals from time to time.

Some liberalistic philosophers, such as Descartes, were of the opinion that consciousness comprised the nucleus of the subject, and that free will existed alongside imagination in consciousness. It has been said of Freud that he "decentered" the subject by pointing out that the center of the subject did not lie in consciousness but in the unconscious. The "feeling of freedom" experienced by consciousness when it chooses between two possibilities is an illusion according to Freud, because consciousness does not know where its "spontaneous" impulses, inspirations, and sensations come from. Freud believed they came from the unconscious and that the subject had to learn to think of the unconscious as part of its identity in order to achieve a comprehensive understanding of itself.

(2) Many consider the humanistic subject concept to be identical with the psychoanalytic subject concept. It is striking how much of what, for example, the romantics said about feeling corresponded to what psychoanalysts later said about sexuality. Feelings/sexuality were suppressed, thus causing both nervous afflictions and mental disorders. Consequently, the best guarantee for mental as well as physical health could be obtained by releasing feelings/sexuality from suppression.

However, Freud himself was particularly reticent to exploit the possibility of making propaganda for psychoanalysis with the help of well-known humanist slogans. He seldom made any attempt to imagine what sexual liberation would imply, and in any case he expected nothing of the sexual drives in the way of a blueprint for the future development of mankind. On the contrary, his theory of the death drive suggests that drives do not necessarily suffer from the consequences of earlier suppression, but that some are by nature destructive and asocial.

(3) Freud's overall appraisal of the subject is reminiscent of the mechanistic subject concept. After completing "A Project for a Scientific Psychology" in the fall of 1895, Freud wrote to Fliess that the neuron model was now a machine that would soon function independently. Several years later, when he had elaborated his fictive psychological model, he still laid great emphasis on presenting all partial processes as an unbroken chain of causal relations, and it could therefore be argued that the basis of his subject concept was still mechanistic. Other statements made in his later writings, such as the rejection of the idea of free will, pointed in the same direction. Nothing in the psyche was left to chance, said Freud; even the choice of a random number turned out, upon closer analysis, to be determined by unconscious motives.

In his clinical-therapeutic writings, however, Freud followed another line of thought; here, only the causes and effects of illnesses were considered to be causally related. Illiness was a vicious circle of compulsion that had to be broken, and the goal of therapy was to abolish the compulsion and give freedom back to the patient. The therapeutic effect was related to consciousness raising, and on this point Freud seemed to partially rehabilitate an otherwise rather depreciated consciousness.

This brief outline of Freud's positions on the three subject concepts has not given us an answer to the question concerning the nature of his own subject concept. Conflicting tendencies in his work have even led some to state that Freud did not have a general subject concept, that his theoretical work was an extension of the line of thought known from the natural sciences and mechanism, while he was a humanist in clinical-therapeutic practice. In other words, Freud the theorist supposedly adopted an objective and explanatory attitude to the subject, while Freud the therapist was empathetic and understanding toward the subject.

We find this splitting of Freud's work unfortunate and misleading. Demanding that the subject be described in one specific way or from one specific point of view only is tantamount to maintaining that the subject is an undivided whole. This, however, contradicts everyday experience, where we one moment use emotional language to speak of our emotional problems, and the next discuss our health problems in purely medical terms, even when they influence our emotional life. We are able to understand our bodies without humanizing their processes, and only to children do we say things like "your tummy would like something to eat now." Since few bodily processes ever become conscious, a certain amount of knowledge and some training are necessary to understand their meaning. We are even accustomed to consult a physician when we experience unfamiliar sensations.

Pursuing this line of reasoning with respect to the unconscious will lead us to similar conclusions. The existence of unconscious processes is established by the existence of symptoms (genuine neurotic symptoms or simply dreams, lapses of memory, slips of the tongue, and so on) that cannot be understood on the basis of consciousness alone. We do not, however, have the same insight into these processes as we do into bodily ones; therefore it would be wrong to place the unconscious as a whole into one or the other type of model. Freud rejected both the purely neurophysiological and the purely humanistic models because neither could provide a satisfying explanation for all aspects of the unconscious. It is obvious that Freud, faced with patients who knew little of either psychological or psychoanalytic matters, was forced to humanize the unconscious, that is, to describe the unconscious for them as a being with its own thoughts, feelings, and wishes. However, no less that the pediatrician who speaks of the stomach as if it were a person, did Freud thereby commit himself to a humanistic theory of the unconscious. Conversely, when Freud used a topographical economic-dynamic model in his metapsychological considerations, he did not claim to have described the unconscious as it really was. In Freud's mind, the metapsychological model was also fictive and only represented an approximation of the truth.

Let us again define the problem. There is no doubt that Freud used mechanistic and partly vitalistic terminology when describing bodily processes on the physical-biological level, and that he used predominantly humanistic terminology in his descriptions of phenomena of consciousness on the level of psychic qualities (see the introduction to the division of levels, V.A). The question remaining is Freud's basic view of unconscious processes at the level of psychic quantities. By dividing the subject into three parts, choosing between humanism and mechanism might not be necessary. A third possibility may be envisioned.

The incontrovertibly mechanical and involuntary aspects of unconscious processes refute any purely humanistic conception of them. It makes no sense to place free will in the unconscious where the compulsion to repeat exerts a pervasive influence and when we generally associate freedom with consciousness. It is possible to give a humanistic interpretation of the most egoistical and narcissistic wishes, which is how Freud understood his own dreams, but the approach is less useful for understanding the repetition of painful and destructive acts. How is it possible for the conscious subject to recognize such a repetition compulsion as its own? It is often difficult to present descriptions of unconscious fantasies as if they were conscious. It is debatable whether it is reasonable to attribute to a child the fantasy that the mother has a penis she has taken from the father before placing it inside of her belly where it remains until it is transformed into a child that leaves her body through the anus along with excrement. The truth is more likely to be a complex of ideas forming constellations never reaching the syntax and ideational precision suggested above. In such cases, a more structural description based less on a psychology of consciousness would be appropriate. With regard to the therapeutic effect, let us repeat that it is not necessary to present the patient with an image of the unconscious as if it were another conscious subject. The humanization of the unconscious may be a good teaching method, but it is not absolutely essential.

We have already commented on the weaknesses of Freud's mechanistic (topographical-economic-dynamic) model of the unconscious (see V.A.1.b). There is no benefit to be gained from imagining the topographical memory systems as consisting of simple ideational elements connected by associational paths. Even the earliest established memory systems continuously change character, which explains why several versions of the id and reality ego are encountered during development (see the model in V.B.2.b). Regression is therefore not merely a return to an earlier stage of development, but a withdrawal of libido to the fantasies in the id that are formed retroactively.

The third concept of the unconscious emerging alongside the humanistic and the mechanistic is the structural. This concept of the unconscious holds that elements are determined by their mutual relations, further implying that unconscious determination is not one of linear causality, but an over-determination, where an element of perception in the present retroactively exerts influence on a memory idea. The self-reflection psychoanalysis has to offer, with or without an analyst, is based on the subject's conscious understanding of itself, in the best cases leading to a recognition of the state of dependence between conscious and unconscious components of identity. The interdependency is structural and comparable to a system of weights and pulleys; if you hang a weight somewhere on the system, it will affect the entire system until a new balance is attained. Regarding the subject, this means that if the conscious identity is adjusted with a single element the fantasy constellation in the unconscious causing symptoms will be influenced and perhaps dissolved.

The structural understanding of the subject's identity first emphasizes a certain complementarity between subject and object. In fantasy the loved one is related in a very precise manner to one's own identity. One of the poles cannot change character without affecting the other. In the section on the development of psychic structures, we saw how the subject/object relation on the narcissistic developmental stage is unequivocally overdetermined by the unpleasure polarity. The subject is thereby induced to take the form of a pleasure ego, while the object is relegated to an extraneous remainder consisting of unpleasurable ideas. We then saw how the pleasure/unpleasure polarity in turn becomes overdetermined by the active/passive polarity during the oedipal stage. Regardless of its previous content, the quality of pleasure becomes related to activity, unpleasure with passivity. The oedipal ego is thus characterized by the firm relationship between subject-pleasure-activity, whereas its object represents unpleasure and passivity. If no narcissistic love had been tied to the object, the ego would only hate it. Instead, the overall result is sadism and ambivalent object love.

The three successive developmental stages witness the increasing complexity of the subject's identity:

1st STAGE:	subject/object				
2d STAGE:	subject/object	⇐	pleasure/unpleasure		
3d STAGE:	subject/object	⇐	pleasure/unpleasure	⇐	active/passive

As we have seen, the greatest difficulties are encountered in incorporating the active/passive polarity in the subject's identity. In practice, the Oedipus complex is never entirely mastered, but continues to rummage as fantasies of power: possession, humiliation, castration, and so on.

Freud said that the mental life is dominated by the three aforementioned polarities (1915c, p. 133). They also form the basis for the differentiation into id, superego, ego, and object generally considered to constitute the definitive psychic structure. Many of the central concepts of psychoanalysis are directly derived from one or more of the polarities affording us the opportunity to discuss them transgressing the various metapsychological viewpoints. It could be argued that the three psychic polarities should really be analyzed separately on each of the three descriptive levels, since Freud first presented them in their conscious form. We can only begin to draw the contours of such an analysis, however, since it goes beyond Freud's own clarifications, which are, after all, the object of our presentation. In the section on the subject's genesis, we went back to birth and followed development forward. In the present section on the subject's structure, we will follow a similar procedure and go back to the fundamental psychic polarity, active/passive, without which the two other polarities, pleasure/unpleasure and subject/object, cannot be imagined, at least not in the adult subject.

1. ACTIVITY AND PASSIVITY

Freud considered active/passive polarity to be a fundamental biological polarity (1915c), part of the organism from birth. On the other hand, activity/passivity is first established as a psychic polarity in the oedipal developmental stage, in which the ego sees itself as active and the object as passive.

Freud had two suggestions for a biological definition. The first suggestion was related to the sensorimotor reflex; the organism was passive when it received stimuli from the outside world (the sensory aspect), active when it reacted to these stimuli (the motor aspect). The second suggestion was associated with the distinction between external and internal stimuli; the organism was passive in relation to external stimuli, but active by virtue of its own drives.

The first definition was apparently based on a similarity between activity and movement. Muscular movement expressed activity, regardless of its cause. The second definition limited the first, insofar as only movements activated by drives were considered active, whereas reactions triggered from the outside were not really active.

Freud's vacillation between the two definitions can be understood on the basis of his psychological definition of activity/passivity. As we have seen, the polarity was used here to differentiate between two types of drive aims: the active and the passive. In this connection, Freud also said that all drives were active and that there was no such thing as a passive drive. Regardless of whether the drive goal was active or passive, a minimum of activity was necessary to attain it. In this sense, the polarity is based on the second biological definition. On the other hand, the first biological definition is decisive for the division of active and passive drive aims. Drives with passive aims develop in anaclisis with sensory processes, which means that their aim is to procure a certain sensory stimulus. When the drive later finds an object, the object must procure sensory stimulus with the help of motor activity. An autoerotic drive display can only partly have a passive aim, first because its deployment necessitates the child's being active, second because the child is unable to determine whether pleasure is derived from activity or from sensory stimulation. Hence, real passive drive aims must conform to the following formula: the child wishes his mother, father, or someone else to touch and stimulate his anus, penis, clitoris, or some other organ. It follows from these considerations that drives with active aims develop in anaclisis to motor processes, and the aims of the drives thus also include motor activity of some kind. Like the passive aim, the active drive aim necessitates an object in order not to coalesce with the passive aim, for example, the active retention of excrement inevitably implies a passive stimulation of the intestinal mucosa. The typical formula of the active drive aim is thus that the child wishes to touch or stimulate specific body areas of other persons.

As long as the drive aims are predominatly sensual (that is, both sensory and motor), it is not possible to distinguish sharply between active and passive, since sensory and motor activity can never be totally separated. Stimuli cannot be accumulated in a specific organ interminably without resulting in a motor abreaction, and it is also impossible to touch or strike an object without having some sensory stimulation. It is only when the sensual drive aims are inhibited and internalized as affectionate drive aims that their active and passive aspects form a stable psychic polarity. The supreme active drive aim is then to love, whereas the passive aim is to be loved and, in ambivalent ties, also to hate and be hated). In subsequent development, it can be imagined that the affectionate drive aims have a structuring effect on the sensual, in such a way that these behave more unambiguously than before, for example, as when men exclusively cultivate their active drive aims and women their passive aims.

(a) Drive Aims and Intersubjectivity

Freud's analyses and examples suggested that the psychic active/passive polarity had other than biologically defined foundations. What we have in mind is the structure that comprises the relationship between two subjects, so-called intersubjectivity. When a child realizes that the object is a person like himself, he becomes conscious of the structural dissymmetry of the relation. When he strikes the other, the other is being struck; when he looks at the other, the other is being looked at. But he also learns that he is himself passive in a number of situations, and this discovery generates persistent attempts to conquer the active position in all matters. The child will not accept passivity, identifying instead with active persons whenever possible. We have argued above that this one-sided use of the active/passive polarity is a deep cause of the Oedipus complex (see V.B.2.b), and we believe that its rapid diffusion to all sectors of the child's psychic universe is due to the structure of language. All transitive sentences have a subject, a verb, either active or passive, and an object. It is difficult to say which object relations first become conscious to the child, but power relationships seem in any case to play a key role in the Oedipus complex; the child gives orders and the parents obey. A related object relation has to do with possession or having; the child receives something from others of which they are consequently deprived. The modality of knowledge also plays a great role for the child. The child does not care to be observed or watched over, but does everything in his power to observe his parents and gain knowledge of them and their secret sexuality.

The dissolution of the Oedipus complex is a necessary step in the psychic and social development of the child. Within the complete complex of active/passive relations, the crisis of the Oedipus complex arises around a single one of them, which invariably comes to represent the others. The only form Freud worked with was the castration complex, in which possession of the penis becomes a general symbol for power and activity, whereas the absence of the penis symbolizes powerlessness and passivity. The Oedipus complex, however, cannot be dissolved without leaving a lasting imprint on the structure of the subject, and above all, the active/passive polarity cannot be annulled once established. The child must continue to make use of the same language, in which every sentence reminds him of the active/passive relation, as well as continue to partake in intersubjective relations.

Generally, in boys, as the Oedipus complex is dissolved, activity is isolated in the superego, and the ego becomes passive (see V.B.2.C). From this position the ego can reconquer some of its activity vis-à-vis the object and thereby only remain passive toward the superego. The activity of the superego covers several areas: it is an internal voice addressing and giving orders to the ego, issuing prohibitions while the ego is the passive listener who obeys. The ego constantly feels watched by the superego, an observing eye that literally sees through the ego's thoughts and intentions. The superego is the internalized parental agency with respect to which the ego can neither escape, hide, nor turn a deaf ear. If it does not obey the superego, it will invariably be punished with guilt feelings and anxiety of conscience. In the treatment of neuroses, in which the superego is particularly severe and cruel, it is evident that the ego cannot simply refuse to obey the superego, since the resulting unpleasure and anxiety are not imagined, but real affects.

In girls, the superego is a less dominant and stable agency because of the experienced lack of a penis (see V.B.2.c). Consequently, stabilization of the personality of girls often consists of relinquishing the active position to the object, from where activity is more difficult to reintroduce into the ego. The active/passive polarity continues to be tied to the modality of possession or having: but whereas the castration complex causes girls to imagine that an active person has *deprived* them of a penis (or another object), during the passive Oedipus complex, passivity is transformed into an expectation of receiving a present of some kind. The giver is then active and the receiver passive. In the sexual pattern, the woman receives a penis and a child from the man, while she in the social pattern lets herself be dominated and supported by him. A man disposed to passive object choice in such a relationship finds his female partner demanding and feels exploited.

In the third constellation of the active/passive polarity, the ego maintains its active position in the same way as in the Oedipus complex. In other words, the oedipal ego is not divided into a superego and a true ego. That is known from certain perversions, such as sadism. In Freud's work, sadism appears mainly in its repressed and neurotic form and even if he generally characterized perversions as positive extensions of infantile sexual aims, his analytic experience on the subject remained somewhat limited. His articles on homosexuality, masochism, and fetishism treated cases where the differentiation between ego and superego had occurred. In psychiatry, a unilaterally active (amoral, vacillating) ego is seen as psychopathy or character deviation. Freud analyzed mania as a somewhat different example of an active ego. Here, ego and superego merge by way of regression, forming an ego with obvious resemblance to the oedipal ego; it throws itself with great vigor into new object relations and symbolically or ritualistically liquidates any father image it might encounter.

Regarding the fourth possibility, the id's taking an active position in the subject's structure, we must first remember a distinction introduced earlier. It can be said that the id is active insofar as all drives are essentially active. The question is, however, whether the ego experiencing itself as passive is able to localize the active agency by which it is dominated in the id (as opposed to the superego and the object). With this limitation, the activity of the id consists exclusively of its ability to create symptoms in the ego. The ego sometimes feels impulses and sees itself performing actions it is unable to understand or unable to accept as being its own. Freud observed, just before introducing the id in his conceptual apparatus, that "what we call our ego behaves essentially passively in life, and that . . . , we are 'lived' by unknown and uncontrollable forces" (Freud 1923b, p. 23). The (in this sense) active agency of the id is the repressed fantasies comprising a substantial part of the subject's identity, even if they cannot be integrated into the ego. During psychoanalytic treatment, fantasies find expression in the form of transference. The specific object relations contained in fantasies are enacted in an intense and concrete manner by what the patient expects of his analyst and by the accusations he levels against him.

(b) Freedom and Determination

The active/passive polarity generally plays a very substantial role in discussions of the subject's freedom or determination. A subject is said to be active or free when it causes its own actions, and passive or determined when causes are found outside the subject. What conclusions are formed as a result of this naturally depend on how the subject is defined. If the subject is defined from a materialistic-mechanistic point of view as a phys-ical-biological individual, many impulses for action obviously come from the outside and the subject must then be seen as determined. If the essence of the subject, defined from a romantic-humanistic point of view, is feelings and drives, then the subject must be called free, if it is able to realize its feelings. The dividing line between subject and object is of less importance because unperverted feelings are believed to be in harmony with nature. Finally, from a rational-liberalistic viewpoint, reason and consciousness are seen as the core of the subject, and its freedom dependent upon whether it is able to act according to the rules of reason or not. The subject, under the influence of its passions, is considered to be unfree and passive (note the presence of the idea of passivity in the word *passion*). Reason too crosses the line between subject and object and was defined by Spinoza, for in-stance, as insight into universal necessity. The measure of freedom thus becomes the degree of insight into necessity. Since the universe is the cause of all possible effects, the subject must identify with the universe in order to be free, that is, in order to become the cause of its own actions. Con-versely, it is unfree when controlled by feelings, because these are tied to the changing states of the body, and because the body is a very small part of the universe.

Each of the three viewpoints on determinism may be found in pure form in Freud's writings. His topographical-economic-dynamic model is basi-cally mechanistic and deterministic and leaves no room for a free subject. Consciousness is here a passive sense organ for the reception of external and internal impulses. On the other hand, as we saw above, he defined drives as active, which can be interpreted to mean that the subject is nonetheless free when fulfilling its drives. Finally, in the adaptive register, there was a tendency in Freud to consider the reality principle, that is, optimal insight into external and internal causes, as a measure of a subject's freedom.

In our opinion, there is nothing original in Freud's statement of these three viewpoints. Their appearance side by side is more confusing than clarifying. Freud's original contribution to the subject is his division of drive aims into two groups, the active and the passive. As we have seen, the active/passive polarity is established by the oedipal object relation, and later marks all intersubjective relations as well as the ego's relation to the superego and the id. In all three relations, the ego is passive after the repression of the Oedipus complex.

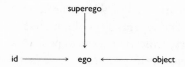

Freud's analysis of "the dependencies of the ego" has to do with these three relations (see in particular *The Ego And The Id,* chapter 5 (1923b, pp. 48–59), and the ego's passivity is consistently regarded as compulsion or determination. Since we are dealing with intrapsychic relations, that is relations within the subject's own ideational world, the nature of determination will always be psychic. The oppression of the subject turns out to be self-oppression, but therapy can turn it into a positive experience, inasmuch as the subject's determination is also a kind of self-determination, if only it does not see itself too narrowly as an ego.

The declared goal of both psychoanalytic therapy and psychoanalytically inspired self-reflection is to remove the subject's self-oppression. It must be pointed out that the resulting liberation is more subjective than real. On the other hand, subjective liberation is arguably the necessary condition for real liberation, or as Freud himself expresses it at the end of his studies on hysteria, much is won if the patient's hysterical misery is successfully transformed into common unhappiness, because with a cured mental life, the patient has the best possibility to defend himself against a really unhappy situation (1895d, p. 312).

We have earlier reviewed the basic principles governing the psychotherapeutic technique of psychoanalysis (see IV.B). Keeping in mind the standpoint we have now advanced, the analyst's task may be summarized in the following manner: to displace the patient's focus on the active/passive polarity to the modality of knowledge. Neurotic suffering often reaches a deadlock because it is articulated within the modality of having. On the basis of the castration complex, the ego experiences its passivity and powerlessness as a result of its lack of a penis, regardless whether the penis is seen to have been taken (from girls) retroactively, or the idea of the penis has been repressed (in boy's). As we saw earlier, the ego is placed under the control of the agency or agencies where the idea of the penis is located. The symptom of the ego often consists of speaking of lost objects, of gathering objects of various kind, and of waiting for conclusive presents or prizes. Obviously, the fee patients pay their analysts may itself become part of the transference neurosis.

Among the symptoms that generally manifest themselves alongside the lost object is a lack of knowledge, where the ego feels superego and analyst see right through it. The superego and the analyst are attributed knowledge greater than the ego's, which experiences powerlessness and mystification because of its ignorance of the processes in the id. It is this extra knowledge, located outside the ego, which the ego is unable to acquire, that paralyzes and pacifies it. The effect of analysis consists of giving this knowledge to the ego, thus redressing its lack. This effect cannot be obtained in any other way. The ego cannot be cured by being given presents or even love by the analyst, since the neurotic ego's craving for love is insatiable. The analytic knowledge provided for the ego is characteristically knowledge concerning the ego's own determination. The ego learns as precisely as possible why it is that it feels inferior and determined. The paradoxical effect of liberation has to do with the fact that the ego cannot be given knowledge of its own determination without at the same time becoming conscious of its ability to break this determination. By becoming conscious, the ego regains its momentarily lost freedom. The greater the knowledge it acquires concerning its own determination, the greater its potential freedom. One could even simply imagine a scientist who had studied a given person so thoroughly that he was able to tell the person what his next move would be; but the information would, of course, enable the person to do something else. Perhaps this too could be predicted, but the ego would nevertheless always be able to raise itself above any concrete prophecy presented to it in an understandable form. In keeping with this example, the goal of psychoanalysis is to produce knowledge in the form of liberating prophecies. Such interventions have the opposite effect of what are called self-fulfilling prophecies.

Analysis and self-reflection do not result in a total elimination of the id, superego, and object from the structure of the subject. Psychoanalysis does not seek the asocial freedom of manic, psychotic, and psychopathic states. Instead, self-reflection leads to a series of breaks with prior valid determination until the determining agencies have been altered to such an extent that the ego's identity has been stabilized on new foundations. The ego that no longer changes during analysis or self-reflection when presented with knowledge concerning its own determination is in a sense the only standard with which to measure the degree of freedom achieved by an ego. In this sense, the subject's freedom is its insight into necessity, as Spinoza thought. Only Freud's theory supposes that the drives will never cease to push the ego in new directions, which is why self-reflection must more or less become a life style and not something that stops after analysis. To some extent Freud also reached this conclusion in his discussion of the terminable and interminable analysis (see IV.B.3.a).

2. PLEASURE AND UNPLEASURE

Freud called pleasure/unpleasure the economic polarity (Freud 1915c, p. 140), thereby suggesting its kinship to the economic viewpoint of metapsychology and to the theory of drives. In the section dealing with this (see V.A.2), we saw how Freud distinguished between stimulation at the physical-biological level, quanta of affect or drive excitation at the level of psychic quantities, and affect or quality of affect at the level of psychic qualities. In this section, we will focus on conscious affects. In keeping with traditional thought, Freud considered these to be outgrowths of the pleasure/unpleasure polarity. Pleasure and unpleasure are the most elementary affects, and elements of pleasure and unpleasure are part of all more complex affects (hate, love, anxiety, desire, mourning, joy, envy, and pity). With the pleasure and reality principles, Freud concurred with the belief of the hedonists that the actions of the human subject are aimed at attaining pleasure and avoiding unpleasure. In part 1 we reviewed similar theories in Hobbes (see I.B.1), Fechner (see I.B.4), and Meynert (see I.B.3.b), among others. What stood out in Freud compared to other writers was his discovery of processes *not* controlled by affects, but lying beyond the principles of pleasure and reality. Because they lie beyond the pleasure principle does not mean, of course, that they do not express themselves as affects; therefore they rightfully belong to this section as well. A closer look at Freud's theory of affects shows that it contains many exciting views pointing beyond traditional hedonism. We will review these views in the first subsection. The second subsection will focus on those parts of the affect theory worked out in greatest detail, namely those dealing with the concepts of anxiety and defense.

(a) Fundamental Hypotheses in the Theory of Affect

In *Beyond the Pleasure Principle,* Freud characterized pleasurable and unpleasureable sensations as "the most obscure and inaccessible region of the mind" (Freud 1920g, p. 7), and in *Inhibitions, Symptoms and Anxiety* he even stated that he did not know what an affect was (1926d, p. 132). This hesitation must be seen in the light of Freud's being gradually forced to revise his first hypotheses concerning the relationship between affect and psychic energy. First there was the hypothesis that affect could be deduced from the level of excitation of psychic energy (unpleasure = high level of excitation; pleasure = low level of excitation), which was the opinion of most nineteenth-century neurophysiologists. Second there was the hypothesis that affect was identical to psychic energy, because affect, like energy, was displaced from idea to idea. The second hypothesis corresponded to the viewpoint of moral philosophers who described conflicts of the soul as clashes between various affects (desire, fear, shame, and so on). There are good reasons to quantify these affects, because the preponderance of one over another must depend on the relative strength of the two (see our reference to Spinoza's comment in *Ethics* [Spinoza 1677] in I.B.1.a).

The two hypotheses appeared in Freud's writings from the 1890s and invariably presented difficulties, because they were contradictory. The first hypothesis was purely quantitative, only concerned with these thresholds that put the sensory appartus out of function because of overloading (for example, when fire is no longer sensed as warmth or light, but as pain), and the threshold where sensations were too weak to be conscious. Affects were therefore placed on a quantitative scale above and below the threshold where sensations and ideas become conscious. According to the second hypothesis, energies have qualitative traits determining the nature of affects. An affect such as love can be displaced from one idea to another so that the ego consequently displaces its love from one person to another. Under certain circumstances however, the affect can change character or be directly transformed into its opposite. Freud thus worked with the idea that unsatisfied libido was transformed into anxiety. On the other hand, he also believed in the relative constancy of affects in dreams; their character remained unchanged in spite of the displacement and condensation occasioned by the dream work. In Freud's two drive dualism the qualitative difference between drive categories was used to explain the qualitative difference between affects. The "love" of sexual drives stood in relation to the "hunger" of the drives of self-preservation as the "love" of life drives stood in relation to the "hate" of death drives (see V.A.2.a).

It is untenable, of course, to work with contradictory hypotheses, but instead of choosing one or the other, we will outline a general view attempting to give each its proper weight. We will do so by formulating three new hypotheses based for the most part on Freud's later writings.

(1) *All affects correspond to discharge processes.* Freud reached this conclusion in "The Unconscious" (1915e, pp. 177–80). An affect is not only a specific quantity of energy or a state corresponding to a specific level of excitation, but also a product of both factors. The quantity of energy and the level of excitation determine the mode of discharge, but without discharge there is no affect. Before an affect may be called an affect, it must be conscious. If the energy as such is identical with an affect, the possibility for an energy quantum to be discharged in one of several ways, and thus produce different, affects will be overlooked. On the other hand, experience from clinical practice that the *same* affect continues to exist as a psychic formation and can be displaced from one idea to another cannot be disregarded. Apparently, this speaks for retaining the concept of affect as displaceable psychic energy. It is possible, however, to explain the phenomenon with the main hypothesis. In cases of the affect of nutritional need (hunger) the affect will remain constant because from the outset few modes of discharge are capable of fulfilling the need. One may hunger for anything to eat or only for delicacies, but more variation is hardly conceivable, since the affect is tied to a specific bodily state. In examining affects such as love, sorrow, and envy, which are not directly anchored to bodily states, Freud gradually came to the conclusion that the affect was constant because it was generated by a memory image (see for example lecture 25 Freud (1916–17) and *Inhibitions, Symptoms, Anxiety* (1926d), chapters 2 and 7–8). All affective experiences are in principle reproduced by the memory of earlier affective experiences, and the displaceability of affects consequently results from the possibility of freely associating the idea of an affect to other ideas. This leaves the question of how the first affects are formed, to which we will return later.

We have established that all affects correspond to discharge processes, although the reverse is not true; not all discharge processes lead to the formation of affects. According to Freud's theory, both thinking and action are discharge processes, and it is perfectly possible to think and to act without experiencing affect. This fact is the basis of the distinction between feelings and reason, which plays an important role in all of the psychological theories we have discussed. Consequently, some discharge processes must lead to affects, while others lead to thinking and action. We have earlier compared this state of affairs with the use of steam in the steam engine; some of the steam is released through the steam whistle, whereas most of it contributes to the motion of the pistons. A steam engine that leaks cannot function properly, but whines and whistles as stream leaks out where it shouldn't. This corresponds to when generation of affect in a given person takes the upper hand to such an extent that most psychic energy is used to generate more affect. In Freud's terminology, the motor discharge processes lead to "external change," while the affectogenic (vasomotor and secretory) discharge processes lead to "internal change."

It is natural to ask what characterizes those discharge processes that generate affects. The closest one may come to an answer based on Freud's writings is that a quantitative disparity exists between the amount of psychic energy discharged and the number of available discharge channels. Unpleasureable affects result from an overloading of discharge channels. In infants, it can be observed how supplementary discharge channels are enlisted to relieve those under pressure. When an infant is hungry or in pain, he attempts to abreact the excitation by crying and wriggling. We may suppose that the characteristic involuntary physiological manifestations of affects, for example, palpitations, shortness of breath, sweating spells, trembling, blushing, paralysis, and, for that matter, erection, appear in the same manner. A common reaction when faced with these often unpleasant affects is to produce symptoms, such as compulsive actions or phobic evasive actions, whose function is precisely to hinder the expression of affects. Conversely, with the pleasurable affects, the inhibition or the resistance holding psychic energy in check is suddenly removed, thus discharging vast amounts of energy. Orgasm not only causes excitation in the psyche to drop (to a level bordering on unconsciousness), but also temporarily removes muscle tension in various organs.

If we maintain the hypothesis that affects correspond to discharge processes, we must modify some of Freud's statements about pleasure and unpleasure. A high level of excitation in the psychic apparatus does not necessarily generate unpleasure. If the level of excitation is kept constant, there is no affect at all. Similarly, unpleasure cannot be defined as increase in excitation. It is true that a sudden increase in excitation generally results in unpleasure (a traumatic experience or penetration of the stimulation shield), but the unpleasure is not caused by increase in excitation itself, but by overloading the channels of discharge. Pleasureable affects are related to a decrease in excitation, not with the consistently low level of excitation that would characterize a state with no affect. In *Beyond the Pleasure Principle* (1920g), when Freud introduced the distinction between the pleasure principle and the Nirvana principle, he imagined that the affectless state of

Nirvana could be a goal in itself, lying beyond considerations of pleasure and unpleasure. We are not of the opinion, however, that the Nirvana principle can be equated with the regulation of affects in the psychic processes. Regulation of affects occurs at the level of psychic qualities, where it reigns supreme, whereas the principle of Nirvana and the principle of inertia belong to the physical-biological level and to the level of psychic quantities, respectively (see V.A.3.a).

(2) *There are two types of affects, bodily and internalized.* This categorization is not Freud's creation but he used it in a new way. Bodily affects are affects that can be localized in specific parts of the body, for example, pain in a big toe, a headache, hunger pangs in the stomach, and excitation in the genitals. In any case, the affect is related to the consciousness of a bodily locality. On the other hand, the internalized, affectionate affects can only be ascribed to an imaginary psychic locality. This is true of the entire spectrum of sentimental feelings and emotional ties in which the ego and not the body feels pain, thirsting for love, or longs for future bliss.

All adaptive affects are in principle bodily affects, since they arise from bodily needs and from the dangers and obstacles threatening the body's existence from the outside. Even if they can have psychic representations, they can never be cut off from their bodily source. What a baby feels as an unspecific and unpleasant sensation in the stomach, becomes hunger to the adult as hunger is worked into ideational structures, but the affect is still the same, and cannot be suppressed or transformed into another affect even by vigorous psychic activity. Another example the distressing affect of accumulation of feces in the bowels which is only relieved by defecation. This painful affect will necessarily remain associated with the idea of the stomach; its only adequate discharge consists of ridding the bowels of feces. It is worth noting that the affect theories influenced by the natural sciences prior to Freud dealt almost exclusively with bodily affects, in particular affects provoked externally such as fear and anger. Assuming the existence of phylogenetically inherited reflex paths, Darwin, for example, was able to explain the physiological expression of affects (specific mimickry, blushing, trembling, and so on). There is no doubt that Freud found inspiration in Darwin, but his work with psychosexual affects took him much further, and he somewhat lost interest in the visible physiological expressions of affects.

Psychosexual affects are originally bodily, like adaptive affects; however, unlike them psychosexual affects can be "internalized." Earlier, we reviewed Freud's theory of how sexual drives develop in attachment to the drives of self-preservation. The first psychosexual affects are expressed as sensations in specific organs or zones (the mouth, the bowels, and the sexual organs). They are so-called co-excitations, demanding discharge like all other excitations.

Coexcitation in the mouth zone may, to a certain extent, be discharged through sucking, but this and similar forms of discharge may not be entirely satisfactory for several reasons. Unlike the production of excitations of need, the production of coexcitation is not constant, and intensified sucking supposedly creates new coexcitations in an endless self-reinforcing process. Furthermore, external hindrances to the child's autoerotism may exist, and particularly with what pertains to phallic/clitoral autoerotism, the child has no true motor path of discharge, insofar as the orgasm reflex is still absent. All in all, then, the excess sexual coexcitations that have not found immediate discharge begin exerting influence on the remaining psychic processes, and unlike excitation determined by needs, psychosexual excitations are not obliged to carry out specific tasks. Although they must be either discharged or abstracted, this need not take place immediately or in any predetermined manner. They are genuinely free energies.

Let us attempt to follow the vicissitude of coexcitations in the psychic apparatus a little more closely. On first sight, they seem to cathect ideas of the body zone from which they are derived, as well as associated for example, of objects that have contact with the body zone in question, the activity carried out by the body zone, and the sensations of pleasure and unpleasure that result from this activity. When alternative discharge channels must be found, cathexes must be displaced to related structures, that is, object ideas, activity ideas and affect ideas having traits in common with them. The psychic meaning of the new structure is thus enforced and the pleasure-producing discharge processes of the original structure are sought to be imposed upon the new structure. This is particularly true of the oedipal active/passive structure, where both anal and phallic affects are transformed into a general sadistic and domineering attitude toward others. Through the function of displacement, the bodily sources of drive are gradually camouflaged in that the child feels that his motives for actions stem from his own ego, and we say that the bodily affects have been "internalized." It is no longer possible to establish their bodily location precisely. Internalization is completed when the bodily autoerotic activities are directly suppressed, as is the case during the period of latency. During this period, affectionate feelings predominate in the psychic life of the child.

One must be cautious when making quantitative comparisons of psychic energies, since they are, after all, purely fictitious concepts. It seems, however, to concur with Freud's thought that channels of direct motor discharge remove comparatively greater quantities of psychic energy than affectogenic ones, regardless of whether the latter are manifested openly or not. Inhibition and restriction of the motor expressions of sexual drives therefore inevitably set the stage for the expression of strong affects. When a high level of sexual excitation has been reached, the energy must be tied either with idealistic ideas of a religious or aesthetic nature, which can be pleasurable to some extent, or discharged as unpleasurable affects. In the second case, it is understandable that the neurotic discharge channels are employed to help reduce or prevent unpleasure; in the first case, the drive has perhaps been sublimated, which does not preclude neurotic traits from influencing behavior. Many of the people who have been acclaimed as saints because they have accomplished unusual deeds, such as spending most of their lives living on top of a column, have certainly been quite neurotic. In general, it is difficult to decide with certainty when we are confronted with genuine sublimations.

Some internalized affects are based on what might be called internal discharge processes, that is, the transferral of cathexes between agencies of the psychic apparatus. It is not always clear how Freud imagined these processes. Sometimes he used phrases such as "the superego hates the ego" and "the id loves the ego" (Freud 1923b). We must insist, however, that these are purely descriptive phrases, since the psychic agencies in question are not the seat of any affect production. The ego alone is "the subject of affect," inasmuch as consciousness is related to ego. If we take the ideational object not necessarily representing a real object, it is meaningless to say that it loves the ego. The true affect is the one generated by the ego when it feels loved by the object, that is, when libido is displaced from the ideational object to the ego. The other phrases must be translated in a similar manner. "The superego hates the ego" really means "the ego feels hated by the superego."

(3) *Ideas on affects influence affect production.* When one experiences a strongly pleasurable or unpleasurable affect, one seldom later remembers the precise conditions surrounding it. Consciousness ceases to register common perceptions and ideas, because it is invaded by affect impulses. In a traffic accident one may see the moon and the stars, but not much else. A far more precise memory of the affect brought on by experience would be related to the unprecise memory of the experience. In such cases,

the usual opposition between idea and affect would be abolished because ideas on affects can partake in the psychic structure on par with all other ideas. Genetically speaking, the strongly cathected affect ideas participate in the formation of the ego. They cannot be forgotten again, but retain their cathexes and furnish the ego with a store of energy (affect preparedness) necessary for it to carry out its functions.

In adaptive psychology affect memories are viewed as effective teachers. When an affect has been associated with a specific idea, the idea will remain linked in memory to the affect until a new association has been formed. A child who burns himself on a hot stove will associate the unpleasurable experience with the stove and will in the future avoid stoves. Regardless of whether there is a teacher present with specific goals in mind or whether reality is the teacher, memories of pleasure and unpleasure will influence both thoughts and actions. Freud worked with a special anxiety preparedness, aimed at ideas in the vicinity of the original umpleasurable idea. When a lesser amount of anxiety or unpleasure appears on the outskirts of the danger zone, the latter functions as a signal activating a reaction. Adaptation between the individual and the world depends in part on how effective the anxiety signal is. The unadapted child will manifest an incomplete way of functioning. He will be afraid of things only superficially reminiscent of a dangerous situation, even though they in fact pose no real danger. At other times he will expose himself without fear to situations, posing serious danger of which he neither knows nor understands.

This idea of affects as tools at the service of education and adaptation outlined here is not a discovery that can be attributed to Freud, of course, but he pointed out the essential difference between psychosexual and adaptive affects. During the upbringing of children as well as in the self-knowledge of adults, psychosexual affects are often treated as if they were adaptive, that is, as if the simple use of punishment and reward could make them follow the same course as adaptive affects. When people suffer from hunger, they can learn to work, stock up reserves, and find new ways to reach their goal when the shortest path is blocked. Hunger will remain hunger no matter what. Sexual desire is less robust. When its means of expression are inhibited or perhaps punished, lasting neuroses can easily result. It is impossible to discipline desire in the same way as hunger, because it sets new goals for itself to replace the old ones. Carrying out symptomatic actions may keep the original affects from being expressed.

In this section, we have wanted to point out the difference between the memory or the idea of the affectogenic (traumatic) experience and the memory or idea of the affect itself. In a traumatic experience excitation in the psychic apparatus suddenly increases. Freud observed that the external stimulus barrier had been penetrated, thus permitting external stimuli to gain free access to the psychic apparatus. An experience of this kind will only leave an unclear and imprecise memory. One might say that the corresponding affect simply consists of a painful overloading of the sensory apparatuses. Freud, however, insisted that affects corresponded to discharge processes (see 1 above), and what generated the affect should therefore be the discharge of the added amount of excitation. This amount of excitation is substantial enough to seek discharge not only through the ordinary channels passing through consciousness, but also by breaking new irregular channels and manifesting itself as, for example, palpitations and shortness of breath. The affect is therefore comprised of both the experience of pain and the secondary perception of heart and lung activities, which consequently also become part of the memory of the affect. After the traumatic experience, the memory of the experience and the memory of the affect will be closely associated, but the latter will gradually free itself from the former and form an affect preparedness making it possible to *think* about the affect without activating its specific channels of discharge and thus *feeling* them.

Freud was initially of the opinion that the unsatisfied libido was directly transformed into anxiety. He later modified this standpoint, claiming that all affects, including anxiety, develop by the reutilization of earlier affectogenic discharge channels. If an experience in the present is similar to affectogenic experiences in childhood, regression occurs. This is common in hysterical attacks where an abundance of the same cramps, paralyses, and other somatic symptoms used earlier in life in an attempt to abreact a traumatic experience can be observed. In Freud's opinion, all present affects involved a regressive return to memories of earlier traumatic experiences, and he even stated that all affects could be compared to hysterical attacks (Freud 1916–1917 lecture 25), albeit affects were phylogenetically acquired. On this point, we can see the influence of Darwin's affect theory (see I.B.3.b).

The regression of psychic energy to the memory of the traumatic experience takes place especially when the experience in the present for some reason cannot be integrated into the overall ideational structure. Conversely, regressive development of affect can be precluded if the traumatic experience becomes connected to other ideas. The raising of consciousness occurring during psychoanalytic treatment consists precisely of such an associative integration of the trauma. This does not necessarily mean that the traumatic experience as such becomes conscious, but merely that the conditions and circumstances surrounding it may be reconstructed in consciousness in such a way that their future cathexes will be transferred to conscious ideas instead of being discharged either along the affectogenic channels of discharge or as symptoms. During psychoanalytic treatment, embarrassing affects cannot be avoided but the more thoroughly they are analyzed the weaker they will be each time they are repeated, and the better the patient will be able to deal with them without recourse to pathological defense mechanisms. For unpleasurable affects, there is good correlation between psychoanalytic therapy and Spinoza's tenet that "a passive feeling ceases to be so as soon as we have formed a clear and explicit idea about it" (Spinoza 1677, p. 199).

For pleasurable affects, the picture becomes more complicated. At first sight, the same tenets are also valid for them. If one repeats a pleasurable experience a number of times, the pleasure will gradually fade and finally disappear entirely. This problem is well known from newspaper columns about marital sex life. We may ascertain that there are strong psychic forces that oppose the neutralization of affect mentioned by Spinoza to the extent that everyone attempts to repeat original and undiminished experiences of pleasure. Freud anticipated another law when he said that "it is the difference in amount between the pleasure of satisfaction which is *demanded* and that which is actually *achieved* that provides the driving factor which will permit of no halting at any position attained" (1920g, p. 42).

The pleasure of satisfaction demanded is the affect memory associated with the original experiences of pleasure. One could say that this cathexis comprises a pleasure preparedness whose goal is to repeat the experience of pleasure. It must thus by association incorporate the basis of pleasure within itself, including the unpleasurable states of excitation preceding the experience of pleasure. The first consequence of this is that being associated with ideas of pleasure, the experiences of unpleasure take on a false quality of pleasure, which Freud called forepleasure. The pleasure obtained from discharge diminishes in intensity each time it is repeated, because the cathexes are spread out over all the ideas concerned with pleasure instead of being discharged regressively. In this way the tendency to intensify forepleasure develops. In order for end pleasure to retain its strength, accumulation of excitation becomes an ever-more-complicated process. In masochism, this process entails inflicting unpleasurable experiences upon oneself. The sexual drive of the masochist takes on the form of the death drive, because death (the process of dying, not being dead) is for him synonymous with the definitive end pleasure. In a sense, masochism contains the prototype of "the driving factor" mentioned by Freud, (1920g, p. 42) and hence of sexual desire, which curiously enough is always located in the field of excitation between experiences of pleasure and experiences of unpleasure. Desire exists both as bodily forepleasure and as internalized longing automatically investing any future goal with nostalgic value, reminiscent of a return to an earlier experience, whose characteristics, however, can only be found in fantasy.

(b) Anxiety and Defense

The concept of defense originated during the second phase of the inception of psychoanalysis (1892–1895), when Freud introduced it to replace Breuer's concept of hypnoid states (see II.B.2). Freud was probably inspired by Meynert, who made use of three parallel conceptual polarities in his textbook of psychiatry Meynert (1884): defense/attack, unpleasure/pleasure, and inhibition/absence of inhibition. The German term *Abwehr* really means *warding off* but considering that the concept must cover a spectrum ranging from primitive reflex mechanisms to highly evolved strategies, we have chosen to use the term *defense*. It is more neutral and less derogatory than *warding off*, and furthermore has been the term most widely used internationally (for example defense is used in French).

In the 1890s, Freud distinguished between a normal and a pathological defense. He also called the latter repression, and this term gradually acquired a very important place in psychoanalytic theory, while *defense* receded somewhat into the background. In the 1920s, however, the concept of defense reappeared in Freud's writings and was given a central place. Henceforward, the concept became very much in vogue within the psychoanalytic movement. Most psychic processes could be regarded as defense processes and classified on the basis of various criteria (such as what was defending, what was being defended, that at which the defense was aimed, and so on). This tendency culminated in 1936 with the publication of Anna Freud's book on the ego and defense mechanisms, a book such acclaimed by those who would later be called ego psychologists. In what follows, however, we will confine ourselves to aspects of the concept of defense in Sigmund Freud's own writings.

The decathexis of an idea that takes place as a result of an unpleasurable affect is the fundamental aspect of the concept of defense. The primary function of defense is to remove unpleasure, whereas its secondary function is to remove the source or the cause of unpleasure. Such a broad definition of defense obviously indicates that there are many more defense processes than the pathological ones. The inclusion of normal defense at this point helps put pathological defenses in perspective.

Defense aimed at unpleasure coming from the outside is easiest to understand. If one has gotten a thorn in one's finger, one can alleviate the pain somewhat by jumping around and screaming (children are often seen using this primary function), but the cause of the pain will not disappear until the thorn is taken out. When experiences of pain are repeated several times an unpleasure, anxiety preparedness, develops, making it possible to anticipate painful experiences and prevent them from taking place. Anxiety functions as a signal that already is triggered by the danger of a painful experience, that is, triggered before the experience of pain itself. It is far from certain, however, that anxiety preparedness stands at the disposal of the secondary function as might be expected of it. If one is attacked by a dangerous animal, the entire anxiety preparedness may be discharged as an anxiety affect, that is, one begins to tremble and is paralyzed and unable to defend oneself. One may end up defending oneself against the anxiety instead of against the danger. Legend has it that the ostrich buries its head in the sand in an attempt to deny the existence of danger. This kind of psychic mechanism is particularly characteristic of psychotic patients, who tell themselves that certain unhappy events have never taken place. If the psychotic was left to himself, he would be unable to survive with this ostrich defense.

Like external stimuli, need stimuli can cause unpleasure, and we have mentioned several times how need must necessarily enforce a secondary function for the individual to survive. Abstracting or denying hunger is no help; it is necessary to be able to overcome the dangers connected with searching for food, that is, to build an effective anxiety preparedness.

Like need stimuli, sexual drives give rise to internal unpleasure. When an attempt is made to remove unpleasure, unpleasure coming from the outside, perhaps as punishment becomes an added danger. An anxiety preparedness is therefore also associated with the sexual drives; on given occasions it triggers signal anxiety or a true anxiety attack. So there are two essentially different sources of unpleasure that can provoke a defense process: the discomfort resulting from unsatisfied drive excitation, and pain or anxiety coming from the outside. Freud had great difficulty keeping the two sources of unpleasure separate in his theory of defense, which is evident from his discussion of whether anxiety has an unpleasure originating from inside or from outside. In his early writings, he believed that unsatisfied libido was immediately transformed into anxiety, whereas in his later writings he was inclined to believe that anxiety in one form or another came from the anxiety preparedness established in the psychic organization by various traumatic experiences. In the end, however, Freud recognized that there was a connection between the two explanations. It was true that anxiety only arose from the memories of earlier traumatic experiences, but drive excitation was nonetheless able to trigger the anxiety preparedness and thereby create such memories. This may be illustrated by a concrete example: the stronger the oedipal demands a boy makes on his parents, the greater the danger of castration in his mind, and the more drastic the defense against castration anxiety will be.

Within the adaptive register, adaptation between the individual and the surrounding world consists of gradually coordinating internal and external impulses as well as gradually weighing the unpleasure coming from inside against that coming from outside. The resulting interdependence may briefly be described as follows: either spontaneous satisfaction of a need provoke external reprisals of some kind (unpleasure coming from the outside), or else satisfaction has to be postponed to avoid these reprisals (triggering unpleasure from the inside). The secondary function consists of a permanent removal of the external source of unpleasure and a regular satisfaction of the need. In order to accede to secondary function, satisfaction must be postponed and the subsequent unpleasure tolerated for shorter or longer periods of time.

A genuine secondary function is impossible in the psychosexual register. Where external stimuli are concerned, it is possible to imagine that excessive reprisals against sexuality can be limited by criticism of the sexual oppression that undoubtedly takes place, but we do not find the secondary function as obvious necessity for the stimuli of the sexual drives, since an absence of feedback to the source of the drive is not life threatening, and since drive energy may very well be discharged without influencing the source of the drive. Ultimately, it can even be said that the secondary function is impossible since drive in the form of desire never settles for any regular or foreseeable satisfaction, not even when it takes into unlimited consideration the bodily drive sources (oral, anal, or genital). From the time a drive first finds new channels (and it always does, for example, by internalization), it can never return to its original mode of satisfaction.

The most primitive defenses within the psychosexual register are characterized by the insufficient coordination of unpleasure coming from outside and inside and by accomplishing merely primary function. These defenses are the prototypes of psychotic defense, in which Freud had a casual interest. A child first defends himself against pain coming from the outside by abreacting or fleeing; he is unable to judge whether the pain belongs to the adaptive or to the psychosexual register. The defense is the same in both cases, and traumatic experiences exert influence on both drives of self-preservation and sexual drives. After a sexual object has been established, psychotic defense is characterized by various degrees of disavowal of the loss of a sexual object, disavowal of the danger of castration, and even disavowal of the reality of the world). It is an attempt to combat unpleasure or anxiety directly while disregarding their cause (see what we earlier called the ostrich defense). Projection is the most primitive psychosexual defense against the unpleasure resulting from drive satisfaction and drive accumulation. At first, this projection has the character of expulsion and annihilation, but as the object becomes established, unpleasure is attributed to it; at first, the ego will both love and hate the object (ambivalence), and then, when it does not succeed in abreacting hate as sadism, the ego will feel threatened and persecuted by the object (paranoia). Severe psychotic afflictions can often be traced back to irrefutable traumatic events during the first years of life, the definitive loss of the object of love, for example. Less severe traumatic experiences will also be able to influence subsequent development, even when isolated on the narcissistic developmental stage as the extraneous remainder (see V.B.2.b). A bad relationship to the mother will increase anxiety preparedness and trigger anxiety in all later situations where there is danger of separation. Freud even believed that the trauma of birth could contribute to this anxiety preparedness, and that there has a structural similarity between birth (separation of the child from its mother), weaning from the breast (another form of separation between mother and child), and castration (separation between the child and the sexual organ of the male).

The specifically neurotic defense mechanism of repression is more complicated than the psychotic defenses and is functionally placed somewhere between primary and secondary function. Repression can first become operational when the third stage in adaptive development has been reached (see V.B.1), more specifically, when the original thing presentations have been doubled by word presentations, when causal relations can be distinguished from other more primitive associations, and when reality testing has been established. The adaptive structures form a hierarchy in which the newest ones modify and adjust the older ones. The transition between layers of the hierarchy is gradual, that is, they shade into each other without sharp boundaries anywhere. It is within this hierarchy that repression causes a split and, it can even be said, initiates the unconscious as a separate system. The first repression, primal repression, as Freud called it, keeps a group of thing presentations from becoming conscious by preventing their translation into word presentations. This group constitutes the primally repressed, that is, the core of the unconscious. The primally repressed has an organizing effect on the ideas around it. It attracts new ideas, including word presentations, that are then said to be afterrepressed, and is also associated with the group of thing presentations that form part of the unconscious without being repressed. In the late topographic model (see V.A.1.a), Freud attempted to combine adaptive and psychosexual lines of thinking by letting part of the id merge with the ego, while another part of the id (the repressed) was sharply distinguished from the repressing ideas in the superego and the ego.

Repression results from an interplay of various processes. In the following model, which can advantageously be compared to the topographical model on page 332, we have attempted to illustrate the most important of these processes:

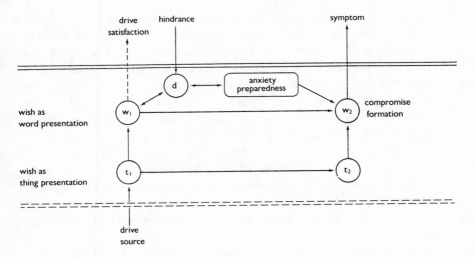

Repression interrupts the process beginning at the drive source and ending with drive satisfaction. The memory of the original satisfaction takes on the character of a wish when it is recathected, and during child development, wish a word presentation (w_1) becomes coupled with wish as a thing presentation (t_1). The specific action satisfying the drive proceeds from the word presentation, which is at first pleasurable because it is associated with the thing presentation.

Repression originally develops from the anxiety preparedness established by unpleasurable or directly traumatic experiences. The anxiety (or unpleasure) preparedness generally works by activating inhibition or another defense mechanism when there is a danger that previously unpleasurable experiences are going to be repeated. In a "Project for a Scientific Psychology," Freud spoke of a side cathexis that could exert influence on the course of psychic processes (see V.B.1). Correspondingly in repression, a countercathexis emanates from the anxiety preparedness influencing the cathexis of the wish presentation (w_1). The anxiety preparedness normally cathects a number of ideas associated with danger, and we have illustrated one of these as idea d, which could, for example, be the threat of castration. When this idea is further associated with the wish presentation, repression is possible. The association of w_1 with d is a causal relation, that is, satisfaction of the drive is punished with castration. The anxiety preparedness controls w_1 and d, which will be associated with anxiety and unpleasure in the future. The wish idea w_1 has undergone a transformation of affect from pleasure to unpleasure.

If the defense had accomplished its secondary function, an action would have proceeded from the anxiety preparedness to remove the external hindrance to drive satisfaction. In repression, however, d is primarily a fantasy, the product of earlier traumatic experiences, the wish presentation and misjudged external threats. Since the anxiety is as much related to memory as it is related to the actual threat, no outwardly directed defense will be able to oppose or remove the danger, and therefore the secondary function of the defense is impossible. The trauma of the past cannot be removed, and consequently the defense must limit itself to the task of removing the anxiety, that is, to fulfilling the primary function. The overpowering anxiety that arises in d is removed by completely decathecting d. Cathexis is pulled back to the anxiety preparedness where it functions countercathectically to help prevent d from being cathected by something else.

The essential operation of repression is certainly the defense against anxiety, and the other aspects of repression are after effects of this essential one. First, the decathexis of d forces w_1 to be decathected too, because the two ideas are closely associated. The cathexis is displaced from w_1 to w_2 instead of triggering anxiety where w_2 joins up with the anxiety preparedness supplying countercathexes to the cathexis of the wish idea. When w_2 became a lasting character trait of the ego structure, Freud called it a reaction formation. Reaction formation is often the exact opposite of the drive wish. Excessive care and tenderness correspond to sadistic drive wishes, excessive cleanliness and meticulousness to anal drive wishes. Second, t_1 is prevented from realeasing its constantly added cathexes through w_1 and this cathexis must consequently find new paths of discharge. Primary processes displace it to nonrepressed thing presentations, which have the possibility of gaining access to consciousness. The idea t_2 is a substitute by displacement or substitute formation of t_1. Innumerable substitute formations can be produced in the unconscious, since even the most remote resemblance can justify an association.

As a rule, there will be interaction between the drive cathexes from t_1, w_1, and d in such a way that they will cooperate in cathecting a specific idea. In our schematic model, w_2 is this compromise formation, which respects the interests of both the id, the ego, and the superego. Dream formation is a fine example of compromise formation (see III.A.1.b), and in neuroses symptoms result from compromise formation. Substitute formation characterizes more severe neuroses, and reaction formation less severe ones. We will give brief examples of repression in each of the three types of transference neuroses.

In anxiety hysteria or phobia, the decathexis of d does not entirely eliminate anxiety, which is instead discharged by the cathexis of w_2. In the case history of "Little Hans," castration anxiety determined the fear of being bitten by a horse (w_2). The ambivalent oedipal attitude to the father was another determinant (t_1, w_1), since intense intellectual preoccupation with horses offered a substitute satisfaction for this attitude. The horse symbolized the father. Defense against castration anxiety only fulfilled the primary function, since a flight from the father or an attack upon him was not induced. The defense against the anxiety of horses was more effective, since Hans was able to avoid them simply by staying indoors. Defense against castration anxiety led to the repression of the oedipal tie to the father (and of the entire Oedipus complex). The idea w_1 was decathected along with d; the idea t_1 retained its cathexis but later had to give it up in the form of symptoms. Freud called the contribution to symptom formation of the cathexis of t_1 the return of the repressed.

In conversion hysteria, anxiety is generally quite successfully eliminated, and compromise formation crystalizes around a factor related to the repressed as well as to the repressing. Conversion symptoms consist of apparently unexplainable sensory or motor innervations: bodily pains, paralyses, cramps, and hallucinations. In each single case, one will see that the symptom is a masked satisfaction of the repressed wish, at the same time as the hysteric punishes herself with the symptom for this improper wish satisfaction. In Dora's case history, there are oedipal identifications with both her mother and father that satisfy her wish to assume their sexual roles, but as punishment she also assumes their symptoms (see IV.C.1). If the mother's own symptoms are also hysterical, it is sometimes necessary to go back several generations to find the origin of a given symptom. Hysteria can thus manifest itself as an epidemic where the "infection" is of purely psychic nature.

In obsessional neurosis, three different processes related to repression can be distinguished: (1) Defense against castration anxiety does not totally eliminate the latter, but replaces it as in phobia with another form of anxiety, namely the anxiety of conscience emanating from the superego. (2) The decathexis of w_1 leads to a reaction formation against the repressed wish. The reaction formation becomes a lasting characteristic of the ego which more or less lives up to the demands of the superego. (3) The t_1 cathexes of the id are displaced to various substitute formations that are the true driving force behind symptoms of compulsion. Conscience anxiety only develops if the rules of compulsion are disobeyed. For example, stepping on cracks in the pavement when one has vowed not to do so immediately provokes anxiety. Reaction formations are a kind of shadow image of repressed wish impulses. The "Rat Man's" and the "Wolf Man's" oedipal aggressions against their fathers were kept repressed by excesses of the opposite attitude, which functioned as countercathexis, that is a gentle and antiaggressive attitude.

The common element of all three transference neuroses is that the repressed is comprised of oedipal wishes while repression itself is carried out in reaction to castration anxiety or to the intolerable affect attending the girl's experience of having been castrated. One may now well ask if the repression of the Oedipus complex and the simultaneous establishment of the superego are not identical with primal repression. The answer at first sight is no, since Freud apparently imagined a very early repression preceding the repression of the Oedipus complex. However, such a primal repression cannot be placed in relation to the known developmental stages. There is no reason to expect to find primal repression on the dividing line between the narcissistic and the oedipal developmental stages. The key to the solution probably lies in Freud's statement that countercathexis is the sole mechanism of primal repression. Countercathexes are established in reaction to all traumatic experiences, and primal repression may be traced all the way back to the birth trauma. But in psychosexual development countercathexis only becomes active in the narcissistic developmental stage, in which all unpleasurable ideas are excluded from the pleasure ego. This mechanism is only possible through countercathexis of the given ideas. Frustrating experiences related to the mother are projected into the unconscious void outside of the pleasure ego (the extraneous remainder). This cannot be primal repression either, if repression presupposes an established secondary system. All possibilities have now apparently been excluded, but this should not lead to the conclusion that primal repression does not exist. We suggest that primal repression be considered as the repression of the Oedipus complex, while adding that the reaction to the idea of castration is a deferred discharge of the anxiety preparedness already in part established by the oral frustration of the narcissistic developmental stage.

3. SUBJECT AND OBJECT

Freud called the last of the three polarities, subject/object, the real polarity (1915c, p. 140). The name is related to his idea of the subject of the adaptive register as a reality ego, representing the body and its characteristics in relation to the world. Reality testing constantly helps to monitor the boundary between body and world, determining where a given impulse originates. After adaptive development has ended the boundary remains fixed.

In the psychosexual register, the subject/object polarity is incomparably more flexible. The subject as a psychic category is not necessarily synomymous with the image of body, just as the idea of an object or objects need not be very "objective." In the course of a child's psychosexual development a number of exchanges and complications occur that turn out to be irreversible. The subject becomes permanently split into systems, each containing specific ideational groups and types of processes.

We have previously used the term *subject* to mean two different things. Freud spoke of the subject as one pole of the psychic polarity subject/object, which has prompted us to attempt to define the subject as the psychic structure representing the individual, and the object as the psychic structure representing external things or persons. In this sense, the subject includes the id, the ego, and the superego, whereas the object must be separated from them as a fourth psychic agency. The addition of the object to the usual conceptual tripartite may seem strange, since Freud sometimes included the object in the ego. While there was no object in Freud's three versions of the late topographical model (see V.A.1.a), the ideational object was separated from the ego and the ego ideal in another one of Freud's models from the period (1921c, p. 116). We must add that the entire theory of identification is unpresentable if a distinction between subject and object is not made.

The second meaning of the term *subject,* which we preferred in part 1 of the book, includes the corporeally defined individual as well as the psychic subject/object polarity. The first meaning is thus included as an important part of the second. The subject's self-concept is itself part of the subject, and the subject therefore also changes when its self-knowledge changes. Of course, self-knowledge can be more or less well founded. One can judge oneself more or less realistically. But this is not the only decisive criterion for self-knowledge, since it also includes wishes, expectations, desire, and fantasy. In part 1, we attempted to show how in specific situations the different subject concepts had an organizing effect on the subject's life. The liberalistic subject concept may be said to provide the ego with a number of defense mechanisms against desire and fantasy, whereby the subject is trained to function in the sphere of circulation. Contrariwise, the human-istic-romantic subject concept presents a psychotic-like defense against the anxiety and unpleasure associated with social reality. Although this defense cannot be said to make the sphere of intimacy perform smoothly, it does somewhat lessen symptoms of crisis and gives desire a compensatory sat-isfaction. In both cases, ideological self-knowledge contributes to the sub-ject's self-suppression since larger parts of the subject are a priori relegated to the unconscious in the service of a greater cause: capitalism. The spheres isolate themselves through the postulate of their own internal self-suffi-ciency, of which the subject's being is the basis, and this means contrarily that the insufficient flexibility of the subject's self-knowledge contributes to the maintainance of structures already established in each of the spheres of society.

The core of Freud's therapeutic insight can be stated as follows: a change in the patient's self-knowledge will also lead to a change in his behavior. Suggestion therapy advances a similar insight: the patient is made to believe something about his condition. Freud, however, had an important addition to make to this line of thought, since he in principle expected the impulses for change in self-knowledge to come from the patient himself. The patient's new and expanded self-knowledge was thought to be present in the unconscious before the beginning of treatment, and the analyst's task therefore limited itself to helping the patient make this self-knowledge conscious. But it would of course be naive to think that the patient would go far in his self-reflection without a theoretical knowledge of the unconscious, and in fact it is psychoanalytic theory that provides therapy with its scope. For instance, it is up to the analyst to decide when the analysis has come to an end, and Freud recognized more and more how difficult it was to finish an analysis at all. No matter how many unconscious traits are brought to light, others remain. The subject cannot find his own essence as he would a buried treasure, because the treasure is in reality a fata morgana. What is to be found in the unconscious are the fantasies that generate longing and desire. It is quite true that the activation of fantasies effects changes in the subject's self-knowledge, but these change-inducing forces are themselves changeable, as several of the concepts of psychoanalysis prove.

Uppermost in our minds is the concept of anaclisis (attachment, leaning on, *Anlehnung*) that in the final analysis transfers the origin of the drive from the subject to the object. Already in caring for a child, the object-person inculcates him with the sexual drive. The rhythm of satisfaction and frustration the first times he is cared for invariably reappears in the drives. If some consider drives to be the true essence of a child's being, then it might be useful to add that drives are themselves under the influence of processes that vary socially and historically. According to Freud, not only do drives develop during childhood, but they are also attached throughout life to psychic and physical changes in excitation to which the subject is exposed. Although Freud focused his attention on the influence of traumatic experiences, he did not exclude work, for example, as a source of excitation. With the concept of overdetermination (or multiple determination) Freud emphasized that several heterogeneous factors always contribute to a given mental illness, symptom, or other psychic phenomenon. The effect is generally the unpredictable result of a combination of chains of causes. The subject cannot find his way back to the essence of his being by tracing any single chain of causes back to its origin, but must in principle trace them all. Freud probably got his inspiration for the concept of overdetermination from Griesinger (see I.B.5.a), who employed the concept of multiple determination in connection with the etiology of mental illnesses. Freud expanded the concept to apply to all psychic processes, and he often made use of it in his analyses. The scope of the concept emerges most clearly from the dream work (see III.A.1.b), but the compromise formation of neurosis is also a good example of overdetermination. In the model in V.C.2.b we cannot even fully demonstrate the principle of over-determination because the arrows suggest that the choice of w_2 is a one-way determination. The truth is rather that numerous possibilities are explored until w_2 is found as a compromise, in which the associational possibilities of both the system *Ucs* and the system *Pcs* are taken into consideration.

The concept of Freud's that most clearly rejects the idea of an unchanging and unique point of reference for the subject's identity is probably imple-mentation by deferred action or retroaction (*Nachtraglichtkeit*). Linear temporal causality is replaced by one of circularity insofar as the subject is able to change the character of past events stored in his memory by the actions he carries out and the experiences he acquires in the present. The active structures in the unconscious are not real childhood memories, but fantasies resulting from encounters between present and past experiences. Determination following a circular time axis is a further example of overdetermination.

(a) Identification and Object Cathexis

The transformations of a subject's identity have many variations, there are insane subjects who imagine being Jesus or Napoleon, moviegoers who after having seen a film pretend they are the hero of the story, children who attempt to imitate the most striking traits in adults in order to be adults themselves. Before Freud, such imitations and identity changes were almost always considered to be a sign of illness, because of the belief that a subject's identity was innate and unalterable. If someone imitated some-one else, he was not himself any more and that was regarded as bad. Freud was among the first for whom identification processes were a completely normal part of the way a subject forged his identity. His presentations of the development of psychic structures were full of identifications, but identifications also played a role in his descriptions of the various types of diseases.

Freud used a number of concepts related to the concept of identification, which often leads to confusion. We will start by defining these concepts and their mutual relationships, without analyzing them fully.

(1) Incorporation (*Einverleibung*) describes any form of real or fantasized assimilation of an object into the body. The incorporation can be oral, anal, or vaginal, or by direct penetration of the body through the skin (gunshot wound, irradiation, lacerations, and so on). A child's fantasies of incorporation are based on the concrete experience of having had the breast put into its mouth. The opposite incorporation is expulsion, which is based on a child's experiences of defecation (expulsion of excrement) and spitting out what it doesn't like. This conceptual polarity is only useful as long as the ego is still mostly a body ego. However, it is common to speak of incorporation and expulsion in connection with the purified pleasure ego, actually a very misrepresented body ego.

(2) Introjection is any form of assimilation of ideas in the ego, not only into the body ego or the pleasure ego, but also into the definitive reality ego and the superego. Genetically speaking, introjection is a further development of incorporation. Later in this section we will discuss different types of introjections. The opposite of introjection is projection, which means that an object is attributed characteristics of the id, the ego, or the superego. In the preceding section, we referred to projection as a defense mechanism (see V.C.2.b); we may project traits that awaken unpleasure or anxiety, just as we spit out something that does not taste good. Projection is genetically speaking a further development of expulsion.

(3) Internalization (*Verinnerlichung*) was often used by Freud as a German equivalent of the word *introjection*. There is a tendency, however, for the meaning of the word to be expanded to include all the changes the subject imposes upon itself in order to adapt to the surrounding world. In an earlier section we particularly used the term in connection with drive aims; when the sensual drive aims are internalized, they become affectionate (see V.C.2.a). In affect theory, we have distinguished between bodily and internalized affects (see V.C.2.a). Externalization, the opposite of internalization, seems to come into play with the establishment of the genital drive aim during puberty.

(4) Introversion is a term Jung introduced to describe any form of withdrawal of the libido from an external object to the subject. Freud adopted the term, but changed its meaning to include only the change in libido cathexis that takes place when the subject turns away from the object or when the object disappears, that is, when libido is withdrawn from the

real object to an ideational or fantasy object. The object is kept in memory while the subject yearns for the real object to return. The withdrawal of libido from the real object is, after all, a theoretical impossibility, since libido never cathects the external object as such, but only the idea of it. In a metapsychologically consistent description, the subject refrains from starting the motor actions that should have led it to its aims along with the real object (Freud 1914c, p. 74). This omission leads to the accumulation of libido in the fantasy idea, which in the long run may cause pathological manifestations. In Freud, the approximate opposite of introversion is transference, with the addition that transference also involves a displacement from an earlier to an actual ideational object. In Jungian psychology, the opposite of introversion is extraversion, or extroversion.

(5) On the basis of his definition of the concept of introversion, Freud defines the process of withdrawal of libido from the ideational object to the ego. The state in which the ego relinquishes the object both in reality and in the world of imagination is called narcissism. This state is again abolished if libido is dispatched from the ego to the ideational object. The two states of libido are complementary: when object libido is increased, ego libido is impoverished, and vice versa. This is the kernel of Freud's narcissicism theory from the second metapsychological thrust. Two additions from the third metapsychological thrust are of more questionable value. First, Freud suggested that the id, not the ego, was the reservoir of libido from which all cathexes were dispatched, and to which they ultimately were withdrawn. This could have relevance for the adaptive register where the id is a kind of "original subject," but not for the psychosexual register where the id primarily consists of repressed ideas and other structures organized by them. Second, Freud suggested that withdrawal of libido to the subject structure (the id, the ego, or the superego), aim inhibition of the drives, and desexualization or sublimation were finally three aspects of the same matter. Even so, we must add that isolated examples of each of these three processes may be found that do not involve the other two.

(6) Identification and object cathexis are the most comprehensive and the most complicated of this series of conceptual pairs. This pair is related to several of the other pairs without, however, coinciding with any of them. Applying a genetic point of view to the new concepts will probably afford us the clearest picture of their scope. But before doing so, we will briefly consider them from the three metapsychological viewpoints.

From the topographical viewpoint, the relationship between identification and object cathexis is determined by the boundary between the intrapsychic subject and the object. An idea in the ego concerns what the subject *is* and is the expression of identification, whereas the ideational object concerns what the subject *has* and is the expression of object cathexis. Identification is most striking when the boundary between the two is moved, that is, when an earlier ideational object is introduced into the ego (for example, when instead of thinking of Humphrey Bogart as a movie star one begins thinking one is Humphrey Bogart and takes on all his mannerisms). This assimilation of the object's identity is the same as an introjection (see above). The change consists of the idea concerned's being constantly cathected and brought into associative connection with the other ideas of the ego. The opposite process, the exclusion of an idea from the ego, is known from projection, where the idea is unpleasurable. An exclusion of a pleasurable idea leading to positive sexual object cathexis is known from narcissistic object choice, where according to Freud one loves "a) what one is (oneself), b) what one was, c) what one would have liked to be, d) the person who was part of oneself"(Freud 1914c, p. 190).

From the economic viewpoint, Freud spoke of the static cathexes of given ideas in terms of identification and object cathexis. In this sense, he also called them emotional ties. The identification need not be a short-lived or transitional emotional tie forced upon the subject from the outside. Closer analysis shows that many of the subject's most stable character traits turn out to consist of identifications, in particular, early identifications with family members. The same goes for object cathexis. Even though real objects are often changed, they are often of the same type. They have all been chosen on the basis of their resemblance to either an earlier object or a fantasized ideal object.

From the dynamic viewpoint, it is possible to describe how libido displacement influences identifications and object choices. The withdrawal of libido from the ideational object to the ego will strengthen the ego's identifications, whereas dispatching libido from the ego to an ideational object will either reinforce an already existing object cathexis or create a new one. These processes must not be confused with introjection or projection. Freud himself, however, contributed to the confusion surrounding these terms when he described the result of the loss of the object in melancholia as follows:

> The result was not the normal one of a withdrawal of the libido from this object and a displacement of it to a new one, but something different, for whose coming about various conditions seem to be necessary. The object-

cathexis proved to have little power of resistance and was brought to an end. But the free libido was not displaced on to another object; it was withdrawn into the ego. There however, it was not employed in any unspecified way, but served to establish an *identification* of the ego with the abandoned object" (Freud 1917e, p. 249).

We maintain that the withdrawal of libido to the ego and the introjection of the ideational object into the ego are two different processes. In the first process, libido is displaced. In the second, the boundary between the ego and the ideational object is displaced.

For the time being, note that identification and object cathexis constitute two very different methods the subject can use to take possession of an object sexually. They each provide their own form of satisfaction, and the one need not necessarily be better than the other. However, identification functions in a number of cases as compensation for an earlier object cathexis. Freud pointed out that identification and object cathexis could not genetically be distinguished from each other during the early oral phase (1923b, p. 31f). This means that it makes no difference to a child whether he *is* or *has* the object. Oral incorporation is the basis of both methods of object possesesion later acquired by the subject, and the central question in a genetic examination is therefore how differentiation between identification and object cathexis takes place.

Let us first examine object cathexis. The absence of symmetry between the two conceptual pairs incorporation/expulsion and identification/object cathexis may seem surprising at first. Incorporation points directly to introjection and identification, whereas expulsion is more like the opposite of an object cathexis. Oral incorporation obviously also points to object cathexis. A child takes possession of the breast as if it were an object and not part of the ego. Adaptive development exerts decisive influence on the detachment of the idea of the breast from the ego and its rise to the status of an ideational object. When this has happened, the sexual tie is also transformed into a true object cathexis, an object choice of the anaclitic type has thus been made (see Freud 1914c, p. 90f.). One could be tempted to say that expulsion and projection had nothing to do with object cathexis, but this would not be entirely correct. In adaptive development, the object is mastered aggressively as the result of the attempted motor abreaction of internal unpleasure (hunger). While a child can sometimes escape from external stimuli, he cannot escape internal ones, and therefore reacts to them as if, they were external. Unable to attack the internal source of stimuli, he attacks the breast mistakenly thinking it is the source of unpleasure. Insofar as attacking the breast removes unpleasure and satisfies hunger, the mechanism is maintained. The tie of the sexual drives to the idea of the breast is very ambivalent, which is still true even after the breast acquires the status of an object. Already in the narcissistic stage, however, the breast is expulsed and hated as a source of sexual frustration, and the idea of the bad breast therefore becomes an important part of the extraneous remainder, that is, the counterpart of the pleasure ego. So saying, we must conclude that the expelled extraneous remainder leaves its mark on the object cathexis by being a source of hate in the ambivalent tie. The greater the sexual frustration and the greater the traumatic experiences a child has been subjected to in the narcissistic developmental stage, the greater also the sadistic component of the oral and anal urge to master. This tendency can eventually dominate to such an extent that the child isolates the mechanism of expulsion and only expresses disgust when offered the breast, even when hungering for both food and love. In the child's fantasy, the breast has then acquired the same status as things that cause pain or food that tastes bad. As we mentioned in the preceding section on anxiety and defense, early traumatic experiences contribute in establishing a strong anxiety preparedness, and it is obvious especially at the end of the oedipal phase that the child's sadism, in conjunction with a reversal of the active/passive polarity triggers intolerable anxiety (anxiety of being castrated, anxiety of having been castrated, and anxiety of losing the object), forcing it to revise its former object cathexes. Freud did not believe ambivalence was surmounted until the genital phase, at which time the subject becomes able to feel unmingled hate and love for other persons, that is, love for some and hate for others.

The development of identification is no less complicated than the development of object cathexis and object choice. This is primarily due to the splitting of the intrapsychic subject into id, ego, and superego. When we identify with another person, the idea of this person may in principle be associated with each of the three agencies. Genetically, there is a tendency for the earliest identifications to become part of the id and the superego, whereas the identifications of the ego seldom can be traced further back than to the period immediately after the dissolution of the Oedipus complex.

(a) *The Identification of the superego.* The emergence of the superego, or ego ideal, led Freud back to primary identification (Freud 1923b, p. 31f). There are different and nearly incompatable ways of understanding this concept. As mentioned earlier, we have chosen to disregard Freud's phylogenetic considerations, and exclude therefore from the outset the possibility that primary identification originates from a biologically inherited memory of the murder of the primal father of a primal horde (see III.C.1.a). The mechanism of identification is itself the result of oral incorporation. Freud made an obvious comparison with cannibals who took over the identities of their murdered enemies and dead family members after having eaten them. A baby does not eat his mother's breast, but incorporates it in fantasy. Of course, the baby's identification with the breast does not mean that he begins to imitate the breast's behavior, which is the usual consequence of identification. What is assimilated to the pleasure ego in fantasy is the breast's ability to give satisifaction. In the narcissistic developmental stage, a child consequently experiences himself as omnipotent and perfect.

One may now ask if the incorporation of the breast, the ideal partial object, is the same as primary identification. The answer is no, since Freud maintained that primary identification was an identification with a total object, a person. The incorporation of the breast is thus only a preliminary stage of primary identification, a trial run so-to-speak. Let us now try to take a closer look at the texts in which Freud defined primary identification. By way of introduction, he said that the effects of the first and earliest identifications were general and lasting, and continued:

> This leads us back to the origin of the ego ideal; for behind it there lies hidden an individual's first and most important identification, his identification with the father in his own personal prehistory. (Freud added in a footnote: "Perhaps it would be safer to say 'with the parents'; for before a child has arrived at definite knowledge of the difference between the sexes, the lack of a penis, it does not distinguish in value between its father and its mother".) This is apparently not in the first instance the consequence or outcome of an object-cathexis; it is a direct and immediate identification and takes place earlier than any object-cathexis. But the object-choices belonging to the first sexual period and relating to the father and mother seem normally to find their outcome in an identification of this kind, and would thus reinforce the primary one (Freud 1923b, p. 31).

It may seem surprising that Freud placed primary identification "earlier than any object cathexis," when he had already established in the same section that identification and object cathexis could not be distinguished from each other in the early oral phase (1923b, p. 29). The statement can therefore only be understood to mean that primary identification is not the result of a relinquished object cathexis. It is as if a child were able to imitate his father or his parents with regard to some characteristics independent of their use as sexual objects. What actually takes place is the child's initiation to the active/passive polarity and the establishment of oedipal emotional ties. Freud was right in questioning the regularity with which the oedipal ego ascribed activity to itself and passivity to the object, since its basis was the intersubjective structure itself more than imitation of the parents (see V.C.1). In the concrete object relation to his parents, the child attempts to promote his own activity at their expense in spite of the actual conditions. The subject *is* active because of its identification and *has* a passive object because of its object cathexis.

The Oedipus complex takes on its familiar triangular form when a child realizes that in fact the parents can be very active. At first, he attempts to defy their injunctions, reprimands, and threats, as if he could, relying on his own ego, take a stand against them. Next, he must assimilate the idea of the active and dangerous parents, and this idea, it will be recalled, exerts decisive influence on the further development of psychic structure. To begin with, this idea supplants the narcissistic and oedipal ego's status as omnipotent and perfect. Mediated by the threat of castration, it then triggers the anxiety preparedness, which causes the repression of the oedipal emotional ties, while only a reduced reality ego retains the right to maintain its connection to consciousness. The assimilated idea of the parents is the superego itself. The superego, however, does not accurately reflect the severity of the parents, since as already mentioned, it derives a number of its characteristics from already existing psychic agencies (the pleasure ego, the oedipal ego, and the expelled extraneous remainder). Furthermore, Freud said that it was not the parents themselves but their superego that served as the model of the superego of the child (1933a, p. 67). The superego contains a new kind of emotional tie besides identification and object cathexis, since it neither expresses what a child (in reality or in his own imagination) *is* or *has,* but something else that cannot easily be described.

The status of the superego can best be explained through the tasks it is able to accomplish. The superego contains the subject's ideals, the aforementioned omnipotence and perfection, and it therefore functions as a standard of comparison and norm for the subject's actions and characteristics. The strength of the superego comes from the anxiety preparedness, which when triggered can cause the decathexis of any idea. This means that the superego, in containing the idea of castration, is the source of repression, censorship, conscience, and morality. Finally, Freud mentioned self-observation as another of the functions of the superego. It originates from the observation of the child by his parents and in pathological cases develops into a delusion of observation, where the patient complains that his every thought is being read and his every action observed.

The superego is the heir of the Oedipus complex, though the former never ceases changing after the repression of the latter. Under certain circumstances, new ideational introjects may become part of the superego. Freud's description of the process of introjection started with enamoring. The sexual object is able to replace the ego ideal when it is overestimated as a result of having taken over the ego's narcissistic libido, and when only affectionate feelings are manifested because the satisfaction of the sensual ones is out of the question. Freud noted that the enamored ego not only attended to the slightest wishes of the loved one, but was also ready to commit serious crimes, clashing with the norms and ideals hitherto valid for its superego, in order to satisfy the loved one. Something similar takes place in pure form in hypnosis, where the hypnotized person is so paralyzed and fascinated that the hypnotist can suggest himself into superego, and give orders having the same authority and conviction as the inner voice of conscience. We can note Freud's analyses of group psychology (see also III.C.1.b), showing how leaders consolidate their power by introjecting themselves by projective identification, so to speak into the superego of each member of the group they lead.

It is perhaps not quite correct to speak of identifications in connection with the superego, since introjected ideas never become part of the subject's being or identity. It is also common to use the term *internalization* in this context. The subject is not allowed to imitate the persons who are the models of its ego ideal, but only to obey them. On the other hand, the superego is also an extension of the active oedipal ego, and if it says nothing about the subject's true identity, it nonetheless says something about the repressed wishes in the id, and about what the subject would have liked to be if given the chance.

(b) *The identification of the ego.* The reality ego remains after the formation of the superego has been completely purged of illusions. It contains a relatively realistic picture of the five-year-old child, but is also receptive to new identifications, and the ego of the adult will generally bear the mark of lasting identificational ties to other. Thus, the role of the parents has not yet been played out. Freud talked about how they were first introjected into the superego and later into the ego. Leaving out primary identification here, we will review the two types of identifications Freud employed.

The first type is based on the libidinal object cathexis preceding the identification. There are special cases where identification and object cathexis can even exist side by side. Freud claimed to have observed this in the relationships of married women to their husbands, whom they both loved and imitated. The general rule is, however, that identification replaces an abandoned object cathexis. Identification is consequently one of the possible reactions to object loss. As a classic example, Freud mentioned the little boy who had lost his beloved kitten. The boy took over the cat's identity, began to crawl on all fours, demanded to eat out of the cat's bowl, and so on. The best examples from psychopathology of similar identifications can be found in melancholia and depression. The person who experiences unrequited love for someone takes revenge on his earlier love object by introjecting it in his ego; there, the object will be subjected to love in earnest by means of the merciless criticism of the superego. A melancholy person accuses himself of having all sorts of unfavorable attributes that in fact belong to the other. Revenge is particularly refined when aimed at the spouse. Here again, Freud pointed to the married woman who could literally torment her husband to death by forcing him to listen to self-accusations that were really directed at him. In mania, a regression takes place which reverses the earlier relationships. The superego and the ego merge to form an agency reminiscent of the active oedipal ego. A manic person takes revenge in another way, against the superego, breaking all its rules and carrying out more or less symbolic executions of restrictive parental images. The manic person abandons all restrictions and willingly plunges headlong into new love relationships until depression again sets in. Freud accurately compared mania with the yearly orgies, celebrations, and carnivals known in many types of societies (see III.C.1.a).

The second group of identifications distinguishes itself from the first by not presupposing a libidinous object tie to the person who is the object of identification, but rather a competitive relationship. In a group, members compete to gain the leader's love, and they identify with each other because they have all introjected the figure of the leader in their superego. Such an identification can temporarily suspend competition and sometimes leads to strong bonds of solidarity. Freud found the same structure in women who habitually gravitated toward renowned artists; they had all given up hope of becoming the exclusive object of affection and were therefore able to demonstrate some measure of solidarity (somewhat like that seen in fan clubs). Freud's most unusual example of this type of identification is identification by a common symptom. When all members of a group have the same unconscious and repressed emotional preparedness, a symptom of this in one of its members will function as a core around which identification will crystalize. Everyone suddenly manifests the same symptom without knowing exactly what it signifies, but all members of the group have the unmistakable impression of having established a bond of solidarity. Group hysteria and group psychosis are well-known phenomena, and according to Freud, panic is also a sign that members of a group have lost their leader at the same time.

(c) *The identification of the id.* This category contains repressed identifications. They are first of all identifications belonging to the Oedipus complex, that is, identifications with the active parents. Freud also employed a general identification with a passive person in the id, so that there were focal points for both male and female unconscious identities. Just as everyone harbors a repressed homosexual object choice, so everyone harbors a repressed identification with the opposite sex. Unconscious identifications contribute to symptom formation in the neurotic, and it is easy to discern such identifications especially in hysterical people. The choice of a unique trait of the person who is the object of identification is usually what is repressed, for example, a specific sign of disease, which itself can perhaps be neurotic (we have discussed such a case above in V.C.2.b).

(b) Fantasy and Reality

Within the adaptive register, the relationship between fantasy and reality constitutes a significant polarity. The psychic life of the child is dominated by fantasies contrasting sharply with the reality-oriented thinking of the adult. Not only can a child be carried away by wishful thinking, but he is even able to obtain hallucinatory wishful satisfaction in agreement with the pleasure principle. He lacks the ability to distinguish between fantasy and reality. This ability (the ability to test reality), on the other hand, is present in the adult, and its loss is one of the surest signs of mental illiness.

Within the psychosexual register, the polarity fantasy/reality is abolished on one very important point. We are referring to the so-called primal fantasies to which Freud attributed a psychic reality. Primal fantasies are unconscious fantasies with psychic consistency as substantial as the memory of real events. They are at the same time wish-fantasies and wish-fulfilling fantasies. As wish fantasies they can trigger real actions whose goal is to fulfill the wish. As wish-fulfilling fantasies, they can also form the basis of dreams and hallucinations. In both cases, a certain distortion of the primal fantasies must be taken into account, which, however, does not affect their psychic consistency. Normally, a wish fantasy will arise in connection with the recathexis of the memory of a past experience of satisfaction, making repetition of the satisfaction possible. This is the most elementary form of repetition compulsion known. What is particular about the repetition compulsion activated by primal fantasies is that the event a person wishes to repeat has never taken place.

In an earlier section (see V.B.3), we reviewed how the primal fantasy is formed retroactively as an idea of a traumatic event. We used the castration of the girl as an example of a primal fantasy. In the model illustrating this in section V.B.3, experience 1 is the experience of oral frustration in the autoerotic and narcissistic developmental stage, whereas experience 2 is the discovery of gender differences and related thoughts in the phallic phase. The primal fantasy is formed on the basis of these two experiences to the extent that the real experience 1 relinquishes its cathexis to the "false" or fictive experience 1 (written "1" in the model). The girl unconsciously explains the cause of her gender by imagining that her mother has castrated her or failed to give her a penis. Experience "1" is founded on a "first lie" (*proton pseudos*), which by pointing development in a new direction nonetheless becomes part of the real basis of further psychosexual development.

Another primal fantasy is the so-called primal scene, that is, a child's idea of the sexual intercourse of the parents. In this case, it is highly probable that the child has in fact seen his parents during intercourse (experience 1), either because the parents did not think the child understood what was happening, or because they thought he was asleep. The primal scene is nonetheless regarded as a fantasy (experience "1"), because a particular meaning is attributed to it in the unconscious; a fight, a punishment, even a castration. Freud believed that everyone had traumatic primal scenes, even people who as children had not witnessed intercourse. This made him assume that primal fantasies could be based on biologically inherited memories. He did, however, leave open the possibility that events other than intercourse could function as the real experience 1, for example, copulation between animals (see the case history of the "Wolf Man, IV.C.5). In any event, Freud assumed that the child consciously or unconsciously related the primal scene to birth, not necessarily in the sense that it understood that intercourse led to pregnancy, but perhaps through a supposition that the mother's severed penis was transformed into a child.

A third primal fantasy concerns child seduction. In part 2, we reviewed how Freud changed his views on seduction throughout the 1890s (see II.B.4). At first he considered the sexual abuse adult hysterics had suffered as children an important cause of hysteria. He later learned that such seductions need not necessarily have been real. The traumatic memory can be a fantasy functioning as a defense against the memory of having masturbated during childhood. The hysterical adult who does not want to accept his or her own sexuality creates a seduction fantasy to explain how sexuality has been implanted into his or her body by others. Freud finally summarized the two conceptions in his theory of infantile sexuality. The real experience can be a seduction but need not be so, since the occasions to implant partial drives in babies as they are under care are numerous (the theory of anaclisis). Parents invariably awaken sexual feelings in their children, whether they want to or not.

The psychic reality of primal fantasies manifests itself in their ability to create symptoms. We can therefore emphasize the topographical aspect of the earlier model by adding symptoms, which enable psychosexual directional determination of the subject's development alongside adaptive determination.

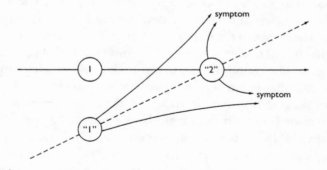

The number 2 is meant to be read in the model both with and without quotation mark, that is, both as experience 2 and experience "2". The idea of the model is that experience 2, which is related to the castration complex, is itself transformed into a fantasy by experience "1". Thus, the circle is closed, since experience "1" is created by the actual experience 2 via the memory of experience 1. The cathexis from experience "1" accentuates castration anxiety in experience 2, leading to the repression of experience

"1". The castration anxiety of experience 2, which now also has the status of an experience "2", deflects impulses from experience "1" whereby they acquire the status of symptoms (the return of the repressed).

The illustration we have chosen to give here affords us the opportunity to make two theoretical comments. First, we are now able to tangibly emphasize the difference between adaptive and psychosexual development. Adaptive development is directed by the real events an individual faces in the different developmental stages, that is, difficulties to be overcome, pleasurable experiences to be repeated, unpleasurable experiences to be counteracted. In the illustration, adaptive development is the horizontal arrow passing through 1 and 2, and psychosexual development the dotted arrow passing through "1" and "2". Neither of these arrows ever definitively dominates the other. The overall development of the subject cannot be reduced either to an adaptive development directed toward higher goals or to psychosexual development aiming to repeat the primal fantasy in reality. In a sense, one cannot even speak of conflict between the two registers, since their mere existence would be unthinkable were it not for the influence they exert on and the way they complement each other. More far-reaching conclusions cannot be drawn from Freud's writings.

The second theoretical comment touches upon the relationship between primal repression and primal fantasies. By choosing the word *primal,* Freud suggested something truly primordial, something that eventually could be explained biologically and phylogenetically. In contradiction to this, we have emphasized the relationship of both concepts to the repression of the Oedipus complex, and have even asserted that primal fantasies are aspects of the primally repressed Oedipus complex. Primal fantasies cannot be reduced to narcissistic fantasies, since they obviously have oedipal traits and consist of both pleasurable and unpleasurable ideas. The two fundamental types of affects of the psychosexual register, anxiety, and desire, are both based on the pleasurable and unpleasurable ideas of primal fantasies. Anxiety preparedness introduces systematic limitations of all pleasurable experiences in view of anticipating unpleasure. In desire, unpleasure and anxiety are sought precisely in order to increase the ending pleasurable experience. Whereas anxiety preparedness in principle neutralizes affect, desire generates it. At best, the two tendencies will balance each other in a way permitting some fluctuation of the affects. At worst, one of the tendencies prevails. In obsessional neurosis, anxiety preparedness is so extensive that the most elementary manifestation of self-expression is impossible. In masochism, on the other hand, desire prevails to such a degree that life itself is endangered. In the analytic examples reviewed in parts 3 and 4, we may now place, by way of deferred action, so to speak, the concept of primal fantasy where we have generally spoken of unconscious wishes or repressed wish fantasies as the unconscious basis for symptom formation. This does not mean, of course, that primal fantasies are the only types of fantasies that exist. On the contrary, the creation of fantasies can be said to be part of all parts of the psychic apparatus. This is particularly obvious in the model we used to illustrate the three phases of dream formation (see III.A.1.a). A primal fantasy is at the starting point (1) of the zig-zag movement. Fantasies repressed later may have been added to it. Repressed ideas in censorship or in the superego are fantasies too, for example, exaggerated ideas concerning the punishment that would be incurred if an unconscious wish were realized. In the system *Pcs,* a new wish fantasy is formed, becoming the starting point of both the second and third phases of dream formation, whose way stations may also be characterized as fantasies. Finally, the manifest dream as it appears in the system *Cs* is also a fantasy, of course, and one that lies closest to what we normally think of as a fantasy. Daydreams, poetic fantasies, and fictions also belong to the group of conscious fantasies. Daydreams express the accomplishment of wishes even more transparently than nocturnal dreams do, since they radically exclude all unpleasant characteristics. For this reason, they are not very reliable phenomena upon which to base an understanding of primal fantasies. Poetic, fantasies, on the other hand, are reliable sources upon which to base an understanding of such fantasies, at least insofar as the poet or writer succeeds in keeping at bay censorship as well as the influence of secondary revision. Primal fantasies and conscious fantasies can never be identical for many reasons. The same goes for psychoanalytic interpretations; to speak about primal fantasies using expressions such as "castration," "seduction," and "primal scene" represents an attempt to reconstruct something that in a final analysis will always remain unknown to consciousness.

Although daydreams are not valid representatives of the unconscious, they can still tell us a great deal about what types of wishes fantasies are able to satisfy. The most elementary sexual fantasies are sensual ones directly traceable to partial drives. Judging from pornography, there is a general interest in most partial drives and not just in genital copulation. There will be oedipal traits in most fantasies, regardless whether they have sensually sexual themes or not. Their core is the active subject and the passive object, that is, the subject who sees itself as conqueror, seducer, and master. In the elaborated oedipal universe, there will also be a rival or opponent who must be eliminated, as well as various helpers. In the passive ("female") universe, a reversal has made the subject passive and the object active, and the roles as giver and taker are strongly cathected. Under the influence of the active/passive polarity, the sensual wishes are combined with wishes for power and possession; daydreams demonstrate ideally that there are associative connections from power and wealth to potency and beauty.

In an earlier section, we discussed the problems related to the working-through and dissolution of the Oedipus complex. Wishes within the modality *having* have a tendency to fortify or confirm the Oedipus complex, and the goal of therapeutic analysis is consequently to displace some of these wishes to modality *knowledge*. The ego can never put itself entirely outside of the active/passive polarity, but systematic self-reflection may permit it to acquire so much knowledge about its own determination to enable it to break this determination momentarily. The wish for knowledge is obviously not an invention of psychoanalysis, and it is only possible to appeal to an analysand's wish for knowledge because among the partial drives there is a drive for knowledge that can be further developed. This drive does not occupy a central place in Freud's developmental theory, but it nonetheless plays a role in connection with infantile sexual investigation, that is, a child's attempt to reach some measure of clarity concerning the basic aspects of sexual life. A typical example of infantile sexual investigation is the child's conviction that children are born through the anus. Another example is their idea of intercourse as an act of violence. In fact, these attempts to understand sexuality are distorted derivatives or offshoots of the primal fantasies that as wish-fulfilling fantasies satisfy the drive for knowledge on a number of points. The three primal fantasies we have mentioned answer the question pertaining to a child's origin (the fantasy of the primal scene), the question pertaining to the origin of gender differences (the castration fantasy), and the origin of sexuality (seduction fantasy). *These three mythological sources determine the direction of a child's psychosexual development and shape both his anxiety and his desire.* In a way, there is obvious continuity between infantile sexual investigation and psychoanalytic sexual investigation. In psychoanalytic self-reflection, psychic reality is attributed to primal fantasies, while an attempt is made to circumscribe the conditions for their appearance. Through psychoanalytic self-reflection the subject learns to exert retroactive influence on primal fantasies, to create a new origin for himself, and thus also to determine the goal of his own life history.

BIBLIOGRAPHY

The bibliography is divided into three sections: 1. bibliographical notes, in which we review the book section by section, indicating the most important primary and secondary literature; 2. a complete Freud bibliography, including the books, articles, letters, and posthumous works published to date; 3. bibliography covering the secondary literature to which we have referred (both in the text itself and in the bibliographical notes).

We generally refer to a work by its author and date of publication. A number of special questions are covered in the introductions of each of the three sections of the bibliography.

1.
BIBLIOGRAPHICAL NOTES

The main purpose of these notes is to help the reader find more literature on the subjects treated in each section. We have accordingly limited our list of references to Freud's own work to the five to ten most important titles on each subject, believing a longer list would only contribute to making further study more confused and insurmountable. Where the secondary literature is concerned, we have likewise made an effort to limit ourselves to the essential sources, nonetheless attempting (1) to include surveys and anthologies themselves containing a number of references, (2) to make sure that the points of view of various psychoanalytic schools were represented, and (3) to find texts with reasonable educational qualitities.

In the present edition, we have deleted all references to Scandinavian literature that has not been translated into one of the major languages. Furthermore, we have attempted to find English and American translations of the German and French works we have quoted. Finally, we have added a number of English and American titles to replace those deleted.

Three works are especially important as general adjuncts to a further study of Freud's psychoanalysis:

(1) James Strachey's *Standard Edition* of Freud's most important works (see bibliography 2). In this edition each title is given its own introduction, defining the work's content and placing it in historical perspective. The edition furthermore includes a special index in which all of the entries are listed. Last but not least, the edition also includes numerous notes, in which, for example, cross-references can be found to other texts and an account given of changes and additions made by Freud in all of the editions of the same work. A separate index to the *Standard Edition* in six large volumes by Guttman et al, was published in 1980.

(2) Laplanche and Pontalis 1967 presents fundamental psychoanalytic concepts in dictionary form. The penetrating analyses of the metapsychol-

ogical concepts in particular are a hallmark of the book. It is interesting to note how the entire conceptual apparatus of psychoanalysis changes character as the authors underscore three interrelated concepts in Freud, that is, *Anlehnung* (anaclisis), Nachtraglichkeit (deferred action), and *Phantasie* (fantasy).

(3) Grinstein 1956–1975 is a bibliography covering psychoanalytic literature. In the fourteen volumes issued to date one is able to look up both authors and topics, thus making it possible to find supplementary references covering the topics we treat on the pages that follow.

Part I. *The Historical Origins of Psychoanalysis*

It is our basic contention that there is a close connection between the historical development of society and social spheres on one side and the historical development of sciences and ideologies on the other. However, we do not believe that either the conditions reigning in the sphere of intimacy or a science like psychoanalysis can be explained from the point of view of "capital logic." Freud's writings are in themselves a key to understanding some of the psychological, and thus also societal, organizational forms not analyzed by Marx or within Marxism.

A. THE SHAPING OF THE SUBJECT IN CAPITALIST SOCIETY

The relationship between the shaping of the subject and the shaping of subject concepts within given social contexts is taken up in this section. Although Habermas 1962 is our most important source of inspiration when it comes to focusing on the social spheres as the primary genial soil of the various subject concepts, we can also recommend Althusser 1970 for its analysis of the function of ideology where socially formative institutions and the individual subject's constraints are concerned. See Elias 1978, Foucault 1975, and Braudel 1979 on the development of the real historical subject. Horkheimer 1936, Ussel 1970, Hunt 1970, Ariès 1960, Shorter 1975, Flandrin 1976, Donzelot 1977, and Rosenbaum 1982 deserve mention as special background literature on the history of the family and of the sphere of intimacy.

B. THE SUBJECT IN PHILOSOPHY, NATURAL SCIENCE, AND LITERATURE

We will begin by mentioning works on the history of science characterized by their application of an overall societal point of view on development. Bernal 1954 is a standard work on the general history of science (for which reason the 1800s only play a limited role in the presentation). The separation among the natural sciences, the humanistic sciences, and the social sciences is related to socially determined interests in Habermas 1968, Apel 1968, and Radnitzky 1968. Althusser 1974 presents a model with which to analyze the relationship between the ideological and the scientific elements of a researcher's theories. Young 1973 represents a newer British Marxism and treats biology and neurophysiology during the same period we do. Hauser 1951 is the standard work on the history of art and literature using the sociological approach. Finally, Kuhn 1962 deserves mention because of the undeniable qualities of his hypotheses on paradigm shift.

1. Philosophy

The philosophical works we have discussed in the text may be found in bibliography 3. The historical development of associationism is reviewed in Warren 1921 and Rapaport 1974. The theme of Freud and philosophy is treated in innumerable texts, and on many different levels. We will content ourselves with references to two collections of articles where more literature may be found: Wollheim 1974 and Gedo and Pollock 1976. Whyte 1960 is an attempt to determine the unconscious before Freud in philosophers from Descartes to Nietzsche.

2. Physics and Biology

The concepts of vitalism and mechanism are discussed in Hall 1969, Mendelsohn 1964, Temkin 1946, and Pickstone 1976. Virchow 1856 is of historical interest (see also literature under I.C. in this bibliography). Concerning the exploration of nerve energy, see du Bois-Reymond 1848 and Home 1970, as well as Mendelsohn 1963, Holmes 1963, and Maienschein 1978 concerning cell theory. The theory of energy constancy is becoming a classic chapter in the history of science, see, for example, Elkana 1974 and Helmholtz 1854. Freud's relationship to the Helmholtz school is treated in two completely different ways in Bernfeld 1944 and Wilden 1972. The theory of evolution is another classic theme. Primary literature on it includes Darwin 1859, Weismann 1882 and 1892, Haeckel 1889, as well as Meynert 1887. Secondary literature includes Ayala and Dobzhansky 1974, Gould 1977, and Bowler 1984. Freud and the theory of evolution is treated, for example, in Ritvo 1965 and 1974.

3. Neurophysiology and Neuroanatomy

Fearing 1930 and Liddell 1960 are classic presentations of the historical development of neurophysiology. Where primary sources are concerned, Wagner 1842–1846 may profitably be placed alongside Müller 1834–1840. A complete review of the knowledge available on the nervous system at the turn of the century may be found in Barker 1899. Special secondary literature on Müller's reflex model is E. Marx 1937–1938 and d'Irsay 1928. Young 1970 may be singled out for its treatment of reflexes and localization, as well as Stevens 1973 for a more popular introduction to the same subject. The primary literature referred to in the text is Meynert 1869 and 1884, Griesinger 1843, Broca 1861, and Jackson 1879–1880, 1882, and 1884. Freud's relationship to neurophysiology is discussed in Amacher 1965, Brun 1936, Riese 1958a, and 1958b, and Pribram and Gill 1976. Køppe 1983 treats associationism and the concept of neuron. Primary sources to the theme of instinct, drive, and affect are: Darwin 1872, Lotze 1844 and 1852, Bastian 1880, and Exner 1894.

4. Psychology

Boring 1950 is the most well-known presentation of the history of experimental psychology. It may profitably be supplemented by Jaroschewski 1975 (Russian) and Jaeger and Staeuble 1978, in which prescientific psychology is anchored to social history. Fechner's psychophysics (1860) must be seen against the background of, for instance, Weber's investigations (1842) and Müller's theory of specific nerve energies (1826). It should also be noted that Helmholtz studied the physiology and psychology of sensation for a period of forty years (see Helmholtz 1878), and that Wundt further developed Fechner's psychophysics (see Wundt 1874). Fechner's theory of cosmic regulatory principles was developed in the following works: Fechner 1846, 1848, 1873, and 1879. Hering (1880) held similar views on periodicity and wave movements applied to the concept of memory. Freud's relationship to Herbart and Fechner is discussed in Dorer 1932.

5. Psychiatry

The history of psychiatry and of psychiatric diseases has become the object of significant interest, especially during recent years, but a standard work in the field does not yet exist. The social historical perspective is variously considered in Foucault 1961, Dörner 1969, and Castel 1976, but these works stop at Pinel and Griesinger. Shorter periods of psychiatric history and delimited disease categories receive historical treatment in Veith 1965, Fischer-Homberger 1970 and 1975, Werlinder 1978, Wallace and Pressley 1980, Scull 1981, Donelly 1983, and Drinka 1984. The decidedly historical surveys, such as Kraepelin 1918, Jaspers 1948, Ackerknecht 1957, and Hunter and MacAlpine 1963, are by and large too superficial and recitative. Kolle 1956–1963 includes longer articles on the foremost psychiatrists and neuropathologists of the period. The theme of hypnosis and hysteria is elucidated quite well. Ellenberger 1970 and Chertok and Saussure 1973 make detailed reviews of its development from Mesmer to Freud. Furthermore it is possible to get an impression of Freud's relationship to his predecessors by reading his commented translations of Charcot (Freud 1886e, 1886f, and 1892–1894) and Bernheim (Freud 1888–1889 and 1892). Nassif 1977 pays particular attention to the relationship among Charcot, Jackson, Bernheim, and Freud. The development of the sexual sciences up to the time of Freud is treated in Wettley 1959 and Sulloway 1979, the latter presenting much new material. Foucault 1976 is an attempt to give an overall view of the history of both sexuality and sexual research. The book has a negative attitude toward Freud and psychoanalysis. Finally, Freud's relationship to psychiatry is stressed in Binswanger 1936.

6. Literature

In many ways, Freud fits the picture of the literature of the 1800s drawn by the Danish literary critic Georg Brandes (see Brandes 1872–1890 and 1886). Brückner 1975 makes a thorough study of Freud's *Privatlektüre* (private reading).

C. THE CRISIS OF THE SUBJECT AND CRITIQUE OF SIMPLIFIED SUBJECT CONCEPTS

Du Bois-Reymond (1872, 1880) clearly voiced the doubts besetting the natural sciences that paved the way for empiriocriticism and positivism. Kraepelin and Wundt have been mentioned as representatives of a positivistic conception of science. Kraepelin received his training at Wundt's psychological laboratory, where he carried out a number of experiments and measurements, notably on the influence of tea and coffee on the psyche (Kraepelin 1892). Lecourt 1973 reiterates Lenin's criticism of empiriocriticism in the light of the present. Lukacs 1923 is an example of Marxist theory of consciousness. The subjective consequences of the historical changes effectuated within the sphere of intimacy may best be seen in the imaginative literature of the period. A striking example worth adding to the works of the authors treated in section I.B.6 is the work of August Strindberg. A theoretical discussion of the altered status of the sphere of intimacy is to be found in Prokop 1976.

Part II. Freud and the Development of Psychoanalysis

There are innumerable books on Freud's life and work. Jones 1953, 1955, and 1957 is by far the best biographical account of Freud's personal life. Jones knew Freud for three decades and had access to a great deal of material that is not yet publicly available. His treatment of Freud's writings is less remarkable than that of his life, however. Robert 1964 and Wollheim 1971 are smaller works in which Freud's writings are reviewed in a chronological manner. Ernst Freud et al. 1976 is a good supplement to Freud's biography in that it has both photographs and text.

A. FREUD'S BACKGROUND

Barea 1966 describes the political and cultural life of Vienna as it was during Freud's lifetime, and Schorske 1980 focuses on the Vienna of the end of the last century. Biographical information concerning Freud before the inception of psychoanalysis has been gathered by Siegfried Bernfeld, although most of it has been incorporated in Jones 1953. Later titles shedding light on Freud's academic career are: Gicklhorn and Gicklhorn 1960, Lesky 1965, and Eissler 1964 and 1966. About Freud's Jewish background, Robert 1974 offers a useful study. Freud's most important writings until 1886 can be divided into groups. Articles related to his work at Brücke's laboratory are Freud 1877a, 1878, and 1882; articles especially related to methods for staining nerve tissue are Freud 1879, 1884b, 1884c, and 1884d. Neuropathological articles on strokes and muscular atrophy, as well as neuroanatomical articles on the acustic nerve are Freud 1884a, 1885c, 1885d, 1886a, 1886b, and 1886c. One of Freud's neurophysiological works, Freud 1884f deserves particular attention since it contains a general view of the nervous system. Special secondary literature on Freud's neuroanatomical, neurophysiological, and neuropathological works include Binswanger 1936, Brun 1936, Jeliffe 1937, Riese 1958a and 1958b, as well as Amacher 1965 and Spehlmann 1953.

B. THE INCEPTION OF PSYCHOANALYSIS

After 1886, Freud began focusing his attention on hypnosis and hysteria, but he continued to write articles on neuropathological topics, such as the series on the nervous diseases of children (Freud 1888a, 1891a, 1893b, 1897a, 1898c, 1899b, and 1900b), and on aphasia (Freud 1888b and 1891b). Secondary literature on Freud's aphasia papers includes O. Marx 1966, Vogel 1954, and Stengel 1954. Holt 1962, 1967 and 1972 take up the relationship between mechanism and vitalism in psychoanalytic theory. Regarding the question of hypnosis and Freud's appraisal of Charcot and Bernheim, their evolutions can be followed in Freud 1888–1889 (the foreword), 1889, 1892–1893, 1893c, and 1893f. Generally speaking, reading the Fliess correspondence (Freud 1950a [first publication], 1985b [complete edition of the letters, but without the Project]) chronologically gives the best idea of the inception of psychoanalysis, since doubts and theoretical innovations are clearly expressed in it. The most important published writings of Freud's from the period are either mentioned in the text itself, or under the corresponding topics in the references of the last three parts.

The secondary literature on the inception of psychoanalysis and on the conditions for its inception is now extensive. We will mention a few titles. Dorer 1932 distinguishes itself by being the first larger work on the scientific sources of psychoanalysis. The main stress is put on Herbart, Fechner, and Meynert, and it is one of the few places where Meynert's theory is treated in detail. Furthermore, the treatment of Freud's papers on aphasia must also be emphasized, since these papers seldom receive serious attention. Freud's neurophysiological and neuroanatomical background are stressed in Amacher 1965. Amacher chose three of Freud's teachers in the field, Brücke, Meynert, and Exner, and emphasized the concepts he believed Freud to have taken over from them. It can be said of both Dorer and Amacher (as well as of many other works on the history of science) that they are primarily collections of quotations with comments and these works seem to assume that mere similarity in the use of concepts and phrasing is taken as proof of direct influence. Spehlmann 1953 is interesting because of his commentaries on all of Freud's relatively unknown neuropathological writings. Nonetheless, it does not live up to the most elementary requirements a work on the history of science must fulfill.

The periods 1886 to 1896 and 1888 to 1898 are covered by Andersson 1962 and Stewart 1967, respectively. Emphasis is put on Freud's concept of neurosis and on his relationship to Charcot and Bernheim, in particular. The same is true of Levin 1978. Of these, Andersson's book is the most detailed and the most carefully worked out. Chertok and Saussure 1973 and Ellenberger 1970 are centered around hypnosis, suggestion, and hysteria. Chertok and Saussure concentrates on the therapeutic techniques of Mesmer and his followers and shows their development into Freud's therapy. Ellenberger's project is somewhat vaster, insofar as he wishes to trace the origin of the concept of the dynamic unconscious and show the form it took in Freud, as well as in Janet, Jung, and Adler. A criticism of the most common ideas concerning the inception of psychoanalysis is also included in the discussion of Freud. This line of thinking was again taken up by Sulloway (1979), who claimed to dispel earlier myths concerning Freud and his creation of psychoanalysis, for example, the myths surrounding his genius and the distances he took from neurophysiology and neu--

ropathology. Sulloway did not get much out of his critical reading of the Freud literature since he one-sidedly emphasized the points that supported his own biologistic interpretation of psychoanalysis. The best sections in the book are those on Fliess and on contemporary theories of infantile sexuality and sexual pathology. Cranefield 1958 and Hirschmüller 1978 deal especially with Freud's relationship with Breuer and Breuer's theoretical work. Freud's self-analysis is treated in Anzieu 1959 and Kanzer and Glenn 1979. A polemical and severely distorted presentation of Freud's abandonment of the seduction theory is to be found in Masson 1984.

C. THE ORGANIZATION OF PSYCHOANALYSIS

Jones 1955 and 1957 are the best introduction to the evolution of the psychoanalytic movement during Freud's lifetime. Reasonable supplements to Jones are Wyss 1961 (review of pupils' own theoretical contributions), Brome 1967 (new material about some of Freud's controversies with his successors), Dahmer 1973 and Jacoby 1983 (development within the psychoanalytic left), as well as Roazen 1971 (the amplest supplement to Jones, also includes a number of pieces of gossip). The minutes of the weekly meetings of the Vienna Psychoanalytic Society 1906 to 1918, as recorded by Otto Rank, have been published in four volumes (Nunberg and Federn 1962–1975). The major psychoanalytic reviews of the period are the *Jahrbuch für psychoanalytische und psychopatologische Forschungen* (1909–1913), the *Zentralblatt für Psychoanalyse* (1911–1914), the *Internationale Zeitschrift für Psychoanalyse* (1912–1943, with slightly changed titles), *Imago: Zeitschrift für Anvendung der Psychoanalyse auf die Geistwissenschaften* (1912–1937, thereafter combined with *Internationale Zeitschrift*), the *International Journal of Psycho-Analysis* (the English language version of *Internationale Zeitschrift,* founded in 1920 and still in existence. Freud published most of his articles in these journals, as did Abraham, Ferenczi, Jones, and others. Furthermore, reviews, debates, lists of members, and more that has not been republished but is still of interest can be found in them. One last group of texts of importance for the period are Freud's letters, in particular the letters to Pfister (Freud 1963), Abraham (Freud 1965a), Lou Andreas-Salomé (Freud 1966a), Groddeck (Freud 1970b), Jung (Freud 1974b), and Arnold Zweig (Freud 1987), as well as a collection of letters to various persons (Freud 1960a).

Part III. The Analytic Work

There are today, roughly speaking, two conceptions of Freud's analytic method, the hermeneutic and the structural. According to the hermeneuticians, the function of language is to express meaning, and the point of analysis or interpretation is to verbalize the meaning present in the unconscious that normally only expresses itself as incomprehensible symptoms. The structuralists, on the other hand, believe that the function of language is to produce meaning, and see the unconscious as a center for the production of meaning. The analytic work, therefore, does not aim at finding one or another meaning for symptoms, but rather aims at describing the concrete system of signs within which meaning is produced and articulated. Condensations and metaphors are examples of the production of new meaning. Ricoeur 1965 is an example of hermeneutics, Lacan 1957b, of structuralism.

A. DREAMS

The Interpretation of Dreams (Freud 1900a) is without comparison the most important text in which Freud dealt with dream analysis, although 1901a, 1916–1917 (lectures 5–15), 1917d, 1933a (lectures 29–30), and 1940a (chapter 5) can also be mentioned. In two of the case histories, Dora (Freud 1905e) and the "Wolf Man" (Freud 1918b), dreams are dealt with in detail. About dream interpretation in analytic therapy, see Freud 1911e and 1923c. Freud analyzed the dreams of the main character in one of W. Jensen's literary texts (Freud 1907a). Freud's own dreams are treated in Anzieu 1959 and Grinstein 1968. Furthermore, Erikson 1954 discusses Freud's Irma dream in detail. The Irma dream is also commented in Lacan 1978. Fromm 1951 offers general considerations on, among other things, the nature of dreams and the history of dream interpretation in easily accessible form.

B. PSYCHIC MALFUNCTIONS

The most important works are Freud's books on the psychopathology of everyday life (1901b) and jokes (1905c). A shorter version of this theme is to be found in Freud 1916–1917 (lectures 2–4), and related subjects are treated in 1910e, 1927d, and 1936a. Bernfeld 1946 assigns the memory of the dandelion to Freud himself. The forgetting of the name Signorelli is commented on by, among others, Wilden 1966 and Rosolato 1968.

C. SOCIETY, RELIGION, AND ART

On the social genesis of the Oedipus complex, including the genesis of religions, see Freud 1912–1913, 1921c, 1927c, and 1939a. On the importance of drives for social dynamics, see Freud 1908b, 1908d, 1930a, and 1932a. On love life seen in social perspective, see Freud 1910h, 1912d, 1914c, 1914f, 1918a, and 1921c. Of the extensive literature on Freud's conception of society and the use of psychoanalytic concepts within sociology and anthropology, three notable titles including further references are Schülein 1975, Bock 1980, and Wallace 1983 (see especially the references to the Freudo-Marxist literature in the notes to part 5). Besides Freud's texts on Leonardo (Freud 1910c) and Hoffmann (1919h), other texts of his on art and literature deserve mention: 1907a, 1908e, 1913f, 1914b, 1916d, 1917b, and 1928b. Secondary literature on Freud's Leonardo analysis includes Laplanche 1980c.

Part IV. The Therapeutic Work

Freud's therapeutic work is not only an important dimension of psychoanalysis, but it is also an important part of the history of psychiatry. Freud delineated the neuroses, inaugurated a special form of psychotherapy (talk therapy), and made the patient's life history part of the treatment.

A. CLASSIFICATION OF DISEASES

Neuropathological and psychiatric disease classification before Freud was not quite as clear-cut as our diagram (see IV.A) suggests, of course. We have diagrammed the main tendencies as they appear in the dominating textbooks of the period: Emminghaus 1878, Krafft-Ebing 1879, 1895, and 1897–1899, Kirchoff 1892, Ziehen 1894, Möbius 1894–1898, and Wernicke 1900. Of Freud's classification of diseases, most psychoanalysts today probably still acknowledge the three psychogenic groups, neuroses, psychoses, and perversions, while the actual neuroses have either been dropped, or else made part of other groups (see Laplanche and Pontalis 1967, the article on neuroses). However, classification is complicated by a number of additions, even in relatively orthodox psychoanalytic texts such as Fenichel 1945, and one is constantly confused by the continuing discussion in modern textbooks of psychiatry on the division of functional ailments into endogenous and psychogenic ones. Traditional disease classification has been pulverized in the newest American list of diagnoses (DSM-III).

1. Actual Neuroses

Freud's earliest ideas on the separation of actual neuroses and psychoneuroses are to be found in Freud 1985a, the Fliess correspondence (for example, the manuscripts B and E Freud 1985b). The official writings in which Freud discussed actual neuroses are Freud 1895b, 1895f, 1896a, and 1898a. The diagnostic category seldom appeared after the turn of the century, but did in Freud 1912f, 1914c, 1916–1917 (lecture 24), and 1926d, for example. Laplanche (1980a, pp. 21–49) discussed the relationship between actual neuroses and psychosomatic ailments.

2. Perversions

Sulloway 1979 indicates Freud's sources on perversions; the major one is probably Krafft-Ebing 1889. Although perversions find "negative" expression in all psychoneuroses, and as such play an important role in Freud's writings, the interest he took in the "positive" perversions was less marked. Important essays include: Freud 1905d (the most important text in which the general status of perversions as well as their different types are discussed), 1914c (narcissism and homosexuality), 1915c (sadism/masochism, voyeurism/exhibitionism), 1916–1917 (lectures 20–21 summarize Freud 1905d), 1919e (masochistic fantasies), 1920a (female homosexuality), 1922b (homosexuality in relation to jealousy and paranoia), 1924c (masochism), and 1927e (fetishism—see also Strachey's introduction to the development of the concept in Freud in 1927e). Listing the vast secondary literature on perversions here would lead us far afield.

3. Transference Neuroses

On the transference neuroses in general and on distinguishing them from each other and from actual neuroses, perversions, and psychoses, see Freud 1894, 1895c, 1896a, 1896b, 1898a, 1906a, 1912c, 1914c, 1915d, 1915e, 1916–1917 (part 3, Freud's most comprehensive presentation of the theory of neuroses), 1924b, 1924d, 1926d, 1950a, and 1985a. In addition, there are special references to each of the three types of neuroses. On obsessional neurosis, see Freud 1894, 1896b, 1907b, 1909d, 1913i, 1915d, 1915e, 1916–1917 (lectures 17–19), 1918b, and 1926d. On conversion hysteria, see Freud 1886d, 1888b, 1893a, 1893h, 1894, 1895d, 1896b, 1896c, 1905e, 1906a, 1908a, 1909a, 1910i, 1915e, 1926d, and 1950a (especially part 2 of the 1895 "Project"). On anxiety hysteria, see Freud 1895c (on phobias), 1908f, 1909b, 1915d, 1915e, 1918b, and 1926d. Fenichel 1945 is the large standard work on neuroses.

4. Psychoses

There is a broad, though somewhat diffuse, interest in psychoses in Freud's writings from the 1890s (see below). During the second metapsychological thrust, the psychoses appeared under the heading "narcissistic neuroses." See in particular the presentation in Freud 1916–1917 (lecture 26). In the third metapsychological thrust, the term *psychosis* was reintroduced to designate schizophrenia and paranoia, while melancholia was still called a "narcissistic neurosis" (see Freud 1924b, 1924e, and 1940). Paranoia is the psychosis about which Freud wrote most; see Freud 1896b, 1911c

(the most important text on the subject), 1914c (discussion of the designation paraphrenia), 1915f, 1922b, 1974b (especially letters 22F and 25F
to Jung, and 1985a (for example, manuscript H, manuscript K, and the
letters dated 30 May 1896, 6 December 1896, and 9 December 1899).
See also Brunswick 1928 on the paranoia of the "Wolf Man." With regard
to dementia praecox/schizophrenia, Freud described related symptoms
(hallucinatory confusion, Meynert's amentia, and hysterical psychosis) in
Freud 1894, and 1950a (for example, manuscript H). The category is
discussed in the correspondence with Jung from about 1907 (Freud
1974b), and Abraham's article (Abraham 1908) must be mentioned as a
catalyst for Freud's subsequent work. See the comments in Freud 1911c,
1914c, 1915e (the most important), and 1917d. Also melancholy appears
regularly in the Fliess correspondence (Freud 1985b, especially manuscript
G). The major text is Freud 1917e, and there are shorter discussions in
1921c and 1923b. Abraham 1924 is an important contribution to the
psychoanalytic description of melancholia.

B. THERAPY

Freud's therapeutic method and his views on the potentialities of therapy
changed throughout his writings. A good sense of this can be obtained by
reading and comparing an early text (Freud 1895d, chapter 4 on the
psychotherapy of hysteria) with a text from the middle of his production
(1916–1917, lectures 27–28), and again with a late text (1937c, in which
a number of unsolved problems are discussed). It may be added that Freud's
contribution to the subject is spread over a long series of shorter texts, of
which the so-called papers on technique from 1911 to 1914 are the most
important. A broad choice of works in chronological order is: Freud 1888–
1889 (foreword), 1889, 1890 (an important text, especially since the
correct date at which it was written has been determined), 1904a, 1905a
(afterword to the Dora case history), 1910d, 1910k, 1911e, 1912b, 1912e,
1913c, 1914a, 1914g, 1915a, 1919a, 1920b, 1920g (chapter 3), 1923c,
1926e, 1927a, 1937d, and 1940a (part 2). Secondary literature includes
Glover 1955 and Greenson 1967, a couple of relatively traditional presentations of psychoanalytic technique and method.

C. CASE HISTORIES

The five case histories we have treated are unquestionably Freud's most important ones, although we could add the four case histories from the hysteria studies (Freud 1895d), a case of paranoia (1915f), a case of homosexuality (1920a), as well as a psychobiographical study of a painter of the 1600s (1923d). In secondary literature on the five large case histories, see Kanzer and Glenn 1980 for a general discussion. On Dora, see Lacan 1952, F. Deutsch 1957 (Dora's later fate), Marcus 1974, and Rogow 1978 (Dora's family relations). On Little Hans, see Fromm 1966, Lorenzer 1970, Loch and Jappe 1974, and Laplanche 1980a. On the "Rat Man," see Laplanche 1980a and Schneiderman 1986. On Schreber, see Baumeyer 1955, Lacan 1959, Niederland 1974, Chabot 1982, as well as comments and notes to the English translation of Schreber's memoirs (Schreber 1903) by MacAlpine and Hunter. On the "Wolf Man," see Brunswick 1928, Lacan 1956, Gardiner 1971, and Obholzer 1980.

Part V. The Theoretical Work

The secondary literature on Freud's metapsychology and the literature on psychoanalytic theory in general is so extensive that most readers will have difficulty finding their bearings in it. Groups centered on special theoretical points of view were formed already during the 1920s and 1930s. After Freud's death, separate schools began making their appearance. Of these, we will focus on three here, because of the notable impact they have had on the theoretical discussion.

English and especially American ego psychology had their heyday in the 1940s and 1950s. They are characterized by their natural scientific approach and by their focus on the adaptation between the individual and his surroundings as the central issue of psychology. The autonomous ego is given prominence as the great intermediary between inside and outside. The leading figures were Heinz Hartmann and David Rapaport, but also Anna Freud had sympathy for ego psychology. Major works are: A. Freud 1936, Hartmann 1939 and 1964, Hartmann et al. 1964, and Rapaport 1960. Ego psychology met opposition from several quarters, probably most significantly from the advocates of a more humanistic psychology within its own ranks. This tendency, already detectable in Erikson 1950, continued in G. S. Klein 1976, Schafer 1976, 1978, and 1983, as well as in Gill 1976. See also Gill and Holtzmann 1976 for a good overview and critical reading. Brenner 1982 is a newer example of traditional ego psychology.

The Marxist and hermeneutic conceptions of psychoanalysis did not originally form a synthesis. So-called Freudo-Marxism is attached to names like Wilhelm Reich and Herbert Marcuse, its line of thinking being roughly to fill the holes in psychoanalysis with the help of Marxism and vice versa, in order to reach a solid global conception of the social subject. Two general surveys are Robinson 1969 and Dahmer 1973. Other, somewhat miscellaneous, examples are Jacoby 1975 and 1983, Cohen 1982, Horowitz 1977, and Lichtman 1982. Hermeneutics is a phenomenologically oriented interpretative science. It became explicitly connected with psychoanalysis around 1960. Its main thesis is that unconscious structures can become understandable through interpretation, and thus be drawn into the meaningful space in which analyst and analysand speak to each other. Hermeneuticians are opposed to causal explanations, as known from ego psychology, on the ground that the human subject is free and therefore not subject to causal laws. An exception is the psychopathological processes of defense, through which human contexts of meaning have been, so to speak, dehumanized in such a way as to create independent causal forces. Ricoeur 1965 is an example of a hermeneutic (though non-Marxist) conception of psychoanalysis. Especially in the 1970s, Alfred Lorenzer and his pupils forged a strong synthesis of Marxist and hermeneutic viewpoints. Lorenzer 1974 combines a subjective analysis of structure based on the therapeutic dialogue and an objective analysis of structure based on a Marxist analysis of socialization. The common designation here is interaction, insofar as both conversation and interplay in other fields can be considered as forms of interaction. Lorenzer supposes that the subjective and objective dimensions can be united in a "dialectic synthesis." See Prætorius 1978 for criticism on grounds of principle of such attempts at synthesis. Another critical discussion may be found in Grünbaum 1984.

The newer French psychoanalysis is primarily represented by Jacques Lacan and the circle around him. When it first drew attention to itself, it was characterized by its structuralistic approach, that is, through the use of Ferdinand de Saussure's structural linguistics in psychoanalysis, although Melanie Klein also deserves mention as one of Lacan's sources of inspiration. Klein and Lacan were among the earliest critics of ego psychology. At the periphery of the Lacan circle and in some opposition to it, we find

Jean Laplanche. We wish to draw attention to Laplanche as a brilliant reader of Freud. Laplanche has documented the existence of a number of perspectives in Freud that Lacan contented himself with postulating. We have on at least three counts been inspired by Lacan and Laplanche in this book:

(1) The three levels of analysis (the physical-biological level, the level of psychic quantities, and the level of psychic qualities) suggest Lacan's three orders (the Real, the Symbolic, and the Imaginary). It seems to us that this tripartite permits a better understanding of the place of the unconscious than the hermeneutic dualisms that put causal and mechanistic connections on one side and meaning and language on another (see Lacan 1959 and 1975b).

(2) While Lacan nearly dismisses the adaptive point of view, it is to Laplanche's credit that he has discussed the relationship between an adaptive and a psychosexual register in Freud's writings. By underlining the importance of the concept of analysis in Freud, he makes further analysis of a drive's dependence on practice possible (see Laplanche 1970 and 1980c).

(3) Both Lacan and Laplanche stress the central position of primal fantasies in the unconscious (see especially Laplanche and Pontalis 1964), and both have done much with Freud's concept of *Nachträglichkeit* (deferred action). In so doing, they stress that the unconscious is formed according to special rules that lie outside of the traditional opposition between drive and society.

A. THE CONCEPTUAL APPARATUS OF METAPSYCHOLOGY

As shown in part 2, we are of the opinion that Freud committed himself to three metapsychological points of view in the 1890s. It was not until Freud 1915e, however, that they were explicitly coordinated. The tripartite viewpoint is most usefully applied to the level of psychic quantities.

1. The Topographical Viewpoint

The important places where Freud discussed topographical concepts are reviewed chronologically in section V.A.1. The texts in question are Freud

492   BIBLIOGRAPHY

1891b, 1894, 1895d, 1900a (chapter 7), 1915e, 1916–1917 (lecture 19), 1920g, 1923b, 1933a, a summary in 1940a, 1950a (especially letters and manuscripts from 1895–1896), and 1970b (the letter to Groddeck dated 17 April 1921). The use of the reflex model as a basis of comparison makes it possible to compare Freud's topographical models with other psychological models. In secondary literature, the most important single essay on the subject is probably Gill 1963, in which the relationship between the early and the late topography are discussed, including the question of topographic regression in the late topography (which is called by Gill and other ego psychologist the structural model). Arlow and Brenner 1964 is a presentation of the same problems; it is easier to read, but less precisely argumented than Gill 1963. Counterparts are, for example, Lacan 1975a and Laplanche 1980a (especially pp. 159–98 and pp. 251–68), where fundamental questions on the theory of science concerning the use of the topographies are taken up in relation to Freud.

2. The Economic Viewpoint

Freud's most important views on economically quantifiable excitation, energy, or drive are to be found in Freud 1895a, 1905d (in which several of the theoretical formulations found in later editions originated), 1914c, 1915c, 1916–1917 (especially lecture 26), 1920g, 1923a, 1923b, (chapter 4), 1924c, 1933a (lecture 32), 1940a, and 1950a (again in the 1895 "Project"). Early discussions of the concept of energy are to be found in Kubie 1947 and 1953, as well as Colby 1955. From the point of view of the levels model, it is striking that many writers are prone to give priority to one of the levels in their discussion of the concepts of drive and energy. Pribram, for example, chose the physical-biological level (Pribram and Gill 1976), Holt (1962 and 1967) chose the level of psychic quantities without wanting to give unequivocal definitions of psychic energy at the other levels (Holt 1967 also includes many references to the energy discussion), and Schafer (1976) expressed his antimetapsychological attitude by accepting only affects and not drive quantities. As attempts are made to translate many natural scientific disciplines into cybernetics and information theory, attempts are also made to replace the psychoanalytic concept of energy with these concepts—see Carroll 1966, Baros 1971, Peterfreund and Schwartz 1971, as well as Rubinstein 1965. Wilden 1972, inspired by Lacan and the newer information theories, shows a tendency to abandon

the concept of energy without at the same time abandonning the unconscious as a psychological category. Lacan has also taken his distance from
the idea that a drive is a quantum of energy, even if his many circuitus
models still imply that something moves from one place to another. Lacan
1973 (pp. 149–200) deals especially with drives and sexuality.

3. The Dynamic Viewpoint

The references of this section are by and large the same as those of the
section on the economic viewpoint. We might, however, add Freud 1900a,
1911b, and 1915c, on primary processes (references concerning defense
processes are grouped below under section V.C.2). As mentioned, Laplanche 1970 has inspired us to oppose the adaptive and psychosexual
registers, and this problem is studied in more detail in Laplanche 1980c,
in which the psychosexual register's retroactive effect on the adaptive
register in sublimation is discussed.

B. THE SUBJECT'S GENESIS

The distinction made in this section between adaptive and psychosexual
development is not generally accepted. For example, ego psychologists and
a number of Freudo-Marxists believe that the adaptive point of view (the
question of adaptation between individual and surroundings) can be applied to the total development. What we call adaptive development here is
what ego psychologists call development within the conflict-free sphere,
while ego psychologists place psychosexual development in the conflict
sphere. The ego of the conflict-free sphere is made autonomous and drive
independent by ego psychologists, whereby the influence of sexuality on
the total subject is, in our opinion, played down (see Hartmann 1939 and
1964 as well as Hartmann et al. 1964).

1. Adaptive Development

The major Freud texts are "A Project for a Scientific Psychology" from
1895 (1950a), 1900a (chapter 7), 1911b, 1915c, 1920g, and 1925h. For
secondary literature (with the above-mentioned reservation) see Hartmann

1939. Especially about the psychology of the "Project," see Endrass 1975 and Pribram and Gill 1976. In general, it is possible to compare Freud's theory of adaptive development with Jean Piaget's developmental theory. It has been emphasized from several quarters that Piaget omitted the affective and thus psychosexual aspect of development. For Piaget, the direction of development was unequivocally determined by goals such as better mastery of psychomotor functions and more effective strategies for problem solving, which is to say, adaptive goals.

2. Psychosexual Development

While Freud gradually lost interest in adaptive development, his works on psychosexual development are still key parts of psychoanalytic theory.

The genesis and development of the various partial drives is treated in Freud 1905d (the major text on the subject because of the additions made in successive editions), 1908b, 1908c, 1915c, 1916–1917 (lectures 20–22), 1917c, and 1923e. Freud also largely included partial drives in his analyses of dreams, works of art, social behavioral patterns, and so on, in his treatment of the etiology of neuroses, psychoses, and perversions, and in the case histories. The developmental sequence oral-anal-phallic-genital—which Freud seldom discussed so schematically—is a part of several attempts at synthesis: see Abraham 1924 (discussed in section V.B.2), Erikson 1950 (part 1), and Fliess 1950 (pp. 254–55, as well as a very large diagram, in which, unfortunately, the choice of categories is not explained very adequately). Laplanche and Pontalis (1967, the article entitled "Libidinal Stage") criticized the schematic coordination of drive development and ego development, and Laplanche (1970) analyzed the genesis of the partial drives in the light of the concept of anaclisis.

Freud's theoretical work on the genesis of psychic structures and development within the psychosexual register seriously gained momentum after the reintroduction of the ego concept in 1910: see Freud 1910i, 1911b, 1911c (the theoretical discussion, chapter 3), 1914c, 1915c, 1917e, 1921c, 1923b, 1925h, and 1933a (lecture 31). In secondary literature, Fenichel 1945 (pp. 33–113) gives a chronological summary of ego development (and drive development) reasonably close to Freud's own point of view, but generally, the secondary literature is marked by the further development of Freud's concepts. Ego psychologists unequivocally place psychosexual ego development in the sphere of conflict (Hartmann 1939), and the defense mechanisms of the ego as a consequence of the incomplete adaptation of nature-given sexuality to the world (A. Freud 1936). Ego development is seen as part of the subject's socialization in the newer German psychoanalysis (Lorenzer 1972). In spite of the criticism aimed at the socially determined socialization ideals, the adaptive point of view is maintained by focusing on adaptation between drive and world (internal and external nature). It is possible to distinguish two parts in Lacan's version of ego development, a further development of Freud's theory of narcissism into a theory of the mirror stage, and a further development of the Oedipus theory based on intersubjectivity and language, where the id, the ego, the superego, and the object are placed in a Z-formed model with the terms S (subject), a (object—o in English), a' (ego—o' in English), and A (the Other or the superego—O in English). See Lacan 1959.

Freud's earliest attempts at formulating a theory of gender-specific development are to be found in the Fliess letters (Freud 1985b), beginning in 1896. He used the term *bisexuality,* a term he had borrowed from Fliess (regardless that the term was not uncommon in the scientific literature of the time, compare Sulloway 1979). Considerations took as their point of departure the idea that the individual was neither just male or female, but both male and female. In women, the female element dominated, whereas the male element dominated in men. It was Fliess's opinion that internal mental conflicts could be explained as conflicts between the male and female elements of each individual, a thought to which Freud sometimes subscribed and one that also appeared in Adler ("the manly protest," Adler 1929) and in Jung ("anima" and "animus," Jung 1958). Freud, however, became increasingly dissatisfied with this explanation, and therefore his thoughts on the subject receded somewhat into the background until after 1915, when in a note to 1905d (pp. 219–20) he introduced a distinction among biological, sociological, and psychological gender polarities, each with its own origin and developmental possibilities. A somewhat provocative article written by Abraham (1921) on the female castration complex started an intense debate, which resulted in significant clarifications of the psychosexual development of both boys and girls. Freud's most important contributions are Freud 1923e, 1924d, 1925j, 1931b, and 1933a (lecture 33). He remained somewhat in agreement with female analysts such as H. Deutsch (1925), Lampl-de Groot (1927 and 1933), and Brunswick (1940), while he did not accept the criticism and divergent standpoints of Horney (1923, 1926, 1932, and 1933), Jones (1927 and 1933), and M. Klein (1928 and 1932). The newer secondary literature is extensive: titles where the possibility of giving a new theoretical basis for the castration complex is explored are Chasseguet-Smirgel 1964, Mitchell 1974, and Laplanche 1980b.

3. Development and Repetition Compulsion

The simple idea that repetition consists of a regressive return to an earlier point of fixation can be found everywhere in Freud's writings, from references to traumas in the early writings, to the etiological model in the lectures from 1916–1917 (especially lectures 22–23). But the more complex thought that traumas are established through deferred action, perhaps as fictions, also shows up regularly (compare the references concerning fantasy in section V.C.3. below). In contrast, the repetition compulsion first appeared thematically as an internal force, the aptitude of a drive to return to an earlier state, in the last phase of Freud's work: 1914g (as a hint), 1919h, and 1920g. One need but read Kierkegaard (1843) to understand that the concept of repetition cannot be used psychologically in any simple way. Consequently, discussions of Freud's concept of repetition compulsion are, in general, very complex, at the same time as they tend to give metapsychology completely new foundations. See, for example, Lacan 1957a and Derrida 1966.

C. THE SUBJECT'S STRUCTURE

It is common among ego psychologists to call Freud's late topographical model the structural model. The psychic functions are placed in a hierarchy corresponding to the structures forming their basis, and these structures are again grouped in an id, an ego, and a superego structure. When we speak of "the subject's structure," we have another meaning in mind. We do not take as our point of departure either functions or representational elements, but the relations existing between the different parts of the psychic apparatus. There is nothing wrong with calling the id, the superego, and the ego psychic structures, but these agencies are themselves formed by other, more fundamental, psychic structures, that is, the polarities subject/object, pleasure/unpleasure, and active/passive. These poles are mutually determinant; one pole is inconceivable without the other. In other words, the positive term is always determined by its absent opposite. This conception of structure is related to the concept of structure in the structural linguistics of Ferdinand de Saussure and of his followers (see Saussure 1916). Although it is true that Freud did not define the polarities as linguistic structures, he did nonetheless take an interest in their linguistic articulations when he described drive vicissitudes as the result of grammatic transformations (Freud 1911c, 1915c, and 1919e), and when he related them to the development of judgmental functions (1925h). Freud's basic language is, of course, less structural than Saussure's linguistic system, less formalistic, and Freud also presupposed a content definition of the basic polarities that is probably unacceptable to the traditional linguists, that is, a body connection (subject/object), an affect polarization (pleasure/un-pleasure), and a power relation or relation of dominance (active/passive). In Freud's opinion, these genetically early content determinations continued to influence language. Melanie Klein's basic language includes three polarities, that are, however, related to Freud's, that is, inner/outer, good/bad, and total object/partial object. The unfinished discussion of these topics can be followed in Lacan and Lorenzer (see bibliography). Where Lacan claims that the unconscious is structured as a language, Lorenzer claims, on the contrary, that the unconscious is nonlinguistic (perhaps even de-symbolized), a point of view that is more traditionally Freudian. Laplanche 1981 expresses a middle standpoint on precisely this question. General questions concerning psychoanalysis and language are discussed in Jappe 1971.

1. Activity and Passivity

Central Freud texts are: 1905d, 1911c, 1913i, 1915c, 1918b, 1919e, 1931b, and (manuscript K from January 1896) in 1985b. Other examples of the theme from Freud's own time are Jekels 1913, Lampl-de Groot 1933, Loewenstein 1935, and Brunswick 1940 (Brunswick introduced the terms *active* and *passive Oedipus complex,* which we have used). Rapaport (1961—written in 1953) showed the inconsistency of earlier attempts to clarify the polarity conceptually, but himself one-sidedly chose the ego's autonomy as the basis of a definition (activity = autonomy; passivity = absence of autonomy of the ego in relationship to the drives and the surrounding world). Schafer 1968 also attempts systematization. La-planche 1970 (chapter 5) is a good example of the emphasis put on the meaning of language and intersubjectivity for the polarity.

2. Pleasure and Unpleasure

The pleasure/unpleasure polarity permeates all of Freud's works, since it is at the basis of every affect (love, hate, anger, desire, envy, guilt, and so on) and every defense mechanism. Freud texts of significance for affect theory in general are: 1900a, 1905d (especially the concept of forepleasure), 1915c, 1915d, 1915e, 1916–1917 (the important lecture 25), 1920g, (chapter 1), 1923b (chapter 2), 1926d (the major work on the subject), and 1950a (manuscript E from 1894 and "Project" from 1895). Secondary literature includes A. Freud 1936 (an attempt to systematize the defense mechanisms) and Rapaport 1953 (takes stock of the psychoanalytic theory of affects and discusses earlier works in the field). Other historical and systematic treatments are Jacobson 1953 and Green 1973 and 1977. Schafer 1976 includes an attempt to replace the metapsychology of affects with an "action language" of which feelings are a part, and Laplanche 1980a attempts to rehabilitate Freud's early anxiety theory to the detriment of his late one.

3. Subject and Object

In Freud, the subject/object polarity is an intrapsychic polarity, in which the object is a representational object and not a real one. This distinction is theoretically suspect where a pure relation of knowledge within the adaptive register is concerned, insofar as it necessitates a "more objective" observer to have any meaning (compare Prætorius 1978). In Freud, we will only refer to it within the psychosexual register, where the sexual object is formed according to rules that cannot in any way be called objective. Freud texts concerning identification and object cathexis (and the related conceptual pairs) are: 1905d, 1914c, 1915c, 1917e, 1921c, 1923b, 1924d, 1925h, and 1933a (lecture 31). Secondary literature includes: Ferenczi 1909, Abraham 1924, Fenichel 1925 and 1926, Federn 1929, Glover 1932, and Erikson 1950. The concepts have been given rich further developments within the school of Melanie Klein, see Heimann 1952 and M. Klein 1955, for example. Freud's view on the concept of fantasy can be pieced together from Freud 1900a, 1907a, 1908e, 1909c, 1911b, 1914c, 1915e, 1915f, 1916–1917 (lecture 23), 1917d, 1918b, 1919e, 1919h, 1926d, and 1950a. In secondary literature, two analyses of the concept of fantasy deserve special mention, Isaacs 1948 and Laplanche and Pontalis 1964.

2.
FREUD
BIBLIOGRAPHY

The bibliography contains a complete list of Freud's writings published before January 1987. The titles are listed in chronological order in accordance with the year of publication, while the letters after the year indicate the succession of publication. If the year of wording is different from the year of publication, it is placed in brackets after the year of publication.

The bibliography is based on *The Standard Edition of the Complete Psychological Works of Sigmund Freud* (James Strachey, ed., 24 vols. London: Hogarth Press, 1960–1974); the bibliographical volume of *Sigmund Freuds Studienausgabe* (A. Mitscherlich, A. Richards, and J. Strachey, eds., 11 vols. Frankfurt: S. Fischer 1969–1975); and R. Dufresne, *Bibliographie des écrits de Freud*. (Paris: Payot, 1973). In accordance with Dufresne we have changed the placement of some of the titles and added the following, which Dufresne found: 1883, 1884g, 1884h, 1933f, 1953–1957, 1956h, 1956i, 1956j, 1956k, 1956l, 1956m, 1956n, 1960c, 1961, 1962, 1964, 1965b, 1965c, 1965d, 1965e, 1966c, 1968a, 1971b. We have ourselves added: 1970b, 1974a, 1974b, 1980, 1985a, 1985b.

In cases in which a title is not translated into English we have cited the original publication.

1877a Über den Ursprung der hinteren Nervenwurzeln im Rückenmarke von Ammocoetes (Petromyzon Planeri). *S.B. Akad. Wiss. Wien* (Math.-Naturwiss. Kl.), 3 Abt., 75.

1877b Beobachtungen über Gestaltung und feineren Bau der als Hoden beschriebenen Lappenorgane des Aals. *S.B. Akad. Wiss. Wien* (Math.-Naturwiss. Kl.), 1 Abt., 75.

1878 Über Spinalganglien und Rückenmark des Petromyzon. *S.B. Akad. Wiss. Wien* (Math.-Naturwiss. Kl.), 3 Abt., 78.

1879 Notiz über eine Methode zur anatomischen Präparation des Nervensystems. *Zbl. med. Wiss.*, 17(26).

1880 Translation of J. S. Mill's "Enfranchisement of Women" (1851); review of Grote's *Plato and the Other Companions of Sokrates* (1866); "Thornton on Labour and its Claims" (1869); "Chapters on Socialism" (1879). Under the titles "Über Frauenemancipation"; "Plato"; "Die Arbeiterfrage"; "Der Sozialismus." In Mill's *Gesammelte Werke*, 12. Leipzig.

1882 [1881] Über den Bau der Nervenfasern und Nervenzellen beim Flusskrebs. *S.B. Akad. Wiss. Wien* (Math.-Naturwiss. Kl.), 3 Abt., 85.

1883 Review of A. Spina's *Studien über Tuberculose*. *Medical News*, 42.

1884a Ein Fall von Hirnblutung mit indirekten basalen Herdsymptomen bei Scorbut. *Wien. med. Wschr.*, 34(9 and 10).

1884b Eine neue Methode zum Studium des Faserverlaufes im Centralnervensystem. *Zbl. med. Wiss.*, 22(11).

1884c A New Histological Method for the Study of Nerve-Tracts in the Brain and Spinal Cord. *Brain*, 7.

1884d Eine neue Methode zum Studium des Faserverlaufes im Centralnervensystem. *Arch. Anat. Physiol., Lpz.*, Anat. Abt.

1884e On Coca. In Freud: *The Cocaine Papers*. Vienna, 1963.

1884f [1882] Die Struktur der Elemente der Nervensystems. *Jb. Psychiat. Neurol.*, 5(3).

1884g Cocaine. *Medical News*, 45.

1884h The Bacillus of Syphilis. *Medical News*, 45.

1885a Contribution to the Knowledge of the Effect of Cocaine. In Freud: *The Cocaine papers*. Vienna, 1963.

1885b On the General Effect of Cocaine. In Freud: *The Cocaine Papers*. Vienna, 1963.

1885c Ein Fall von Muskelathrophie mit ausgebreiteten Sensibilitätsstörungen (Syringomyelie). *Wien. med. Wschr.*, 35(13).

1885d Zur Kenntnis der Olivenzwischenschicht. *Neurol. Zbl.*, 4(12).

1885e Opinion on Parke's Cocaine. In Freud: *The Cocaine Papers*. Vienna, 1963.

1885f Addenda to On Coca (see 1884e).

1886a Akute multiple Neuritis der spinalen und Hirnnerven. *Wien. med. Wschr.*, 36(6).

1886b With L. Darkschewitsch: Über die Beziehung des Strickkörpers zum Hinterstrang und Hinterstrangskern nebst Bemerkungen über zwei Felder der Oblongata. *Neurol. Zbl.*, 5(6).

1886c Über den Ursprung des Nervus acusticus. *Mschr. Ohrenheilk.*, Neue Folge, 20(8 and 9).

1886d Observation of a Severe Case of Hemi-Anaesthesia in a Hysterical Male. *S.E.* 1.

1886e Translation of J.-M. Charcot's "Sur un cas de coxalgie hysterique de cause traumatique chez l'homme." Under the title "Über einen Fall von hysterischer Coxalgie aus traumatischer Ursache bei einem Manne." *Wien. med. Wschr.*, 36. (Incorporated in 1886f).

1886f Translation with preface and footnotes of J.-M. Charcot's *Leçons sur les maladies du système nerveux*, vol. 3, Paris, 1887. Under the title *Neue Vorlesungen über die Krankheiten des Nervensystems insbesondere über Hysterie.* Wien.
English translation of the preface: Preface to the Translation of Charcot's *Lectures on the Diseases of the Nervous System. S.E.* 1.

1887a Review of Averbeck's "Die Akute Neurasthenie." *S.E.* 1.

1887b Review of Weir Mitchell's *Die Behandlung gewisser Formen von Neurasthenie und Hysterie*, Berlin, 1887. *S.E.* 1.

1887c Review of Adamkiewicz's "Monoplegia anaesthetica." *Neurol. Zbl.*, 6(6).

1887d Cravings for and Fear of Cocaine. In Freud: *The Cocaine Papers.* Vienna, 1963.

1887e Review of H. Obersteiner's *Anleitung beim Studium des Baues der nervösen Centralorgane im gesunden und kranken Zustande. Wien. med. Wschr.*, 37(50).

1887f Das Nervensystem. Chapter 5 in Buchheim: *Ärtzliche Versicherungsdiagnostik*, Vienna.

1887g Review of J. Pal's "Ein Beitrag zur Nervenfärbetechnik". *Neurol. Zbl.*, 6(3).

1887h Review of Al. Borgherini's "Beiträge zur Kenntnis der Leitungsbahnen im Rückmarke." *Neurol. Zbl.*, 6(4).

1887i Review of J. Nussbaum's "Über die wechselseitigen Beziehungen zwischen den centralen Ursprungsgebieten der Augenmuskelnerven." *Neurol. Zbl.*, 6(23).

1888a Über Hemianopsie im frühesten Kindesalter. *Wien. med. Wschr.*, 38(32 and 33).

1888b "Aphasie," "Gehirn," "Hysterie," and "Hysteroepilepsie." In Villaret's *Handwörterbuch der gesammten Medizin*, 1. Stuttgart. (Unsigned; authorship uncertain). "Hysteria" and "Hystero-Epilepsy." *S.E.* 1.

1888–1889 [1888] Translation with preface and notes of H. Bernheim's *De la suggestion et de ses applications à la thérapeutique*, Paris, 1886. Under the title *Die Suggestion und ihre Heilwirkungen*. Vienna. (Part 2 trans. O. von. Springer).
Translation of the preface: Preface to the Translation of Bernheim's *Suggestion. S.E.* 1.

1889 Review of August Forel's *Hypnotism. S.E.* 1.

1890 Psychical (or Mental) Treatment. *S.E.* 7. (Formerly considered 1905b).

1891a With O. Rie: *Klinische Studie über die halbseitige Cerebrallähmung der Kinder*, Heft 3 of Kassowitz (ed.): *Beiträge zur Kinderheilkunde*. Vienna.

1891b *On Aphasia*. New York, 1953.

1891c "Kinderlähmung" and "Lähmung." In Villaret's *Handwörterbuch der gesammten Medizin*, 2. Stuttgart. (Unsigned; authorship uncertain).

1891d Hypnosis. *S.E.* 1.

1892 Translation of H. Bernheim's *Hypnotisme, suggestion et psychothérapie: études nouvelles*, Paris, 1891. Under the title *Neue Studien über Hypnotismus, Suggestion und Psychotherapie*. Vienna.

1892–1893 [1892] A Case of Successful Treatment by Hypnotism. *S.E.* 1.

1892–1894 Translation with preface and footnotes of J.-M. Charcot's *Leçons du mardi à la Salpêtrière (1887–1888)*, Paris, 1888. Under the title *Poliklinische Vorträge*, 1. Vienna.
Translation of preface and footnotes: Preface and Footnotes to the Translation of Charcot's *Tuesday Lectures. S.E.* 1.

1893a [1892] With J. Breuer: On the Psychical Mechanism of Hysterical Phenomena: Preliminary Communication. *S.E.* 2.

1893b *Zur Kenntniss der cerebralen Diplegien des Kindesalters (im Ansschluss an die Little'sche Krankheit)*, Heft. 3, Neue Folge, of *Beiträge zur Kinderheilkunde*, ed. Kassowitz. Vienna.

1893c [1888–1893] Some Points for a Comparative Study of Organic and Hysterical Motor Paralysis. *S.E.* 1.

1893d Über familiären Formen von cerebralen Diplegien. *Neurol. Zbl.*, 12(15 and 16).

1893e Les diplégies cérébrales infantiles. *Rev. neurol.*, 1(8).

1893f Charcot. *S.E.* 1.

1893g Über ein Symptom, das häufig die Enuresis nocturna der Kinder begleitet. *Neurol. Zbl.*, 12(21).

1893h On the Psychical Mechanism of Hysterical Phenomena. *S.E.* 3.

1894 The Neuro-Psychoses of Defence. *S.E.* 3.

1895a Review of Edinger's "Eine neue Theorie über die Ursachen einiger Nervenkrankheiten, insbesondere der Neuritis und Tabes. *Wien. klin. Rdsch.*, 9(2).

1895b [1894] On the Grounds for Detaching a Particular Syndrome from Neurasthenia under the Description "Anxiety Neurosis." *S.E.* 3.

1895c [1894] Obsessions and Phobias. *S.E.* 3.

1895d [1893–1895] With J. Breuer: *Studies on Hysteria. S.E.* 2. (Including Breuer's contributions).

1895e Über die Bernhardt'sche Senbsibilitätsstörung am Oberschenkel. *Neurol. Zbl.*, 14(11).

1895f A Reply to Criticisms of My Paper on Anxiety Neurosis. *S.E.* 3.

1895g Über Hysterie. *Wien. klin. Rdsch.*, 9(42–44).

1895h Mechanismus der Zwangsvorstellungen und Phobien. Author's abstract. *Wien. klin. Wschr.*, 8.

1896a Heredity and the Aetiology of the Neuroses. *S.E.* 3.

1896b Further Remarks on the Neuro-Psychoses of Defense. *S.E.* 3.

1896c The Aetiology of Hysteria. *S.E.* 3.

1896d Preface to the second German edition of H. Bernheim's *Suggestion. S.E.* 1.

1897a *Die Infantile Cerebrallähmung,* 2 Theil, 2 Abt. of Nothnagel's *Specielle Pathologie und Therapie,* 9. Vienna.

1897b Abstracts of the Scientific Writings of Dr. Sigmund Freud (1877–1897). *S.E.* 3.

1898a Sexuality in the Aetiology of the Neuroses. *S.E.* 3.

1898b The Psychical Mechanism of Forgetfulness. *S.E.* 3.

1898c Cerebrale Kinderlähmung (1). *Jbr. Leist. Neurol.*, 1 (1897).

1899a Screen Memories. *S.E.* 3.

1899b Cerebrale Kinderlähmung (2). *Jbr. Leist. Neurol.*, 2 (1898).

1900a [1899] *The Interpretation of Dreams. S.E.* 4–5.

1900b Cerebrale Kinderlähmung (3). *Jbr. Leist. Neurol.*, 3.

1901a *On Dreams. S.E.* 5.

1901b *The Psychopathology of Everyday Life. S.E.* 6.

1901c [1899] Autobiographical note. In J. L. Pagel's *Biographisches Lexicon hervorragende Ärtze des neunzehnten Jahrhunderts. S.E.* 3.

1903 Review of George Biedenkapp's *In Kampfe gegen Hirnbacillen. S.E.* 9.

1904a [1903] Freud's Psycho-Analytic Procedure. *S.E.* 7.

1904b Review of John Bigelow's *The Mystery of Sleep. S.E.* 9.

1904c Review of A. Baumgarten's *Neurasthenie, Wesen, Heilung, Vorbeugung. Neu Freie Presse,* 4 Feb., Morgenbl., 22.

1904d Note on "Magnetische Menschen." *Neue Freie Presse,* 6 Nov., Morgenbl., 10.

1904e Obituary of Prof. S. Hammerschlag. *S.E.* 9.

1904f An Unknown Review of Freud. *Int. J. Psycho-Anal.,* 48, 1967.

1905a [1904] On Psychotherapy. *S.E.* 7.

1905b Now shown as 1890a.

1905c *Jokes and Their Relation to the Unconscious. S.E.* 8.

1905d *Three Essays on the Theory of Sexuality. S.E.* 7.

1905e [1901] Fragment of an Analysis of a Case of Hysteria. *S.E.* 7.

1905f Review of R. Wickmann's *Lebensregeln für Neurastheniker. Neue Freie Presse,* 31 Aug., Morgenbl., 21.

1906a [1905] My Views on the Part played by Sexuality in the Aetiology of Neuroses. *S.E.* 7.

1906b Preface to Freud's Shorter Writings 1893–1906. *S.E.* 3.

1906c Psycho-Analysis and the Establishment of the Facts in Legal Proceedings. S.E. 9.

1906d Two Letters to Magnus Hirschfield. *Monatsberichte des wissenschaftlichhumanitären Komites,* 5.

1906e [1904] Two Letters to Wilhelm Fliess. In Richard Pfenning: *Wilhelm Fliess und seine Nachentdecker: O. Weiniger und H. Swoboda.* Berlin.

1906f Contribution to a Questionnaire on Reading. *S.E.* 9. (Formerly considered 1907d).

1907a [1906] *Delusions and Dreams in Jensen's "Gradiva." S.E.* 9.

1907b Obsessive Actions and Religious Practices. *S.E.* 9.

1907c The Sexual Enlightenment of Children. *S.E.* 9.

1907d Now shown as 1906f.

1907e Prospectus for *Schriften zur angewandten Seelenkunde,* in 1907a. *S.E.* 9.

1908a Hysterical Phantasies and their Relation to Bisexuality. *S.E.* 9.

1908b Character and Anal Eroticism. *S.E.* 9.

1908c On the Sexual Theories of Children. *S.E.* 9.

1908d "Civilized" Sexual Morality and Modern Nervous Illness. *S.E.* 9.

1908e Creative Writers and Day-Dreaming. *S.E.* 9.

1908f Preface to Stekel's *Nervöse Angstzustände und ihre Behandlung*. *S.E.* 9.

1909a [1908] Some General Remarks on Hysterical Attacks. *S.E.* 9.

1909b Analysis of a Phobia in a Five-Year-Old Boy. *S.E.* 10.

1909c [1908] Family Romances. *S.E.* 9.

1909d Notes upon a Case of Obsessional Neurosis. *S.E.* 10.

1910a [1909] Five Lectures on Psycho-Analysis. *S.E.* 11.

1910b [1909] Preface to Ferenczi's *Lélekelemzés: Ertekezések a pszichoanalizis köréböl*. *S.E.* 9.

1910c *Leonardo da Vinci and a Memory of His Childhood*. *S.E.* 11.

1910d The Future Prospects of Psycho-Analytic Therapy. *S.E.* 11.

1910e The Antithetical Meaning of Primal Words. *S.E.* 11.

1910f Letter to Dr. Friedrich S. Krauss on *Anthropophyteia*, *S.E.* 11.

1910g Contributions to a Discussion on Suicide. *S.E.* 11.

1910h A Special Type of Choice of Object Made by Men. *S.E.* 11.

1910i The Psycho-Analytic View of Psychogenic Disturbance of Vision. *S.E.* 11.

1910j Two Instances of Pathogenic Phantasies Revealed by the Patients Themselves. *S.E.* 11.

1910k "Wild" Psycho-Analysis. *S.E.* 11.

1910l A Typical Example of a Disguised Oedipus Dream. Included in *The Interpretation of Dreams*. *S.E.* 5.

1910m Review of Wilh. Neutra's "Briefe an nervöse Frauen". *S.E.* 11.

1911a Additions to the Interpretation of Dreams. Incorporated in *The Interpretation of Dreams*. *S.E.* 5.

1911b Formulations on the Two Principles of Mental Functioning. *S.E.* 12.

1911c [1910] Psycho-Analytic Notes on an Autobiographical Account of a Case of Paranoia (Dementia Paranoides). *S.E.* 12.

1911d The Significance of Vowel Sequences. *S.E.* 12.

1911e The Handling of Dream-Interpretation in Psycho-Analysis. *S.E.* 12.

1911f Great is Diana of the Ephesians. *S.E.* 12.

1911g Abstract of G. Greve's "Sobre psicologia y psicoterapia de ciertos estados angustiosos. *Zbl. Psychoan.* 1.

1911h Footnote to Stekel's "Zur Psychologie des Exhibitionismus. *S.E.* 18.

1911i The Forgetting of Proper Names. (In 1901b from 4th ed. onwards.) *S.E.* 6.

1911j Translation with footnote of James J. Putnam's "On the Etiology and Treatment of the Psychoneuroses," 1910. (Translation incorporated in editor's footnote to 1919b.) *S.E.* 17.

1912a [1911] Postscript to the Case of Paranoia. *S.E.* 12.

1912b The Dynamics of Transference. *S.E.* 12.

1912c Types of Onset of Neurosis. *S.E.* 12.

1912d On the Universal Tendency to Debasement in the Sphere of Love. *S.E.* 11.

1912e Recommendations to Physicians Practising Psycho-Analysis. *S.E.* 12.

1912f Contributions to a Discussion on Masturbation. *S.E.* 12.

1912g A Note on the Unconscious in Psycho-Analysis. *S.E.* 12.

1912h Request for Examples of Childhood Dreams. (Translation included in 1918b.) *S.E.* 17.

1912–1913 *Totem and Taboo. S.E.* 13.

1913a An Evidental Dream. *S.E.* 12.

1913b Introduction to Pfister's *Die psychoanalytische Methode. S.E.* 12.

1913c On Beginning the Treatment (Further Recommendations on the Technique of Psycho-Analysis, I). *S.E.* 12.

1913d The Occurrence in Dreams of Material from Fairy Tales. *S.E.* 12.

1913e Preface to Steiner's *Die psychischen Störungen der männlichen Potenz. S.E.* 12.

1913f The Theme of the Three Caskets. *S.E.* 12.

1913g Two Lies Told by Children. *S.E.* 12.

1913h Observations and Examples from Analytic Practice. *S.E.* 13.

1913i The Disposition to Obsessional Neurosis. *S.E.* 12.

1913j The Claims of Psycho-Analysis to Scientific Interest. *S.E.* 13.

1913k Preface to J. G. Bourke's *Scatalogic Rites of all Nations. S.E.* 12.

1913l Childhood Dreams with a Particular Meaning. (Included in 1918b.) *S.E.* 17.

1913m [1911] On Psycho-Analysis. *S.E.* 12.

1914a Fausse Reconnaissance ("déjà reconté") in Psycho-Analytic Treatment. *S.E.* 13.

1914b [1913] The Moses of Michelangelo. *S.E.* 13.

1914c On Narcissism: An Introduction. *S.E.* 14.

1914d On the History of the Psycho-Analytic Movement. *S.E.* 14.

1914e The Representation in a Dream of a "Great Achievement." (Included in 1900a.) *S.E.* 5.

1914f Some Reflections on Schoolboy Psychology. *S.E.* 13.

1914g Remembering, Repeating and Working-Through (Further Recommendations on the Technique of Psycho-Analysis, II). *S.E.* 12.

1915a [1914] Observations on Transference-Love (Further Recommendations on the Technique of Psycho-Analysis, III). *S.E.* 12.

1915b Thoughts for the Times on War and Death. *S.E.* 14.

1915c Instincts and Their Vicissitudes. *S.E.* 14.

1915d Repression. *S.E.* 14.

1915e The Unconscious. *S.E.* 14.

1915f A Case of Paranoia Running Counter to the Psycho-Analytic Theory of Disease. *S.E.* 14.

1915g [1914] Letter to Dr. F. van Eeden. *S.E.* 14.

1916a [1915] On Transcience. *S.E.* 14.

1916b A Mythological Parallel to a Visual Obsession. *S.E.* 14.

1916c A Connection between a Symbol and a Symptom. *S.E.* 14.

1916d Some Character-Types Met with in Psycho-Analytic Work. *S.E.* 14.

1916e Footnote to Ernest Jones's "Professor Janet über Psychoanalyse." *S.E.* 2.

1916–1917 [1915–1917] *Introductory Lectures on Psycho-Analysis. S.E.* 15–16.

1917a A Difficulty in the Path of Psycho-Analysis. *S.E.* 17.

1917b A Childhood Recollection from *Dichtung und Wahrheit. S.E.* 17.

1917c On Transformations of Instincts as Exemplified in Anal Eroticism. *S.E.* 17.

1917d A Metapsychological Supplement to the Theory of Dreams. *S.E.* 14.

1917e Mourning and Melancholia. *S.E.* 14.

1918a [1917] The Taboo of Virginity. *S.E.* 11.

1918b [1914] From the History of an Infantile Neurosis. *S.E.* 17.

1919a Lines of Advance in Psycho-Analytic Therapy. *S.E.* 17.

1919b James J. Putnam. *S.E.* 17.

1919c A Note on Psycho-Analytic Publications and Prizes. *S.E.* 17.

1919d Introduction to *Psycho-Analysis and the War Neuroses. S.E.* 17.

1919e A Child is Being Beaten. *S.E.* 17.

1919f Victor Tausk. *S.E.* 17.

1919g Preface to Reik's *Ritual: Psycho-Analytic Studies*. *S.E.* 17.

1919h The "Uncanny." *S.E.* 17.

1919i [1915] Letter to Dr. Hermine von Hug-Helmuth. *S.E.* 14.

1919j On the Teaching of Psycho-Analysis in Universities. *S.E.* 17.

1919k E. T. A. Hoffmann on the Function of Consciousness. (Included in 1919h.) *S.E.* 17.

1920a The Psychogenesis of a Case of Female Homosexuality. *S.E.* 18.

1920b A Note of the Prehistory of the Technique of Analysis. *S.E.* 18.

1920c Dr. Anton von Freund. *S.E.* 19.

1920d Associations of a Four-Year-Old Child. *S.E.* 18.

1920e Preface to the Fourth Edition of *Three Essays on the Theory of Sexuality*. *S.E.* 17.

1920f Supplements to the Theory of Dreams. *S.E.* 18.

1920g *Beyond the Pleasure Principle*. *S.E.* 18.

1921a English Preface to J. J. Putnam's *Addresses on Psycho-Analysis*. *S.E.* 18.

1921b English Introduction to Varendonck's *The Psychology of Dreams*. *S.E.* 18.

1921c *Group Psychology and the Analysis of the Ego*. *S.E.* 18.

1921d Award of Prizes. (Included in 1919c.) *S.E.* 17.

1921e Extract from a Letter to Claparède. (Included in 1910i.) *S.E.* 11.

1922a Dreams and Telepathy. *S.E.* 18.

1922b [1921] Some Neurotic Mechanisms in Jealousy, Paranoia and Homosexuality. *S.E.* 18.

1922c Postscript to the "Analysis of a Phobia in a Five-Year-Old Boy." *S.E.* 10.

1922d Prize Offer. (Included in 1919c.) *S.E.* 17.

1922e Preface to Raymond de Saussure's *La méthode psychoanalytique*. *S.E.* 19.

1922f Some Remarks on the Unconscious. (Included in 1923b.) *S.E.* 19.

1923a Two Encyclopaedia Articles. *S.E.* 18.

1923b *The Ego and the Id*. *S.E.* 19.

1923c [1922] Remarks on the Theory and Practice of Dream-Interpretation. *S.E.* 19.

1923d A Seventeenth-Century Demonological Neurosis. *S.E.* 19.

1923e The Infantile Genital Organization. *S.E.* 19.

1923f Joseph Popper-Lynkeus and the Theory of Dreams. *S.E.* 19.

1923g Preface to Max Eitington's *Report on the Berlin Psycho-Analytic Policlinic*. *S.E.* 19.

1923h Letter to Senor Luis Lopez-Ballesteros y de Torres. *S.E.* 19.

1923i Dr. Sándor Ferenczi (on His 50th Birthday). *S.E.* 19.

1924a Letter to *Le Sisque Vert. S.E.* 19.

1924b [1923] Neurosis and Psychosis. *S.E.* 19.

1924c The Economic Problem of Masochism. *S.E.* 19.

1924d The Dissolution of the Oedipus Complex. *S.E.* 19.

1924e The Loss of Reality in Neurosis and Psychosis. *S.E.* 19.

1924f [1923] A Short Account of Psycho-Analysis. *S.E.* 19.

1924g [1923] Extracts from a Letter to Wittels. *S.E.* 19.

1924h Editorial Changes in the *Zeitschrift. S.E.* 19.

1924i Letter in *Jewish Observer and Middle East Review,* 3(23).

1925a [1924] A Note upon the "Mystic Writing-Pad." *S.E.* 19.

1925b Letter to the Editor of the *Jüdische Presszentrale, Zurich. S.E.* 19.

1925c Message on the Opening of the Hebrew University. *S.E.* 19.

1925d [1924] *An Autobiographical Study. S.E.* 20.

1925e [1924] The Resistances to Psycho-Analysis. *S.E.* 19.

1925f Preface to Aichorn's *Wayward Youth. S.E.* 19.

1925g Josef Breuer. *S.E.* 19.

1925h Negation. *S.E.* 19.

1925i Some Additional Notes on Dream-Interpretation as a Whole. *S.E.* 19.

1925j Some Psychical Consequences of the Anatomical Distinction between the Sexes. *S.E.* 19.

1926a To Romain Rolland. *S.E.* 20.

1926b Karl Abraham. *S.E.* 20.

1926c Foreword to E. Pickworth Farrow's *A Practical Method of Self-Analysis. S.E.* 20.

1926d [1925] *Inhibitions, Symptoms and Anxiety. S.E.* 20.

1926e *The Question of Lay Analysis. S.E.* 20.

1926f An Article in the *Encyclopaedia Britannica. S.E.* 20.

1926g Footnote on Hering. (Included in 1915e.) *S.E.* 14.

1926h Letter from Freud. In Theodor Reich's *From Thirty Years with Freud.* New York, 1940.

1926i Dr. Reik and the Problem of Quackery. *S.E.* 21.

1927a Postscript to *The Question of Lay Analysis. S.E.* 20.

1927b Supplement to "The Moses of Michelangelo." *S.E.* 13.

1927c *The Future of an Illusion. S.E.* 21.

1927d Humour. *S.E.* 21.

1927e Fetishism. *S.E.* 21.

1928a [1927] A Religious Experience. *S.E.* 21.

1928b [1927] Dostoevsky and Parricide. *S.E.* 21.

1929a Dr. Ernest Jones (on His 50th Birthday). *S.E.* 21.

1929b Letter to Maxime Leroy. *S.E.* 21.

1930a [1929] *Civilization and Its Discontents.* *S.E.* 21.

1930b Preface to *Zehn Jahre Berliner Psychoanalytisches Institut.* *S.E.* 21.

1930c Introduction to the Special Psychopathology Number of *The Medical Review of Reviews.* *S.E.* 21.

1930d Letter to Dr. Alfons Paquet. *S.E.* 21.

1930e Address delivered in the Goethe House at Frankfurt. *S.E.* 21.

1930f [1929] Letter to Theodor Reik. *S.E.* 21.

1931a Libidinal Types. *S.E.* 21.

1931b Female Sexuality. *S.E.* 21.

1931c Introduction to Edoardo Weiss's *Elementi di Psicoanalisi.* *S.E.* 21.

1931d [1930] The Expert Opinion in the Halsmann Case. *S.E.* 21.

1931e Letter to the Burgomaster of Pribor. *S.E.* 21.

1931f Letter to Georg Fuchs. *S.E.* 22.

1932a [1931] The Acquisition and Control of Fire. *S.E.* 22.

1932b [1931] Preface to Hermann Nunberg's *Allgemeine Neurosenlehre auf psychoanalytische Grundlage.* *S.E.* 21.

1932c My Contact with Josef Popper-Lynkeus. *S.E.* 22.

1932d Résumé of first part of lecture 30 of 1933a. *Magyar Hirlap,* 25 Dec.

1932e [1931] Preface to the 3rd edition of *The Interpretation of Dreams.* *S.E.* 4.

1933a [1931] *Neue Folge der Vorlesungen zur Einführung in die Psychoanalyse.* *S.E.* 22.

1933b [1932] *Why War?* *S.E.* 22.

1933c Sándor Ferenczi. *S.E.* 22.

1933d Preface to Marie Bonaparte's *The Life and Works of Edgar Allan Poe.* *S.E.* 22.

1933e [1932] Three Letters to André Breton. *Le surréalisme au service de la révolution,* 5, 10.

1933f Letter to Siegfried Hessing. In S. Hessing's *Spinoza Festschrift.* Heidelberg, 1933.

1934a [1930] Preface to the Hebrew Translation of *Introductory Lectures on Psycho-Analysis.* *S.E.* 15.

1934b [1930] Preface to the Hebrew Translation of *Totem and Taboo.* *S.E.* 13.

1935a Postscript to *An Autobiographical Study*. *S.E.* 20.

1935b The Subtleties of a Faulty Action. *S.E.* 22.

1935c Thomas Mann on His Sixtieth Birthday. *S.E.* 22.

1936a A Disturbance of Memory on the Acropolis. *S.E.* 22.

1936b [1932] Preface to Richard Sterba's *Handwörterbuch der Psychoanalyse*. *S.E.* 22.

1936c [1935] Preface to Czech edition of *Introductory Lectures on Psycho-Analysis*. Prague.

1936d Zum Ableben Professor Brauns. *Mitteilungsblatt der Verinigung jüdischer Ärtzte*, 29(6).

1937a Lou Andreas-Salomé. *S.E.* 23.

1937b Moses an Egyptian. *S.E.* 23.

1937c Analysis Terminable and Interminable. *S.E.* 23.

1937d Construction in Analysis. *S.E.* 23.

1937e If Moses Was an Egyptian. *S.E.* 23.

1938a A Comment on Anti-Semitism. *S.E.* 23.

1938b [1937] Letter to André Breton. Translation in Nicolas Cala's "Surrealist Intentions." *Transformation*, 1(49), 1950.

1938c Anti-Semitism in England. *S.E.* 23.

1939a [1934–1938] *Moses and Monotheism*. *S.E.* 23.

1939b With Anna Freud: Translation of Marie Bonaparte's *Topsy Chow-Chow au Poil d'Or*, Paris, 1937. Under the title *Topsy, der Goldhaarige Chow*. Amsterdam.

1939c (Formerly considered 1948a.) Letter to the Editors of *Das Psychoanalytische Volksbuch*. Printed in *Das Psychoanalytische Volksbuch* (3d ed.). Berne.

1940a [1938] *An Outline of Psycho-Analysis*. *S.E.* 23.

1940b [1938] Some Elementary Lessons in Psycho-Analysis. *S.E.* 23.

1940c [1922] Medusa's Head. *S.E.* 18.

1940d [1892] With J. Breuer: On the Theory of Hysterical Attacks. *S.E.* 1.

1940e [1938] Splitting of the Ego in the Process of Defense. *S.E.* 23.

1940f [1939] Letter to Mrs. Anna Freud Bernays. In Mrs. Bernay's "My Brother Sigmund Freud." *American Mercury*, Nov.

1940g [1938] Preface to Yisrael Doryon's *Lynkeus' New State*. Jerusalem.

1941a [1892] Letter to Josef Breuer. *S.E.* 1.

1941b [1892] Note 3. *S.E.* 1.

1941c [1899] A Premonitory Dream Fulfilled. *S.E.* 5.

1941d [1921] Psycho-Analysis and Telepathy. *S.E.* 18.

1941e [1926] Address to the Members of the *B'nai B'rith*. *S.E.* 20.

1941f [1938] Findings, Ideas, Problems. *S.E.* 23.

1941g [1936] Entwurf zu einem Brief an Thomas Mann. *Int. Z. Psychoan. Imago,* 26.

1941h [1939] Letter to C. Berg. In Berg's *War in the Mind.* London.

1941i [1873] Ein Jugendbrief. Included in 1960a and 1969a.

1942a [1905–1906] Psychopathic Characters on the Stage. *S.E.* 7.

1945a [1939] Foreword to J. Hobman's *David Eder.* London.

1945b [1926] Letter to M. D. Eder. In J. Hobman's *David Eder.* London.

1945c [1936] Letter to Barbara Low. In J. Hobman's *Davis Eder.* London.

1945–1946 [1938] Letter to Yisrael Doryon. In Doryon's *Der Mann Moses.* Jerusalem.

1946 [1938–1939] Two Letters to David Abrahamsen. In Abrahamsen's *The Mind and Death of a Genius.* New York.

1948 Now shown as 1939c.

1950a [1887–1902] *The Origins of Psycho-Analysis* (in part; including "A Project for a Scientific Psychology") *S.E.* 1. (See 1985b).

1950b [1936] Letter to Kurt Hiller. In Hiller's *Köpfe und Tröpfe, Profile aus einem Vierteljahrhundert.* Hamburg.

1951a [1935] A Letter on Homosexuality. *Amer. J. Psychiat.,* 107. (Included in 1960a.)

1951b [1938–1939] Six Letters to Jacob Meitlis. In Meitlis's "The Last Days of Sigmund Freud," *Jewish Frontier,* 20. Sept.

1951c [1930–1932] Two Letters to Richard Flatter. In "Queries and Notes: Sigmund Freud on Shakespeare," *Shakespeare Quarterly,* 2(4).

1952a [1938] Three Letters to Theodor Reik. *Psychoanalysis,* 1(5).

1952b [1931] Letter to Victor Bauer. In Charles Veillon's *Journal de la maison* (Lausanne), 9.

1954a [1933] Three Letters to J. Magnes. In M. Rosenbaum's "Freud-Eitingon-Magnes Correspondence, Psychoanalysis at the Hebrew University," *J. Amer. Psychoan.,* 2(2).

1954b [1929] Letter to Yivo, *News of the Yivo,* 55(9).

1954c [1934] Letter to Havelock Ellis. In J. Wortis's *Fragment of an Analysis with Freud.* New York.

1954d [1932–1935] Four Letters to J. Wortis. In Wortis's *Fragments of an Analysis with Freud.* New York.

1955a [1907–1908] Original Record of the Case of Obsessional Neurosis (the "Rat Man"). *S.E.* 10. (See 1974a.)

1955b [1906–1931] Ten Letters to Arthur Schnitzler, *Die Neue Rundschau*, 66(1).

1955c [1920] Memorandum on the Electrical Treatment of War Neurosis. *S.E.* 17.

1955d [1876] Two Applications for Grants for Biological Research. In J. Gicklhorn's "Wissenschaftsgeschichtliche Notizen zu den Studien von S. Syrski (1874) und S. Freud (1877) über männliche Flussaale," *S.B. Akad. Wiss. Wien* (Math-Naturwiss. Kl.) 1 Abt., 164(1 and 2).

1955e [1930] Letter to Juliette Boutonier. In J. Favez-Boutonier's "Psychoanalyse et philosophie," *Bull. soc. fr. philos.*, 49(3).

1955f [1909–1938] Letters and extracts from letters to Ludwig Binswanger. In Binswanger's *Sigmund Freud: Reminiscences of a Friendship*. New York, 1957.

1955–1956 [1938] Letter to Nandor Fodor. *Psychoanalysis, J. Nat. Psychol. Ass. Psychoanal.*, 4(2).

1956a [1886] Report on My Studies in Paris and Berlin, on a Travelling Bursary Granted from the University Jubilee Fund, 1885–6. *S.E.* 1.

1956b [1916] Letter to Eduard Hitschmann. *Psychoanal. Quart.*, 25.

1956c [1932–1938] Letters to Hilda Aldington (H. D.). In H. D.'s *Tribute to Freud*, New York.

1956d [1923 and 1936] Two Letters to Erich Leyens. *Psychoanal. Quart.*, 25.

1956e [1920] Letter to Wilfrid Lay. *Psychoanal. Quart.*, 25.

1956f [1933] Letter to Xavier Boveda. *Psychoanal. Quart.*, 25.

1956g [1927] Letter to Julie Braun-Vogelstein, *J. Am. Psychoanal. Ass.*, 4.

1956h [1913] Letter to A. Maeder. *Schweizerische Zeitschrift für Psychologie und ihre Anwendungen*, 15.

1956i [1926] Ein unbekannter Freud-Brief. *Aufbau*, 22(21).

1956j [1921–1937] Letter to (and from) Girindrasekhar Bose regarding Psycho-Analysis, *Samiksa, Journal of the Indian Psychoanalytical Society*, 10(2–3).

1956k [1911–1938] Letter to Theodor Reik, 1911–38. In T. Reik's *In Search Within*. New York.

1956l [1922] Letter to Silberer. *Psyche*, 10.

1956m [?] Letter to L. Szondi. *Psyche*, 10.

1956n [?] Letter to Prof. George Fuchs. *Psyche*, 10.

1953–1957 [1882–1939] Selections of letters in E. Jones's *The Life and Work of Sigmund Freud*. 3 vols. London.

1957a [1911] Now 1958.

1957b [1921] Letter to Dr. Hereward Carrington: *Psychoanalysis and the Future. J. Nat. Psychol. Ass. Psychoanal.*, 13.

1957c [1931] Letter to Immanuel Velikowsky, *Psychoanalysis and the Future. J. Nat. Psychol. Ass. Psychoanal.*, 16.

1958 [1911] With D. E. Oppenheim: *Dreams in Folklore. S.E.* 12.

1960a [1873–1939] *Letters 1873–1939.* New York.

1960b [1885] Curriculum vitae. In J. and R. Gicklhorn's *Sigmund Freuds akademische Laufbahn.* Wien.

1960c [1923] Letter to G. Stanley Hall. *Psychoanal. Quart.*, 29.

1961 [1909–1911] Letters to C. G. Jung. In Jung's *Erinnerung, Träume, Gedanken.* Frankfurt am Main.

1962 [1921] Letter to Leonard Blumgarth. In M. Wangh's *Fruition of an Idea.* New York.

1963 [1909–1939] *Psycho-Analysis and Faith. The Letters of Sigmund Freud and Oskar Pfister.* New York.

1964 [1918–1939] Letters to Ernest Simmel. *J. Amer. Psychoanal. Ass.*, 12(1).

1965a [1907–1926] *A Psycho-Analytic Dialogue. The Letters of Sigmund Freud and Karl Abraham.* New York.

1965b [1871–1910] Letter to Eduard Silberstein. *Neue Literatur, Zeitschrift des Schriftstellerverbands der R.V.R.*, 16(3).

1965c [1910–1912] Letter to Eugen Bleuler. Freud-Bleuler Correspondence, *Archives of General Psychiatry*, 12.

1965d [1918] Letter to Hermann Hesse. *Jahrbuch der Deutschen Schillergesellschaft*, 9.

1965e [1930] The Freud-Janet Controversy: An Unpublished Letter. *British Medical Journal*, 5426.

1966a [1912–1936] *Sigmund Freud and Lou Andreas-Salomé: Letters.* London, 1972.

1966b [1938] Introduction to S. Freud and W. C. Bullitt: *Thomas Woodrow Wilson, Twenty-Eighth President of the United States: A Psychological Study, Encounter*, 28(1).

1966c [1920–1934] Letters to Edoardo Weiss. *Psychoanalytic Forum* 1966.

1967 [1928] Letter to Lytton Strachey. *Almanach: Das einundachzigste Jahr.* Frankfurth am Main.

1968a [1927–1939] *The Letters of Sigmund Freud and Arnold Zweig.* New York, 1987.

1968b [1909] American Interview. *The Psychoanalytic Review,* 55(3).

1968c [1938] Letter to Herman M. Serota. *Bulletin of the Philadelphia Association for Psychoanalysis,* 18(1).

1969a [1872–1874] Seven Letters and Two Postcards to Emil Fluss. *Int. J. Psycho.-Anal.,* 50.

1970a [1919–1936] *Sigmund Freud as a Consultant: Recollections of a Pioneer in Psychoanalysis.* Ed. M. Grotjan. New York.

1970b [1917–1934] Letters to George Groddeck. In Groddeck's *Der Mensch und sein Es.* Wiesbaden.

1971a [1909–1911] Letter to James J. Putnam. In *James Jackson Putnam and Psychoanalysis: Letters between Putnam and Sigmund Freud, Ernest Jones, William James, Sandor Ferenczi and Morton Prince, 1877–1917.* Cambridge.

1971b [1883] Letter to Martha Bernays. *J. Amer. Psychoanal. Ass.,* 19(2).

1974a [1907–1908] *L'Homme aux rats. Journal d'une analyse.* Paris. (French-German complete edition of Freud's record of the case of the "Rat Man." See 1955a).

1974b [1906–1923] Letters between Freud and Jung. *Letters.* Princeton.

1980 [1933] Letter to Sigurd Naesgaard. *Scandinavian Psychoanalytic Review.*

1985a [1915] *Übersicht der Übertragungsneurosen. Ein bisher unbekanntes Manuskript.* Frankfurt am Main.

1985b [1887–1904] *The Complete Letters of Sigmund Freud to Wilhelm Fliess 1887–1904.* Ed. J. M. Masson. (not including "A Project for a Scientific Psychology"; see 1950a).

1987 [1927–1939] *The Letters of Sigmund Freud and Arnold Zweig.* Ed. E. Freud. New York

3.

BIBLIOGRAPHY
OF SECONDARY LITERATURE

This bibliography contains authors other than Freud. The date following a title is, as is the case in the Freud bibliography, the date of the first publication of the article or book, although we cannot guarantee this always to be the case. When a new and altered edition of a work has been published, we sometimes use its date of publication as if it were an entirely new work. In cases where the edition used is not the first one, the date of publication is written after the place of publication. We have attempted to find English and American translations of German and French titles for this edition. When this has not been possible, we have cited the original titles.

Abraham, K. (1908). The Psychosexual Differences between Hysteria and Dementia Praecox. *Selected Papers*. London: Hogarth Press, 1965.

Abraham, K. (1921). Manifestations of the Female Castration Complex. *Selected Papers*. London: Hogarth Press, 1965.

Abraham, K. (1924). A Short History of the Development of the Libido. *Selected Papers*. London: Hogarth Press, 1965.

Ackerknecht, E. H. (1957). *A Short History of Psychiatry*. New York: Harper and Row, 1968.

Adler, A. (1929). *Individual Psychology*. New York: Humanities Press.

Alexander, M.; Eisenstein, S.; and Grotjahn, M. (eds.) (1966). *Psychoanalytic Pioneers*. New York: Basic Books.

Althusser, L. (1970). Ideology and Ideological State Apparatuses. *Lenin and Philosophy and Other Essays*. New York: Monthly Review Press, 1971.

Althusser, L. (1974). *Philosophie et philosophie spontanée des savants*. Paris: François Maspero.

Amacher, P. (1965). *Freud's Neurological Education and Its Influence on Psychoanalytic Theory*. New York: International Universities Press.

Andersen, H. C. (1845). *The Snow Queen*. Harmondsworth: Penguin Books, 1981.

Andersson, O. (1962). *Studies in the Prehistory of Psychoanalysis*. Stockholm: Norsteds.

Andkjær Olsen, O., and Køppe, S. (1986). Problems in Freud's Metapsychology. *Scandinavian Journal of Psychology, 27*.

Andkjær Olsen, O., and Køppe, S. (1987). Some Developments in the History of the Concept of Narcissism. *Psychoanalysis and Contemporary Thought, 10*.

Anzieu, D. (1959). *L'auto-analyse de Freud et la découverte de la psychanalyse*. Paris: Presses Universitaires de France, 1975.

Apel, K. O. (1968). Szientistik, Hermenutik, Ideologiekritik. *Wiener Jahrbuch für Philosophie*, bd. I.

Ariès, P. (1960). *Centuries of Childhood*. London: Penguin Books, 1973.

Arlow, J., and Brenner, C. (1964). *Psychoanalytic Concepts and the Structural Theory*. New York: International Universities Press, 1973.

Ayala, F. J., and Dobzhansky, T. (1974). *Studies in the Philosophy of Biology*. Berkeley: University of California Press.

Bang, H. (1886). *Am Wege*. Berlin: G. Fischer, 1910.

Barea, I. (1966). *Vienna. Legend and Reality*. London: Secker and Warburg.

Barker, L. F. (1899). *The Nervous System and Its Constituent Neurones*. New York: D. Appleton.

Baros, C. P. (1971). Thermodynamic and Evolutionary Concepts in the Formal Structure of Freud's Metapsychology. In S. Arieti (ed.). *The World Biennial of Psychiatry and Psychotherapy*. New York: Basic Books.

Bastian, H. C. (1880). *The Brain as Organ of Mind*. London: C. Kegan Paul.

Baumeyer, F. (1955). Der Fall Schreber. *Psyche, 9*.

Beard, G. M. (1869). Neurasthenia or Nervous Exhaustion. *Medical and Surgical Journal, 3*.

Beard, G. M. (1905). *Sexual Neurasthenia*. New York: Treat.

Bernal, J. D. (1954). *Science in History*. Vols. 1–4. London: Pelican Books, 1969.

Bernfeld, S. (1944). Freud's Earliest Theories and the Schools of Helmholtz. *Psychoanalytic Quarterly, 13*.

Bernfeld, S. (1946). An Unknown Autobiographical Fragment by Freud. *The American Imago,* 4.

Bernfeld, S. (1953). Freud's Studies on Cocaine 1884–1887. *International Journal of Psycho-Analysis,* 34.

Bernheim, H. (1888). *Die Suggestion und ihre Heilwirkung.* Wien: Franz Deuticke.

Bernheim, H. (1891). *Neue Studien über Hypnotismus, Suggestion und Psychotherapie.* Wien: Franz Deuticke, 1892.

Binswanger, L. (1936). S. Freud und die Verfassung der klinischen Psychiatrie. *Schweizer Archiv für Neurologie und Psychiatrie,* 37.

Bock, P. K. (1980). *Continuities in Psychological Anthropology.* San Francisco: W. H. Freeman and Company.

Bon, G. le (1895). *Psychologie des foules.* Paris: F. Alcan, 1907.

Boring, E. G. (1950). *A History of Experimental Psychology.* New York: Appleton-Century-Crafts.

Bowler, P. J. (1984). *Evolution. The History of an Idea.* Berkeley: University of California Press.

Brandes, G. (1872–1890). *Main Currents in 19th Century Literature.* New York: Macmillan, 1901–1905.

Brandes, G. (1886). *Creative Spirits of the 19th Century.* New York: Thomas Y. Crowell, 1923.

Braudel, F. (1979). *Civilization and Capitalism. 15th–18th Century.* Vols. 1–3. London: Fontana Press.

Brenner, C. (1982). *The Mind in Conflict.* New York: IUP, 1983.

Broca, P. (1861). Remarks on the Seat of the Faculty of Articulate Language Followed by an Observation of Aphemia. E. G. Bonin (ed.). *Some Papers on the Cerebral Cortes.* Springfield: Charles C. Thomas.

Brome, V. (1967). *Freud and His Early Circle.* London: Heinemann.

Brückner, P. (1975). *Sigmund Freuds Privatlektüre.* Köln: Verlag Rolf Horst.

Brun, R. (1936). Sigmund Freuds Leistungen auf den Gebiete der organischen Neurologie und Psychiatrie. *Schweizer Archiv für Neurologie und Psychiatrie,* 37.

Brunswick, R. M. (1928). A Supplement to Freud's History of an Infantile Neurosis. *International Journal of Psycho-Analysis,* 9.

Brunswick, R. M. (1940). The Pre-Oedipal Phase of the Libido Development. *Psychoanalytic Quarterly,* 9.

Byck, R. (ed.) (1974). *Cocaine Papers by Sigmund Freud.* New York: Stonehill.

Cannon, W. B. (1929). Organization for Physiological Homeostasis. *Physiological Review*, 9.

Carroll, M. D. (1966). General Systems Theory and Psychoanalysis. *Psychoanalytic Quarterly*, 35.

Castel, R. (1976). *L'ordre psychiatrique*. Paris: Les Éditions de Minuit.

Chabot, C. B. (1982). *Freud on Schreber*. Amherst, Mass.: University of Massachusetts Press.

Charcot, J.-M. (1886). *Neue Vorlesungen über die Krankheiten des Nervensystems insbesondere über Hysterie*. Wien: Franz Deuticke.

Charcot, J.-M. (1888). *Poliklinische Vorträge I*. Wien: Franz Deuticke, 1892.

Chasseguet-Smirgel, J. (ed.) (1964). *Female Sexuality*. Ann Arbor: University of Michigan Press, 1970.

Chertok, L., and Saussure, R. de (1973). *The Therapeutic Revolution: From Mesmer to Freud*. New York: Brunner/Mazel, 1979.

Cohen, I. H. (1982). *Ideology and Unconsciousness*. New York: New York University Press.

Colby, K. M. (1955). *Energy and Structure in Psychoanalysis*. New York: Ronald Press.

Cranefield, P. F. (1958). J. Breuer's Evaluation of His Contribution to Psycho-Analysis. *International Journal of Psycho-Analysis*, 39.

Dahmer, H. (1973). *Libido und Gesellschaft*. Frankfurt am Main: Suhrkamp.

Darwin, C. (1859). *On the Origin of Species*. Cambridge, Mass.: Harvard University Press, 1976.

Darwin, C. (1871). *The Descent of Man I-II*. New York: American Home, 1902.

Darwin, C. (1872). *The Expression of the Emotions in Man and Animals*. Chicago: University of Chicago Press, 1974.

Derrida, J. (1966). Freud et la scène de l'écriture. *L'écriture et la différence*. Paris: Éditions du Seuil, 1967.

Descartes, R. (1641). *Meditations on First Philosophy*. Cambridge: Cambridge University Press, 1986.

Deutsch, F. (1957). A Footnote to Freud's "Fragment of an Analysis of a Case of Hysteria." *Psychoanalytic Quarterly*, 26.

Deutsch, H. (1925). The Psychology of Woman in Relation to the Functions of Reproduction. *International Journal of Psycho-Analysis*, 6.

d'Irsay, S. (1928). Der philosophische Hintergrund der Nervenphysiologie im 17. und 18. Jahrhundert. *Archiv für Geschichte der Medizin*, 20.

Donelly, M. (1983). *Managing the Mind*. London: Tavistock.

Donzelot, J. (1977). *The Policing of Families*. New York: Pantheon Books, 1979.

Dorer, M. (1932). *Historische Grundlagen der Psychoanalyse*. Leipzig: Felix Meiner.

Dörner, K. (1969). *Bürger und Irre*. Frankfurt am Main: Europäische Verlagsanstalt.

Drinka, G. F. (1984). *The Birth of Neuroses*. New York: Simon and Schuster.

DSM-III *Diagnostic and Statistical Manual of Mental Disorders [Third Edition]*. Washington: American Psychiatric Association, 1980.

du Bois-Reymond, E. (1848). *Untersuchungen über Thierische Elektricität*. Berlin: G. Reimer.

du Bois-Reymond, E. (1872). *Über die Grenzen des Naturerkennens*. Leipzig: Veit, 1882.

du Bois-Reymond, E. (1880). *Die Sieben Welträtsel*. Leipzig: Veit, 1882.

Eissler, K. R. (1964). *Medical Orthodoxy and the Future of Psychoanalysis*. New York: International Universities Press.

Eissler, K. R. (1966). *S. Freud und die Wiener Universität*. Bern: Hans Huber.

Elias, N. (1978). *The Civilizing Process*. New York: Urizen Books.

Elkana, Y. (1974). *The Discovery of the Conversation of Energy*. London: Hutchinson.

Ellenberger, H. F. (1956). Fechner and Freud. *Bulletin of the Menninger Clinic*, 20.

Ellenberger, H. F. (1957). The Unconscious before Freud. *Bulletin of the Menninger Clinic*, 21.

Ellenberger, H. F. (1970). *The Discovery of the Unconscious*. New York: Basic Books.

Emminghaus, H. (1878). *Allgemeine Psychopathologie zur Einführung in das Studium der Geistesstörungen*. Leipzig: F. C. W. Vogel.

Endrass, G. (1975). *Zur Geschichte und Systematik von Qualität und Quantität in Freuds Metapsychologie*. Basel: Clausthal-Zellerfeld.

Erikson, E. H. (1950). *Childhood and Society*. Harmondsworth: Penguin Books, 1975.

Erikson, E. H. (1954). The Dream Specimen of Psychoanalysis. *Journal of the American Psychoanalytic Association*, 2.

Exner, S. (1894). *Entwurf zu einer physiologischen Erklärung der psychischen Erscheinungen*. Wien: Franz Deuticke.

Fearing, F. (1930). *Reflex Action*. London: M. I. T. Press 1970.

Fechner, G. T. (1846). *Über das höchste Gut*. Leipzig: Breitkopf und Härtel.

Fechner, G. T. (1848). Über das Lustprinzip des Handelns. *Zeitschrift für Philosophie und philosophischen Kritik.*

Fechner, G. T. (1860). *Elemente der Psychophysik.* Leipzig: Breitkopf und Härtel, 1907.

Fechner, G. T. (1873). *Einige Ideen zur Schöpfungs- und Entwicklungsgeschichte der Organismen.* Leipzig: Breitkopf und Härtel.

Fechner, G. T. (1879). *Die Tagesansicht gegenüber der Nachtansicht.* Leipzig: Breitkopf und Härtel.

Federn, P. (1929). Das Ich als Subjekt und Objekt im Narzissmus. *Internationale Zeitschrift für Psychoanalyse,* 15.

Fenichel, O. (1925). Introjection and the Castration Complex. *The Collected Papers of Otto Fenichel 1.* New York: Norton, 1953.

Fenichel, O. (1926). Identification. *The Collected Papers of Otto Fenichel 1.* New York: Norton, 1953.

Fenichel, O. (1945). *The Psychoanalytic Theory of Neurosis.* New York: Norton.

Ferenczi, S. (1909). Introjection and Transference. *Sex in Psycho-Analysis.* New York: Basic Books, 1950.

Ferenczi, S. (1914). On the Nosology of Male Homosexuality. *Further Contributions to the Theory and Technique of Psychoanalysis.* London: Hogarth Press, 1926.

Ferenczi, S. (1924). *Thalassa: A Theory of Genitality.* New York: Norton, 1968.

Fischer-Homberger, E. (1970). *Hypochondrie.* Bern: Hans Huber.

Fischer-Homberger, E. (1975). *Die traumatische Neurose.* Bern: Hans Huber.

Flandrin, J.-L. (1976). *Families in Former Times.* Cambridge: Cambridge University Press, 1980.

Flaubert, G. (1857). *Madame Bovary.* New York: Modern Library, 1982.

Fliess, R. (ed.) (1950). *The Psychoanalytic Reader.* New York: International Universities Press, 1973.

Foucault, M. (1961). *Madness and Civilization.* London: Tavistock, 1971.

Foucault, M. (1975). *Discipline and Punish.* Harmondsworth: Penguin Books.

Foucault, M. (1976). *The History of Sexuality.* Vol. 1. London: Allan Lane, 1978.

Freud, A. (1936). *The Ego and the Mechanisms of Defence.* London: Hogarth Press, 1976.

Freud, E., et al. (1976). *Sigmund Freud: His Life in Pictures and Words.* New York: Norton, 1985.

Fromm, E. (1951). *The Forgotten Language.* London: Victor Gollancz, 1952.

Fromm, E. (1966). The Oedipus Complex: Comments on the Case of Little Hans. *The Crisis of Psychoanalysis.* Harmondsworth: Penguin Books, 1973.

Gardiner, M. (ed.) (1971). *The Wolf-Man.* New York: Basic Books.

Gedo, J. E., and Pollock, G. H. (eds.) (1976). *Freud: The Fusion of Science and Humanism.* New York: International Universities Press.

Gicklhorn, J., and Gicklhorn, R. (1960). *S. Freuds akademische Laufbahn im Lichte der Dokumente.* Wien: Urban und Schwarzenberg.

Gill, M. M. (1963). *Topography and Systems in Psychoanalytic Theory.* New York: International Universities Press.

Gill, M. M. (1976). Metapsychology Is Not Psychology. In M. M. Gill and P. S. Holzman (eds.). *Psychology versus Metapsychology.* New York: International Universities Press.

Gill, M. M., and Holzman, P. S. (eds.) (1976). *Psychology versus Metapsychology.* New York: International Universities Press.

Glover, E. (1932). A Psycho-Analytical Approach to the Classification of Mental Disorders. In *On the Early Development of Mind.* New York: International Universities Press.

Glover, E. (1955). *The Technique of Psycho-Analysis.* New York: International Universities Press.

Goncourt, E. de, and Goncourt, J. de (1865). *Germinie Lacerteux.*

Gould, S. J. (1977). *Ontogeny and Phylogeny.* Cambridge: Belknap Press of Harvard University Press.

Gray, M. (1978). *Neurosis.* New York: Van Nostrand Reinhold.

Green, A. (1973). *Le discours vivant. La conception psychanalytique de l'affect.* Paris: Presses Universitaires de France.

Green, A. (1977). Conceptions of Affect. *International Journal of Psycho-Analysis, 58.*

Greenson, R. R. (1967). *The Technique and Practice of Psychoanalysis.* London: Hogarth Press, 1981.

Griesinger, W. (1843). Ueber psychische Reflexactionen. *Gesammelte Abhandlungen I.* Berlin: August Hirschwald, 1872.

Griesinger, W. (1845). *Die Pathologie und Therapie der psychischen Krankheiten.* Braunschweig: Friedrich Wreden, 1871.

Grinstein, A. (1956–1975). *The Index of Psychoanalytic Writings*. Vols. 1–14. New York: International Universities Press.

Grinstein, A. (1968). *On Sigmund Freud's Dreams*. New York: International Universities Press, 1980.

Grünbaum, A. (1984). *The Foundations of Psychoanalysis*. Berkeley: University of California Press.

Guttman, S. A., Parrish, S. M., and Jones, R. L. (eds.) (1980). *The Concordance to The Standard Edition of The Complete Psychological Works of Sigmund Freud*. Vols. 1–6. Boston: G. K. Hall.

Habermas, J. (1962). *Strukturwandel der Öffentlichkeit*. Darmstadt: Luchterhand, 1978.

Habermas, J. (1968). *Knowledge and Human Interests*. Boston: Beacon Press, 1971.

Haeckel, E. (1889). *The History of Creation*. London: Kegan Paul, 1892.

Hall, T. (1969). *Ideas of Life and Matter*. Chicago: University of Chicago Press.

Hartmann, E. von (1868). *Philosophy of the Unconscious*. London: Trübner, 1884.

Hartmann, H. (1939). *Ego Psychology and the Problem of Adaptation*. New York: International Universities Press, 1975.

Hartmann, H. (1964). *Essays on Ego Psychology*. New York: International Universities Press, 1973.

Hartmann, H.; Kris, E.; and Loewenstein, R. M. (1964). *Papers on Psychoanalytic Psychology*. New York: International Universities Press, 1977.

Hauser, A. (1951). *The Social History of Art*. London: Routledge and Kegan Paul, 1962.

Heimann, P. (1952). Certain Functions of Introjection and Projection in Early Infancy. J. Riviere (ed.). *Developments in Psycho-Analysis*. London: Hogarth Press, 1973.

Helmholtz, H. von (1854). *Über die Wechselwirkung der Naturkräfte*. Königsberg: Gräfe und Unzer.

Helmholtz, H. von (1878). Die Thatsachen in der Wahrnehmung. *Vorträge und Reden*. Vol. 2. Braunschweig: Friedrich Vieweg, 1884.

Herbart, J. F. (1816). *Lehrbuch zur Psychologie*. Leipzig: August Wilhelm Unzer.

Herbart, J. F. (1824–1825). *Psychologie als Wissenschaft neu gegründet*. Leipzig: August Wilhelm Unzer.

Hering, E. (1880). *Über das Gedächtnis*. Leipzig: Wilhelm Engelmann.

Hirschmüller, A. (1978). *Physiologie und Psychoanalyse in Leben und Werk J. Breuers*. Bern: Hans Huber.

Hobbes, T. (1650). *Human Nature or the Fundamental Elements of Policy*. Selected parts in *Body, Man, and Citizen*. New York: Collier Books, 1967.

Hoffmann, E. T. A. (1813–1816). *The Devil's Elixirs*. London: Calder and Boyars, 1963.

Hoffmann, E. T. A. (1817). *The Sandman*. In *Selected Writings of E. T. A. Hoffman*, Volume I. Leonard J. Kent and Elizabeth C. Knight (eds. and trans.). Chicago: University of Chicago Press, 1969.

Holmes, F. L. (1963). The Milieu Interieur and the Cell Theory. *Bulletin of the History of Medicine*, 37.

Holt, R. R. (1962). A Critical Examination of Freud's Concept of Bound vs. Free Cathexis. *Journal of the American Psychoanalytic Association*, 10.

Holt, R. R. (1967). Beyond Vitalism and Mechanism: Freud's Concept of Psychic Energy. *Science and Psychoanalysis*, 11.

Holt, R. R. (1972). Freud's Mechanistic and Humanistic Images of Man. *Psychoanalysis and Contemporary Thought*, 1.

Home, R. W. (1970). Electricity and the Nervous Fluid. *Journal of the History of Biology*, 3.

Horkheimer, M. (1936). Allgemeiner Teil. In M. Horkheimer (ed.). *Studien über Autorität und Familie*. Paris: Librairie Félix Alcan.

Horney, K. (1923). On the Genesis of the Castration Complex in Women. *Feminine Psychology*. New York: Norton, 1973.

Horney, K. (1926). The Flight from Womanhood. *Feminine Psychology*. New York: Norton, 1973.

Horney, K. (1932). The Dread of Woman. *Feminine Psychology*. New York: Norton, 1973.

Horney, K. (1933). The Denial of the Vagina. *Feminine Psychology*. New York: Norton, 1973.

Horowitz, G. (1977). *Repression: Basic and Surplus Repression in Psychoanalytic Theory*. Toronto: University of Toronto Press.

Hunt, D. (1970). *Parents and Children in History*. New York: Basic Books.

Hunter, R. A., and MacAlpine, I. (1963). *Three Hundred Years of Psychiatry 1535–1860*. London: Oxford University Press.

Ibsen, H. (1894). *Little Eyolf*. Harmondsworth: Penguin Classics, 1950.

Ibsen, H. (1877). *Pillars of Society*. Harmondsworth: Penguin Classics, 1950.

Ibsen, H. (1879). *A Doll's House*. Harmondsworth: Penguin Classics, 1950.

Ibsen, H. (1881). *Ghosts*. Harmondsworth: Penguin Classics, 1950.

Ibsen, H. (1882). *An Enemy of the People*. Harmondsworth: Penguin Classics, 1950.

Ibsen, H. (1884). *The Wild Duck*. Harmondsworth: Penguin Classics, 1950.

Ibsen, H. (1886). *Rosmersholm*. Harmondsworth: Penguin Classics, 1950.

Ibsen, H. (1888). *The Lady from the Sea*. Harmondsworth: Penguin Classics, 1950.

Institoris, H., and Sprenger, J. (1485). *Malleus Maleficarum*. London: John Rodker, 1928.

Isaacs, S. (1948). The Nature and Function of Phantasy. In J. Riviere (ed.). *Developments in Psycho-Analysis*. London: Hogarth Press, 1973.

Jackson, J. H. (1879–1880). On Affections of Speech from Disease of the Brain. *Brain*, 1–2.

Jackson, J. H. (1882). On some Implications of Dissolution of the Nervous System. *Selected Writings*. Vol. 2. New York: Basic Books, 1958.

Jackson, J. H. (1884). Evolution and Dissolution of the Nervous System. *Selected Writings*. Vol. 2. New York: Basic Books, 1958.

Jacobsen, J. P. (1876). *Marie Grubbe*. New York: Twayne American-Scandinavian Foundation, 1975.

Jacobsen, J. P. (1880). *Niels Lyhne*. New York: Twayne American-Scandinavian Foundation, 1967.

Jacobson, E. (1953). The Affects and Their Pleasure-Unpleasure Qualities in Relation to the Psychic Discharge Processes. In R. M. Loewenstein (ed.). *Drives, Affects, Behavior*. New York: International Universities Press.

Jacoby, R. (1975). *Social Amnesia*. Boston: Beacon Press.

Jacoby, R. (1983). *The Repression of Psychoanalysis*. New York: Basic Books.

Jaeger, S., and Staeuble, I. (1978). *Die gesellschaftliche Genese der Psychologie*. Frankfurt am Main: Campus.

Jappe, G. (1971). *Über Wort und Sprache in der Psychoanalyse*. Frankfurt am Main: S. Fischer.

Jaroschewski, M. (1975). *Psychologie im 20. Jahrhundert*. Berlin: Volkseigener Verlag.

Jaspers, K. (1948). *Allgemeine Psychopathologie*. Berlin: Springer.

Jekels, L. (1913). Einige Bemerkungen zur Trieblehre. *Internationale Zeitschrift für ärztliche Psychoanalyse*, 1.

Jeliffe, S. E. (1937). Sigmund Freud as a Neurologist. *Journal of Nervous and Mental Disease*, 85.

Jones, E. (1916). The Theory of Symbolism. *Papers on Psycho-Analysis*. London: Maresfield Reprints, 1977.

Jones, E. (1927). The Early Development of Female Sexuality. *Papers on Psycho-Analysis*. London: Maresfield Reprints, 1977.

Jones, E. (1933). The Phallic Phase. *Papers on Psycho-Analysis*. London: Maresfield Reprints.

Jones, E. (1953). *Sigmund Freud. Life and Work I. The Young Freud 1856–1900*. London: Hogarth Press, 1972.

Jones, E. (1955). *Sigmund Freud. Life and Work II. Years of Maturity 1901–1919*. London: Hogarth Press, 1974.

Jones, E. (1957). *Sigmund Freud. Life and Work III. The Last Phase 1919–1939*. London: Hogarth Press, 1974.

Jung, C. G. (1911). *Symbols of Transformation*. New York: Pantheon, 1956.

Jung, C. G. (1958). *Psyche and Symbol*. New York: Doubleday.

Kanzer, M., and Glenn, J. (eds.) (1979). *Freud and His Self-Analysis*. New York: Jason Aronson.

Kanzer, M., and Glenn, J. (eds.). (1980). *Freud and His Patients*. New York: Jason Aronson.

Kierkegaard, S. (1843). *Repetition*. (With: *Fear and Trembling*). Princeton: Princeton University Press, 1983.

Kirchoff, T. (1892). *Lehrbuch der Psychiatrie für Studierende und Aerzte*. Leipzig: S. Hirzel.

Klein, G. S. (1976). *Psychoanalytic Theory*. New York: International Universities Press.

Klein, M. (1928). Early Stages of the Oedipus Conflict. *The Writings of Melanie Klein*. Vol. 1. London: Hogarth Press, 1975.

Klein, M. (1932). *The Psycho-Analysis of Children*. London: Hogarth Press, 1975.

Klein, M. (1955). On Identification. In *The Writings of Melanie Klein*. Vol. 3. London: Hogarth Press, 1975.

Kolle, K. (1956–1963). *Grosse Nervenärzte*. Vols. 1–3. Stuttgart: George Thieme Verlag.

Køppe, S. (1983). The Psychology of the Neuron: Freud, Cajal and Golgi. *Scandinavian Journal of Psychology*, 24.

Kraepelin, E. (1892). *Ueber die Beeinflussung einfacher psychischer Vorgänge*. Jena: Ambr. Abel.

Kraepelin, E. (1918). *Hundert Jahre Psychiatrie*. Berlin: Julius Springer.

Krafft-Ebing, R. von (1879). *Text-Book of Insanity, Based on Clinical Observations*. Philadelphia: F. A. Davis.

Krafft-Ebing, R. von (1889). *Psychopathia Sexualis, with Especial Reference to Antipathic Sexual Instinct: A Medico-Forensich Study*. London: Rebman.

Krafft-Ebing, R. von (1895). *Nervosität und Neurasthenische Zustände*. Wien: Alfred Hölder.

Krafft-Ebing, R. von (1897–1899). *Arbeiten aus dem Gesammtgebiet der Psychiatrie und Neuro-Pathologie*. Vols. 1–4. Leipzig: J. A. Barth.

Kubie, L. S. (1947). The Fallacious Use of Quantitative Concepts in Dynamic Psychology. *Psychoanalytic Quarterly,* 16.

Kubie, L. S. (1953). Some Implications for Psychoanalysis of Modern Concepts of the Organization of the Brain. *Psychoanalytic Quarterly,* 22.

Kuhn, T. S. (1962). *The Structure of Scientific Revolutions*. Chicago: University of Chicago Press.

Lacan, J. (1952). Intervention on Transference. In J. Mitchell and J. Rose (eds.). *Feminine Sexuality*. London: Macmillan Press, 1982.

le Bon, G. *See* Bon, G. le.

Lacan, J. (1956). Réponse au commentaire de Jean Hyppolite sur la "Verneinung" de Freud. In *Ecrits*. Paris: Éditions du Seuil, 1966.

Lacan, J. (1957a). Le séminaire sur "La Lettre volée." In *Ecrits*. Paris: Éditions du Seuil, 1966.

Lacan, J. (1957b). The Agency of the Letter in the Unconscious. In *Ecrits: A Selection*. London: Tavistock, 1977.

Lacan, J. (1959). On a Question Preliminary to any Possible Treatment of Psychosis. In *Ecrits: A Selection*. London: Tavistock, 1977.

Lacan, J. (1973). *The Four Fundamental Concepts of Psycho-Analysis*. Harmondsworth: Penguin Books, 1979.

Lacan, J. (1975a). *Le séminaire, livre I. Les écrits techniques de Freud*. Paris: Éditions du Seuil.

Lacan, J. (1975b). *Le séminaire, livre XX. Encore*. Paris: Éditions du Seuil.

Lacan, J. (1978). *Le séminaire, livre II. Le moi dans la théorie de Freud et dans la technique de la psychanalyse*. Paris: Éditions du Seuil.

Lampl-de Groot, J. (1927). The Evolution of the Oedipus Complex in Women. *International Journal of Psycho-Analysis*, 9, 1928.

Lampl-de Groot, J. (1933). Problems of Femininity. *Psychoanalytic Quarterly*, 2.

Laplanche, J. (1970). *Life and Death in Psychoanalysis*. London: Johns Hopkins University Press, 1979.

Laplanche, J. (1980a). *Problématiques I. L'angoisse*. Paris: Presses Universitaires de France.

Laplanche, J. (1980b). *Problématiques II. Castration—Symbolisations*. Paris: Presses Universitaires de France.

Laplanche, J. (1980c). *Problématiques III. La sublimation*. Paris: Presses Universitaires de France.

Laplanche, J. (1981). *Problématiques IV. L'inconscient et le ça*. Paris: Presses Universitaires de France.

Laplanche, J., and Leclaire, S. (1961). L'inconscient, une étude psychanalytique. In J. Laplanche: *Problématiques IV*. Presses Universitaires de France 1981.

Laplanche, J., and Pontalis, J.-B. (1964). Fantasme originaire, fantasme des origines, origine du fantasme. *Les temps modernes,* 215.

Laplanche, J., and Pontalis, J.-B. (1967). *The Language of Psychoanalysis*. New York: Norton, 1973.

Laughlin, H. P. (1967). *The Neuroses*. Washington: Butterworths.

Lecourt, D. (1973). *Une crise et son enjeu*. Paris: François Maspero.

Lesky, E. (1965). *Die wiener medizinische Schule im 19. Jahrhundert*. Graz: Herman Bühlaus Nachf.

Levin, K. (1978). *Freud's Early Psychology of the Neuroses: A Historical Perspective*. Pittsburgh: University of Pittsburgh Press.

Lichtman, R. (1982). The Production of Desire. New York: The Free Press.

Liddell, E. G. T. (1960). *The Discovery of the Reflexes*. Oxford: Clarendon Press.

Loch, W., and Jappe, G. (1974). Die Konstruktion der Wirklichkeit und die Phantasien. *Psyche,* 28.

Locke, J. (1690). *An Essay Concerning Human Understanding*. London: J. M. Dent and Sons, 1972.

Loewenstein, R. M. (1935). Phallic Passivity in Men. *International Journal of Psycho-Analysis,* 16.

Lorenzer, A. (1970). *Sprachzerstörung und Rekonstruktion*. Frankfurt am Main: Suhrkamp.

Lorenzer, A. (1972). *Zur Begründung einer materialistischen Sozialisationstheorie*. Frankfurt am Main: Suhrkamp, 1973.

Lorenzer, A. (1974). *Die Wahrheit der psychoanalytischen Erkenntnis*. Frankfurt am Main: Suhrkamp, 1976.

Lotze, R. H. (1844). Instinct. In R. Wagner (ed.). *Handwörterbuch der Physiologie*. Vol. 2. Braunschweig: Friedrich Vieweg.

Lotze, R. H. (1852). *Medicinische Psychologie*. Leipzig: Weidmann'sche Buchhandlung.

Lukacs, G. (1923). *Geschichte und Klassenbewusstsein*. Berlin: Halensee.

Madsen, K. B. (1987). *A History of Psychology in Metascientific Perspective*. Amsterdam: North Holland.

Maienschein, J. (1978). Cell Lineage, Ancestral Reminiscence and the Biogenetic Law. *Journal of the History of Biology*, 11.

Marcus, S. (1974). Freud and Dora: Story, History, Case History. *Representations*. New York: Random House, 1976.

Marx, E. (1937–1938). Die Entstehung der Reflexlehre seit A. von Heller bis in die zweite Hälfte des 19. Jahrhundert. *Sitzungsberichte der Heidelberger Akademie der Wissenschaften*, 73.

Marx, K. (1867–1894). *Capital*. New York: International Publishers, 1972.

Marx, K., and Engels, F. (1848). *The Communist Manifesto*. New York: Washington Square Press, 1965.

Marx, O. (1966). Aphasia Studies and the Language Theory in the 19th Century. *Bulletin of the History of Medicine*, 40.

Marx, O. (1967). Freud and Aphasia. American Journal of Psychiatry, 124.

Masson, J. M. (1984). *The Assault on Truth. Freud's Suppression of the Seduction Theory*. New York: Farrar, Straus and Giroux.

McDougall, W. (1920). *The Group Mind*. New York: Putnam.

Mendelsohn, E. (1963). Cell Theory and the Development of General Physiology. *Archives international d'histoire des sciences*, 16.

Mendelsohn, E. (1964). The Biological Sciences in the Nineteenth Century: Some Problems and Sources. *History of Science*, 3.

Mendelsohn, E. (1965). Physical Models and Physiological Concepts: Explanation in Nineteenth-Century Biology. *The British Journal for the History of Science*, 2.

Meynert, T. (1869). *Der Bau der Gross-Hirnrinde*. Leipzig: J. H. Heuser.

Meynert, T. (1884). *Psychiatrie. Klinik der Erkrankungen des Vorderhirns*. Wien: Wilhelm Braumüller.

Meynert, T. (1887). Mechanik der Physionomik. *Sammlung von populärwissenschaftliche Vorträge über den Bau und die Leistungen des Gehirns*. Wien: Wilhelm Braumüller.

Mitchell, J. (1974). *Psychoanalysis and Feminism*. Harmondsworth: Penguin Books, 1975.

Möbius, P. J. (1894–1898). *Neurologische Beiträge*. Vols. 1–5. Leipzig: Ambr. Abel (Arthur Meiner).

Müller, J. (1826). *Zur vergleichenden Physiologie des Gesichtssinnes des Menschen und der Thiere*. Leipzig: G. Gnobloch.

Müller, J. (1834–1840). *Handbuch der Physiologie des Menschen*. Coblenz: J. Hölscher.

Nassif, J. (1977). *Freud—l'inconscient. Sur les commencements de la psychanalyse*. Paris: Éditions Galilée.

Niederland, W. G. (1974). *The Schreber Case*. New York: New York Times Book.

Nunberg, H., and Federn, E. (eds.) (1962–1975). *Minutes of the Vienna Psychoanalytic Society*. Vols. 1–4. New York: International Universities Press.

Obholzer, K. (1980). *The Wolf-Man: Conversations with Freud's Patient: Sixty Years Later*. New York: Continuum, 1982.

Peterfreund, E., and Schwartz, J. T. (1971). *Information, Systems and Psychoanalysis*. New York: International Universities Press.

Pickstone, J. V. (1976). Vital Actions and Organic Physics. *Bulletin of the History of Medicine*, 50.

Prætorius, N. (1978). *Subject and Object. An Essay on the Epistemological Foundation for a Theory of Perception*. Copenhagen: Dansk Psykologisk Forlag.

Pribram, K. H., and Gill, M. M. (1976). *Freud's 'Project' Re-assessed*. New York: Basic Books.

Prokop, U. (1976). *Weiblicher Lebenszusammenhang*. Frankfurt am Main: Suhrkamp, 1977.

Radnitzky, G. (1968). Contemporary Schools of Metascience. Chicago: Henry Regnery.

Rapaport, D. (1953). On the Psychoanalytic Theory of Affects. In M. M. Gill (ed.): *The Collected Papers of David Rapaport*. New York: Basic Books, 1967.

Rapaport, D. (1960). *The Structure of Psychoanalytic Theory*. New York: International Universities Press, 1969.

Rapaport, D. (1961). Some Metapsychological Considerations Concerning Activity and Passivity. In M. M. Gill (ed.): *The Collected Papers of Davis Rapaport*. New York: Basic Books, 1967.

Rapaport, D. (1974). *The History of the Concept of Association of Ideas*. New York: International Universities Press.

Ricoeur, P. (1965). *Freud and Philosophy: An Essay on Interpretation*. New Haven: Yale University Press, 1970.

Riese, W. (1958a). Freudian Concepts of Brain Function and Brain Disease. *Journal of Nervous and Mental Disease*, 127.

Riese, W. (1958b). The Pre-Freudian Origins of Psychoanalysis. *Science and Psychoanalysis*, 1.

Ritvo, L. B. (1965). Darwin as the Source of Freud's Neo-Lamarkianism. *Journal of the American Psychoanalytic Association*, 13.

Ritvo, L. B. (1974). The Impact of Darwin on Freud. *Psychoanalytic Quarterly*, 43.

Roazen, P. (1971). *Freud and His Followers*. New York: New York University Press, 1985.

Robert, M. (1964). *La révolution psychanalytique. La vie et l'oeuvre de Freud*. Vols. 1–2. Paris: Payot, 1979.

Robert, M. (1974). *D'OEdipe à Moïse. Freud et la conscience juive*. Paris: Calmann-Lévy, 1978.

Robinson, P. A. (1969). *The Freudian Left*. New York: Harper and Row.

Rogow, A. A. (1978). A Further Footnote to Freud's "Fragment of an Analysis of a Case of Hysteria." *Journal of the American Psychoanalytic Association*, 26.

Romberg, M. H. (1846). *Lehrbuch der Nervenkrankheiten der Menschen*. Berlin: August Hirschwald.

Rosenbaum, H. (1982). *Formen der Familie*. Frankfurt am Main: Suhrkamp.

Rosolato, G. (1968). *Le sens des oublis. L'Arc*, 34.

Rousseau, J.-J. (1762). *Emile*. New York: Basic Books, 1979.

Rubinstein, B. B. (1965). Psychoanalytic Theory and the Mind-Body Problem. In N. S. Greenfield and W. C. Lewis (eds.): *Psychoanalysis and Current Biological Thought*. Madison: University of Wisconsin Press.

Saussure, F. de (1916). *Course in General Linguistics*. New York: Philosophical Library, 1959.

Schafer, R. (1968). On the Theoretical and Technical Conceptualization of Activity and Passivity. *Psychoanalytic Quarterly*, 37.

Schafer, R. (1976). *A New Language for Psychoanalysis*. New Haven: Yale University Press.

Schafer, R. (1978). *Language and Insight*. New Haven: Yale University Press.

Schafer, R. (1983). *The Analytic Attitude*. London: Hogarth Press.

Scheidt, J. (1973). *Freud und das Kokain*. München: Kindler.

Schneiderman, S. (1986). *Rat Man*. New York: New York University Press.

Schorske, C. E. (1980). *Fin-de-siècle Vienna*. New York: Alfred A. Knopf.

Schreber, D. P. (1903). *Memoirs of My Nervous Illness*. London: W. Dawson, 1955.

Schülein, J. A. (1975). *Das Gesellschaftsbild der freudschen Theorie*. Frankfurt am Main: Campus.

Scull, A. (ed.) (1981). *Madhouses, Mad-Doctors, and Madmen*. Philadelphia: University of Pennsylvania Press.

Shorter, E. (1975). *The Making of the Modern Family*. New York: Basic Books.

Spehlmann, R. (1953). *Sigmund Freuds neurologische Schriften*. Berlin: Springer.

Spinoza, B. (1677). *Ethics*. Malibu Cal.: J. Simon, 1981.

Stendhal (1830). *The Red and the Black*, New York: Modern Library, 1984.

Stengel, E. (1954). A Re-evaluation of Freud's Book "On Aphasia." Its Significance for Psycho-Analysis. *International Journal of Psycho-Analysis*, 35.

Stevens, L. A. (1973). *Explorers of the Brain*. London: Angus.

Stevenson, R. L. (1886). *The Strange Case of Dr. Jekyll and Mr. Hyde*. New York: W. L. Allison, n.d.

Stewart, W. A. (1967). *Psychoanalysis: The First Ten Years 1888–1898*. London: George Allan, 1969.

Strindberg, A. (1886). *The Son of a Servant*. London: W. Rider, 1913.

Sulloway, F. J. (1979). Freud: *Biologist of the Mind*. New York: Basic Books.

Temkin, O. (1946). Materialism in French and German Physiology of the Early Nineteenth Century. *Bulletin of the History of Medicine*, 20.

Ussel, J. van (1970). *Sexualunterdrückung*. Reinbek bei Hamburg: Rowohlt.

Veith, I. (1965). *Hysteria*. Chicago: University of Chicago Press.

Virchow, R. (1856). Alter und neuer Vitalismus. *Virchow Archiv*, 9.

Vogel, P. (1954). Zur Aphasielehre Sigmund Freuds. *Monatschrift für Psychiatrie und Neurologie*, 128.

Wagner, R. (1842–1846). *Handwörterbuch der Physiologie*. Vols. 1–3. Braunschweig: Friedrich Vieweg.

Wallace, E. R. (1983). *Freud and Anthropology*. New York: International Universities Press.

Wallace, E. R., and Pressley, L. C. (eds.) (1980). *Essays in the History of Psychiatry*. Columbia: WM. S. Hall Psychiatric Institute.

Warren, H. C. (1921). *A History of Association Psychology*. New York: Charles Scribner's Sons, 1967.

Weber, E. H. (1842). *Tastsinn und Gemeingefühl*. Leipzig: Weidmannsche Buchhandlung.

Weismann, A. (1882). *Ueber die Dauer des Lebens*. Jena: Gustav Fischer.

Weismann, A. (1892). *Das Keimplasma*. Jena: Gustav Fischer.

Werlinder, H. (1978). *Psychopathy: A History of the Concepts*. Uppsala: Almquist and Wiksell.

Wernicke, C. (1900). *Grundriss der Psychiatrie in klinischen Vorlesungen*. Leipzig: G. Thieme.

Wettley, A. (1959). *Von der "Psychopathia sexualis" zur Sexualwissenschaft*. Stuttgart: Ferdinand Enke.

Whyte, L. L. (1960). *The Unconscious before Freud*. New York: Basic Books.

Wilden, A. (1966). Freud, Signorelli and Lacan: The Repression of the Signifier. *American Imago, 23*.

Wilden, A. (1972). *System and Structure*. 2nd edition. London: Tavistock, 1980.

Wollheim, R. (1971). *Freud*. London: Fontana Books, 1975.

Wollheim, R. (ed.) (1974). *Freud. A Collection of Critical Essays*. New York: Anchor Books.

Wundt, W. (1874). *Grundzüge der physiologischen Psychologie*. Leipzig: W. Engelmann.

Wyss, D. (1961). *Die tiefenpsychologischen Schulen von den Anfängen bis zur Gegenwart*. Göttingen: Vandenhoeck und Ruprecht, 1970.

Young, R. (1970). *Mind, Brain and Adaptation in the Nineteenth Century*. Oxford: Clarendon Press.

Young, R. (1973). The Historiographic and Ideological Contexts of the Nineteenth Century Debate on Man's Place in Nature. In M. Teich and R. Young (ed.): *Changing Perspectives in the History of Science*. London: Heinemann.

Ziehen, T. (1894). *Psychiatrie für Aerzte und Studierenden*. Leipzig: S. Hirzel.

NAME INDEX

SUBJECT INDEX